RUGGLES

MERTON OF THE MOVIES

BUNKER BEAN

THREE MASTERPIECES OF HUMOR

Harry Leon Wilson

CONTENTS

BOOK ONE
RUGGLES OF RED GAP

TO HELEN COOKE WILSON

CHAPTER ONE

At 6:30 in our Paris apartment I had finished the Honourable George, performing those final touches that make the difference between a man well turned out and a man merely dressed. In the main I was not dissatisfied. His dress waistcoats, it is true, no longer permit the inhalation of anything like a full breath, and his collars clasp too closely. (I have always held that a collar may provide quite ample room for the throat without sacrifice of smartness if the depth be at least two and one quarter inches.) And it is no secret to either the Honourable George or our intimates that I have never approved his fashion of beard, a reddish, enveloping, brushlike affair never nicely enough trimmed. I prefer, indeed, no beard at all, but he stubbornly refuses to shave, possessing a difficult chin. Still, I repeat, he was not nearly impossible as he now left my hands.

"Dining with the Americans," he remarked, as I conveyed the hat, gloves, and stick to him in their proper order.

"Yes, sir," I replied. "And might I suggest, sir, that your choice be a grilled undercut or something simple, bearing in mind the undoubted effects of shell-fish upon one's complexion?" The hard truth is that after even a very little lobster the Honourable George has a way of coming out in spots. A single oyster patty, too, will often spot him quite all over.

"What cheek! Decide that for myself," he retorted with a lame effort at dignity which he was unable to sustain. His eyes fell from mine. "Besides, I'm almost quite certain that the last time it was the melon. Wretched things, melons!"

Then, as if to divert me, he rather fussily refused the correct evening stick I had chosen for him and seized a knobby bit of thornwood suitable only for moor and upland work, and brazenly quite discarded the gloves.

"Feel a silly fool wearing gloves when there's no reason!" he exclaimed pettishly.

"Quite so, sir," I replied, freezing instantly.

"Now, don't play the juggins," he retorted. "Let me be comfortable. And I don't mind telling you I stand to win a hundred quid this very evening."

"I dare say," I replied. The sum was more than needed, but I had cause to be thus cynical.

"From the American Johnny with the eyebrows," he went on with a quite pathetic enthusiasm. "We're to play their American game of poker—drawing poker as they call it. I've watched them play for near a fortnight. It's beastly simple. One has only to know when to bluff."

"A hundred pounds, yes, sir. And if one loses——"

He flashed me a look so deucedly queer that it fair chilled me.

"I fancy you'll be even more interested than I if I lose," he remarked in tones of a curious evenness that were somehow rather deadly. The words seemed pregnant with meaning, but before I could weigh them I heard him noisily descending the stairs. It was only then I recalled having noticed that he had not changed to his varnished boots, having still on his feet the doggish and battered pair he most favoured. It was a trick of his to evade me with them. I did for them each day all that human boot-cream could do, but they were things no sensitive gentleman would endure with evening dress. I was glad to reflect that doubtless only Americans would observe them.

So began the final hours of a 14th of July in Paris that must ever be memorable. My own birthday, it is also chosen by the French as one on which to celebrate with carnival some one of those regrettable events in their own distressing past.

To begin with, the day was marked first of all by the breezing in of his lordship the Earl of Brinstead, brother of the Honourable George, on his way to England from the Engadine. More peppery than usual had his lordship been, his grayish side-whiskers in angry upheaval and his inflamed words exploding quite all over the place, so that the Honourable George and I had both perceived it to be no time for admitting our recent financial reverse at the gaming tables of Ostend. On the contrary, we had gamely affirmed the last quarter's allowance to be practically untouched—a desperate stand, indeed! But there was that in his lordship's manner to urge us to it, though even so he appeared to be not more than half deceived.

"No good greening me!" he exploded to both of us. "Tell in a flash—gambling, or a woman—typing-girl, milliner, dancing person, what, what! Guilty faces, both of you. Know you too well. My word, what, what!"

Again we stoutly protested while his lordship on the hearthrug rocked in his boots and glared. The Honourable George gamely rattled some loose coin of the baser sort in his pockets and tried in return for a glare of innocence foully aspersed. I dare say he fell short of it. His histrionic gifts are but meagre.

"Fools, quite fools, both of you!" exploded his lordship anew. "And, make it worse, no longer young fools. Young and a fool, people make excuses. Say, 'Fool? Yes, but so young!' But old and a fool—not a word to say, what, what! Silly rot at forty." He clutched his side-whiskers with frenzied hands. He seemed to comb them to a more bristling rage.

"Dare say you'll both come croppers. Not surprise me. Silly old George, course, course! Hoped better of Ruggles, though. Ruggles different from old George. Got a brain. But can't use it. Have old George wed to a charwoman presently. Hope she'll be a worker. Need to be—support you both, what, what!"

I mean to say, he was coming it pretty thick, since he could not have forgotten that each time I had warned him so he could hasten to save his brother from distressing mésalliances. I refer to the affair with the typing-girl and to the later entanglement with a Brixton milliner encountered informally under the portico of a theatre in Charing Cross Road. But he was in no mood to concede that I had thus far shown a scrupulous care in these emergencies. Peppery he was, indeed. He gathered hat and stick, glaring indignantly at each of them and then at us.

"Greened me fair, haven't you, about money? Quite so, quite so! Not hear from you then till next quarter. No telegraphing—no begging letters. Shouldn't a bit know what to make of them. Plenty you got to last. Say so yourselves." He laughed villainously here. "Morning," said he, and was out.

"Old Nevil been annoyed by something," said the Honourable George after a long silence. "Know the old boy too well. Always tell when he's been annoyed. Rather wish he hadn't been."

So we had come to the night of this memorable day, and to the Honourable George's departure on his mysterious words about the hundred pounds.

Left alone, I began to meditate profoundly. It was the closing of a day I had seen dawn with the keenest misgiving, having had reason to believe it might be fraught with significance if not disaster to myself. The year before a gypsy at Epsom had solemnly warned me that a great change would come into my life on or before my fortieth birthday. To this I might have paid less heed but for its disquieting confirmation on a later day at a psychic parlour in Edgware Road. Proceeding there in company with my eldest brother-in-law, a plate-layer and surfaceman on the Northern (he being uncertain about the Derby winner for that year), I was told by the person for a trifle of two shillings that I was soon to cross water and to meet many strange adventures. True, later events proved her to have been psychically unsound as to the Derby winner (so that my brother-in-law, who was out two pounds ten, thereby threatened to have an action against her); yet her reference to myself had confirmed the words of the gypsy; so it will be plain why I had been anxious the whole of this birthday.

For one thing, I had gone on the streets as little as possible, though I should naturally have done that, for the behaviour of the French on this bank holiday of theirs is repugnant in the extreme to the sane English point of view—I mean their frivolous public dancing and marked conversational levity. Indeed, in their soberest moments, they have too little of British weight. Their best-dressed men are apparently turned out not by menservants but by modistes. I will not say their women are without a gift for wearing gowns, and their chefs have unquestionably got at the inner meaning of food, but as a people at large they would never do with us. Even their language is not based on reason. I have had occasion, for example, to acquire their word for bread, which is "pain." As if that were not wild enough, they mispronounce it atrociously. Yet for years these people have been separated from us only by a narrow strip of water!

By keeping close to our rooms, then, I had thought to evade what of evil might have been in store for me on this day. Another evening I might have ventured

4

abroad to a cinema palace, but this was no time for daring, and I took a further precaution of locking our doors. Then, indeed, I had no misgiving save that inspired by the last words of the Honourable George. In the event of his losing the game of poker I was to be even more concerned than he. Yet how could evil come to me, even should the American do him in the eye rather frightfully? In truth, I had not the faintest belief that the Honourable George would win the game. He fancies himself a card-player, though why he should, God knows. At bridge with him every hand is a no-trumper. I need not say more. Also it occurred to me that the American would be a person not accustomed to losing. There was that about him.

More than once I had deplored this rather Bohemian taste of the Honourable George which led him to associate with Americans as readily as with persons of his own class; and especially had I regretted his intimacy with the family in question. Several times I had observed them, on the occasion of bearing messages from the Honourable George—usually his acceptance of an invitation to dine. Too obviously they were rather a handful. I mean to say, they were people who could perhaps matter in their own wilds, but they would never do with us.

Their leader, with whom the Honourable George had consented to game this evening, was a tall, careless-spoken person, with a narrow, dark face marked with heavy black brows that were rather tremendous in their effect when he did not smile. Almost at my first meeting him I divined something of the public man in his bearing, a suggestion, perhaps, of the confirmed orator, a notion in which I was somehow further set by the gesture with which he swept back his carelessly falling forelock. I was not surprised, then, to hear him referred to as the "Senator." In some unexplained manner, the Honourable George, who is never as reserved in public as I could wish him to be, had chummed up with this person at one of the race-tracks, and had thereafter been almost quite too pally with him and with the very curious other members of his family—the name being Floud.

The wife might still be called youngish, a bit florid in type, plumpish, with yellow hair, though to this a stain had been applied, leaving it in deficient consonance with her eyebrows; these shading grayish eyes that crackled with determination. Rather on the large side she was, forcible of speech and manner, yet curiously eager, I had at once detected, for the exactly correct thing in dress and deportment.

The remaining member of the family was a male cousin of the so-called Senator, his senior evidently by half a score of years, since I took him to have reached the late fifties. "Cousin Egbert" he was called, and it was at once apparent to me that he had been most direly subjugated by the woman whom he addressed with great respect as "Mrs. Effie." Rather a seamed and drooping chap he was, with mild, whitish-blue eyes like a porcelain doll's, a mournfully drooped gray moustache, and a grayish jumble of hair. I early remarked his hunted look in the presence of the woman. Timid and soft-stepping he was beyond measure.

Such were the impressions I had been able to glean of these altogether queer people during the fortnight since the Honourable George had so lawlessly taken them up. Lodged they were in an hotel among the most expensive situated near what would have been our Trafalgar Square, and I later recalled that I had been most interestedly studied by the so-called "Mrs. Effie" on each of the few occasions I appeared there. I mean to say, she would not be above putting to me intimate questions concerning my term of service with the Honourable George Augustus Vane-Basingwell, the precise nature of the duties I performed for him, and even the exact sum of my honourarium. On the last occasion she had remarked—and too well I recall a strange glitter in her competent eyes—"You are just the man needed by poor Cousin Egbert there—you could make something of him. Look at the way he's tied that cravat after all I've said to him."

The person referred to here shivered noticeably, stroked his chin in a manner enabling him to conceal the cravat, and affected nervously to be taken with a sight in the street below. In some embarrassment I withdrew, conscious of a cold, speculative scrutiny bent upon me by the woman.

If I have seemed tedious in my recital of the known facts concerning these extraordinary North American natives, it will, I am sure, be forgiven me in the light of those tragic developments about to ensue.

Meantime, let me be pictured as reposing in fancied security from all evil predictions while I awaited the return of the Honourable George. I was only too certain he would come suffering from an acute acid dyspepsia, for I had seen lobster in his shifty eyes as he left me; but beyond this I apprehended nothing poignant, and I gave myself up to meditating profoundly upon our situation.

Frankly, it was not good. I had done my best to cheer the Honourable George, but since our brief sojourn at Ostend, and despite the almost continuous hospitality of the Americans, he had been having, to put it bluntly, an awful hump. At Ostend, despite my remonstrance, he had staked and lost the major portion of his quarter's allowance in testing a system at the wheel which had been warranted by the person who sold it to him in London to break any bank in a day's play. He had meant to pause but briefly at Ostend, for little more than a test of the system, then proceed to Monte Carlo, where his proposed terrific winnings would occasion less alarm to the managers. Yet at Ostend the system developed such grave faults in the first hour of play that we were forced to lay up in Paris to economize.

For myself I had entertained doubts of the system from the moment of its purchase, for it seemed awfully certain to me that the vendor would have used it himself instead of parting with it for a couple of quid, he being in plain need of fresh linen and smarter boots, to say nothing of the quite impossible lounge-suit he wore the night we met him in a cab shelter near Covent Garden. But the Honourable George had not listened to me. He insisted the chap had made it all enormously clear; that those mathematical Johnnies never valued money for its own sake, and that we should presently be as right as two sparrows in a crate.

Fearfully annoyed I was at the dénouement. For now we were in Paris, rather meanly lodged in a dingy hotel on a narrow street leading from what with us might have been Piccadilly Circus. Our rooms were rather a good height with a carved cornice and plaster enrichments, but the furnishings were musty and the general air depressing, notwithstanding the effect of a few good mantel ornaments which I have long made it a rule to carry with me.

Then had come the meeting with the Americans. Glad I was to reflect that this had occurred in Paris instead of London. That sort of thing gets about so. Even from Paris I was not a little fearful that news of his mixing with this raffish set might get to the ears of his lordship either at the town house or at Chaynes-Wotten. True, his lordship is not over-liberal with his brother, but that is small reason for affronting the pride of a family that attained its earldom in the fourteenth century. Indeed the family had become important quite long before this time, the first Vane-Basingwell having been beheaded by no less a personage than William the Conqueror, as I learned in one of the many hours I have been privileged to browse in the Chaynes-Wotten library.

It need hardly be said that in my long term of service with the Honourable George, beginning almost from the time my mother nursed him, I have endeavoured to keep him up to his class, combating a certain laxness that has hampered him. And most stubborn he is, and wilful. At games he is almost quite a duffer. I once got him to play outside left on a hockey eleven and he excited much comment, some of which was of a favourable nature, but he cares little for hunting or shooting and, though it is scarce a matter to be gossiped of, he loathes cricket. Perhaps I have disclosed enough concerning him. Although the Vane-Basingwells have quite almost always married the right people, the Honourable George was beyond question born queer.

Again, in the matter of marriage, he was difficult. His lordship, having married early into a family of *poor lifes*, was now long a widower, and meaning to remain so he had been especially concerned that the Honourable George should contract a proper alliance. Hence our constant worry lest he prove too susceptible out of his class. More than once had he shamefully funked his fences. There was the distressing instance of the Honourable Agatha Cradleigh. Quite all that could be desired of family and dower she was, thirty-two years old, a bit faded though still eager, with the rather immensely high forehead and long, thin, slightly curved Cradleigh nose.

The Honourable George at his lordship's peppery urging had at last consented to a betrothal, and our troubles for a time promised to be over, but it came to precisely nothing. I gathered it might have been because she wore beads on her gown and was interested in uplift work, or that she bred canaries, these birds being loathed by the Honourable George with remarkable intensity, though it might equally have been that she still mourned a deceased fiancé of her early girlhood, a curate, I believe, whose faded letters she had preserved and would read to the Honourable George at intimate moments, weeping bitterly the while. Whatever may have been his fancied objection—that is the time we disappeared and were not heard of for near a twelvemonth.

Wondering now I was how we should last until the next quarter's allowance. We always had lasted, but each time it was a different way. The Honourable George at a crisis of this sort invariably spoke of entering trade, and had actually talked of selling motor-cars, pointing out to me that even certain rulers of Europe had frankly entered this trade as agents. It might have proved remunerative had he known anything of motor-cars, but I was more than glad he did not, for I have always considered machinery to be unrefined. Much I preferred that he be a company promoter or something of that sort in the city, knowing about bonds and debentures, as many of the best of our families are not above doing. It seemed all he could do with propriety, having failed in examinations for the army and the church, and being incurably hostile to politics, which he declared silly rot.

Sharply at midnight I aroused myself from these gloomy thoughts and breathed a long sigh of relief. Both gipsy and psychic expert had failed in their prophecies. With a lightened heart I set about the preparations I knew would be needed against the Honourable George's return. Strong in my conviction that he would not have been able to resist lobster, I made ready his hot foot-bath with its solution of brine-crystals and put the absorbent fruit-lozenges close by, together with his sleeping-suit, his bed-cap, and his knitted night-socks. Scarcely was all ready when I heard his step.

He greeted me curtly on entering, swiftly averting his face as I took his stick, hat, and top-coat. But I had seen the worst at one glance. The Honourable George was more than spotted—he was splotchy. It was as bad as that.

"Lobster *and* oysters," I made bold to remark, but he affected not to have heard, and proceeded rapidly to disrobe. He accepted the foot-bath without demur, pulling a blanket well about his shoulders, complaining of the water's temperature, and demanding three of the fruit-lozenges.

"Not what you think at all," he then said. "It was that cursed bar-le-duc jelly. Always puts me this way, and you quite well know it."

"Yes, sir, to be sure," I answered gravely, and had the satisfaction of noting that he looked quite a little foolish. Too well he knew I could not be deceived, and even now I could surmise that the lobster had been supported by sherry. How many times have I not explained to him that sherry has double the tonic vinosity of any other wine and may not be tampered with by the sensitive. But he chose at present to make light of it, almost as if he were chaffing above his knowledge of some calamity.

"Some book Johnny says a chap is either a fool or a physician at forty," he remarked, drawing the blanket more closely about him.

"I should hardly rank you as a Harley Street consultant, sir," I swiftly retorted, which was slanging him enormously because he had turned forty. I mean to say, there was but one thing he could take me as meaning him to be, since at forty I considered him no physician. But at least I had not been too blunt, the touch about the Harley Street consultant being rather neat, I thought, yet not too subtle for him.

He now demanded a pipe of tobacco, and for a time smoked in silence. I could see that his mind worked painfully.

"Stiffish lot, those Americans," he said at last.

"They do so many things one doesn't do," I answered.

"And their brogue is not what one could call top-hole, is it now? How often they say 'I guess!' I fancy they must say it a score of times in a half-hour."

"I fancy they do, sir," I agreed.

"I fancy that Johnny with the eyebrows will say it even oftener."

"I fancy so, sir. I fancy I've counted it well up to that."

"I fancy you're quite right. And the chap 'guesses' when he awfully well knows, too. That's the essential rabbit. To-night he said 'I guess I've got you beaten to a pulp,' when I fancy he wasn't guessing at all. I mean to say, I swear he knew it perfectly."

"You lost the game of drawing poker?" I asked coldly, though I knew he had carried little to lose.

"I lost——" he began. I observed he was strangely embarrassed. He strangled over his pipe and began anew: "I said that to play the game soundly you've only to know when to bluff. Studied it out myself, and jolly well right I was, too, as far as I went. But there's further to go in the silly game. I hadn't observed that to play it greatly one must also know when one's opponent is bluffing."

"Really, sir?"

"Oh, really; quite important, I assure you. More important than one would have believed, watching their silly ways. You fancy a chap's bluffing when he's doing nothing of the sort. I'd enormously have liked to know it before we played. Things would have been so awfully different for us"—he broke off curiously, paused, then added—"for you."

"Different for me, sir?" His words seemed gruesome. They seemed open to some vaguely sinister interpretation. But I kept myself steady.

"We live and learn, sir," I said, lightly enough.

"Some of us learn too late," he replied, increasingly ominous.

"I take it you failed to win the hundred pounds, sir?"

"I have the hundred pounds; I won it—by losing."

Again he evaded my eye.

"Played, indeed, sir," said I.

"You jolly well won't believe that for long."

Now as he had the hundred pounds, I couldn't fancy what the deuce and all he meant by such prattle. I was half afraid he might be having me on, as I have known him do now and again when he fancied he could get me. I fearfully wanted to ask questions. Again I saw the dark, absorbed face of the gipsy as he studied my future.

"Rotten shift, life is," now murmured the Honourable George quite as if he had forgotten me. "If I'd have but put through that Monte Carlo affair I dare say I'd have chucked the whole business—gone to South Africa, perhaps, and set up a mine or a plantation. Shouldn't have come back. Just cut off, and good-bye to this mess. But no capital. Can't do things without capital. Where these American Johnnies have the pull of us. Do anything. Nearly do what they jolly well like to. No sense to money. Stuff that runs blind. Look at the silly beggars that have it——" On he went quite alarmingly with his tirade. Almost as violent he was as an ugly-headed chap I once heard ranting when I went with my brother-in-law to a meeting of the North Brixton Radical Club. Quite like an anarchist he was. Presently he quieted. After a long pull at his pipe he regarded me with an entire change of manner. Well I knew something was coming; coming swift as a rocketing woodcock. Word for word I put down our incredible speeches:

"You are going out to America, Ruggles."

"Yes, sir; North or South, sir?"

"North, I fancy; somewhere on the West coast—Ohio, Omaha, one of those Indian places."

"Perhaps Indiana or the Yellowstone Valley, sir."

"The chap's a sort of millionaire."

"The chap, sir?"

"Eyebrow chap. Money no end—mines, lumber, domestic animals, that sort of thing."

"Beg pardon, sir! I'm to go——"

"Chap's wife taken a great fancy to you. Would have you to do for the funny, sad beggar. So he's won you. Won you in a game of drawing poker. Another man would have done as well, but the creature was keen for you. Great strength of character. Determined sort. Hope you won't think I didn't play soundly, but it's not a forthright game. Think they're bluffing when they aren't. When they are you mayn't think it. So far as hiding one's intentions, it's a most rottenly immoral game. Low, animal cunning—that sort of thing."

"Do I understand I was the stake, sir?" I controlled myself to say. The heavens seemed bursting about my head.

"Ultimately lost you were by the very trifling margin of superiority that a hand known as a club flush bears over another hand consisting of three of the eights—not quite all of them, you understand, only three, and two other quite meaningless cards."

I could but stammer piteously, I fear. I heard myself make a wretched failure of words that crowded to my lips.

"But it's quite simple, I tell you. I dare say I could show it you in a moment if you've cards in your box."

"Thank you, sir, I'll not trouble you. I'm certain it was simple. But would you mind telling me what exactly the game was played for?"

"Knew you'd not understand at once. My word, it was not too bally simple. If I won I'd a hundred pounds. If I lost I'd to give you up to them but still to receive a hundred pounds. I suspect the Johnny's conscience pricked him. Thought you were worth a hundred pounds, and guessed all the time he could do me awfully in the eye with his poker. Quite set they were on having you. Eyebrow chap seemed to think it a jolly good wheeze. She didn't, though. Quite off her head at having you for that glum one who does himself so badly."

Dazed I was, to be sure, scarce comprehending the calamity that had befallen us.

"Am I to understand, sir, that I am now in the service of the Americans?"

"Stupid! Of course, of course! Explained clearly, haven't I, about the club flush and the three eights. Only three of them, mind you. If the other one had been in my hand, I'd have done him. As narrow a squeak as that. But I lost. And you may be certain I lost gamely, as a gentleman should. No laughing matter, but I laughed with them—except the funny, sad one. He was worried and made no secret of it. They were good enough to say I took my loss like a dead sport."

More of it followed, but always the same. Ever he came back to the sickening, concise point that I was to go out to the American wilderness with these grotesque folk who had but the most elementary notions of what one does and what one does not do. Always he concluded with his boast that he had taken his loss like a dead sport. He became vexed at last by my painful efforts to understand how, precisely, the dreadful thing had come about. But neither could I endure more. I fled to my room. He had tried again to impress upon me that three eights are but slightly inferior to the flush of clubs.

I faced my glass. My ordinary smooth, full face seemed to have shrivelled. The marks of my anguish were upon me. Vainly had I locked myself in. The gipsy's warning had borne its evil fruit. Sold, I'd been; even as once the poor blackamoors were sold into American bondage. I recalled one of their pathetic folk-songs in which the wretches were wont to make light of their lamentable estate; a thing I had often heard sung by a black with a banjo on the pier at Brighton; not a genuine black, only dyed for the moment he was, but I had never lost the plaintive quality of the verses:

"Away down South in Michigan,

Where I was so happy and so gay,

'Twas there I mowed the cotton and the cane—"

How poignantly the simple words came back to me! A slave, day after day mowing his owner's cotton and cane, plucking the maize from the savannahs, yet happy and gay! Should I be equal to this spirit? The Honourable George had lost; so I, his pawn, must also submit like a dead sport.

How little I then dreamed what adventures, what adversities, what ignominies—yes, and what triumphs were to be mine in those back blocks of North America! I saw but a bleak wilderness, a distressing contact with people who never for a moment would do with us. I shuddered. I despaired.

And outside the windows gay Paris laughed and sang in the dance, ever unheeding my plight!

CHAPTER TWO

In that first sleep how often do we dream that our calamity has been only a dream. It was so in my first moments of awakening. Vestiges of some grotesquely hideous nightmare remained with me. Wearing the shackles of the slave, I had been mowing the corn under the fierce sun that beats down upon the American savannahs. Sickeningly, then, a wind of memory blew upon me and I was alive to my situation.

Nor was I forgetful of the plight in which the Honourable George would now find himself. He is as good as lost when not properly looked after. In the ordinary affairs of life he is a simple, trusting, incompetent duffer, if ever there was one. Even in so rudimentary a matter as collar-studs he is like a storm-tossed mariner—I mean to say, like a chap in a boat on the ocean who doesn't know what sails to pull up nor how to steer the silly rudder.

One rather feels exactly that about him.

And now he was bound to go seedy beyond description—like the time at Mentone when he dreamed a system for playing the little horses, after which for a fortnight I was obliged to nurse a well-connected invalid in order that we might last over till next remittance day. The havoc he managed to wreak among his belongings in that time would scarce be believed should I set it down—not even a single boot properly treed—and his appearance when I was enabled to recover him (my client having behaved most handsomely on the eve of his departure for Spain) being such that I passed him in the hotel lounge without even a nod—climbing-boots, with trousers from his one suit of boating flannels, a blazered golfing waistcoat, his best morning-coat with the wide braid, a hunting-stock and a motoring-cap, with his beard more than discursive, as one might say, than I had ever seen it. If I disclose this thing it is only that my fears for him may be comprehended when I pictured him being permanently out of hand.

Meditating thus bitterly, I had but finished dressing when I was startled by a knock on my door and by the entrance, to my summons, of the elder and more subdued Floud, he of the drooping mustaches and the mournful eyes of pale blue. One glance at his attire brought freshly to my mind the atrocious difficulties of my new situation. I may be credited or not, but combined with tan boots and wretchedly fitting trousers of a purple hue he wore a black frock-coat, revealing far, far too much of a blue satin "made" cravat on which was painted a cluster of tiny white flowers—lilies of the valley, I should say. Unbelievably above this monstrous mélange was a rather low-crowned bowler hat.

Hardly repressing a shudder, I bowed, whereupon he advanced solemnly to me and put out his hand. To cover the embarrassing situation tactfully I extended my own, and we actually shook hands, although the clasp was limply quite formal.

"How do you do, Mr. Ruggles?" he began.

I bowed again, but speech failed me.

"She sent me over to get you," he went on. He uttered the word "She" with such profound awe that I knew he could mean none other than Mrs. Effie. It was most extraordinary, but I dare say only what was to have been expected from persons of this sort. In any good-class club or among gentlemen at large it is customary to allow one at least twenty-four hours for the payment of one's gambling debts. Yet there I was being collected by the winner at so early an hour as half-after seven. If I had been a five-pound note instead of myself, I fancy it would have been quite the same. These Americans would most indecently have sent for their winnings before the Honourable George had awakened. One would have thought they had expected him to refuse payment of me after losing me the night before. How little they seemed to realize that we were both intending to be dead sportsmen.

"Very good, sir," I said, "but I trust I may be allowed to brew the Honourable George his tea before leaving? I'd hardly like to trust to him alone with it, sir."

"Yes, sir," he said, so respectfully that it gave me an odd feeling. "Take your time, Mr. Ruggles. I don't know as I am in any hurry on my own account. It's only account of Her."

I trust it will be remembered that in reporting this person's speeches I am making an earnest effort to set them down word for word in all their terrific peculiarities. I mean to say, I would not be held accountable for his phrasing, and if I corrected his speech, as of course the tendency is, our identities might become confused. I hope this will be understood when I report him as saying things in ways one doesn't word them. I mean to say that it should not be thought that I would say them in this way if it chanced that I were saying the same things in my proper person. I fancy this should now be plain.

"Very well, sir," I said.

"If it was me," he went on, "I wouldn't want you a little bit. But it's Her. She's got her mind made up to do the right thing and have us all be somebody, and when she makes her mind up——" He hesitated and studied the ceiling for some seconds. "Believe me," he continued, "Mrs. Effie is some wildcat!"

"Yes, sir—some wildcat," I repeated.

"Believe *me*, Bill," he said again, quaintly addressing me by a name not my own—"believe me, she'd fight a rattlesnake and give it the first two bites."

Again let it be recalled that I put down this extraordinary speech exactly as I heard it. I thought to detect in it that grotesque exaggeration with which the Americans so distressingly embellish their humour. I mean to say, it could hardly have been meant in all seriousness. So far as my researches have extended, the rattlesnake is an invariably poisonous reptile. Fancy giving one so downright an advantage as the first two bites, or even one bite, although I believe the thing does not in fact bite at all, but does one down with its forked tongue, of which there is an excellent drawing in my little volume, "Inquire Within; 1,000 Useful Facts."

"Yes, sir," I replied, somewhat at a loss; "quite so, sir!"

"I just thought I'd wise you up beforehand."

"Thank you, sir," I said, for his intention beneath the weird jargon was somehow benevolent. "And if you'll be good enough to wait until I have taken tea to the Honourable George——"

"How is the Judge this morning?" he broke in.

"The Judge, sir?" I was at a loss, until he gestured toward the room of the Honourable George.

"The Judge, yes. Ain't he a justice of the peace or something?"

"But no, sir; not at all, sir."

"Then what do you call him 'Honourable' for, if he ain't a judge or something?"

"Well, sir, it's done, sir," I explained, but I fear he was unable to catch my meaning, for a moment later (the Honourable George, hearing our voices, had thrown a boot smartly against the door) he was addressing him as "Judge" and thereafter continued to do so, nor did the Honourable George seem to make any moment of being thus miscalled.

I served the Ceylon tea, together with biscuits and marmalade, the while our caller chatted nervously. He had, it appeared, procured his own breakfast while on his way to us.

"I got to have my ham and eggs of a morning," he confided. "But she won't let me have anything at that hotel but a continental breakfast, which is nothing but coffee and toast and some of that there sauce you're eating. She says when I'm on the continent I got to eat a continental breakfast, because that's the smart thing to do, and not stuff myself like I was on the ranch; but I got that game beat both ways from the jack. I duck out every morning before she's up. I found a place where you can get regular ham and eggs."

"Regular ham and eggs?" murmured the Honourable George.

"French ham and eggs is a joke. They put a slice of boiled ham in a little dish, slosh a couple of eggs on it, and tuck the dish into the oven a few minutes. Say, they won't ever believe that back in Red Gap when I tell it. But I found this here little place where they do it right, account of Americans having made trouble so much over the other way. But, mind you, don't let on to her," he warned me suddenly.

"Certainly not, sir," I said. "Trust me to be discreet, sir."

"All right, then. Maybe we'll get on better than what I thought we would. I was looking for trouble with you, the way she's been talking about what you'd do for me."

"I trust matters will be pleasant, sir," I replied.

"I can be pushed just so far," he curiously warned me, "and no farther—not by any man that wears hair."

"Yes, sir," I said again, wondering what the wearing of hair might mean to this process of pushing him, and feeling rather absurdly glad that my own face is smoothly shaven.

"You'll find Ruggles fairish enough after you've got used to his ways," put in the Honourable George.

"All right, Judge; and remember it wasn't my doings," said my new employer, rising and pulling down to his ears his fearful bowler hat. "And now we better report to her before she does a hot-foot over here. You can pack your grip later in the day," he added to me.

"Pack my grip—yes, sir," I said numbly, for I was on the tick of leaving the Honourable George helpless in bed. In a voice that I fear was broken I spoke of clothes for the day's wear which I had laid out for him the night before. He waved a hand bravely at us and sank back into his pillow as my new employer led me forth. There had been barely a glance between us to betoken the dreadfulness of the moment.

At our door I was pleased to note that a taximetre cab awaited us. I had acutely dreaded a walk through the streets, even of Paris, with my new employer garbed as he was. The blue satin cravat of itself would have been bound to insure us more attention than one would care for.

I fear we were both somewhat moody during the short ride. Each of us seemed to have matters of weight to reflect upon. Only upon reaching our destination did my companion brighten a bit. For a fare of five francs forty centimes he gave the driver a ten-franc piece and waited for no change.

"I always get around them that way," he said with an expression of the brightest cunning. "She used to have the laugh on me because I got so much counterfeit money handed to me. Now I don't take any change at all."

"Yes, sir," I said. "Quite right, sir."

"There's more than one way to skin a cat," he added as we ascended to the Floud's drawing-room, though why his mind should have flown to this brutal sport, if it be a sport, was quite beyond me. At the door he paused and hissed at me: "Remember, no matter what she says, if you treat me white I'll treat you white." And before I could frame any suitable response to this puzzling announcement he had opened the door and pushed me in, almost before I could remove my cap.

16

Seated at the table over coffee and rolls was Mrs. Effie. Her face brightened as she saw me, then froze to disapproval as her glance rested upon him I was to know as Cousin Egbert. I saw her capable mouth set in a straight line of determination.

"You did your very worst, didn't you?" she began. "But sit down and eat your breakfast. He'll soon change *that*." She turned to me. "Now, Ruggles, I hope you understand the situation, and I'm sure I can trust you to take no nonsense from him. You see plainly what you've got to do. I let him dress to suit himself this morning, so that you could know the worst at once. Take a good look at him— shoes, coat, hat—that dreadful cravat!"

"I call this a right pretty necktie," mumbled her victim over a crust of toast. She had poured coffee for him.

"You hear that?" she asked me. I bowed sympathetically.

"What does he look like?" she insisted. "Just tell him for his own good, please."

But this I could not do. True enough, during our short ride he had been reminding me of one of a pair of cross-talk comedians I had once seen in a music-hall. This, of course, was not a thing one could say.

"I dare say, Madam, he could be smartened up a bit. If I might take him to some good-class shop——"

"And burn the things he's got on——" she broke in.

"Not this here necktie," interrupted Cousin Egbert rather stubbornly. "It was give to me by Jeff Tuttle's littlest girl last Christmas; and this here Prince Albert coat—what's the matter of it, I'd like to know? It come right from the One Price Clothing Store at Red Gap, and it's plenty good to go to funerals in——"

"And then to a barber-shop with him," went on Mrs. Effie, who had paid no heed to his outburst. "Get him done right for once."

Her relative continued to nibble nervously at a bit of toast.

"I've done something with him myself," she said, watching him narrowly. "At first he insisted on having the whole bill-of-fare for breakfast, but I put my foot down, and now he's satisfied with the continental breakfast. That goes to show he has something in him, if we can only bring it out."

"Something in him, indeed, yes, Madam!" I assented, and Cousin Egbert, turning to me, winked heavily.

"I want him to look like some one," she resumed, "and I think you're the man can make him if you're firm with him; but you'll have to be firm, because he's full of tricks. And if he starts any rough stuff, just come to me."

"Quite so, Madam," I said, but I felt I was blushing with shame at hearing one of my own sex so slanged by a woman. That sort of thing would never do with us.

And yet there was something about this woman—something weirdly authoritative. She showed rather well in the morning light, her gray eyes crackling as she talked. She was wearing a most elaborate peignoir, and of course she should not have worn the diamonds; it seemed almost too much like the morning hour of a stage favourite; but still one felt that when she talked one would do well to listen.

Hereupon Cousin Egbert startled me once more.

"Won't you set up and have something with us, Mr. Ruggles?" he asked me.

I looked away, affecting not to have heard, and could feel Mrs. Effie scowling at him. He coughed into his cup and sprayed coffee well over himself. His intention had been obvious in the main, though exactly what he had meant by "setting up" I couldn't fancy—as if I had been a performing poodle!

The moment's embarrassment was well covered by Mrs. Effie, who again renewed her instructions, and from an escritoire brought me a sheaf of the pretentiously printed sheets which the French use in place of our banknotes.

"You will spare no expense," she directed, "and don't let me see him again until he looks like some one. Try to have him back here by five. Some very smart friends of ours are coming for tea."

"I won't drink tea at that outlandish hour for any one," said Cousin Egbert rather snappishly.

"You will at least refuse it like a man of the world, I hope," she replied icily, and he drooped submissive once more. "You see?" she added to me.

"Quite so, Madam," I said, and resolved to be firm and thorough with Cousin Egbert. In a way I was put upon my mettle. I swore to make him look like some one. Moreover, I now saw that his half-veiled threats of rebellion to me had been pure swank. I had in turn but to threaten to report him to this woman and he would be as clay in my hands.

I presently had him tucked into a closed taxicab, half-heartedly muttering expostulations and protests to which I paid not the least heed. During my strolls I had observed in what would have been Regent Street at home a rather good-class shop with an English name, and to this I now proceeded with my charge. I am afraid I rather hustled him across the pavement and into the shop, not knowing what tricks he might be up to, and not until he was well to the back did I attempt to explain myself to the shop-walker who had followed us. To him I then gave details of my charge's escape from a burning hotel the previous night, which accounted for his extraordinary garb of the moment, he having been obliged to accept the loan of garments that neither fitted him nor harmonized with one another. I mean to say, I did not care to have the chap suspect we would don tan boots, a frock-coat, and bowler hat except under the most tremendous compulsion.

Cousin Egbert stared at me open mouthed during this recital, but the shop-walker was only too readily convinced, as indeed who would not have been, and called an intelligent assistant to relieve our distress. With his help I swiftly selected an outfit that was not half bad for ready-to-wear garments. There was a black morning-coat, snug at the waist, moderately broad at the shoulders, closing with two buttons, its skirt sharply cut away from the lower button and reaching to the bend of the knee. The lapels were, of course, soft-rolled and joined the collar with a triangular notch. It is a coat of immense character when properly worn, and I was delighted to observe in the trying on that Cousin Egbert filled it rather smartly. Moreover, he submitted more meekly than I had hoped. The trousers I selected were of gray cloth, faintly striped, the waistcoat being of the same material as the coat, relieved at the neck-opening by an edging of white.

With the boots I had rather more trouble, as he refused to wear the patent leathers that I selected, together with the pearl gray spats, until I grimly requested the telephone assistant to put me through to the hotel, desiring to speak to Mrs. Senator Floud. This brought him around, although muttering, and I had less trouble with shirts, collars, and cravats. I chose a shirt of white piqué, a wing collar with small, square-cornered tabs, and a pearl ascot.

Then in a cabinet I superintended Cousin Egbert's change of raiment. We clashed again in the matter of sock-suspenders, which I was astounded to observe he did not possess. He insisted that he had never worn them—garters he called them—and never would if he were shot for it, so I decided to be content with what I had already gained.

By dint of urging and threatening I at length achieved my ground-work and was more than a little pleased with my effect, as was the shop-assistant, after I had tied the pearl ascot and adjusted a quiet tie-pin of my own choosing.

"Now I hope you're satisfied!" growled my charge, seizing his bowler hat and edging off.

"By no means," I said coldly. "The hat, if you please, sir."

He gave it up rebelliously, and I had again to threaten him with the telephone before he would submit to a top-hat with a moderate bell and broad brim. Surveying this in the glass, however, he became perceptibly reconciled. It was plain that he rather fancied it, though as yet he wore it consciously and would turn his head slowly and painfully, as if his neck were stiffened.

Having chosen the proper gloves, I was, I repeat, more than pleased with this severely simple scheme of black, white, and gray. I felt I had been wise to resist any tendency to colour, even to the most delicate of pastel tints. My last selection was a smartish Malacca stick, the ideal stick for town wear, which I thrust into the defenceless hands of my client.

"And now, sir," I said firmly, "it is but a step to a barber's stop where English is spoken." And ruefully he accompanied me. I dare say that by that time he had discovered that I was not to be trifled with, for during his hour in the barber's chair he did not once rebel openly. Only at times would he roll his eyes to mine in dumb appeal. There was in them something of the utter confiding helplessness I had noted in the eyes of an old setter at Chaynes-Wotten when I had been called upon to assist the undergardener in chloroforming him. I mean to say, the dog had jolly well known something terrible was being done to him, yet his eyes seemed to say he knew it must be all for the best and that he trusted us. It was this look I caught as I gave directions about the trimming of the hair, and especially when I directed that something radical should be done to the long, grayish moustache that fell to either side of his chin in the form of a horseshoe. I myself was puzzled by this difficulty, but the barber solved it rather neatly, I thought, after a whispered consultation with me. He snipped a bit off each end and then stoutly waxed the whole affair until the ends stood stiffly out with distinct military implications. I shall never forget, and indeed I was not a little touched by the look of quivering anguish in the eyes of my client when he first beheld this novel effect. And yet when we were once more in the street I could not but admit that the change was worth all that it had cost him in suffering. Strangely, he now looked like some one, especially after I had persuaded him to a carnation for his buttonhole. I cannot say that his carriage was all that it should have been, and he was still conscious of his smart attire, but I nevertheless felt a distinct thrill of pride in my own work, and was eager to reveal him to Mrs. Effie in his new guise.

But first he would have luncheon—dinner he called it—and I was not averse to this, for I had put in a long and trying morning. I went with him to the little restaurant where Americans had made so much trouble about ham and eggs, and there he insisted that I should join him in chops and potatoes and ale. I thought it only proper then to point out to him that there was certain differences in our walks of life which should be more or less denoted by his manner of addressing me. Among other things he should not address me as Mr. Ruggles, nor was it customary for a valet to eat at the same table with his master. He seemed much interested in these distinctions and thereupon addressed me as "Colonel," which was of course quite absurd, but this I could not make him see. Thereafter, I may say, that he called me impartially either "Colonel" or "Bill." It was a situation that I had never before been obliged to meet, and I found it trying in the extreme. He was a chap who seemed ready to pal up with any one, and I could not but recall the strange assertion I had so often heard that in America one never knows who is one's superior. Fancy that! It would never do with us. I could only determine to be on my guard.

Our luncheon done, he consented to accompany me to the hotel of the Honourable George, whence I wished to remove my belongings. I should have preferred to go alone, but I was too fearful of what he might do to himself or his clothes in my absence.

We found the Honourable George still in bed, as I had feared. He had, it seemed, been unable to discover his collar studs, which, though I had placed them in a fresh shirt for him, he had carelessly covered with a blanket. Begging Cousin Egbert to be seated in my room, I did a few of the more obvious things required by my late master.

"You'd leave me here like a rat in a trap," he said reproachfully, which I thought almost quite a little unjust. I mean to say, it had all been his own doing, he having lost me in the game of drawing poker, so why should he row me about it now? I silently laid out the shirt once more.

"You might have told me where I'm to find my brown tweeds and the body linen."

Again he was addressing me as if I had voluntarily left him without notice, but I observed that he was still mildly speckled from the night before, so I handed him the fruit-lozenges, and went to pack my own box. Cousin Egbert I found sitting as I had left him, on the edge of a chair, carefully holding his hat, stick, and gloves, and staring into the wall. He had promised me faithfully not to fumble with his cravat, and evidently he had not once stirred. I packed my box swiftly—my "grip," as he called it—and we were presently off once more, without another sight of the Honourable George, who was to join us at tea. I could hear him moving about, using rather ultra-frightful language, but I lacked heart for further speech with him at the moment.

An hour later, in the Floud drawing-room, I had the supreme satisfaction of displaying to Mrs. Effie the happy changes I had been able to effect in my charge. Posing him, I knocked at the door of her chamber. She came at once and drew a long breath as she surveyed him, from varnished boots, spats, and coat to top-hat, which he still wore. He leaned rather well on his stick, the hand to his hip, the elbow out, while the other hand lightly held his gloves. A moment she looked, then gave a low cry of wonder and delight, so that I felt repaid for my trouble. Indeed, as she faced me to thank me I could see that her eyes were dimmed.

"Wonderful!" she exclaimed. "Now he looks like some one!" And I distinctly perceived that only just in time did she repress an impulse to grasp me by the hand. Under the circumstances I am not sure that I wouldn't have overlooked the lapse had she yielded to it. "Wonderful!" she said again.

Hereupon Cousin Egbert, much embarrassed, leaned his stick against the wall; the stick fell, and in reaching down for it his hat fell, and in reaching for that he dropped his gloves; but I soon restored him to order and he was safely seated where he might be studied in further detail, especially as to his moustaches, which I had considered rather the supreme touch.

"He looks exactly like some well-known clubman," exclaimed Mrs. Effie.

Her relative growled as if he were quite ready to savage her.

"Like a man about town," she murmured. "Who would have thought he had it in him until you brought it out?" I knew then that we two should understand each other.

21

The slight tension was here relieved by two of the hotel servants who brought tea things. At a nod from Mrs. Effie I directed the laying out of these.

At that moment came the other Floud, he of the eyebrows, and a cousin cub called Elmer, who, I understood, studied art. I became aware that they were both suddenly engaged and silenced by the sight of Cousin Egbert. I caught their amazed stares, and then terrifically they broke into gales of laughter. The cub threw himself on a couch, waving his feet in the air, and holding his middle as if he'd suffered a sudden acute dyspepsia, while the elder threw his head back and shrieked hysterically. Cousin Egbert merely glared at them and, endeavouring to stroke his moustache, succeeded in unwaxing one side of it so that it once more hung limply down his chin, whereat they renewed their boorishness. The elder Floud was now quite dangerously purple, and the cub on the couch was shrieking: "No matter how dark the clouds, remember she is still your stepmother," or words to some such silly effect as that. How it might have ended I hardly dare conjecture—perhaps Cousin Egbert would presently have roughed them—but a knock sounded, and it became my duty to open our door upon other guests, women mostly; Americans in Paris; that sort of thing.

I served the tea amid their babble. The Honourable George was shown up a bit later, having done to himself quite all I thought he might in the matter of dress. In spite of serious discrepancies in his attire, however, I saw that Mrs. Effie meant to lionize him tremendously. With vast ceremony he was presented to her guests— the Honourable George Augustus Vane-Basingwell, brother of his lordship the Earl of Brinstead. The women fluttered about him rather, though he behaved moodily, and at the first opportunity fell to the tea and cakes quite wholeheartedly.

In spite of my aversion to the American wilderness, I felt a bit of professional pride in reflecting that my first day in this new service was about to end so auspiciously. Yet even in that moment, being as yet unfamiliar with the room's lesser furniture, I stumbled slightly against a hassock hid from me by the tray I carried. A cup of tea was lost, though my recovery was quick. Too late I observed that the hitherto self-effacing Cousin Egbert was in range of my clumsiness.

"There goes tea all over my new pants!" he said in a high, pained voice.

"Sorry, indeed, sir," said I, a ready napkin in hand. "Let me dry it, sir!"

"Yes, sir, I fancy quite so, sir," said he.

I most truly would have liked to shake him smartly for this. I saw that my work was cut out for me among these Americans, from whom at their best one expects so little.

CHAPTER THREE

As I brisked out of bed the following morning at half-after six, I could not but wonder rather nervously what the day might have in store for me. I was obliged to admit that what I was in for looked a bit thick. As I opened my door I heard stealthy footsteps down the hall and looked out in time to observe Cousin Egbert entering his own room. It was not this that startled me. He would have been abroad, I knew, for the ham and eggs that were forbidden him. Yet I stood aghast, for with the lounge-suit of tweeds I had selected the day before he had worn his top-hat! I am aware that these things I relate of him may not be credited. I can only put them down in all sincerity.

I hastened to him and removed the thing from his head. I fear it was not with the utmost deference, for I have my human moments.

"It's not done, sir," I protested. He saw that I was offended.

"All right, sir," he replied meekly. "But how was I to know? I thought it kind of set me off." He referred to it as a "stove-pipe" hat. I knew then that I should find myself overlooking many things in him. He was not a person one could be stern with, and I even promised that Mrs. Effie should not be told of his offence, he promising in turn never again to stir abroad without first submitting himself to me and agreeing also to wear sock-suspenders from that day forth. I saw, indeed, that diplomacy might work wonders with him.

At breakfast in the drawing-room, during which Cousin Egbert earned warm praise from Mrs. Effie for his lack of appetite (he winking violently at me during this), I learned that I should be expected to accompany him to a certain art gallery which corresponds to our British Museum. I was a bit surprised, indeed, to learn that he largely spent his days there, and was accustomed to make notes of the various objects of interest.

"I insisted," explained Mrs. Effie, "that he should absorb all the culture he could on his trip abroad, so I got him a notebook in which he puts down his impressions, and I must say he's done fine. Some of his remarks are so good that when he gets home I may have him read a paper before our Onwards and Upwards Club."

Cousin Egbert wriggled modestly at this and said: "Shucks!" which I took to be a term of deprecation.

"You needn't pretend," said Mrs. Effie. "Just let Ruggles here look over some of the notes you have made," and she handed me a notebook of ruled paper in which there was a deal of writing. I glanced, as bidden, at one or two of the paragraphs, and confess that I, too, was amazed at the fluency and insight displayed along lines in which I should have thought the man entirely uninformed. "This choice work represents the first or formative period of the Master," began one note, "but distinctly foreshadows that later method which

23

made him at once the hope and despair of his contemporaries. In the 'Portrait of the Artist by Himself' we have a canvas that well repays patient study, since here is displayed in its full flower that ruthless realism, happily attenuated by a superbly subtle delicacy of brush work——" It was really quite amazing, and I perceived for the first time that Cousin Egbert must be "a diamond in the rough," as the well-known saying has it. I felt, indeed, that I would be very pleased to accompany him on one of his instructive strolls through this gallery, for I have always been of a studious habit and anxious to improve myself in the fine arts.

"You see?" asked Mrs. Effie, when I had perused this fragment. "And yet folks back home would tell you that he's just a——" Cousin Egbert here coughed alarmingly. "No matter," she continued. "He'll show them that he's got something in him, mark my words."

"Quite so, Madam," I said, "and I shall consider it a privilege to be present when he further prosecutes his art studies."

"You may keep him out till dinner-time," she continued. "I'm shopping this morning, and in the afternoon I shall motor to have tea in the Boy with the Senator and Mr. Nevil Vane-Basingwell."

Presently, then, my charge and I set out for what I hoped was to be a peaceful and instructive day among objects of art, though first I was obliged to escort him to a hatter's and glover's to remedy some minor discrepancies in his attire. He was very pleased when I permitted him to select his own hat. I was safe in this, as the shop was really artists in gentlemen's headwear, and carried only shapes, I observed, that were confined to exclusive firms so as to insure their being worn by the right set. As to gloves and a stick, he was again rather pettish and had to be set right with some firmness. He declared he had lost his stick and gloves of the previous day. I discovered later that he had presented them to the lift attendant. But I soon convinced him that he would not be let to appear without these adjuncts to a gentleman's toilet.

Then, having once more stood by at the barber's while he was shaved and his moustaches firmly waxed anew, I saw that he was fit at last for his art studies. The barber this day suggested curling the moustaches with a heated iron, but at this my charge fell into so unseemly a rage that I deemed it wise not to insist. He, indeed, bluntly threatened a nameless violence to the barber if he were so much as touched with the iron, and revealed an altogether shocking gift for profanity, saying loudly: "I'll be—dashed—if you will!" I mean to say, I have written "dashed" for what he actually said. But at length I had him once more quieted.

"Now, sir," I said, when I had got him from the barber's shop, to the barber's manifest relief: "I fancy we've time to do a few objects of art before luncheon. I've the book here for your comments," I added.

"Quite so," he replied, and led me at a rapid pace along the street in what I presumed was the direction of the art museum. At the end of a few blocks he paused at one of those open-air public houses that disgracefully line the streets of the French capital. I mean to say that chairs and tables are set out upon the pavement in the most brazen manner and occupied by the populace, who there drink their silly beverages and idle away their time. After scanning the score or so of persons present, even at so early an hour as ten of the morning, he fell into one of the iron chairs at one of the iron tables and motioned me to another at his side.

When I had seated myself he said "Beer" to the waiter who appeared, and held up two fingers.

"Now, look at here," he resumed to me, "this is a good place to do about four pages of art, and then we can go out and have some recreation somewhere." Seeing that I was puzzled, he added: "This way—you take that notebook and write in it out of this here other book till I think you've done enough, then I'll tell you to stop." And while I was still bewildered, he drew from an inner pocket a small, well-thumbed volume which I took from him and saw to be entitled "One Hundred Masterpieces of the Louvre."

"Open her about the middle," he directed, "and pick out something that begins good, like 'Here the true art-lover will stand entranced——' You got to write it, because I guess you can write faster than what I can. I'll tell her I dictated to you. Get a hustle on now, so's we can get through. Write down about four pages of that stuff."

Stunned I was for a moment at his audacity. Too plainly I saw through his deception. Each day, doubtless, he had come to a low place of this sort and copied into the notebook from the printed volume.

"But, sir," I protested, "why not at least go to the gallery where these art objects are stored? Copy the notes there if that must be done."

"I don't know where the darned place is," he confessed. "I did start for it the first day, but I run into a Punch and Judy show in a little park, and I just couldn't get away from it, it was so comical, with all the French kids hollering their heads off at it. Anyway, what's the use? I'd rather set here in front of this saloon, where everything is nice."

"It's very extraordinary, sir," I said, wondering if I oughtn't to cut off to the hotel and warn Mrs. Effie so that she might do a heated foot to him, as he had once expressed it.

"Well, I guess I've got my rights as well as anybody," he insisted. "I'll be pushed just so far and no farther, not if I never get any more cultured than a jack-rabbit. And now you better go on and write or I'll be—dashed—if I'll ever wear another thing you tell me to."

He had a most bitter and dangerous expression on his face, so I thought best to humour him once more. Accordingly I set about writing in his notebook from the volume of criticism he had supplied.

"Change a word now and then and skip around here and there," he suggested as I wrote, "so's it'll sound more like me."

"Quite so, sir," I said, and continued to transcribe from the printed page. I was beginning the fifth page in the notebook, being in the midst of an enthusiastic description of the bit of statuary entitled "The Winged Victory," when I was startled by a wild yell in my ear. Cousin Egbert had leaped to his feet and now danced in the middle of the pavement, waving his stick and hat high in the air and shouting incoherently. At once we attracted the most undesirable attention from the loungers about us, the waiters and the passers-by in the street, many of whom stopped at once to survey my charge with the liveliest interest. It was then I saw that he had merely wished to attract the attention of some one passing in a cab. Half a block down the boulevard I saw a man likewise waving excitedly, standing erect in the cab to do so. The cab thereupon turned sharply, came back on the opposite side of the street, crossed over to us, and the occupant alighted.

He was an American, as one might have fancied from his behaviour, a tall, dark-skinned person, wearing a drooping moustache after the former style of Cousin Egbert, supplemented by an imperial. He wore a loose-fitting suit of black which had evidently received no proper attention from the day he purchased it. Under a folded collar he wore a narrow cravat tied in a bowknot, and in the bosom of his white shirt there sparkled a diamond such as might have come from a collection of crown-jewels. This much I had time to notice as he neared us. Cousin Egbert had not ceased to shout, nor had he paid the least attention to my tugs at his coat. When the cab's occupant descended to the pavement they fell upon each other and did for some moments a wild dance such as I imagine they might have seen the red Indians of western America perform. Most savagely they punched each other, calling out in the meantime: "Well, old horse!" and "Who'd ever expected to see you here, darn your old skin!" (Their actual phrases, be it remembered.)

The crowd, I was glad to note, fell rapidly away, many of them shrugging their shoulders in a way the French have, and even the waiters about us quickly lost interest in the pair, as if they were hardened to the sight of Americans greeting one another. The two were still saying: "Well! well!" rather breathlessly, but had become a bit more coherent.

"Jeff Tuttle, you—dashed—old long-horn!" exclaimed Cousin Egbert.

"Good old Sour-dough!" exploded the other. "Ain't this just like old home week!"

"I thought mebbe you wouldn't know me with all my beadwork and my new war-bonnet on," continued Cousin Egbert.

"Know you, why, you knock-kneed old Siwash, I could pick out your hide in a tanyard!"

"Well, well, well!" replied Cousin Egbert.

26

"Well, well, well!" said the other, and again they dealt each other smart blows.

"Where'd you turn up from?" demanded Cousin Egbert.

"Europe," said the other. "We been all over Europe and Italy—just come from some place up over the divide where they talk Dutch, the Madam and the two girls and me, with the Reverend Timmins and his wife riding line on us. Say, he's an out-and-out devil for cathedrals—it's just one church after another with him— Baptist, Methodist, Presbyterian, Lutheran, takes 'em all in—never overlooks a bet. He's got Addie and the girls out now. My gosh! it's solemn work! Me? I ducked out this morning."

"How'd you do it?"

"Told the little woman I had to have a tooth pulled—I was working it up on the train all day yesterday. Say, what you all rigged out like that for, Sour-dough, and what you done to your face?"

Cousin Egbert here turned to me in some embarrassment. "Colonel Ruggles, shake hands with my friend Jeff Tuttle from the State of Washington."

"Pleased to meet you, Colonel," said the other before I could explain that I had no military title whatever, never having, in fact, served our King, even in the ranks. He shook my hand warmly.

"Any friend of Sour-dough Floud's is all right with me," he assured me. "What's the matter with having a drink?"

"Say, listen here! I wouldn't have to be blinded and backed into it," said Cousin Egbert, enigmatically, I thought, but as they sat down I, too, seated myself. Something within me had sounded a warning. As well as I know it now I knew then in my inmost soul that I should summon Mrs. Effie before matters went farther.

"Beer is all I know how to say," suggested Cousin Egbert.

"Leave that to me," said his new friend masterfully. "Where's the boy? Here, boy! Veesky-soda! That's French for high-ball," he explained. "I've had to pick up a lot of their lingo."

Cousin Egbert looked at him admiringly. "Good old Jeff!" he said simply. He glanced aside to me for a second with downright hostility, then turned back to his friend. "Something tells me, Jeff, that this is going to be the first happy day I've had since I crossed the state line. I've been pestered to death, Jeff—what with Mrs. Effie after me to improve myself so's I can be a social credit to her back in Red Gap, and learn to wear clothes and go without my breakfast and attend art galleries. If you'd stand by me I'd throw her down good and hard right now, but you know what she is——"

"I sure do," put in Mr. Tuttle so fervently that I knew he spoke the truth. "That woman can bite through nails. But here's your drink, Sour-dough. Maybe it will cheer you up."

Extraordinary! I mean to say, biting through nails.

"Three rousing cheers!" exclaimed Cousin Egbert with more animation than I had ever known him display.

"Here's looking at you, Colonel," said his friend to me, whereupon I partook of the drink, not wishing to offend him. Decidedly he was not vogue. His hat was remarkable, being of a black felt with high crown and a wide and flopping brim. Across his waistcoat was a watch-chain of heavy links, with a weighty charm consisting of a sculptured gold horse in full gallop. That sort of thing would never do with us.

"Here, George," he immediately called to the waiter, for they had quickly drained their glasses, "tell the bartender three more. By gosh! but that's good, after the way I've been held down."

"Me, too," said Cousin Egbert. "I didn't know how to say it in French."

"The Reverend held me down," continued the Tuttle person. "'A glass of native wine,' he says, 'may perhaps be taken now and then without harm.' 'Well,' I says, 'leave us have ales, wines, liquors, and cigars,' I says, but not him. I'd get a thimbleful of elderberry wine or something about every second Friday, except when I'd duck out the side door of a church and find some caffy. Here, George, foomer, foomer—bring us some seegars, and then stay on that spot—I may want you."

"Well, well!" said Cousin Egbert again, as if the meeting were still incredible.

"You old stinging-lizard!" responded the other affectionately. The cigars were brought and I felt constrained to light one.

"The State of Washington needn't ever get nervous over the prospect of losing me," said the Tuttle person, biting off the end of his cigar.

I gathered at once that the Americans have actually named one of our colonies "Washington" after the rebel George Washington, though one would have thought that the indelicacy of this would have been only too apparent. But, then, I recalled, as well, the city where their so-called parliament assembles, Washington, D. C. Doubtless the initials indicate that it was named in "honour" of another member of this notorious family. I could not but reflect how shocked our King would be to learn of this effrontery.

Cousin Egbert, who had been for some moments moving his lips without sound, here spoke:

"I'm going to try it myself," he said. "Here, Charley, veesky-soda! He made me right off," he continued as the waiter disappeared. "Say, Jeff, I bet I could have learned a lot of this language if I'd had some one like you around."

"Well, it took me some time to get the accent," replied the other with a modesty which I could detect was assumed. More acutely than ever was I conscious of a psychic warning to separate these two, and I resolved to act upon it with the utmost diplomacy. The third whiskey and soda was served us.

"Three rousing cheers!" said Cousin Egbert.

"Here's looking at you!" said the other, and I drank. When my glass was drained I arose briskly and said:

"I think we should be getting along now, sir, if Mr. Tuttle will be good enough to excuse us." They both stared at me.

"Yes, sir—I fancy not, sir," said Cousin Egbert.

"Stop your kidding, you fat rascal!" said the other.

"Old Bill means all right," said Cousin Egbert, "so don't let him irritate you. Bill's our new hired man. He's all right—just let him talk along."

"Can't he talk setting down?" asked the other. "Does he have to stand up every time he talks? Ain't that a good chair?" he demanded of me. "Here, take mine," and to my great embarrassment he arose and offered me his chair in such a manner that I felt moved to accept it. Thereupon he took the chair I had vacated and beamed upon us, "Now that we're all home-folks, together once more, I would suggest a bit of refreshment. Boy, veesky-soda!"

"I fancy so, sir," said Cousin Egbert, dreamily contemplating me as the order was served. I was conscious even then that he seemed to be studying my attire with a critical eye, and indeed he remarked as if to himself: "What a coat!" I was rather shocked by this, for my suit was quite a decent lounge-suit that had become too snug for the Honourable George some two years before. Yet something warned me to ignore the comment.

"Three rousing cheers!" he said as the drink was served.

"Here's looking at you!" said the Tuttle person.

And again I drank with them, against my better judgment, wondering if I might escape long enough to be put through to Mrs. Floud on the telephone. Too plainly the situation was rapidly getting out of hand, and yet I hesitated. The Tuttle person under an exterior geniality was rather abrupt. And, moreover, I now recalled having observed a person much like him in manner and attire in a certain cinema drama of the far Wild West. He had been a constable or sheriff in the piece and had subdued a band of armed border ruffians with only a small pocket pistol. I thought it as well not to cross him.

When they had drunk, each one again said, "Well! well!"

"You old maverick!" said Cousin Egbert.

"You—dashed—old horned toad!" responded his friend.

"What's the matter with a little snack?"

"Not a thing on earth. My appetite ain't been so powerful craving since Heck was a pup."

29

These were their actual words, though it may not be believed. The Tuttle person now approached his cabman, who had waited beside the curb.

"Say, Frank," he began, "Ally restorong," and this he supplemented with a crude but informing pantomime of one eating. Cousin Egbert was already seated in the cab, and I could do nothing but follow. "Ally restorong!" commanded our new friend in a louder tone, and the cabman with an explosion of understanding drove rapidly off.

"It's a genuine wonder to me how you learned the language so quick," said Cousin Egbert.

"It's all in the accent," protested the other. I occupied a narrow seat in the front. Facing me in the back seat, they lolled easily and smoked their cigars. Down the thronged boulevard we proceeded at a rapid pace and were passing presently before an immense gray edifice which I recognized as the so-called Louvre from its illustration on the cover of Cousin Egbert's art book. He himself regarded it with interest, though I fancy he did not recognize it, for, waving his cigar toward it, he announced to his friend:

"The Public Library." His friend surveyed the building with every sign of approval.

"That Carnegie is a hot sport, all right," he declared warmly. "I'll bet that shack set him back some."

"Three rousing cheers!" said Cousin Egbert, without point that I could detect.

We now crossed their Thames over what would have been Westminster Bridge, I fancy, and were presently bowling through a sort of Battersea part of the city. The streets grew quite narrow and the shops smaller, and I found myself wondering not without alarm what sort of restaurant our abrupt friend had chosen.

"Three rousing cheers!" said Cousin Egbert from time to time, with almost childish delight.

Debouching from a narrow street again into what the French term a boulevard, we halted before what was indeed a restaurant, for several tables were laid on the pavement before the door, but I saw at once that it was anything but a nice place. "Au Rendezvous des Cochers Fideles," read the announcement on the flap of the awning, and truly enough it was a low resort frequented by cabbies— "The meeting-place of faithful coachmen." Along the curb half a score of horses were eating from their bags, while their drivers lounged before the place, eating, drinking, and conversing excitedly in their grotesque jargon.

We descended, in spite of the repellent aspect of the place, and our driver went to the foot of the line, where he fed his own horse. Cousin Egbert, already at one of the open-air tables, was rapping smartly for a waiter.

"What's the matter with having just one little one before grub?" asked the Tuttle person as we joined him. He had a most curious fashion of speech. I mean to say, when he suggested anything whatsoever he invariably wished to know what might be the matter with it.

"Veesky-soda!" demanded Cousin Egbert of the serving person who now appeared, "and ask your driver to have one," he then urged his friend.

The latter hereupon addressed the cabman who had now come up.

"Vooley-voos take something!" he demanded, and the cabman appeared to accept.

"Vooley-voos your friends take something, too?" he demanded further, with a gesture that embraced all the cabmen present, and these, too, appeared to accept with the utmost cordiality.

"You're a wonder, Jeff," said Cousin Egbert. "You talk it like a professor."

"It come natural to me," said the fellow, "and it's a good thing, too. If you know a little French you can go all over Europe without a bit of trouble."

Inside the place was all activity, for many cabmen were now accepting the proffered hospitality, and calling "votry santy!" to their host, who seemed much pleased. Then to my amazement Cousin Egbert insisted that our cabman should sit at table with us. I trust I have as little foolish pride as most people, but this did seem like crowding it on a bit thick. In fact, it looked rather dicky. I was glad to remember that we were in what seemed to be the foreign quarter of the town, where it was probable that no one would recognize us. The drink came, though our cabman refused the whiskey and secured a bottle of native wine.

"Three rousing cheers!" said Cousin Egbert as we drank once more, and added as an afterthought, "What a beautiful world we live in!"

"Vooley-voos make-um bring dinner!" said the Tuttle person to the cabman, who thereupon spoke at length in his native tongue to the waiter. By this means we secured a soup that was not half bad and presently a stew of mutton which Cousin Egbert declared was "some goo." To my astonishment I ate heartily, even in such raffish surroundings. In fact, I found myself pigging it with the rest of them. With coffee, cigars were brought from the tobacconist's next-door, each cabman present accepting one. Our own man was plainly feeling a vast pride in his party, and now circulated among his fellows with an account of our merits.

"This is what I call life," said the Tuttle person, leaning back in his chair.

"I'm coming right back here every day," declared Cousin Egbert happily.

"What's the matter with a little drive to see some well-known objects of interest?" inquired his friend.

"Not art galleries," insisted Cousin Egbert.

"And not churches," said his friend. "Every day's been Sunday with me long enough."

"And not clothing stores," said Cousin Egbert firmly. "The Colonel here is awful fussy about my clothes," he added.

"Is, heh?" inquired his friend. "How do you like this hat of mine?" he asked, turning to me. It was that sudden I nearly fluffed the catch, but recovered myself in time.

"I should consider it a hat of sound wearing properties, sir," I said.

He took it off, examined it carefully, and replaced it.

"So far, so good," he said gravely. "But why be fussy about clothes when God has given you only one life to live?"

"Don't argue about religion," warned Cousin Egbert.

"I always like to see people well dressed, sir," I said, "because it makes such a difference in their appearance."

He slapped his thigh fiercely. "My gosh! that's true. He's got you there, Sourdough. I never thought of that."

"He makes me wear these chest-protectors on my ankles," said Cousin Egbert bitterly, extending one foot.

"What's the matter of taking a little drive to see some well-known objects of interest?" said his friend.

"Not art galleries," said Cousin Egbert firmly.

"We said that before—and not churches."

"And not gents' furnishing goods."

"You said that before."

"Well, you said not churches before."

"Well, what's the matter with taking a little drive?"

"Not art galleries," insisted Cousin Egbert. The thing seemed interminable. I mean to say, they went about the circle as before. It looked to me as if they were having a bit of a spree.

"We'll have one last drink," said the Tuttle person.

"No," said Cousin Egbert firmly, "not another drop. Don't you see the condition poor Bill here is in?" To my amazement he was referring to me. Candidly, he was attempting to convey the impression that I had taken a drop too much. The other regarded me intently.

"Pickled," he said.

"Always affects him that way," said Cousin Egbert. "He's got no head for it."

"Beg pardon, sir," I said, wishing to explain, but this I was not let to do.

"Don't start anything like that here," broke in the Tuttle person, "the police wouldn't stand for it. Just keep quiet and remember you're among friends."

"Yes, sir; quite so, sir," said I, being somewhat puzzled by these strange words. "I was merely——"

"Look out, Jeff," warned Cousin Egbert, interrupting me; "he's a devil when he starts."

"Have you got a knife?" demanded the other suddenly.

"I fancy so, sir," I answered, and produced from my waistcoat pocket the small metal-handled affair I have long carried. This he quickly seized from me.

"You can keep your gun," he remarked, "but you can't be trusted with this in your condition. I ain't afraid of a gun, but I am afraid of a knife. You could have backed me off the board any time with this knife."

"Didn't I tell you?" asked Cousin Egbert.

"Beg pardon, sir," I began, for this was drawing it quite too thick, but again he interrupted me.

"We'd better get him away from this place right off," he said.

"A drive in the fresh air might fix him," suggested Cousin Egbert. "He's as good a scout as you want to know when he's himself." Hereupon, calling our waiting cabman, they both, to my embarrassment, assisted me to the vehicle.

"Ally caffy!" directed the Tuttle person, and we were driven off, to the raised hats of the remaining cabmen, through many long, quiet streets.

"I wouldn't have had this happen for anything," said Cousin Egbert, indicating me.

"Lucky I got that knife away from him," said the other.

To this I thought it best to remain silent, it being plain that the men were both well along, so to say.

The cab now approached an open square from which issued discordant blasts of music. One glance showed it to be a street fair. I prayed that we might pass it, but my companions hailed it with delight and at once halted the cabby.

"Ally caffy on the corner," directed the Tuttle person, and once more we were seated at an iron table with whiskey and soda ordered. Before us was the street fair in all its silly activity. There were many tinselled booths at which games of chance or marksmanship were played, or at which articles of ornament or household decoration were displayed for sale, and about these were throngs of low-class French idling away their afternoon in that mad pursuit of pleasure which is so characteristic of this race. In the centre of the place was a carrousel from which came the blare of a steam orchestrion playing the "Marseillaise," one of their popular songs. From where I sat I could perceive the circle of gaudily painted beasts that revolved about this musical atrocity. A fashion of horses seemed to predominate, but there was also an ostrich (a bearded Frenchman being astride this bird for the moment), a zebra, a lion, and a gaudily emblazoned giraffe. I shuddered as I thought of the evil possibilities that might be suggested to my two companions by this affair. For the moment I was pleased to note that they had forgotten my supposed indisposition, yet another equally absurd complication ensued when the drink arrived.

"Say, don't your friend ever loosen up?" asked the Tuttle person of Cousin Egbert.

"Tighter than Dick's hatband," replied the latter.

"And then some! He ain't bought once. Say, Bo," he continued to me as I was striving to divine the drift of these comments, "have I got my fingers crossed or not?"

Seeing that he held one hand behind him I thought to humour him by saying, "I fancy so, sir."

"He means 'yes,'" said Cousin Egbert.

The other held his hand before me with the first two fingers spread wide apart. "You lost," he said. "How's that, Sour-dough? We stuck him the first rattle out of the box."

"Good work," said Cousin Egbert. "You're stuck for this round," he added to me. "Three rousing cheers!"

I readily perceived that they meant me to pay the score, which I accordingly did, though I at once suspected the fairness of the game. I mean to say, if my opponent had been a trickster he could easily have rearranged his fingers to defeat me before displaying them. I do not say it was done in this instance. I am merely pointing out that it left open a way to trickery. I mean to say, one would wish to be assured of his opponent's social standing before playing this game extensively.

No sooner had we finished the drink than the Tuttle person said to me:

"I'll give you one chance to get even. I'll guess your fingers this time." Accordingly I put one hand behind me and firmly crossed the fingers, fancying that he would guess them to be uncrossed. Instead of which he called out "Crossed," and I was obliged to show them in that wise, though, as before pointed out, I could easily have defeated him by uncrossing them before revealing my hand. I mean to say, it is not on the face of it a game one would care to play with casual acquaintances, and I questioned even then in my own mind its prevalence in the States. (As a matter of fact, I may say that in my later life in the States I could find no trace of it, and now believe it to have been a pure invention on the part of the Tuttle person. I mean to say, I later became convinced that it was, properly speaking, not a game at all.)

Again they were hugely delighted at my loss and rapped smartly on the table for more drink, and now to my embarrassment I discovered that I lacked the money to pay for this "round" as they would call it.

"Beg pardon, sir," said I discreetly to Cousin Egbert, "but if you could let me have a bit of change, a half-crown or so——" To my surprise he regarded me coldly and shook his head emphatically in the negative.

"Not me," he said; "I've been had too often. You're a good smooth talker and you may be all right, but I can't take a chance at my time of life."

"What's he want now?" asked the other.

"The old story," said Cousin Egbert: "come off and left his purse on the hatrack or out in the woodshed some place." This was the height of absurdity, for I had said nothing of the sort.

"I was looking for something like that," said the other "I never make a mistake in faces. You got a watch there haven't you?"

"Yes, sir," I said, and laid on the table my silver English half-hunter with Albert. They both fell to examining this with interest, and presently the Tuttle person spoke up excitedly:

"Well, darn my skin if he ain't got a genuine double Gazottz. How did you come by this, my man?" he demanded sharply.

"It came from my brother-in-law, sir," I explained, "six years ago as security for a trifling loan."

"He sounds honest enough," said the Tuttle person to Cousin Egbert.

"Yes, but maybe it ain't a regular double Gazottz," said the latter. "The market is flooded with imitations."

"No, sir, I can't be fooled on them boys," insisted the other. "Blindfold me and I could pick a double Gazottz out every time. I'm going to take a chance on it, anyway." Whereupon the fellow pocketed my watch and from his wallet passed me a note of the so-called French money which I was astounded to observe was for the equivalent of four pounds, or one hundred francs, as the French will have it. "I'll advance that much on it," he said, "but don't ask for another cent until I've had it thoroughly gone over by a plumber. It may have moths in it."

It seemed to me that the chap was quite off his head, for the watch was worth not more than ten shillings at the most, though what a double Gazottz might be I could not guess. However, I saw it would be wise to appear to accept the loan, and tendered the note in payment of the score.

When I had secured the change I sought to intimate that we should be leaving. I thought even the street fair would be better for us than this rapid consumption of stimulants.

"I bet he'd go without buying," said Cousin Egbert.

"No, he wouldn't," said the other. "He knows what's customary in a case like this. He's just a little embarrassed. Wait and see if I ain't right." At which they both sat and stared at me in silence for some moments until at last I ordered more drink, as I saw was expected of me.

"He wants the cabman to have one with him," said Cousin Egbert, whereat the other not only beckoned our cabby to join us, but called to two labourers who were passing, and also induced the waiter who served us to join in the "round."

"He seems to have a lot of tough friends," said Cousin Egbert as we all drank, though he well knew I had extended none of these invitations.

"Acts like a drunken sailor soon as he gets a little money," said the other.

"Three rousing cheers!" replied Cousin Egbert, and to my great chagrin he leaped to his feet, seized one of the navvies about the waist, and there on the public pavement did a crude dance with him to the strain of the "Marseillaise" from the steam orchestrion. Not only this, but when the music had ceased he traded hats with the navvy, securing a most shocking affair in place of the new one, and as they parted he presented the fellow with the gloves and stick I had purchased for him that very morning. As I stared aghast at this *faux pas* the navvy, with his new hat at an angle and twirling the stick, proceeded down the street with mincing steps and exaggerated airs of gentility, to the applause of the entire crowd, including Cousin Egbert.

"This ain't quite the hat I want," he said as he returned to us, "but the day is young. I'll have other chances," and with the help of the public-house window as a mirror he adjusted the unmentionable thing with affectations of great nicety.

"He always was a dressy old scoundrel," remarked the Tuttle person. And then, as the music came to us once more, he continued: "Say, Sour-dough, let's go over to the rodeo—they got some likely looking broncs over there."

Arm in arm, accordingly, they crossed the street and proceeded to the carrousel, first warning the cabby and myself to stay by them lest harm should come to us. What now ensued was perhaps their most remarkable behaviour at the day. At the time I could account for it only by the liquor they had consumed, but later experience in the States convinced me that they were at times consciously spoofing. I mean to say, it was quite too absurd—their seriously believing what they seemed to believe.

The carrousel being at rest when we approached, they gravely examined each one of the painted wooden effigies, looking into such of the mouths as were open, and cautiously feeling the forelegs of the different mounts, keeping up an elaborate pretence the while that the beasts were real and that they were in danger of being kicked. One absurdly painted horse they agreed would be the most difficult to ride. Examining his mouth, they disputed as to his age, and called the cabby to have his opinion of the thing's fetlocks, warning each other to beware of his rearing. The cabby, who was doubtless also intoxicated, made an equal pretence of the beast's realness, and indulged, I gathered, in various criticisms of its legs at great length.

"I think he's right," remarked the Tuttle person when the cabby had finished. "It's a bad case of splints. The leg would be blistered if I had him."

"I wouldn't give him corral room," said Cousin Egbert. "He's a bad actor. Look at his eye! Whoa! there—you would, would you!" Here he made a pretence that the beast had seized him by the shoulder. "He's a man-eater! What did I tell you? Keep him away!"

"I'll take that out of him," said the Tuttle person. "I'll show him who's his master."

"You ain't never going to try to ride him, Jeff? Think of the wife and little ones!"

"You know me, Sour-dough. No horse never stepped out from under me yet. I'll not only ride him, but I'll put a silver dollar in each stirrup and give you a thousand for each one I lose and a thousand for every time I touch leather."

Cousin Egbert here began to plead tearfully:

"Don't do it, Jeff—come on around here. There's a big five-year-old roan around here that will be safe as a church for you. Let that pinto alone. They ought to be arrested for having him here."

But the other seemed obdurate.

"Start her up, Professor, when I give the word!" he called to the proprietor, and handed him one of the French banknotes. "Play it all out!" he directed, as this person gasped with amazement.

Cousin Egbert then proceeded to the head of the beast.

"You'll have to blind him," he said.

"Sure!" replied the other, and with loud and profane cries to the animal they bound a handkerchief about his eyes.

"I can tell he's going to be a twister," warned Cousin Egbert. "I better ear him," and to my increased amazement he took one of the beast's leather ears between his teeth and held it tightly. Then with soothing words to the supposedly dangerous animal, the Tuttle person mounted him.

"Let him go!" he called to Cousin Egbert, who released the ear from between his teeth.

"Wait!" called the latter. "We're all going with you," whereupon he insisted that the cabby and I should enter a sort of swan-boat directly in the rear. I felt a silly fool, but I saw there was nothing else to be done. Cousin Egbert himself mounted a horse he had called a "blue roan," waved his hand to the proprietor, who switched a lever, the "Marseillaise" blared forth, and the platform began to revolve. As we moved, the Tuttle person whisked the handkerchief from off the eyes of his mount and with loud, shrill cries began to beat the sides of its head with his soft hat, bobbing about in his saddle, moreover, as if the beast were most unruly and like to dismount him. Cousin Egbert joined in the yelling, I am sorry to say, and lashed his beast as if he would overtake his companion. The cabman also became excited and shouted his utmost, apparently in the way of encouragement. Strange to say, I presume on account of the motion, I felt the thing was becoming infectious and was absurdly moved to join in the shouts, restraining myself with difficulty. I could distinctly imagine we were in the hunting field and riding the tails off the hounds, as one might say.

In view of what was later most unjustly alleged of me, I think it as well to record now that, though I had partaken freely of the stimulants since our meeting with the Tuttle person, I was not intoxicated, nor until this moment had I felt even the slightest elation. Now, however, I did begin to feel conscious of a mild exhilaration, and to be aware that I was viewing the behaviour of my companions with a sort of superior but amused tolerance. I can account for this only by supposing that the swift revolutions of the carrousel had in some occult manner intensified or consummated, as one might say, the effect of my previous potations. I mean to say, the continued swirling about gave me a frothy feeling that was not unpleasant.

As the contrivance came to rest, Cousin Egbert ran to the Tuttle person, who had dismounted, and warmly shook his hand, as did the cabby.

"I certainly thought he had you there once, Jeff," said Cousin Egbert. "Of all the twisters I ever saw, that outlaw is the worst."

"Wanted to roll me," said the other, "but I learned him something."

It may not be credited, but at this moment I found myself examining the beast and saying: "He's crocked himself up, sir—he's gone tender at the heel." I knew perfectly, it must be understood, that this was silly, and yet I further added, "I fancy he's picked up a stone." I mean to say, it was the most utter rot, pretending seriously that way.

"You come away," said Cousin Egbert. "Next thing you'll be thinking you can ride him yourself." I did in truth experience an earnest craving for more of the revolutions and said as much, adding that I rode at twelve stone.

"Let him break his neck if he wants to," urged the Tuttle person.

"It wouldn't be right," replied Cousin Egbert, "not in his condition. Let's see if we can't find something gentle for him. Not the roan—I found she ain't bridle-wise. How about that pheasant?"

"It's an ostrich, sir," I corrected him, as indeed it most distinctly was, though at my words they both indulged in loud laughter, affecting to consider that I had misnamed the creature.

"Ostrich!" they shouted. "Poor old Bill—he thinks it's an ostrich!"

38

"Quite so, sir," I said, pleasantly but firmly, determining not to be hoaxed again.

"Don't drivel that way," said the Tuttle person.

"Leave it to the driver, Jeff—maybe he'll believe *him*," said Cousin Egbert almost sadly, whereupon the other addressed the cabby:

"Hey, Frank," he began, and continued with some French words, among which I caught "vooley-vous, ally caffy, foomer"; and something that sounded much like "kafoozleum," at which the cabby spoke at some length in his native language concerning the ostrich. When he had done, the Tuttle person turned to me with a superior frown.

"Now I guess you're satisfied," he remarked. "You heard what Frank said— it's an Arabian muffin bird." Of course I was perfectly certain that the chap had said nothing of the sort, but I resolved to enter into the spirit of the thing, so I merely said: "Yes, sir; my error; it was only at first glance that it seemed to be an ostrich."

"Come along," said Cousin Egbert. "I won't let him ride anything he can't guess the name of. It wouldn't be right to his folks."

"Well, what's that, then?" demanded the other, pointing full at the giraffe.

"It's a bally ant-eater, sir," I replied, divining that I should be wise not to seem too obvious in naming the beast.

"Well, well, so it is!" exclaimed the Tuttle person delightedly.

"He's got the eye with him this time," said Cousin Egbert admiringly.

"He's sure a wonder," said the other. "That thing had me fooled; I thought at first it was a Russian mouse hound."

"Well, let him ride it, then," said Cousin Egbert, and I was practically lifted into the saddle by the pair of them.

"One moment," said Cousin Egbert. "Can't you see the poor thing has a sore throat? Wait till I fix him." And forthwith he removed his spats and in another moment had buckled them securely high about the throat of the giraffe. It will be seen that I was not myself when I say that this performance did not shock me as it should have done, though I was, of course, less entertained by it than were the remainder of our party and a circle of the French lower classes that had formed about us.

"Give him his head! Let's see what time you can make!" shouted Cousin Egbert as the affair began once more to revolve. I saw that both my companions held opened watches in their hands.

It here becomes difficult for me to be lucid about the succeeding events of the day. I was conscious of a mounting exhilaration as my beast swept me around the circle, and of a marked impatience with many of the proprieties of behaviour that ordinarily with me matter enormously. I swung my cap and joyously urged my strange steed to a faster pace, being conscious of loud applause each time I passed my companions. For certain lapses of memory thereafter I must wholly blame this insidious motion.

For example, though I believed myself to be still mounted and whirling (indeed I was strongly aware of the motion), I found myself seated again at the corner public house and rapping smartly for drink, which I paid for. I was feeling remarkably fit, and suffered only a mild wonder that I should have left the carrousel without observing it. Having drained my glass, I then remember asking Cousin Egbert if he would consent to change hats with the cabby, which he willingly did. It was a top-hat of some strange, hard material brightly glazed. Although many unjust things were said of me later, this is the sole incident of the day which causes me to admit that I might have taken a glass too much, especially as I undoubtedly praised Cousin Egbert's appearance when the exchange had been made, and was heard to wish that we might all have hats so smart.

It was directly after this that young Mr. Elmer, the art student, invited us to his studio, though I had not before remarked his presence, and cannot recall now where we met him. The occurrence in the studio, however, was entirely natural. I wished to please my friends and made no demur whatever when asked to don the things—a trouserish affair, of sheep's wool, which they called "chapps," a flannel shirt of blue (they knotted a scarlet handkerchief around my neck), and a wide-brimmed white hat with four indentations in the crown, such as one may see worn in the cinema dramas by cow-persons and other western-coast desperadoes. When they had strapped around my waist a large pistol in a leather jacket, I considered the effect picturesque in the extreme, and my friends were loud in their approval of it.

I repeat, it was an occasion when it would have been boorish in me to refuse to meet them halfway. I even told them an excellent wheeze I had long known, which I thought they might not, have heard. It runs: "Why is Charing Cross? Because the Strand runs into it." I mean to say, this is comic providing one enters wholly into the spirit of it, as there is required a certain nimbleness of mind to get the point, as one might say. In the present instance some needed element was lacking, for they actually drew aloof from me and conversed in low tones among themselves, pointedly ignoring me. I repeated the thing to make sure they should see it, whereat I heard Cousin Egbert say. "Better not irritate him—he'll get mad if we don't laugh," after which they burst into laughter so extravagant that I knew it to be feigned. Hereupon, feeling quite drowsy, I resolved to have forty winks, and with due apologies reclined upon the couch, where I drifted into a refreshing slumber.

Later I inferred that I must have slept for some hours. I was awakened by a light flashed in my eyes, and beheld Cousin Egbert and the Tuttle person, the latter wishing to know how late I expected to keep them up. I was on my feet at once with apologies, but they instantly hustled me to the door, down a flight of steps, through a court-yard, and into the waiting cab. It was then I noticed that I was wearing the curious hat of the American Far-West, but when I would have gone back to leave it, and secure my own, they protested vehemently, wishing to know if I had not given them trouble enough that day.

In the cab I was still somewhat drowsy, but gathered that my companions had left me, to dine and attend a public dance-hall with the cubbish art student. They had not seemed to need sleep and were still wakeful, for they sang from time to time, and Cousin Egbert lifted the cabby's hat, which he still wore, bowing to imaginary throngs along the street who were supposed to be applauding him. I at once became conscience-stricken at the thought of Mrs. Effie's feelings when she should discover him to be in this state, and was on the point of suggesting that he seek another apartment for the night, when the cab pulled up in front of our own hotel.

Though I protest that I was now entirely recovered from any effect that the alcohol might have had upon me, it was not until this moment that I most horribly discovered myself to be in the full cow-person's regalia I had donned in the studio in a spirit of pure frolic. I mean to say, I had never intended to wear the things beyond the door and could not have been hired to do so. What was my amazement then to find my companions laboriously lifting me from the cab in this impossible tenue. I objected vehemently, but little good it did me.

"Get a policeman if he starts any of that rough stuff," said the Tuttle person, and in sheer horror of a scandal I subsided, while one on either side they hustled me through the hotel lounge—happily vacant of every one but a tariff manager— and into the lift. And now I perceived that they were once more pretending to themselves that I was in a bad way from drink, though I could not at once suspect the full iniquity of their design.

As we reached our own floor, one of them still seeming to support me on either side, they began loud and excited admonitions to me to be still, to come along as quickly as possible, to stop singing, and not to shoot. I mean to say, I was entirely quiet, I was coming along as quickly as they would let me, I had not sung, and did not wish to shoot, yet they persisted in making this loud ado over my supposed intoxication, aimlessly as I thought, until the door of the Floud drawing-room opened and Mrs. Effie appeared in the hallway. At this they redoubled their absurd violence with me, and by dint of tripping me they actually made it appear that I was scarce able to walk, nor do I imagine that the costume I wore was any testimonial to my sobriety.

"Now we got him safe," panted Cousin Egbert, pushing open the door of my room.

"Get his gun, first!" warned the Tuttle person, and this being taken from me, I was unceremoniously shoved inside.

"What does all this mean?" demanded Mrs. Effie, coming rapidly down the hall. "Where have you been till this time of night? I bet it's your fault, Jeff Tuttle—you've been getting him going."

They were both voluble with denials of this, and though I could scarce believe my ears, they proceeded to tell a story that laid the blame entirely on me.

"No, ma'am, Mis' Effie," began the Tuttle person. "It ain't that way at all. You wrong me if ever a man was wronged."

"You just seen what state he was in, didn't you?" asked Cousin Egbert in tones of deep injury. "Do you want to take another look at him?" and he made as if to push the door farther open upon me.

"Don't do it—don't get him started again!" warned the Tuttle person. "I've had trouble enough with that man to-day."

"I seen it coming this morning," said Cousin Egbert, "when we was at the art gallery. He had a kind of wild look in his eyes, and I says right then: 'There's a man ought to be watched,' and, well, one thing led to another—look at this hat he made me wear—nothing would satisfy him but I should trade hats with some cab-driver——"

"I was coming along from looking at two or three good churches," broke in the Tuttle person, "when I seen Sour-dough here having a kind of a mix-up with this man because of him insisting he must ride a kangaroo or something on a merry-go-round, and wanting Sour-dough to ride an ostrich with him, and then when we got him quieted down a little, nothing would do him but he's got to be a cowboy—you seen his clothes, didn't you? And of course I wanted to get back to Addie and the girls, but I seen Sour-dough here was in trouble, so I stayed right by him, and between us we got the maniac here."

"He's one of them should never touch liquor," said Cousin Egbert; "it makes a demon of him."

"I got his knife away from him early in the game," said the other.

"I don't suppose I got to wear this cabman's hat just because he told me to, have I?" demanded Cousin Egbert.

"And here I'd been looking forward to a quiet day seeing some well-known objects of interest," came from the other, "after I got my tooth pulled, that is."

"And me with a tooth, too, that nearly drove me out of my mind," said Cousin Egbert suddenly.

I could not see Mrs. Effie, but she had evidently listened to this outrageous tale with more or less belief, though not wholly credulous.

"You men have both been drinking yourselves," she said shrewdly.

"We had to take a little; he made us," declared the Tuttle person brazenly.

"He got so he insisted on our taking something every time he did," added Cousin Egbert. "And, anyway, I didn't care so much, with this tooth of mine aching like it does."

"You come right out with me and around to that dentist I went to this morning," said the Tuttle person. "You'll suffer all night if you don't."

"Maybe I'd better," said Cousin Egbert, "though I hate to leave this comfortable hotel and go out into the night air again."

"I'll have the right of this in the morning," said Mrs. Effie. "Don't think it's going to stop here!" At this my door was pulled to and the key turned in the lock.

Frankly I am aware that what I have put down above is incredible, yet not a single detail have I distorted. With a quite devilish ingenuity they had fastened upon some true bits: I had suggested the change of hats with the cabby, I had wished to ride the giraffe, and the Tuttle person had secured my knife, but how monstrously untrue of me was the impression conveyed by these isolated facts. I could believe now quite all the tales I had ever heard of the queerness of Americans. Queerness, indeed! I went to bed resolving to let the morrow take care of itself.

Again I was awakened by a light flashing in my eyes, and became aware that Cousin Egbert stood in the middle of the room. He was reading from his notebook of art criticisms, with something of an oratorical effect. Through the half-drawn curtains I could see that dawn was breaking. Cousin Egbert was no longer wearing the cabby's hat. It was now the flat cap of the Paris constable or policeman.

CHAPTER FOUR

The sight was a fair crumpler after the outrageous slander that had been put upon me by this elderly inebriate and his accomplice. I sat up at once, prepared to bully him down a bit. Although I was not sure that I engaged his attention, I told him that his reading could be very well done without and that he might take himself off. At this he became silent and regarded me solemnly.

"Why did Charing Cross the Strand? Because three rousing cheers," said he.

Of course he had the wheeze all wrong and I saw that he should be in bed. So with gentle words I lured him to his own chamber. Here, with a quite unexpected perversity, he accused me of having kept him up the night long and begged now to be allowed to retire. This he did with muttered complaints of my behaviour, and was almost instantly asleep. I concealed the constable's cap in one of his boxes, for I feared that he had not come by this honestly. I then returned to my own room, where for a long time I meditated profoundly upon the situation that now confronted me.

It seemed probable that I should be shopped by Mrs. Effie for what she had been led to believe was my rowdyish behaviour. However dastardly the injustice to me, it was a solution of the problem that I saw I could bring myself to meet with considerable philosophy. It meant a return to the quiet service of the Honourable George and that I need no longer face the distressing vicissitudes of life in the back blocks of unexplored America. I would not be obliged to muddle along in the blind fashion of the last two days, feeling a frightful fool. Mrs. Effie would surely not keep me on, and that was all about it. I had merely to make no defence of myself. And even if I chose to make one I was not certain that she would believe me, so cunning had been the accusations against me, with that tiny thread of fact which I make no doubt has so often enabled historians to give a false colouring to their recitals without stating downright untruths. Indeed, my shameless appearance in the garb of a cow person would alone have cast doubt upon the truth as I knew it to be.

Then suddenly I suffered an illumination. I perceived all at once that to make any sort of defence of myself would not be cricket. I mean to say, I saw the proceedings of the previous day in a new light. It is well known that I do not hold with the abuse of alcoholic stimulants, and yet on the day before, in moments that I now confess to have been slightly elevated, I had been conscious of a certain feeling of fellowship with my two companions that was rather wonderful. Though obviously they were not university men, they seemed to belong to what in America would be called the landed gentry, and yet I had felt myself on terms of undoubted equality with them. It may be believed or not, but there had been brief spaces when I forgot that I was a gentleman's man. Astoundingly I had experienced the confident ease of a gentleman among his equals. I was obliged to admit now that this might have been a mere delusion of the cup, and yet I wondered, too, if perchance I might not have caught something of that American spirit of equality which is said to be peculiar to republics. Needless to say I had never believed in the existence of this spirit, but had considered it rather a ghastly jest, having been a reader of our own periodical press since earliest youth. I mean to say, there could hardly be a stable society in which one had no superiors, because in that case one would not know who were one's inferiors. Nevertheless, I repeat that I had felt a most novel enlargement of myself; had, in fact, felt that I was a gentleman among gentlemen, using the word in its strictly technical sense. And so vividly did this conviction remain with me that I now saw any defence of my course to be out of the question.

I perceived that my companions had meant to have me on toast from the first. I mean to say, they had started a rag with me—a bit of chaff—and I now found myself rather preposterously enjoying the manner in which they had chivied me. I mean to say, I felt myself taking it as one gentleman would take a rag from other gentlemen—not as a bit of a sneak who would tell the truth to save his face. A couple of chaffing old beggars they were, but they had found me a topping dead sportsman of their own sort. Be it remembered I was still uncertain whether I had caught something of that alleged American spirit, or whether the drink had made me feel equal at least to Americans. Whatever it might be, it was rather great, and I was prepared to face Mrs. Effie without a tremor—to face her, of course, as one overtaken by a weakness for spirits.

When the bell at last rang I donned my service coat and, assuming a look of profound remorse, I went to the drawing-room to serve the morning coffee. As I suspected, only Mrs. Effie was present. I believe it has been before remarked that she is a person of commanding presence, with a manner of marked determination. She favoured me with a brief but chilling glance, and for some moments thereafter affected quite to ignore me. Obviously she had been completely greened the night before and was treating me with a proper contempt. I saw that it was no use grousing at fate and that it was better for me not to go into the American wilderness, since a rolling stone gathers no moss. I was prepared to accept instant dismissal without a character.

She began upon me, however, after her first cup of coffee, more mildly than I had expected.

"Ruggles, I'm horribly disappointed in you."

"Not more so than I myself, Madam," I replied.

"I am more disappointed," she continued, "because I felt that Cousin Egbert had something in him——"

"Something in him, yes, Madam," I murmured sympathetically.

"And that you were the man to bring it out. I was quite hopeful after you got him into those new clothes. I don't believe any one else could have done it. And

45

now it turns out that you have this weakness for drink. Not only that, but you have a mania for insisting that other men drink with you. Think of those two poor fellows trailing you over Paris yesterday trying to save you from yourself."

"I shall never forget it, Madam," I said.

"Of course I don't believe that Jeff Tuttle always has to have it forced on him. Jeff Tuttle is an Indian. But Cousin Egbert is different. You tore him away from that art gallery where he was improving his mind, and led him into places that must have been disgusting to him. All he wanted was to study the world's masterpieces in canvas and marble, yet you put a cabman's hat on him and made him ride an antelope, or whatever the thing was. I can't think where you got such ideas."

"I was not myself. I can only say that I seemed to be subject to an attack." And the Tuttle person was one of their Indians! This explained so much about him.

"You don't look like a periodical souse," she remarked.

"Quite so, Madam."

"But you must be a wonder when you do start. The point is: am I doing right to intrust Cousin Egbert to you again?"

"Quite so, Madam."

"It seems doubtful if you are the person to develop his higher nature."

Against my better judgment I here felt obliged to protest that I had always been given the highest character for quietness and general behaviour and that I could safely promise that I should be guilty of no further lapses of this kind. Frankly, I was wishing to be shopped, and yet I could not resist making this mild defence of myself. Such I have found to be the way of human nature. To my surprise I found that Mrs. Effie was more than half persuaded by these words and was on the point of giving me another trial. I cannot say that I was delighted at this. I was ready to give up all Americans as problems one too many for me, and yet I was strangely a little warmed at thinking I might not have seen the last of Cousin Egbert, whom I had just given a tuckup.

"You shall have your chance," she said at last, "and just to show you that I'm not narrow, you can go over to the sideboard there and pour yourself out a little one. It ought to be a lifesaver to you, feeling the way you must this morning."

"Thank you, Madam," and I did as she suggested. I was feeling especially fit, but I knew that I ought to play in character, as one might say.

"Three rousing cheers!" I said, having gathered the previous day that this was a popular American toast. She stared at me rather oddly, but made no comment other than to announce her departure on a shopping tour. Her bonnet, I noted, was quite wrong. Too extremely modish it was, accenting its own lines at the expense of a face to which less attention should have been called. This is a mistake common to the sex, however. They little dream how sadly they mock and betray

46

their own faces. Nothing I think is more pathetic than their trustful unconsciousness of the tragedy—the rather plainish face under the contemptuous structure that points to it and shrieks derision. The rather plain woman who knows what to put upon her head is a woman of genius. I have seen three, perhaps.

I now went to the room of Cousin Egbert. I found him awake and cheerful, but disinclined to arise. It was hard for me to realize that his simple, kindly face could mask the guile he had displayed the night before. He showed no sign of regret for the false light in which he had placed me. Indeed he was sitting up in bed as cheerful and independent as if he had paid two-pence for a park chair.

"I fancy," he began, "that we ought to spend a peaceful day indoors. The trouble with these foreign parts is that they don't have enough home life. If it isn't one thing it's another."

"Sometimes it's both, sir," I said, and he saw at once that I was not to be wheedled. Thereupon he grinned brazenly at me, and demanded:

"What did she say?"

"Well, sir," I said, "she was highly indignant at me for taking you and Mr. Tuttle into public houses and forcing you to drink liquor, but she was good enough, after I had expressed my great regret and promised to do better in the future, to promise that I should have another chance. It was more than I could have hoped, sir, after the outrageous manner in which I behaved."

He grinned again at this, and in spite of my resentment I found myself grinning with him. I am aware that this was a most undignified submission to the injustice he had put upon me, and it was far from the line of stern rebuke that I had fully meant to adopt with him, but there seemed no other way. I mean to say, I couldn't help it.

"I'm glad to hear you talk that way," he said. "It shows you may have something in you after all. What you want to do is to learn to say no. Then you won't be so much trouble to those who have to look after you."

"Yes, sir," I said, "I shall try, sir."

"Then I'll give you another chance," he said sternly.

I mean to say, it was all spoofing, the way we talked. I am certain he knew it as well as I did, and I am sure we both enjoyed it. I am not one of those who think it shows a lack of dignity to unbend in this manner on occasion. True, it is not with every one I could afford to do so, but Cousin Egbert seemed to be an exception to almost every rule of conduct.

At his earnest request I now procured for him another carafe of iced water (he seemed already to have consumed two of these), after which he suggested that I read to him. The book he had was the well-known story, "Robinson Crusoe," and I began a chapter which describes some of the hero's adventures on his lonely island.

Cousin Egbert, I was glad to note, was soon sleeping soundly, so I left him and retired to my own room for a bit of needed rest. The story of "Robinson Crusoe" is one in which many interesting facts are conveyed regarding life upon remote islands where there are practically no modern conveniences and one is put to all sorts of crude makeshifts, but for me the narrative contains too little dialogue.

For the remainder of the day I was left to myself, a period of peace that I found most welcome. Not until evening did I meet any of the family except Cousin Egbert, who partook of some light nourishment late in the afternoon. Then it was that Mrs. Effie summoned me when she had dressed for dinner, to say:

"We are sailing for home the day after to-morrow. See that Cousin Egbert has everything he needs."

The following day was a busy one, for there were many boxes to be packed against the morrow's sailing, and much shopping to do for Cousin Egbert, although he was much against this.

"It's all nonsense," he insisted, "her saying all that truck helps to 'finish' me. Look at me! I've been in Europe darned near four months and I can't see that I'm a lick more finished than when I left Red Gap. Of course it may show on me so other people can see it, but I don't believe it does, at that." Nevertheless, I bought him no end of suits and smart haberdashery.

When the last box had been strapped I hastened to our old lodgings on the chance of seeing the Honourable George once more. I found him dejectedly studying an ancient copy of the "Referee." Too evidently he had dined that night in a costume which would, I am sure, have offended even Cousin Egbert. Above his dress trousers he wore a golfing waistcoat and a shooting jacket. However, I could not allow myself to be distressed by this. Indeed, I knew that worse would come. I forebore to comment upon the extraordinary choice of garments he had made. I knew it was quite useless. From any word that he let fall during our chat, he might have supposed himself to be dressed as an English gentleman should be.

He bade me seat myself, and for some time we smoked our pipes in a friendly silence. I had feared that, as on the last occasion, he would row me for having deserted him, but he no longer seemed to harbour this unjust thought. We spoke of America, and I suggested that he might some time come out to shoot big game along the Ohio or the Mississippi. He replied moodily, after a long interval, that if he ever did come out it would be to set up a cattle plantation. It was rather agreed that he would come should I send for him. "Can't sit around forever waiting for old Nevil's toast crumbs," said he.

We chatted for a time of home politics, which was, of course, in a wretched state. There was a time when we might both have been won to a sane and reasoned liberalism, but the present so-called government was coming it a bit too thick for us. We said some sharp things about the little Welsh attorney who was beginning to be England's humiliation. Then it was time for me to go.

The moment was rather awkward, for the Honourable George, to my great embarrassment, pressed upon me his dispatch-case, one that we had carried during all our travels and into which tidily fitted a quart flask. Brandy we usually carried in it. I managed to accept it with a word of thanks, and then amazingly he shook hands twice with me as we said good-night. I had never dreamed he could be so greatly affected. Indeed, I had always supposed that there was nothing of the sentimentalist about him.

So the Honourable George and I were definitely apart for the first time in our lives.

It was with mingled emotions that I set sail next day for the foreign land to which I had been exiled by a turn of the cards. Not only was I off to a wilderness where a life of daily adventure was the normal life, but I was to mingle with foreigners who promised to be quite almost impossibly queer, if the family of Flouds could be taken as a sample of the native American—knowing Indians like the Tuttle person; that sort of thing. If some would be less queer, others would be even more queer, with queerness of a sort to tax even my *savoir faire*, something which had been sorely taxed, I need hardly say, since that fatal evening when the Honourable George's intuitions had played him false in the game of drawing poker. I was not the first of my countrymen, however, to find himself in desperate straits, and I resolved to behave as England expects us to.

I have said that I was viewing the prospect with mingled emotions. Before we had been out many hours they became so mingled that, having crossed the Channel many times, I could no longer pretend to ignore their true nature. For three days I was at the mercy of the elements, and it was then I discovered a certain hardness in the nature of Cousin Egbert which I had not before suspected. It was only by speaking in the sharpest manner to him that I was able to secure the nursing my condition demanded. I made no doubt he would actually have left me to the care of a steward had I not been firm with him. I have known him leave my bedside for an hour at a time when it seemed probable that I would pass away at any moment. And more than once, when I summoned him in the night to administer one of the remedies with which I had provided myself, or perhaps to question him if the ship were out of danger, he exhibited something very like irritation. Indeed he was never properly impressed by my suffering, and at times when he would answer my call it was plain to be seen that he had been passing idle moments in the smoke-room or elsewhere, quite as if the situation were an ordinary one.

It is only fair to say, however, that toward the end of my long and interesting illness I had quite broken his spirit and brought him to be as attentive as even I could wish. By the time I was able with his assistance to go upon deck again he was bringing me nutritive wines and jellies without being told, and so attentive did he remain that I overheard a fellow-passenger address him as Florence Nightingale. I also overheard the Senator tell him that I had got his sheep, whatever that may have meant—a sheep or a goat—some domestic animal. Yet with all his willingness he was clumsy in his handling of me; he seemed to take nothing with any proper seriousness, and in spite of my sharpest warning he would never wear the proper clothes, so that I always felt he was attracting undue attention to us. Indeed, I should hardly care to cross with him again, and this I told him straight.

Of the so-called joys of ship-life, concerning which the boat companies speak so enthusiastically in their folders, the less said the better. It is a childish mind, I think, that can be impressed by the mere wabbly bulk of water. It is undoubtedly tremendous, but nothing to kick up such a row about. The truth is that the prospect from a ship's deck lacks that variety which one may enjoy from almost any English hillside. One sees merely water, and that's all about it.

It will be understood, therefore, that I hailed our approach to the shores of foreign America with relief if not with enthusiasm. Even this was better than an ocean which has only size in its favour and has been quite too foolishly overrated.

We were soon steaming into the harbour of one of their large cities. Chicago, I had fancied it to be, until the chance remark of an American who looked to be a well-informed fellow identified it as New York. I was much annoyed now at the behaviour of Cousin Egbert, who burst into silly cheers at the slightest excuse, a passing steamer, a green hill, or a rusty statue of quite ungainly height which seemed to be made of crude iron. Do as I would, I could not restrain him from these unseemly shouts. I could not help contrasting his boisterousness with the fine reserve which, for example, the Honourable George would have maintained under these circumstances.

A further relief it was, therefore, when we were on the dock and his mind was diverted to other matters. A long time we were detained by customs officials who seemed rather overwhelmed by the gowns and millinery of Mrs. Effie, but we were at last free and taken through the streets of the crude new American city of New York to a hotel overlooking what I dare say in their simplicity they call their Hyde Park.

CHAPTER FIVE

I must admit that at this inn they did things quite nicely, doubtless because it seemed to be almost entirely staffed by foreigners. One would scarce have known within its walls that one had come out to North America, nor that savage wilderness surrounded one on every hand. Indeed I was surprised to learn that we were quite at the edge of the rough Western frontier, for in but one night's journey we were to reach the American mountains to visit some people who inhabited a camp in their dense wilds.

A bit of romantic thrill I felt in this adventure, for we should encounter, I inferred, people of the hardy pioneer stock that has pushed the American civilization, such as it is, ever westward. I pictured the stalwart woodsman, axe in hand, braving the forest to fell trees for his rustic home, while at night the red savages prowled about to scalp any who might stray from the blazing campfire. On the day of our landing I had read something of this—of depredations committed by their Indians at Arizona.

From what would, I take it, be their Victoria station, we three began our journey in one of the Pullman night coaches, the Senator of this family having proceeded to their home settlement of Red Gap with word that he must "look after his fences," referring, doubtless, to those about his cattle plantation.

As our train moved out Mrs. Effie summoned me for a serious talk concerning the significance of our present visit; not of the wilderness dangers to which we might be exposed, but of its social aspects, which seemed to be of prime importance. We were to visit, I learned, one Charles Belknap-Jackson of Boston and Red Gap, he being a person who mattered enormously, coming from one of the very oldest families of Boston, a port on their east coast, and a place, I gathered, in which some decent attention is given to the matter of who has been one's family. A bit of a shock it was to learn that in this rough land they had their castes and precedences. I saw I had been right to suspect that even a crude society could not exist without its rules for separating one's superiors from the lower sorts. I began to feel at once more at home and I attended the discourse of Mrs. Effie with close attention.

The Boston person, in one of those irresponsibly romantic moments that sometimes trap the best of us, had married far beneath him, espousing the simple daughter of one of the crude, old-settling families of Red Gap. Further, so inattentive to details had he been, he had neglected to secure an ante-nuptial settlement as our own men so wisely make it their rule to do, and was now suffering a painful embarrassment from this folly; for the mother-in-law, controlling the rather sizable family fortune, had harshly insisted that the pair reside in Red Gap, permitting no more than an occasional summer visit to his native Boston, whose inhabitants she affected not to admire.

"Of course the poor fellow suffers frightfully," explained Mrs. Effie, "shut off there away from all he'd been brought up to, but good has come of it, for his presence has simply done wonders for us. Before he came our social life was too awful for words—oh, a *mixture*! Practically every one in town attended our dances; no one had ever told us any better. The Bohemian set mingled freely with the very oldest families—oh, in a way that would never be tolerated in London society, I'm sure. And everything so crude! Why, I can remember when no one thought of putting doilies under the finger-bowls. No tone to it at all. For years we had no country club, if you can believe that. And even now, in spite of the efforts of Charles and a few of us, there are still some of the older families that are simply sloppy in their entertaining. And promiscuous. The trouble I've had with the Senator and Cousin Egbert!"

"The Flouds are an old family?" I suggested, wishing to understand these matters deeply.

"The Flouds," she answered impressively, "were living in Red Gap before the spur track was ever run out to the canning factory—and I guess you know what that means!"

"Quite so, Madam," I suggested; and, indeed, though it puzzled me a bit, it sounded rather tremendous, as meaning with us something like since the battle of Hastings.

"But, as I say, Charles at once gave us a glimpse of the better things. Thanks to him, the Bohemian set and the North Side set are now fairly distinct. The scraps we've had with that Bohemian set! He has a real genius for leadership, Charles has, but I know he often finds it so discouraging, getting people to know their places. Even his own mother-in-law, Mrs. Lysander John Pettengill—but you'll see to-morrow how impossible she is, poor old soul! I shouldn't talk about her, I really shouldn't. Awfully good heart the poor old dear has, but—well, I don't see why I shouldn't tell you the exact truth in plain words—you'd find it out soon enough. She is simply a confirmed *mixer*. The trial she's been and is to poor Charles! Almost no respect for any of the higher things he stands for—and temper? Well, I've heard her swear at him till you'd have thought it was Jeff Tuttle packing a green cayuse for the first time. Words? Talk about words! And Cousin Egbert always standing in with her. He's been another awful trial, refusing to play tennis at the country club, or to take up golf, or do any of those smart things, though I got him a beautiful lot of sticks. But no: when he isn't out in the hills, he'd rather sit down in that back room at the Silver Dollar saloon, playing cribbage all day with a lot of drunken loafers. But I'm so hoping that will be changed, now that I've made him see there are better things in life. Don't you really think he's another man?"

"To an extent, Madam, I dare say," I replied cautiously.

"It's chiefly what I got you for," she went on. "And then, in a general way you will give tone to our establishment. The moment I saw you I knew you could be an influence for good among us. No one there has ever had anything like you. Not even Charles. He's tried to have American valets, but you never can get them to understand their place. Charles finds them so offensively familiar. They don't seem to realize. But of course you realize."

I inclined my head in sympathetic understanding.

"I'm looking forward to Charles meeting you. I guess he'll be a little put out at our having you, but there's no harm letting him see I'm to be reckoned with. Naturally his wife, Millie, is more or less mentioned as a social leader, but I never could see that she is really any more prominent than I am. In fact, last year after our Bazaar of All Nations our pictures in costume were in the Spokane paper as 'Red Gap's Rival Society Queens,' and I suppose that's what we are, though we work together pretty well as a rule. Still, I must say, having you puts me a couple of notches ahead of her. Only, for heaven's sake, keep your eye on Cousin Egbert!"

"I shall do my duty, Madam," I returned, thinking it all rather morbidly interesting, these weird details about their county families.

"I'm sure you will," she said at parting. "I feel that we shall do things right this year. Last year the Sunday Spokane paper used to have nearly a column under the heading 'Social Doings of Red Gap's Smart Set.' This year we'll have a good two columns, if I don't miss my guess."

In the smoking-compartment I found Cousin Egbert staring gloomily into vacancy, as one might say, the reason I knew being that he had vainly pleaded with Mrs. Effie to be allowed to spend this time at their Coney Island, which is a sort of Brighton. He transferred his stare to me, but it lost none of its gloom.

"Hell begins to pop!" said he.

"Referring to what, sir?" I rejoined with some severity, for I have never held with profanity.

"Referring to Charles Belknap Hyphen Jackson of Boston, Mass.," said he, "the greatest little trouble-maker that ever crossed the hills—with a bracelet on one wrist and a watch on the other and a one-shot eyeglass and a gold cigareet case and key chains, rings, bangles, and jewellery till he'd sink like lead if he ever fell into the crick with all that metal on."

"You are speaking, sir, about a person who matters enormously," I rebuked him.

"If I hadn't been afraid of getting arrested I'd have shot him long ago."

"It's not done, sir," I said, quite horrified by his rash words.

"It's liable to be," he insisted. "I bet Ma Pettengill will go in with me on it any time I give her the word. Say, listen! there's one good mixer."

"The confirmed Mixer, sir?" For I remembered the term.

"The best ever. Any one can set into her game that's got a stack of chips." He uttered this with deep feeling, whatever it might exactly mean.

"I can be pushed just so far," he insisted sullenly. It struck me then that he should perhaps have been kept longer in one of the European capitals. I feared his brief contact with those refining influences had left him less polished than Mrs. Effie seemed to hope. I wondered uneasily if he might not cause her to miss her guess. Yet I saw he was in no mood to be reasoned with, and I retired to my bed which the blackamoor guard had done out. Here I meditated profoundly for some time before I slept.

Morning found our coach shunted to a siding at a backwoods settlement on the borders of an inland sea. The scene was wild beyond description, where quite almost anything might be expected to happen, though I was a bit reassured by the presence of a number of persons of both sexes who appeared to make little of the dangers by which we were surrounded. I mean to say since they thus took their women into the wilds so freely, I would still be a dead sportsman.

After a brief wait at a rude quay we embarked on a launch and steamed out over the water. Mile after mile we passed wooded shores that sloped up to mountains of prodigious height. Indeed the description of the Rocky Mountains, of which I take these to be a part, have not been overdrawn. From time to time, at the edge of the primeval forest, I could make out the rude shelters of hunter and trapper who braved these perils for the sake of a scanty livelihood for their hardy wives and little ones.

Cousin Egbert, beside me, seemed unimpressed, making no outcry at the fearsome wildness of the scene, and when I spoke of the terrific height of the mountains he merely admonished me to "quit my kidding." The sole interest he had thus far displayed was in the title of our craft—*Storm King*.

"Think of the guy's imagination, naming this here chafing dish the *Storm King*!" said he; but I was impatient of levity at so solemn a moment, and promptly rebuked him for having donned a cravat that I had warned him was for town wear alone; whereat he subsided and did not again intrude upon me.

Far ahead, at length, I could descry an open glade at the forest edge, and above this I soon spied floating the North American flag, or national emblem. It is, of course, known to us that the natives are given to making rather a silly noise over this flag of theirs, but in this instance—the pioneer fighting his way into the wilderness and hoisting it above his frontier home—I felt strangely indisposed to criticise. I understood that he could be greatly cheered by the flag of the country he had left behind.

We now neared a small dock from which two ladies brandished handkerchiefs at us, and were presently welcomed by them. I had no difficulty in identifying the Mrs. Charles Belknap-Jackson, a lively featured brunette of neutral tints, rather stubby as to figure, but modishly done out in white flannels.

She surveyed us interestedly through a lorgnon, observing which Mrs. Effie was quick with her own. I surmised that neither of them was skilled with this form of glass (which must really be raised with an air or it's no good); also that each was not a little chagrined to note that the other possessed one.

Nor was it less evident that the other lady was the mother of Mrs. Belknap-Jackson; I mean to say, the confirmed Mixer—an elderly person of immense bulk in gray walking-skirt, heavy boots, and a flowered blouse that was overwhelming. Her face, under her grayish thatch of hair, was broad and smiling, the eyes keen, the mouth wide, and the nose rather a bit blobby. Although at every point she was far from vogue, she impressed me not unpleasantly. Even her voice, a magnificently hoarse rumble, was primed with a sort of uncouth good-will which one might accept in the States. Of course it would never do with us.

I fancied I could at once detect why they had called her the "Mixer." She embraced Mrs. Effie with an air of being about to strangle the woman; she affectionately wrung the hands of Cousin Egbert, and had grasped my own tightly before I could evade her, not having looked for that sort of thing.

"That's Cousin Egbert's man!" called Mrs. Effie. But even then the powerful creature would not release me until her daughter had called sharply, "Maw! Don't you hear? He's a *man*!" Nevertheless she gave my hand a parting shake before turning to the others.

"Glad to see a human face at last!" she boomed. "Here I've been a month in this dinky hole," which I thought strange, since we were surrounded by league upon league of the primal wilderness. "Cooped up like a hen in a barrel," she added in tones that must have carried well out over the lake.

"Cousin Egbert's man," repeated Mrs. Effie, a little ostentatiously, I thought. "Poor Egbert's so dependent on him—quite helpless without him."

Cousin Egbert muttered sullenly to himself as he assisted me with the bags. Then he straightened himself to address them.

"Won him in a game of freeze-out," he remarked quite viciously.

"Does he doll Sour-dough up like that all the time?" demanded the Mixer, "or has he just come from a masquerade? What's he represent, anyway?" And these words when I had taken especial pains and resorted to all manner of threats to turn him smartly out in the walking-suit of a pioneer!

"Maw!" cried our hostess, "do try to forget that dreadful nickname of Egbert's."

"I sure will if he keeps his disguise on," she rumbled back. "The old horned toad is most as funny as Jackson."

Really, I mean to say, they talked most amazingly. I was but too glad when they moved on and we could follow with the bags.

55

"Calls her 'Maw' all right now," hissed Cousin Egbert in my ear, "but when that begoshed husband of hers is around the house she calls her 'Mater.'"

His tone was vastly bitter. He continued to mutter sullenly to himself—a way he had—until we had disposed of the luggage and I was laying out his afternoon and evening wear in one of the small detached houses to which we had been assigned. Nor did he sink his grievance on the arrival of the Mixer a few moments later. He now addressed her as "Ma" and asked if she had "the makings," which puzzled me until she drew from the pocket of her skirt a small cloth sack of tobacco and some bits of brown paper, from which they both fashioned cigarettes.

"The smart set of Red Gap is holding its first annual meeting for the election of officers back there," she began after she had emitted twin jets of smoke from the widely separated corners of her set mouth.

"I say, you know, where's Hyphen old top?" demanded Cousin Egbert in a quite vile imitation of one speaking in the correct manner.

"Fishing," answered the Mixer with a grin. "In a thousand dollars' worth of clothes. These here Eastern trout won't notice you unless you dress right." I thought this strange indeed, but Cousin Egbert merely grinned in his turn.

"How'd he get you into this awfully horrid rough place?" he next demanded.

"Made him. 'This or Red Gap for yours,' I says. The two weeks in New York wasn't so bad, what with Millie and me getting new clothes, though him and her both jumped on me that I'm getting too gay about clothes for a party of my age. 'What's age to me,' I says, 'when I like bright colours?' Then we tried his home-folks in Boston, but I played that string out in a week.

"Two old-maid sisters, thin noses and knitted shawls! Stick around in the back parlour talking about families—whether it was Aunt Lucy's Abigail or the Concord cousin's Hester that married an Adams in '78 and moved out west to Buffalo. I thought first I could liven them up some, *you* know. Looked like it would help a lot for them to get out in a hack and get a few shots of hooch under their belts, stop at a few roadhouses, take in a good variety show; get 'em to feeling good, understand? No use. Wouldn't start. Darn it! they held off from me. Don't know why. I sure wore clothes for them. Yes, sir. I'd get dressed up like a broken arm every afternoon; and, say, I got one sheath skirt, black and white striped, that just has to be looked at. Never phased them, though.

"I got to thinking mebbe it was because I made my own smokes instead of using those vegetable cigarettes of Jackson's, or maybe because I'd get parched and demand a slug of booze before supper. Like a Sunday afternoon all the time, when you eat a big dinner and everybody's sleepy and mad because they can't take a nap, and have to set around and play a few church tunes on the organ or look through the album again."

"Ain't that right? Don't it fade you?" murmured Cousin Egbert with deep feeling.

"And little Lysander, my only grandson, poor kid, getting the fidgets because they try to make him talk different, and raise hell every time he knocks over a vase or busts a window. Say, would you believe it? they wanted to keep him there—yes, sir—make him refined. Not for me! 'His father's about all he can survive in those respects,' I says. What do you think? Wanted to let his hair grow so he'd have curls. Some dames, yes? I bet they'd have give the kid lovely days. 'Boston may be all O.K. for grandfathers,' I says; 'not for grandsons, though.'

"Then Jackson was set on Bar Harbor, and I had to be firm again. Darn it! that man is always making me be firm. So here we are. He said it was a camp, and that sounded good. But my lands! he wears his full evening dress suit for supper every night, and you had ought to heard him go on one day when the patent ice-machine went bad."

"My good gosh!" said Cousin Egbert quite simply.

I had now finished laying out his things and was about to withdraw.

"Is he always like that?" suddenly demanded the Mixer, pointing at me.

"Oh, Bill's all right when you get him out with a crowd," explained the other. "Bill's really got the makings of one fine little mixer."

They both regarded me genially. It was vastly puzzling. I mean to say, I was at a loss how to take it, for, of course, that sort of thing would never do with us. And yet I felt a queer, confused sort of pleasure in the talk. Absurd though it may seem, I felt there might come moments in which America would appear almost not impossible.

As I went out Cousin Egbert was telling her of Paris. I lingered to hear him disclose that all Frenchmen have "M" for their first initial, and that the Louer family must be one of their wealthiest, the name "A. Louer" being conspicuous on millions of dollars' worth of their real estate. This family, he said, must be like the Rothschilds. Of course the poor soul was absurdly wrong. I mean to say, the letter "M" merely indicates "Monsieur," which is their foreign way of spelling Mister, while "A Louer" signifies "to let." I resolved to explain this to him at the first opportunity, not thinking it right that he should spread such gross error among a race still but half-enlightened.

Having now a bit of time to myself, I observed the construction of this rude homestead, a dozen or more detached or semi-detached structures of the native log, yet with the interiors more smartly done out than I had supposed was common even with the most prosperous of their scouts and trappers. I suspected a false idea of this rude life had been given by the cinema dramas. I mean to say, with pianos, ice-machines, telephones, objects of art, and servants, one saw that these woodsmen were not primitive in any true sense of the word.

The butler proved to be a genuine blackamoor, a Mr. Waterman, he informed me, his wife, also a black, being the cook. An elderly creature of the utmost gravity of bearing, he brought to his professional duties a finish, a dignity, a manner in short that I have scarce known excelled among our own serving people. And a creature he was of the most eventful past, as he informed me at our first encounter. As a slave he had commanded an immensely high price, some twenty thousand dollars, as the American money is called, and two prominent slaveholders had once fought a duel to the death over his possession. Not many, he assured me, had been so eagerly sought after, they being for the most part held cheaper—"common black trash," he put it.

Early tiring of the life of slavery, he had fled to the wilds and for some years led a desperate band of outlaws whose crimes soon put a price upon his head. He spoke frankly and with considerable regret of these lawless years. At the outbreak of the American war, however, with a reward of fifty thousand dollars offered for his body, he had boldly surrendered to their Secretary of State for War, receiving a full pardon for his crimes on condition that he assist in directing the military operations against the slaveholding aristocracy. Invaluable he had been in this service, I gathered, two generals, named respectively Grant and Sherman, having repeatedly assured him that but for his aid they would more than once in sheer despair have laid down their swords.

I could readily imagine that after these years of strife he had been glad to embrace the peaceful calling in which I found him engaged. He was, as I have intimated, a person of lofty demeanour, with a vein of high seriousness. Yet he would unbend at moments as frankly as a child and play at a simple game of chance with a pair of dice. This he was good enough to teach to myself and gained from me quite a number of shillings that I chanced to have. For his consort, a person of tremendous bulk named Clarice, he showed a most chivalric consideration, and even what I might have mistaken for timidity in one not a confessed desperado. In truth, he rather flinched when she interrupted our chat from the kitchen doorway by roundly calling him "an old black liar." I saw that his must indeed be a complex nature.

From this encounter I chanced upon two lads who seemed to present the marks of the backwoods life as I had conceived it. Strolling up a woodland path, I discovered a tent pitched among the trees, before it a smouldering campfire, over which a cooking-pot hung. The two lads, of ten years or so, rushed from the tent to regard me, both attired in shirts and leggings of deerskin profusely fringed after the manner in which the red Indians decorate their outing or lounge-suits. They were armed with sheath knives and revolvers, and the taller bore a rifle.

"Howdy, stranger?" exclaimed this one, and the other repeated the simple American phrase of greeting. Responding in kind, I was bade to seat myself on a fallen log, which I did. For some moments they appeared to ignore me, excitedly discussing an adventure of the night before, and addressing each other as Dead Shot and Hawk Eye. From their quaint backwoods speech I gathered that Dead Shot, the taller lad, had the day before been captured by a band of hostile redskins who would have burned him at the stake but for the happy chance that the chieftain's daughter had become enamoured of him and cut his bonds.

They now planned to return to the encampment at nightfall to fetch away the daughter, whose name was White Fawn, and cleaned and oiled their weapons for the enterprise. Dead Shot was vindictive in the extreme, swearing to engage the chieftain in mortal combat and to cut his heart out, the same chieftain in former years having led his savage band against the forest home of Dead Shot while he was yet too young to defend it, and scalped both of his parents. "I was a mere stripling then, but now the coward will feel my steel!" he coldly declared.

It had become absurdly evident as I listened that the whole thing was but spoofing of a silly sort that lads of this age will indulge in, for I had seen the younger one take his seat at the luncheon table. But now they spoke of a raid on the settlement to procure "grub," as the American slang for food has it. Bidding me stop on there and to utter the cry of the great horned owl if danger threatened, they stealthily crept toward the buildings of the camp. Presently came a scream, followed by a hoarse shout of rage. A second later the two dashed by me into the dense woods, Hawk Eye bearing a plucked fowl. Soon Mr. Waterman panted up the path brandishing a barge pole and demanding to know the whereabouts of the marauders. As he had apparently for the moment reverted to his primal African savagery, I deliberately misled him by indicating a false direction, upon which he went off, muttering the most frightful threats.

The two culprits returned, put their fowl in the pot to boil, and swore me eternal fidelity for having saved them. They declared I should thereafter be known as Keen Knife, and that, needing a service, I might call upon them freely.

"Dead Shot never forgets a friend," affirmed the taller lad, whereupon I formally shook hands with the pair and left them to their childish devices. They were plotting as I left to capture "that nigger," as they called him, and put him to death by slow torture.

But I was now shrewd enough to suspect that I might still be far from the western frontier of America. The evidence had been cumulative but was no longer questionable. I mean to say, one might do here somewhat after the way of our own people at a country house in the shires. I resolved at the first opportunity to have a look at a good map of our late colonies.

Late in the afternoon our party gathered upon the small dock and I understood that our host now returned from his trouting. Along the shore of the lake he came, propelled in a native canoe by a hairy backwoods person quite wretchedly gotten up, even for a wilderness. Our host himself, I was quick to observe, was vogue to the last detail, with a sense of dress and equipment that can never be acquired, having to be born in one. As he stepped from his frail craft I saw that he was rather slight of stature, dark, with slender moustaches, a finely sensitive nose, and eyes of an almost austere repose. That he had much of the real manner was at once apparent. He greeted the Flouds and his own family with just

59

that faint touch of easy superiority which would stamp him to the trained eye as one that really mattered. Mrs. Effie beckoned me to the group.

"Let Ruggles take your things—Cousin Egbert's man," she was saying. After a startled glance at Cousin Egbert, our host turned to regard me with flattering interest for a moment, then transferred to me his oddments of fishing machinery: his rod, his creel, his luncheon hamper, landing net, small scales, ointment for warding off midges, a jar of cold cream, a case containing smoked glasses, a rolled map, a camera, a book of flies. As I was stowing these he explained that his sport had been wretched; no fish had been hooked because his guide had not known where to find them. I here glanced at the backwoods person referred to and at once did not like the look in his eyes. He winked swiftly at Cousin Egbert, who coughed rather formally.

"Let Ruggles help you to change," continued Mrs. Effie. "He's awfully handy. Poor Cousin Egbert is perfectly helpless now without him."

So I followed our host to his own detached hut, though feeling a bit queer at being passed about in this manner, I mean to say, as if I were a basket of fruit. Yet I found it a grateful change to be serving one who knew our respective places and what I should do for him. His manner of speech, also, was less barbarous than that of the others, suggesting that he might have lived among our own people a fortnight or so and have tried earnestly to correct his deficiencies. In fact he remarked to me after a bit: "I fancy I talk rather like one of yourselves, what?" and was pleased as Punch when I assured him that I had observed this. He questioned me at length regarding my association with the Honourable George, and the houses at which we would have stayed, being immensely particular about names and titles.

"You'll find us vastly different here," he said with a sigh, as I held his coat for him. "Crude, I may say. In truth, Red Gap, where my interests largely confine me, is a town of impossible persons. You'll see in no time what I mean."

"I can already imagine it, sir," I said sympathetically.

"It's not for want of example," he added. "Scores of times I show them better ways, but they're eaten up with commercialism—money-grubbing."

I perceived him to be a person of profound and interesting views, and it was with regret I left him to bully Cousin Egbert into evening dress. It is undoubtedly true that he will never wear this except it have the look of having been forced upon him by several persons of superior physical strength.

The evening passed in a refined manner with cards and music, the latter being emitted from a phonograph which I was asked to attend to and upon which I reproduced many of their quaint North American folksongs, such as "Everybody Is Doing It," which has a rare native rhythm. At ten o'clock, it being noticed by the three playing dummy bridge that Cousin Egbert and the Mixer were absent, I accompanied our host in search of them. In Cousin Egbert's hut we found them, seated at a bare table, playing at cards—a game called seven-upwards, I learned. Cousin Egbert had removed his coat, collar, and cravat, and his sleeves were rolled to his elbows like a navvy's. Both smoked the brown paper cigarettes.

"You see?" murmured Mr. Belknap-Jackson as we looked in upon them.

"Quite so, sir," I said discreetly.

The Mixer regarded her son-in-law with some annoyance, I thought.

"Run off to bed, Jackson!" she directed. "We're busy. I'm putting a nick in Sour-dough's bank roll."

Our host turned away with a contemptuous shrug that I dare say might have offended her had she observed it, but she was now speaking to Cousin Egbert, who had stared at us brazenly.

"Ring that bell for the coon, Sour-dough. I'll split a bottle of Scotch with you."

It queerly occurred to me that she made this monstrous suggestion in a spirit of bravado to annoy Mr. Belknap-Jackson.

CHAPTER SIX

There are times when all Nature seems to smile, yet when to the sensitive mind it will be faintly brought that the possibilities are quite tremendously otherwise if one will consider them pro and con. I mean to say, one often suspects things may happen when it doesn't look so.

The succeeding three days passed with so ordered a calm that little would any but a profound thinker have fancied tragedy to lurk so near their placid surface. Mrs. Effie and Mrs. Belknap-Jackson continued to plan the approaching social campaign at Red Gap. Cousin Egbert and the Mixer continued their card game for the trifling stake of a shilling a game, or "two bits," as it is known in the American monetary system. And our host continued his recreation.

Each morning I turned him out in the smartest of fishing costumes and each evening I assisted him to change. It is true I was now compelled to observe at these times a certain lofty irritability in his character, yet I more than half fancied this to be queerly assumed in order to inform me that he was not unaccustomed to services such as I rendered him. There was that about him. I mean to say, when he sharply rebuked me for clumsiness or cried out "Stupid!" it had a perfunctory languor, as if meant to show me he could address a servant in what he believed to be the grand manner. In this, to be sure, he was so oddly wrong that the pathos of it quite drowned what I might otherwise have felt of resentment.

But I next observed that he was sharp in the same manner with the hairy backwoods person who took him to fish each day, using words to him which I, for one, would have employed, had I thought them merited, only after the gravest hesitation. I have before remarked that I did not like the gleam in this person's eyes: he was very apparently a not quite nice person. Also I more than once observed him to wink at Cousin Egbert in an evil manner.

As I have so truly said, how close may tragedy be to us when life seems most correct! It was Belknap-Jackson's custom to raise a view halloo each evening when he returned down the lake, so that we might gather at the dock to oversee his landing. I must admit that he disembarked with somewhat the manner of a visiting royalty, demanding much attention and assistance with his impedimenta. Undoubtedly he liked to be looked at. This was what one rather felt. And I can fancy that this very human trait of his had in a manner worn upon the probably undisciplined nerves of the backwoods josser—had, in fact, deprived him of his "goat," as the native people have it.

Be this as it may, we gathered at the dock on the afternoon of the third day of our stay to assist at the return. As the native log craft neared the dock our host daringly arose to a graceful kneeling posture in the bow and saluted us charmingly, the woods person in the stern wielding his single oar in gloomy silence. At the moment a most poetic image occurred to me—that he was like a dull grim figure of Fate that fetches us low at the moment of our highest seeming. I mean to say, it was a silly thought, perhaps, yet I afterward recalled it most vividly.

Holding his creel aloft our host hailed us:

"Full to-day, thanks to going where I wished and paying no attention to silly guides' talk." He beamed upon us in an unquestionably superior manner, and again from the moody figure at the stern I intercepted the flash of a wink to Cousin Egbert. Then as the frail craft had all but touched the dock and our host had half risen, there was a sharp dipping of the thing and he was ejected into the chilling waters, where he almost instantly sank. There were loud cries of alarm from all, including the woodsman himself, who had kept the craft upright, and in these Mr. Belknap-Jackson heartily joined the moment his head appeared above the surface, calling "Help!" in the quite loudest of tones, which was thoughtless enough, as we were close at hand and could easily have heard his ordinary speaking voice.

The woods person now stepped to the dock, and firmly grasping the collar of the drowning man hauled him out with but little effort, at the same time becoming voluble with apologies and sympathy. The rescued man, however, was quite off his head with rage and bluntly berated the fellow for having tried to assassinate him. Indeed he put forth rather a torrent of execration, but to all of this the fellow merely repeated his crude protestations of regret and astonishment, seeming to be sincerely grieved that his intentions should have been doubted.

From his friends about him the unfortunate man was receiving the most urgent advice to seek dry garments lest he perish of chill, whereupon he turned abruptly to me and cried: "Well, Stupid, don't you see the state that fellow has put me in? What are you doing? Have you lost your wits?"

Now I had suffered a very proper alarm and solicitude for him, but the injustice of this got a bit on me. I mean to say, I suddenly felt a bit of temper myself, though to be sure retaining my control.

"Yes, sir; quite so, sir," I replied smoothly. "I'll have you right as rain in no time at all, sir," and started to conduct him off the dock. But now, having gone a little distance, he began to utter the most violent threats against the woods person, declaring, in fact, he would pull the fellow's nose. However, I restrained him from rushing back, as I subtly felt I was wished to do, and he at length consented again to be led toward his hut.

But now the woods person called out: "You're forgetting all your pretties!" By which I saw him to mean the fishing impedimenta he had placed on the dock. And most unreasonably at this Mr. Belknap-Jackson again turned upon me, wishing anew to be told if I had lost my wits and directing me to fetch the stuff. Again I was conscious of that within me which no gentleman's man should confess to. I mean to say, I felt like shaking him. But I hastened back to fetch the rod, the creel, the luncheon hamper, the midge ointment, the camera, and other articles which the woods fellow handed me.

With these somewhat awkwardly carried, I returned to our still turbulent host. More like a volcano he was than a man who has had a narrow squeak from drowning, and before we had gone a dozen feet more he again turned and declared he would "go back and thrash the unspeakable cad within an inch of his life." Their relative sizes rendering an attempt of this sort quite too unwise, I was conscious of renewed irritation toward him; indeed, the vulgar words, "Oh, stow that piffle!" swiftly formed in the back of my mind, but again I controlled myself, as the chap was now sneezing violently.

"Best hurry on, sir," I said with exemplary tact. "One might contract a severe head-cold from such a wetting," and further endeavoured to sooth him while I started ahead to lead him away from the fellow. Then there happened that which fulfilled my direst premonitions. Looking back from a moment of calm, the psychology of the crisis is of a rudimentary simplicity.

Enraged beyond measure at the woods person, Mr. Belknap-Jackson yet retained a fine native caution which counselled him to attempt no violence upon that offender; but his mental tension was such that it could be relieved only by his attacking some one; preferably some one forbidden to retaliate. I walked there temptingly but a pace ahead of him, after my well-meant word of advice.

I make no defence of my own course. I am aware there can be none. I can only plead that I had already been vexed not a little by his unjust accusations of stupidity, and dismiss with as few words as possible an incident that will ever seem to me quite too indecently criminal. Briefly, then, with my well-intended "Best not lower yourself, sir," Mr. Belknap-Jackson forgot himself and I forgot myself. It will be recalled that I was in front of him, but I turned rather quickly. (His belongings I had carried were widely disseminated.)

Instantly there were wild outcries from the others, who had started toward the main, or living house.

"He's killed Charles!" I heard Mrs. Belknap-Jackson scream; then came the deep-chested rumble of the Mixer, "Jackson kicked him first!" They ran for us. They had reached us while our host was down, even while my fist was still clenched. Now again the unfortunate man cried "Help!" as his wife assisted him to his feet.

"Send for an officer!" cried she.

"The man's an anarchist!" shouted her husband.

"Nonsense!" boomed the Mixer. "Jackson got what he was looking for. Do it myself if he kicked me!"

"Oh, Maw! Oh, Mater!" cried her daughter tearfully.

"Gee! He done it in one punch!" I heard Cousin Egbert say with what I was aghast to suspect was admiration.

Mrs. Effie, trembling, could but glare at me and gasp. Mercifully she was beyond speech for the moment.

Mr. Belknap-Jackson was now painfully rubbing his right eye, which was not what he should have done, and I said as much.

"Beg pardon, sir, but one does better with a bit of raw beef."

"How dare you, you great hulking brute!" cried his wife, and made as if to shield her husband from another attack from me, which I submit was unjust.

"Bill's right," said Cousin Egbert casually. "Put a piece of raw steak on it. Gee! with one wallop!" And then, quite strangely, for a moment we all amiably discussed whether cold compresses might not be better. Presently our host was led off by his wife. Mrs. Effie followed them, moaning: "Oh, oh, oh!" in the keenest distress.

At this I took to my own room in dire confusion, making no doubt I would presently be given in charge and left to languish in gaol, perhaps given six months' hard.

Cousin Egbert came to me in a little while and laughed heartily at my fear that anything legal would be done. He also made some ill-timed compliments on the neatness of the blow I had dealt Mr. Belknap-Jackson, but these I found in wretched taste and was begging him to desist, when the Mixer entered and began to speak much in the same strain.

"Don't you ever dare do a thing like that again," she warned me, "unless I got a ringside seat," to which I remained severely silent, for I felt my offence should not be made light of.

"Three rousing cheers!" exclaimed Cousin Egbert, whereat the two most unfeelingly went through a vivid pantomime of cheering.

Our host, I understood, had his dinner in bed that night, and throughout the evening, as I sat solitary in remorse, came the mocking strains of another of their American folksongs with the refrain:

> "You made me what I am to-day,   I hope
> you're satisfied!"

I conceived it to be the Mixer and Cousin Egbert who did this and, considering the plight of our host, I thought it in the worst possible taste. I had raised my hand against the one American I had met who was at all times vogue. And not only this: For I now recalled a certain phrase I had flung out as I stood over him, ranting indeed no better than an anarchist, a phrase which showed my poor culture to be the flimsiest veneer.

Late in the night, as I lay looking back on the frightful scene, I recalled with wonder a swift picture of Cousin Egbert caught as I once looked back to the dock. He had most amazingly shaken the woods person by the hand, quickly but with marked cordiality. And yet I am quite certain he had never been presented to the fellow.

Promptly the next morning came the dreaded summons to meet Mrs. Effie. I was of course prepared to accept instant dismissal without a character, if indeed I were not to be given in charge. I found her wearing an expression of the utmost sternness, erect and formidable by the now silent phonograph. Cousin Egbert, who was present, also wore an expression of sternness, though I perceived him to wink at me.

"I really don't know what we're to do with you, Ruggles," began the stricken woman, and so done out she plainly was that I at once felt the warmest sympathy for her as she continued: "First you lead poor Cousin Egbert into a drunken debauch——"

Cousin Egbert here coughed nervously and eyed me with strong condemnation.

"—then you behave like a murderer. What have you to say for yourself?"

At this I saw there was little I could say, except that I had coarsely given way to the brute in me, and yet I knew I should try to explain.

"I dare say, Madam, it may have been because Mr. Belknap-Jackson was quite sober at the unfortunate moment."

"Of course Charles was sober. The idea! What of it?"

"I was remembering an occasion at Chaynes-Wotten when Lord Ivor Cradleigh behaved toward me somewhat as Mr. Belknap-Jackson did last night and when my own deportment was quite all that could be wished. It occurs to me now that it was because his lordship was, how shall I say?—quite far gone in liquor at the time, so that I could without loss of dignity pass it off as a mere prank. Indeed, he regarded it as such himself, performing the act with a good nature that I found quite irresistible, and I am certain that neither his lordship nor I have ever thought the less of each other because of it. I revert to this merely to show that I have not always acted in a ruffianly manner under these circumstances. It seems rather to depend upon how the thing is done—the mood of the performer—his mental state. Had Mr. Belknap-Jackson been—pardon me—quite drunk, I feel that the outcome would have been happier for us all. So far as I have thought along these lines, it seems to me that if one is to be kicked at all, one must be kicked good-naturedly. I mean to say, with a certain camaraderie, a lightness, a gayety, a genuine good-will that for the moment expresses itself uncouthly—an element, I regret to say, that was conspicuously lacking from the brief activities of Mr. Belknap-Jackson."

"I never heard such crazy talk," responded Mrs. Effie, "and really I never saw such a man as you are for wanting people to become disgustingly drunk. You made poor Cousin Egbert and Jeff Tuttle act like beasts, and now nothing will satisfy you but that Charles should roll in the gutter. Such dissipated talk I never did hear,

66

and poor Charles rarely taking anything but a single glass of wine, it upsets him so; even our reception punch he finds too stimulating!"

I mean to say, the woman had cleanly missed my point, for never have I advocated the use of fermented liquors to excess; but I saw it was no good trying to tell her this.

"And the worst of it," she went rapidly on, "Cousin Egbert here is acting stranger than I ever knew him to act. He swears if he can't keep you he'll never have another man, and you know yourself what that means in his case—and Mrs. Pettengill saying she means to employ you herself if we let you go. Heaven knows what the poor woman can be thinking of! Oh, it's awful—and everything was going so beautifully. Of course Charles would simply never be brought to accept an apology——"

"I am only too anxious to make one," I submitted.

"Here's the poor fellow now," said Cousin Egbert almost gleefully, and our host entered. He carried a patch over his right eye and was not attired for sport on the lake, but in a dark morning suit of quietly beautiful lines that I thought showed a fine sense of the situation. He shot me one superior glance from his left eye and turned to Mrs. Effie.

"I see you still harbour the ruffian?"

"I've just given him a call-down," said Mrs. Effie, plainly ill at ease, "and he says it was all because you were sober; that if you'd been in the state Lord Ivor Cradleigh was the time it happened at Chaynes-Wotten he wouldn't have done anything to you, probably."

"What's this, what's this? Lord Ivor Cradleigh—Chaynes-Wotten?" The man seemed to be curiously interested by the mere names, in spite of himself. "His lordship was at Chaynes-Wotten for the shooting, I suppose?" This, most amazingly, to me.

"A house party at Whitsuntide, sir," I explained.

"Ah! And you say his lordship was——"

"Oh, quite, quite in his cups, sir. If I might explain, it was that, sir—its being done under circumstances and in a certain entirely genial spirit of irritation to which I could take no offence, sir. His lordship is a very decent sort, sir. I've known him intimately for years."

"Dear, dear!" he replied. "Too bad, too bad! And I dare say you thought me out of temper last night? Nothing of the sort. You should have taken it in quite the same spirit as you did from Lord Ivor Cradleigh."

"It seemed different, sir," I said firmly. "If I may take the liberty of putting it so, I felt quite offended by your manner. I missed from it at the most critical moment, as one might say, a certain urbanity that I found in his lordship, sir."

"Well, well, well! It's too bad, really. I'm quite aware that I show a sort of brusqueness at times, but mind you, it's all on the surface. Had you known me as long as you've known his lordship, I dare say you'd have noticed the same rough urbanity in me as well. I rather fancy some of us over here don't do those things so very differently. A few of us, at least."

"I'm glad, indeed, to hear it, sir. It's only necessary to understand that there is a certain mood in which one really cannot permit one's self to be—you perceive, I trust."

"Perfectly, perfectly," said he, "and I can only express my regret that you should have mistaken my own mood, which, I am confident, was exactly the thing his lordship might have felt."

"I gladly accept your apology, sir," I returned quickly, "as I should have accepted his lordship's had his manner permitted any misapprehension on my part. And in return I wish to apologize most contritely for the phrase I applied to you just after it happened, sir. I rarely use strong language, but——"

"I remember hearing none," said he.

"I regret to say, sir, that I called you a blighted little mug——"

"You needn't have mentioned it," he replied with just a trace of sharpness, "and I trust that in future——"

"I am sure, sir, that in future you will give me no occasion to misunderstand your intentions—no more than would his lordship," I added as he raised his brows.

Thus in a manner wholly unexpected was a frightful situation eased off.

"I'm so glad it's settled!" cried Mrs. Effie, who had listened almost breathlessly to our exchange.

"I fancy I settled it as Cradleigh would have—eh, Ruggles?" And the man actually smiled at me.

"Entirely so, sir," said I.

"If only it doesn't get out," said Mrs. Effie now. "We shouldn't want it known in Red Gap. Think of the talk!"

"Certainly," rejoined Mr. Belknap-Jackson jauntily, "we are all here above gossip about an affair of that sort. I am sure—" He broke off and looked uneasily at Cousin Egbert, who coughed into his hand and looked out over the lake before he spoke.

"What would I want to tell a thing like that for?" he demanded indignantly, as if an accusation had been made against him. But I saw his eyes glitter with an evil light.

An hour later I chanced to be with him in our detached hut, when the Mixer entered.

"What happened?" she demanded.

"What do you reckon happened?" returned Cousin Egbert. "They get to talking about Lord Ivy Craddles, or some guy, and before we know it Mr. Belknap Hyphen Jackson is apologizing to Bill here."

"No?" bellowed the Mixer.

"Sure did he!" affirmed Cousin Egbert.

Here they grasped each other's arms and did a rude native dance about the room, nor did they desist when I sought to explain that the name was not at all Ivy Craddles.

CHAPTER SEVEN

Now once more it seemed that for a time I might lead a sanely ordered existence. Not for long did I hope it. I think I had become resigned to the unending series of shocks that seemed to compose the daily life in North America. Few had been my peaceful hours since that fatal evening in Paris. And the shocks had become increasingly violent. When I tried to picture what the next might be I found myself shuddering. For the present, like a stag that has eluded the hounds but hears their distant baying, I lay panting in momentary security, gathering breath for some new course. I mean to say, one couldn't tell what might happen next. Again and again I found myself coming all over frightened.

Wholly restored I was now in the esteem of Mr. Belknap-Jackson, who never tired of discussing with me our own life and people. Indeed he was quite the most intelligent foreigner I had encountered. I may seem to exaggerate in the American fashion, but I doubt if a single one of the others could have named the counties of England or the present Lord Mayor of London. Our host was not like that. Also he early gave me to know that he felt quite as we do concerning the rebellion of our American colonies, holding it a matter for the deepest regret; and justly proud he was of the circumstance that at the time of that rebellion his own family had put all possible obstacles in the way of the traitorous Washington. To be sure, I dare say he may have boasted a bit in this.

It was during the long journey across America which we now set out upon that I came to this sympathetic understanding of his character and of the chagrin he constantly felt at being compelled to live among people with whom he could have as little sympathy as I myself had.

This journey began pleasantly enough, and through the farming counties of Philadelphia, Ohio, and Chicago was not without interest. Beyond came an incredibly large region, much like the steppes of Siberia, I fancy: vast uninhabited stretches of heath and down, with but here and there some rude settlement about which the poor peasants would eagerly assemble as our train passed through. I could not wonder that our own travellers have always spoken so disparagingly of the American civilization. It is a country that would never do with us.

Although we lived in this train a matter of nearly four days, I fancy not a single person dressed for dinner as one would on shipboard. Even Belknap-Jackson dined in a lounge-suit, though he wore gloves constantly by day, which was more than I could get Cousin Egbert to do.

As we went ever farther over these leagues of fen and fell and rolling veldt, I could but speculate unquietly as to what sort of place the Red Gap must be. A residential town for gentlemen and families, I had understood, with a little colony of people that really mattered, as I had gathered from Mrs. Effie. And yet I was unable to divine their object in going so far away to live. One goes to distant places for the winter sports or for big game shooting, but this seemed rather grotesquely perverse.

Little did I then dream of the spiritual agencies that were to insure my gradual understanding of the town and its people. Unsuspectingly I fronted a future so wildly improbable that no power could have made me credit it had it then been foretold by the most rarely endowed gypsy. It is always now with a sort of terror that I look back to those last moments before my destiny had unfolded far enough to be actually alarming. I was as one floating in fancied security down the calm river above their famous Niagara Falls—to be presently dashed without warning over the horrible verge. I mean to say, I never suspected.

Our last day of travel arrived. We were now in a roughened and most untidy welter of mountain and jungle and glen, with violent tarns and bleak bits of moorland that had all too evidently never known the calming touch of the landscape gardener; a region, moreover, peopled by a much more lawless appearing peasantry than I had observed back in the Chicago counties, people for the most part quite wretchedly gotten up and distinctly of the lower or working classes.

Late in the afternoon our train wound out of a narrow cutting and into a valley that broadened away on every hand to distant mountains. Beyond doubt this prospect could, in a loose way of speaking, be called scenery, but of too violent a character it was for cultivated tastes. Then, as my eye caught the vague outlines of a settlement or village in the midst of this valley, Cousin Egbert, who also looked from, the coach window, amazed me by crying out:

"There she is—little old Red Gap! The fastest growing town in the State, if any one should ask you."

"Yes, sir; I'll try to remember, sir," I said, wondering why I should be asked this.

"Garden spot of the world," he added in a kind of ecstasy, to which I made no response, for this was too preposterous. Nearing the place our train passed an immense hoarding erected by the roadway, a score of feet high, I should say, and at least a dozen times as long, upon which was emblazoned in mammoth red letters on a black ground, "*Keep Your Eye on Red Gap!*" At either end of this lettering was painted a gigantic staring human eye. Regarding this monstrosity with startled interest, I heard myself addressed by Belknap-Jackson:

"The sort of vulgarity I'm obliged to contend with," said he, with a contemptuous gesture toward the hoarding. Indeed the thing lacked refinement in its diction, while the painted eyes were not Art in any true sense of the word. "The work of our precious Chamber of Commerce," he added, "though I pleaded with them for days and days."

"It's a sort of thing would never do with us, sir," I said.

"It's what one has to expect from a commercialized bourgeoise," he returned bitterly. "And even our association, 'The City Beautiful,' of which I was president, helped to erect the thing. Of course I resigned at once."

"Naturally, sir; the colours are atrocious."

"And the words a mere blatant boast!" He groaned and left me, for we were now well into a suburb of detached villas, many of them of a squalid character, and presently we had halted at the station. About this bleak affair was the usual gathering of peasantry and the common people, villagers, agricultural labourers, and the like, and these at once showed a tremendous interest in our party, many of them hailing various members of us with a quite offensive familiarity.

Belknap-Jackson, of course, bore himself through this with a proper aloofness, as did his wife and Mrs. Effie, but I heard the Mixer booming salutations right and left. It was Cousin Egbert, however, who most embarrassed me by the freedom of his manner with these persons. He shook hands warmly with at least a dozen of them and these hailed him with rude shouts, dealt him smart blows on the back and, forming a circle about him, escorted him to a carriage where Mrs. Effie and I awaited him. Here the driver, a loutish and familiar youth, also seized his hand and, with some crude effect of oratory, shouted to the crowd.

"What's the matter with Sour-dough?" To this, with a flourish of their impossible hats, they quickly responded in unison,

"He's all right!" accenting the first word terrifically.

Then, to the immense relief of Mrs. Effie and myself, he was released and we were driven quickly off from the raffish set. Through their Regent and Bond streets we went, though I mean to say they were on an unbelievably small or village scale, to an outlying region of detached villas that doubtless would be their St. John's Wood, but my efforts to observe closely were distracted by the extraordinary freedom with which our driver essayed to chat with us, saying he "guessed" we were glad to get back to God's country, and things of a similar intimate nature. This was even more embarrassing to Mrs. Effie than it was to me, since she more than once felt obliged to answer the fellow with a feigned cordiality.

Relieved I was when we drew up before the town house of the Flouds. Set well back from the driveway in a faded stretch of common, it was of rather a garbled architecture, with the Tudor, late Gothic, and French Renaissance so intermixed that one was puzzled to separate the periods. Nor was the result so vast as this might sound. Hardly would the thing have made a wing of the manor house at Chaynes-Wotten. The common or small park before it was shielded from the main thoroughfare by a fence of iron palings, and back of this on either side of a gravelled walk that led to the main entrance were two life-sized stags not badly sculptured from metal.

Once inside I began to suspect that my position was going to be more than a bit dicky. I mean to say, it was not an establishment in our sense of the word, being staffed, apparently, by two China persons who performed the functions of cook, housemaids, footmen, butler, and housekeeper. There was not even a billiard room.

During the ensuing hour, marked by the arrival of our luggage and the unpacking of boxes, I meditated profoundly over the difficulties of my situation. In a wilderness, beyond the confines of civilization, I would undoubtedly be compelled to endure the hardships of the pioneer; yet for the present I resolved to let no inkling of my dismay escape.

The evening meal over—dinner in but the barest technical sense—I sat alone in my own room, meditating thus darkly. Nor was I at all cheered by the voice of Cousin Egbert, who sang in his own room adjoining. I had found this to be a habit of his, and his songs are always dolorous to the last degree. Now, for example, while life seemed all too black to me, he sang a favourite of his, the pathetic ballad of two small children evidently begging in a business thoroughfare:

> "Lone and weary through the streets we wander,
> For we have no place to lay our head;   Not a friend
> is left on earth to shelter us,   For both our
> parents now are dead."

It was a fair crumpler in my then mood. It made me wish to be out of North America—made me long for London; London with a yellow fog and its greasy pavements, where one knew what to apprehend. I wanted him to stop, but still he atrociously sang in his high, cracked voice:

> "Dear mother died when we were both young,
> And father built for us a home,   But now he's killed
> by falling timbers,   And we are left here all
> alone."

I dare say I should have rushed madly into the night had there been another verse, but now he was still. A moment later, however, he entered my room with the suggestion that I stroll about the village streets with him, he having a mission to perform for Mrs. Effie. I had already heard her confide this to him. He was to proceed to the office of their newspaper and there leave with the press chap a notice of our arrival which from day to day she had been composing on the train.

"I just got to leave this here piece for the *Recorder*," he said; "then we can sasshay up and down for a while and meet some of the boys."

How profoundly may our whole destiny be affected by the mood of an idle moment; by some superficial indecision, mere fruit of a transient unrest. We lightly debate, we hesitate, we yawn, unconscious of the brink. We half-heartedly decline a suggested course, then lightly accept from sheer ennui, and "life," as I have read in a quite meritorious poem, "is never the same again." It was thus I now toyed there with my fate in my hands, as might a child have toyed with a bauble. I mean to say, I was looking for nothing thick.

"She's wrote a very fancy piece for that newspaper," Cousin Egbert went on, handing me the sheets of manuscript. Idly I glanced down the pages.

"Yesterday saw the return to Red Gap of Mrs. Senator James Knox Floud and Egbert G. Floud from their extensive European tour," it began. Farther I caught vagrant lines, salient phrases: "—the well-known social leader of our North Side set ... planning a series of entertainments for the approaching social season that promise to eclipse all previous gayeties of Red Gap's smart set ... holding the reins of social leadership with a firm grasp ... distinguished for her social graces and tact as a hostess ... their palatial home on Ophir Avenue, the scene of so much of the smart social life that has distinguished our beautiful city."

It left me rather unmoved from my depression, even the concluding note: "The Flouds are accompanied by their English manservant, secured through the kind offices of the brother of his lordship Earl of Brinstead, the well-known English peer, who will no doubt do much to impart to the coming functions that air of smartness which distinguishes the highest social circles of London, Paris, and other capitals of the great world of fashion."

"Some mess of words, that," observed Cousin Egbert, and it did indeed seem to be rather intimately phrased.

"Better come along with me," he again urged. There was a moment's fateful silence, then, quite mechanically, I arose and prepared to accompany him. In the hall below I handed him his evening stick and gloves, which he absently took from me, and we presently traversed that street of houses much in the fashion of the Floud house and nearly all boasting some sculptured bit of wild life on their terraces.

It was a calm night of late summer; all Nature seemed at peace. I looked aloft and reflected that the same stars were shining upon the civilization I had left so far behind. As we walked I lost myself in musing pensively upon this curious astronomical fact and upon the further vicissitudes to which I would surely be exposed. I compared myself whimsically to an explorer chap who has ventured among a tribe of natives and who must seem to adopt their weird manners and customs to save himself from their fanatic violence.

From this I was aroused by Cousin Egbert, who, with sudden dismay regarding his stick and gloves, uttered a low cry of anguish and thrust them into my hands before I had divined his purpose.

"You'll have to tote them there things," he swiftly explained. "I forgot where I was." I demurred sharply, but he would not listen.

"I didn't mind it so much in Paris and Europe, where I ain't so very well known, but my good gosh! man, this is my home town. You'll have to take them. People won't notice it in you so much, you being a foreigner, anyway."

Without further objection I wearily took them, finding a desperate drollery in being regarded as a foreigner, whereas I was simply alone among foreigners; but I knew that Cousin Egbert lacked the subtlety to grasp this point of view and made no effort to lay it before him. It was clear to me then, I think, that he would forever remain socially impossible, though perhaps no bad sort from a mere human point of view.

We continued our stroll, turning presently from this residential avenue to a street of small unlighted shops, and from this into a wider and brilliantly lighted thoroughfare of larger shops, where my companion presently began to greet native acquaintances. And now once more he affected that fashion of presenting me to his friends that I had so deplored in Paris. His own greeting made, he would call out heartily: "Shake hands with my friend Colonel Ruggles!" Nor would he heed my protests at this, so that in sheer desperation I presently ceased making them, reflecting that after all we were encountering the street classes of the town.

At a score of such casual meetings I was thus presented, for he seemed to know quite almost every one and at times there would be a group of natives about us on the pavement. Twice we went into "saloons," as they rather pretentiously style their public houses, where Cousin Egbert would stand the drinks for all present, not omitting each time to present me formally to the bar-man. In all these instances I was at once asked what I thought of their town, which was at first rather embarrassing, as I was confident that any frank disclosure of my opinion, being necessarily hurried, might easily be misunderstood. I at length devised a conventional formula of praise which, although feeling a frightful fool, I delivered each time thereafter.

Thus we progressed the length of their commercial centre, the incidents varying but little.

"Hello, Sour-dough, you old shellback! When did you come off the trail?"

"Just got in. My lands! but it's good to be back. Billy, shake hands with my friend Colonel Ruggles."

I mean to say, the persons were not all named "Billy," that being used only by way of illustration. Sometimes they would be called "Doc" or "Hank" or "Al" or "Chris." Nor was my companion invariably called "shellback." "Horned-toad" and "Stinging-lizard" were also epithets much in favour with his friends.

At the end of this street we at length paused before the office, as I saw, of "The Red Gap *Recorder*; Daily and Weekly." Cousin Egbert entered here, but came out almost at once.

"Henshaw ain't there, and she said I got to be sure and give him this here piece personally; so come on. He's up to a lawn-feet."

"A social function, sir?" I asked.

"No; just a lawn-feet up in Judge Ballard's front yard to raise money for new uniforms for the band—that's what the boy said in there."

"But would it not be highly improper for me to appear there, sir?" I at once objected. "I fear it's not done, sir."

"Shucks!" he insisted, "don't talk foolish that way. You're a peach of a little mixer all right. Come on! Everybody goes. They'll even let me in. I can give this here piece to Henshaw and then we'll spend a little money to help the band-boys along."

My misgivings were by no means dispelled, yet as the affair seemed to be public rather than smart, I allowed myself to be led on.

Into another street of residences we turned, and after a brisk walk I was able to identify the "front yard" of which my companion had spoken. The strains of an orchestra came to us and from the trees and shrubbery gleamed the lights of paper lanterns. I could discern tents and marquees, a throng of people moving among them. Nearer, I observed a refreshment pavilion and a dancing platform.

Reaching the gate, Cousin Egbert paid for us an entrance fee of two shillings to a young lady in gypsy costume whom he greeted cordially as Beryl Mae, not omitting to present me to her as Colonel Ruggles.

We moved into the thick of the crowd. There was much laughter and hearty speech, and it at once occurred to me that Cousin Egbert had been right: it would not be an assemblage of people that mattered, but rather of small tradesmen, artisans, tenant-farmers and the like with whom I could properly mingle.

My companion was greeted by several of the throng, to whom he in turn presented me, among them after a bit to a slight, reddish-bearded person wearing thick nose-glasses whom I understood to be the pressman we were in search of. Nervous of manner he was and preoccupied with a notebook in which he frantically scribbled items from time to time. Yet no sooner was I presented to him than he began a quizzing sort of conversation with me that lasted near a half-hour, I should say. Very interested he seemed to hear of my previous life, having in full measure that naïve curiosity about one which Americans take so little pains to hide. Like the other natives I had met that evening, he was especially concerned to know what I thought of Red Gap. The chat was not at all unpleasant, as he seemed to be a well-informed person, and it was not without regret that I noted the approach of Cousin Egbert in company with a pleasant-faced, middle-aged lady in Oriental garb, carrying a tambourine.

"Mrs. Ballard, allow me to make you acquainted with my friend Colonel Ruggles!" Thus Cousin Egbert performed his ceremony. The lady grasped my hand with great cordiality.

"You men have monopolized the Colonel long enough," she began with a large coquetry that I found not unpleasing, and firmly grasping my arm she led me off in the direction of the refreshment pavilion, where I was playfully let to know that

I should purchase her bits of refreshment, coffee, plum-cake, an ice, things of that sort. Through it all she kept up a running fire of banter, from time to time presenting me to other women young and old who happened about us, all of whom betrayed an interest in my personality that was not unflattering, even from this commoner sort of the town's people.

Nor would my new friend release me when she had refreshed herself, but had it that I must dance with her. I had now to confess that I was unskilled in the native American folk dances which I had observed being performed, whereupon she briskly chided me for my backwardness, but commanded a valse from the musicians, and this we danced together.

I may here say that I am not without a certain finesse on the dancing-floor and I rather enjoyed the momentary abandon with this village worthy. Indeed I had rather enjoyed the whole affair, though I felt that my manner was gradually marking me as one apart from the natives; made conscious I was of a more finished, a suaver formality in myself—the Mrs. Ballard I had met came at length to be by way of tapping me coquettishly with her tambourine in our lighter moments. Also my presence increasingly drew attention, more and more of the village belles and matrons demanding in their hearty way to be presented to me. Indeed the society was vastly more enlivening, I reflected, than I had found it in a similar walk of life at home.

Rather regretfully I left with Cousin Egbert, who found me at last in one of the tents having my palm read by the gypsy young person who had taken our fees at the gate. Of course I am aware that she was probably without any real gifts for this science, as so few are who undertake it at charity bazaars, yet she told me not a few things that were significant: that my somewhat cold exterior and air of sternness were but a mask to shield a too-impulsive nature; that I possessed great firmness of character and was fond of Nature. She added peculiarly at the last "I see trouble ahead, but you are not to be downcast—the skies will brighten."

It was at this point that Cousin Egbert found me, and after he had warned the young woman that I was "some mixer" we departed. Not until we had reached the Floud home did he discover that he had quite forgotten to hand the press-chap Mrs. Effie's manuscript.

"Dog on the luck!" said he in his quaint tone of exasperation, "here I've went and forgot to give Mrs. Effie's piece to the editor." He sighed ruefully. "Well, to-morrow's another day."

And so the die was cast. To-morrow was indeed another day!

Yet I fell asleep on a memory of the evening that brought me a sort of shamed pleasure—that I had falsely borne the stick and gloves of Cousin Egbert. I knew they had given me rather an air.

CHAPTER EIGHT

I have never been able to recall the precise moment the next morning when I began to feel a strange disquietude but the opening hours of the day were marked by a series of occurrences slight in themselves yet so cumulatively ominous that they seemed to lower above me like a cloud of menace.

Looking from my window, shortly after the rising hour, I observed a paper boy pass through the street, whistling a popular melody as he ran up to toss folded journals into doorways. Something I cannot explain went through me even then; some premonition of disaster slinking furtively under my casual reflection that even in this remote wild the public press was not unknown.

Half an hour later the telephone rang in a lower room and I heard Mrs. Effie speak in answer. An unusual note in her voice caused me to listen more attentively. I stepped outside my door. To some one she was expressing amazement, doubt, and quick impatience which seemed to culminate, after she had again, listened, in a piercing cry of consternation. The term is not too strong. Evidently by the unknown speaker she had been first puzzled, then startled, then horrified; and now, as her anguished cry still rang in my ears, that snaky premonition of evil again writhed across my consciousness.

Presently I heard the front door open and close. Peering into the hallway below I saw that she had secured the newspaper I had seen dropped. Her own door now closed upon her. I waited, listening intently. Something told me that the incident was not closed. A brief interval elapsed and she was again at the telephone, excitedly demanding to be put through to a number.

"Come at once!" I heard her cry. "It's unspeakable! There isn't a moment to lose! Come as you are!" Hereupon, banging the receiver into its place with frenzied roughness, she ran halfway up the stairs to shout:

"Egbert Floud! Egbert Floud! You march right down here this minute, sir!"

From his room I heard an alarmed response, and a moment later knew that he had joined her. The door closed upon them, but high words reached me. Mostly the words of Mrs. Effie they were, though I could detect muffled retorts from the other. Wondering what this could portend, I noted from my window some ten minutes later the hurried arrival of the C. Belknap-Jacksons. The husband clenched a crumpled newspaper in one hand and both he and his wife betrayed signs to the trained eye of having performed hasty toilets for this early call.

As the door of the drawing-room closed upon them there ensued a terrific outburst carrying a rich general effect of astounded rage. Some moments the sinister chorus continued, then a door sharply opened and I heard my own name cried out by Mrs. Effie in a tone that caused me to shudder. Rapidly descending the stairs, I entered the room to face the excited group. Cousin Egbert crouched on a sofa in a far corner like a hunted beast, but the others were standing, and all glared at me furiously.

The ladies addressed me simultaneously, one of them, I believe, asking me what I meant by it and the other demanding how dared I, which had the sole effect of adding to my bewilderment, nor did the words of Cousin Egbert diminish this.

"Hello, Bill!" he called, adding with a sort of timid bravado: "Don't you let 'em bluff you, not for a minute!"

"Yes, and it was probably all that wretched Cousin Egbert's fault in the first place," snapped Mrs. Belknap-Jackson almost tearfully.

"Say, listen here, now; I don't see as how I've done anything wrong," he feebly protested. "Bill's human, ain't he? Answer me that!"

"One sees it all!" This from Belknap-Jackson in bitter and judicial tones. He flung out his hands at Cousin Egbert in a gesture of pitiless scorn. "I dare say," he continued, "that poor Ruggles was merely a tool in his hands—weak, possibly, but not vicious."

"May I inquire——" I made bold to begin, but Mrs. Effie shut me off, brandishing the newspaper before me.

"Read it!" she commanded in hoarse, tragic tones. "There!" she added, pointing at monstrous black headlines on the page as I weakly took it from her. And then I saw. There before them, divining now the enormity of what had come to pass, I controlled myself to master the following screed:

> RED GAP'S DISTINGUISHED VISITOR   Colonel
> Marmaduke Ruggles of London and Paris, late of the
> British army, bon-vivant and man of the world, is in
> our midst   for an indefinite stay, being at present
> the honoured house   guest of Senator and Mrs. James
> Knox Floud, who returned from   foreign parts on the
> 5:16 flyer yesterday afternoon. Colonel   Ruggles
> has long been intimately associated with the family
> of his lordship the Earl of Brinstead, and especially
> with   his lordship's brother, the Honourable George
> Augustus   Vane-Basingwell, with whom he has recently
> been sojourning   in la belle France. In a brief
> interview which the Colonel   genially accorded ye
> scribe, he expressed himself as delighted   with our
> thriving little city.   "It's somewhat a town—if
> I've caught your American slang,"   he said with a
> merry twinkle in his eyes. "You have the garden   spot
> of the West, if not of the civilized world, and your
> people display a charm that must be, I dare say,
> typically   American. Altogether, I am enchanted
> with the wonders I have   beheld since landing at
> your New York, particularly with the   habit your
> best people have of roughing it in camps like that
> of Mr. C. Belknap-Jackson among the mountains of New

York, where   I was most pleasantly entertained by
himself and his delightful   wife. The length of my
stay among you is uncertain, though I   have been
pressed by the Flouds, with whom I am stopping, and
by the C. Belknap-Jacksons to prolong it indefinitely,
and in   fact to identify myself to an extent with
your social life."   The Colonel is a man of
distinguished appearance, with the   seasoned bearing
of an old campaigner, and though at moments   he
displays that cool reserve so typical of the English
gentleman, evidence was not lacking last evening that
he can   unbend on occasion. At the lawn fête held
in the spacious   grounds of Judge Ballard, where a
myriad Japanese lanterns   made the scene a veritable
fairyland, he was quite the most   sought-after
notable present, and gayly tripped the light
fantastic toe with the élite of Red Gap's smart set
there   assembled.   From his cordial manner of
entering into the spirit of the   affair we predict
that Colonel Ruggles will be a decided   acquisition
to our social life, and we understand that a   series
of recherché entertainments in his honour has already
been planned by Mrs. County Judge Ballard, who took
the   distinguished guest under her wing the moment
he appeared   last evening. Welcome to our city,
Colonel! And may the warm   hearts of Red Gap cause
you to forget that European world of   fashion of
which you have long been so distinguished an
ornament!

In a sickening silence I finished the thing. As the absurd sheet fell from my nerveless fingers Mrs. Effie cried in a voice hoarse with emotion:

"Do you realize the dreadful thing you've done to us?"

Speechless I was with humiliation, unequal even to protesting that I had said nothing of the sort to the press-chap. I mean to say, he had wretchedly twisted my harmless words.

"Have you nothing to say for yourself?" demanded Mrs. Belknap-Jackson, also in a voice hoarse with emotion. I glanced at her husband. He, too, was pale with anger and trembling, so that I fancied he dared not trust himself to speak.

"The wretched man," declared Mrs. Effie, addressing them all, "simply can't realize—how disgraceful it is. Oh, we shall never be able to live it down!"

"Imagine those flippant Spokane sheets dressing up the thing," hissed Belknap-Jackson, speaking for the first time. "Imagine their blackguardly humour!"

"And that awful Cousin Egbert," broke in Mrs. Effie, pointing a desperate finger toward him. "Think of the laughing-stock he'll become! Why, he'll simply never be able to hold up his head again."

"Say, you listen here," exclaimed Cousin Egbert with sudden heat; "never you mind about my head. I always been able to hold up my head any time I felt like it." And again to me he threw out, "Don't you let 'em bluff you, Bill!"

"I gave him a notice for the paper," explained Mrs. Effie plaintively; "I'd written it all nicely out to save them time in the office, and that would have prevented this disgrace, but he never gave it in."

"I clean forgot it," declared the offender. "What with one thing and another, and gassing back and forth with some o' the boys, it kind of went out o' my head."

"Meeting our best people—actually dancing with them!" murmured Mrs. Belknap-Jackson in a voice vibrant with horror. "My dear, I truly am so sorry for you."

"You people entertained him delightfully at your camp," murmured Mrs. Effie quickly in her turn, with a gesture toward the journal.

"Oh, we're both in it, I know. I know. It's appalling!"

"We'll never be able to live it down!" said Mrs. Effie. "We shall have to go away somewhere."

"Can't you imagine what Jen' Ballard will say when she learns the truth?" asked the other bitterly. "Say we did it on purpose to humiliate her, and just as all our little scraps were being smoothed out, so we could get together and put that Bohemian set in its place. Oh, it's so dreadful!" On the verge of tears she seemed.

"And scarcely a word mentioned of our own return—when I'd taken such pains with the notice!"

"Listen here!" said Cousin Egbert brightly. "I'll take the piece down now and he can print it in his paper for you to-morrow."

"You can't understand," she replied impatiently. "I casually mentioned our having brought an English manservant. Print that now and insult all our best people who received him!"

"Pathetic how little the poor chap understands," sighed Belknap-Jackson. "No sense at all of our plight—naturally, naturally!"

"'A series of entertainments being planned in his honour!'" quavered Mrs. Belknap-Jackson.

"'The most sought-after notable present!'" echoed Mrs. Effie viciously.

Again and again I had essayed to protest my innocence, only to provoke renewed outbursts. I could but stand there with what dignity I retained and let them savage me. Cousin Egbert now spoke again:

"Shucks! What's all the fuss? Just because I took Bill out and give him a good time! Didn't you say yourself in that there very piece that he'd impart to coming functions an air of smartness like they have all over Europe? Didn't you write them very words? And ain't he already done it the very first night he gets here,

81

right at that there lawn-feet where I took him? What for do you jump on me then? I took him and he done it; he done it good. Bill's a born mixer. Why, he had all them North Side society dames stung the minute I flashed him; after him quicker than hell could scorch a feather; run out from under their hats to get introduced to him—and now you all turn on me like a passel of starved wolves." He finished with a note of genuine irritation I had never heard in his voice.

"The poor creature's demented," remarked Mrs. Belknap-Jackson pityingly.

"Always been that way," said Mrs. Effie hopelessly.

Belknap-Jackson contented himself with a mere clicking sound of commiseration.

"All right, then, if you're so smart," continued Cousin Egbert. "Just the same Bill, here, is the most popular thing in the whole Kulanche Valley this minute, so all I got to say is if you want to play this here society game you better stick close by him. First thing you know, some o' them other dames'll have him won from you. That Mis' Ballard's going to invite him to supper or dinner or some other doings right away. I heard her say so."

To my amazement a curious and prolonged silence greeted this amazing tirade. The three at length were regarding each other almost furtively. Belknap-Jackson began to pace the floor in deep thought.

"After all, no one knows except ourselves," he said in curiously hushed tones at last.

"Of course it's one way out of a dreadful mess," observed his wife.

"Colonel Marmaduke Ruggles of the British army," said Mrs. Effie in a peculiar tone, as if she were trying over a song.

"It may indeed be the best way out of an impossible situation," continued Belknap-Jackson musingly. "Otherwise we face a social upheaval that might leave us demoralized for years—say nothing of making us a laughingstock with the rabble. In fact, I see nothing else to be done."

"Cousin Egbert would be sure to spoil it all again," objected Mrs. Effie, glaring at him.

"No danger," returned the other with his superior smile. "Being quite unable to realize what has happened, he will be equally unable to realize what is going to happen. We may speak before him as before a babe in arms; the amenities of the situation are forever beyond him."

"I guess I always been able to hold up my head when I felt like it," put in Cousin Egbert, now again both sullen and puzzled. Once more he threw out his encouragement to me: "Don't let 'em run any bluffs, Bill! They can't touch you, and they know it."

"'Touch him,'" murmured Mrs. Belknap-Jackson with an able sneer. "My dear, what a trial he must have been to you. I never knew. He's as bad as the mater, actually."

"And such hopes I had of him in Paris," replied Mrs. Effie, "when he was taking up Art and dressing for dinner and everything!"

"I can be pushed just so far!" muttered the offender darkly.

There was now a ring at the door which I took the liberty of answering, and received two notes from a messenger. One bore the address of Mrs. Floud and the other was quite astonishingly to myself, the name preceded by "Colonel."

"That's Jen' Ballard's stationery!" cried Mrs. Belknap-Jackson. "Trust her not to lose one second in getting busy!"

"But he mustn't answer the door that way," exclaimed her husband as I handed Mrs. Effie her note.

They were indeed both from my acquaintance of the night before. Receiving permission to read my own, I found it to be a dinner invitation for the following Friday. Mrs. Effie looked up from hers.

"It's all too true," she announced grimly. "We're asked to dinner and she earnestly hopes dear Colonel Ruggles will have made no other engagement. She also says hasn't he the darlingest English accent. Oh, isn't it a mess!"

"You see how right I am," said Belknap-Jackson.

"I guess we've got to go through with it," conceded Mrs. Effie.

"The pushing thing that Ballard woman is!" observed her friend.

"Ruggles!" exclaimed Belknap-Jackson, addressing me with sudden decision.

"Yes, sir."

"Listen carefully—I'm quite serious. In future you will try to address me as if I were your equal. Ah! rather you will try to address me as if you were *my* equal. I dare say it will come to you easily after a bit of practice. Your employers will wish you to address them in the same manner. You will cultivate toward us a manner of easy friendliness—remember I'm entirely serious—quite as if you were one of us. You must try to be, in short, the Colonel Marmaduke Ruggles that wretched penny-a-liner has foisted upon these innocent people. We shall thus avert a most humiliating contretemps."

The thing fair staggered me. I fell weakly into the chair by which I had stood, for the first time in a not uneventful career feeling that my *savoir faire* had been overtaxed.

"Quite right," he went on. "Be seated as one of us," and he amazingly proffered me his cigarette case. "Do take one, old chap," he insisted as I weakly waved it away, and against my will I did so. "Dare say you'll fancy them—a non-throat cigarette especially prescribed for me." He now held a match so that I was obliged to smoke. Never have I been in less humour for it.

"There, not so hard, is it? You see, we're getting on famously."

"Ain't I always said Bill was a good mixer?" called Cousin Egbert, but his gaucherie was pointedly ignored.

"Now," continued Belknap-Jackson, "suppose you tell us in a chatty, friendly way just what you think about this regrettable affair." All sat forward interestedly.

"But I met what I supposed were your villagers," I said; "your small tradesmen, your artisans, clerks, shop-assistants, tenant-farmers, and the like, I'd no idea in the world they were your county families. Seemed quite a bit too jolly for that. And your press-chap—preposterous, quite! He quizzed me rather, I admit, but he made it vastly different. Your pressmen are remarkable. That thing is a fair crumpler."

"But surely," put in Mrs. Effie, "you could see that Mrs. Judge Ballard must be one of our best people."

"I saw she was a goodish sort," I explained, "but it never occurred to me one would meet her in your best houses. And when she spoke of entertaining me I fancied I might stroll by her cottage some fair day and be asked in to a slice from one of her own loaves and a dish of tea. There was that about her."

"Mercy!" exclaimed both ladies, Mrs. Belknap-Jackson adding a bit maliciously I thought, "Oh, don't you awfully wish she could hear him say it just that way?"

"As to the title," I continued, "Mr. Egbert has from the first had a curious American tendency to present me to his many friends as 'Colonel.' I am sure he means as little by it as when he calls me 'Bill,' which I have often reminded him is not a name of mine."

"Oh, we understand the poor chap is a social incompetent," said Belknap-Jackson with a despairing shrug.

"Say, look here," suddenly exclaimed Cousin Egbert, a new heat in his tone, "what I call Bill ain't a marker to what I call you when I really get going. You ought to hear me some day when I'm feeling right!"

"Really!" exclaimed the other with elaborate sarcasm.

"Yes, sir. Surest thing you know. I could call you a lot of good things right now if so many ladies wasn't around. You don't think I'd be afraid, do you? Why, Bill there had you licked with one wallop."

"But really, really!" protested the other with a helpless shrug to the ladies, who were gasping with dismay.

"You ruffian!" cried his wife.

"Egbert Floud," said Mrs. Effie fiercely, "you will apologize to Charles before you leave this room. The idea of forgetting yourself that way. Apologize at once!"

"Oh, very well," he grumbled, "I apologize like I'm made to." But he added quickly with even more irritation, "only don't you get the idea it's because I'm afraid of you."

"Tush, tush!" said Belknap-Jackson.

"No, sir; I apologize, but it ain't for one minute because I'm afraid of you."

"Your bare apology is ample; I'm bound to accept it," replied the other, a bit uneasily I thought.

"Come right down to it," continued Cousin Egbert, "I ain't afraid of hardly any person. I can be pushed just so far." Here he looked significantly at Mrs. Effie.

"After all I've tried to do for him!" she moaned. "I thought he had something in him."

"Darn it all, I like to be friendly with my friends," he bluntly persisted. "I call a man anything that suits me. And I ain't ever apologized yet because I was afraid. I want all parties here to get that."

"Say no more, please. It's quite understood," said Belknap-Jackson hastily. The other subsided into low mutterings.

"I trust you fully understand the situation, Ruggles—Colonel Ruggles," he continued to me.

"It's preposterous, but plain as a pillar-box," I answered. "I can only regret it as keenly as any right-minded person should. It's not at all what I've been accustomed to."

"Very well. Then I suggest that you accompany me for a drive this afternoon. I'll call for you with the trap, say at three."

"Perhaps," suggested his wife, "it might be as well if Colonel Ruggles were to come to us as a guest." She was regarding me with a gaze that was frankly speculative.

"Oh, not at all, not at all!" retorted Mrs. Effie crisply. "Having been announced as our house guest—never do in the world for him to go to you so soon. We must be careful in this. Later, perhaps, my dear."

Briefly the ladies measured each other with a glance. Could it be, I asked myself, that they were sparring for the possession of me?

"Naturally he will be asked about everywhere, and there'll be loads of entertaining to do in return."

"Of course," returned Mrs. Effie, "and I'd never think of putting it off on to you, dear, when we're wholly to blame for the awful thing."

"That's so thoughtful of you, dear," replied her friend coldly.

"At three, then," said Belknap-Jackson as we arose.

"I shall be delighted," I murmured.

"I bet you won't," said Cousin Egbert sourly. "He wants to show you off." This, I could see, was ignored as a sheer indecency.

"We shall have to get a reception in quick," said Mrs. Effie, her eyes narrowed in calculation.

"I don't see what all the fuss was about," remarked Cousin Egbert again, as if to himself; "tearing me to pieces like a passel of wolves!"

The Belknap-Jacksons left hastily, not deigning him a glance. And to do the poor soul justice, I believe he did not at all know what the "fuss" had been about. The niceties of the situation were beyond him, dear old sort though he had shown himself to be. I knew then I was never again to be harsh with him, let him dress as he would.

"Say," he asked, the moment we were alone, "you remember that thing you called him back there that night—'blighted little mug,' was it?"

"It's best forgotten, sir," I said.

"Well, sir, some way it sounded just the thing to call him. It sounded bully. What does it mean?"

So far was his darkened mind from comprehending that I, in a foreign land, among a weird people, must now have a go at being a gentleman; and that if I fluffed my catch we should all be gossipped to rags!

Alone in my room I made a hasty inventory of my wardrobe. Thanks to the circumstance that the Honourable George, despite my warning, had for several years refused to bant, it was rather well stocked. The evening clothes were irreproachable; so were the frock coat and a morning suit. Of waistcoats there were a number showing but slight wear. The three lounge-suits of tweed, though slightly demoded, would still be vogue in this remote spot. For sticks, gloves, cravats, and body-linen I saw that I should be compelled to levy on the store I had laid in for Cousin Egbert, and I happily discovered that his top-hat set me quite effectively.

Also in a casket of trifles that had knocked about in my box I had the good fortune to find the monocle that the Honourable George had discarded some years before on the ground that it was "bally nonsense." I screwed the glass into my eye. The effect was tremendous.

Rather a lark I might have thought it but for the false military title. That was rank deception, and I have always regarded any sort of wrongdoing as detestable. Perhaps if he had introduced me as a mere subaltern in a line regiment—but I was powerless.

For the afternoon's drive I chose the smartest of the lounge-suits, a Carlsbad hat which Cousin Egbert had bitterly resented for himself, and for top-coat a light weight, straight-hanging Chesterfield with velvet collar which, although the cut studiously avoids a fitted effect, is yet a garment that intrigues the eye when carried with any distinction. So many top-coats are but mere wrappings! I had, too, gloves of a delicately contrasting tint.

Altogether I felt I had turned myself out well, and this I found to be the verdict of Mrs. Effie, who engaged me in the hall to say that I was to have anything in the way of equipment I liked to ask for. Belknap-Jackson also, arriving now in a smart trap to which he drove two cobs tandem, was at once impressed and made me compliments upon my tenue. I was aware that I appeared not badly beside him. I mean to say, I felt that I was vogue in the finest sense of the word.

Mrs. Effie waved us a farewell from the doorway, and I was conscious that from several houses on either side of the avenue we attracted more than a bit of attention. There were doors opened, blinds pushed aside, faces—that sort of thing.

At a leisurely pace we progressed through the main thoroughfares. That we created a sensation, especially along the commercial streets, where my host halted at shops to order goods, cannot be denied. Furore is perhaps the word. I mean to say, almost quite every one stared. Rather more like a parade it was than I could have wished, but I was again resolved to be a dead sportsman.

Among those who saluted us from time to time were several of the lesser townsmen to whom Cousin Egbert had presented me the evening before, and I now perceived that most of these were truly persons I must not know in my present station—hodmen, road-menders, grooms, delivery-chaps, that sort. In responding to the often florid salutations of such, I instilled into my barely perceptible nod a certain frigidity that I trusted might be informing. I mean to say, having now a position to keep up, it would never do at all to chatter and pal about loosely as Cousin Egbert did.

When we had done a fairish number of streets, both of shops and villas, we drove out a winding roadway along a tarn to the country club. The house was an unpretentious structure of native wood, fronting a couple of tennis courts and a golf links, but although it was tea-time, not a soul was present. Having unlocked the door, my host suggested refreshment and I consented to partake of a glass of sherry and a biscuit. But these, it seemed, were not to be had; so over pegs of ginger ale, found in an ice-chest, we sat for a time and chatted.

"You will find us crude, Ruggles, as I warned you," my host observed. "Take this deserted clubhouse at this hour. It tells the story. Take again the matter of sherry and a biscuit—so simple! Yet no one ever thinks of them, and what you mean by a biscuit is in this wretched hole spoken of as a cracker."

I thanked him for the item, resolving to add it to my list of curious Americanisms. Already I had begun a narrative of my adventures in this wild land, a thing I had tentatively entitled, "Alone in North America."

"Though we have people in abundance of ample means," he went on, "you will regret to know that we have not achieved a leisured class. Barely once in a fortnight will you see this club patronized, after all the pains I took in its organization. They simply haven't evolved to the idea yet; sometimes I have moments in which I despair of their ever doing so."

As usual he grew depressed when speaking of social Red Gap, so that we did not tarry long in the silent place that should have been quite alive with people smartly having their tea. As we drove back he touched briefly and with all delicacy on our changed relations.

"What made me only too glad to consent to it," he said, "is the sodden depravity of that Floud chap. Really he's a menace to the community. I saw from the degenerate leer on his face this morning that he will not be able to keep silent about that little affair of ours back there. Mark my words, he'll talk. And fancy how embarrassing had you continued in the office for which you were engaged. Fancy it being known I had been assaulted by a—you see what I mean. But now, let him talk his vilest. What is it? A mere disagreement between two gentlemen, generous, hot-tempered chaps, followed by mutual apologies. A mere nothing!"

I was conscious of more than a little irritation at his manner of speaking of Cousin Egbert, but this in my new character I could hardly betray.

When he set me down at the Floud house, "Thanks for the breeze-out," I said; then, with an easy wave of the hand and in firm tones, "Good day, Jackson! See you again, old chap!"

I had nerved myself to it as to an icy tub and was rewarded by a glow such as had suffused me that morning in Paris after the shameful proceedings with Cousin Egbert and the Indian Tuttle. I mean to say, I felt again that wonderful thrill of equality—quite as if my superiors were not all about me.

Inside the house Mrs. Effie addressed the last of a heap of invitations for an early reception—"To meet Colonel Marmaduke Ruggles," they read.

CHAPTER NINE

Of the following fortnight I find it difficult to write coherently. I found myself in a steady whirl of receptions, luncheons, dinners, teas, and assemblies of rather a pretentious character, at the greater number of which I was obliged to appear as the guest of honour. It began with the reception of Mrs. Floud, at which I may be said to have made my first formal bow to the smarter element of Red Gap, followed by the dinner of the Mrs. Ballard, with whom I had formed acquaintance on that first memorable evening.

I was during this time like a babe at blind play with a set of chess men, not knowing king from pawn nor one rule of the game. Senator Floud—who was but a member of their provincial assembly, I discovered—sought an early opportunity to felicitate me on my changed estate, though he seemed not a little amused by it.

"Good work!" he said. "You know I was afraid our having an English valet would put me in bad with the voters this fall. They're already saying I wear silk stockings since I've been abroad. My wife did buy me six pair, but I've never worn any. Shows how people talk, though. And even now they'll probably say I'm making up to the British army. But it's better than having a valet in the house. The plain people would never stand my having a valet and I know it."

I thought this most remarkable, that his constituency should resent his having proper house service. American politics were, then, more debased than even we of England had dreamed.

"Good work!" he said again. "And say, take out your papers—become one of us. Be a citizen. Nothing better than an American citizen on God's green earth. Read the Declaration of Independence. Here——" From a bookcase at his hand he reached me a volume. "Read and reflect, my man! Become a citizen of a country where true worth has always its chance and one may hope to climb to any heights whatsoever." Quite like an advertisement he talked, but I read their so-called Declaration, finding it snarky in the extreme and with no end of silly rot about equality. In no way at all did it solve the problems by which I had been so suddenly confronted.

Social lines in the town seemed to have been drawn by no rule whatever. There were actually tradesmen who seemed to matter enormously; on the other hand, there were those of undoubted qualifications, like Mrs. Pettengill, for example, and Cousin Egbert, who deliberately chose not to matter, and mingled as freely with the Bohemian set as they did with the county families. Thus one could never be quite certain whom one was meeting. There was the Tuttle person. I had learned from Mrs. Effie in Paris that he was an Indian (accounting for much that was startling in his behaviour there) yet despite his being an aborigine I now learned that his was one of the county families and he and his white American wife were guests at that first dinner. Throughout the meal both Cousin Egbert and he winked atrociously at me whenever they could catch my eye.

There was, again, an English person calling himself Hobbs, a baker, to whom Cousin Egbert presented me, full of delight at the idea that as compatriots we were bound to be congenial. Yet it needed only a glance and a moment's listening to the fellow's execrable cockney dialect to perceive that he was distinctly low-class, and I was immensely relieved, upon inquiry, to learn that he affiliated only with the Bohemian set. I felt a marked antagonism between us at that first meeting; the fellow eyed me with frank suspicion and displayed a taste for low chaffing which I felt bound to rebuke. He it was, I may now disclose, who later began a fashion of referring to me as "Lord Algy," which I found in the worst possible taste. "Sets himself up for a gentleman, does he? He ain't no more a gentleman than wot I be!" This speech of his reported to me will show how impossible the creature was. He was simply a person one does not know, and I was not long in letting him see it.

And there was the woman who was to play so active a part in my later history, of whom it will be well to speak at once. I had remarked her on the main street before I knew her identity. I am bound to say she stood out from the other women of Red Gap by reason of a certain dash, not to say beauty. Rather above medium height and of pleasingly full figure, her face was piquantly alert, with long-lashed eyes of a peculiar green, a small nose, the least bit raised, a lifted chin, and an abundance of yellowish hair. But it was the expertness of her gowning that really held my attention at that first view, and the fact that she knew what to put on her head. For the most part, the ladies I had met were well enough gotten up yet looked curiously all wrong, lacking a genius for harmony of detail.

This person, I repeat, displayed a taste that was faultless, a knowledge of the peculiar needs of her face and figure that was unimpeachable. Rather with regret it was I found her to be a Mrs. Kenner, the leader of the Bohemian set. And then came the further items that marked her as one that could not be taken up. Perhaps a summary of these may be conveyed when I say that she had long been known as Klondike Kate. She had some years before, it seemed, been a dancing person in the far Alaska north and had there married the proprietor of one of the resorts in which she disported herself—a man who had accumulated a very sizable fortune in his public house and who was shot to death by one of his patrons who had alleged unfairness in a game of chance. The widow had then purchased a townhouse in Red Gap and had quickly gathered about her what was known as the Bohemian set, the county families, of course, refusing to know her.

After that first brief study of her I could more easily account for the undercurrents of bitterness I had felt in Red Gap society. She would be, I saw, a dangerous woman in any situation where she was opposed; there was that about her—a sort of daring disregard of the established social order. I was not surprised to learn that the men of the community strongly favoured her, especially the younger dancing set who were not restrained by domestic considerations. Small wonder then that the women of the "old noblesse," as I may call them, were outspokenly bitter in their comments upon her. This I discovered when I attended an afternoon meeting of the ladies' "Onwards and Upwards Club," which, I had been told, would be devoted to a study of the English Lake poets, and where, it having been discovered that I read rather well, I had consented to favour the assembly with some of the more significant bits from these bards. The meeting, I regret to say, after a formal enough opening was diverted from its original purpose, the time being occupied in a quite heated discussion of a so-called "Dutch Supper" the Klondike person had given the evening before, the same having been attended, it seemed, by the husbands of at least three of those present, who had gone incognito, as it were. At no time during the ensuing two hours was there a moment that seemed opportune for the introduction of some of our noblest verse.

And so, by often painful stages, did my education progress. At the country club I played golf with Mr. Jackson. At social affairs I appeared with the Flouds. I played bridge. I danced the more dignified dances. And, though there was no proper church in the town—only dissenting chapels, Methodist, Presbyterian, and such outlandish persuasions—I attended services each Sabbath, and more than once had tea with what at home would have been the vicar of the parish.

It was now, when I had begun to feel a bit at ease in my queer foreign environment, that Mr. Belknap-Jackson broached his ill-starred plan for amateur theatricals. At the first suggestion of this I was immensely taken with the idea, suspecting that he would perhaps present "Hamlet," a part to which I have devoted long and intelligent study and to which I feel that I could bring something which has not yet been imparted to it by even the most skilled of our professional actors. But at my suggestion of this Mr. Belknap-Jackson informed me that he had already played Hamlet himself the year before, leaving nothing further to be done in that direction, and he wished now to attempt something more difficult; something, moreover, that would appeal to the little group of thinking people about us—he would have "a little theatre of ideas," as he phrased it—and he had chosen for his first offering a play entitled "Ghosts" by the foreign dramatist Ibsen.

I suspected at first that this might be a farce where a supposititious ghost brings about absurd predicaments in a country house, having seen something along these lines, but a reading of the thing enlightened me as to its character, which, to put it bluntly, is rather thick. There is a strain of immorality running through it which I believe cannot be too strongly condemned if the world is to be made better, and this is rendered the more repugnant to right-thinking people by the fact that the participants are middle-class persons who converse in quite commonplace language such as one may hear any day in the home.

Wrongdoing is surely never so objectionable as when it is indulged in by common people and talked about in ordinary language, and the language of this play is not stage language at all. Immorality such as one gets in Shakespeare is of so elevated a character that one accepts it, the language having a grandeur incomparably above what any person was ever capable of in private life, being always elegant and unnatural.

Though I felt this strongly, I was in no position to urge my objections, and at length consented to take a part in the production, reflecting that the people depicted were really foreigners and the part I would play was that of a clergyman whose behaviour throughout is above reproach. For himself Mr. Jackson had chosen the part of Oswald, a youth who goes quite dotty at the last for reasons which are better not talked about. His wife was to play the part of a serving-maid, who was rather a baggage, while Mrs. Judge Ballard was to enact his mother. (I may say in passing I have learned that the plays of this foreigner are largely concerned with people who have been queer at one time or another, so that one's parentage is often uncertain, though they always pay for it by going off in the head before the final curtain. I mean to say, there is too much neighbourhood scandal in them.)

There remained but one part to fill, that of the father of the serving-maid, an uncouth sort of drinking-man, quite low-class, who, in my opinion, should never have been allowed on the stage at all, since no moral lesson is taught by him. It was in the casting of this part that Mr. Jackson showed himself of a forgiving nature. He offered it to Cousin Egbert, saying he was the true "type"—"with his weak, dissolute face"—and that "types" were all the rage in theatricals.

At first the latter heatedly declined the honour, but after being urged and browbeaten for three days by Mrs. Effie he somewhat sullenly consented, being shown that there were not many lines for him to learn. From the first, I think, he was rendered quite miserable by the ordeal before him, yet he submitted to the rehearsals with a rather pathetic desire to please, and for a time all seemed well. Many an hour found him mugging away at the book, earnestly striving to memorize the part, or, as he quaintly expressed it, "that there piece they want me to speak." But as the day of our performance drew near it became evident to me, at least, that he was in a desperately black state of mind. As best I could I cheered him with words of praise, but his eye met mine blankly at such times and I could see him shudder poignantly while waiting the moment of his entrance.

And still all might have been well, I fancy, but for the extremely conscientious views of Mr. Jackson in the matter of our costuming and make-up. With his lines fairly learned, Cousin Egbert on the night of our dress rehearsal was called upon first to don the garb of the foreign carpenter he was to enact, the same involving shorts and gray woollen hose to his knees, at which he protested violently. So far as I could gather, his modesty was affronted by this revelation of his lower legs. Being at length persuaded to this sacrifice, he next submitted his face to Mr. Jackson, who adjusted it to a labouring person's beard and eyebrows, crimsoning the cheeks and nose heavily with grease-paint and crowning all with an unkempt wig.

The result, I am bound to say, was artistic in the extreme. No one would have suspected the identity of Cousin Egbert, and I had hopes that he would feel a new courage for his part when he beheld himself. Instead, however, after one quick glance into the glass he emitted a gasp of horror that was most eloquent, and thereafter refused to be comforted, holding himself aloof and glaring hideously at all who approached him. Rather like a mad dog he was.

Half an hour later, when all was ready for our first act, Cousin Egbert was not to be found. I need not dwell upon the annoyance this occasioned, nor upon how a substitute in the person of our hall's custodian, or janitor, was impressed to read the part. Suffice it to tell briefly that Cousin Egbert, costumed and bedizened as he was, had fled not only the theatre but the town as well. Search for him on the morrow was unavailing. Not until the second day did it become known that he had been seen at daybreak forty miles from Red Gap, goading a spent horse into the wilds of the adjacent mountains. Our informant disclosed that one side of his face was still bearded and that he had kept glancing back over his shoulder at frequent intervals, as if fearful of pursuit. Something of his frantic state may also be gleaned from the circumstance that the horse he rode was one he had found hitched in a side street near the hall, its ownership being unknown to him.

For the rest it may be said that our performance was given as scheduled, announcement being made of the sudden illness of Mr. Egbert Floud, and his part being read from the book in a rich and cultivated voice by the superintendent of the high school. Our efforts were received with respectful attention by a large audience, among whom I noted many of the Bohemian set, and this I took as an especial tribute to our merits. Mr. Belknap-Jackson, however, to whom I mentioned the circumstance, was pessimistic.

"I fear," said he, "we have not heard the last of it. I am sure they came for no good purpose."

"They were quite orderly in their behaviour," I suggested

"Which is why I suspect them. That Kenner woman, Hobbs, the baker, the others of their set—they're not thinking people; I dare say they never consider social problems seriously. And you may have noticed that they announce an amateur minstrel performance for a week hence. I'm quite convinced that they mean to be vulgar to the last extreme—there has been so much talk of the behaviour of the wretched Floud, a fellow who really has no place in our modern civilization. He should be compelled to remain on his ranche."

And indeed these suspicions proved to be only too well founded. That which followed was so atrociously personal that in any country but America we could have had an action against them. As Mr. Belknap-Jackson so bitterly said when all was over, "Our boasted liberty has degenerated into license."

It is best told in a few words, this affair of the minstrel performance, which I understood was to be an entertainment wherein the participants darkened themselves to resemble blackamoors. Naturally, I did not attend, it being agreed that the best people should signify their disapproval by staying away, but the disgraceful affair was recounted to me in all its details by more than one of the large audience that assembled. In the so-called "grand first part" there seemed to have been little that was flagrantly insulting to us, although in their exchange of conundrums, which is a peculiar feature of this form of entertainment, certain names were bandied about with a freedom that boded no good.

It was in the after-piece that the poltroons gave free play to their vilest fancies. Our piece having been announced as "Ghosts; a Drama for Thinking People," this part was entitled on their programme, "Gloats; a Dram for Drinking People," a transposition that should perhaps suffice to show the dreadful lengths to which they went; yet I feel that the thing should be set down in full.

The stage was set as our own had been, but it would scarce be credited that the Kenner woman in male attire had made herself up in a curiously accurate resemblance to Belknap-Jackson as he had rendered the part of Oswald, copying not alone his wig, moustache, and fashion of speech, but appearing in a golfing suit which was recognized by those present as actually belonging to him.

Nor was this the worst, for the fellow Hobbs had copied my own dress and make-up and persisted in speaking in an exaggerated manner alleged to resemble mine. This, of course, was the most shocking bad taste, and while it was quite to have been expected of Hobbs, I was indeed rather surprised that the entire assembly did not leave the auditorium in disgust the moment they perceived his base intention. But it was Cousin Egbert whom they had chosen to rag most unmercifully, and they were not long in displaying their clumsy attempts at humour.

As the curtain went up they were searching for him, affecting to be unconscious of the presence of their audience, and declaring that the play couldn't go on without him. "Have you tried all the saloons?" asked one, to which another responded, "Yes, and he's been in all of them, but now he has fled. The sheriff has put bloodhounds on his trail and promises to have him here, dead or alive."

"Then while we are waiting," declared the character supposed to represent myself, "I will tell you a wheeze," whereupon both the female characters fell to their knees shrieking, "Not that! My God, not that!" while Oswald sneered viciously and muttered, "Serves me right for leaving Boston."

To show the infamy of the thing, I must here explain that at several social gatherings, in an effort which I still believe was praiseworthy, I had told an excellent wheeze which runs: "Have you heard the story of the three holes in the ground?" I mean to say, I would ask this in an interested manner, as if I were about to relate the anecdote, and upon being answered "No!" I would exclaim with mock seriousness, "Well! Well! Well!" This had gone rippingly almost quite every time I had favoured a company with it, hardly any one of my hearers failing to get the joke at a second telling. I mean to say, the three holes in the ground being three "Wells!" uttered in rapid succession.

Of course if one doesn't see it at once, or finds it a bit subtle, it's quite silly to attempt to explain it, because logically there is no adequate explanation. It is merely a bit of nonsense, and that's quite all to it. But these boors now fell upon it with their coarse humour, the fellow Hobbs pretending to get it all wrong by asking if they had heard the story about the three wells and the others replying: "No, tell us the hole thing," which made utter nonsense of it, whereupon they all began to cry, "Well! well! well!" at each other until interrupted by a terrific noise in the wings, which was followed by the entrance of the supposed Cousin Egbert, a part enacted by the cab-driver who had conveyed us from the station the day of our arrival. Dragged on he was by the sheriff and two of the town constables, the latter being armed with fowling-pieces and the sheriff holding two large dogs in leash. The character himself was heavily manacled and madly rattled his chains, his face being disguised to resemble Cousin Egbert's after the beard had been adjusted.

"Here he is!" exclaimed the supposed sheriff; "the dogs ran him into the third hole left by the well-diggers, and we lured him out by making a noise like sour dough." During this speech, I am told, the character snarled continuously and tried to bite his captors. At this the woman, who had so deplorably unsexed herself for the character of Mr. Belknap-Jackson as he had played Oswald, approached the prisoner and smartly drew forth a handful of his beard which she stuffed into a pipe and proceeded to smoke, after which they pretended that the play went on. But no more than a few speeches had been uttered when the supposed Cousin Egbert eluded his captors and, emitting a loud shriek of horror, leaped headlong through the window at the back of the stage, his disappearance being followed by the sounds of breaking glass as he was supposed to fall to the street below.

"How lovely!" exclaimed the mimic Oswald. "Perhaps he has broken both his legs so he can't run off any more," at which the fellow Hobbs remarked in his affected tones: "That sort of thing would never do with us."

This I learned aroused much laughter, the idea being that the remark had been one which I am supposed to make in private life, though I dare say I have never uttered anything remotely like it.

"The fellow is quite impossible," continued the spurious Oswald, with a doubtless rather clever imitation of Mr. Belknap-Jackson's manner. "If he is killed, feed him to the goldfish and let one of the dogs read his part. We must get along with this play. Now, then. 'Ah! why did I ever leave Boston where every one is nice and proper?'" To which his supposed mother replied with feigned emotion: "It was because of your father, my poor boy. Ah, what I had to endure through those years when he cursed and spoke disrespectfully of our city. 'Scissors and white aprons,' he would cry out, 'Why is Boston?' But I bore it all for your sake, and now you, too, are smoking—you will go the same way."

"But promise me, mother," returns Oswald, "promise me if I ever get dusty in the garret, that Lord Algy here will tell me one of his funny wheezes and put me out of pain. You could not bear to hear me knocking Boston as poor father did. And I feel it coming—already my mother-in-law has bluffed me into admitting that Red Gap has a right to be on the same map with Boston if it's a big map."

And this was the coarsely wretched buffoonery that refined people were expected to sit through! Yet worse followed, for at their climax, the mimic Oswald having gone quite off his head, the Hobbs person, still with the preposterous affectation of taking me off in speech and manner, was persuaded by the stricken mother to sing. "Sing that dear old plantation melody from London," she cried, "so that my poor boy may know there are worse things than death." And all this witless piffle because of a quite natural misunderstanding of mine.

I have before referred to what I supposed was an American plantation melody which I had heard a black sing at Brighton, meaning one of the English blacks who colour themselves for the purpose, but on reciting the lines at an evening affair, when the American folksongs were under discussion, I was told that it could hardly have been written by an American at all, but doubtless by one of our own composers who had taken too little trouble with his facts. I mean to say, the song as I had it, betrayed misapprehensions both of a geographical and faunal nature, but I am certain that no one thought the worse of me for having been deceived, and I had supposed the thing forgotten. Yet now what did I hear but that a garbled version of this song had been supposedly sung by myself, the Hobbs person meantime mincing across the stage and gesturing with a monocle which he had somehow procured, the words being quite simply:

"Away down south in Michigan,

Where I was a slave, so happy and so gay,

'Twas there I mowed the cotton and the cane.

I used to hunt the elephants, the tigers, and giraffes,

And the alligators at the break of day.

But the blooming Injuns prowled about my cabin every night,

So I'd take me down my banjo and I'd play,

And I'd sing a little song and I'd make them dance with glee,

On the banks of the Ohio far away."

I mean to say, there was nothing to make a dust about even if the song were not of a true American origin, yet I was told that the creature who sang it received hearty applause and even responded to an encore.

CHAPTER TEN

I need hardly say that this public ridicule left me dazed. Desperately I recalled our calm and orderly England where such things would not be permitted. There we are born to our stations and are not allowed to forget them. We matter from birth, or we do not matter, and that's all to it. Here there seemed to be no stations to which one was born; the effect was sheer anarchy, and one might ridicule any one whomsoever. As was actually said in that snarky manifesto drawn up by the rebel leaders at the time our colonies revolted, "All men are created free and equal"—than which absurdity could go no farther—yet the lower middle classes seemed to behave quite as if it were true.

And now through no fault of my own another awkward circumstance was threatening to call further attention to me, which was highly undesirable at this moment when the cheap one-and-six Hobbs fellow had so pointedly singled me out for his loathsome buffoonery.

Some ten days before, walking alone at the edge of town one calm afternoon, where I might commune with Nature, of which I have always been fond, I noted an humble vine-clad cot, in the kitchen garden of which there toiled a youngish, neat-figured woman whom I at once recognized as a person who did occasional charring for the Flouds on the occasion of their dinners or receptions. As she had appeared to be cheerful and competent, of respectful manners and a quite marked intelligence, I made nothing of stopping at her gate for a moment's chat, feeling a quite decided relief in the thought that here was one with whom I need make no pretence, her social position being sharply defined.

We spoke of the day's heat, which was bland, of the vegetables which she watered with a lawn hose, particularly of the tomatoes of which she was pardonably proud, and of the flowering vine which shielded her piazza from the sun. And when she presently and with due courtesy invited me to enter, I very affably did so, finding the atmosphere of the place reposeful and her conversation of a character that I could approve. She was dressed in a blue print gown that suited her no end, the sleeves turned back over her capable arms; her brown hair was arranged with scrupulous neatness, her face was pleasantly flushed from her agricultural labours, and her blue eyes flashed a friendly welcome and a pleased acknowledgment of the compliments I made her on the garden. Altogether, she was a person with whom I at once felt myself at ease, and a relief, I confess it was, after the strain of my high social endeavours.

After a tour of the garden I found myself in the cool twilight of her little parlour, where she begged me to be seated while she prepared me a dish of tea, which she did in the adjoining kitchen, to a cheerful accompaniment of song, quite with an honest, unpretentious good-heartedness. Glad I was for the moment to forget the social rancors of the town, the affronted dignities of the North Side set, and the pernicious activities of the Bohemians, for here all was of a simple humanity such as I would have found in a farmer's cottage at home.

As I rested in the parlour I could not but approve its general air of comfort and good taste—its clean flowered wall-paper, the pair of stuffed birds on the mantel, the comfortable chairs, the neat carpet, the pictures, and, on a slender-legged stand, the globe of goldfish. These I noted with an especial pleasure, for I have always found an intense satisfaction in their silent companionship. Of the pictures I noted particularly a life-sized drawing in black-and-white in a large gold frame, of a man whom I divined was the deceased husband of my hostess. There was also a spirited reproduction of "The Stag at Bay" and some charming coloured prints of villagers, children, and domestic animals in their lighter moments.

Tea being presently ready, I genially insisted that it should be served in the kitchen where it had been prepared, though to this my hostess at first stoutly objected, declaring that the room was in no suitable state. But this was a mere womanish hypocrisy, as the place was spotless, orderly, and in fact quite meticulous in its neatness. The tea was astonishingly excellent, so few Americans I had observed having the faintest notion of the real meaning of tea, and I was offered with it bread and butter and a genuinely satisfying compote of plums of which my hostess confessed herself the fabricator, having, as she quaintly phrased the thing, "put it up."

And so, over this collation, we chatted for quite all of an hour. The lady did, as I have intimated, a bit of charring, a bit of plain sewing, and also derived no small revenue from her vegetables and fruit, thus managing, as she owned the free-hold of the premises, to make a decent living for herself and child. I have said that she was cheerful and competent, and these epithets kept returning to me as we talked. Her husband—she spoke of him as "poor Judson"—had been a carter and odd-job fellow, decent enough, I dare say, but hardly the man for her, I thought, after studying his portrait. There was a sort of foppish weakness in his face. And indeed his going seemed to have worked her no hardship, nor to have left any incurable sting of loss.

Three cups of the almost perfect tea I drank, as we talked of her own simple affairs and of the town at large, and at length of her child who awakened noisily from slumber in an adjacent room and came voraciously to partake of food. It was a male child of some two and a half years, rather suggesting the generous good-nature of the mother, but in the most shocking condition, a thing I should have spoken strongly to her about at once had I known her better. Queer it seemed to me that a woman of her apparently sound judgment should let her offspring reach this terrible state without some effort to alleviate it. The poor thing, to be blunt, was grossly corpulent, legs, arms, body, and face being wretchedly fat, and yet she now fed it a large slice of bread thickly spread with butter and loaded to overflowing with the fattening sweet. Banting of the strictest sort was of course what it needed. I have had but the slightest experience with children, but there could be no doubt of this if its figure was to be maintained. Its waistline was quite impossible, and its eyes, as it owlishly scrutinized me over its superfluous food, showed from a face already quite as puffy as the Honourable George's. I did, indeed, venture so far as suggesting that food at untimely hours made for a too-rounded outline, but to my surprise the mother took this as a tribute to the creature's grace, crying, "Yes, he wuzzum wuzzums a fatty ole sing," with an air of most fatuous pride, and followed this by announcing my name to it with concerned precision.

"Ruggums," it exclaimed promptly, getting the name all wrong and staring at me with cold detachment; then "Ruggums-Ruggums-Ruggums!" as if it were a game, but still stuffing itself meanwhile. There was a sort of horrid fascination in the sight, but I strove as well as I could to keep my gaze from it, and the mother and I again talked of matters at large.

I come now to speak of an incident which made this quite harmless visit memorable and entailed unforeseen consequences of an almost quite serious character.

As we sat at tea there stalked into the kitchen a nondescript sort of dog, a creature of fairish size, of a rambling structure, so to speak, coloured a puzzling grayish brown with underlying hints of yellow, with vast drooping ears, and a long and most saturnine countenance.

Quite a shock it gave me when I looked up to find the beast staring at me with what I took to be the most hearty disapproval. My hostess paused in silence as she noted my glance. The beast then approached me, sniffed at my boots inquiringly, then at my hands with increasing animation, and at last leaped into my lap and had licked my face before I could prevent it.

I need hardly say that this attention was embarrassing and most distasteful, since I have never held with dogs. They are doubtless well enough in their place, but there is a vast deal of sentiment about them that is silly, and outside the hunting field the most finely bred of them are too apt to be noisy nuisances. When I say that the beast in question was quite an American dog, obviously of no breeding whatever, my dismay will be readily imagined. Rather impulsively, I confess, I threw him to the floor with a stern, "Begone, sir!" whereat he merely crawled to my feet and whimpered, looking up into my eyes with a most horrid and sickening air of devotion. Hereupon, to my surprise, my hostess gayly called out:

"Why, look at Mr. Barker—he's actually taken up with you right away, and him usually so suspicious of strangers. Only yesterday he bit an agent that was calling with silver polish to sell—bit him in the leg so I had to buy some from the poor fellow—and now see! He's as friendly with you as you could wish. They do say that dogs know when people are all right. Look at him trying to get into your lap again." And indeed the beast was again fawning upon me in the most abject manner, licking my hands and seeming to express for me some hideous admiration. Seeing that I repulsed his advances none too gently, his owner called to him:

"Down, Mr. Barker, down, sir! Get out!" she continued, seeing that he paid her no attention, and then she thoughtfully seized him by the collar and dragged him to a safe distance where she held him, he nevertheless continuing to regard me with the most servile affection.

"Ruggums, Ruggums, Ruggums!" exploded the child at this, excitedly waving the crust of its bread.

"Behave, Mr. Barker!" called his owner again. "The gentleman probably doesn't want you climbing all over him."

The remainder of my visit was somewhat marred by the determination of Mr. Barker, as he was indeed quite seriously called, to force his monstrous affections upon me, and by the well-meant but often careless efforts of his mistress to restrain him. She, indeed, appeared to believe that I would feel immensely pleased at these tokens of his liking.

As I took my leave after sincere expressions of my pleasure in the call, the child with its face one fearful smear of jam again waved its crust and shouted, "Ruggums!" while the dog was plainly bent on departing with me. Not until he had been secured by a rope to one of the porch stanchions could I safely leave, and as I went he howled dismally after violent efforts to chew the detaining rope apart.

I finished my stroll with the greatest satisfaction, for during the entire hour I had been enabled to forget the manifold cares of my position. Again it seemed to me that the portrait in the little parlour was not that of a man who had been entirely suited to this worthy and energetic young woman. Highly deserving she seemed, and when I knew her better, as I made no doubt I should, I resolved to instruct her in the matter of a more suitable diet for her offspring, the present one, as I have said, carrying quite too large a preponderance of animal fats. Also, I mused upon the extraordinary tolerance she accorded to the sad-faced but too demonstrative Mr. Barker. He had been named, I fancied, by some one with a primitive sense of humour, I mean to say, he might have been facetiously called "Barker" because he actually barked a bit, though adding the "Mister" to it seemed to be rather forcing the poor drollery. At any rate, I was glad to believe I should see little of him in his free state.

And yet it was precisely the curious fondness of this brute for myself that now added to my embarrassments. On two succeeding days I paused briefly at Mrs. Judson's in my afternoon strolls, finding the lady as wholesomely reposeful as ever in her effect upon my nature, but finding the unspeakable dog each time more lavish of his disgusting affection for me.

Then, one day, when I had made back to the town and was in fact traversing the main commercial thoroughfare in a dignified manner, I was made aware that the brute had broken away to follow me. Close at my heels he skulked. Strong words hissed under my breath would not repulse him, and to blows I durst not proceed, for I suddenly divined that his juxtaposition to me was exciting amused comment among certain of the natives who observed us. The fellow Hobbs, in the doorway of his bake-shop, was especially offensive, bursting into a shout of boorish laughter and directing to me the attention of a nearby group of loungers, who likewise professed to become entertained. So situated, I was of course obliged to affect unconsciousness of the awful beast, and he was presently running joyously at my side as if secure in my approval, or perhaps his brute intelligence divined that for the moment I durst not turn upon him with blows.

Nor did the true perversity of the situation at once occur to me. Not until we had gained one of the residence avenues did I realize the significance of the ill-concealed merriment we had aroused. It was not that I had been followed by a random cur, but by one known to be the dog of the lady I had called upon. I mean to say, the creature had advertised my acquaintance with his owner in a way that would lead base minds to misconstrue its extent.

Thoroughly maddened by this thought, and being now safely beyond close observers, I turned upon the animal to give it a hearty drubbing with my stick, but it drew quickly off, as if divining my intention, and when I hurled the stick at it, retrieved it, and brought it to me quite as if it forgave my hostility. Discovering at length that this method not only availed nothing but was bringing faces to neighbouring windows, and that it did not the slightest good to speak strongly to the beast, I had perforce to accompany it to its home, where I had the satisfaction of seeing its owner once more secure it firmly with the rope.

Thus far a trivial annoyance one might say, but when the next day the creature bounded up to me as I escorted homeward two ladies from the Onwards and Upwards Club, leaping upon me with extravagant manifestations of delight and trailing a length of gnawed rope, it will be seen that the thing was little short of serious.

"It's Mr. Barker," exclaimed one of the ladies, regarding me brightly.

At a cutlery shop I then bought a stout chain, escorted the brute to his home, and saw him tethered. The thing was rather getting on me. The following morning he waited for me at the Floud door and was beside himself with rapture when I appeared. He had slipped his collar. And once more I saw him moored. Each time I had apologized to Mrs. Judson for seeming to attract her pet from home, for I could not bring myself to say that the beast was highly repugnant to me, and least of all could I intimate that his public devotion to me would be seized upon by the coarser village wits to her disadvantage.

"I never saw him so fascinated with any one before," explained the lady as she once more adjusted his leash. But that afternoon, as I waited in the trap for Mr. Jackson before the post-office, the beast seemed to appear from out the earth to leap into the trap beside me. After a rather undignified struggle I ejected him, whereupon he followed the trap madly to the country club and made a farce of my golf game by retrieving the ball after every drive. This time, I learned, the child had released him.

It is enough to add that for those remaining days until the present the unspeakable creature's mad infatuation for me had made my life well-nigh a torment, to say nothing of its being a matter of low public jesting. Hardly did I dare show myself in the business centres, for as surely as I did the animal found me and crawled to fawn upon me, affecting his release each day in some novel manner. Each morning I looked abroad from my window on arising, more than likely detecting his outstretched form on the walk below, patiently awaiting my appearance, and each night I was liable to dreams of his coming upon me, a monstrous creature, sad-faced but eager, tireless, resolute, determined to have me for his own.

Musing desperately over this impossible state of affairs, I was now surprised to receive a letter from the wretched Cousin Egbert, sent by the hand of the Tuttle person. It was written in pencil on ruled sheets apparently torn from a cheap notebook, quite as if proper pens and decent stationery were not to be had, and ran as follows:

> DEAR FRIEND BILL: Well, Bill, I know God hates a quitter, but I guess I got   a streak of yellow in me wider than the Comstock lode. I was kicking at my stirrups even before I seen that bunch of whiskers,   and when I took a flash of them and seen he was intending I   should go out before folks without any regular pants on, I says   I can be pushed just so far. Well, Bill, I beat it like a bat out of hell, as I guess you know by this time, and I would like   to seen them catch me as I had a good bronc. If you know whose   bronc it was tell him I will make it all O.K. The bronc will be   all right when he rests up some. Well, Bill, I am here on the ranche, where everything is nice, and I would never come back   unless certain parties agree to do what is right. I would not   speak pieces that way for the President of the U.S. if he ask   me to on his bended knees. Well, Bill, I wish you would come   out here yourself, where everything is nice. You can't tell what   that bunch of crazies would be wanting you to do next thing with   false whiskers and no right pants. I would tell them "I can be   pushed just so far, and now I will go out to the ranche with   Sourdough for some time, where things are nice." Well, Bill,   if you will come out Jeff Tuttle will bring you Wednesday when   he comes with more grub, and you will find everything nice. I   have told Jeff to bring you, so no more at present, with kind   regards and   hoping   to   see   you   here   soon.
> Your   true   friend,

E.G. FLOUD.   P.S. Mrs. Effie said she would broaden
me out. Maybe she did,   because I felt pretty flat.
Ha! ha!

Truth to tell, this wild suggestion at once appealed to me. I had an impulse to withdraw for a season from the social whirl, to seek repose among the glens and gorges of this cattle plantation, and there try to adjust myself more intelligently to my strange new environment. In the meantime, I hoped, something might happen to the dog of Mrs. Judson; or he might, perhaps, in my absence outlive his curious mania for me.

Mrs. Effie, whom I now consulted, after reading the letter of Cousin Egbert, proved to be in favour of my going to him to make one last appeal to his higher nature.

"If only he'd stick out there in the brush where he belongs, I'd let him stay," she explained. "But he won't stick; he gets tired after awhile and drops in perhaps on the very night when we're entertaining some of the best people at dinner—and of course we're obliged to have him, though he's dropped whatever manners I've taught him and picked up his old rough talk, and he eats until you wonder how he can. It's awful! Sometimes I've wondered if it couldn't be adenoids—there's a lot of talk about those just now—some very select people have them, and perhaps they're what kept him back and made him so hopelessly low in his tastes, but I just know he'd never go to a doctor about them. For heaven's sake, use what influence you have to get him back here and to take his rightful place in society."

I had a profound conviction that he would never take his rightful place in society, be it the fault of adenoids or whatever; that low passion of his for being pally with all sorts made it seem that his sense of values must have been at fault from birth, and yet I could not bring myself to abandon him utterly, for, as I have intimated, something in the fellow's nature appealed to me. I accordingly murmured my sympathy discreetly and set about preparations for my journey.

Feeling instinctively that Cousin Egbert would not now be dressing for dinner, I omitted evening clothes from my box, including only a morning-suit and one of form-fitting tweeds which I fancied would do me well enough. But no sooner was my box packed than the Tuttle person informed me that I could take no box whatever. It appeared that all luggage would be strapped to the backs of animals and thus transported. Even so, when I had reduced myself to one park riding-suit and a small bundle of necessary adjuncts, I was told that the golf-sticks must be left behind. It appeared there would be no golf.

And so quite early one morning I started on this curious pilgrimage from what was called a "feed corral" in a low part of the town. Here the Tuttle person had assembled a goods-train of a half-dozen animals, the luggage being adjusted to their backs by himself and two assistants, all using language of the most disgraceful character throughout the process. The Tuttle person I had half expected to appear garbed in his native dress—Mrs. Effie had once more referred to "that Indian Jeff Tuttle"—but he wore instead, as did his two assistants, the outing or lounge suit of the Western desperado, nor, though I listened closely, could I hear him exclaim, "Ugh! Ugh!" in moments of emotional stress as my reading had informed me that the Indian frequently does.

The two assistants, solemn-faced, ill-groomed fellows, bore the curious American names of Hank and Buck, and furiously chewed the tobacco plant at all times. After betraying a momentary interest in my smart riding-suit, they paid me little attention, at which I was well pleased, for their manners were often repellent and their abrupt, direct fashion of speech quite disconcerting.

The Tuttle person welcomed me heartily and himself adjusted the saddle to my mount, expressing the hope that I would "get my fill of scenery," and volunteering the information that my destination was "one sleep" away.

CHAPTER ELEVEN

Although fond of rural surroundings and always interested in nature, the adventure in which I had become involved is not one I can recommend to a person of refined tastes. I found it little enough to my own taste even during the first two hours of travel when we kept to the beaten thoroughfare, for the sun was hot, the dust stifling, and the language with which the goods-animals were berated coarse in the extreme.

Yet from this plain roadway and a country of rolling down and heather which was at least not terrifying, our leader, the Tuttle person, swerved all at once into an untried jungle, in what at the moment I supposed to be a fit of absent-mindedness, following a narrow path that led up a fearsomely slanted incline among trees and boulders of granite thrown about in the greatest disorder. He was followed, however, by the goods-animals and by the two cow-persons, so that I soon saw the new course must be intended.

The mountains were now literally quite everywhere, some higher than others, but all of a rough appearance, and uninviting in the extreme. The narrow path, moreover, became more and more difficult, and seemed altogether quite insane with its twistings and fearsome declivities. One's first thought was that at least a bit of road-metal might have been put upon it. But there was no sign of this throughout our toilsome day, nor did I once observe a rustic seat along the way, although I saw an abundance of suitable nooks for these. Needless to say, in all England there is not an estate so poorly kept up.

There being no halt made for luncheon, I began to look forward to tea-time, but what was my dismay to observe that this hour also passed unnoted. Not until night was drawing upon us did our caravan halt beside a tarn, and here I learned that we would sup and sleep, although it was distressing to observe how remote we were from proper surroundings. There was no shelter and no modern conveniences; not even a wash-hand-stand or water-jug. There was, of course, no central heating, and no electricity for one's smoothing-iron, so that one's clothing must become quite disreputable for want of pressing. Also the informal manner of cooking and eating was not what I had been accustomed to, and the idea of sleeping publicly on the bare ground was repugnant in the extreme. I mean to say, there was no *vie intime*. Truly it was a coarser type of wilderness than that which I had encountered near New York City.

The animals, being unladen, were fitted with a species of leather bracelet about their forefeet and allowed to stray at their will. A fire was built and coarse food made ready. It is hardly a thing to speak of, but their manner of preparing tea was utterly depraved, the leaves being flung into a tin of boiling water and allowed to *stew*. The result was something that I imagine etchers might use in making lines upon their metal plates. But for my day's fast I should have been unequal to this, or to the crude output of their frying-pans.

Yet I was indeed glad that no sign of my dismay had escaped me, for the cow-persons, Hank and Buck, as I discovered, had given unusual care to the repast on my account, and I should not have liked to seem unappreciative. Quite by accident I overheard the honest fellows quarrelling about an oversight: they had, it seemed, left the finger-bowls behind; each was bitterly blaming the other for this, seeming to feel that the meal could not go forward. I had not to be told that they would not ordinarily carry finger-bowls for their own use, and that the forgotten utensils must have been meant solely for my comfort. Accordingly, when the quarrel was at its highest I broke in upon it, protesting that the oversight was of no consequence, and that I was quite prepared to roughen it with them in the best of good fellowship. They were unable to conceal their chagrin at my having overheard them, and slunk off abashed to the cooking-fire. It was plain that under their repellent exteriors they concealed veins of the finest chivalry, and I took pains during the remainder of the evening to put them at their ease, asking them many questions about their wild life.

Of the dangers of the jungle by which we were surrounded the most formidable, it seemed, was not the grizzly bear, of which I had read, but an animal quaintly called the "high-behind," which lurks about camping-places such as ours and is often known to attack man in its search for tinned milk of which it is inordinately fond. The spoor of one of these beasts had been detected near our campfire by the cow-person called Buck, and he now told us of it, though having at first resolved to be silent rather than alarm us.

As we carried a supply of the animal's favourite food, I was given two of the tins with instructions to hurl them quickly at any high-behind that might approach during the night, my companions arming themselves in a similar manner. It appears that the beast has tushes similar in shape to tin openers with which it deftly bites into any tins of milk that may be thrown at it. The person called Hank had once escaped with his life only by means of a tin of milk which had caught on the sabrelike tushes of the animal pursuing him, thus rendering him harmless and easy of capture.

Needless to say, I was greatly interested in this animal of the quaint name, and resolved to remain on watch during the night in the hope of seeing one, but at this juncture we were rejoined by the Tuttle person, who proceeded to recount to Hank and Buck a highly coloured version of my regrettable encounter with Mr. C. Belknap-Jackson back in the New York wilderness, whereat they both lost interest in the high-behind and greatly embarrassed me with their congratulations upon this lesser matter. Cousin Egbert, it seemed, had most indiscreetly talked of the thing, which was now a matter of common gossip in Red Gap. Thereafter I could get from them no further information about the habits of the high-behind, nor did I remain awake to watch for one as I had resolved to, the fatigues of the day proving too much for me. But doubtless none approached during the night, as the two tins of milk with which I was armed were untouched when I awoke at dawn.

Again we set off after a barbarous breakfast, driving our laden animals ever deeper into the mountain fastness, until it seemed that none of us could ever emerge, for I had ascertained that there was not a compass in the party. There was now a certain new friendliness in the manner of the two cow-persons toward me, born, it would seem, of their knowledge of my assault upon Belknap-Jackson, and I was somewhat at a loss to know how to receive this, well intentioned though it was. I mean to say, they were undoubtedly of the servant-class, and of course one must remember one's own position, but I at length decided to be quite friendly and American with them.

The truth must be told that I was now feeling in quite a bit of a funk and should have welcomed any friendship offered me; I even found myself remembering with rather a pensive tolerance the attentions of Mr. Barker, though doubtless back in Red Gap I should have found them as loathsome as ever. My hump was due, I made no doubt, first, to my precarious position in the wilderness, but more than that to my anomalous social position, for it seemed to me now that I was neither fish nor fowl. I was no longer a gentleman's man—the familiar boundaries of that office had been swept away; on the other hand, I was most emphatically not the gentleman I had set myself up to be, and I was weary of the pretence. The friendliness of these uncouth companions, then, proved doubly welcome, for with them I could conduct myself in a natural manner, happily forgetting my former limitations and my present quite fictitious dignities.

I even found myself talking to them of cricket as we rode, telling them I had once hit an eight—fully run out it was and not an overthrow—though I dare say it meant little to them. I also took pains to describe to them the correct method of brewing tea, which they promised thereafter to observe, though this I fear they did from mere politeness.

Our way continued adventurously upward until mid-afternoon, when we began an equally adventurous descent through a jungle of pine trees, not a few of which would have done credit to one of our own parks, though there were, of course, too many of them here to be at all effective. Indeed, it may be said that from a scenic standpoint everything through which we had passed was overdone: mountains, rocks, streams, trees, all sounding a characteristic American note of exaggeration.

Then at last we came to the wilderness abode of Cousin Egbert. A rude hut of native logs it was, set in this highland glen beside a tarn. From afar we descried its smoke, and presently in the doorway observed Cousin Egbert himself, who waved cheerfully at us. His appearance gave me a shock. Quite aware of his inclination to laxness, I was yet unprepared for his present state. Never, indeed, have I seen a man so badly turned out. Too evidently unshaven since his disappearance, he was gotten up in a faded flannel shirt, open at the neck and without the sign of cravat, a pair of overalls, also faded and quite wretchedly spotty, and boots of the most shocking description. Yet in spite of this dreadful tenue he greeted me without embarrassment and indeed with a kind of artless pleasure. Truly the man was impossible, and when I observed the placard he had allowed to remain on the waistband of his overalls, boastfully alleging their indestructibility, my sympathies flew back to Mrs. Effie. There was a cartoon emblazoned on this placard, depicting the futile efforts of two teams of stout horses, each attached to a leg of the garment, to wrench it in twain. I mean to say, one might be reduced to overalls, but this blatant emblem was not a thing any gentleman need have retained. And again, observing his footgear, I was glad to recall that I had included a plentiful supply of boot-cream in my scanty luggage.

Three of the goods-animals were now unladen, their burden of provisions being piled beside the door while Cousin Egbert chatted gayly with the cow-persons and the Indian Tuttle, after which these three took their leave, being madly bent, it appeared, upon penetrating still farther into the wilderness to another cattle farm. Then, left alone with Cousin Egbert, I was not long in discovering that, strictly speaking, he had no establishment. Not only were there no servants, but there were no drains, no water-taps, no ice-machine, no scullery, no central heating, no electric wiring. His hut consisted of but a single room, and this without a floor other than the packed earth, while the appointments were such as in any civilized country would have indicated the direst poverty. Two beds of the rudest description stood in opposite corners, and one end of the room was almost wholly occupied by a stone fireplace of primitive construction, over which the owner now hovered in certain feats of cookery.

Thanks to my famished state I was in no mood to criticise his efforts, which he presently set forth upon the rough deal table in a hearty but quite inelegant manner. The meal, I am bound to say, was more than welcome to my now indiscriminating palate, though at a less urgent moment I should doubtless have found the bread soggy and the beans a pernicious mass. There was a stew of venison, however, which only the most skilful hands could have bettered, though how the man had obtained a deer was beyond me, since it was evident he possessed no shooting or deer-stalking costume. As to the tea, I made bold to speak my mind and succeeded in brewing some for myself.

Throughout the repast Cousin Egbert was constantly attentive to my needs and was more cheerful of demeanour than I had ever seen him. The hunted look about his eyes, which had heretofore always distinguished him, was now gone, and he bore himself like a free man.

"Yes, sir," he said, as we smoked over the remains of the meal, "you stay with me and I'll give you one swell little time. I'll do the cooking, and between whiles we can sit right here and play cribbage day in and day out. You can get a taste of real life without moving."

I saw then, if never before, that his deeper nature would not be aroused. Doubtless my passing success with him in Paris had marked the very highest stage of his spiritual development. I did not need to be told now that he had left off sock-suspenders forever, nor did I waste words in trying to recall him to his better self. Indeed for the moment I was too overwhelmed by fatigue even to remonstrate about his wretched lounge-suit, and I early fell asleep on one of the beds while he was still engaged in washing the metal dishes upon which we had eaten, singing the while the doleful ballad of "Rosalie, the Prairie Flower."

It seemed but a moment later that I awoke, for Cousin Egbert was again busy among the dishes, but I saw that another day had come and his song had changed to one equally sad but quite different. "In the hazel dell my Nellie's sleeping," he sang, though in a low voice and quite cheerfully. Indeed his entire repertoire of ballads was confined to the saddest themes, chiefly of desirable maidens taken off untimely either by disease or accident. Besides "Rosalie, the Prairie Flower," there was "Lovely Annie Lisle," over whom the willows waved and earthly music could not waken; another named "Sweet Alice Ben Bolt" lying in the churchyard, and still another, "Lily Dale," who was pictured "'neath the trees in the flowery vale," with the wild rose blossoming o'er the little green grave.

His face was indeed sad as he rendered these woful ballads and yet his voice and manner were of the cheeriest, and I dare say he sang without reference to their real tragedy. It was a school of American balladry quite at variance with the cheerful optimism of those I had heard from the Belknap-Jackson phonograph, where the persons are not dead at all but are gayly calling upon one another to come on and do a folkdance, or hear a band or crawl under—things of that sort. As Cousin Egbert bent over a frying pan in which ham was cooking he crooned softly:

"In the hazel dell my Nellie's sleeping,
Nellie loved so long,
While my lonely, lonely watch I'm keeping,
Nellie lost and gone."

I could attribute his choice only to that natural perversity which prompted him always to do the wrong thing, for surely this affecting verse was not meant to be sung at such a moment.

Attempting to arise, I became aware that the two days' journey had left me sadly lame and wayworn, also that my face was burned from the sun and that I had been awakened too soon. Fortunately I had with me a shilling jar of Ridley's Society Complexion Food, "the all-weather wonder," which I applied to my face with cooling results, and I then felt able to partake of a bit of the breakfast which Cousin Egbert now brought to my bedside. The ham was of course not cooked correctly and the tea was again a mere corrosive, but so anxious was my host to please me that I refrained from any criticism, though at another time I should have told him straight what I thought of such cookery.

When we had both eaten I slept again to the accompaniment of another sad song and the muted rattle of the pans as Cousin Egbert did the scullery work, and it was long past the luncheon hour when I awoke, still lame from the saddle, but greatly refreshed.

It was now that another blow befell me, for upon arising and searching through my kit I discovered that my razors had been left behind. By any thinking man the effect of this oversight will be instantly perceived. Already low in spirits, the prospect of going unshaven could but aggravate my funk. I surrendered to the wave of homesickness that swept over me. I wanted London again, London with its yellow fog and greasy pavements, I wished to buy cockles off a barrow, I longed for toasted crumpets, and most of all I longed for my old rightful station; longed to turn out a gentleman, longed for the Honourable George and our peaceful if sometimes precarious existence among people of the right sort. The continued shocks since that fateful night of the cards had told upon me. I knew now that I had not been meant for adventure. Yet here I had turned up in the most savage of lands after leading a life of dishonest pretence in a station to which I had not been born—and, for I knew not how many days, I should not be able to shave my face.

But here again a ferment stirred in my blood, some electric thrill of anarchy which had come from association with these Americans, a strange, lawless impulse toward their quite absurd ideals of equality, a monstrous ambition to be in myself some one that mattered, instead of that pretended Colonel Ruggles who, I now recalled, was to-day promised to bridge at the home of Mrs. Judge Ballard, where he would talk of hunting in the shires, of the royal enclosure at Ascot, of Hurlingham and Ranleigh, of Cowes in June, of the excellence of the converts at Chaynes-Wotten. No doubt it was a sort of madness now seized me, consequent upon the lack of shaving utensils.

I wondered desperately if there was a true place for me in this life. I had tasted their equality that day of debauch in Paris, but obviously the sensation could not permanently be maintained upon spirits. Perhaps I might obtain a post in a bank; I might become a shop-assistant, bag-man, even a pressman. These moody and unwholesome thoughts were clouding my mind as I surveyed myself in the wrinkled mirror which had seemed to suffice the uncritical Cousin Egbert for his toilet. It hung between the portrait of a champion middle-weight crouching in position and the calendar advertisement of a brewery which, as I could not fancy Cousin Egbert being in the least concerned about the day of the month, had too evidently been hung on his wall because of the coloured lithograph of a blond creature in theatrical undress who smirked most immorally.

Studying the curiously wavy effect this glass produced upon my face, I chanced to observe in a corner of the frame a printed card with the heading "Take Courage!" To my surprise the thing, when I had read it, capped my black musings upon my position in a rather uncanny way. Briefly it recited the humble beginnings of a score or more of the world's notable figures.

"Demosthenes was the son of a cutler," it began. "Horace was the son of a shopkeeper. Virgil's father was a porter. Cardinal Wolsey was the son of a butcher.

Shakespeare the son of a wool-stapler." Followed the obscure parentage of such well-known persons as Milton, Napoleon, Columbus, Cromwell. Even Mohammed was noted as a shepherd and camel-driver, though it seemed rather questionable taste to include in the list one whose religion, as to family life, was rather scandalous. More to the point was the citation of various Americans who had sprung from humble beginnings: Lincoln, Johnson, Grant, Garfield, Edison. It is true that there was not, apparently, a gentleman's servant among them; they were rail-splitters, boatmen, tailors, artisans of sorts, but the combined effect was rather overwhelming.

From the first moment of my encountering the American social system, it seemed, I had been by way of becoming a rabid anarchist—that is, one feeling that he might become a gentleman regardless of his birth—and here were the disconcerting facts concerning a score of notables to confirm me in my heresy. It was not a thing to be spoken lightly of in loose discussion, but there can be no doubt that at this moment I coldly questioned the soundness of our British system, the vital marrow of which is to teach that there is a difference between men and men. To be sure, it will have been seen that I was not myself, having for a quarter year been subjected to a series of nervous shocks, and having had my mind contaminated, moreover, by being brought into daily contact with this unthinking American equality in the person of Cousin Egbert, who, I make bold to assert, had never for one instant since his doubtless obscure birth considered himself the superior of any human being whatsoever.

This much I advance for myself in extenuation of my lawless imaginings, but of them I can abate no jot; it was all at once clear to me, monstrous as it may seem, that Nature and the British Empire were at variance in their decrees, and that somehow a system was base which taught that one man is necessarily inferior to another. I dare say it was a sort of poisonous intoxication—that I should all at once declare:

"His lordship tenth Earl of Brinstead and Marmaduke Ruggles are two men; one has made an acceptable peer and one an acceptable valet, yet the twain are equal, and the system which has made one inferior socially to the other is false and bad and cannot endure." For a moment, I repeat, I saw myself a gentleman in the making—a clear fairway without bunkers from tee to green—meeting my equals with a friendly eye; and then the illumining shock, for I unconsciously added to myself, "Regarding my inferiors with a kindly tolerance." It was there I caught myself. So much a part of the system was I that, although I could readily conceive a society in which I had no superiors, I could not picture one in which I had not inferiors. The same poison that ran in the veins of their lordships ran also in the veins of their servants. I was indeed, it appeared, hopelessly inoculated. Again I read the card. Horace was the son of a shopkeeper, but I made no doubt that, after he became a popular and successful writer of Latin verse, he looked down upon his own father. Only could it have been otherwise, I thought, had he been born in this fermenting America to no station whatever and left to achieve his rightful one.

So I mused thus licentiously until one clear conviction possessed me: that I would no longer pretend to the social superiority of one Colonel Marmaduke Ruggles. I would concede no inferiority in myself, but I would not again, before Red Gap's county families vaunt myself as other than I was. That this was more than a vagrant fancy on my part will be seen when I aver that suddenly, strangely, alarmingly, I no longer cared that I was unshaven and must remain so for an untold number of days. I welcomed the unhandsome stubble that now projected itself upon my face; I curiously wished all at once to be as badly gotten up as Cousin Egbert, with as little thought for my station in life. I would no longer refrain from doing things because they were "not done." My own taste would be the law.

It was at this moment that Cousin Egbert appeared in the doorway with four trout from the stream nearby, though how he had managed to snare them I could not think, since he possessed no correct equipment for angling. I fancy I rather overwhelmed him by exclaiming, "Hello, Sour-dough!" since never before had I addressed him in any save a formal fashion, and it is certain I embarrassed him by my next proceeding, which was to grasp his hand and shake it heartily, an action that I could explain no more than he, except that the violence of my self-communion was still upon me and required an outlet. He grinned amiably, then regarded me with a shrewd eye and demanded if I had been drinking.

"This," I said; "I am drunk with this," and held the card up to him. But when he took it interestedly he merely read the obverse side which I had not observed until now. "Go to Epstein's for Everything You Wear," it said in large type, and added, "The Square Deal Mammoth Store."

"They carry a nice stock," he said, still a bit puzzled by my tone, "though I generally trade at the Red Front." I turned the card over for him and he studied the list of humble-born notables, though from a point of view peculiarly his own. "I don't see," he began, "what right they got to rake up all that stuff about people that's dead and gone. Who cares what their folks was!" And he added, "'Horace was the son of a shopkeeper'—Horace who?" Plainly the matter did not excite him, and I saw it would be useless to try to convey to him what the items had meant to me.

"I mean to say, I'm glad to be here with you," I said.

"I knew you'd like it," he answered. "Everything is nice here."

"America is some country," I said.

"She is, she is," he answered. "And now you can bile up a pot of tea in your own way while I clean these here fish for sapper."

I made the tea. I regret to say there was not a tea cozy in the place; indeed the linen, silver, and general table equipment were sadly deficient, but in my reckless mood I made no comment.

"Your tea smells good, but it ain't got no kick to it," he observed over his first cup. "When I drench my insides with tea I sort of want it to take a hold." And still I made no effort to set him right. I now saw that in all true essentials he did not need me to set him right. For so uncouth a person he was strangely commendable and worthy.

As we sipped our tea in companionable silence, I busy with my new and disturbing thoughts, a long shout came to us from the outer distance. Cousin Egbert brightened.

"I'm darned if that ain't Ma Pettengill!" he exclaimed. "She's rid over from the Arrowhead."

We rushed to the door, and in the distance, riding down upon us at terrific speed, I indeed beheld the Mixer. A moment later she reigned in her horse before us and hoarsely rumbled her greetings. I had last seen her at a formal dinner where she was rather formidably done out in black velvet and diamonds. Now she appeared in a startling tenue of khaki riding-breeches and flannel shirt, with one of the wide-brimmed cow-person hats. Even at the moment of greeting her I could not but reflect how shocked our dear Queen would be at the sight of this riding habit.

She dismounted with hearty explanations of how she had left her "round-up" and ridden over to visit, having heard from the Tuttle person that we were here. Cousin Egbert took her horse and she entered the hut, where to my utter amazement she at once did a feminine thing. Though from her garb one at a little distance might have thought her a man, a portly, florid, carelessly attired man, she made at once for the wrinkled mirror where, after anxiously scanning her burned face for an instant, she produced powder and puff from a pocket of her shirt and daintily powdered her generous blob of a nose. Having achieved this to her apparent satisfaction, she unrolled a bundle she had carried at her saddle and donned a riding skirt, buttoning it about the waist and smoothing down its folds—before I could retire.

"There, now," she boomed, as if some satisfying finality had been brought about. Such was the Mixer. That sort of thing would never do with us, and yet I suddenly saw that she, like Cousin Egbert, was strangely commendable and worthy. I mean to say, I no longer felt it was my part to set her right in any of the social niceties. Some curious change had come upon me. I knew then that I should no longer resist America.

CHAPTER TWELVE

With a curious friendly glow upon me I set about helping Cousin Egbert in the preparation of our evening meal, a work from which, owing to the number and apparent difficulty of my suggestions, he presently withdrew, leaving me in entire charge. It is quite true that I have pronounced views as to the preparation and serving of food, and I dare say I embarrassed the worthy fellow without at all meaning to do so, for too many of his culinary efforts betray the fumbling touch of the amateur. And as I worked over the open fire, doing the trout to a turn, stirring the beans, and perfecting the stew with deft touches of seasoning, I worded to myself for the first time a most severe indictment against the North American cookery, based upon my observations across the continent and my experience as a diner-out in Red Gap.

I saw that it would never do with us, and that it ought, as a matter of fact, to be uplifted. Even then, while our guest chattered gossip of the town over her brown paper cigarettes, I felt the stirring of an impulse to teach Americans how to do themselves better at table. For the moment, of course, I was hampered by lack of equipment (there was not even a fish slice in the establishment), but even so I brewed proper tea and was able to impart to the simple viands a touch of distinction which they had lacked under Cousin Egbert's all-too-careless manipulation.

As I served the repast Cousin Egbert produced a bottle of the brown American whiskey at which we pegged a bit before sitting to table.

"Three rousing cheers!" said he, and the Mixer responded with "Happy days!"

As on that former occasion, the draught of spirits flooded my being with a vast consciousness of personal worth and of good feeling toward my companions. With a true insight I suddenly perceived that one might belong to the great lower middle-class in America and still matter in the truest, correctest sense of the term.

As we fell hungrily to the food, the Mixer did not fail to praise my cooking of the trout, and she and Cousin Egbert were presently lamenting the difficulty of obtaining a well-cooked meal in Red Gap. At this I boldly spoke up, declaring that American cookery lacked constructive imagination, making only the barest use of its magnificent opportunities, following certain beaten and all-too-familiar roads with a slavish stupidity.

"We nearly had a good restaurant," said the Mixer. "A Frenchman came and showed us a little flash of form, but he only lasted a month because he got homesick. He had half the people in town going there for dinner, too, to get away from their Chinamen—and after I spent a lot of money fixing the place up for him, too."

I recalled the establishment, on the main street, though I had not known that our guest was its owner. Vacant it was now, and looking quite as if the bailiffs had been in.

"He couldn't cook ham and eggs proper," suggested Cousin Egbert. "I tried him three times, and every time he done something French to 'em that nobody had ought to do to ham and eggs."

Hereupon I ventured to assert that a too-intense nationalism would prove the ruin of any chef outside his own country; there must be a certain breadth of treatment, a blending of the best features of different schools. One must know English and French methods and yet be a slave to neither; one must even know American cookery and be prepared to adapt its half-dozen or so undoubted excellencies. From this I ventured further into a general criticism of the dinners I had eaten at Red Gap's smartest houses. Too profuse they were, I said, and too little satisfying in any one feature; too many courses, constructed, as I had observed, after photographs printed in the back pages of women's magazines; doubtless they possessed a certain artistic value as sights for the eye, but considered as food they were devoid of any inner meaning.

"Bill's right," said Cousin Egbert warmly. "Mrs. Effie, she gets up about nine of them pictures, with nuts and grated eggs and scrambled tomatoes all over 'em, and nobody knowing what's what, and even when you strike one that tastes good they's only a dab of it and you mustn't ask for any more. When I go out to dinner, what I want is to have 'em say, 'Pass up your plate, Mr. Floud, for another piece of the steak and some potatoes, and have some more squash and help yourself to the quince jelly.' That's how it had ought to be, but I keep eatin' these here little plates of cut-up things and waiting for the real stuff, and first thing I know I get a spoonful of coffee in something like you put eye medicine into, and I know it's all over. Last time I was out I hid up a dish of these here salted almuns under a fern and et the whole lot from time to time, kind of absent like. It helped some, but it wasn't dinner."

"Same here," put in the Mixer, saturating half a slice of bread in the sauce of the stew. "I can't afford to act otherwise than like I am a lady at one of them dinners, but the minute I'm home I beat it for the icebox. I suppose it's all right to be socially elegant, but we hadn't ought to let it contaminate our food none. And even at that New York hotel this summer you had to make trouble to get fed proper. I wanted strawberry shortcake, and what do you reckon they dealt me? A thing looking like a marble palace—sponge cake and whipped cream with a few red spots in between. Well, long as we're friends here together, I may say that I raised hell until I had the chef himself up and told him exactly what to do; biscuit dough baked and prized apart and buttered, strawberries with sugar on 'em in between and on top, and plenty of regular cream. Well, after three days' trying he finally managed to get simple—he just couldn't believe I meant it at first, and kept building on the whipped cream—and the thing cost eight dollars, but you can bet he had me, even then; the bonehead smarty had sweetened the cream and grated nutmeg into it. I give up.

"And if you can't get right food in New York, how can you expect to here? And Jackson, the idiot, has just fired the only real cook in Red Gap. Yes, sir; he's let the coons go. It come out that Waterman had sneaked out that suit of his golf clothes that Kate Kenner wore in the minstrel show, so he fired them both, and now I got to support 'em, because, as long as we're friends here, I don't mind telling you I egged the coon on to do it."

I saw that she was referring to the black and his wife whom I had met at the New York camp, though it seemed quaint to me that they should be called "coons," which is, I take it, a diminutive for "raccoon," a species of ground game to be found in America.

Truth to tell, I enjoyed myself immensely at this simple but satisfying meal, feeling myself one with these homely people, and I was sorry when we had finished.

"That was some little dinner itself," said the Mixer as she rolled a cigarette; "and now you boys set still while I do up the dishes." Nor would she allow either of us to assist her in this work. When she had done, Cousin Egbert proceeded to mix hot toddies from the whiskey, and we gathered about the table before the open fire.

"Now we'll have a nice home evening," said the Mixer, and to my great embarrassment she began at once to speak to myself.

"A strong man like him has got no business becoming a social butterfly," she remarked to Cousin Egbert.

"Oh, Bill's all right," insisted the latter, as he had done so many times before.

"He's all right so far, but let him go on for a year or so and he won't be a darned bit better than what Jackson is, mark my words. Just a social butterfly, wearing funny clothes and attending afternoon affairs."

"Well, I don't say you ain't right," said Cousin Egbert thoughtfully; "that's one reason I got him out here where everything is nice. What with speaking pieces like an actor, I was afraid they'd have him making more kinds of a fool of himself than what Jackson does, him being a foreigner, and his mind kind o' running on what clothes a man had ought to wear."

Hereupon, so flushed was I with the good feeling of the occasion, I told them straight that I had resolved to quit being Colonel Ruggles of the British army and associate of the nobility; that I had determined to forget all class distinctions and to become one of themselves, plain, simple, and unpretentious. It is true that I had consumed two of the hot grogs, but my mind was clear enough, and both my companions applauded this resolution.

"If he can just get his mind off clothes for a bit he might amount to something," said Cousin Egbert, and it will scarcely be credited, but at the moment I felt actually grateful to him for this admission.

"We'll think about his case," said the Mixer, taking her own second toddy, whereupon the two fell to talking of other things, chiefly of their cattle plantations and the price of beef-stock, which then seemed to be six and one half, though what this meant I had no notion. Also I gathered that the Mixer at her own cattle-farm had been watching her calves marked with her monogram, though I would never have credited her with so much sentiment.

When the retiring hour came, Cousin Egbert and I prepared to take our blankets outside to sleep, but the Mixer would have none of this.

"The last time I slept in here," she remarked, "mice was crawling over me all night, so you keep your shack and I'll bed down outside. I ain't afraid of mice, understand, but I don't like to feel their feet on my face."

And to my great dismay, though Cousin Egbert took it calmly enough, she took a roll of blankets and made a crude pallet on the ground outside, under a spreading pine tree. I take it she was that sort. The least I could do was to secure two tins of milk from our larder and place them near her cot, in case of some lurking high-behind, though I said nothing of this, not wishing to alarm her needlessly.

Inside the hut Cousin Egbert and I partook of a final toddy before retiring. He was unusually thoughtful and I had difficulty in persuading him to any conversation. Thus having noted a bearskin before my bed, I asked him if he had killed the animal.

"No," said he shortly, "I wouldn't lie for a bear as small as that." As he was again silent, I made no further approaches to him.

From my first sleep I was awakened by a long, booming yell from our guest outside. Cousin Egbert and I reached the door at the same time.

"I've got it!" bellowed the Mixer, and we went out to her in the chill night. She sat up with the blankets muffled about her.

"We start Bill in that restaurant," she began. "It come to me in a flash. I judge he's got the right ideas, and Waterman and his wife can cook for him."

"Bully!" exclaimed Cousin Egbert. "I was thinking he ought to have a gents' furnishing store, on account of his mind running to dress, but you got the best idea."

"I'll stake him to the rent," she put in.

"And I'll stake him to the rest," exclaimed Cousin Egbert delightedly, and, strange as it may seem, I suddenly saw myself a licensed victualler.

"I'll call it the 'United States Grill,'" I said suddenly, as if by inspiration.

"Three rousing cheers for the U.S. Grill!" shouted Cousin Egbert to the surrounding hills, and repairing to the hut he brought out hot toddies with which we drank success to the new enterprise. For a half-hour, I dare say, we discussed details there in the cold night, not seeing that it was quite preposterously bizarre. Returning to the hut at last, Cousin Egbert declared himself so chilled that he must have another toddy before retiring, and, although I was already feeling myself the equal of any American, I consented to join him.

Just before retiring again my attention centred a second time upon the bearskin before my bed and, forgetting that I had already inquired about it, I demanded of him if he had killed the animal. "Sure," said he; "killed it with one shot just as it was going to claw me. It was an awful big one."

Morning found the three of us engrossed with the new plan, and by the time our guest rode away after luncheon the thing was well forward and I had the Mixer's order upon her estate agent at Red Gap for admission to the vacant premises. During the remainder of the day, between games of cribbage, Cousin Egbert and I discussed the venture. And it was now that I began to foresee a certain difficulty.

How, I asked myself, would the going into trade of Colonel Marmaduke Ruggles be regarded by those who had been his social sponsors in Red Gap? I mean to say, would not Mrs. Effie and the Belknap-Jacksons feel that I had played them false? Had I not given them the right to believe that I should continue, during my stay in their town, to be one whom their county families would consider rather a personage? It was idle, indeed, for me to deny that my personality as well as my assumed origin and social position abroad had conferred a sort of prestige upon my sponsors; that on my account, in short, the North Side set had been newly armed in its battle with the Bohemian set. And they relied upon my continued influence. How, then, could I face them with the declaration that I meant to become a tradesman? Should I be doing a caddish thing, I wondered?

Putting the difficulty to Cousin Egbert, he dismissed it impatiently by saying: "Oh, shucks!" In truth I do not believe he comprehended it in the least. But then it was that I fell upon my inspiration. I might take Colonel Marmaduke Ruggles from the North Side set, but I would give them another and bigger notable in his place. This should be none other than the Honourable George, whom I would now summon. A fortnight before I had received a rather snarky letter from him demanding to know how long I meant to remain in North America and disclosing that he was in a wretched state for want of some one to look after him. And he had even hinted that in the event of my continued absence he might himself come out to America and fetch me back. His quarter's allowance, would, I knew, be due in a fortnight, and my letter would reach him, therefore, before some adventurer had sold him a system for beating the French games of chance. And my letter would be compelling. I would make it a summons he could not resist. Thus, when I met the reproachful gaze of the C. Belknap-Jacksons and of Mrs. Effie, I should be able to tell them: "I go from you, but I leave you a better man in my place." With the Honourable George Augustus Vane-Basingwell, next Earl of Brinstead, as their house guest, I made no doubt that the North Side set would at once prevail as it never had before, the Bohemian set losing at once such of its members as really mattered, who would of course be sensible of the tremendous social importance of the Honourable George.

Yet there came moments in which I would again find myself in no end of a funk, foreseeing difficulties of an insurmountable character. At such times Cousin Egbert strove to cheer me with all sorts of assurances, and to divert my mind he took me upon excursions of the roughest sort into the surrounding jungle, in search either of fish or ground game. After three days of this my park-suit became almost a total ruin, particularly as to the trousers, so that I was glad to borrow a pair of overalls such as Cousin Egbert wore. They were a tidy fit, but, having resolved not to resist America any longer, I donned them without even removing the advertising placard.

With my ever-lengthening stubble of beard it will be understood that I now appeared as one of their hearty Western Americans of the roughest type, which was almost quite a little odd, considering my former principles. Cousin Egbert, I need hardly say, was immensely pleased with my changed appearance, and remarked that I was "sure a live wire." He also heartened me in the matter of the possible disapproval of C. Belknap-Jackson, which he had divined was the essential rabbit in my moodiness.

"I admit the guy uses beautiful language," he conceded, "and probably he's top-notched in education, but jest the same he ain't the whole seven pillars of the house of wisdom, not by a long shot. If he gets fancy with you, sock him again. You done it once." So far was the worthy fellow from divining the intimate niceties involved in my giving up a social career for trade. Nor could he properly estimate the importance of my plan to summon the Honourable George to Red Gap, merely remarking that the "Judge" was all right and a good mixer and that the boys would give him a swell time.

Our return journey to Red Gap was made in company with the Indian Tuttle, and the two cow-persons, Hank and Buck, all of whom professed themselves glad to meet me again, and they, too, were wildly enthusiastic at hearing from Cousin Egbert of my proposed business venture. Needless to say they were of a class that would bother itself little with any question of social propriety involved in my entering trade, and they were loud in their promises of future patronage. At this I again felt some misgiving, for I meant the United States Grill to possess an atmosphere of quiet refinement calculated to appeal to particular people that really mattered; and yet it was plain that, keeping a public house, I must be prepared to entertain agricultural labourers and members of the lower or working classes. For a time I debated having an ordinary for such as these, where they could be shut away from my selecter patrons, but eventually decided upon a tariff that would be prohibitive to all but desirable people. The rougher or Bohemian element, being required to spring an extra shilling, would doubtless seek other places.

For two days we again filed through mountain gorges of a most awkward character, reaching Red Gap at dusk. For this I was rather grateful, not only because of my beard and the overalls, but on account of a hat of the most shocking description which Cousin Egbert had pressed upon me when my own deer-stalker was lost in a glen. I was willing to roughen it in all good-fellowship with these worthy Americans, but I knew that to those who had remarked my careful taste in dress my present appearance would seem almost a little singular. I would rather I did not shock them to this extent.

Yet when our animals had been left in their corral, or rude enclosure, I found it would be ungracious to decline the hospitality of my new friends who wished to drink to the success of the U.S. Grill, and so I accompanied them to several public houses, though with the shocking hat pulled well down over my face. Also, as the dinner hour passed, I consented to dine with them at the establishment of a Chinese, where we sat on high stools at a counter and were served ham and eggs and some of the simpler American foods.

The meal being over, I knew that we ought to cut off home directly, but Cousin Egbert again insisted upon visiting drinking-places, and I had no mind to leave him, particularly as he was growing more and more bitter in my behalf against Mr. Belknap-Jackson. I had a doubtless absurd fear that he would seek the gentleman out and do him a mischief, though for the moment he was merely urging me to do this. It would, he asserted, vastly entertain the Indian Tuttle and the cow-persons if I were to come upon Mr. Belknap-Jackson and savage him without warning, or at least with only a paltry excuse, which he seemed proud of having devised.

"You go up to the guy," he insisted, "very polite, you understand, and ask him what day this is. If he says it's Tuesday, sock him."

"But it is Tuesday," I said.

"Sure," he replied, "that's where the joke comes in."

Of course this was the crudest sort of American humour and not to be given a moment's serious thought, so I redoubled my efforts to detach him from our honest but noisy friends, and presently had the satisfaction of doing so by pleading that I must be up early on the morrow and would also require his assistance. At parting, to my embarrassment, he insisted on leading the group in a cheer. "What's the matter with Ruggles?" they loudly demanded in unison, following the query swiftly with: "He's all right!" the "he" being eloquently emphasized.

But at last we were away from them and off into the darker avenue, to my great relief, remembering my garb. I might be a living wire, as Cousin Egbert had

120

said, but I was keenly aware that his overalls and hat would rather convey the impression that I was what they call in the States a bad person from a bitter creek.

To my further relief, the Floud house was quite dark as we approached and let ourselves in. Cousin Egbert, however, would enter the drawing-room, flood it with light, and seat himself in an easy-chair with his feet lifted to a sofa. He then raised his voice in a ballad of an infant that had perished, rendering it most tearfully, the refrain being, "Empty is the cradle, baby's gone!" Apprehensive at this, I stole softly up the stairs and had but reached the door of my own room when I heard Mrs. Effie below. I could fancy the chilling gaze which she fastened upon the singer, and I heard her coldly demand, "Where are your feet?" Whereupon the plaintive voice of Cousin Egbert arose to me, "Just below my legs." I mean to say, he had taken the thing as a quiz in anatomy rather than as the rebuke it was meant to be. As I closed my door, I heard him add that he could be pushed just so far.

CHAPTER THIRTEEN

Having written and posted my letter to the Honourable George the following morning, I summoned Mr. Belknap-Jackson, conceiving it my first duty to notify him and Mrs. Effie of my trade intentions. I also requested Cousin Egbert to be present, since he was my business sponsor.

All being gathered at the Floud house, including Mrs. Belknap-Jackson, I told them straight that I had resolved to abandon my social career, brilliant though it had been, and to enter trade quite as one of their middle-class Americans. They all gasped a bit at my first words, as I had quite expected them to do, but what was my surprise, when I went on to announce the nature of my enterprise, to find them not a little intrigued by it, and to discover that in their view I should not in the least be lowering myself.

"Capital, capital!" exclaimed Belknap-Jackson, and the ladies emitted little exclamations of similar import.

"At last," said Mrs. Belknap-Jackson, "we shall have a place with tone to it. The hall above will be splendid for our dinner dances, and now we can have smart luncheons and afternoon teas."

"And a red-coated orchestra and after-theatre suppers," said Mrs. Effie.

"Only," put in Belknap-Jackson thoughtfully, "he will of course be compelled to use discretion about his patrons. The rabble, of course——" He broke off with a wave of his hand which, although not pointedly, seemed to indicate Cousin Egbert, who once more wore the hunted look about his eyes and who sat by uneasily. I saw him wince.

"Some people's money is just as good as other people's if you come right down to it," he muttered, "and Bill is out for the coin. Besides, we all got to eat, ain't we?"

Belknap-Jackson smiled deprecatingly and again waved his hand as if there were no need for words.

"That rowdy Bohemian set——" began Mrs. Effie, but I made bold to interrupt. There might, I said, be awkward moments, but I had no doubt that I should be able to meet them with a flawless tact. Meantime, for the ultimate confusion of the Bohemian set of Red Gap, I had to announce that the Honourable George Augustus Vane-Basingwell would presently be with us. With him as a member of the North Side set, I pointed out, it was not possible to believe that any desirable members of the Bohemian set would longer refuse to affiliate with the smartest people.

My announcement made quite all the sensation I had anticipated. Belknap-Jackson, indeed, arose quickly and grasped me by the hand, echoing, "The

Honourable George Augustus Vane-Basingwell, brother of the Earl of Brinstead," with little shivers of ecstasy in his voice, while the ladies pealed their excitement incoherently, with "Really! really!" and "Actually coming to Red Gap—the brother of a lord!"

Then almost at once I detected curiously cold glances being darted at each other by the ladies.

"Of course we will be only too glad to put him up," said Mrs. Belknap-Jackson quickly.

"But, my dear, he will of course come to us first," put in Mrs. Effie. "Afterward, to be sure——"

"It's so important that he should receive a favourable impression," responded Mrs. Belknap-Jackson.

"That's exactly why——" Mrs. Effie came back with not a little obvious warmth. Belknap-Jackson here caught my eye.

"I dare say Ruggles and I can be depended upon to decide a minor matter like that," he said.

The ladies both broke in at this, rather sputteringly, but Cousin Egbert silenced them.

"Shake dice for him," he said—"poker dice, three throws, aces low."

"How shockingly vulgar!" hissed Mrs. Belknap-Jackson.

"Even if there were no other reason for his coming to us," remarked her husband coldly, "there are certain unfortunate associations which ought to make his entertainment here quite impossible."

"If you're calling me 'unfortunate associations,'" remarked Cousin Egbert, "you want to get it out of your head right off. I don't mind telling you, the Judge and I get along fine together. I told him when I was in Paris and Europe to look me up the first thing if ever he come here, and he said he sure would. The Judge is some mixer, believe me!"

"The 'Judge'!" echoed the Belknap-Jacksons in deep disgust.

"You come right down to it—I bet a cookie he stays just where I tell him to stay," insisted Cousin Egbert. The evident conviction of his tone alarmed his hearers, who regarded each other with pained speculation.

"Right where I tell him to stay and no place else," insisted Cousin Egbert, sensing the impression he had made.

"But this is too monstrous!" said Mr. Jackson, regarding me imploringly.

"The Honourable George," I admitted, "has been known to do unexpected things, and there have been times when he was not as sensitive as I could wish to the demands of his caste——"

"Bill is stalling—he knows darned well the Judge is a mixer," broke in Cousin Egbert, somewhat to my embarrassment, nor did any reply occur to me. There was a moment's awkward silence during which I became sensitive to a radical change in the attitude which these people bore to Cousin Egbert. They shot him looks of furtive but unmistakable respect, and Mrs. Effie remarked almost with tenderness: "We must admit that Cousin Egbert has a certain way with him."

"I dare say Floud and I can adjust the matter satisfactorily to all," remarked Belknap-Jackson, and with a jaunty affection of good-fellowship, he opened his cigarette case to Cousin Egbert.

"I ain't made up my mind yet where I'll have him stay," announced the latter, too evidently feeling his newly acquired importance. "I may have him stay one place, then again I may have him stay another. I can't decide things like that off-hand."

And here the matter was preposterously left, the aspirants for this social honour patiently bending their knees to the erstwhile despised Cousin Egbert, and the latter being visibly puffed up. By rather awkward stages they came again to a discussion of the United States Grill.

"The name, of course, might be thought flamboyant," suggested Belknap-Jackson delicately.

"But I have determined," I said, "no longer to resist America, and so I can think of no name more fitting."

"Your determination," he answered, "bears rather sinister implications. One may be vanquished by America as I have been. One may even submit; but surely one may always resist a little, may not one? One need not abjectly surrender one's finest convictions, need one?"

"Oh, shucks," put in Cousin Egbert petulantly, "what's the use of all that 'one' stuff? Bill wants a good American name for his place. Me? I first thought the 'Bon Ton Eating House' would be kind of a nice name for it, but as soon as he said the 'United States Grill' I knew it was a better one. It sounds kind of grand and important."

Belknap-Jackson here made deprecating clucks, but not too directly toward Cousin Egbert, and my choice of a name was not further criticised. I went on to assure them that I should have an establishment quietly smart rather than noisily elegant, and that I made no doubt the place would give a new tone to Red Gap, whereat they all expressed themselves as immensely pleased, and our little conference came to an end.

In company with Cousin Egbert I now went to examine the premises I was to take over. There was a spacious corner room, lighted from the front and side, which would adapt itself well to the decorative scheme I had in mind. The kitchen with its ranges I found would be almost quite suitable for my purpose, requiring but little alteration, but the large room was of course atrociously impossible in the

124

American fashion, with unsightly walls, the floors covered with American cloth of a garish pattern, and the small, oblong tables and flimsy chairs vastly uninviting.

As to the gross ideals of the former tenant, I need only say that he had made, as I now learned, a window display of foods, quite after the manner of a draper's window: moulds of custard set in a row, flanked on either side by "pies," as the natives call their tarts, with perhaps a roast fowl or ham in the centre. Artistic vulgarity could of course go little beyond this, but almost as offensive were the abundant wall-placards pathetically remaining in place.

"Coffee like mother used to make," read one. Impertinently intimate this, professing a familiarity with one's people that would never do with us. "Try our Boston Baked Beans," pleaded another, quite abjectly. And several others quite indelicately stated the prices at which different dishes might be had: "Irish Stew, 25 cents"; "Philadelphia Capon, 35 cents"; "Fried Chicken, Maryland, 50 cents"; "New York Fancy Broil, 40 cents." Indeed the poor chap seemed to have been possessed by a geographical mania, finding it difficult to submit the simplest viands without crediting them to distant towns or provinces.

Upon Cousin Egbert's remarking that these bedizened placards would "come in handy," I took pains to explain to him just how different the United States Grill would be. The walls would be done in deep red; the floor would be covered with a heavy Turkey carpet of the same tone; the present crude electric lighting fixtures must be replaced with indirect lighting from the ceiling and electric candlesticks for the tables. The latter would be massive and of stained oak, my general colour-scheme being red and brown. The chairs would be of the same style, comfortable chairs in which patrons would be tempted to linger. The windows would be heavily draped. In a word, the place would have atmosphere; not the loud and blaring, elegance which I had observed in the smartest of New York establishments, with shrieking decorations and tables jammed together, but an atmosphere of distinction which, though subtle, would yet impress shop-assistants, plate-layers and road-menders, hodmen, carters, cattle-persons—in short the middle-class native.

Cousin Egbert, I fear, was not properly impressed with my plan, for he looked longingly at the wall-placards, yet he made the most loyal pretence to this effect, even when I explained further that I should probably have no printed menu, which I have always regarded as the ultimate vulgarity in a place where there are any proper relations between patrons and steward. He made one wistful, timid reference to the "Try Our Merchant's Lunch for 35 cents," after which he gave in entirely, particularly when I explained that ham and eggs in the best manner would be forthcoming at his order, even though no placard vaunted them or named their price. Advertising one's ability to serve ham and eggs, I pointed out to him, would be quite like advertising that one was a member of the Church of England.

After this he meekly enough accompanied me to his bank, where he placed a thousand pounds to my credit, adding that I could go as much farther as I liked, whereupon I set in motion the machinery for decorating and furnishing the place, with particular attention to silver, linen, china, and glassware, all of which, I was resolved, should have an air of its own.

Nor did I neglect to seek out the pair of blacks and enter into an agreement with them to assist in staffing my place. I had feared that the male black might have resolved to return to his adventurous life of outlawry after leaving the employment of Belknap-Jackson, but I found him peacefully inclined and entirely willing to accept service with me, while his wife, upon whom I would depend for much of the actual cooking, was wholly enthusiastic, admiring especially my colour-scheme of reds. I observed at once that her almost exclusive notion of preparing food was to fry it, but I made no doubt that I would be able to broaden her scope, since there are of course things that one simply does not fry.

The male black, or raccoon, at first alarmed me not a little by reason of threats he made against Belknap-Jackson on account of having been shopped. He nursed an intention, so he informed me, of putting snake-dust in the boots of his late employer and so bringing evil upon him, either by disease or violence, but in this I discouraged him smartly, apprising him that the Belknap-Jacksons would doubtless be among our most desirable patrons, whereupon his wife promised for him that he would do nothing of the sort. She was a native of formidable bulk, and her menacing glare at her consort as she made this promise gave me instant confidence in her power to control him, desperate fellow though he was.

Later in the day, at the door of the silversmith's, Cousin Egbert hailed the pressman I had met on the evening of my arrival, and insisted that I impart to him the details of my venture. The chap seemed vastly interested, and his sheet the following morning published the following:

> THE DELMONICO OF THE WEST   Colonel
> Marmaduke Ruggles of London and Paris, for the past
> two months a social favourite in Red Gap's select North
> Side   set, has decided to cast his lot among us and
> will henceforth   be reckoned as one of our leading
> business men. The plan of   the Colonel is nothing
> less than to give Red Gap a truly élite   and
> recherché restaurant after the best models of London
> and   Paris, to which purpose he will devote a
> considerable portion   of his ample means. The
> establishment will occupy the roomy   corner store
> of the Pettengill block, and orders have already
> been placed for its decoration and furnishing, which
> will be   sumptuous beyond anything yet seen in our
> thriving metropolis.   In speaking of his enterprise
> yesterday, the Colonel remarked,   with a sly twinkle
> in his eye, "Demosthenes was the son of a   cutler,
> Cromwell's father was a brewer, your General Grant was

a tanner, and a Mr. Garfield, who held, I gather, an important   post in your government, was once employed on a canal-ship, so   I trust that in this land of equality it will not be presumptuous   on my part to seek to become the managing owner of a restaurant   that will be a credit to the fastest growing town in the state.   "You Americans have," continued the Colonel in his dry, inimitable manner, "a bewildering variety of foodstuffs, but I trust I may   be forgiven for saying that you have used too little constructive   imagination in the cooking of it. In the one matter of tea,   for example, I have been obliged to figure in some episodes that were profoundly regrettable. Again, amid the profusion of   fresh vegetables and meats, you are becoming a nation of tinned   food eaters, or canned food as you prefer to call it. This,   I need hardly say, adds to your cost of living and also makes   you liable to one of the most dreaded of modern diseases, a   disease whose rise can be traced to the rise of the tinned-food   industry. Your tin openers rasp into the tin with the result   that a fine sawdust of metal must drop into the contents and   so enter the human system. The result is perhaps negligible in a large majority of cases, but that it is not universally so   is proved by the prevalence of appendicitis. Not orange or   grape pips, as was so long believed, but the deadly fine rain   of metal shavings must be held responsible for this scourge. I need hardly say that at the United States Grill no tinned   food will be used."   This latest discovery of the Colonel's is important if true.   Be that as it may, his restaurant will fill a long-felt want,   and will doubtless prove to be an important factor in the social   gayeties of our smart set. Due notice of its opening will be   given in the news and doubtless in the advertising columns of this journal.

Again I was brought to marvel at a peculiarity of the American press, a certain childish eagerness for marvels and grotesque wonders. I had given but passing thought to my remarks about appendicitis and its relation to the American tinned-food habit, nor, on reading the chap's screed, did they impress me as being fraught with vital interest to thinking people; in truth, I was more concerned with the comparison of myself to a restaurateur of the crude new city of New York, which might belittle rather than distinguish me, I suspected. But what was my astonishment to perceive in the course of a few days that I had created rather a sensation, with attending newspaper publicity which, although bizarre enough, I am bound to say contributed not a little to the consideration in which I afterward came to be held by the more serious-minded persons of Red Gap.

127

Busied with the multitude of details attending my installation, I was called upon by another press chap, representing a Spokane sheet, who wished me to elaborate my views concerning the most probable cause of appendicitis, which I found myself able to do with some eloquence, reciting among other details that even though the metal dust might be of an almost microscopic fineness, it could still do a mischief to one's appendix. The press chap appeared wholly receptive to my views, and, after securing details of my plan to smarten Red Gap with a restaurant of real distinction, he asked so civilly for a photographic portrait of myself that I was unable to refuse him. The thing was a snap taken of me one morning at Chaynes-Wotten by Higgins, the butler, as I stood by his lordship's saddle mare. It was not by any means the best likeness I have had, but there was a rather effective bit of background disclosing the driveway and the façade of the East Wing.

This episode I had well-nigh forgotten when on the following Sunday I found the thing emblazoned across a page of the Spokane sheet under a shrieking headline: "Can Opener Blamed for Appendicitis." A secondary heading ran, "Famous British Sportsman and Bon Vivant Advances Novel Theory." Accompanying this was a print of the photograph entitled, "Colonel Marmaduke Ruggles with His Favourite Hunter, at His English Country Seat."

Although the article made suitable reference to myself and my enterprise, it was devoted chiefly to a discussion of my tin-opening theory and was supplemented by a rather snarky statement signed by a physician declaring it to be nonsense. I thought the fellow might have chosen his words with more care, but again dismissed the matter from my mind. Yet this was not to be the last of it. In due time came a New York sheet with a most extraordinary page. "Titled Englishman Learns Cause of Appendicitis," read the heading in large, muddy type. Below was the photograph of myself, now entitled, "Sir Marmaduke Ruggles and His Favourite Hunter." But this was only one of the illustrations. From the upper right-hand corner a gigantic hand wielding a tin-opener rained a voluminous spray of metal, presumably, upon a cowering wretch in the lower left-hand corner, who was quite plainly all in. There were tables of statistics showing the increase, side by side of appendicitis and the tinned-food industry, a matter to which I had devoted, said the print, years of research before announcing my discovery. Followed statements from half a dozen distinguished surgeons, each signed autographically, all but one rather bluntly disagreeing with me, insisting that the tin-opener cuts cleanly and, if not man's best friend, should at least be considered one of the triumphs of civilization. The only exception announced that he was at present conducting laboratory experiments with a view to testing my theory and would disclose his results in due time. Meantime, he counselled the public to be not unduly alarmed.

Of the further flood of these screeds, which continued for the better part of a year, I need not speak. They ran the gamut from serious leaders in medical journals to paid ridicule of my theory in advertisements printed by the foodtinning persons, and I have to admit that in the end the public returned to a full confidence in its tinned foods. But that is beside the point, which was that Red Gap had become intensely interested in the United States Grill, and to this I was not averse, though I would rather I had been regarded as one of their plain, common sort, instead of the fictitious Colonel which Cousin Egbert's well-meaning stupidity had foisted upon the town. The "Sir Marmaduke Ruggles and His Favourite Hunter" had been especially repugnant to my finer taste, particularly as it was seized upon by the cheap one-and-six fellow Hobbs for some of his coarsest humour, he more than once referring to that detestable cur of Mrs. Judson's, who had quickly resumed his allegiance to me, as my "hunting pack."

The other tradesmen of the town, I am bound to say, exhibited a friendly interest in my venture which was always welcome and often helpful. Even one of my competitors showed himself to be a dead sport by coming to me from time to time with hints and advice. He was an entirely worthy person who advertised his restaurant as "Bert's Place." "Go to Bert's Place for a Square Meal," was his favoured line in the public prints. He, also, I regret to say, made a practice of displaying cooked foods in his show-window, the window carrying the line in enamelled letters, "Tables Reserved for Ladies."

Of course between such an establishment and my own there could be little in common, and I was obliged to reject a placard which he offered me, reading, "No Checks Cashed. This Means You!" although he and Cousin Egbert warmly advised that I display it in a conspicuous place. "Some of them dead beats in the North Side set will put you sideways if you don't," warned the latter, but I held firmly to the line of quiet refinement which I had laid down, and explained that I could allow no such inconsiderate mention of money to be obtruded upon the notice of my guests. I would devise some subtler protection against the dead beet-roots.

In the matter of music, however, I was pleased to accept the advice of Cousin Egbert. "Get one of them musical pianos that you put a nickel in," he counselled me, and this I did, together with an assorted repertoire of selections both classical and popular, the latter consisting chiefly of the ragging time songs to which the native Americans perform their folkdances.

And now, as the date of my opening drew near, I began to suspect that its social values might become a bit complicated. Mrs. Belknap-Jackson, for example, approached me in confidence to know if she might reserve all the tables in my establishment for the opening evening, remarking that it would be as well to put the correct social cachet upon the place at once, which would be achieved by her inviting only the desirable people. Though she was all for settling the matter at once, something prompted me to take it under consideration.

The same evening Mrs. Effie approached me with a similar suggestion, remarking that she would gladly take it upon herself to see that the occasion was unmarred by the presence of those one would not care to meet in one's own home. Again I was non-committal, somewhat to her annoyance.

The following morning I was sought by Mrs. Judge Ballard with the information that much would depend upon my opening, and if the matter were left entirely in her hands she would be more than glad to insure its success. Of her, also, I begged a day's consideration, suspecting then that I might be compelled to ask these three social leaders to unite amicably as patronesses of an affair that was bound to have a supreme social significance. But as I still meditated profoundly over the complication late that afternoon, overlooking in the meanwhile an electrician who was busy with my shaded candlesticks, I was surprised by the self-possessed entrance of the leader of the Bohemian set, the Klondike person of whom I have spoken. Again I was compelled to observe that she was quite the most smartly gowned woman in Red Gap, and that she marvellously knew what to put on her head.

She coolly surveyed my decorations and such of the furnishings as were in place before addressing me.

"I wish to engage one of your best tables," she began, "for your opening night—the tenth, isn't it?—this large one in the corner will do nicely. There will be eight of us. Your place really won't be half bad, if your food is at all possible."

The creature spoke with a sublime effrontery, quite as if she had not helped a few weeks before to ridicule all that was best in Red Gap society, yet there was that about her which prevented me from rebuking her even by the faintest shade in my manner. More than this, I suddenly saw that the Bohemian set would be a factor in my trade which I could not afford to ignore. While I affected to consider her request she tapped the toe of a small boot with a correctly rolled umbrella, lifting her chin rather attractively meanwhile to survey my freshly done ceiling. I may say here that the effect of her was most compelling, and I could well understand the bitterness with which the ladies of the Onwards and Upwards Society had gossiped her to rags. Incidently, this was the first correctly rolled umbrella, saving my own, that I had seen in North America.

"I shall be pleased," I said, "to reserve this table for you—eight places, I believe you said?"

She left me as a duchess might have. She was that sort. I felt almost quite unequal to her. And the die was cast. I faced each of the three ladies who had previously approached me with the declaration that I was a licensed victualler, bound to serve all who might apply. That while I was keenly sensitive to the social aspects of my business, it was yet a business, and I must, therefore, be in supreme control. In justice to myself I could not exclusively entertain any faction of the North Side set, nor even the set in its entirety. In each instance, I added that I could not debar from my tables even such members of the Bohemian set as conducted themselves in a seemly manner. It was a difficult situation, calling out all my tact, yet I faced it with a firmness which was later to react to my advantage in ways I did not yet dream of.

So engrossed for a month had I been with furnishers, decorators, char persons, and others that the time of the Honourable George's arrival drew on quite before I realized it. A brief and still snarky note had apprised me of his intention to come out to North America, whereupon I had all but forgotten him, until a telegram from Chicago or one of those places had warned me of his imminence. This I displayed to Cousin Egbert, who, much pleased with himself, declared that the Honourable George should be taken to the Floud home directly upon his arrival.

"I meant to rope him in there on the start," he confided to me, "but I let on I wasn't decided yet, just to keep 'em stirred up. Mrs. Effie she butters me up with soft words every day of my life, and that Jackson lad has offered me about ten thousand of them vegetable cigarettes, but I'll have to throw him down. He's the human flivver. Put him in a car of dressed beef and he'd freeze it between here and Spokane. Yes, sir; you could cut his ear off and it wouldn't bleed. I ain't going to run the Judge against no such proposition like that." Of course the poor chap was speaking his own backwoods metaphor, as I am quite sure he would have been incapable of mutilating Belknap-Jackson, or even of imprisoning him in a goods van of beef. I mean to say, it was merely his way of speaking and was not to be taken at all literally.

As a result of his ensuing call upon the pressman, the sheet of the following morning contained word of the Honourable George's coming, the facts being not garbled more than was usual with this chap.

> RED GAP'S NOTABLE GUEST   En route for our thriving metropolis is a personage no   less distinguished than the Honourable George Augustus Vane-Basingwell, only brother and next in line of succession to his lordship the Earl of Brinstead, the well-known British peer of London, England. Our noble visitor will be the house guest of Senator and Mrs. J. K. Floud, at their palatial residence on Ophir Avenue,   where he will be extensively entertained, particularly by   our esteemed fellow-townsman, Egbert G. Floud, with whom   he recently hobnobbed during the latter's stay in Paris,   France. His advent will doubtless prelude a season of unparalleled gayety, particularly as Mr. Egbert Floud assures us that the "Judge," as he affectionately calls him, is "sure some mixer." If this be true, the gentleman   has selected a community where his talent will find ample   scope, and we bespeak for his lordship a hearty welcome.

CHAPTER FOURTEEN

I must do Cousin Egbert the justice to say that he showed a due sense of his responsibility in meeting the Honourable George. By general consent the honour had seemed to fall to him, both the Belknap-Jacksons and Mrs. Effie rather timidly conceding his claim that the distinguished guest would prefer it so. Indeed, Cousin Egbert had been loudly arrogant in the matter, speaking largely of his European intimacy with the "Judge" until, as he confided to me, he "had them all bisoned," or, I believe, "buffaloed" is the term he used, referring to the big-game animal that has been swept from the American savannahs.

At all events no one further questioned his right to be at the station when the Honourable George arrived, and for the first time almost since his own homecoming he got himself up with some attention to detail. If left to himself I dare say he would have donned frock-coat and top-hat, but at my suggestion he chose his smartest lounge-suit, and I took pains to see that the minor details of hat, boots, hose, gloves, etc., were studiously correct without being at all assertive.

For my own part, I was also at some pains with my attire going consciously a bit further with details than Cousin Egbert, thinking it best the Honourable George should at once observe a change in my bearing and social consequence so that nothing in his manner toward me might embarrassingly publish our former relations. The stick, gloves, and monocle would achieve this for the moment, and once alone I meant to tell him straight that all was over between us as master and man, we having passed out of each other's lives in that respect. If necessary, I meant to read to him certain passages from the so-called "Declaration of Independence," and to show him the fateful little card I had found, which would acquaint him, I made no doubt, with the great change that had come upon me, after which our intimacy would rest solely upon the mutual esteem which I knew to exist between us. I mean to say, it would never have done for one moment at home, but finding ourselves together in this wild and lawless country we would neither of us try to resist America, but face each other as one equal native to another.

Waiting on the station platform with Cousin Egbert, he confided to the loungers there that he was come to meet his friend Judge Basingwell, whereat all betrayed a friendly interest, though they were not at all persons that mattered, being of the semi-leisured class who each day went down, as they put it, "to see Number Six go through." There was thus a rather tense air of expectancy when the train pulled in. From one of the Pullman night coaches emerged the Honourable George, preceded by a blackamoor or raccoon bearing bags and bundles, and followed by another uniformed raccoon and a white guard, also bearing bags and bundles, and all betraying a marked anxiety.

One glance at the Honourable George served to confirm certain fears I had suffered regarding his appearance. Topped by a deer-stalking fore-and-aft cap in an inferior state of preservation, he wore the jacket of a lounge-suit, once possible, doubtless, but now demoded, and a blazered golfing waistcoat, striking for its poisonous greens, trousers from an outing suit that I myself had discarded after it came to me, and boots of an entirely shocking character. Of his cravat I have not the heart to speak, but I may mention that all his garments were quite horrid with wrinkles and seemed to have been slept in repeatedly.

Cousin Egbert at once rushed forward to greet his guest, while I busied myself in receiving the hand-luggage, wishing to have our guest effaced from the scene and secluded, with all possible speed. There were three battered handbags, two rolls of travelling rugs, a stick-case, a dispatch-case, a pair of binoculars, a hat-box, a top-coat, a storm-coat, a portfolio of correspondence materials, a camera, a medicine-case, some of these lacking either strap or handle. The attendants all emitted hearty sighs of relief when these articles had been deposited upon the platform. Without being told, I divined that the Honourable George had greatly worried them during the long journey with his fretful demands for service, and I tipped them handsomely while he was still engaged with Cousin Egbert and the latter's station-lounging friends to whom he was being presented. At last, observing me, he came forward, but halted on surveying the luggage, and screamed hoarsely to the last attendant who was now boarding the train. The latter vanished, but reappeared, as the train moved off, with two more articles, a vacuum night-flask and a tin of charcoal biscuits, the absence of which had been swiftly detected by their owner.

It was at that moment that one of the loungers nearby made a peculiar observation. "Gee!" said he to a native beside him, "it must take an awful lot of trouble to be an Englishman." At the moment this seemed to me to be pregnant with meaning, though doubtless it was because I had so long been a resident of the North American wilds.

Again the Honourable George approached me and grasped my hand before certain details of my attire and, I fancy, a certain change in my bearing, attracted his notice. Perhaps it was the single glass. His grasp of my hand relaxed and he rubbed his eyes as if dazed from a blow, but I was able to carry the situation off quite nicely under cover of the confusion attending his many bags and bundles, being helped also at the moment by the deeply humiliating discovery of a certain omission from his attire. I could not at first believe my eyes and was obliged to look again and again, but there could be no doubt about it: the Honourable George was wearing a single spat!

I cried out at this, pointing, I fancy, in a most undignified manner, so terrific had been the shock of it, and what was my amazement to hear him say: "But I *had* only one, you silly! How could I wear 'em both when the other was lost in that bally rabbit-hutch they put me in on shipboard? No bigger than a parcels-lift!" And he had too plainly crossed North America in this shocking state! Glad I was then that Belknap-Jackson was not present. The others, I dare say, considered it a mere freak of fashion. As quickly as I could, I hustled him into the waiting carriage, piling his luggage about him to the best advantage and hurrying Cousin Egbert after him as rapidly as I could, though the latter, as on the occasion of my own arrival, halted our departure long enough to present the Honourable George to the driver.

"Judge, shake hands with my friend Eddie Pierce." adding as the ceremony was performed, "Eddie keeps a good team, any time you want a hack-ride."

"Sure, Judge," remarked the driver cordially. "Just call up Main 224, any time. Any friend of Sour-dough's can have anything they want night or day." Whereupon he climbed to his box and we at last drove away.

The Honourable George had continued from the moment of our meeting to glance at me in a peculiar, side-long fashion. He seemed fascinated and yet unequal to a straight look at me. He was undoubtedly dazed, as I could discern from his absent manner of opening the tin of charcoal biscuits and munching one. I mean to say, it was too obviously a mere mechanical impulse.

"I say," he remarked to Cousin Egbert, who was beaming fondly at him, "how strange it all is! It's quite foreign."

"The fastest-growing little town in the State," said Cousin Egbert.

"But what makes it grow so silly fast?" demanded the other.

"Enterprise and industries," answered Cousin Egbert loftily.

"Nothing to make a dust about," remarked the Honourable George, staring glassily at the main business thoroughfare. "I've seen larger towns—scores of them."

"You ain't begun to see this town yet," responded Cousin Egbert loyally, and he called to the driver, "Has he, Eddie?"

"Sure, he ain't!" said the driver person genially. "Wait till he sees the new waterworks and the sash-and-blind factory!"

"Is he one of your gentleman drivers?" demanded the Honourable George. "And why a blind factory?"

"Oh, Eddie's good people all right," answered the other, "and the factory turns out blinds and things."

"Why turn them out?" he left this and continued: "He's like that American Johnny in London that drives his own coach to Brighton, yes? Ripping idea! Gentleman driver. But I say, you know, I'll sit on the box with him. Pull up a bit, old son!"

To my consternation the driver chap halted, and before I could remonstrate the Honourable George had mounted to the box beside him. Thankful I was we had left the main street, though in the residence avenue where the change was made we attracted far more attention than was desirable. "Didn't I tell you he was some mixer?" demanded Cousin Egbert of me, but I was too sickened to make any suitable response. The Honourable George's possession of a single spat was now flaunted, as it were, in the face of Red Gap's best families.

"How foreign it all is!" he repeated, turning back to us, yet with only his side-glance for me. "But the American Johnny in London had a much smarter coach than this, and better animals, too. You're not up to his class yet, old thing!"

"That dish-faced pinto on the off side," remarked the driver, "can outrun anything in this town for fun, money, or marbles."

"Marbles!" called the Honourable George to us; "why marbles? Silly things! It's all bally strange! And why do your villagers stare so?"

"Some little mixer, all right, all right," murmured Cousin Egbert in a sort of ecstasy, as we drew up at the Floud home. "And yet one of them guys back there called him a typical Britisher. You bet I shut him up quick—saying a thing like that about a plumb stranger. I'd 'a' mixed it with him right there except I thought it was better to have things nice and not start something the minute the Judge got here."

With all possible speed I hurried the party indoors, for already faces were appearing at the windows of neighbouring houses. Mrs. Effie, who met us, allowed her glare at Cousin Egbert, I fancy, to affect the cordiality of her greeting to the Honourable George; at least she seemed to be quite as dazed as he, and there was a moment of constraint before he went on up to the room that had been prepared for him. Once safely within the room I contrived a moment alone with him and removed his single spat, not too gently, I fear, for the nervous strain since his arrival had told upon me.

"You have reason to be thankful," I said, "that Belknap-Jackson was not present to witness this."

"They cost seven and six," he muttered, regarding the one spat wistfully. "But why Belknap-Jackson?"

"Mr. C. Belknap-Jackson of Boston and Red Gap," I returned sternly. "He does himself perfectly. To think he might have seen you in this rowdyish state!" And I hastened to seek a presentable lounge-suit from his bags.

"Everything is so strange," he muttered again, quite helplessly. "And why the mural decoration at the edge of the settlement? Why keep one's eye upon it? Why should they do such things? I say, it's all quite monstrous, you know."

I saw that indeed he was quite done for with amazement, so I ran him a bath and procured him a dish of tea. He rambled oddly at moments of things the guard on the night-coach had told him of North America, of Niagara Falls, and Missouri and other objects of interest. He was still almost quite a bit dotty when I was obliged to leave him for an appointment with the raccoon and his wife to discuss the menu of my opening dinner, but Cousin Egbert, who had rejoined us, was listening sympathetically. As I left, the two were pegging it from a bottle of hunting sherry which the Honourable George had carried in his dispatch-case. I was about to warn him that he would come out spotted, but instantly I saw that there must be an end to such surveillance. I could not manage an enterprise of the magnitude of the United States Grill and yet have an eye to his meat and drink. I resolved to let spots come as they would.

On all hands I was now congratulated by members of the North Side set upon the master-stroke I had played in adding the Honourable George to their number. Not only did it promise to reunite certain warring factions in the North Side set itself, but it truly bade fair to disintegrate the Bohemian set. Belknap-Jackson wrung my hand that afternoon, begging me to inform the Honourable George that he would call on the morrow to pay his respects. Mrs. Judge Ballard besought me to engage him for an early dinner, and Mrs. Effie, it is needless to say, after recovering from the shock of his arrival, which she attributed to Cousin Egbert's want of taste, thanked me with a wealth of genuine emotion.

Only by slight degrees, then, did it fall to be noticed that the Honourable George did not hold himself to be too strictly bound by our social conventions as to whom one should be pally with. Thus, on the morrow, at the hour when the Belknap-Jacksons called, he was regrettably absent on what Cousin Egbert called "a hack-ride" with the driver person he had met the day before, nor did they return until after the callers had waited the better part of two hours. Cousin Egbert, as usual, received the blame for this, yet neither of the Belknap-Jacksons nor Mrs. Effie dared to upbraid him.

Being presented to the callers, I am bound to say that the Honourable George showed himself to be immensely impressed by Belknap-Jackson, whom I had never beheld more perfectly vogue in all his appointments. He became, in fact, rather moody in the presence of this subtle niceness of detail, being made conscious, I dare say, of his own sloppy lounge-suit, rumpled cravat, and shocking boots, and despite Belknap-Jackson's amiable efforts to draw him into talk about hunting in the shires and our county society at home, I began to fear that they would not hit it off together. The Honourable George did, however, consent to drive with his caller the following day, and I relied upon the tandem to recall him to his better self. But when the callers had departed he became quite almost plaintive to me.

"I say, you know, I shan't be wanted to pal up much with that chap, shall I? I mean to say, he wears so many clothes. They make me writhe as if I wore them myself. It won't do, you know."

I told him very firmly that this was piffle of the most wretched sort. That his caller wore but the prescribed number of garments, each vogue to the last note, and that he was a person whom one must know. He responded pettishly that he vastly preferred the gentleman driver with whom he had spent the afternoon, and "Sour-dough," as he was now calling Cousin Egbert.

"Jolly chaps, with no swank," he insisted. "We drove quite almost everywhere—waterworks, cemetery, sash-and-blind factory. You know I thought 'blind factory' was some of their bally American slang for the shop of a chap who made eyeglasses and that sort of thing, but nothing of the kind. They saw up timbers there quite all over the place and nail them up again into articles. It's all quite foreign."

Nor was his account of his drive with Belknap-Jackson the following day a bit more reassuring.

"He wouldn't stop again at the sash-and-blind factory, where I wished to see the timbers being sawed and nailed, but drove me to a country club which was not in the country and wasn't a club; not a human there, not even a barman. Fancy a club of that sort! But he took me to his own house for a glass of sherry and a biscuit, and there it wasn't so rotten. Rather a mother-in-law I think, she is—bally old booming grenadier—topping sort—no end of fun. We palled up immensely and I quite forgot the Jackson chap till it was time for him to drive me back to these diggings. Rather sulky he was, I fancy; uppish sort. Told him the old one was quite like old Caroline, dowager duchess of Clewe, but couldn't tell if it pleased him. Seemed to like it and seemed not to: rather uncertain.

"Asked him why the people of the settlement pronounced his name 'Belknap Hyphen Jackson,' and that seemed to make him snarky again. I mean to say names with hyphen marks in 'em—I'd never heard the hyphen pronounced before, but everything is so strange. He said only the lowest classes did it as a form of coarse wit, and that he was wasting himself here. Wouldn't stay another day if it were not for family reasons. Queer sort of wheeze to say 'hyphen' in a chap's name as if it were a word, when it wasn't at all. The old girl, though—bellower she is—perfectly top-hole; familiar with cattle—all that sort of thing. Sent away the chap's sherry and had 'em bring whiskey and soda. The hyphen chap fidgeted a good bit—nervous sort, I take it. Looked through a score of magazines, I dare say, when he found we didn't notice him much; turned the leaves too fast to see anything, though; made noises and coughed—that sort of thing. Fine old girl. Daughter, hyphen chap's wife, tried to talk, too, some rot about the season being well on here, and was there a good deal of society in London, and would I be free for dinner on the ninth?

"Silly chatter! old girl talked sense: cattle, mines, timber, blind factory, two-year olds, that kind of thing. Shall see her often. Not the hyphen chap, though; too much like one of those Bond Street milliner-chap managers."

Vague misgivings here beset me as to the value of the Honourable George to the North Side set. Nor could I feel at all reassured on the following day when Mrs. Effie held an afternoon reception in his honour. That he should be unaware of the event's importance was to be expected, for as yet I had been unable to get him to take the Red Gap social crisis seriously. At the hour when he should have been dressed and ready I found him playing at cribbage with Cousin Egbert in the latter's apartment, and to my dismay he insisted upon finishing the rubber although guests were already arriving.

Even when the game was done he flatly refused to dress suitably, declaring that his lounge-suit should be entirely acceptable to these rough frontier people, and he consented to go down at all only on condition that Cousin Egbert would accompany him. Thereafter for an hour the two of them drank tea uncomfortably as often as it was given them, and while the Honourable George undoubtedly made his impression, I could not but regret that he had so few conversational graces.

How different, I reflected, had been my own entrée into this county society! As well as I might I again carried off the day for the Honourable George, endeavouring from time to time to put him at his ease, yet he breathed an unfeigned sigh of relief when the last guest had left and he could resume his cribbage with Cousin Egbert. But he had received one impression of which I was glad: an impression of my own altered social quality, for I had graced the occasion with an urbanity which was as far beyond him as it must have been astonishing. It was now that he began to take seriously what I had told him of my business enterprise, so many of the guests having mentioned it to him in terms of the utmost enthusiasm. After my first accounts to him he had persisted in referring to it as a tuck-shop, a sort of place where schoolboys would exchange their halfpence for toffy, sweet-cakes, and marbles.

Now he demanded to be shown the premises and was at once duly impressed both with their quiet elegance and my own business acumen. How it had all come about, and why I should be addressed as "Colonel Ruggles" and treated as a person of some importance in the community, I dare say he has never comprehended to this day. As I had planned to do, I later endeavoured to explain to him that in North America persons were almost quite equal to one another—being born so—but at this he told me not to be silly and continued to regard my rise as an insoluble part of the strangeness he everywhere encountered, even after I added that Demosthenes was the son of a cutler, that Cardinal Wolsey's father had been a pork butcher, and that Garfield had worked on a canal-boat. I found him quite hopeless. "Chaps go dotty talkin' that piffle," was his comment.

At another time, I dare say, I should have been rather distressed over this inability of the Honourable George to comprehend and adapt himself to the peculiarities of American life as readily as I had done, but just now I was quite too taken up with the details of my opening to give it the deeper consideration it deserved. In fact, there were moments when I confessed to myself that I did not care tuppence about it, such was the strain upon my executive faculties. When decorators and furnishers had done their work, when the choice carpet was laid, when the kitchen and table equipments were completed to the last detail, and when the lighting was artistically correct, there was still the matter of service.

As to this, I conceived and carried out what I fancy was rather a brilliant stroke, which was nothing less than to eliminate the fellow Hobbs as a social factor of even the Bohemian set. In contracting with him for my bread and rolls, I took an early opportunity of setting the chap in his place, as indeed it was not difficult to do when he had observed the splendid scale on which I was operating. At our second interview he was removing his hat and addressing me as "sir."

While I have found that I can quite gracefully place myself on a level with the middle-class American, there is a serving type of our own people to which I shall eternally feel superior; the Hobbs fellow was of this sort, having undeniably the soul of a lackey. In addition to jobbing his bread and rolls, I engaged him as pantry man, and took on such members of his numerous family as were competent. His wife was to assist my raccoon cook in the kitchen, three of his sons were to serve as waiters, and his youngest, a lad in his teens, I installed as vestiare, garbing him in a smart uniform and posting him to relieve my gentleman patrons of their hats and top-coats. A daughter was similarly installed as maid, and the two achieved an effect of smartness unprecedented in Red Gap, an effect to which I am glad to say that the community responded instantly.

In other establishments it was the custom for patrons to hang their garments on hat-pegs, often under a printed warning that the proprietor would disclaim responsibility in case of loss. In the one known as "Bert's Place" indeed the warning was positively vulgar: "Watch Your Overcoat." Of course that sort of coarseness would have been impossible in my own place.

As another important detail I had taken over from Mrs. Judson her stock of jellies and compotes which I had found to be of a most excellent character, and had ordered as much more as she could manage to produce, together with cut flowers from her garden for my tables. She, herself, being a young woman of the most pleasing capabilities, had done a bit of charring for me and was now to be in charge of the glassware, linen, and silver. I had found her, indeed, highly sympathetic with my highest aims, and not a few of her suggestions as to management proved to be entirely sound. Her unspeakable dog continued his quite objectionable advances to me at every opportunity, in spite of my hitting him about, rather, when I could do so unobserved, but the sinister interpretation that might be placed upon this by the baser-minded was now happily answered by the circumstance of her being in my employment. Her child, I regret to say, was still grossly overfed, seldom having its face free from jam or other smears. It persisted, moreover, in twisting my name into "Ruggums," which I found not a little embarrassing.

The night of my opening found me calmly awaiting the triumph that was due me. As some one has said of Napoleon, I had won my battle in my tent before the firing of a single shot. I mean to say, I had looked so conscientiously after details, even to assuring myself that Cousin Egbert and the Honourable George would appear in evening dress, my last act having been to coerce each of them into purchasing varnished boots, the former submitting meekly enough, though the Honourable George insisted it was a silly fuss.

At seven o'clock, having devoted a final inspection to the kitchen where the female raccoon was well on with the dinner, and having noted that the members of my staff were in their places, I gave a last pleased survey of my dining-room, with its smartly equipped tables, flower-bedecked, gleaming in the softened light from my shaded candlesticks. Truly it was a scene of refined elegance such as Red Gap had never before witnessed within its own confines, and I had seen to it that the dinner as well would mark an epoch in the lives of these simple but worthy people.

Not a heavy nor a cloying repast would they find. Indeed, the bare simplicity of my menu, had it been previously disclosed, would doubtless have disappointed more than one of my dinner-giving patronesses; but each item had been perfected to an extent never achieved by them. Their weakness had ever been to serve a profusion of neutral dishes, pleasing enough to the eye, but unedifying except as a spectacle. I mean to say, as food it was noncommittal; it failed to intrigue.

I should serve only a thin soup, a fish, small birds, two vegetables, a salad, a sweet and a savoury, but each item would prove worthy of the profoundest consideration. In the matter of thin soup, for example, the local practice was to serve a fluid of which, beyond the circumstance that it was warmish and slightly tinted, nothing of interest could ever be ascertained. My own thin soup would be a revelation to them. Again, in the matter of fish. This course with the hostesses of Red Gap had seemed to be merely an excuse for a pause. I had truly sympathized with Cousin Egbert's bitter complaint: "They hand you a dab of something about the size of a watch-charm with two strings of potato."

For the first time, then, the fish course in Red Gap was to be an event, an abundant portion of native fish with a lobster sauce which I had carried out to its highest power. My birds, hot from the oven, would be food in the strictest sense of the word, my vegetables cooked with a zealous attention, and my sweet immensely appealing without being pretentiously spectacular. And for what I believed to be quite the first time in the town, good coffee would be served. Disheartening, indeed, had been the various attenuations of coffee which had been imposed upon me in my brief career as a diner-out among these people. Not one among them had possessed the genius to master an acceptable decoction of the berry, the bald simplicity of the correct formula being doubtless incredible to them.

The blare of a motor horn aroused me from this musing, and from that moment I had little time for meditation until the evening, as the *Journal* recorded the next morning, "had gone down into history." My patrons arrived in groups, couples, or singly, almost faster than I could seat them. The Hobbs lad, as vestiare, would halt them for hats and wraps, during which pause they would emit subdued cries of surprise and delight at my beautifully toned ensemble, after which, as they walked to their tables, it was not difficult to see that they were properly impressed.

Mrs. Effie, escorted by the Honourable George and cousin Egbert, was among the early arrivals; the Senator being absent from town at a sitting of the House. These were quickly followed by the Belknap-Jacksons and the Mixer, resplendent in purple satin and diamonds, all being at one of my large tables, so that the Honourable George sat between Mrs. Belknap-Jackson and Mrs. Effie, though he at first made a somewhat undignified essay to seat himself next the Mixer. Needless to say, all were in evening dress, though the Honourable George had fumbled grossly with his cravat and rumpled his shirt, nor had he submitted to having his beard trimmed, as I had warned him to do. As for Belknap-Jackson, I had never beheld him more truly vogue in every detail, and his slightly austere manner in any Red Gap gathering had never set him better. Both Mrs. Belknap-Jackson and Mrs. Effie wielded their lorgnons upon the later comers, thus giving their table quite an air.

Mrs. Judge Ballard, who had come to be one of my staunchest adherents, occupied an adjacent table with her family party and two or three of the younger dancing set. The Indian Tuttle with his wife and two daughters were also among the early comers, and I could not but marvel anew at the red man's histrionic powers. In almost quite correct evening attire, and entirely decorous in speech and gesture, he might readily have been thought some one that mattered, had he not at an early opportunity caught my eye and winked with a sly significance.

Quite almost every one of the North Side set was present, imparting to my room a general air of distinguished smartness, and in addition there were not a few of what Belknap-Jackson had called the "rabble," persons of no social value, to be sure, but honest, well-mannered folk, small tradesmen, shop-assistants, and the like. These plain people, I may say, I took especial pains to welcome and put at their ease, for I had resolved, in effect, to be one of them, after the manner prescribed by their Declaration thing.

With quite all of them I chatted easily a moment or two, expressing the hope that they would be well pleased with their entertainment. I noted while thus engaged that Belknap-Jackson eyed me with frank and superior cynicism, but this affected me quite not at all and I took pains to point my indifference, chatting with increased urbanity with the two cow-persons, Hank and Buck, who had entered rather uncertainly, not in evening dress, to be sure, but in decent black as befitted their stations. When I had prevailed upon them to surrender their hats to the vestiare and had seated them at a table for two, they informed me in hoarse undertones that they were prepared to "put a bet down on every card from soda to hock," so that I at first suspected they had thought me conducting a gaming establishment, but ultimately gathered that they were merely expressing a cordial determination to enter into the spirit of the occasion.

There then entered, somewhat to my uneasiness, the Klondike woman and her party. Being almost the last, it will be understood that they created no little sensation as she led them down the thronged room to her table. She was wearing an evening gown of lustrous black with the apparently simple lines that are so baffling to any but the expert maker, with a black picture hat that suited her no end. I saw more than one matron of the North Side set stiffen in her seat, while Mrs. Belknap-Jackson and Mrs. Effie turned upon her the chilling broadside of their lorgnons. Belknap-Jackson merely drew himself up austerely. The three other women of her party, flutterers rather, did little but set off their hostess. The four men were of a youngish sort, chaps in banks, chemists' assistants, that sort of thing, who were constantly to be seen in her train. They were especially reprobated by the matrons of the correct set by reason of their deliberately choosing to ally themselves with the Bohemian set.

Acutely feeling the antagonism aroused by this group, I was momentarily discouraged in a design I had half formed of using my undoubted influence to unite the warring social factions of Red Gap, even as Bismarck had once brought the warring Prussian states together in a federated Germany. I began to see that the Klondike woman would forever prove unacceptable to the North Side set. The cliques would unite against her, even if one should find in her a spirit of reconciliation, which I supremely doubted.

The bustle having in a measure subsided, I gave orders for the soup to be served, at the same time turning the current into the electric pianoforte. I had wished for this opening number something attractive yet dignified, which would in a manner of speaking symbolize an occasion to me at least highly momentous. To this end I had chosen Handel's celebrated Largo, and at the first strains of this highly meritorious composition I knew that I had chosen surely. I am sure the piece was indelibly engraved upon the minds of those many dinner-givers who were for the first time in their lives realizing that a thin soup may be made a thing to take seriously.

Nominally, I occupied a seat at the table with the Belknap-Jacksons and Mrs. Effie, though I apprehended having to be more or less up and down in the direction of my staff. Having now seated myself to soup, I was for the first time made aware of the curious behaviour of the Honourable George. Disregarding his own soup, which was of itself unusual with him, he was staring straight ahead with a curious intensity. A half turn of my head was enough. He sat facing the Klondike woman. As I again turned a bit I saw that under cover of her animated converse with her table companions she was at intervals allowing her very effective eyes to rest, as if absently, upon him. I may say now that a curious chill seized me, bringing with it a sudden psychic warning that all was not going to be as it should be. Some calamity impended. The man was quite apparently fascinated, staring with a fixed, hypnotic intensity that had already been noted by his companions on either side.

With a word about the soup, shot quickly and directly at him, I managed to divert his gaze, but his eyes had returned even before the spoon had gone once to his lips. The second time there was a soup stain upon his already rumpled shirt front. Presently it became only too horribly certain that the man was out of himself, for when the fish course was served he remained serenely unconscious that none of the lobster sauce accompanied his own portion. It was a rich sauce, and the almost immediate effect of shell-fish upon his complexion being only too well known to me, I had directed that his fish should be served without it, though I had fully expected him to row me for it and perhaps create a scene. The circumstance of his blindly attacking the unsauced fish was eloquent indeed.

The Belknap-Jacksons and Mrs. Effie were now plainly alarmed, and somewhat feverishly sought to engage his attention, with the result only that he snapped monosyllables at them without removing his gaze from its mark. And the woman was now too obviously pluming herself upon the effect she had achieved; upon us all she flashed an amused consciousness of her power, yet with a fine affectation of quite ignoring us. I was here obliged to leave the table to oversee the serving of the wine, returning after an interval to find the situation unchanged, save that the woman no longer glanced at the Honourable George. Such were her tactics. Having enmeshed him, she confidently left him to complete his own undoing. I had returned with the serving of the small birds. Observing his own before him, the Honourable George wished to be told why he had not been served with fish, and only with difficulty could be convinced that he had partaken of this. "Of course in public places one must expect to come into contact with persons of that sort," remarked Mrs. Effie.

"Something should be done about it," observed Mrs. Belknap-Jackson, and they both murmured "Creature!" though it was plain that the Honourable George had little notion to whom they referred. Observing, however, that the woman no longer glanced at him, he fell to his bird somewhat whole-heartedly, as indeed did all my guests.

From every side I could hear eager approval of the repast which was now being supplemented at most of the tables by a sound wine of the Burgundy type which I had recommended or by a dry champagne. Meantime, the electric pianoforte played steadily through a repertoire that had progressed from the Largo to more vivacious pieces of the American folkdance school. As was said in the press the following day, "Gayety and good-feeling reigned supreme, and one and all felt that it was indeed good to be there."

Through the sweet and the savoury the dinner progressed, the latter proving to be a novelty that the hostesses of Red Gap thereafter slavishly copied, and with the advent of the coffee ensued a noticeable relaxation. People began to visit one another's tables and there was a blithe undercurrent of praise for my efforts to smarten the town's public dining.

The Klondike woman, I fancy, was the first to light a cigarette, though quickly followed by the ladies of her party. Mrs. Belknap-Jackson and Mrs. Effie, after a period of futile glaring at her through the lorgnons, seemed to make their resolves simultaneously, and forthwith themselves lighted cigarettes.

"Of course it's done in the smart English restaurants," murmured Belknap-Jackson as he assisted the ladies to their lights. Thereupon Mrs. Judge Ballard, farther down the room, began to smoke what I believe was her first cigarette, which proved to be a signal for other ladies of the Onwards and Upwards Society to do the same, Mrs. Ballard being their president. It occurred to me that these ladies were grimly bent on showing the Klondike woman that they could trifle quite as gracefully as she with the lesser vices of Bohemia; or perhaps they wished to demonstrate to the younger dancing men in her train that the North Side set was not desolately austere in its recreation. The Honourable George, I regret to say, produced a smelly pipe which he would have lighted; but at a shocked and cold glance from me he put it by and allowed the Mixer to roll him one of the yellow paper cigarettes from a sack of tobacco which she had produced from some secret recess of her costume.

Cousin Egbert had been excitedly happy throughout the meal and now paid me a quaint compliment upon the food. "Some eats, Bill!" he called to me. "I got to hand it to you," though what precisely it was he wished to hand me I never ascertained, for the Mixer at that moment claimed my attention with a compliment of her own. "That," said she, "is the only dinner I've eaten for a long time that was composed entirely of food."

This hour succeeding the repast I found quite entirely agreeable, more than one person that mattered assuring me that I had assisted Red Gap to a notable advance in the finest and correctest sense of the word, and it was with a very definite regret that I beheld my guests departing. Returning to our table from a group of these who had called me to make their adieus, I saw that a most regrettable incident had occurred—nothing less than the formal presentation of the Honourable George to the Klondike woman. And the Mixer had appallingly done it!

"Everything is so strange here," I heard him saying as I passed their table, and the woman echoed, "Everything!" while her glance enveloped him with a curious effect of appraisal. The others of her party were making much of him, I could see, quite as if they had preposterous designs of wresting him from the North Side set to be one of themselves. Mrs. Belknap-Jackson and Mrs. Effie affected to ignore the meeting. Belknap-Jackson stared into vacancy with a quite shocked expression as if vandals had desecrated an altar in his presence. Cousin Egbert having drawn off one of his newly purchased boots during the dinner was now replacing it with audible groans, but I caught his joyous comment a moment later: "Didn't I tell you the Judge was some mixer?"

"Mixing, indeed," snapped the ladies.

A half-hour later the historic evening had come to an end. The last guest had departed, and all of my staff, save Mrs. Judson and her male child. These I begged to escort to their home, since the way was rather far and dark. The child, incautiously left in the kitchen at the mercy of the female black, had with criminal stupidity been stuffed with food, traces of almost every course of the dinner being apparent upon its puffy countenance. Being now in a stupor from overfeeding, I was obliged to lug the thing over my shoulder. I resolved to warn the mother at an early opportunity of the perils of an unrestricted diet, although the deluded creature seemed actually to glory in its corpulence. I discovered when halfway to her residence that the thing was still tightly clutching the gnawed thigh-bone of a fowl which was spotting the shoulder of my smartest top-coat. The mother, however, was so ingenuously delighted with my success and so full of prattle concerning my future triumphs that I forbore to instruct her at this time. I may say that of all my staff she had betrayed the most intelligent understanding of my ideals, and I bade her good-night with a strong conviction that she would greatly assist me in the future. She also promised that Mr. Barker should thereafter be locked in a cellar at such times as she was serving me.

Returning through the town, I heard strains of music from the establishment known as "Bert's Place," and was shocked on staring through his show window to observe the Honourable George and Cousin Egbert waltzing madly with the cow-persons, Hank and Buck, to the strains of a mechanical piano. The Honourable George had exchanged his top-hat for his partner's cow-person hat, which came down over his ears in a most regrettable manner.

I thought it best not to intrude upon their coarse amusement and went on to the grill to see that all was safe for the night. Returning from my inspection some half-hour later, I came upon the two, Cousin Egbert in the lead, the Honourable George behind him. They greeted me somewhat boisterously, but I saw that they were now content to return home and to bed. As they walked somewhat mincingly, I noticed that they were in their hose, carrying their varnished boots in either hand.

Of the Honourable George, who still wore the cow-person's hat, I began now to have the gravest doubts. There had been an evil light in the eyes of the Klondike woman and her Bohemian cohorts as they surveyed him. As he preceded me I heard him murmur ecstatically: "Sush is life."

CHAPTER FIFTEEN

Launched now upon a business venture that would require my unremitting attention if it were to prosper, it may be imagined that I had little leisure for the social vagaries of the Honourable George, shocking as these might be to one's finer tastes. And yet on the following morning I found time to tell him what. To put it quite bluntly, I gave him beans for his loose behaviour the previous evening, in publicly ogling and meeting as an equal one whom one didn't know.

To my amazement, instead of being heartily ashamed of his licentiousness, I found him recalcitrant. Stubborn as a mule he was and with a low animal cunning that I had never given him credit for. "Demosthenes was the son of a cutler," said he, "and Napoleon worked on a canal-boat, what? Didn't you say so yourself, you juggins, what? Fancy there being upper and lower classes among natives! What rot! And I like North America. I don't mind telling you straight I'm going to take it up."

Horrified by these reckless words, I could only say "Noblesse oblige," meaning to convey that whatever the North Americans did, the next Earl of Brinstead must not meet persons one doesn't know, whereat he rejoined tartly that I was "to stow that piffle!"

Being now quite alarmed, I took the further time to call upon Belknap-Jackson, believing that he, if any one, could recall the Honourable George to his better nature. He, too, was shocked, as I had been, and at first would have put the blame entirely upon the shoulders of Cousin Egbert, but at this I was obliged to admit that the Honourable George had too often shown a regrettable fondness for the society of persons that did not matter, especially females, and I cited the case of the typing-girl and the Brixton millinery person, with either of whom he would have allied himself in marriage had not his lordship intervened. Belknap-Jackson was quite properly horrified at these revelations.

"Has he no sense of 'Noblesse oblige'?" he demanded, at which I quoted the result of my own use of this phrase to the unfortunate man. Quite too plain it was that "Noblesse oblige!" would never stop him from yielding to his baser impulses.

"We must be tactful, then," remarked Belknap-Jackson. "Without appearing to oppose him we must yet show him who is really who in Red Gap. We shall let him see that we have standards which must be as rigidly adhered to as those of an older civilization. I fancy it can be done."

Privately I fancied not, yet I forbore to say this or to prolong the painful interview, particularly as I was due at the United States Grill.

The *Recorder* of that morning had done me handsomely, declaring my opening to have been a social event long to be remembered, and describing the costumes of a dozen or more of the smartly gowned matrons, quite as if it had been an assembly ball. My task now was to see that the Grill was kept to the high level of its opening, both as a social ganglion, if one may use the term, and as a place to which the public would ever turn for food that mattered. For my first luncheon the raccoons had prepared, under my direction, a steak-and-kidney pie, in addition to which I offered a thick soup and a pudding of high nutritive value.

To my pleased astonishment the crowd at midday was quite all that my staff could serve, several of the Hobbs brood being at school, and the luncheon was received with every sign of approval by the business persons who sat to it. Not only were there drapers, chemists, and shop-assistants, but solicitors and barristers, bankers and estate agents, and all quite eager with their praise of my fare. To each of these I explained that I should give them but few things, but that these would be food in the finest sense of the word, adding that the fault of the American school lay in attempting a too-great profusion of dishes, none of which in consequence could be raised to its highest power.

So sound was my theory and so nicely did my simple-dished luncheon demonstrate it that I was engaged on the spot to provide the bi-monthly banquet of the Chamber of Commerce, the president of which rather seriously proposed that it now be made a monthly affair, since they would no longer be at the mercy of a hotel caterer whose ambition ran inversely to his skill. Indeed, after the pudding, I was this day asked to become a member of the body, and I now felt that I was indubitably one of them—America and I had taken each other as seriously as could be desired.

More than once during the afternoon I wondered rather painfully what the Honourable George might be doing. I knew that he had been promised to a meeting of the Onwards and Upwards Club through the influence of Mrs. Effie, where it had been hoped that he would give a talk on Country Life in England. At least she had hinted to them that he might do this, though I had known from the beginning that he would do nothing of the sort, and had merely hoped that he would appear for a dish of tea and stay quiet, which was as much as the North Side set could expect of him. Induced to speak, I was quite certain he would tell them straight that Country Life in England was silly rot, and that was all to it. Now, not having seen him during the day, I could but hope that he had attended the gathering in suitable afternoon attire, and that he would have divined that the cattle-person's hat did not coordinate with this.

At four-thirty, while I was still concerned over the possible misadventures of the Honourable George, my first patrons for tea began to arrive, for I had let it be known that I should specialize in this. Toasted crumpets there were, and muffins, and a tea cake rich with plums, and tea, I need not say, which was all that tea could be. Several tables were filled with prominent ladies of the North Side set, who were loud in their exclamations of delight, especially at the finished smartness of my service, for it was perhaps now that the profoundly serious thought I had given to my silver, linen, and glassware showed to best advantage. I suspect that this was the first time many of my guests had encountered a tea cozy, since from that day they began to be prevalent in Red Gap homes. Also my wagon containing the crumpets, muffins, tea cake, jam and bread-and-butter, which I now used for the first time created a veritable sensation.

There was an agreeable hum of chatter from these early comers when I found myself welcoming Mrs. Judge Ballard and half a dozen members of the Onwards and Upwards Club, all of them wearing what I made out to be a baffled look. From these I presently managed to gather that their guest of honour for the afternoon had simply not appeared, and that the meeting, after awaiting him for two hours, had dissolved in some resentment, the time having been spent chiefly in an unflattering dissection of the Klondike woman's behaviour the evening before.

"He is a naughty man to disappoint us so cruelly!" declared Mrs. Judge Ballard of the Honourable George, but the coquetry of it was feigned to cover a very real irritation. I made haste with possible excuses. I said that he might be ill, or that important letters in that day's post might have detained him. I knew he had been astonishingly well that morning, also that he loathed letters and almost practically never received any; but something had to be said.

"A naughty, naughty fellow!" repeated Mrs. Ballard, and the members of her party echoed it. They had looked forward rather pathetically, I saw, to hearing about Country Life in England from one who had lived it.

I was now drawn to greet the Belknap-Jacksons, who entered, and to the pleasure of winning their hearty approval for the perfection of my arrangements. As the wife presently joined Mrs. Ballard's group, the husband called me to his table and disclosed that almost the worst might be feared of the Honourable George. He was at that moment, it appeared, with a rabble of cow-persons and members of the lower class gathered at a stockade at the edge of town, where various native horses fresh from the wilderness were being taught to be ridden.

"The wretched Floud is with him," continued my informant, "also the Tuttle chap, who continues to be received by our best people in spite of my remonstrances, and he yells quite like a demon when one of the riders is thrown. I passed as quickly as I could. The spectacle was—of course I make allowances for Vane-Basingwell's ignorance of our standards—it was nothing short of disgusting; a man of his position consorting with the herd!"

"He told me no longer ago than this morning," I said, "that he was going to take up America."

"He *has*!" said Belknap-Jackson with bitter emphasis. "You should see what he has on—a cowboy hat and chapps! And the very lowest of them are calling him 'Judge'!"

"He flunked a meeting of the Onwards and Upwards Society," I added.

"I know! I know! And who could have expected it in one of his lineage? At this very moment he should be conducting himself as one of his class. Can you wonder at my impatience with the West? Here at an hour when our social life should be in evidence, when all trade should be forgotten, I am the only man in the town who shows himself in a tea-room; and Vane-Basingwell over there debasing himself with our commonest sort!"

All at once I saw that I myself must bear the brunt of this scandal. I had brought hither the Honourable George, promising a personage who would for once and all unify the North Side set and perhaps disintegrate its rival. I had been felicitated upon my master-stroke. And now it seemed I had come a cropper. But I resolved not to give up, and said as much now to Belknap-Jackson.

"I may be blamed for bringing him among you, but trust me if things are really as bad as they seem, I'll get him off again. I'll not let myself be bowled by such a silly lob as that. Trust me to devote profound thought to this problem."

"We all have every confidence in you," he assured me, "but don't be too severe all at once with the chap. He might recover a sane balance even yet."

"I shall use discretion," I assured him, "but if it proves that I have fluffed my catch, rely upon me to use extreme measures."

"Red Gap needs your best effort," he replied in a voice that brimmed with feeling.

At five-thirty, my rush being over, I repaired to the neighbourhood where the Honourable George had been reported. The stockade now contained only a half-score of the untaught horses, but across the road from it was a public house, or saloon, from which came unmistakable sounds of carousing. It was an unsavoury place, frequented only by cattle and horse persons, the proprietor being an abandoned character named Spilmer, who had once done a patron to death in a drunken quarrel. Only slight legal difficulties had been made for him, however, it having been pleaded that he acted in self-defence, and the creature had at once resumed his trade as publican. There was even public sympathy for him at the time on the ground that he possessed a blind mother, though I have never been able to see that this should have been a factor in adjudging him.

I paused now before the low place, imagining I could detect the tones of the Honourable George high above the chorus that came out to me. Deciding that in any event it would not become me to enter a resort of this stamp, I walked slowly back toward the more reputable part of town, and was presently rewarded by seeing the crowd emerge. It was led, I saw, by the Honourable George. The cattle-hat was still down upon his ears, and to my horror he had come upon the public thoroughfare with his legs encased in the chapps—a species of leathern pantalettes covered with goat's wool—a garment which I need not say no gentleman should be seen abroad in. As worn by the cow-persons in their daily toil they are only just possible, being as far from true vogue as anything well could be.

Accompanying him were Cousin Egbert, the Indian Tuttle, the cow-persons, Hank and Buck, and three or four others of the same rough stamp. Unobtrusively I followed them to our main thoroughfare, deeply humiliated by the atrocious spectacle the Honourable George was making of himself, only to observe them turn into another public house entitled "The Family Liquor Store," where it seemed only too certain, since the bearing of all was highly animated, that they would again carouse.

At once seeing my duty, I boldly entered, finding them aligned against the American bar and clamouring for drink. My welcome was heartfelt, even enthusiastic, almost every one of them beginning to regale me with incidents of the afternoon's horse-breaking. The Honourable George, it seemed, had himself briefly mounted one of the animals, having fallen into the belief that the cow-persons did not try earnestly enough to stay on their mounts. I gathered that one experience had dissuaded him from this opinion.

"That there little paint horse," observed Cousin Egbert genially, "stepped out from under the Judge the prettiest you ever saw."

"He sure did," remarked the Honourable George, with a palpable effort to speak the American brogue. "A most flighty beast he was—nerves all gone—I dare say a hopeless neurasthenic."

And then when I would have rebuked him for so shamefully disappointing the ladies of the Onwards and Upwards Society, he began to tell me of the public house he had just left.

"I say, you know that Spilmer chap, he's a genuine murderer—he let me hold the weapon with which he did it—and he has blind relatives dependent upon him, or something of that sort, otherwise I fancy they'd have sent him to the gallows. And, by God! he's a witty scoundrel, what! Looking at his sign—leaving the settlement it reads, 'Last Chance,' but entering the settlement it reads, 'First Chance.' Last chance and first chance for a peg, do you see what I mean? I tried it out; walked both ways under the sign and looked up; it worked perfectly. Enter the settlement, 'First Chance'; leave the settlement, 'Last Chance.' Do you see what I mean? Suggestive, what! Witty! You'd never have expected that murderer-Johnny to be so subtle. Our own murderers aren't that way. I say, it's a tremendous wheeze. I wonder the press-chaps don't take it up. It's better than the blind factory, though the chap's mother or something is blind. What ho! But that's silly! To be sure one has nothing to do with the other. I say, have another, you chaps! I've not felt so fit in ages. I'm going to take up America!"

Plainly it was no occasion to use serious words to the man. He slapped his companions smartly on their backs and was slapped in turn by all of them. One or two of them called him an old horse! Not only was I doing no good for the North Side set, but I had felt obliged to consume two glasses of spirits that I did not wish. So I discreetly withdrew. As I went, the Honourable George was again telling them that he was "going in" for North America, and Cousin Egbert was calling "Three rousing cheers!"

Thus luridly began, I may say, a scandal that was to be far-reaching in its dreadful effects. Far from feeling a proper shame on the following day, the Honourable George was as pleased as Punch with himself, declaring his intention of again consorting with the cattle and horse persons and very definitely declining an invitation to play at golf with Belknap-Jackson.

"Golf!" he spluttered. "You do it, and then you've directly to do it all over again. I mean to say, one gets nowhere. A silly game—what!"

Wishing to be in no manner held responsible for his vicious pursuits, I that day removed my diggings from the Floud home to chambers in the Pettengill block above the Grill, where I did myself quite nicely with decent mantel ornaments, some vivacious prints of old-world cathedrals, and a few good books, having for body-servant one of the Hobbs lads who seemed rather teachable. I must admit, however, that I was frequently obliged to address him more sharply than one should ever address one's servant, my theory having always been that a serving person should be treated quite as if he were a gentleman temporarily performing menial duties, but there was that strain of lowness in all the Hobbses which often forbade this, a blending of servility with more or less skilfully dissembled impertinence, which I dare say is the distinguishing mark of our lower-class serving people.

Removed now from the immediate and more intimate effects of the Honourable George's digressions, I was privileged for days at a time to devote my attention exclusively to my enterprise. It had thriven from the beginning, and after a month I had so perfected the minor details of management that everything was right as rain. In my catering I continued to steer a middle course between the British school of plain roast and boiled and a too often piffling French complexity, seeking to retain the desirable features of each. My luncheons for the tradesmen rather held to a cut from the joint with vegetables and a suitable sweet, while in my dinners I relaxed a bit into somewhat imaginative salads and entrées. For the tea-hour I constantly strove to provide some appetizing novelty, often, I confess, sacrificing nutrition to mere sightliness in view of my almost exclusive feminine patronage, yet never carrying this to an undignified extreme.

As a result of my sound judgment, dinner-giving in Red Gap began that winter to be done almost entirely in my place. There might be small informal affairs at home, but for dinners of any pretension the hostesses of the North Side set came to me, relying almost quite entirely upon my taste in the selection of the menu. Although at first I was required to employ unlimited tact in dissuading them from strange and laboured concoctions, whose photographs they fetched me from their women's magazines, I at length converted them from this unwholesome striving for novelty and laid the foundations for that sound scheme of gastronomy which to-day distinguishes this fastest-growing town in the state, if not in the West of America.

It was during these early months, I ought perhaps to say, that I rather distinguished myself in the matter of a relish which I compounded one day when there was a cold round of beef for luncheon. Little dreaming of the magnitude of the moment, I brought together English mustard and the American tomato catsup, in proportions which for reasons that will be made obvious I do not here disclose, together with three other and lesser condiments whose identity also must remain a secret. Serving this with my cold joint, I was rather amazed at the sensation it created. My patrons clamoured for it repeatedly and a barrister wished me to prepare a flask of it for use in his home. The following day it was again demanded and other requests were made for private supplies, while by the end of the week my relish had become rather famous. Followed a suggestion from Mrs. Judson as she overlooked my preparation of it one day from her own task of polishing the glassware.

"Put it on the market," said she, and at once I felt the inspiration of her idea. To her I entrusted the formula. I procured a quantity of suitable flasks, while in her own home she compounded the stuff and filled them. Having no mind to claim credit not my own, I may now say that this rather remarkable woman also evolved the idea of the label, including the name, which was pasted upon the bottles when our product was launched.

"Ruggles' International Relish" she had named it after a moment's thought. Below was a print of my face taken from an excellent photographic portrait, followed by a brief summary of the article's unsurpassed excellence, together with a list of the viands for which it was commended. As the International Relish is now a matter of history, the demand for it having spread as far east as Chicago and those places, I may add that it was this capable woman again who devised the large placard for hoardings in which a middle-aged but glowing bon-vivant in evening dress rebukes the blackamoor who has served his dinner for not having at once placed Ruggles' International Relish upon the table. The genial annoyance of the diner and the apologetic concern of the black are excellently depicted by the artist, for the original drawing of which I paid a stiffish price to the leading artist fellow of Spokane. This now adorns the wall of my sitting-room.

It must not be supposed that I had been free during these months from annoyance and chagrin at the manner in which the Honourable George was conducting himself. In the beginning it was hoped both by Belknap-Jackson and myself that he might do no worse than merely consort with the rougher element of the town. I mean to say, we suspected that the apparent charm of the raffish cattle-persons might suffice to keep him from any notorious alliance with the dreaded Bohemian set. So long as he abstained from this he might still be received at our best homes, despite his regrettable fondness for low company. Even when he brought the murderer Spilmer to dine with him at my place, the thing was condoned as a freakish grotesquerie in one who, of unassailable social position, might well afford to stoop momentarily.

I must say that the murderer—a heavy-jowled brute of husky voice, and quite lacking a forehead—conducted himself on this occasion with an entirely decent restraint of manner, quite in contrast to the Honourable George, who betrayed an expansively naïve pride in his guest, seeming to wish the world to know of the event. Between them they consumed a fair bottle of the relish. Indeed, the Honourable George was inordinately fond of this, as a result of which he would often come out quite spotty again. Cousin Egbert was another who became so addicted to it that his fondness might well have been called a vice. Both he and the Honourable George would drench quite every course with the sauce, and Cousin Egbert, with that explicit directness which distinguished his character, would frankly sop his bread-crusts in it, or even sip it with a coffee-spoon.

As I have intimated, in spite of the Honourable George's affiliations with the slum-characters of what I may call Red Gap's East End, he had not yet publicly identified himself with the Klondike woman and her Bohemian set, in consequence of which—let him dine and wine a Spilmer as he would—there was yet hope that he would not alienate himself from the North Side set.

At intervals during the early months of his sojourn among us he accepted dinner invitations at the Grill from our social leaders; in fact, after the launching of the International Relish, I know of none that he declined, but it was evident to me that he moved but half-heartedly in this higher circle. On one occasion, too, he appeared in the trousers of a lounge-suit of tweeds instead of his dress trousers, and with tan boots. The trousers, to be sure, were of a sombre hue, but the brown boots were quite too dreadfully unmistakable. After this I may say that I looked for anything, and my worst fears were soon confirmed.

It began as the vaguest sort of gossip. The Honourable George, it was said, had been a guest at one of the Klondike woman's evening affairs. The rumour crystallized. He had been asked to meet the Bohemian set at a Dutch supper and had gone. He had lingered until a late hour, dancing the American folkdances (for which he had shown a surprising adaptability) and conducting himself generally as the next Earl of Brinstead should not have done. He had repeated his visit, repairing to the woman's house both afternoon and evening. He had become a constant visitor. He had spoken regrettably of the dulness of a meeting of the Onwards and Upwards Society which he had attended. He was in the woman's toils.

With gossip of this sort there was naturally much indignation, and yet the leaders of the North Side set were so delicately placed that there was every reason for concealing it. They redoubled their attentions to the unfortunate man, seeking to leave him not an unoccupied evening or afternoon. Such was the gravity of the crisis. Belknap-Jackson alone remained finely judicial.

"The situation is of the gravest character," he confided to me, "but we must be wary. The day isn't lost so long as he doesn't appear publicly in the creature's train. For the present we have only unverified rumour. As a man about town Vane-Basingwell may feel free to consort with vicious companions and still maintain his proper standing. Deplore it as all right-thinking people must, under present social conditions he is undoubtedly free to lead what is called a double life. We can only wait."

Such was the state of the public mind, be it understood, up to the time of the notorious and scandalous defection of this obsessed creature, an occasion which I cannot recall without shuddering, and which inspired me to a course that was later to have the most inexplicable and far-reaching consequences.

Theatrical plays had been numerous with us during the season, with the natural result of many after-theatre suppers being given by those who attended, among them the North Side leaders, and frequently the Klondike woman with her following. On several of these occasions, moreover, the latter brought as supper guests certain representatives of the theatrical profession, both male and female, she apparently having a wide acquaintance with such persons. That this sort of thing increased her unpopularity with the North Side set will be understood when I add that now and then her guests would be of undoubted respectability in their private lives, as theatrical persons often are, and such as our smartest hostesses would have been only too glad to entertain.

To counteract this effect Belknap-Jackson now broached to me a plan of undoubted merit, which was nothing less than to hold an afternoon reception at his home in honour of the world's greatest pianoforte artist, who was presently to give a recital in Red Gap.

"I've not met the chap myself," he began, "but I knew his secretary and travelling companion quite well in a happier day in Boston. The recital here will be Saturday evening, which means that they will remain here on Sunday until the evening train East. I shall suggest to my friend that his employer, to while away the tedium of the Sunday, might care to look in upon me in the afternoon and meet a few of our best people. Nothing boring, of course. I've no doubt he will arrange it. I've written him to Portland, where they now are."

"Rather a card that will be," I instantly cried. "Rather better class than entertaining strolling players." Indeed the merit of the proposal rather overwhelmed me. It would be dignified and yet spectacular. It would show the Klondike woman that we chose to have contact only with artists of acknowledged preëminence and that such were quite willing to accept our courtesies. I had hopes, too, that the Honourable George might be aroused to advantages which he seemed bent upon casting to the American winds.

A week later Belknap-Jackson joyously informed me that the great artist had consented to accept his hospitality. There would be light refreshments, with which I was charged. I suggested tea in the Russian manner, which he applauded.

"And everything dainty in the way of food," he warned me. "Nothing common, nothing heavy. Some of those tiny lettuce sandwiches, a bit of caviare, macaroons—nothing gross—a decanter of dry sherry, perhaps, a few of the lightest wafers; things that cultivated persons may trifle with—things not repugnant to the artist soul."

I promised my profoundest consideration to these matters.

"And it occurs to me," he thoughtfully added, "that this may be a time for Vane-Basingwell to silence the slurs upon himself that are becoming so common. I shall beg him to meet our guest at his hotel and escort him to my place. A note to my friend, 'the bearer, the Honourable George Augustus Vane-Basingwell, brother of his lordship the Earl of Brinstead, will take great pleasure in escorting to my home——' You get the idea? Not bad!"

Again I applauded, resolving that for once the Honourable George would be suitably attired even if I had to bully him. And so was launched what promised to be Red Gap's most notable social event of the season. The Honourable George, being consulted, promised after a rather sulky hesitation to act as the great artist's escort, though he persisted in referring to him as "that piano Johnny," and betrayed a suspicion that Belknap-Jackson was merely bent upon getting him to perform without price.

"But no," cried Belknap-Jackson, "I should never think of anything so indelicate as asking him to play. My own piano will be tightly closed and I dare say removed to another room."

At this the Honourable George professed to wonder why the chap was desired if he wasn't to perform. "All hair and bad English—silly brutes when they don't play," he declared. In the end, however, as I have said, he consented to act as he was wished to. Cousin Egbert, who was present at this interview, took somewhat the same view as the Honourable George, even asserting that he should not attend the recital.

"He don't sing, he don't dance, he don't recite; just plays the piano. That ain't any kind of a show for folks to set up a whole evening for," he protested bitterly, and he went on to mention various theatrical pieces which he had considered worthy, among them I recall being one entitled "The Two Johns," which he regretted not having witnessed for several years, and another called "Ben Hur," which was better than all the piano players alive, he declared. But with the Honourable George enlisted, both Belknap-Jackson and I considered the opinions of Cousin Egbert to be quite wholly negligible.

Saturday's *Recorder*, in its advance notice of the recital, announced that the Belknap-Jacksons of Boston and Red Gap would entertain the artist on the following afternoon at their palatial home in the Pettengill addition, where a select few of the North Side set had been invited to meet him. Belknap-Jackson himself was as a man uplifted. He constantly revised and re-revised his invitation list; he sought me out each day to suggest subtle changes in the very artistic menu I had prepared for the affair. His last touch was to supplement the decanter of sherry with a bottle of vodka. About the caviare he worried quite fearfully until it proved upon arrival to be fresh and of prime quality. My man, the Hobbs boy, had under my instructions pressed and smarted the Honourable George's suit for afternoon wear. The carriage was engaged. Saturday night it was tremendously certain that no hitch could occur to mar the affair. We had left no detail to chance.

The recital itself was quite all that could have been expected, but underneath the enthusiastic applause there ran even a more intense fervour among those fortunate ones who were to meet the artist on the morrow.

Belknap-Jackson knew himself to be a hero. He was elaborately cool. He smiled tolerantly at intervals and undoubtedly applauded with the least hint of languid proprietorship in his manner. He was heard to speak of the artist by his first name. The Klondike woman and many of her Bohemian set were prominently among those present and sustained glances of pitying triumph from those members of the North Side set so soon to be distinguished above her.

The morrow dawned auspiciously, very cloudy with smartish drives of wind and rain. Confined to the dingy squalor of his hotel, how gladly would the artist, it was felt, seek the refined cheer of one of our best homes where he would be enlivened by an hour or so of contact with our most cultivated people. Belknap-Jackson telephoned me with increasing frequency as the hour drew near, nervously seeming to dread that I would have overlooked some detail of his refined refreshments, or that I would not have them at his house on time. He telephoned often to the Honourable George to be assured that the carriage with its escort would be prompt. He telephoned repeatedly to the driver chap, to impress upon him the importance of his mission.

His guests began to arrive even before I had decked his sideboard with what was, I have no hesitation in declaring, the most superbly dainty buffet collation that Red Gap had ever beheld. The atmosphere at once became tense with expectation.

At three o'clock the host announced from the telephone: "Vane-Basingwell has started from the Floud house." The guests thrilled and hushed the careless chatter of new arrivals. Belknap-Jackson remained heroically at the telephone, having demanded to be put through to the hotel. He was flushed with excitement. A score of minutes later he announced with an effort to control his voice: "They have left the hotel—they are on the way."

The guests stiffened in their seats. Some of them nervously and for no apparent reason exchanged chairs with others. Some late arrivals bustled in and were immediately awed to the same electric silence of waiting. Belknap-Jackson placed the sherry decanter where the vodka bottle had been and the vodka bottle where the sherry decanter had been. "The effect is better," he remarked, and went to stand where he could view the driveway. The moments passed.

156

At such crises, which I need not say have been plentiful in my life, I have always known that I possessed an immense reserve of coolness. Seldom have I ever been so much as slightly flustered. Now I was calmness itself, and the knowledge brought me no little satisfaction as I noted the rather painful distraction of our host. The moments passed—long, heavy, silent moments. Our host ascended trippingly to an upper floor whence he could see farther down the drive. The guests held themselves in smiling readiness. Our host descended and again took up his post at a lower window.

The moments passed—stilled, leaden moments. The silence had become intolerable. Our host jiggled on his feet. Some of the quicker-minded guests made a pretence of little conversational flurries: "That second movement—oh, exquisitely rendered!... No one has ever read Chopin so divinely.... How his family must idolize him!... They say.... That exquisite concerto!... Hasn't he the most stunning hair.... Those staccato passages left me actually limp—I'm starting Myrtle in Tuesday to take of Professor Gluckstein. She wants to take stenography, but I tell her.... Did you think the preludes were just the tiniest bit idealized.... I always say if one has one's music, and one's books, of course—He must be very, *very* fond of music!"

Such were the hushed, tentative fragments I caught.

The moments passed. Belknap-Jackson went to the telephone. "What? But they're not here! Very strange! They should have been here half an hour ago. Send some one—yes, at once." In the ensuing silence he repaired to the buffet and drank a glass of vodka. Quite distraught he was.

The moments passed. Again several guests exchanged seats with other guests. It seemed to be a device for relieving the strain. Once more there were scattering efforts at normal talk. "Myrtle is a strange girl—a creature of moods, I call her. She wanted to act in the moving pictures until papa bought the car. And she knows every one of the new tango steps, but I tell her a few lessons in cooking wouldn't—Beryl Mae is just the same puzzling child; one thing one day, and another thing the next; a mere bundle of nerves, and so sensitive if you say the least little thing to her ... If we could only get Ling Wong back—this Jap boy is always threatening to leave if the men don't get up to breakfast on time, or if Gertie makes fudge in his kitchen of an afternoon ... Our boy sends all his wages to his uncle in China, but I simply can't get him to say, 'Dinner is served.' He just slides in and says, 'All right, you come!' It's very annoying, but I always tell the family, 'Remember what a time we had with the Swede——'"

I mean to say, things were becoming rapidly impossible. The moments passed. Belknap-Jackson again telephoned: "You did send a man after them? Send some one after him, then. Yes, at once!" He poured himself another peg of the vodka. Silence fell again. The waiting was terrific. We had endured an hour of it, and but little more was possible to any sensitive human organism. All at once, as if the very last possible moment of silence had passed, the conversation broke loudly and generally: "And did you notice that slimpsy thing she wore last night? Indecent, if you ask me, with not a petticoat under it, I'll be bound!... Always wears shoes twice too small for her ... What men can see in her ... How they can endure that perpetual smirk!..." They were at last discussing the Klondike woman, and whatever had befallen our guest of honour I knew that those present would never regain their first awe of the occasion. It was now unrestrained gabble.

The second hour passed quickly enough, the latter half of it being enlivened by the buffet collation which elicited many compliments upon my ingenuity and good taste. Quite almost every guest partook of a glass of the vodka. They chattered of everything but music, I dare say it being thought graceful to ignore the afternoon's disaster.

Belknap-Jackson had sunk into a mood of sullen desperation. He drained the vodka bottle. Perhaps the liquor brought him something of the chill Russian fatalism. He was dignified but sodden, with a depression that seemed to blow from the bleak Siberian steppes. His wife was already receiving the adieus of their guests. She was smouldering ominously, uncertain where the blame lay, but certain there was blame. Criminal blame! I could read as much in her narrowed eyes as she tried for aplomb with her guests.

My own leave I took unobtrusively. I knew our strangely missing guest was to depart by the six-two train, and I strolled toward the station. A block away I halted, waiting. It had been a time of waiting. The moments passed. I heard the whistle of the approaching train. At the same moment I was startled by the approach of a team that I took to be running away.

I saw it was the carriage of the Pierce chap and that he was driving with the most abandoned recklessness. His passengers were the Honourable George, Cousin Egbert, and our missing guest. The great artist as they passed me seemed to feel a vast delight in his wild ride. He was cheering on the driver. He waved his arms and himself shouted to the maddened horses. The carriage drew up to the station with the train, and the three descended.

The artist hurriedly shook hands in the warmest manner with his companions, including the Pierce chap, who had driven them. He beckoned to his secretary, who was waiting with his bags. He mounted the steps of the coach, and as the train pulled out he waved frantically to the three. He kissed his hand to them, looking far out as the train gathered momentum. Again and again he kissed his hand to the hat-waving trio.

It was too much. The strain of the afternoon had told even upon my own iron nerves. I felt unequal at that moment to the simplest inquiry, and plainly the situation was not one to attack in haste. I mean to say, it was too pregnant with meaning. I withdrew rapidly from the scene, feeling the need for rest and silence.

As I walked I meditated profoundly.

CHAPTER SIXTEEN

From the innocent lips of Cousin Egbert the following morning there fell a tale of such cold-blooded depravity that I found myself with difficulty giving it credit. At ten o'clock, while I still mused pensively over the events of the previous day, he entered the Grill in search of breakfast, as had lately become his habit. I greeted him with perceptible restraint, not knowing what guilt might be his, but his manner to me was so unconsciously genial that I at once acquitted him of any complicity in whatever base doings had been forward.

He took his accustomed seat with a pleasant word to me. I waited.

"Feeling a mite off this morning," he began, "account of a lot of truck I eat yesterday. I guess I'll just take something kind of dainty. Tell Clarice to cook me up a nice little steak with plenty of fat on it, and some fried potatoes, and a cup of coffee and a few waffles to come. The Judge he wouldn't get up yet. He looked kind of mottled and anguished, but I guess he'll pull around all right. I had the chink take him up about a gallon of strong tea. Say, listen here, the Judge ain't so awful much of a stayer, is he?"

Burning with curiosity I was to learn what he could tell me of the day before, yet I controlled myself to the calmest of leisurely questioning in order not to alarm him. It was too plain that he had no realization of what had occurred. It was always the way with him, I had noticed. Events the most momentous might culminate furiously about his head, but he never knew that anything had happened.

"The Honourable George," I began, "was with you yesterday? Perhaps he ate something he shouldn't."

"He did, he did; he done it repeatedly. He et pretty near as much of that sauerkraut and frankfurters as the piano guy himself did, and that's some tribute, believe me, Bill! Some tribute!"

"The piano guy?" I murmured quite casually.

"And say, listen here, that guy is all right if anybody should ask you. You talk about your mixers!"

This was a bit puzzling, for of course I had never "talked about my mixers." I shouldn't a bit know how to go on. I ventured another query.

"Where was it this mixing and that sort of thing took place?"

"Why, up at Mis' Kenner's, where we was having a little party: frankfurters and sauerkraut and beer. My stars! but that steak looks good. I'm feeling better already." His food was before him, and he attacked it with no end of spirit.

"Tell me quite all about it," I amiably suggested, and after a moment's hurried devotion to the steak, he slowed up a bit to talk.

"Well, listen here, now. The Judge says to me when Eddie Pierce comes, 'Sour-dough,' he says, 'look in at Mis' Kenner's this afternoon if you got nothing else on; I fancy it will repay you.' Just like that. 'Well,' I says, 'all right, Judge, I fancy I will. I fancy I ain't got anything else on,' I says. 'And I'm always glad to go there,' I says, because no matter what they're always saying about this here Bohemian stuff, Kate Kenner is one good scout, take it from me. So in a little while I slicked up some and went on around to her house. Then hitched outside I seen Eddie Pierce's hack, and I says, 'My lands! that's a funny thing,' I says. 'I thought the Judge was going to haul this here piano guy out to the Jackson place where he could while away the tejum, like Jackson said, and now it looks as if they was here. Or mebbe it's just Eddie himself that has fancied to look in, not having anything else on.'

"Well, so anyway I go up on the stoop and knock, and when I get in the parlour there the piano guy is and the Judge and Eddie Pierce, too, Eddie helping the Jap around with frankfurters and sauerkraut and beer and one thing and another.

"Besides them was about a dozen of Mis' Kenner's own particular friends, all of 'em good scouts, let me tell you, and everybody laughing and gassing back and forth and cutting up and having a good time all around. Well, so as soon as they seen me, everybody says, 'Oh, here comes Sour-dough—good old Sour-dough!' and all like that, and they introduced me to the piano guy, who gets up to shake hands with me and spills his beer off the chair arm on to the wife of Eddie Fosdick in the Farmers' and Merchants' National, and so I sat down and et with 'em and had a few steins of beer, and everybody had a good time all around."

The wonderful man appeared to believe that he had told me quite all of interest concerning this monstrous festivity. He surveyed the mutilated remnant of his steak and said: "I guess Clarice might as well fry me a few eggs. I'm feeling a lot better." I directed that this be done, musing upon the dreadful menu he had recited and recalling the exquisite finish of the collation I myself had prepared. Sausages, to be sure, have their place, and beer as well, but sauerkraut I have never been able to regard as an at all possible food for persons that really matter. Germans, to be sure!

Discreetly I renewed my inquiry: "I dare say the Honourable George was in good form?" I suggested.

"Well, he et a lot. Him and the piano guy was bragging which could eat the most sausages."

I was unable to restrain a shudder at the thought of this revolting contest.

"The piano guy beat him out, though. He'd been at the Palace Hotel for three meals and I guess his appetite was right craving."

"And afterward?"

"Well, it was like Jackson said: this lad wanted to while away the tejum of a Sunday afternoon, and so he whiled it, that's all. Purty soon Mis' Kenner set down to the piano and sung some coon songs that tickled him most to death, and then she got to playing ragtime—say, believe me, Bill, when she starts in on that rag stuff she can make a piano simply stutter itself to death.

"Well, at that the piano guy says it's great stuff, and so he sets down himself to try it, and he catches on pretty good, I'll say that for him, so we got to dancing while he plays for us, only he don't remember the tunes good and has to fake a lot. Then he makes Mis' Kenner play again while he dances with Mis' Fosdick that he spilled the beer on, and after that we had some more beer and this guy et another plate of kraut and a few sausages, and Mis' Kenner sings 'The Robert E. Lee' and a couple more good ones, and the guy played some more ragtime himself, trying to get the tunes right, and then he played some fancy pieces that he'd practised up on, and we danced some and had a few more beers, with everybody laughing and cutting up and having a nice home afternoon.

"Well, the piano guy enjoyed himself every minute, if anybody asks you, being lit up like a main chandelier. They made him feel like he was one of their own folks. You certainly got to hand it to him for being one little good mixer. Talk about whiling away the tejum! He done it, all right, all right. He whiled away so much tejum there he darned near missed his train. Eddie Pierce kept telling him what time it was, only he'd keep asking Mis' Kenner to play just one more rag, and at last we had to just shoot him into his fur overcoat while he was kissing all the women on their hands, and we'd have missed the train at that if Eddie hadn't poured the leather into them skates of his all the way down to the dee-po. He just did make it, and he told the Judge and Eddie and me that he ain't had such a good time since he left home. I kind of hated to see him go."

He here attacked the eggs with what seemed to be a freshening of his remarkable appetite. And as yet, be it noted, I had detected no consciousness on his part that a foul betrayal of confidence had been committed. I approached the point.

"The Belknap-Jacksons were rather expecting him, you know. My impression was that the Honourable George had been sent to escort him to the Belknap-Jackson house."

"Well, that's what I thought, too, but I guess the Judge forgot it, or mebbe he thinks the guy will mix in better with Mis' Kenner's crowd. Anyway, there they was, and it probably didn't make any difference to the guy himself. He likely thought he could while away the tejum there as well as he could while it any place, all of them being such good scouts. And the Judge has certainly got a case on Mis' Kenner, so mebby she asked him to drop in with any friend of his. She's got him bridle-wise and broke to all gaits." He visibly groped for an illumining phrase. "He—he just looks at her."

The simple words fell upon my ears with a sickening finality. "He just looks at her." I had seen him "just look" at the typing-girl and at the Brixton milliner. All too fearfully I divined their preposterous significance. Beyond question a black infamy had been laid bare, but I made no effort to convey its magnitude to my guileless informant. As I left him he was mildly bemoaning his own lack of skill on the pianoforte.

"Darned if I don't wish I'd 'a' took some lessons on the piano myself like that guy done. It certainly does help to while away the tejum when you got friends in for the afternoon. But then I was just a hill-billy. Likely I couldn't have learned the notes good."

It was a half-hour later that I was called to the telephone to listen to the anguished accents of Belknap-Jackson.

"Have you heard it?" he called. I answered that I had.

"The man is a paranoiac. He should be at once confined in an asylum for the criminal insane."

"I shall row him fiercely about it, never fear. I've not seen him yet."

"But the creature should be watched. He may do harm to himself or to some innocent person. They—they run wild, they kill, they burn—set fire to buildings—that sort of thing. I tell you, none of us is safe."

"The situation," I answered, "has even more shocking possibilities, but I've an idea I shall be equal to it. If the worst seems to be imminent I shall adopt extreme measures." I closed the interview. It was too painful. I wished to summon all my powers of deliberation.

To my amazement who should presently appear among my throng of luncheon patrons but the Honourable George. I will not say that he slunk in, but there was an unaccustomed diffidence in his bearing. He did not meet my eye, and it was not difficult to perceive that he had no wish to engage my notice. As he sought a vacant table I observed that he was spotted quite profusely, and his luncheon order was of the simplest.

Straight I went to him. He winced a bit, I thought, as he saw me approach, but then he apparently resolved to brass it out, for he glanced full at me with a terrific assumption of bravado and at once began to give me beans about my service.

"Your bally tea shop running down, what! Louts for waiters, cloddish louts! Disgraceful, my word! Slow beggars! Take a year to do you a rasher and a bit of toast, what!"

To this absurd tirade I replied not a word, but stood silently regarding him. I dare say my gaze was of the most chilling character and steady. He endured it but a moment. His eyes fell, his bravado vanished, he fumbled with the cutlery. Quite abashed he was.

162

"Come, your explanation!" I said curtly, divining that the moment was one in which to adopt a tone with him. He wriggled a bit, crumpling a roll with panic fingers.

"Come, come!" I commanded.

His face brightened, though with an intention most obviously false. He coughed—a cough of pure deception. Not only were his eyes averted from mine, but they were glassed to an uncanny degree. The fingers wrought piteously at the now plastic roll.

"My word, the chap was taken bad; had to be seen to, what! Revived, I mean to say. All piano Johnnies that way—nervous wrecks, what! Spells! Spells, man—spells!"

"Come, come!" I said crisply. The glassed eyes were those of one hypnotized.

"In the carriage—to the hyphen chap's place, to be sure. Fainting spell—weak heart, what! No stimulants about. Passing house! Perhaps have stimulants—heart tablets, er—beer—things of that sort. Lead him in. Revive him. Quite well presently, but not well enough to go on. Couldn't let a piano Johnny die on our hands, what! Inquest, evidence, witnesses—all that silly rot. Save his life, what! Presence of mind! Kind hearts, what! Humanity! Do as much for any chap. Not let him die like a dog in the gutter, what! Get no credit, though——" His curiously mechanical utterance trailed off to be lost in a mere husky murmur. The glassy stare was still at my wall.

I have in the course of my eventful career had occasion to mark the varying degrees of plausibility with which men speak untruths, but never, I confidently aver, have I beheld one lie with so piteous a futility. The art—and I dare say with diplomat chaps and that sort it may properly be called an art—demands as its very essence that the speaker seem to be himself convinced of the truth of that which he utters. And the Honourable George in his youth mentioned for the Foreign Office!

I turned away. The exhibition was quite too indecent. I left him to mince at his meagre fare. As I glanced his way at odd moments thereafter, he would be muttering feverishly to himself. I mean to say, he no longer *was* himself. He presently made his way to the street, looking neither to right nor left. He had, in truth, the dazed manner of one stupefied by some powerful narcotic. I wondered pityingly when I should again behold him—if it might be that his poor wits were bedevilled past mending.

My period of uncertainty was all too brief. Some two hours later, full into the tide of our afternoon shopping throng, there issued a spectacle that removed any lingering doubt of the unfortunate man's plight. In the rather smart pony-trap of the Klondike woman, driven by the person herself, rode the Honourable George. Full in the startled gaze of many of our best people he advertised his defection from all that makes for a sanely governed stability in our social organism. He had gone flagrantly over to the Bohemian set.

I could detect that his eyes were still glassy, but his head was erect. He seemed to flaunt his shame. And the guilty partner of his downfall drove with an affectation of easy carelessness, yet with a lift of the chin which, though barely perceptible, had all the effect of binding the prisoner to her chariot wheels; a prisoner, moreover, whom it was plain she meant to parade to the last ignominious degree. She drove leisurely, and in the little infrequent curt turns of her head to address her companion she contrived to instill so finished an effect of boredom that she must have goaded to frenzy any matron of the North Side set who chanced to observe her, as more than one of them did.

Thrice did she halt along our main thoroughfare for bits of shopping, a mere running into of shops or to the doors of them where she could issue verbal orders, the while she surveyed her waiting and drugged captive with a certain half-veiled but good-humoured insolence. At these moments—for I took pains to overlook the shocking scene—the Honourable George followed her with eyes no longer glassed; the eyes of helpless infatuation. "He looks at her," Cousin Egbert had said. He had told it all and told it well. The equipage graced our street upon one paltry excuse or another for the better part of an hour, the woman being minded that none of us should longer question her supremacy over the next and eleventh Earl of Brinstead.

Not for another hour did the effects of the sensation die out among tradesmen and the street crowds. It was like waves that recede but gradually. They talked. They stopped to talk. They passed on talking. They hissed vivaciously; they rose to exclamations. I mean to say, there was no end of a gabbling row about it.

There was in my mind no longer any room for hesitation. The quite harshest of extreme measures must be at once adopted before all was too late. I made my way to the telegraph office. It was not a time for correspondence by post.

Afterward I had myself put through by telephone to Belknap-Jackson. With his sensitive nature he had stopped in all day. Although still averse to appearing publicly, he now consented to meet me at my chambers late that evening.

"The whole town is seething with indignation," he called to me. "It was disgraceful. I shall come at ten. We rely upon you."

Again I saw that he was concerned solely with his humiliation as a would-be host. Not yet had he divined that the deluded Honourable George might go to the unspeakable length of a matrimonial alliance with the woman who had enchained him. And as to his own disaster, he was less than accurate when he said that the whole town was seething with indignation. The members of the North Side set, to be sure, were seething furiously, but a flippant element of the baser sort was quite openly rejoicing. As at the time of that most slanderous minstrel performance, it was said that the Bohemian set had again, if I have caught the phrase, "put a thing

164

over upon" the North Side set. Many persons of low taste seemed quite to enjoy the dreadful affair, and the members of the Bohemian set, naturally, throughout the day had been quite coarsely beside themselves with glee.

Little they knew, I reflected, what power I could wield nor that I had already set in motion its deadly springs. Little did the woman dream, flaunting her triumph up and down our main business thoroughfare, that one who watched her there had but to raise his hand to wrest the victim from her toils. Little did she now dream that he would stop at no half measures. I mean to say, she would never think I could bowl her out as easy as buying cockles off a barrow.

At the hour for our conference Belknap-Jackson arrived at my chambers muffled in an ulster and with a soft hat well over his face. I gathered that he had not wished to be observed.

"I feel that this is a crisis," he began as he gloomily shook my hand. "Where is our boasted twentieth-century culture if outrages like this are permitted? For the first time I understand how these Western communities have in the past resorted to mob violence. Public feeling is already running high against the creature and her unspeakable set."

I met this outburst with the serenity of one who holds the winning cards in his hand, and begged him to be seated. Thereupon I disclosed to him the weakly, susceptible nature of the Honourable George, reciting the incidents of the typing-girl and the Brixton milliner. I added that now, as before, I should not hesitate to preserve the family honour.

"A dreadful thing, indeed," he murmured, "if that adventuress should trap him into a marriage. Imagine her one day a Countess of Brinstead! But suppose the fellow prove stubborn; suppose his infatuation dulls all his finer instincts?"

I explained that the Honourable George, while he might upon the spur of the moment commit a folly, was not to be taken too seriously; that he was, I believed, quite incapable of a grand passion. I mean to say, he always forgot them after a few days. More like a child staring into shop-windows he was, rapidly forgetting one desired object in the presence of others. I added that I had adopted the extremest measures.

Thereupon, perceiving that I had something in my sleeve, as the saying is, my caller besought me to confide in him. Without a word I handed him a copy of my cable message sent that afternoon to his lordship:

> "Your immediate presence required to prevent a monstrous folly."

He brightened as he read it.

"You actually mean to say——" he began.

"His lordship," I explained, "will at once understand the nature of what is threatened. He knows, moreover, that I would not alarm him without cause. He will come at once, and the Honourable George will be told what. His lordship has never failed. He tells him what perfectly, and that's quite all to it. The poor chap will be saved."

My caller was profoundly stirred. "Coming here—to Red Gap—his lordship the Earl of Brinstead—actually coming here! My God! This is wonderful!" He paused; he seemed to moisten his dry lips; he began once more, and now his voice trembled with emotion: "He will need a place to stay; our hotel is impossible; had you thought——" He glanced at me appealingly.

"I dare say," I replied, "that his lordship will be pleased to have you put him up; you would do him quite nicely."

"You mean it—seriously? That would be—oh, inexpressible. He would be our house guest! The Earl of Brinstead! I fancy that would silence a few of these serpent tongues that are wagging so venomously to-day!"

"But before his coming," I insisted, "there must be no word of his arrival. The Honourable George would know the meaning of it, and the woman, though I suspect now that she is only making a show of him, might go on to the bitter end. They must suspect nothing."

"I had merely thought of a brief and dignified notice in our press," he began, quite wistfully, "but if you think it might defeat our ends——"

"It must wait until he has come."

"Glorious!" he exclaimed. "It will be even more of a blow to them." He began to murmur as if reading from a journal, "'His lordship the Earl of Brinstead is visiting for a few days'—it will surely be as much as a few days, perhaps a week or more—'is visiting for a few days the C. Belknap-Jacksons of Boston and Red Gap.'" He seemed to regard the printed words. "Better still, 'The C. Belknap-Jacksons of Boston and Red Gap are for a few days entertaining as their honoured house guest his lordship the Earl of Brinstead——' Yes, that's admirable."

He arose and impulsively clasped my hand. "Ruggles, dear old chap, I shan't know at all how to repay you. The Bohemian set, such as are possible, will be bound to come over to us. There will be left of it but one unprincipled woman— and she wretched and an outcast. She has made me absurd. I shall grind her under my heel. The east room shall be prepared for his lordship; he shall breakfast there if he wishes. I fancy he'll find us rather more like himself than he suspects. He shall see that we have ideals that are not half bad."

He wrung my hand again. His eyes were misty with gratitude.

CHAPTER SEVENTEEN

Three days later came the satisfying answer to my cable message:

"Damn! Sailing Wednesday.—BRINSTEAD."

Glad I was he had used the cable. In a letter there would doubtless have been still other words improper to a peer of England.

Belknap-Jackson thereafter bore himself with a dignity quite tremendous even for him. Graciously aloof, he was as one carrying an inner light. "We hold them in the hollow of our hand," said he, and both his wife and himself took pains on our own thoroughfare to cut the Honourable George dead, though I dare say the poor chap never at all noticed it. They spoke of him as "a remittance man"— the black sheep of a noble family. They mentioned sympathetically the trouble his vicious ways had been to his brother, the Earl. Indeed, so mysteriously important were they in allusions of this sort that I was obliged to caution them, lest they let out the truth. As it was, there ran through the town an undercurrent of puzzled suspicion. It was intimated that we had something in our sleeves.

Whether this tension was felt by the Honourable George, I had no means of knowing. I dare say not, as he is self-centred, being seldom aware of anything beyond his own immediate sensations. But I had reason to believe that the Klondike woman had divined some menace in our attitude of marked indifference. Her own manner, when it could be observed, grew increasingly defiant, if that were possible. The alliance of the Honourable George with the Bohemian set had become, of course, a public scandal after the day of his appearance in her trap and after his betrayal of the Belknap-Jacksons had been gossiped to rags. He no longer troubled himself to pretend any esteem whatever for the North Side set. Scarce a day passed but he appeared in public as the woman's escort. He flagrantly performed her commissions, and at their questionable Bohemian gatherings, with their beer and sausages and that sort of thing, he was the gayest of that gay, mad set.

Indeed, of his old associates, Cousin Egbert quite almost alone seemed to find him any longer desirable, and him I had no heart to caution, knowing that I should only wound without enlightening him, he being entirely impervious to even these cruder aspects of class distinction. I dare say he would have considered the marriage of the Honourable George as no more than the marriage of one of his cattle-person companions. I mean to say, he is a dear old sort and I should never fail to defend him in the most disheartening of his vagaries, but he is undeniably insensitive to what one does and does not do.

The conviction ran, let me repeat, that we had another pot of broth on the fire. I gleaned as much from the Mixer, she being one of the few others besides Cousin Egbert in whose liking the Honourable George had not terrifically descended. She made it a point to address me on the subject over a dish of tea at the Grill one afternoon, choosing a table sufficiently remote from my other feminine guests, who doubtless, at their own tables, discussed the same complication. I was indeed glad that we were remote from other occupied tables, because in the course of her remarks she quite forcefully uttered an oath, which I thought it as well not to have known that I cared to tolerate in my lady patrons.

"As to what Jackson feels about the way it was handed out to him that Sunday," she bluntly declared, "I don't care a——" The oath quite dazed me for a moment, although I had been warned that she would use language on occasion. "What I do care about," she went on briskly, "is that I won't have this girl pestered by Jackson or by you or by any man that wears hair! Why, Jackson talks so silly about her sometimes you'd think she was a bad woman—and he keeps hinting about something he's going to put over till I can hardly keep my hands off him. I just know some day he'll make me forget I'm a lady. Now, take it from me, Bill, if you're setting in with him, don't start anything you can't finish."

Really she was quite fierce about it. I mean to say, the glitter in her eyes made me recall what Cousin Egbert had said of Mrs. Effie, her being quite entirely willing to take on a rattlesnake and give it the advantage of the first two assaults. Somewhat flustered I was, yet I hastened to assure her that, whatever steps I might feel obliged to take for the protection of the Honourable George, they would involve nothing at all unfair to the lady in question.

"Well, they better hadn't!" she resumed threateningly. "That girl had a hard time all right, but listen here—she's as right as a church. She couldn't fool me a minute if she wasn't. Don't you suppose I been around and around quite some? Just because she likes to have a good time and outdresses these dames here—is that any reason they should get out their hammers? Ain't she earned some right to a good time, tell me, after being married when she was a silly kid to Two-spot Kenner, the swine—and God bless the trigger finger of the man that bumped him off! As for the poor old Judge, don't worry. I like the old boy, but Kate Kenner won't do anything more than make a monkey of him just to spite Jackson and his band of lady knockers. Marry him? Say, get me right, Bill—I'll put it as delicate as I can—the Judge is too darned far from being a mental giant for that."

I dare say she would have slanged me for another half-hour but for the constant strain of keeping her voice down. As it was, she boomed up now and again in a way that reduced to listening silence the ladies at several distant tables.

As to the various points she had raised, I was somewhat confused. About the Honourable George, for example: He was, to be sure, no mental giant. But one occupying his position is not required to be. Indeed, in the class to which he was born one well knows that a mental giant would be quite as distressingly bizarre as any other freak. I regretted not having retorted this to her, for it now occurred to me that she had gone it rather strong with her "poor old Judge." I mean to say, it was almost quite a little bit raw for a native American to adopt this patronizing tone toward one of us.

And yet I found that my esteem for the Mixer had increased rather than diminished by reason of her plucky defence of the Klondike woman. I had no reason to suppose that the designing creature was worth a defence, but I could only admire the valour that made it. Also I found food for profound meditation in the Mixer's assertion that the woman's sole aim was to "make a monkey" of the Honourable George. If she were right, a mésalliance need not be feared, at which thought I felt a great relief. That she should achieve the lesser and perhaps equally easy feat with the poor chap was a calamity that would be, I fancied, endured by his lordship with a serene fortitude.

Curiously enough, as I went over the Mixer's tirade point by point, I found in myself an inexplicable loss of animus toward the Klondike woman. I will not say I was moved to sympathy for her, but doubtless that strange ferment of equality stirred me toward her with something less than the indignation I had formerly felt. Perhaps she was an entirely worthy creature. In that case, I merely wished her to be taught that one must not look too far above one's station, even in America, in so serious an affair as matrimony. With all my heart I should wish her a worthy mate of her own class, and I was glad indeed to reflect upon the truth of my assertion to the Mixer, that no unfair advantage would be taken of her. His lordship would remove the Honourable George from her toils, a made monkey, perhaps, but no husband.

Again that day did I listen to a defence of this woman, and from a source whence I could little have expected it. Meditating upon the matter, I found myself staring at Mrs. Judson as she polished some glassware in the pantry. As always, the worthy woman made a pleasing picture in her neat print gown. From staring at her rather absently I caught myself reflecting that she was one of the few women whose hair is always perfectly coiffed. I mean to say, no matter what the press of her occupation, it never goes here and there.

From the hair, my meditative eye, still rather absently, I believe, descended her quite good figure to her boots. Thereupon, my gaze ceased to be absent. They were not boots. They were bronzed slippers with high heels and metal buckles and of a character so distinctive that I instantly knew they had once before been impressed upon my vision. Swiftly my mind identified them: they had been worn by the Klondike woman on the occasion of a dinner at the Grill, in conjunction with a gown to match and a bluish scarf—all combining to achieve an immense effect.

My assistant hummed at her task, unconscious of my scrutiny. I recall that I coughed slightly before disclosing to her that my attention had been attracted to her slippers. She took the reference lightly, affecting, as the sex will, to belittle any prized possession in the face of masculine praise.

"I have seen them before," I ventured.

"She gives me all of hers. I haven't had to buy shoes since baby was born. She gives me—lots of things—stockings and things. She likes me to have them."

"I didn't know you knew her."

"Years! I'm there once a week to give the house a good going over. That Jap of hers is the limit. Dust till you can't rest. And when I clean he just grins."

I mused upon this. The woman was already giving half her time to superintending two assistants in the preparation of the International Relish.

"Her work is too much in addition to your own," I suggested.

"Me? Work too hard? Not in a thousand years. I do all right for you, don't I?"

It was true; she was anything but a slacker. I more nearly approached my real objection.

"A woman in your position," I began, "can't be too careful as to the associations she forms——" I had meant to go on, but found it quite absurdly impossible. My assistant set down the glass she had and quite venomously brandished her towel at me.

"So that's it?" she began, and almost could get no farther for mere sputtering. I mean to say, I had long recognized that she possessed character, but never had I suspected that she would have so inadequate a control of her temper.

"So that's it?" she sputtered again, "And I thought you were too decent to join in that talk about a woman just because she's young and wears pretty clothes and likes to go out. I'm astonished at you, I really am. I thought you were more of a man!" She broke off, scowling at me most furiously.

Feeling all at once rather a fool, I sought to conciliate her. "I have joined in no talk," I said. "I merely suggested——" But she shut me off sharply.

"And let me tell you one thing: I can pick out my associates in this town without any outside help. The idea! That girl is just as nice a person as ever walked the earth, and nobody ever said she wasn't except those frumpy old cats that hate her good looks because the men all like her."

"Old cats!" I echoed, wishing to rebuke this violence of epithet, but she would have none of me.

"Nasty old spite-cats," she insisted with even more violence, and went on to an almost quite blasphemous absurdity. "A prince in his palace wouldn't be any too good for her!"

"Tut, tut!" I said, greatly shocked.

"Tut nothing!" she retorted fiercely. "A regular prince in his palace, that's what she deserves. There isn't a single man in this one-horse town that's good enough to pick up her glove. And she knows it, too. She's carrying on with your silly Englishman now, but it's just to pay those old cats back in their own coin. She'll carry on with him—yes! But marry? Good heavens and earth! Marriage is serious!" With this novel conclusion she seized another glass and began to wipe it viciously. She glared at me, seeming to believe that she had closed the interview. But I couldn't stop. In some curious way she had stirred me rather out of myself— but not about the Klondike woman nor about the Honourable George. I began most illogically, I admit, to rage inwardly about another matter.

"You have other associates," I exclaimed quite violently, "those cattle-persons—I know quite all about it. That Hank and Buck—they come here on the chance of seeing you; they bring you boxes of candy, they bring you little presents. Twice they've escorted you home at night when you quite well knew I was only too glad to do it——" I felt my temper most curiously running away with me, ranting about things I hadn't meant to at all. I looked for another outburst from her, but to my amazement she flashed me a smile with a most enigmatic look back of it. She tossed her head, but resumed her wiping of the glass with a certain demureness. She spoke almost meekly:

"They're very old friends, and I'm sure they always act right. I don't see anything wrong in it, even if Buck Edwards has shown me a good deal of attention."

But this very meekness of hers seemed to arouse all the violence in my nature.

"I won't have it!" I said. "You have no right to receive presents from men. I tell you I won't have it! You've no right!"

"Haven't I?" she suddenly said in the most curious, cool little voice, her eyes falling before mine. "Haven't I? I didn't know."

It was quite chilling, her tone and manner. I was cool in an instant. Things seemed to mean so much more than I had supposed they did. I mean to say, it was a fair crumpler. She paused in her wiping of the glass but did not regard me. I was horribly moved to go to her, but coolly remembered that that sort of thing would never do.

"I trust I have said enough," I remarked with entirely recovered dignity.

"You have," she said.

"I mean I won't have such things," I said.

"I hear you," she said, and fell again to her work. I thereupon investigated an ice-box and found enough matter for complaint against the Hobbs boy to enable me to manage a dignified withdrawal to the rear. The remarkable creature was humming again as I left.

I stood in the back door of the Grill giving upon the alley, where I mused rather excitedly. Here I was presently interrupted by the dog, Mr. Barker. For weeks now I had been relieved of his odious attentions, by the very curious circumstance that he had transferred them to the Honourable George. Not all my kicks and cuffs and beatings had sufficed one whit to repulse him. He had kept after me, fawned upon me, in spite of them. And then on a day he had suddenly, with glad cries, become enamoured of the Honourable George, waiting for him at doors, following him, hanging upon his every look. And the Honourable George had rather fancied the beast and made much of him.

And yet this animal is reputed by poets and that sort of thing to be man's best friend, faithfully sharing his good fortune and his bad, staying by his side to the bitter end, even refusing to leave his body when he has perished—starving there with a dauntless fidelity. How chagrined the weavers of these tributes would have been to observe the fickle nature of the beast in question! For weeks he had hardly deigned me a glance. It had been a relief, to be sure, but what a sickening disclosure of the cur's trifling inconstancy. Even now, though he sniffed hungrily at the open door, he paid me not the least attention—me whom he had once idolized!

I slipped back to the ice-box and procured some slices of beef that were far too good for him. He fell to them with only a perfunctory acknowledgment of my agency in procuring them.

"Why, I thought you hated him!" suddenly said the voice of his owner. She had tiptoed to my side.

"I do," I said quite savagely, "but the unspeakable beast can't be left to starve, can he?"

I felt her eyes upon me, but would not turn. Suddenly she put her hand upon my shoulder, patting it rather curiously, as she might have soothed her child. When I did turn she was back at her task. She was humming again, nor did she glance my way. Quite certainly she was no longer conscious that I stood about. She had quite forgotten me. I could tell as much from her manner. "Such," I reflected, with an unaccustomed cynicism, "is the light inconsequence of women and dogs." Yet I still experienced a curiously thrilling determination to protect her from her own good nature in the matter of her associates.

At a later and cooler moment of the day I reflected upon her defence of the Klondike woman. A "prince in his palace" not too good for her! No doubt she had meant me to take these remarkable words quite seriously. It was amazing, I thought, with what seriousness the lower classes of the country took their dogma of equality, and with what naïve confidence they relied upon us to accept it. Equality in North America was indeed praiseworthy; I had already given it the full weight of my approval and meant to live by it. But at home, of course, that sort of thing would never do. The crude moral worth of the Klondike woman might be all that her two defenders had alleged, and indeed I felt again that strange little thrill of almost sympathy for her as one who had been unjustly aspersed. But I could only resolve that I would be no party to any unfair plan of opposing her. The Honourable George must be saved from her trifling as well as from her serious designs, if such she might have; but so far as I could influence the process it should cause as little chagrin as possible to the offender. This much the Mixer and my charwoman had achieved with me. Indeed, quite hopeful I was that when the

172

creature had been set right as to what was due one of our oldest and proudest families she would find life entirely pleasant among those of her own station. She seemed to have a good heart.

As the day of his lordship's arrival drew near, Belknap-Jackson became increasingly concerned about the precise manner of his reception and the details of his entertainment, despite my best assurances that no especially profound thought need be given to either, his lordship being quite that sort, fussy enough in his own way but hardly formal or pretentious.

His prospective host, after many consultations with me, at length allowed himself to be dissuaded from meeting his lordship in correct afternoon garb of frock-coat and top-hat, consenting, at my urgent suggestion, to a mere lounge-suit of tweeds with a soft-rolled hat and a suitable rough day stick. Again in the matter of the menu for his lordship's initial dinner which we had determined might well be tendered him at my establishment. Both husband and wife were rather keen for an elaborate repast of many courses, feeling that anything less would be doing insufficient honour to their illustrious guest, but I at length convinced them that I quite knew what his lordship would prefer: a vegetable soup, an abundance of boiled mutton with potatoes, a thick pudding, a bit of scientifically correct cheese, and a jug of beer. Rather trying they were at my first mention of this—a dinner quite without finesse, to be sure, but eminently nutritive—and only their certainty that I knew his lordship's ways made them give in.

The affair was to be confined to the family, his lordship the only guest, this being thought discreet for the night of his arrival in view of the peculiar nature of his mission. Belknap-Jackson had hoped against hope that the Mixer might not be present, and even so late as the day of his lordship's arrival he was cheered by word that she might be compelled to keep her bed with a neuralgia.

To the afternoon train I accompanied him in his new motor-car, finding him not a little distressed because the chauffeur, a native of the town, had stoutly—and with some not nice words, I gathered—refused to wear the smart uniform which his employer had provided.

"I would have shopped the fellow in an instant," he confided to me, "had it been at any other time. He was most impertinent. But as usual, here I am at the mercy of circumstances. We couldn't well subject Brinstead to those loathsome public conveyances."

We waited in the usual throng of the leisured lower-classes who are so naïvely pleased at the passage of a train. I found myself picturing their childish wonder had they guessed the identity of him we were there to meet. Even as the train appeared Belknap-Jackson made a last moan of complaint.

"Mrs. Pettengill," he observed dejectedly, "is about the house again and I fear will be quite well enough to be with us this evening." For a moment I almost quite disapproved of the fellow. I mean to say, he was vogue and all that, and no doubt had been wretchedly mistreated, but after all the Mixer was not one to be wished ill to.

A moment later I was contrasting the quiet arrival of his lordship with the clamour and confusion that had marked the advent among us of the Honourable George. He carried but one bag and attracted no attention whatever from the station loungers. While I have never known him be entirely vogue in his appointments, his lordship carries off a lounge-suit and his gray-cloth hat with a certain manner which the Honourable George was never known to achieve even in the days when I groomed him. The grayish rather aggressive looking side-whiskers first caught my eye, and a moment later I had taken his hand. Belknap-Jackson at the same time took his bag, and with a trepidation so obvious that his lordship may perhaps have been excusable for a momentary misapprehension. I mean to say, he instantly and crisply directed Belknap-Jackson to go forward to the luggage van and recover his box.

A bit awkward it was, to be sure, but I speedily took the situation in hand by formally presenting the two men, covering the palpable embarrassment of the host by explaining to his lordship the astounding ingenuity of the American luggage system. By the time I had deprived him of his check and convinced him that his box would be admirably recovered by a person delegated to that service, Belknap-Jackson, again in form, was apologizing to him for the squalid character of the station and for the hardships he must be prepared to endure in a crude Western village. Here again the host was annoyed by having to call repeatedly to his mechanician in order to detach him from a gossiping group of loungers. He came smoking a quite fearfully bad cigar and took his place at the wheel entirely without any suitable deference to his employer.

His lordship during the ride rather pointedly surveyed me, being impressed, I dare say, by something in my appearance and manner quite new to him. Doubtless I had been feeling equal for so long that the thing was to be noticed in my manner. He made no comment upon me, however. Indeed almost the only time he spoke during our passage was to voice his astonishment at not having been able to procure the London *Times* at the press-stalls along the way. His host made clucking noises of sympathy at this. He had, he said, already warned his lordship that America was still crude.

"Crude? Of course, what, what!" exclaimed his lordship. "But naturally they'd have the *Times*! I dare say the beggars were too lazy to look it out. Laziness, what, what!"

"We've a job teaching them to know their places," ventured Belknap-Jackson, moodily regarding the back of his chauffeur which somehow contrived to be eloquent with disrespect for him.

"My word, what rot!" rejoined his lordship. I saw that he had arrived in one of his peppery moods. I fancy he could not have recited a multiplication table

174

without becoming fanatically assertive about it. That was his way. I doubt if he had ever condescended to have an opinion. What might have been opinions came out on him like a rash in form of the most violent convictions.

"What rot not to know their places, when they must know them!" he snappishly added.

"Quite so, quite so!" his host hastened to assure him.

"A—dashed—fine big country you have," was his only other observation.

"Indeed, indeed," murmured his host mildly. I had rather dreaded the oath which his lordship is prone to use lightly.

Reaching the Belknap-Jackson house, his lordship was shown to the apartment prepared for him.

"Tea will be served in half an hour, your—er—Brinstead," announced his host cordially, although seemingly at a loss how to address him.

"Quite so, what, what! Tea, of course, of course! Why wouldn't it be? Meantime, if you don't mind, I'll have a word with Ruggles. At once."

Belknap-Jackson softly and politely withdrew at once.

Alone with his lordship, I thought it best to acquaint him instantly with the change in my circumstances, touching lightly upon the matter of my now being an equal with rather most of the North Americans. He listened with exemplary patience to my brief recital and was good enough to felicitate me.

"Assure you, glad to hear it—glad no end. Worthy fellow; always knew it. And equal, of course, of course! Take up their equality by all means if you take 'em up themselves. Curious lot of nose-talking beggars, and putting r's every place one shouldn't, but don't blame you. Do it myself if I could—England gone to pot. Quite!"

"Gone to pot, sir?" I gasped.

"Don't argue. Course it has. Women! Slasher fiends and firebrands! Pictures, churches, golf-greens, cabinet members—nothing safe. Pouring their beastly filth into pillar boxes. Women one knows. Hussies, though! Want the vote—rot! Awful rot! Don't blame you for America. Wish I might, too. Good thing, my word! No backbone in Downing Street. Let the fiends out again directly they're hungry. No system! No firmness! No dash! Starve 'em proper, I would."

He was working himself into no end of a state. I sought to divert him.

"About the Honourable George, sir——" I ventured.

"What's the silly ass up to now? Dancing girl got him—yes? How he does it, I can't think. No looks, no manner, no way with women. Can't stand him myself. How ever can they? Frightful bore, old George is. Well, well, man, I'm waiting. Tell me, tell me, tell me!"

Briefly I disclosed to him that his brother had entangled himself with a young person who had indeed been a dancing girl or a bit like that in the province of Alaska. That at the time of my cable there was strong reason to believe she would stop at nothing—even marriage, but that I had since come to suspect that she might be bent only on making a fool of her victim, she being, although an honest enough character, rather inclined to levity and without proper respect for established families.

I hinted briefly at the social warfare of which she had been a storm centre. I said again, remembering the warm words of the Mixer and of my charwoman, that to the best of my knowledge her character was without blemish. All at once I was feeling preposterously sorry for the creature.

His lordship listened, though with a cross-fire of interruptions. "Alaska dancing girl. Silly! Nothing but snow and mines in Alaska." Or, again, "Make a fool of old George? What silly piffle! Already done it himself, what, what! Waste her time!" And if she wasn't keen to marry him, had I called him across the ocean to intervene in a vulgar village squabble about social precedence? "Social precedence silly rot!"

I insisted that his brother should be seen to. One couldn't tell what the woman might do. Her audacity was tremendous, even for an American. To this he listened more patiently.

"Dare say you're right. You don't go off your head easily. I'll rag him proper, now I'm here. Always knew the ass would make a silly marriage if he could. Yes, yes, I'll break it up quick enough. I say I'll break it up proper. Dancers and that sort. Dangerous. But I know their tricks."

A summons to tea below interrupted him.

"Hungry, my word! Hardly dared eat in that dining-coach. Tinned stuff all about one. Appendicitis! American journal—some Colonel chap found it out. Hunting sort. Looked a fool beside his silly horse, but seemed to know. Took no chances. Said the tin-opener slays its thousands. Rot, no doubt. Perhaps not."

I led him below, hardly daring at the moment to confess my own responsibility for his fears. Another time, I thought, we might chat of it.

Belknap-Jackson with his wife and the Mixer awaited us. His lordship was presented, and I excused myself.

"Mrs. Pettengill, his lordship the Earl of Brinstead," had been the host's speech of presentation to the Mixer.

"How do do, Earl; I'm right glad to meet you," had been the Mixer's acknowledgment, together with a hearty grasp of the hand. I saw his lordship's face brighten.

"What ho!" he cried with the first cheerfulness he had exhibited, and the Mixer, still vigorously pumping his hand, had replied, "Same here!" with a vast smile of good nature. It occurred to me that they, at least, were quite going to "get" each other, as Americans say.

"Come right in and set down in the parlour," she was saying at the last. "I don't eat between meals like you English folks are always doing, but I'll take a shot of hooch with you."

The Belknap-Jacksons stood back not a little distressed. They seemed to publish that their guest was being torn from them.

"A shot of hooch!" observed his lordship "I dare say your shooting over here is absolutely top-hole—keener sport than our popping at driven birds. What, what!"

CHAPTER EIGHTEEN

At a latish seven, when the Grill had become nicely filled with a representative crowd, the Belknap-Jacksons arrived with his lordship. The latter had not dressed and I was able to detect that Belknap-Jackson, doubtless noting his guest's attire at the last moment, had hastily changed back to a lounge-suit of his own. Also I noted the absence of the Mixer and wondered how the host had contrived to eliminate her. On this point he found an opportunity to enlighten me before taking his seat.

"Mark my words, that old devil is up to something," he darkly said, and I saw that he was genuinely put about, for not often does he fall into strong language.

"After pushing herself forward with his lordship all through tea-time in the most brazen manner, she announces that she has a previous dinner engagement and can't be with us. I'm as well pleased to have her absent, of course, but I'd pay handsomely to know what her little game is. Imagine her not dining with the Earl of Brinstead when she had the chance! That shows something's wrong. I don't like it. I tell you she's capable of things."

I mused upon this. The Mixer was undoubtedly capable of things. Especially things concerning her son-in-law. And yet I could imagine no opening for her at the present moment and said as much. And Mrs. Belknap-Jackson, I was glad to observe, did not share her husband's evident worry. She had entered the place plumingly, as it were, sweeping the length of the room before his lordship with quite all the manner her somewhat stubby figure could carry off. Seated, she became at once vivacious, chatting to his lordship brightly and continuously, raking the room the while with her lorgnon. Half a dozen ladies of the North Side set were with parties at other tables. I saw she was immensely stimulated by the circumstance that these friends were unaware of her guest's identity. I divined that before the evening was over she would contrive to disclose it.

His lordship responded but dully to her animated chat. He is never less urbane than when hungry, and I took pains to have his favourite soup served quite almost at once. This he fell upon. I may say that he has always a hearty manner of attacking his soup. Not infrequently he makes noises. He did so on this occasion. I mean to say, there was no finesse. I hovered near, anxious that the service should be without flaw.

His head bent slightly over his plate, I saw a spoonful of soup ascending with precision toward his lips. But curiously it halted in mid-air, then fell back. His lordship's eyes had become fixed upon some one back of me. At once, too, I noted looks of consternation upon the faces of the Belknap-Jacksons, the hostess freezing in the very midst of some choice phrase she had smilingly begun.

I turned quickly. It was the Klondike person, radiant in the costume of black and the black hat. She moved down the hushed room with well-lifted chin, eyes straight ahead and narrowed to but a faint offended consciousness of the staring crowd. It was well done. It was superior. I am able to judge those things.

Reaching a table the second but one from the Belknap-Jacksons's, she relaxed finely from the austere note of her progress and turned to her companions with a pretty and quite perfect confusion as to which chair she might occupy. Quite awfully these companions were the Mixer, overwhelming in black velvet and diamonds, and Cousin Egbert, uncomfortable enough looking but as correctly enveloped in evening dress as he could ever manage by himself. His cravat had been tied many times and needed it once more.

They were seated by the raccoon with quite all his impressiveness of manner. They faced the Belknap-Jackson party, yet seemed unconscious of its presence. Cousin Egbert, with a bored manner which I am certain he achieved only with tremendous effort, scanned my simple menu. The Mixer settled herself with a vast air of comfort and arranged various hand-belongings about her on the table.

Between them the Klondike woman sat with a restraint that would actually not have ill-become one of our own women. She did not look about; her hands were still, her head was up. At former times with her own set she had been wont to exhibit a rather defiant vivacity. Now she did not challenge. Finely, eloquently, there pervaded her a reserve that seemed almost to exhale a fragrance. But of course that is silly rot. I mean to say, she drew the attention without visible effort. She only waited.

The Earl of Brinstead, as we all saw, had continued to stare. Thrice slowly arose the spoon of soup, for mere animal habit was strong upon him, yet at a certain elevation it each time fell slowly back. He was acting like a mechanical toy. Then the Mixer caught his eye and nodded crisply. He bobbed in response.

"What ho! The dowager!" he exclaimed, and that time the soup was successfully resumed.

"Poor old mater!" sighed his hostess. "She's constantly taking up people. One does, you know, in these queer Western towns."

"Jolly old thing, awfully good sort!" said his lordship, but his eyes were not on the Mixer.

Terribly then I recalled the Honourable George's behaviour at that same table the night he had first viewed this Klondike person. His lordship was staring in much the same fashion. Yet I was relieved to observe that the woman this time was quite unconscious of the interest she had aroused. In the case of the Honourable George, who had frankly ogled her—for the poor chap has ever lacked the finer shades in these matters—she had not only been aware of it but had deliberately played upon it. It is not too much to say that she had shown herself to be a creature of blandishments. More than once she had permitted her eyes to rest upon him with that peculiarly womanish gaze which, although superficially of a blank innocence, is yet all-seeing and even shoots little fine arrows of questions from its ambuscade. But now she was ignoring his lordship as utterly as she did the Belknap-Jacksons.

To be sure she may later have been in some way informed that his eyes were seeking her, but never once, I am sure, did she descend to even a veiled challenge of his glance or betray the faintest discreet consciousness of it. And this I was indeed glad to note in her. Clearly she must know where to draw the line, permitting herself a malicious laxity with a younger brother which she would not have the presumption to essay with the holder of the title. Pleased I was, I say, to detect in her this proper respect for his lordship's position. It showed her to be not all unworthy.

The dinner proceeded, his lordship being good enough to compliment me on the fare which I knew was done to his liking. Yet, even in the very presence of the boiled mutton, his eyes were too often upon his neighbour. When he behaved thus in the presence of a dish of mutton I had not to be told that he was strongly moved. I uneasily recalled now that he had once been a bit of a dog himself. I mean to say, there was talk in the countryside, though of course it had died out a score of years ago. I thought it as well, however, that he be told almost immediately that the person he honoured with his glance was no other than the one he had come to subtract his unfortunate brother from.

The dinner progressed—somewhat jerkily because of his lordship's inattention—through the pudding and cheese to coffee. Never had I known his lordship behave so languidly in the presence of food he cared for. His hosts ate even less. They were worried. Mrs. Belknap-Jackson, however, could simply no longer contain within herself the secret of their guest's identity. With excuses to the deaf ears of his lordship she left to address a friend at a distant table. She addressed others at other tables, leaving a flutter of sensation in her wake.

Belknap-Jackson, having lighted one of his non-throat cigarettes, endeavoured to engross his lordship with an account of their last election of officers to the country club. His lordship was not properly attentive to this. Indeed, with his hostess gone he no longer made any pretence of concealing his interest in the other table. I saw him catch the eye of the Mixer and astonishingly intercepted from her a swift but most egregious wink.

"One moment," said his lordship to the host. "Must pay my respects to the dowager, what, what! Jolly old muggins, yes!" And he was gone.

I heard the Mixer's amazing presentation speech.

"Mrs. Kenner, Mr. Floud, his lordship—say, listen here, is your right name Brinstead, or Basingwell, like your brother's?"

The Klondike person acknowledged the thing with a faintly gracious nod. It carried an air, despite the slightness of it. Cousin Egbert was more cordial.

"Pleased to meet you, Lord!" said he, and grasped the newcomer's hand. "Come on, set in with us and have some coffee and a cigar. Here, Jeff, bring the

180

lord a good cigar. We was just talking about you that minute. How do you like our town? Say, this here Kulanche Valley——" I lost the rest. His lordship had seated himself. At his own table Belknap-Jackson writhed acutely. He was lighting a second cigarette—the first not yet a quarter consumed!

At once the four began to be thick as thieves, though it was apparent his lordship had eyes only for the woman. Coffee was brought. His lordship lighted his cigar. And now the word had so run from Mrs. Belknap-Jackson that all eyes were drawn to this table. She had created her sensation and it had become all at once more of one than she had thought. From Mrs. Judge Ballard's table I caught her glare at her unconscious mother. It was not the way one's daughter should regard one in public.

Presently contriving to pass the table again, I noted that Cousin Egbert had changed his form of address.

"Have some brandy with your coffee, Earl. Here, Jeff, bring Earl and all of us some lee-cures." I divined the monstrous truth that he supposed himself to be calling his lordship by his first name, and he in turn must have understood my shocked glance of rebuke, for a bit later, with glad relief in his tones, he was addressing his lordship as "Cap!" And myself he had given the rank of colonel!

The Klondike person in the beginning finely maintained her reserve. Only at the last did she descend to vivacity or the use of her eyes. This later laxness made me wonder if, after all, she would feel bound to pay his lordship the respect he was wont to command from her class.

"You and poor George are rather alike," I overheard, "except that he uses the single 'what' and you use the double. Hasn't he any right to use the double 'what' yet, and what does it mean, anyway? Tell us."

"What, what!" demanded his lordship, a bit puzzled.

"But that's it! What do you say 'What, what' for? It can't do you any good."

"What, what! But I mean to say, you're having me on. My word you are—spoofing, I mean to say. What, what! To be sure. Chaffing lot, you are!" He laughed. He was behaving almost with levity.

"But poor old George is so much younger than you—you must make allowances," I again caught her saying; and his lordship replied:

"Not at all; not at all! Matter of a half-score years. Barely a half-score; nine and a few months. Younger? What rot! Chaffing again."

Really it was a bit thick, the creature saying "poor old George" quite as if he were something in an institution, having to be wheeled about in a bath-chair with rugs and water-bottles!

Glad I was when the trio gave signs of departure. It was woman's craft dictating it, I dare say. She had made her effect and knew when to go.

"Of course we shall have to talk over my dreadful designs on your poor old George," said the amazing woman, intently regarding his lordship at parting.

"Leave it to me," said he, with a scarcely veiled significance.

"Well, see you again, Cap," said Cousin Egbert warmly. "I'll take you around to meet some of the boys. We'll see you have a good time."

"What ho!" his lordship replied cordially. The Klondike person flashed him one enigmatic look, then turned to precede her companions. Again down the thronged room she swept, with that chin-lifted, drooping-eyed, faintly offended half consciousness of some staring rabble at hand that concerned her not at all. Her alert feminine foes, I am certain, read no slightest trace of amusement in her unwavering lowered glance. So easily she could have been crude here!

Belknap-Jackson, enduring his ignominious solitude to the limit of his powers, had joined his wife at the lower end of the room. They had taken the unfortunate development with what grace they could. His lordship had dropped in upon them quite informally—charming man that he was. Of course he would quickly break up the disgraceful affair. Beginning at once. They would doubtless entertain for him in a quiet way——

At the deserted table his lordship now relieved a certain sickening apprehension that had beset me.

"What, what! Quite right to call me out here. Shan't forget it. Dangerous creature, that. Badly needed, I was. Can't think why you waited so long! Anything might have happened to old George. Break it up proper, though. Never do at all. Impossible person for him. Quite!"

I saw they had indeed taken no pains to hide the woman's identity from him nor their knowledge of his reason for coming out to the States, though with wretchedly low taste they had done this chaffingly. Yet it was only too plain that his lordship now realized what had been the profound gravity of the situation, and I was glad to see that he meant to end it without any nonsense.

"Silly ass, old George, though," he added as the Belknap-Jacksons approached. "How a creature like that could ever have fancied him! What, what!"

His hosts were profuse in their apologies for having so thoughtlessly run away from his lordship—they carried it off rather well. They were keen for sitting at the table once more, as the other observant diners were lingering on, but his lordship would have none of this.

"Stuffy place!" said he. "Best be getting on." And so, reluctantly, they led him down the gauntlet of widened eyes. Even so, the tenth Earl of Brinstead had dined publicly with them. More than repaid they were for the slight the Honourable George had put upon them in the affair of the pianoforte artist.

An hour later Belknap-Jackson had me on by telephone. His voice was not a little worried.

"I say, is his lordship, the Earl, subject to spells of any sort? We were in the library where I was showing him some photographic views of dear old Boston, and right over a superb print of our public library he seemed to lose consciousness. Might it be a stroke? Or do you think it's just a healthy sleep? And shall I venture to shake him? How would he take that? Or should I merely cover him with a travelling rug? It would be so dreadful if anything happened when he's been with us such a little time."

I knew his lordship. He has the gift of sleeping quite informally when his attention is not too closely engaged. I suggested that the host set his musical phonograph in motion on some one of the more audible selections. As I heard no more from him that night I dare say my plan worked.

Our town, as may be imagined, buzzed with transcendent gossip on the morrow. The *Recorder* disclosed at last that the Belknap-Jacksons of Boston and Red Gap were quietly entertaining his lordship, the Earl of Brinstead, though since the evening before this had been news to hardly any one. Nor need it be said that a viciously fermenting element in the gossip concerned the apparently cordial meeting of his lordship with the Klondike person, an encounter that had been watched with jealous eyes by more than one matron of the North Side set. It was even intimated that if his lordship had come to put the creature in her place he had chosen a curious way to set about it.

Also there were hard words uttered of the Belknap-Jacksons by Mrs. Effie, and severe blame put upon myself because his lordship had not come out to the Flouds'.

"But the Brinsteads have always stopped with us before," she went about saying, as if there had been a quite long succession of them. I mean to say, only the Honourable George had stopped on with them, unless, indeed, the woman actually counted me as one. Between herself and Mrs. Belknap-Jackson, I understood, there ensued early that morning by telephone a passage of virulent acidity, Mrs. Effie being heard by Cousin Egbert to say bluntly that she would get even.

Undoubtedly she did not share the annoyance of the Belknap-Jacksons at certain eccentricities now developed by his lordship which made him at times a trying house guest. That first morning he arose at five sharp, a custom of his which I deeply regretted not having warned his host about. Discovering quite no one about, he had ventured abroad in search of breakfast, finding it at length in the eating establishment known as "Bert's Place," in company with engine-drivers, plate-layers, milk persons, and others of a common sort.

Thereafter he had tramped furiously about the town and its environs for some hours, at last encountering Cousin Egbert who escorted him to the Floud home for his first interview with the Honourable George. The latter received his lordship in bed, so Cousin Egbert later informed me. He had left the two together, whereupon for an hour there were heard quite all over the house words of the most explosive character. Cousin Egbert, much alarmed at the passionate beginning of the interview, suspected they might do each other a mischief, and for some moments hovered about with the aim, if need be, of preserving human life. But as the uproar continued evenly, he at length concluded they would do no more than talk, the outcome proving the accuracy of his surmise.

Mrs. Effie, meantime, saw her opportunity and seized it with a cool readiness which I have often remarked in her. Belknap-Jackson, distressed beyond measure at the strange absence of his guest, had communicated with me by telephone several times without result. Not until near noon was I able to give him any light. Mrs. Effie had then called me to know what his lordship preferred for luncheon. Replying that cold beef, pickles, and beer were his usual mid-day fancy, I hastened to allay the fears of the Belknap-Jacksons, only to find that Mrs. Effie had been before me.

"She says," came the annoyed voice of the host, "that the dear Earl dropped in for a chat with his brother and has most delightfully begged her to give him luncheon. She says he will doubtless wish to drive with them this afternoon, but I had already planned to drive him myself—to the country club and about. The woman is high-handed, I must say. For God's sake, can't you do something?"

I was obliged to tell him straight that the thing was beyond me, though I promised to recover his guest promptly, should any opportunity occur. The latter did not, however, drive with the Flouds that afternoon. He was observed walking abroad with Cousin Egbert, and it was later reported by persons of unimpeachable veracity that they had been seen to enter the Klondike person's establishment.

Evening drew on without further news. But then certain elated members of the Bohemian set made it loosely known that they were that evening to dine informally at their leader's house to meet his lordship. It seemed a bit extraordinary to me, yet I could not but rejoice that he should thus adopt the peaceful methods of diplomacy for the extrication of his brother.

Belknap-Jackson now telephoning to know if I had heard this report— "canard" he styled it—I confirmed it and remarked that his lordship was undoubtedly by way of bringing strong pressure to bear on the woman.

"But I had expected him to meet a few people here this evening," cried the host pathetically. I was then obliged to tell him that the Brinsteads for centuries had been bluntly averse to meeting a few people. It seemed to run in the blood.

The Bohemian dinner, although quite informal, was said to have been highly enjoyed by all, including the Honourable George, who was among those present, as well as Cousin Egbert. The latter gossiped briefly of the affair the following day.

"Sure, the Cap had a good time all right," he said. "Of course he ain't the mixer the Judge is, but he livens up quite some, now and then. Talks like a bunch of firecrackers going off all to once, don't he? Funny guy. I walked with him to the Jacksons' about twelve or one. He's going back to Mis' Kenner's house today. He says it'll take a lot of talking back and forth to get this thing settled right, and it's got to be right, he says. He seen that right off." He paused as if to meditate profoundly.

"If you was to ask me, though, I'd say she had him—just like that!"

He held an open hand toward me, then tightly clenched it.

Suspecting he might spread absurd gossip of this sort, I explained carefully to him that his lordship had indeed at once perceived her to be a dangerous woman; and that he was now taking his own cunning way to break off the distressing affair between her and his brother. He listened patiently, but seemed wedded to some monstrous view of his own.

"Them dames of that there North Side set better watch out," he remarked ominously. "First thing they know, what that Kate Kenner'll hand them—they can make a lemonade out of!"

I could make but little of this, save its general import, which was of course quite shockingly preposterous. I found myself wishing, to be sure, that his lordship had been able to accomplish his mission to North America without appearing to meet the person as a social equal, as I feared indeed that a wrong impression of his attitude would be gained by the undiscerning public. It might have been better, I was almost quite certain, had he adopted a stern and even brutal method at the outset, instead of the circuitous and diplomatic. Belknap-Jackson shared this view with me.

"I should hate dreadfully to have his lordship's reputation suffer for this," he confided to me.

The first week dragged to its close in this regrettable fashion. Oftener than not his hosts caught no glimpse of his lordship throughout the day. The smart trap and the tandem team were constantly ready, but he had not yet been driven abroad by his host. Each day he alleged the necessity of conferring with the woman.

"Dangerous creature, my word! But dangerous!" he would announce. "Takes no end of managing. Do it, though; do it proper. Take a high hand with her. Can't have silly old George in a mess. Own brother, what, what! Time needed, though. Not with you at dinner, if you don't mind. Creature has a way of picking up things not half nasty."

But each day Belknap-Jackson met him with pressing offers of such entertainment as the town afforded. Three times he had been obliged to postpone the informal evening affair for a few smart people. Yet, though patient, he was determined. Reluctantly at last he abandoned the design of driving his guest about in the trap, but he insistently put forward the motor-car. He would drive it himself. They would spend pleasant hours going about the country. His lordship continued elusive. To myself he confided that his host was a nagger.

"Awfully nagging sort, yes. Doesn't know the strain I'm under getting this silly affair straight. Country interesting no doubt, what, what! But, my word! saw nothing but country coming out. Country quite all about, miles and miles both sides of the metals. Seen enough country. Seen motor-cars, too, my word. Enough of both, what, what!"

Yet it seemed that on the Saturday after his arrival he could no longer decently put off his insistent host. He consented to accompany him in the motor-car. Rotten judging it was on the part of Belknap-Jackson. He should have listened to me. They departed after luncheon, the host at the wheel. I had his account of such following events as I did not myself observe.

"Our country club," he observed early in the drive. "No one there, of course. You'd never believe the trouble I've had——"

"Jolly good club," replied his lordship. "Drive back that way."

"Back that way," it appeared, would take them by the detached villa of the Klondike person.

"Stop here," directed his lordship. "Shan't detain you a moment."

This was at two-thirty of a fair afternoon. I am able to give but the bare facts, yet I must assume that the emotions of Belknap-Jackson as he waited there during the ensuing two hours were of a quite distressing nature. As much was intimated by several observant townspeople who passed him. He was said to be distrait; to be smoking his cigarettes furiously.

At four-thirty his lordship reappeared. With apparent solicitude he escorted the Klondike person, fetchingly gowned in a street costume of the latest mode. They chatted gayly to the car.

"Hope I've not kept you waiting, old chap," said his lordship genially. "Time slips by one so. You two met, of course, course!" He bestowed his companion in the tonneau and ensconced himself beside her.

"Drive," said he, "to your goods shops, draper's, chemist's—where was it?"

"To the Central Market," responded the lady in bell-like tones, "then to the Red Front store, and to that dear little Japanese shop, if he doesn't mind."

"Mind! Mind! Course not, course not! Are you warm? Let me fasten the robe."

I confess to have felt a horrid fascination for this moment as I was able to reconstruct it from Belknap-Jackson's impassioned words. It was by way of being one of those scenes we properly loathe yet morbidly cannot resist overlooking if opportunity offers.

Into the flood tide of our Saturday shopping throng swept the car and its remarkably assembled occupants. The street fair gasped. The woman's former parade of the Honourable George had been as nothing to this exposure.

"Poor Jackson's face was a study," declared the Mixer to me later.

I dare say. It was still a study when my own turn came to observe it. The car halted before the shops that had been designated. The Klondike person dispatched her commissions in a superbly leisured manner, attentively accompanied by the Earl of Brinstead bearing packages for her.

Belknap-Jackson, at the wheel, stared straight ahead. I am told he bore himself with dignity even when some of our more ingenuous citizens paused to converse with him concerning his new motor-car. He is even said to have managed a smile when his passengers returned.

"I have it," exclaimed his lordship now. "Deuced good plan—go to that Ruggles place for a jolly fat tea. No end of a spree, what, what!"

It is said that on three occasions in turning his car and traversing the short block to the Grill the owner escaped disastrous collision with other vehicles only by the narrowest possible margin. He may have courted something of the sort. I dare say he was desperate.

"Join us, of course!" said his lordship, as he assisted his companion to alight. Again I am told the host managed to illumine his refusal with a smile. He would take no tea—the doctor's orders.

The surprising pair entered at the height of my tea-hour and were served to an accompaniment of stares from the ladies present. To this they appeared oblivious, being intent upon their conference. His lordship was amiable to a degree. It now occurred to me that he had found the woman even more dangerous than he had at first supposed. He was being forced to play a deep game with her and was meeting guile with guile. He had, I suspected, found his poor brother far deeper in than any of us had thought. Doubtless he had written compromising letters that must be secured—letters she would hold at a price.

And yet I had never before had excuse to believe his lordship possessed the diplomatic temperament. I reflected that I must always have misread him. He was deep, after all. Not until the two left did I learn that Belknap-Jackson awaited them with his car. He loitered about in adjacent doorways, quite like a hired fellow. He was passionately smoking more cigarettes than were good for him.

I escorted my guests to the car. Belknap-Jackson took his seat with but one glance at me, yet it was eloquent of all the ignominy that had been heaped upon him.

"Home, I think," said the lady when they were well seated. She said it charmingly.

"Home," repeated his lordship. "Are you quite protected by the robe?"

An incautious pedestrian at the next crossing narrowly escaped being run down. He shook a fist at the vanishing car and uttered a stream of oaths so vile that he would instantly have been taken up in any well-policed city.

Half an hour later Belknap-Jackson called me.

"He got out with that fiend! He's staying on there. But, my God! can nothing be done?"

"His lordship is playing a most desperate game," I hastened to assure him. "He's meeting difficulties. She must have her dupe's letters in her possession. Blackmail, I dare say. Best leave his lordship free. He's a deep character."

"He presumed far this afternoon—only the man's position saved him with me!" His voice seemed choked with anger. Then, remotely, faint as distant cannonading, a rumble reached me. It was hoarse laughter of the Mixer, perhaps in another room. The electric telephone has been perfected in the States to a marvellous delicacy of response.

I now found myself observing Mrs. Effie, who had been among the absorbed onlookers while the pair were at their tea, she having occupied a table with Mrs. Judge Ballard and Mrs. Dr. Martingale. Deeply immersed in thought she had been, scarce replying to her companions. Her eyes had narrowed in a way I well knew when she reviewed the social field.

Still absorbed she was when Cousin Egbert entered, accompanied by the Honourable George. The latter had seen but little of his brother since their first stormy interview, but he had also seen little of the Klondike woman. His spirits, however, had seemed quite undashed. He rarely missed his tea. Now as they seated themselves they were joined quickly by Mrs. Effie, who engaged her relative in earnest converse. It was easy to see that she begged a favour. She kept a hand on his arm. She urged. Presently, seeming to have achieved her purpose, she left them, and I paused to greet the pair.

"I guess that there Mrs. Effie is awful silly," remarked Cousin Egbert enigmatically. "No, sir; she can't ever tell how the cat is going to jump." Nor would he say more, though he most elatedly held a secret.

With this circumstance I connected the announcement in Monday's *Recorder* that Mrs. Senator Floud would on that evening entertain at dinner the members of Red Gap's Bohemian set, including Mrs. Kate Kenner, the guest of honour being his lordship the Earl of Brinstead, "at present visiting in this city. Covers," it added, "would be laid for fourteen." I saw that Cousin Egbert would have been made the ambassador to conduct what must have been a business of some delicacy.

Among the members of the North Side set the report occasioned the wildest alarm. And yet so staunch were known to be the principles of Mrs. Effie that but few accused her of downright treachery. It seemed to be felt that she was but lending herself to the furtherance of some deep design of his lordship's. Blackmail, the recovery of compromising letters, the avoidance of legal proceedings—these were hinted at. For myself I suspected that she had merely misconstrued the seeming cordiality of his lordship toward the woman and, at the expense of the Belknap-Jacksons, had sought the honour of entertaining him. If, to do that, she must entertain the woman, well and good. She was not one to funk her fences with the game in sight.

Consulting me as to the menu for her dinner, she allowed herself to be persuaded to the vegetable soup, boiled mutton, thick pudding, and cheese which I recommended, though she pleaded at length for a chance to use the new fish set and for a complicated salad portrayed in her latest woman's magazine. Covered with grated nuts it was in the illustration. I was able, however, to convince her that his lordship would regard grated nuts as silly.

From Belknap-Jackson I learned by telephone (during these days, being sensitive, he stopped in almost quite continuously) that Mrs. Effie had profusely explained to his wife about the dinner. "Of course, my dear, I couldn't have the presumption to ask you and your husband to sit at table with the creature, even if he did think it all right to drive her about town on a shopping trip. But I thought we ought to do something to make the dear Earl's visit one to be remembered—he's *so* appreciative! I'm sure you understand just how things are——"

In reciting this speech to me Belknap-Jackson essayed to simulate the tone and excessive manner of a woman gushing falsely. The fellow was quite bitter about it.

"I sometimes think I'll give up," he concluded. "God only knows what things are coming to!"

It began to seem even to me that they were coming a bit thick. But I knew that his lordship was a determined man. He was of the bulldog breed that has made old England what it is. I mean to say, I knew he would put the woman in her place.

CHAPTER NINETEEN

Echoes of the Monday night dinner reached me the following day. The affair had passed off pleasantly enough, the members of the Bohemian set conducting themselves quite as persons who mattered, with the exception of the Klondike woman herself, who, I gathered, had descended to a mood of most indecorous liveliness considering who the guest of honour was. She had not only played and sung those noisy native folksongs of hers, but she had, it seemed, conducted herself with a certain facetious familiarity toward his lordship.

"Every now and then," said Cousin Egbert, my principal informant, "she'd whirl in and josh the Cap all over the place about them funny whiskers he wears. She told him out and out he'd just got to lose them."

"Shocking rudeness!" I exclaimed.

"Oh, sure, sure!" he agreed, yet without indignation. "And the Cap just hated her for it—you could tell that by the way he looked at her. Oh, he hates her something terrible. He just can't bear the sight of her."

"Naturally enough," I observed, though there had been an undercurrent to his speech that I thought almost quite a little odd. His accents were queerly placed. Had I not known him too well I should have thought him trying to be deep. I recalled his other phrases, that Mrs. Effie was seeing which way a cat would leap, and that the Klondike person would hand the ladies of the North Side set a lemon squash. I put them all down as childish prattle and said as much to the Mixer later in the day as she had a dish of tea at the Grill.

"Yes, Sour-dough's right," she observed. "That Earl just hates the sight of her—can't bear to look at her a minute." But she, too, intoned the thing queerly.

"He's putting pressure to bear on her," I said.

"Pressure!" said the Mixer; and then, "Hum!" very dryly.

With this news, however, it was plain as a pillar-box that things were going badly with his lordship's effort to release the Honourable George from his entanglement. The woman, doubtless with his compromising letters, would be holding out for a stiffish price; she would think them worth no end. And plainly again, his lordship had thrown off his mask; was unable longer to conceal his aversion for her. This, to be sure, was more in accordance with his character as I had long observed it. If he hated her it was like him to show it when he looked at her. I mean he was quite like that with almost any one. I hoped, however, that diplomacy might still save us all sorts of a nasty row.

To my relief when the pair appeared for tea that afternoon—a sight no longer causing the least sensation—I saw that his lordship must have returned to his first or diplomatic manner. Doubtless he still hated her, but one would little have suspected it from his manner of looking at her. I mean to say, he looked at her another way. The opposite way, in fact. He was being subtle in the extreme. I fancied it must have been her wretched levity regarding his beard that had goaded him into the exhibitions of hatred noted by Cousin Egbert and the Mixer. Unquestionably his lordship may be goaded in no time if one deliberately sets about it. At the time, doubtless, he had sliced a drive or two, as one might say, but now he was back in form.

Again I confess I was not a little sorry for the creature, seeing her there so smartly taken in by his effusive manner. He was having her on in the most obvious way and she, poor dupe, taking it all quite seriously. Prime it was, though, considering the creature's designs; and I again marvelled that in all the years of my association with his lordship I had never suspected what a topping sort he could be at this game. His mask was now perfect. It recalled, indeed, Cousin Egbert's simple but telling phrase about the Honourable George—"He looks at her!" It could now have been said of his lordship with the utmost significance to any but those in the know.

And so began, quite as had the first, the second week of his lordship's stay among us. Knowing he had booked a return from Cooks, I fancied that results of some sort must soon ensue. The pressure he was putting on the woman must begin to tell. And this was the extreme of the encouragement I was able to offer the Belknap-Jacksons. Both he and his wife were of course in a bit of a state. Nor could I blame them. With an Earl for house guest they must be content with but a glimpse of him at odd moments. Rather a barren honour they were finding it.

His lordship's conferences with the woman were unabated. When not secluded with her at her own establishment he would be abroad with her in her trap or in the car of Belknap-Jackson. The owner, however, no longer drove his car. He had never taken another chance. And well I knew these activities of his lordship's were being basely misconstrued by the gossips.

"The Cap is certainly some queener," remarked Cousin Egbert, which perhaps reflected the view of the deceived public at this time, the curious term implying that his lordship was by way of being a bit of a dog. But calm I remained under these aspersions, counting upon a clean-cut vindication of his lordship's methods when he should have got the woman where he wished her.

I remained, I repeat, serenely confident that a signal triumph would presently crown his lordship's subtly planned attack. And then, at midweek, I was rudely shocked to the suspicion that all might not be going well with his plan. I had not seen the pair for a day, and when they did appear for their tea I instantly detected a profound change in their mutual bearing. His lordship still looked at the woman, but the raillery of their past meetings had gone. Too plainly something momentous had occurred. Even the woman was serious. Had they fought to the last stand? Would she have been too much for him? I mean to say, was the Honourable George cooked?

I now recalled that I had observed an almost similar change in the latter's manner. His face wore a look of wildest gloom that might have been mitigated perhaps by a proper trimming of his beard, but even then it would have been remarked by those who knew him well. I divined, I repeat, that something momentous had now occurred and that the Honourable George was one not least affected by it.

Rather a sleepless night I passed, wondering fearfully if, after all, his lordship would have been unable to extricate the poor chap from this sordid entanglement. Had the creature held out for too much? Had she refused to compromise? Would there be one of those appalling legal things which our best families so often suffer? What if the victim were to cut off home?

Nor was my trepidation allayed by the cryptic remark of Mrs. Judson as I passed her at her tasks in the pantry that morning:

"A prince in his palace not too good—that's what I said!"

She shot the thing at me with a manner suspiciously near to flippancy. I sternly demanded her meaning.

"I mean what I mean," she retorted, shutting her lips upon it in a definite way she has. Well enough I knew the import of her uncivil speech, but I resolved not to bandy words with her, because in my position it would be undignified; because, further, of an unfortunate effect she has upon my temper at such times.

"She's being terrible careful about *her* associates," she presently went on, with a most irritating effect of addressing only herself; "nothing at all but just dukes and earls and lords day in and day out!" Too often when the woman seems to wish it she contrives to get me in motion, as the American saying is.

"And it is deeply to be regretted," I replied with dignity, "that other persons must say less of themselves if put to it."

Well she knew what I meant. Despite my previous clear warning, she had more than once accepted small gifts from the cattle-persons, Hank and Buck, and had even been seen brazenly in public with them at a cinema palace. One of a more suspicious nature than I might have guessed that she conducted herself thus for the specific purpose of enraging me, but I am glad to say that no nature could be more free than mine from vulgar jealousy, and I spoke now from the mere wish that she should more carefully guard her reputation. As before, she exhibited a surprising meekness under this rebuke, though I uneasily wondered if there might not be guile beneath it.

"Can I help it," she asked, "if they like to show me attentions? I guess I'm a free woman." She lifted her head to observe a glass she had polished. Her eyes were curiously lighted. She had this way of embarrassing me. And invariably, moreover, she aroused all that is evil in my nature against the two cattle-persons, especially the Buck one, actually on another occasion professing admiration for "his wavy chestnut hair!" I saw now that I could not trust myself to speak of the fellow. I took up another matter.

"That baby of yours is too horribly fat," I said suddenly. I had long meant to put this to her. "It's too fat. It eats too much!"

To my amazement the creature was transformed into a vixen.

"It—it! Too fat! You call my boy 'it' and say he's too fat! Don't you dare! What does a creature like you know of babies? Why, you wouldn't even know——"

But the thing was too painful. Let her angry words be forgotten. Suffice to say, she permitted herself to cry out things that might have given grave offence to one less certain of himself than I. Rather chilled I admit I was by her frenzied outburst. I was shrewd enough to see instantly that anything in the nature of a criticism of her offspring must be led up to, rather; perhaps couched in less direct phrases than I had chosen. Fearful I was that she would burst into another torrent of rage, but to my amazement she all at once smiled.

"What a fool I am!" she exclaimed. "Kidding me, were you? Trying to make me mad about the baby. Well, I'll give you good. You did it. Yes, sir, I never would have thought you had a kidding streak in you—old glum-face!"

"Little you know me," I retorted, and quickly withdrew, for I was then more embarrassed than ever, and, besides, there were other and graver matters forward to depress and occupy me.

In my fitful sleep of the night before I had dreamed vividly that I saw the Honourable George being dragged shackled to the altar. I trust I am not superstitious, but the vision had remained with me in all its tormenting detail. A veiled woman had grimly awaited him as he struggled with his uniformed captors. I mean to say, he was being hustled along by two constables.

That day, let me now put down, was to be a day of the most fearful shocks that a man of rather sensitive nervous organism has ever been called upon to endure. There are now lines in my face that I make no doubt showed then for the first time.

And it was a day that dragged interminably, so that I became fair off my head with the suspense of it, feeling that at any moment the worst might happen. For hours I saw no one with whom I could consult. Once I was almost moved to call up Belknap-Jackson, so intolerable was the menacing uncertainty; but this I knew bordered on hysteria, and I restrained the impulse with an iron will.

But I wretchedly longed for a sight of Cousin Egbert or the Mixer, or even of the Honourable George; some one to assure me that my horrid dream of the night before had been a baseless fabric, as the saying is. The very absence of these people and of his lordship was in itself ominous.

Nervously I kept to a post at one of my windows where I could survey the street. And here at mid-day I sustained my first shock. Terrific it was. His lordship had emerged from the chemist's across the street. He paused a moment, as if to recall his next mission, then walked briskly off. And this is what I had been stupefied to note: he was clean shaven! The Brinstead side-whiskers were gone! Whiskers that had been worn in precisely that fashion by a tremendous line of the Earls of Brinstead! And the tenth of his line had abandoned them. As well, I thought, could he have defaced the Brinstead arms.

It was plain as a pillar-box, indeed. The woman had our family at her mercy, and she would show no mercy. My heart sank as I pictured the Honourable George in her toils. My dream had been prophetic. Then I reflected that this very circumstance of his lordship's having pandered to her lawless whim about his beard would go to show he had not yet given up the fight. If the thing were hopeless I knew he would have seen her—dashed—before he would have relinquished it. There plainly was still hope for poor George. Indeed his lordship might well have planned some splendid coup; this defacement would be a part of his strategy, suffered in anguish for his ultimate triumph. Quite cheered I became at the thought. I still scanned the street crowd for some one who could acquaint me with developments I must have missed.

But then a moment later came the call by telephone of Belknap-Jackson. I answered it, though with little hope than to hear more of his unending complaints about his lordship's negligence. Startled instantly I was, however, for his voice was stranger than I had known it even in moments of his acutest distress. Hoarse it was, and his words alarming but hardly intelligible.

"Heard?—My God!—Heard?—My God!—Marriage! Marriage! God!" But here he broke off into the most appalling laughter—the blood-curdling laughter of a chained patient in a mad-house. Hardly could I endure it and grateful I was when I heard the line close. Even when he attempted vocables he had sounded quite like an inferior record on a phonographic machine. But I had heard enough to leave me aghast. Beyond doubt now the very worst had come upon our family. His lordship's tremendous sacrifice would have been all in vain. Marriage! The Honourable George was done for. Better had it been the typing-girl, I bitterly reflected. Her father had at least been a curate!

Thankful enough I now was for the luncheon-hour rush: I could distract myself from the appalling disaster. That day I took rather more than my accustomed charge of the serving. I chatted with our business chaps, recommending the joint in the highest terms; drawing corks; seeing that the relish was abundantly stocked at every table. I was striving to forget.

Mrs. Judson alone persisted in reminding me of the impending scandal. "A prince in his palace," she would maliciously murmur as I encountered her. I think she must have observed that I was bitter, for she at last spoke quite amiably of our morning's dust-up.

"You certainly got my goat," she said in the quaint American fashion, "telling me little No-no was too fat. You had me going there for a minute, thinking you meant it!"

The creature's name was Albert, yet she persisted in calling it "No-no," because the child itself would thus falsely declare its name upon being questioned, having in some strange manner gained this impression. It was another matter I meant to bring to her attention, but at this crisis I had no heart for it.

My crowd left. I was again alone to muse bitterly upon our plight. Still I scanned the street, hoping for a sight of Cousin Egbert, who, I fancied, would be informed as to the wretched details. Instead, now, I saw the Honourable George. He walked on the opposite side of the thoroughfare, his manner of dejection precisely what I should have expected. Followed closely as usual he was by the Judson cur. A spirit of desperate mockery seized me. I called to Mrs. Judson, who was gathering glasses from a table. I indicated the pair.

"Mr. Barker," I said, "is dogging his footsteps." I mean to say, I uttered the words in the most solemn manner. Little the woman knew that one may often be moved in the most distressing moments to a jest of this sort. She laughed heartily, being of quick discernment. And thus jauntily did I carry my knowledge of the lowering cloud. But I permitted myself no further sallies of that sort. I stayed expectantly by the window, and I dare say my bearing would have deceived the most alert. I was steadily calm. The situation called precisely for that.

The hours sped darkly and my fears mounted. In sheer desperation, at length, I had myself put through to Belknap-Jackson. To my astonishment he seemed quite revived, though in a state of feverish gayety. He fair bubbled.

"Just leaving this moment with his lordship to gather up some friends. We meet at your place. Yes, yes—all the uncertainty is past. Better set up that largest table—rather a celebration."

Almost more confusing it was than his former message, which had been confined to calls upon his Maker and to maniac laughter. Was he, I wondered, merely making the best of it? Had he resolved to be a dead sportsman? A few moments later he discharged his lordship at my door and drove rapidly on. (Only a question of time it is when he will be had heavily for damages due to his reckless driving.)

His lordship bustled in with a cheerfulness that staggered me. He, too, was gay; almost debonair. A gardenia was in his lapel. He was vogue to the last detail in a form-fitting gray morning-suit that had all the style essentials. Almost it seemed as if three valets had been needed to groom him. He briskly rubbed his hands.

"Biggest table—people. Tea, that sort of thing. Have a go of champagne, too, what, what! Beard off, much younger appearing? Of course, course! Trust women, those matters. Tea cake, toast, crumpets, marmalade—things like that. Plenty champagne! Not happen every day! Ha! ha!"

To my acute distress he here thumbed me in the ribs and laughed again. Was he, too, I wondered, madly resolved to be a dead sportsman in the face of the unavoidable? I sought to edge in a discreet word of condolence, for I knew that between us there need be no pretence.

"I know you did your best, sir," I observed. "And I was never quite free of a fear that the woman would prove too many for us. I trust the Honourable George——"

But I had said as much as he would let me. He interrupted me with his thumb again, and on his face was what in a lesser person I should unhesitatingly have called a leer.

"You dog, you! Woman prove too many for us, what, what! Dare say you knew what to expect. Silly old George! Though how she could ever have fancied the juggins——"

I was about to remark that the creature had of course played her game from entirely sordid motives and I should doubtless have ventured to applaud the game spirit in which he was taking the blow. But before I could shape my phrases on this delicate ground Mrs. Effie, the Senator, and Cousin Egbert arrived. They somewhat formally had the air of being expected. All of them rushed upon his lordship with an excessive manner. Apparently they were all to be dead sportsmen together. And then Mrs. Effie called me aside.

"You can do me a favour," she began. "About the wedding breakfast and reception. Dear Kate's place is so small. It wouldn't do. There will be a crush, of course. I've had the loveliest idea for it—our own house. You know how delighted we'd be. The Earl has been so charming and everything has turned out so splendidly. Oh, I'd love to do them this little parting kindness. Use your influence like a good fellow, won't you, when the thing is suggested?"

"Only too gladly," I responded, sick at heart, and she returned to the group. Well I knew her motive. She was by way of getting even with the Belknap-Jacksons. As Cousin Egbert in his American fashion would put it, she was trying to pass them a bison. But I was willing enough she should house the dreadful affair. The more private the better, thought I.

A moment later Belknap-Jackson's car appeared at my door, now discharging the Klondike woman, effusively escorted by the Mixer and by Mrs. Belknap-Jackson. The latter at least, I had thought, would show more principle. But she had buckled atrociously, quite as had her husband, who had quickly, almost merrily, followed them. There was increased gayety as they seated themselves about the large table, a silly noise of pretended felicitation over a calamity that not even the tenth Earl of Brinstead had been able to avert. And then Belknap-Jackson beckoned me aside.

"I want your help, old chap, in case it's needed," he began.

"The wedding breakfast and reception?" I said quite cynically.

"You've thought of it? Good! Her own place is far too small. Crowd, of course. And it's rather proper at our place, too, his lordship having been our house guest. You see? Use what influence you have. The affair will be rather widely commented on—even the New York papers, I dare say."

"Count upon me," I answered blandly, even as I had promised Mrs. Effie. Disgusted I was. Let them maul each other about over the wretched "honour." They could all be dead sports if they chose, but I was now firmly resolved that for myself I should make not a bit of pretence. The creature might trick poor George into a marriage, but I for one would not affect to regard it as other than a blight upon our house. I was just on the point of hoping that the victim himself might have cut off to unknown parts when I saw him enter. By the other members of the party he was hailed with cries of delight, though his own air was finely honest, being dejected in the extreme. He was dressed as regrettably as usual, this time in parts of two lounge-suits.

As he joined those at the table I constrained myself to serve the champagne. Senator Floud arose with a brimming glass.

"My friends," he began in his public-speaking manner, "let us remember that Red Gap's loss is England's gain—to the future Countess of Brinstead!"

To my astonishment this appalling breach of good taste was received with the loudest applause, nor was his lordship the least clamorous of them. I mean to say, the chap had as good as wished that his lordship would directly pop off. It was beyond me. I walked to the farthest window and stood a long time gazing pensively out; I wished to be away from that false show. But they noticed my absence at length and called to me. Monstrously I was desired to drink to the happiness of the groom. I thought they were pressing me too far, but as they quite gabbled now with their tea and things, I hoped to pass it off. The Senator, however, seemed to fasten me with his eye as he proposed the toast—"To the happy man!"

I drank perforce.

"A body would think Bill was drinking to the Judge," remarked Cousin Egbert in a high voice.

"Eh?" I said, startled to this outburst by his strange words.

"Good old George!" exclaimed his lordship. "Owe it all to the old juggins, what, what!"

The Klondike person spoke. I heard her voice as a bell pealing through breakers at sea. I mean to say, I was now fair dazed.

"Not to old George," said she. "To old Ruggles!"

"To old Ruggles!" promptly cried the Senator, and they drank.

Muddled indeed I was. Again in my eventful career I felt myself tremble; I knew not what I should say, any *savoir faire* being quite gone. I had received a crumpler of some sort—but what *sort?*

My sleeve was touched. I turned blindly, as in a nightmare. The Hobbs cub who was my vestiare was handing me our evening paper. I took it from him, staring—staring until my knees grew weak. Across the page in clarion type rang the unbelievable words:

BRITISH PEER WINS AMERICAN BRIDE

His Lordship Tenth Earl of Brinstead to Wed One of Red Gap's Fairest Daughters

My hands so shook that in quick subterfuge I dropped the sheet, then stooped for it, trusting to control myself before I again raised my face. Mercifully the others were diverted by the journal. It was seized from me, passed from hand to hand, the incredible words read aloud by each in turn. They jested of it!

"Amazing chaps, your pressmen!" Thus the tenth Earl of Brinstead, while I pinched myself viciously to bring back my lost aplomb. "Speedy beggars, what, what! Never knew it myself till last night. She would and she wouldn't."

"I think you knew," said the lady. Stricken as I was I noted that she eyed him rather strangely, quite as if she felt some decent respect for him.

"Marriage is serious," boomed the Mixer.

"Don't blame her, don't blame her—swear I don't!" returned his lordship. "Few days to think it over—quite right, quite right. Got to know their own minds, my word!"

While their attention was thus mercifully diverted from me, my own world by painful degrees resumed its stability. I mean to say, I am not the fainting sort, but if I were, then I should have keeled over at my first sight of that journal. But now I merely recovered my glass of champagne and drained it. Rather pigged it a bit, I fancy. Badly needing a stimulant I was, to be sure.

They now discussed details: the ceremony—that sort of thing.

"Before a registrar, quickest way," said his lordship.

"Nonsense! Church, of course!" rumbled the Mixer very arbitrarily.

"Quite so, then," assented his lordship. "Get me the rector of the parish—a vicar, a curate, something of that sort."

"Then the breakfast and reception," suggested Mrs. Effie with a meaning glance at me before she turned to the lady. "Of course, dearest, your own tiny nest would never hold your host of friends——"

"I've never noticed," said the other quickly. "It's always seemed big enough," she added in pensive tones and with downcast eyes.

"Oh, not large enough by half," put in Belknap-Jackson, "Most charming little home-nook but worlds too small for all your well-wishers." With a glance at me he narrowed his eyes in friendly calculation. "I'm somewhat puzzled myself— Suppose we see what the capable Ruggles has to suggest."

"Let Ruggles suggest something by all means!" cried Mrs. Effie.

I mean to say, they both quite thought they knew what I would suggest, but it was nothing of the sort. The situation had entirely changed. Quite another sort of thing it was. Quickly I resolved to fling them both aside. I, too, would be a dead sportsman.

"I was about to suggest," I remarked, "that my place here is the only one at all suitable for the breakfast and reception. I can promise that the affair will go off smartly."

The two had looked up with such radiant expectation at my opening words and were so plainly in a state at my conclusion that I dare say the future Countess of Brinstead at once knew what. She flashed them a look, then eyed me with quick understanding.

"Great!" she exclaimed in a hearty American manner. "Then that's settled," she continued briskly, as both Belknap-Jackson and Mrs. Effie would have interposed "Ruggles shall do everything: take it off our shoulders—ices, flowers, invitations."

"The invitation list will need great care, of course," remarked Belknap-Jackson with a quite savage glance at me.

"But you just called him 'the capable Ruggles,'" insisted the fiancée. "We shall leave it all to him. How many will you ask, Ruggles?" Her eyes flicked from mine to Belknap-Jackson.

"Quite almost every one," I answered firmly.

"Fine!" she said.

"Ripping!" said his lordship.

"His lordship will of course wish a best man," suggested Belknap-Jackson. "I should be only too glad——"

"You're going to suggest Ruggles again!" cried the lady. "Just the man for it! You're quite right. Why, we owe it all to Ruggles, don't we?"

She here beamed upon his lordship. Belknap-Jackson wore an expression of the keenest disrelish.

"Of course, course!" replied his lordship. "Dashed good man, Ruggles! Owe it all to him, what, what!"

I fancy in the cordial excitement of the moment he was quite sincere. As to her ladyship, I am to this day unable to still a faint suspicion that she was having me on. True, she owed it all to me. But I hadn't a bit meant it and well she knew it. Subtle she was, I dare say, but bore me no malice, though she was not above setting Belknap-Jackson back a pace or two each time he moved up.

A final toast was drunk and my guests drifted out. Belknap-Jackson again glared savagely at me as he went, but Mrs. Effie rather outglared him. Even I should hardly have cared to face her at that moment.

And I was still in a high state of muddle. It was all beyond me. Had his lordship, I wondered, too seriously taken my careless words about American equality? Of course I had meant them to apply only to those stopping on in the States.

Cousin Egbert lingered to the last, rather with a troubled air of wishing to consult me. When I at length came up with him he held the journal before me, indicating lines in the article—"relict of an Alaskan capitalist, now for some years one of Red Gap's social favourites."

"Read that there," he commanded grimly. Then with a terrific earnestness I had never before remarked in him: "Say, listen here! I better go round right off and mix it up with that fresh guy. What's he hinting around at by that there word 'relict'? Why, say, she was married to him——"

I hastily corrected his preposterous interpretation of the word, much to his relief.

I was still in my precious state of muddle. Mrs. Judson took occasion to flounce by me in her work of clearing the table.

"A prince in his palace," she taunted. I laughed in a lofty manner.

"Why, you poor thing, I've known it all for some days," I said.

"Well, I must say you're the deep one if you did—never letting on!"

She was unable to repress a glance of admiration at me as she moved off.

I stood where she had left me, meditating profoundly.

CHAPTER TWENTY

Two days later at high noon was solemnized the marriage of his lordship to the woman who, without a bit meaning it, I had so curiously caused to enter his life. The day was for myself so crowded with emotions that it returns in rather a jumble: patches of incidents, little floating clouds of memory; some meaningless and one at least to be significant to my last day.

The ceremony was had in our most nearly smart church. It was only a Methodist church, but I took pains to assure myself that a ceremony performed by its curate would be legal. I still seem to hear the organ, strains of "The Voice That Breathed Through Eden," as we neared the altar; also the Mixer's rumbling whisper about a lost handkerchief which she apparently found herself needing at that moment.

The responses of bride and groom were unhesitating, even firm. Her ladyship, I thought, had never appeared to better advantage than in the pearl-tinted lustreless going-away gown she had chosen. As always, she had finely known what to put on her head.

Senator Floud, despite Belknap-Jackson's suggestion of himself for the office, had been selected to give away the bride, as the saying is. He performed his function with dignity, though I recall being seized with horror when the moment came; almost certain I am he restrained himself with difficulty from making a sort of a speech.

The church was thronged. I had seen to that. I had told her ladyship that I should ask quite almost every one, and this I had done, squarely in the face of Belknap-Jackson's pleading that discretion be used. For a great white light, as one might say, had now suffused me. I had seen that the moment was come when the warring factions of Red Gap should be reunited. A Bismarck I felt myself, indeed. That I acted ably was later to be seen.

Even for the wedding breakfast, which occurred directly after the ceremony, I had shown myself a dictator in the matter of guests. Covers were laid in my room for seventy and among these were included not only the members of the North Side set and the entire Bohemian set, but many worthy persons not hitherto socially existent yet who had been friends or well-wishers of the bride.

I am persuaded to confess that in a few of these instances I was not above a snarky little wish to correct the social horizon of Belknap-Jackson; to make it more broadly accord, as I may say, with the spirit of American equality for which their forefathers bled and died on the battlefields of Boston, New York, and Vicksburg.

Not the least of my reward, then, was to see his eyebrows more than once eloquently raise, as when the cattle-persons, Hank and Buck, appeared in suits of decent black, or when the driver chap Pierce entered with his quite obscure mother on his arm, or a few other cattle and horse persons with whom the Honourable George had palled up during his process of going in for America.

This laxity I felt that the Earl of Brinstead and his bride could amply afford, while for myself I had soundly determined that Red Gap should henceforth be without "sets." I mean to say, having frankly taken up America, I was at last resolved to do it whole-heartedly. If I could not take up the whole of it, I would not take up a part. Quite instinctively I had chosen the slogan of our Chamber of Commerce: "Don't Knock—Boost; and Boost Altogether." Rudely worded though it is, I had seen it to be sound in spirit.

These thoughts ran in my mind during the smart repast that now followed. Insidiously I wrought among the guests to amalgamate into one friendly whole certain elements that had hitherto been hostile. The Bohemian set was not segregated. Almost my first inspiration had been to scatter its members widely among the conservative pillars of the North Side set. Left in one group, I had known they would plume themselves quite intolerably over the signal triumph of their leader; perhaps, in the American speech, "start something." Widely scattered, they became mere parts of the whole I was seeking to achieve.

The banquet progressed gayly to its finish. Toasts were drunk no end, all of them proposed by Senator Floud who, toward the last, kept almost constantly on his feet. From the bride and groom he expanded geographically through Red Gap, the Kulanche Valley, the State of Washington, and the United States to the British Empire, not omitting the Honourable George—who, I noticed, called for the relish and consumed quite almost an entire bottle during the meal. Also I was proposed—"through whose lifelong friendship for the illustrious groom this meeting of hearts and hands has been so happily brought about."

Her ladyship's eyes rested briefly upon mine as her lips touched the glass to this. They conveyed the unspeakable. Rather a fool I felt, and unable to look away until she released me. She had been wondrously quiet through it all. Not dazed in the least, as might have been looked for in one of her lowly station thus prodigiously elevated; and not feverishly gay, as might also have been anticipated. Simple and quiet she was, showing a complete but perfectly controlled awareness of her position.

For the first time then, I think, I did envision her as the Countess of Brinstead. She was going to carry it off. Perhaps quite as well as even I could have wished his lordship's chosen mate to do. I observed her look at his lordship with those strange lights in her eyes, as if only half realizing yet wholly believing all that he believed. And once at the height of the gayety I saw her reach out to touch his sleeve, furtively, swiftly, and so gently he never knew.

It occurred to me there were things about the woman we had taken too little trouble to know. I wondered what old memories might be coming to her now; what staring faces might obtrude, what old, far-off, perhaps hated, voices might be sounding to her; what of remembered hurts and heartaches might newly echo back to make her flinch and wonder if she dreamed. She touched the sleeve again, as it might have been in protection from them, her eyes narrowed, her gaze fixed. It queerly occurred to me that his lordship might find her as difficult to know as we had—and yet would keep always trying more than we had, to be sure. I mean to say, she was no gabbler.

The responses to the Senator's toasts increased in volume. His final flight, I recall, involved terms like "our blood-cousins of the British Isles," and introduced a figure of speech about "hands across the sea," which I thought striking, indeed. The applause aroused by this was noisy in the extreme, a number of the cattle and horse persons, including the redskin Tuttle, emitting a shrill, concerted "yipping" which, though it would never have done with us, seemed somehow not out of place in North America, although I observed Belknap-Jackson to make gestures of extreme repugnance while it lasted.

There ensued a rather flurried wishing of happiness to the pair. A novel sight it was, the most austere matrons of the North Side set vying for places in the line that led past them. I found myself trying to analyze the inner emotions of some of them I best knew as they fondly greeted the now radiant Countess of Brinstead. But that way madness lay, as Shakespeare has so aptly said of another matter. I recalled, though, the low-toned comment of Cousin Egbert, who stood near me.

"Don't them dames stand the gaff noble!" It was quite true. They were heroic. I recalled then his other quaint prophecy that her ladyship would hand them a bottle of lemonade. As is curiously usual with this simple soul, he had gone to the heart of the matter.

The throng dwindled to the more intimate friends. Among those who lingered were the Belknap-Jacksons and Mrs. Effie. Quite solicitous they were for the "dear Countess," as they rather defiantly called her to one another. Belknap-Jackson casually mentioned in my hearing that he had been asked to Chaynes-Wotten for the shooting. Mrs. Effie, who also heard, swiftly remarked that she would doubtless run over in the spring—the dear Earl was so insistent. They rather glared at each other. But in truth his lordship had insisted that quite almost every one should come and stop on with him.

"Of course, course, what, what! Jolly party, no end of fun. Week-end, that sort of thing. Know she'll like her old friends best. Wouldn't be keen for the creature if she'd not. Have 'em all, have 'em all. Capital, by Jove!"

To be sure it was a manner of speaking, born of the expansive good feeling of the moment. Yet I believe Cousin Egbert was the only invited one to decline. He did so with evident distress at having to refuse.

"I like your little woman a whole lot," he observed to his lordship, "but Europe is too kind of uncomfortable for me; keeps me upset all the time, what with all the foreigners and one thing and another. But, listen here, Cap! You pack the little woman back once in a while. Just to give us a flash at her. We'll give you both a good time."

"What ho!" returned his lordship. "Of course, course! Fancy we'd like it vastly, what, what!"

"Yes, sir, I fancy you would, too," and rather startlingly Cousin Egbert seized her ladyship and kissed her heartily. Whereupon her ladyship kissed the fellow in return.

"Yes, sir, I dare say I fancy you would," he called back a bit nervously as he left.

Belknap-Jackson drove the party to the station, feeling, I am sure, that he scored over Mrs. Effie, though he was obliged to include the Mixer, from whom her ladyship bluntly refused to be separated. I inferred that she must have found the time and seclusion in which to weep a bit on the Mixer's shoulder. The waist of the latter's purple satin gown was quite spotty at the height of her ladyship's eyes.

Belknap-Jackson on this occasion drove his car with the greatest solicitude, proceeding more slowly than I had ever known him do. As I attended to certain luggage details at the station he was regretting to his lordship that they had not had a longer time at the country club the day it was exhibited.

"Look a bit after silly old George," said his lordship to me at parting. "Chap's dotty, I dare say. Talking about a plantation of apple trees now. For his old age—that sort of thing. Be something new in a fortnight, though. Like him, of course, course!"

Her ladyship closed upon my hand with a remarkable vigour of grip.

"We owe it all to you," she said, again with dancing eyes. Then her eyes steadied queerly. "Maybe you won't be sorry."

"Know I shan't." I fancy I rather growled it, stupidly feeling I was not rising to the occasion. "Knew his lordship wouldn't rest till he had you where he wanted you. Glad he's got you." And curiously I felt a bit of a glad little squeeze in my throat for her. I groped for something light—something American.

"You are some Countess," I at last added in a silly way.

"What, what!" said his lordship, but I had caught her eyes. They brimmed with understanding.

With the going of that train all life seemed to go. I mean to say, things all at once became flat. I turned to the dull station.

"Give you a lift, old chap," said Belknap-Jackson. Again he was cordial. So firmly had I kept the reins of the whole affair in my grasp, such prestige he knew it would give me, he dared not broach his grievance.

Some half-remembered American phrase of Cousin Egbert's ran in my mind. I had put a buffalo on him!

"Thank you," I said, "I'm needing a bit of a stretch and a breeze-out."

I wished to walk that I might the better meditate. With Belknap-Jackson one does not sufficiently meditate.

A block up from the station I was struck by the sight of the Honourable George. Plodding solitary down that low street he was, heeled as usual by the Judson cur. He came to the Spilmer public house and for a moment stared up, quite still, at the "Last Chance" on its chaffing signboard. Then he wheeled abruptly and entered. I was moved to follow him, but I knew it would never do. He would row me about the service of the Grill—something of that sort. I dare say he had fancied her ladyship as keenly as one of his volatile nature might. But I knew him!

Back on our street the festival atmosphere still lingered. Groups of recent guests paused to discuss the astounding event. The afternoon paper was being scanned by many of them. An account of the wedding was its "feature," as they say. I had no heart for that, but on the second page my eye caught a minor item:

> "A special meeting of the Ladies Onwards and Upwards Club is called for to-morrow afternoon at two sharp at the residence of Mrs. Dr. Percy Hailey Martingale, for the transaction of important business."

One could fancy, I thought, what the meeting would discuss. Nor was I wrong, for I may here state that the evening paper of the following day disclosed that her ladyship the Countess of Brinstead had unanimously been elected to a life honorary membership in the club.

Back in the Grill I found the work of clearing the tables well advanced, and very soon its before-dinner aspect of calm waiting was restored. Surveying it I reflected that one might well wonder if aught momentous had indeed so lately occurred here. A motley day it had been.

I passed into the linen and glass pantry.

Mrs. Judson, polishing my glassware, burst into tears at my approach, frankly stanching them with her towel. I saw it to be a mere overflow of the meaningless emotion that women stock so abundantly on the occasion of a wedding. She is an almost intensely feminine person, as can be seen at once by any one who understands women. In a goods box in the passage beyond I noted her nipper fast asleep, a mammoth beef-rib clasped to its fat chest. I debated putting this abuse to her once more but feared the moment was not propitious. She dried her eyes and smiled again.

"A prince in his palace," she murmured inanely. "She thought first he was going to be as funny as the other one; then she found he wasn't. I liked him, too. I didn't blame her a bit. He's one of that kind—his bark's worse than his bite. And to think you knew all the time what was coming off. My, but you're the Mr. Deep-one!"

I saw no reason to stultify myself by denying this. I mean to say, if she thought it, let her!

"The last thing yesterday she gave me this dress."

I had already noted the very becoming dull blue house gown she wore. Quite with an air she carried it. To be sure, it was not suitable to her duties. The excitements of the day, I suppose, had rendered me a bit sterner than is my wont. Perhaps a little authoritative.

"A handsome gown," I replied icily, "but one would hardly choose it for the work you are performing."

"Rubbish!" she retorted plainly. "I wanted to look nice—I had to go in there lots of times. And I wanted to be dressed for to-night."

"Why to-night, may I ask?" I was all at once uncomfortably curious.

"Why, the boys are coming for me. They're going to take No-no home, then we're all going to the movies. They've got a new bill at the Bijou, and Buck Edwards especially wants me to see it. One of the cowboys in it that does some star riding looks just like Buck—wavy chestnut hair. Buck himself is one of the best riders in the whole Kulanche."

The woman seemed to have some fiendish power to enrage me. As she prattled thus, her eyes demurely on the glass she dried, I felt a deep flush mantle my brow. She could never have dreamed that she had this malign power, but she was now at least to suspect it.

"Your Mr. Edwards," I began calmly enough, "may be like the cinema actor: the two may be as like each other as makes no difference—but you are not going." I was aware that the latter phrase was heated where I had merely meant it to be impressive. Dignified firmness had been the line I intended, but my rage was mounting. She stared at me. Astonished beyond words she was, if I can read human expressions.

"I am!" she snapped at last.

"You are not!" I repeated, stepping a bit toward her. I was conscious of a bit of the rowdy in my manner, but I seemed powerless to prevent it. All my culture was again but the flimsiest veneer.

"I am, too!" she again said, though plainly dismayed.

"No!" I quite thundered it, I dare say. "No, no! No, no!"

The nipper cried out from his box. Not until later did it occur to me that he had considered himself to be addressed in angry tones.

"No, no!" I thundered again. I couldn't help myself, though silly rot I call it now. And then to my horror the mother herself began to weep.

"I will!" she sobbed. "I will! I will! I will!"

"No, no!" I insisted, and I found myself seizing her shoulders, not knowing if I mightn't shake her smartly, so drawn-out had the woman got me; and still I kept shouting my senseless "No, no!" at which the nipper was now yelling.

She struggled her best as I clutched her, but I seemed to have the strength of a dozen men; the woman was nothing in my grasp, and my arms were taking their blind rage out on her.

Secure I held her, and presently she no longer struggled, and I was curiously no longer angry, but found myself soothing her in many strange ways. I mean to say, the passage between us had fallen to be of the very shockingly most sentimental character.

"You are so masterful!" she panted.

"I'll have my own way," I threatened; "I've told you often enough."

"Oh, you're so domineering!" she murmured. I dare say I am a bit that way.

"I'll show you who's to be master!"

"But I never dreamed you meant this," she answered. True, I had most brutally taken her by surprise. I could easily see how, expecting nothing of the faintest sort, she had been rudely shocked.

"I meant it all along," I said firmly, "from the very first moment." And now again she spoke in almost awed tones of my "deepness." I have never believed in that excessive intuition which is so widely boasted for woman.

"I never dreamed of it," she said again, and added: "Mrs. Kenner and I were talking about this dress only last night and I said—I never, never dreamed of such a thing!" She broke off with sudden inconsequence, as women will.

We had now to quiet the nipper in his box. I saw even then that, domineering though I may be, I should probably never care to bring the child's condition to her notice again. There was something about her—something volcanic in her femininity. I knew it would never do. Better let the thing continue to be a monstrosity! I might, unnoticed, of course, snatch a bun from its grasp now and then.

Our evening rush came and went quite as if nothing had happened. I may have been rather absent, reflecting pensively. I mean to say, I had at times considered this alliance as a dawning possibility, but never had I meant to be sudden. Only for the woman's remarkably stubborn obtuseness I dare say the understanding might have been deferred to a more suitable moment and arranged in a calm and orderly manner. But the die was cast. Like his lordship, I had chosen an American bride—taken her by storm and carried her off her feet before she knew it. We English are often that way.

At ten o'clock we closed the Grill upon a day that had been historic in the truest sense of the word. I shouldered the sleeping nipper. He still passionately clutched the beef-rib and for some reason I felt averse to depriving him of it, even though it would mean a spotty top-coat.

Strangely enough, we talked but little in our walk. It seemed rather too tremendous to talk of.

When I gave the child into her arms at the door it had become half awake.

"Ruggums!" it muttered sleepily.

"Ruggums!" echoed the mother, and again, very softly in the still night: "Ruggums—Ruggums!"

That in the few months since that rather agreeable night I have acquired the title of Red Gap's social dictator cannot be denied. More than one person of discernment may now be heard to speak of my "reign," though this, of course, is coming it a bit thick.

The removal by his lordship of one who, despite her sterling qualities, had been a source of discord, left the social elements of the town in a state of the wildest disorganization. And having for myself acquired a remarkable prestige from my intimate association with the affair, I promptly seized the reins and drew the scattered forces together.

First, at an early day I sought an interview with Belknap-Jackson and Mrs. Effie and told them straight precisely why I had played them both false in the matter of the wedding breakfast. With the honour granted to either of them, I explained, I had foreseen another era of cliques, divisions, and acrimony. Therefore I had done the thing myself, as a measure of peace.

Flatly then I declared my intention of reconciling all those formerly opposed elements and of creating a society in Red Gap that would be a social union in the finest sense of the word. I said that contact with their curious American life had taught me that their equality should be more than a name, and that, especially in the younger settlements, a certain relaxation from the rigid requirements of an older order is not only unavoidable but vastly to be desired. I meant to say, if we were going to be Americans it was silly rot trying to be English at the same time.

I pointed out that their former social leaders had ever been inspired by the idea of exclusion; the soul of their leadership had been to cast others out; and that the campaign I planned was to be one of inclusion—even to the extent of Bohemians and well-behaved cattle-persons—-which I believed to be in the finest harmony with their North American theory of human association. It might be thought a naïve theory, I said, but so long as they had chosen it I should staunchly abide by it.

I added what I dare say they did not believe: that the position of leader was not one I should cherish for any other reason than the public good. That when one better fitted might appear they would find me the first to rejoice.

I need not say that I was interrupted frequently and acridly during this harangue, but I had given them both a buffalo and well they knew it. And I worked swiftly from that moment. I gave the following week the first of a series of subscription balls in the dancing hall above the Grill, and both Mrs. Belknap-Jackson and Mrs. Effie early enrolled themselves as patronesses, even after I had made it plain that I alone should name the guests.

The success of the affair was all I could have wished. Red Gap had become a social unit. Nor was appreciation for my leadership wanting. There will be malcontents, I foresee, and from the informed inner circles I learn that I have already been slightingly spoken of as a foreigner wielding a sceptre over native-born Americans, but I have the support of quite all who really matter, and I am confident these rebellions may be put down by tact alone. It is too well understood by those who know me that I have Equality for my watchword.

I mean to say, at the next ball of the series I may even see that the fellow Hobbs has a card if I can become assured that he has quite freed himself from certain debasing class-ideals of his native country. This to be sure is an extreme case, because the fellow is that type of our serving class to whom equality is unthinkable. They must, from their centuries of servility, look either up or down; and I scarce know in which attitude they are more offensive to our American point of view. Still I mean to be broad. Even Hobbs shall have his chance with us!

It is late June. Mrs. Ruggles and I are comfortably installed in her enlarged and repaired house. We have a fowl-run on a stretch of her free-hold, and the kitchen-garden thrives under the care of the Japanese agricultural labourer I have employed.

Already I have discharged more than half my debt to Cousin Egbert, who exclaims, "Oh, shucks!" each time I make him a payment. He and the Honourable George remain pally no end and spend much of their abundant leisure at Cousin Egbert's modest country house. At times when they are in town they rather consort with street persons, but such is the breadth of our social scheme that I shall never exclude them from our gayeties, though it is true that more often than not they decline to be present.

Mrs. Ruggles, I may say, is a lady of quite amazing capacities combined strangely with the commonest feminine weaknesses. She has acute business judgment at most times, yet would fly at me in a rage if I were to say what I think of the nipper's appalling grossness. Quite naturally I do not push my unquestioned mastery to this extreme. There are other matters in which I amusedly let her have her way, though she fondly reminds me almost daily of my brutal self-will.

On one point I have just been obliged to assert this. She came running to me with a suggestion for economizing in the manufacture of the relish. She had devised a cheaper formula. But I was firm.

"So long as the inventor's face is on that flask," I said, "its contents shall not be debased a tuppence. My name and face will guarantee its purity."

She gave in nicely, merely declaring that I needn't growl like one of their bears with a painful foot.

At my carefully mild suggestion she has just brought the nipper in from where he was cattying the young fowls, much to their detriment. But she is now heaping compote upon a slice of thickly buttered bread for him, glancing meanwhile at our evening newspaper.

"Ruggums always has his awful own way, doesn't ums?" she remarks to the nipper.

Deeply ignoring this, I resume my elocutionary studies of the Declaration of Independence. For I should say that a signal honour of a municipal character has just been done me. A committee of the Chamber of Commerce has invited me to participate in their exercises on an early day in July—the fourth, I fancy—when they celebrate the issuance of this famous document. I have been asked to read it, preceding a patriotic address to be made by Senator Floud.

I accepted with the utmost pleasure, and now on my vine-sheltered porch have begun trying it out for the proper voice effects. Its substance, I need not say, is already familiar to me.

The nipper is horribly gulping at its food, jam smears quite all about its countenance. Mrs. Ruggles glances over her journal.

"How would you like it," she suddenly demands, "if I went around town like these English women—burning churches and houses of Parliament and cutting up fine oil paintings. How would that suit your grouchy highness?"

"This is not England," I answer shortly. "That sort of thing would never do with us."

"My, but isn't he the fierce old Ruggums!" she cries in affected alarm to the now half-suffocated nipper.

Once more I take up the Declaration of Independence. It lends itself rather well to reciting. I feel that my voice is going to carry.

THE END

BOOK
TWO

MERT
ON OF
THE
MOVIE
S

To George Ade

CHAPTER I. DIRTY WORK AT THE BORDER

At the very beginning of the tale there comes a moment of puzzled hesitation. One way of approach is set beside another for choice, and a third contrived for better choice. Still the puzzle persists, all because the one precisely right way might seem—shall we say intense, high keyed, clamorous? Yet if one way is the only right way, why pause? Courage! Slightly dazed, though certain, let us be on, into the shrill thick of it. So, then—

Out there in the great open spaces where men are men, a clash of primitive hearts and the coming of young love into its own! Well had it been for Estelle St. Clair if she had not wandered from the Fordyce ranch. A moment's delay in the arrival of Buck Benson, a second of fear in that brave heart, and hers would have been a fate worse than death.

Had she not been warned of Snake le Vasquez, the outlaw—his base threat to win her by fair means or foul? Had not Buck Benson himself, that strong, silent man of the open, begged her to beware of the half-breed? Perhaps she had resented the hint of mastery in Benson's cool, quiet tones as he said, "Miss St. Clair, ma'am, I beg you not to endanger your welfare by permitting the advances of this viper. He bodes no good to such as you."

Perhaps—who knows?—Estelle St. Clair had even thought to trifle with the feelings of Snake le Vasquez, then to scorn him for his presumption. Although the beautiful New York society girl had remained unsullied in the midst of a city's profligacy, she still liked "to play with fire," as she laughingly said, and at the quiet words of Benson—Two-Gun Benson his comrades of the border called him—she had drawn herself to her full height, facing him in all her blond young beauty, and pouted adorably as she replied, "Thank you! But I can look out for myself."

Yet she had wandered on her pony farther than she meant to, and was not without trepidation at the sudden appearance of the picturesque halfbreed, his teeth flashing in an evil smile as he swept off his broad sombrero to her. Above her suddenly beating heart she sought to chat gayly, while the quick eyes of the outlaw took in the details of the smart riding costume that revealed every line of her lithe young figure. But suddenly she chilled under his hot glance that now spoke all too plainly.

"I must return to my friends," she faltered. "They will be anxious." But the fellow laughed with a sinister leer. "No—ah, no, the lovely senorita will come with me," he replied; but there was the temper of steel in his words. For Snake le Vasquez, on the border, where human life was lightly held, was known as the Slimy Viper. Of all the evil men in that inferno, Snake was the foulest. Steeped in vice, he feared neither God nor man, and respected no woman. And now, Estelle St. Clair, drawing-room pet, pampered darling of New York society, which she ruled with an iron hand from her father's Fifth Avenue mansion, regretted bitterly that she had not given heed to honest Buck Benson. Her prayers, threats, entreaties, were in vain. Despite her struggles, the blows her small fists rained upon the scoundrel's taunting face, she was borne across the border, on over the mesa, toward the lair of the outlaw.

"Have you no mercy?" she cried again and again. "Can you not see that I loathe and despise you, foul fiend that you are? Ah. God in heaven, is there no help at hand?" The outlaw remained deaf to these words that should have melted a heart of stone. At last over the burning plain was seen the ruined hovel to which the scoundrel was dragging his fair burden. It was but the work of a moment to dismount and bear her half-fainting form within the den. There he faced her, repellent with evil intentions.

"Ha, senorita, you are a beautiful wildcat, yes? But Snake le Vasquez will tame you! Ha, ha!" laughed he carelessly.

With a swift movement the beautiful girl sought to withdraw the small silver-mounted revolver without which she never left the ranch. But Snake le Vasquez, with a muttered oath, was too quick for her. He seized the toy and contemptuously hurled it across his vile den.

"Have a care, my proud beauty!" he snarled, and the next moment she was writhing in his grasp.

Little availed her puny strength. Helpless as an infant was the fair New York society girl as Snake le Vasquez, foulest of the viper breed, began to force his attention upon her. The creature's hot kisses seared her defenseless cheek. "Listen!" he hissed. "You are mine, mine at last. Here you shall remain a prisoner until you have consented to be my wife." All seemed, indeed, lost.

"Am I too late, Miss St. Clair?"

Snake le Vasquez started at the quiet, grim voice.

"Sapristi!" he snarled. "You!"

"Me!" replied Buck Benson, for it was, indeed, no other.

"Thank God, at last!" murmured Estelle St. Clair, freeing herself from the foul arms that had enfolded her slim young beauty and staggering back from him who would so basely have forced her into a distasteful marriage. In an instant she had recovered the St. Clair poise, had become every inch the New York society leader, as she replied, "Not too late, Mr. Benson! Just in time, rather. Ha, ha! This—this gentleman has become annoying. You are just in time to mete out the punishment he so justly deserves, for which I shall pray that heaven reward you."

She pointed an accusing finger at the craven wretch who had shrunk from her and now cowered at the far side of the wretched den. At that moment she was strangely thrilled. What was his power, this strong, silent man of the open with his deep reverence for pure American womanhood? True, her culture demanded a gentleman, but her heart demanded a man. Her eyes softened and fell before his cool, keen gaze, and a blush mantled her fair cheek. Could he but have known it, she stood then in meek surrender before this soft-voiced master. A tremor swept the honest rugged face of Buck Benson as heart thus called to heart. But his keen eyes flitted to Snake le Vasquez.

"Now, curse you, viper that you are, you shall fight me, by heaven! in American fashion, man to man, for, foul though you be, I hesitate to put a bullet through your craven heart."

The beautiful girl shivered with new apprehension, the eyes of Snake le Vasquez glittered with new hope. He faced his steely eyed opponent for an instant only, then with a snarl like that of an angry beast sprang upon him. Benson met the cowardly attack with the flash of a powerful fist, and the outlaw fell to the floor with a hoarse cry of rage and pain. But he was quickly upon his feet again, muttering curses, and again he attacked his grim-faced antagonist. Quick blows rained upon his defenseless face, for the strong, silent man was now fairly aroused. He fought like a demon, perhaps divining that here strong men battled for a good woman's love. The outlaw was proving to be no match for his opponent. Arising from the ground where a mighty blow had sent him, he made a lightning-like effort to recover the knife which Benson had taken from him.

"Have a care!" cried the girl in quick alarm. "That fiend in human form would murder you!"

But Buck Benson's cool eye had seen the treachery in ample time. With a muttered "Curse you, fiend that you are!" he seized the form of the outlaw in a powerful grasp, raised him high aloft as if he had been but a child, and was about to dash him to the ground when a new voice from the doorway froze him to immobility. Statute-like he stood there, holding aloft the now still form of Snake le Vasquez.

The voice from the doorway betrayed deep amazement and the profoundest irritation:

"Merton Gill, what in the sacred name of Time are you meanin' to do with that dummy? For the good land's sake! Have you gone plumb crazy, or what? Put that thing down!"

The newcomer was a portly man of middle age dressed in ill-fitting black. His gray hair grew low upon his brow and he wore a parted beard.

The conqueror of Snake le Vasquez was still frozen, though he had instantly ceased to be Buck Benson, the strong, silent, two-gun man of the open spaces. The irritated voice came again:

"Put that dummy down, you idiot! What you think you're doin', anyway? And say, what you got that other one in here for, when it ought to be out front of the store showin' that new line of gingham house frocks? Put that down and handle it careful! Mebbe you think I got them things down from Chicago just for you to play horse with. Not so! Not so at all! They're to help show off goods, and that's what I want 'em doin' right now. And for Time's sake, what's that revolver lyin' on the floor for? Is it loaded? Say, are you really out of your senses, or ain't you? What's got into you lately? Will you tell me that? Skyhootin' around in here, leavin' the front of the store unpertected for an hour or two, like your time was your own. And don't tell me you only been foolin' in here for three minutes, either, because when I come back from lunch just now there was Mis' Leffingwell up at the notions counter wanting some hooks and eyes, and she tells me she's waited there a good thutty minutes if she's waited one. Nice goin's on, I must say, for a boy drawin' down the money you be! Now you git busy! Take that one with the gingham frock out and stand her in front where she belongs, and then put one them new raincoats on the other and stand him out where he belongs, and then look after a few customers. I declare, sometimes I git clean out of patience with you! Now, for gosh's sake, stir your stumps!"

"Oh, all right—yes, sir," replied Merton Gill, though but half respectfully. The "Oh, all right" had been tainted with a trace of sullenness. He was tired of this continual nagging and fussing over small matters; some day he would tell the old grouch so.

And now, gone the vivid tale of the great out-of-doors, the wide plains of the West, the clash of primitive-hearted men for a good woman's love. Gone, perhaps, the greatest heart picture of a generation, the picture at which you laugh with a lump in your throat and smile with a tear in your eye, the story of plausible punches, a big, vital theme masterfully handled—thrills, action, beauty, excitement—carried to a sensational finish by the genius of that sterling star of the shadowed world, Clifford Armytage—once known as Merton Gill in the little hamlet of Simsbury, Illinois, where for a time, ere yet he was called to screen triumphs, he served as a humble clerk in the so-called emporium of Amos G. Gashwiler—Everything For The Home. Our Prices Always Right.

Merton Gill—so for a little time he must still be known—moodily seized the late Estelle St. Clair under his arm and withdrew from the dingy back storeroom. Down between the counters of the emporium he went with his fair burden and left her outside its portals, staring from her very definitely lashed eyes across the slumbering street at the Simsbury post office. She was tastefully arrayed in one of those new checked gingham house frocks so heatedly mentioned a moment since by her lawful owner, and across her chest Merton Gill now imposed, with no tenderness of manner, the appealing legend, "Our Latest for Milady; only $6.98." He returned for Snake le Vasquez. That outlaw's face, even out of the picture, was evil. He had been picked for the part because of this face—plump, pinkly tinted cheeks, lustrous, curling hair of some repellent composition, eyes with a hard glitter, each lash distinct in blue-black lines, and a small, tip-curled black mustache that lent the whole an offensive smirk. Garbed now in a raincoat, he, too, was posed before the emporium front, labelled "Rainproof or You Get Back Your Money." So frankly evil was his mien that Merton Gill, pausing to regard him, suffered a brief relapse into artistry.

"You fiend!" he muttered, and contemptuously smote the cynical face with an open hand.

Snake le Vasquez remained indifferent to the affront, smirking insufferably across the slumbering street at the wooden Indian proffering cigars before the establishment of Selby Brothers, Confectionery and Tobaccos.

Within the emporium the proprietor now purveyed hooks and eyes to an impatient Mrs. Leffingwell. Merton Gill, behind the opposite counter, waited upon a little girl sent for two and a quarter yards of stuff to match the sample crumpled in her damp hand. Over the suave amenities of this merchandising Amos Gashwiler glared suspiciously across the store at his employee. Their relations were still strained. Merton also glared at Amos, but discreetly, at moments when the other's back was turned or when he was blandly wishing to know of Mrs. Leffingwell if there would be something else to-day. Other customers entered. Trade was on.

Both Merton and Amos wore airs of cheerful briskness that deceived the public. No one could have thought that Amos was fearing his undoubtedly crazed clerk might become uncontrollable at any moment, or that the clerk was mentally parting from Amos forever in a scene of tense dramatic value in which his few dignified but scathing words would burn themselves unforgettably into the old man's brain. Merton, to himself, had often told Amos these things. Some day he'd say them right out, leaving his victim not only in the utmost confusion but in black despair of ever finding another clerk one half as efficient as Merton Gill.

The afternoon wore to closing time in a flurry of trade, during which, as Merton continued to behave sanely, the apprehension of his employer in a measure subsided. The last customer had departed from the emporium. The dummies were brought inside. The dust curtains were hung along the shelves of dry goods. There remained for Merton only the task of delivering a few groceries. He gathered these and took them out to the wagon in front. Then he changed from his store coat to his street coat and donned a rakish plush hat.

Amos was also changing from his store coat to his street coat and donning his frayed straw hat.

"See if you can't keep from actin' crazy while you make them deliveries," said Amos, not uncordially, as he lighted a choice cigar from the box which he kept hidden under a counter.

Merton wished to reply: "See here, Mr. Gashwiler, I've stood this abuse long enough! The time has come to say a few words to you—" But aloud he merely responded, "Yes, sir!"

The circumstance that he also had a cigar from the same box, hidden not so well as Amos thought, may have subdued his resentment. He would light the cigar after the first turn in the road had carried him beyond the eagle eye of its owner.

The delivery wagon outside was drawn by an elderly horse devoid of ambition or ideals. His head was sunk in dejection. He was gray at the temples, and slouched in the shafts in a loafing attitude, one forefoot negligently crossed in front of the other. He aroused himself reluctantly and with apparent difficulty when Merton Gill seized the reins and called in commanding tones, "Get on there, you old skate!" The equipage moved off under the gaze of Amos, who was locking the doors of his establishment.

Turning the first corner into a dusty side street, Merton dropped the reins and lighted the filched cigar. Other Gashwiler property was sacred to him. From all the emporium's choice stock he would have abstracted not so much as a pin; but the Gashwiler cigars, said to be "The World's Best 10c Smoke," with the picture of a dissipated clubman in evening dress on the box cover, were different, in that they were pointedly hidden from Merton. He cared little for cigars, but this was a challenge; the old boy couldn't get away with anything like that. If he didn't want his cigars touched let him leave the box out in the open like a man. Merton drew upon the lighted trophy, moistened and pasted back the wrapper that had broken when the end was bitten off, and took from the bottom of the delivery wagon the remains of a buggy whip that had been worn to half its length. With this he now tickled the bony ridges of the horse. Blows meant nothing to Dexter, but he could still be tickled into brief spurts of activity. He trotted with swaying head, sending up an effective dust screen between the wagon and a still possibly observing Gashwiler.

His deliveries made, Merton again tickled the horse to a frantic pace which continued until they neared the alley on which fronted the Gashwiler barn; there the speed was moderated to a mild amble, for Gashwiler believed his horse should be driven with tenderness, and his equally watchful wife believed it would run away if given the chance.

Merton drove into the barnyard, unhitched the horse, watered it at the half of a barrel before the iron pump, and led it into the barn, where he removed the harness. The old horse sighed noisily and shook himself with relief as the bridle was removed and a halter slipped over his venerable brow.

Ascertaining that the barnyard was vacant, Merton immediately became attentive to his charge. Throughout the late drive his attitude had been one of mild but contemptuous abuse. More than once he had uttered the words "old skate" in tones of earnest conviction, and with the worn end of the whip he had cruelly tickled the still absurdly sensitive sides. Had beating availed he would with no compunction have beaten the drooping wreck. But now, all at once, he was curiously tender. He patted the shoulder softly, put both arms around the bony neck, and pressed his face against the face of Dexter. A moment he stood thus, then spoke in a tear-choked voice:

"Good-by, old pal—the best, the truest pal a man ever had. You and me has seen some tough times, old pard; but you've allus brought me through without a scratch; allus brought me through." There was a sob in the speaker's voice, but he manfully recovered a clear tone of pathos. "And now, old pal, they're a-takin' ye from me—yes, we got to part, you an' me. I'm never goin' to set eyes on ye agin. But we got to be brave, old pal; we got to keep a stiff upper lip—no cryin' now; no bustin' down."

The speaker unclasped his arms and stood with head bowed, his face working curiously, striving to hold back the sobs.

For Merton Gill was once more Clifford Armytage, popular idol of the screen, in his great role of Buck Benson bidding the accustomed farewell to his four-footed pal that had brought him safely through countless dangers. How are we to know that in another couple of hundred feet of the reel Buck will escape the officers of the law who have him for that hold-up of the Wallahoola stage—of which he was innocent—leap from a second-story window of the sheriff's office onto the back of his old pal, and be carried safely over the border where the hellhounds can't touch him until his innocence is proved by Estelle St. Clair, the New York society girl, whose culture demanded a gentleman but whose heart demanded a man. How are we to know this? We only know that Buck Benson always has to kiss his horse good-by at this spot in the drama.

Merton Gill is impressively Buck Benson. His sobs are choking him. And though Gashwiler's delivery horse is not a pinto, and could hardly get over the border ahead of a sheriff's posse, the scene is affecting.

"Good-by, again, old pal, and God bless ye!" sobs Merton.

CHAPTER II. THAT NIGHT—THE APARTMENTS OF CLIFFORD ARMYTAGE

Merton Gill mealed at the Gashwiler home. He ate his supper in moody silence, holding himself above the small gossip of the day that engaged Amos and his wife. What to him meant the announcement that Amos expected a new line of white goods on the morrow, or Mrs. Gashwiler's version of a regrettable incident occurring at that afternoon's meeting of the Entre Nous Five Hundred Club, in which the score had been juggled adversely to Mrs. Gashwiler, resulting in the loss of the first prize, a handsome fern dish, and concerning which Mrs. Gashwiler had thought it best to speak her mind? What importance could he attach to the disclosure of Metta Judson, the Gashwiler hired girl, who chatted freely during her appearances with food, that Doc Cummins had said old Grandma Foutz couldn't last out another day; that the Peter Swansons were sending clear to Chicago for Tilda's trousseau; and that Jeff Murdock had arrested one of the Giddings boys, but she couldn't learn if it was Ferd or Gus, for being drunk as a fool and busting up a bazaar out at the Oak Grove schoolhouse, and the fighting was something terrible.

Scarcely did he listen to these petty recitals. He ate in silence, and when he had finished the simple meal he begged to be excused. He begged this in a lofty, detached, somewhat weary manner, as a man of the world, excessively bored at the dull chatter but still the fastidious gentleman, might have begged it, breaking into one of the many repetitions by his hostess of just what she had said to Mrs. Judge Ellis. He was again Clifford Armytage, enacting a polished society man among yokels. He was so impressive, after rising, in his bow to Mrs. Gashwiler that Amos regarded him with a kindling suspicion.

"Say!" he called, as Merton in the hallway plucked his rakish plush hat from the mirrored rack. "You remember, now, no more o' that skylarkin' with them dummies! Them things cost money."

Merton paused. He wished to laugh sarcastically, a laugh of withering scorn. He wished to reply in polished tones, "Skylarkin'! You poor, dull clod, what do you know of my ambitions, my ideals? You, with your petty life devoted to gaining a few paltry dollars!" But he did not say this, or even register the emotion that would justly accompany such a subtitle. He merely rejoined, "All right, sir, I'm not going to touch them," and went quickly out. "Darned old grouch!" he muttered as he went down the concrete walk to the Gashwiler front gate.

Here he turned to regard the two-story brick house and the square of lawn with a concrete deer on one side of the walk, balanced by a concrete deer on the other. Before the gate was the cast-iron effigy of a small Negro in fantastic uniform, holding an iron ring aloft. The Gashwiler carriage horse had been tethered to this in the days before the Gashwiler touring car had been acquired.

"Dwelling of a country storekeeper!" muttered Merton. "That's all you are!"

This was intended to be scornful. Merton meant that on the screen it would be recognized as this and nothing more. It could not be taken for the mansion of a rich banker, or the country home of a Wall Street magnate. He felt that he had been keen in his dispraise, especially as old Gashwiler would never get the sting of it. Clod!

Three blocks brought him to the heart of the town, still throbbing faintly. He stood, irresolute, before the Giddings House. Chairs in front of this hostelry were now vacant of loafers, and a clatter of dishes came through the open windows of the dining room, where supper was on. Farther down the street Selby Brothers, Cigars and Confectionery, would be open; lights shone from the windows of the Fashion Pool Parlour across the way; the City Drug Store could still be entered; and the post office would stay open until after the mail from No. 4 was distributed. With these exceptions the shops along this mart of trade were tightly closed, including the Gashwiler Emporium, at the blind front of which Merton now glanced with the utmost distaste.

Such citizens as were yet abroad would be over at the depot to watch No. 4 go through. Merton debated joining these sight-seers. Simsbury was too small to be noticed by many trains. It sprawled along the track as if it had been an afterthought of the railroad. Trains like No. 4 were apt to dash relentlessly by it without slackening speed, the mail bag being flung to the depot platform. But sometimes there would be a passenger for Simsbury, and the proud train would slow down and halt reluctantly, with a grinding of brakes, while the passenger alighted. Then a good view of the train could be had; a line of beautiful sleepers terminating in an observation car, its rear platform guarded by a brass-topped railing behind which the privileged lolled at ease; and up ahead a wonderful dining car, where dinner was being served; flitting white-clad waiters, the glitter of silver and crystal and damask, and favoured beings feasting at their lordly ease, perhaps denying even a careless glance at the pitiful hamlet outside, or at most looking out impatient at the halt, or merely staring with incurious eyes while awaiting their choice foods.

Not one of these enviable persons ever betrayed any interest in Simsbury or its little group of citizens who daily gathered on the platform to do them honour. Merton Gill used to fancy that these people might shrewdly detect him to be out of place there—might perhaps take him to be an alien city man awaiting a similar proud train going the other way, standing, as he would, aloof from the obvious villagers, and having a manner, a carriage, an attire, such as further set him apart.

Still, he could never be sure about this. Perhaps no one ever did single him out as a being patently of the greater world. Perhaps they considered that he was rightly of Simsbury and would continue to be a part of it all the days of his life; or perhaps they wouldn't notice him at all. They had been passing Simsburys all day, and all Simsburys and all their peoples must look very much alike to them. Very well—a day would come. There would be at Simsbury a momentous stop of No. 4 and another passenger would be in that dining car, disjoined forever from Simsbury, and he with them would stare out the polished windows at the gaping throng, and he would continue to stare with incurious eyes at still other Simsburys along the right of way, while the proud train bore him off to triumphs never dreamed of by natural-born villagers.

He decided now not to tantalize himself with a glance at this splendid means of escape from all that was sordid. He was still not a little depressed by the late unpleasantness with Gashwiler, who had thought him a crazy fool, with his revolver, his fiercely muttered words, and his holding aloft of a valuable dummy as if to threaten it with destruction. Well, some day the old grouch would eat his words; some day he would be relating to amazed listeners that he had known Merton Gill intimately at the very beginning of his astounding career. That was bound to come. But to-night Merton had no heart for the swift spectacle of No. 4. Nor even, should it halt, did he feel up to watching those indifferent, incurious passengers who little recked that a future screen idol in natty plush hat and belted coat amusedly surveyed them. To-night he must be alone—but a day would come. Resistless Time would strike his hour!

Still he must wait for the mail before beginning his nightly study. Certain of his magazines would come to-night. He sauntered down the deserted street, pausing before the establishment of Selby Brothers. From the door of this emerged one Elmer Huff, clerk at the City Drug Store. Elmer had purchased a package of cigarettes and now offered one to Merton.

"'Lo, Mert! Have a little pill?"

"No, thanks," replied Merton firmly.

He had lately given up smoking—save those clandestine indulgences at the expense of Gashwiler—because he was saving money against his great day.

Elmer lighted one of his own little pills and made a further suggestion.

"Say, how about settin' in a little game with the gang to-night after the store closes—ten-cent limit?"

"No, thanks," replied Merton, again firmly.

He had no great liking for poker at any limit, and he would not subject his savings to a senseless hazard. Of course he might win, but you never could tell.

"Do you good," urged Elmer. "Quit at twelve sharp, with one round of roodles."

"No, I guess not," said Merton.

"We had some game last night, I'll tell the world! One hand we had four jacks out against four aces, and right after that I held four kings against an ace full. Say, one time there I was about two-eighty to the good, but I didn't have enough sense to quit. Hear about Gus Giddings? They got him over in the coop for breaking in on a social out at the Oak Grove schoolhouse last night. Say, he had a peach on when he left here, I'll tell the world! But he didn't get far. Them Grove lads certainly made a believer out of him. You ought to see that left eye of his!"

Merton listened loftily to this village talk, gossip of a rural sport who got a peach on and started something—And the poker game in the back room of the City Drug Store! What diversions were these for one who had a future? Let these clods live out their dull lives in their own way. But not Merton Gill, who held aloof from their low sports, studied faithfully the lessons in his film-acting course, and patiently bided his time.

He presently sauntered to the post office, where the mail was being distributed. Here he found the sight-seers who had returned from the treat of No. 4's flight, and many of the less enterprising citizens who had merely come down for their mail. Gashwiler was among these, smoking one of his choice cigars. He was not allowed to smoke in the house. Merton, knowing this prohibition, strictly enforced by Mrs. Gashwiler, threw his employer a glance of honest pity. Briefly he permitted himself a vision of his own future home—a palatial bungalow in distant Hollywood, with expensive cigars in elaborate humidors and costly gold-tipped cigarettes in silver things on low tables. One might smoke freely there in every room.

Under more of the Elmer Huff sort of gossip, and the rhythmic clump of the cancelling stamp back of the drawers and boxes, he allowed himself a further glimpse of this luxurious interior. He sat on a low couch, among soft cushions, a magnificent bearskin rug beneath his feet. He smoked one of the costly cigarettes and chatted with a young lady interviewer from Photo Land.

"You ask of my wife," he was saying. "But she is more than a wife—she is my best pal, and, I may add, she is also my severest critic."

He broke off here, for an obsequious Japanese butler entered with a tray of cooling drinks. The tray would be gleaming silver, but he was uncertain about the drinks; something with long straws in them, probably. But as to anything alcoholic, now—While he was trying to determine this the general-delivery window was opened and the interview had to wait. But, anyway, you could smoke where you wished in that house, and Gashwiler couldn't smoke any closer to his house than the front porch. Even trying it there he would be nagged, and fussily asked why he didn't go out to the barn. He was a poor fish, Gashwiler; a country storekeeper without a future. A clod!

Merton, after waiting in line, obtained his mail, consisting of three magazines— Photo Land, Silver Screenings, and Camera. As he stepped away he saw that Miss Tessie Kearns stood three places back in the line. He waited at the door for her. Miss Kearns was the one soul in Simsbury who understood him. He had confided to her all his vast ambitions; she had sympathized with them, and her never-failing encouragement had done not a little to stiffen his resolution at odd times when the haven of Hollywood seemed all too distant. A certain community of ambitions had been the foundation of this sympathy between the two, for Tessie Kearns meant to become a scenario writer of eminence, and, like Merton, she was now both studying and practising a difficult art. She conducted the millinery and dressmaking establishment next to the Gashwiler Emporium, but found time, as did Merton, for the worthwhile things outside her narrow life.

She was a slight, spare little figure, sedate and mouselike, of middle age and, to the village, of a quiet, sober way of thought. But, known only to Merton, her real life was one of terrific adventure, involving crime of the most atrocious sort, and contact not only with the great and good, but with loathsome denizens of the underworld who would commit any deed for hire. Some of her scenarios would have profoundly shocked the good people of Simsbury, and she often suffered tremors of apprehension at the thought that one of them might be enacted at the Bijou Palace right there on Fourth Street, with her name brazenly announced as author. Suppose it were Passion's Perils! She would surely have to leave town after that! She would be too ashamed to stay. Still she would be proud, also, for by that time they would be calling her to Hollywood itself. Of course nothing so distressing—or so grand—had happened yet, for none of her dramas had been accepted; but she was coming on. It might happen any time.

She joined Merton, a long envelope in her hand and a brave little smile on her pinched face.

"Which one is it?" he asked, referring to the envelope.

"It's Passion's Perils." she answered with a jaunty affectation of amusement. "The Touchstone-Blatz people sent it back. The slip says its being returned does not imply any lack of merit."

"I should think it wouldn't!" said Merton warmly.

He knew Passion's Perils. A company might have no immediate need for it, but its rejection could not possibly imply a lack of merit, because the merit was there. No one could dispute that.

They walked on to the Bijou Palace. Its front was dark, for only twice a week, on Tuesdays and Saturdays, could Simsbury muster a picture audience; but they could read the bills for the following night. The entrance was flanked on either side by billboards, and they stopped before the first. Merton Gill's heart quickened its beats, for there was billed none other than Beulah Baxter in the ninth installment of her tremendous serial, The Hazards of Hortense.

It was going to be good! It almost seemed that this time the scoundrels would surely get Hortense. She was speeding across a vast open quarry in a bucket attached to a cable, and one of the scoundrels with an ax was viciously hacking at the cable's farther anchorage. It would be a miracle if he did not succeed in his hellish design to dash Hortense to the cruel rocks below. Merton, of course, had not a moment's doubt that the miracle would intervene; he had seen other serials. So he made no comment upon the gravity of the situation, but went at once to the heart of his ecstasy.

"The most beautiful woman on the screen," he murmured.

"Well, I don't know."

Miss Kearns appeared about to advance the claims of rival beauties, but desisted when she saw that Merton was firm.

"None of the rest can touch her," he maintained. "And look at her nerve! Would your others have as much nerve as that?"

"Maybe she has someone to double in those places," suggested the screen-wise Tessie Kearns.

"Not Beulah Baxter. Didn't I see her personal appearance that time I went to Peoria last spring on purpose to see it? Didn't she talk about the risks she look and how the directors were always begging her to use a double and how her artistic convictions wouldn't let her do any such thing? You can bet the little girl is right there in every scene!"

They passed to the other billboard. This would be the comedy. A painfully cross-eyed man in misfitting clothes was doing something supposed to be funny—pushing a lawn mower over the carpet of a palatial home.

"How disgusting!" exclaimed Miss Kearns.

"Ain't it?" said Merton. "How they can have one of those terrible things on the same bill with Miss Baxter—I can't understand it."

"Those censors ought to suppress this sort of buffoonery instead of scenes of dignified passion like they did in Scarlet Sin," declared Tessie. "Did you read about that?"

"They sure ought," agreed Merton. "These comedies make me tired. I never see one if I can help it."

Walking on, they discussed the wretched public taste and the wretched actors that pandered to it. The slap-stick comedy, they held, degraded a fine and beautiful art. Merton was especially severe. He always felt uncomfortable at one of these regrettable exhibitions when people about him who knew no better laughed heartily. He had never seen anything to laugh at, and said as much.

They crossed the street and paused at the door of Miss Kearns' shop, behind which were her living rooms. She would to-night go over Passion's Perils once more and send it to another company.

"I wonder," she said to Merton, "if they keep sending it back because the sets are too expensive. Of course there's the one where the dissipated English nobleman, Count Blessingham, lures Valerie into Westminster Abbey for his own evil purposes on the night of the old earl's murder—that's expensive—but they get a chance to use it again when Valerie is led to the altar by young Lord Stonecliff, the rightful heir. And of course Stonecliff Manor, where Valerie is first seen as governess, would be expensive; but they use that in a lot of scenes, too. Still, maybe I might change the locations around to something they've got built."

"I wouldn't change a line," said Merton. "Don't give in to 'em. Make 'em take it as it is. They might ruin your picture with cheap stuff."

"Well," the authoress debated, "maybe I'll leave it. I'd especially hate to give up Westminster Abbey. Of course the scene where she is struggling with Count Blessingham might easily be made offensive—it's a strong scene—but it all comes right. You remember she wrenches herself loose from his grasp and rushes to throw herself before the altar, which suddenly lights up, and the scoundrel is afraid to pursue her there, because he had a thorough religious training when a boy at Oxford, and he feels it would be sacrilegious to seize her again while the light from the altar shines upon her that way, and so she's saved for the time being. It seems kind of a shame not to use Westminster Abbey for a really big scene like that, don't you think?"

"I should say so!" agreed Merton warmly. "They build plenty of sets as big as that. Keep it in!"

"Well, I'll take your advice. And I shan't give up trying with my other ones. And I'm writing to another set of people—see here." She took from her handbag a clipped advertisement which she read to Merton in the fading light, holding it close to her keen little eyes. "Listen! 'Five thousand photoplay ideas needed. Working girl paid ten thousand dollars for ideas she had thought worthless. Yours may be worth more. Experience unnecessary. Information free. Producers' League 562, Piqua, Ohio.' Doesn't that sound encouraging? And it isn't as if I didn't have some experience. I've been writing scenarios for two years now."

"We both got to be patient," he pointed out. "We can't succeed all at once, just remember that."

"Oh, I'm patient, and I'm determined; and I know you are, too, Merton. But the way my things keep coming back—well, I guess we'd both get discouraged if it wasn't for our sense of humour."

"I bet we would," agreed Merton. "And good-night!"

He went on to the Gashwiler Emporium and let himself into the dark store. At the moment he was bewailing that the next installment of The Hazards of Hortense would be shown on a Saturday night, for on those nights the store kept open until nine and he could see it but once. On a Tuesday night he would have watched it twice, in spite of the so-called comedy unjustly sharing the bill with it.

Lighting a match, he made his way through the silent store, through the stock room that had so lately been the foul lair of Snake le Vasquez, and into his own personal domain, a square partitioned off from the stockroom in which were his cot, the table at which he studied the art of screen acting, and his other little belongings. He often called this his den. He lighted a lamp on the table and drew the chair up to it.

On the boards of the partition in front of him were pasted many presentments of his favourite screen actress, Beulah Baxter, as she underwent the nerve-racking Hazards of Hortense. The intrepid girl was seen leaping from the seat of her high-powered car to the cab of a passing locomotive, her chagrined pursuers in the distant background. She sprang from a high cliff into the chill waters of a storm-tossed sea. Bound to the back of a spirited horse, she was raced down the steep slope of a rocky ravine in the Far West. Alone in a foul den of the underworld she held at bay a dozen villainous Asiatics. Down the fire escape of a great New York hotel she made a perilous way. From the shrouds of a tossing ship she was about to plunge to a watery release from the persecutor who was almost upon her. Upon the roof of the Fifth Avenue mansion of her scoundrelly guardian in the great city of New York she was gaining the friendly projection of a cornice from which she could leap and again escape death—even a fate worse than death, for the girl was pursued from all sorts of base motives. This time, friendless and alone in profligate New York, she would leap from the cornice to the branches of the great eucalyptus tree that grew hard by. Unnerving performances like these were a constant inspiration to Merton Gill. He knew that he was not yet fit to act in such scenes—to appear opportunely in the last reel of each installment and save Hortense for the next one. But he was confident a day would come.

On the same wall he faced also a series of photographs of himself. These were stills to be one day shown to a director who would thereupon perceive his screen merits. There was Merton in the natty belted coat, with his hair slicked back in the approved mode and a smile upon his face; a happy, careless college youth. There was Merton in tennis flannels, his hair nicely disarranged, jauntily holding a borrowed racquet. Here he was in a trench coat and the cap of a lieutenant, grim of face, the jaw set, holding a revolver upon someone unpictured; there in a wide-collared sport shirt lolling negligently upon a bench after a hard game of polo or something. Again he appeared in evening dress, two straightened fingers resting against his left temple. Underneath this was written in a running, angular, distinguished hand, "Very truly yours, Clifford Armytage." This, and prints of it similarly inscribed, would one day go to unknown admirers who besought him for likenesses of himself.

But Merton lost no time in scanning these pictorial triumphs. He was turning the pages of the magazines he had brought, his first hasty search being for new photographs of his heroine. He was quickly rewarded. Silver Screenings proffered some fresh views of Beulah Baxter, not in dangerous moments, but revealing certain quieter aspects of her wondrous life. In her kitchen, apron clad, she stirred something. In her lofty music room she was seated at her piano. In her charming library she was shown "Among Her Books." More charmingly she was portrayed with her beautiful arms about the shoulders of her dear old mother. And these accompanied an interview with the actress.

The writer, one Esther Schwarz, professed the liveliest trepidation at first meeting the screen idol, but was swiftly reassured by the unaffected cordiality of her reception. She found that success had not spoiled Miss Baxter. A sincere artist, she yet absolutely lacked the usual temperament and mannerisms. She seemed more determined than ever to give the public something better and finer. Her splendid dignity, reserve, humanness, high ideals, and patient study of her art had but mellowed, not hardened, a gracious personality. Merton Gill received these assurances without surprise. He knew Beulah Baxter would prove to be these delightful things. He read on for the more exciting bits.

"I'm so interested in my work," prettily observed Miss Baxter to the interviewer; "suppose we talk only of that. Leave out all the rest—my Beverly Hills home, my cars, my jewels, my Paris gowns, my dogs, my servants, my recreations. It is work alone that counts, don't you think? We must learn that success, all that is beautiful and fine, requires work, infinite work and struggle. The beautiful comes only through suffering and sacrifice. And of course dramatic work broadens a girl's viewpoint, helps her to get the real, the worthwhile things out of life, enriching her nature with the emotional experience of her roles. It is through such pressure that we grow, and we must grow, must we not? One must strive for the ideal, for the art which will be but the pictorial expression of that, and for the emotion which must be touched by the illuminating vision of a well-developed imagination if the vital message of the film is to be felt.

"But of course I have my leisure moments from the grinding stress. Then I turn to my books—I'm wild about history. And how I love the great free out-of-doors! I should prefer to be on a simple farm, were I a boy. The public would not have me a boy, you say"—she shrugged prettily—"oh, of course, my beauty, as they are pleased to call it. After all, why should one not speak of that? Beauty is just a stock in trade, you know. Why not acknowledge it frankly? But do come to my delightful kitchen, where I spend many a spare moment, and see the lovely custard I have made for dear mamma's luncheon."

Merton Gill was entranced by this exposition of the quieter side of his idol's life. Of course he had known she could not always be making narrow escapes, and it seemed that she was almost more delightful in this staid domestic life. Here, away from her professional perils, she was, it seemed, "a slim little girl with sad eyes and a wistful mouth."

The picture moved him strongly. More than ever he was persuaded that his day would come. Even might come the day when it would be his lot to lighten the sorrow of those eyes and appease the wistfulness of that tender mouth. He was less sure about this. He had been unable to learn if Beulah Baxter was still unwed. Silver Screenings, in reply to his question, had answered, "Perhaps." Camera, in its answers to correspondents, had said, "Not now." Then he had written to Photo Land: "Is Beulah Baxter unmarried?" The answer had come, "Twice." He had been able to make little of these replies, enigmatic, ambiguous, at best. But he felt that some day he would at least be chosen to act with this slim little girl with the sad eyes and wistful mouth. He, it might be, would rescue her from the branches of the great eucalyptus tree growing hard by the Fifth Avenue mansion of the scoundrelly guardian. This, if he remembered well her message about hard work.

He recalled now the wondrous occasion on which he had travelled the nearly hundred miles to Peoria to see his idol in the flesh. Her personal appearance had been advertised.

It was on a Saturday night, but Merton had silenced old Gashwiler with the tale of a dying aunt in the distant city. Even so, the old grouch had been none too considerate. He had seemed to believe that Merton's aunt should have died nearer to Simsbury, or at least have chosen a dull Monday.

But Merton had held with dignity to the point; a dying aunt wasn't to be hustled about as to either time or place. She died when her time came—even on a Saturday night—and where she happened to be, though it were a hundred miles from some point more convenient to an utter stranger. He had gone and thrillingly had beheld for five minutes his idol in the flesh, the slim little girl of the sorrowful eyes and wistful mouth, as she told the vast audience—it seemed to Merton that she spoke solely to him—by what narrow chance she had been saved from disappointing it. She had missed the train, but had at once leaped into her high-powered roadster and made the journey at an average of sixty-five miles an hour, braving death a dozen times. For her public was dear to her, and she would not have it disappointed, and there she was before them in her trim driving suit, still breathless from the wild ride.

Then she told them—Merton especially—how her directors had again and again besought her not to persist in risking her life in her dangerous exploits, but to allow a double to take her place at the more critical moments. But she had never been able to bring herself to this deception, for deception, in a way, it would be. The directors had entreated in vain. She would keep faith with her public, though full well she knew that at any time one of her dare-devil acts might prove fatal.

Her public was very dear to her. She was delighted to meet it here, face to face, heart to heart. She clasped her own slender hands over her own heart as she said this, and there was a pathetic little catch in her voice as she waved farewell kisses to the throng. Many a heart besides Merton's beat more quickly at knowing that she must rush out to the high-powered roadster and be off at eighty miles an hour to St. Louis, where another vast audience would the next day be breathlessly awaiting her personal appearance.

Merton had felt abundantly repaid for his journey. There had been inspiration in this contact. Little he minded the acid greeting, on his return, of a mere Gashwiler, spawning in his low mind a monstrous suspicion that the dying aunt had never lived.

Now he read in his magazines other intimate interviews by other talented young women who had braved the presence of other screen idols of both sexes. The interviewers approached them with trepidation, and invariably found that success had not spoiled them. Fine artists though they were, applauded and richly rewarded, yet they remained simple, unaffected, and cordial to these daring reporters. They spoke with quiet dignity of their work, their earnest efforts to give the public something better and finer. They wished the countless readers of the interviews to comprehend that their triumphs had come only with infinite work and struggle, that the beautiful comes only through suffering and sacrifice. At lighter moments they spoke gayly of their palatial homes, their domestic pets, their wives or husbands and their charming children. They all loved the great out-of-doors, but their chief solace from toil was in this unruffled domesticity where they could forget the worries of an exacting profession and lead a simple home life. All the husbands and wives were more than that—they were good pals; and of course they read and studied a great deal. Many of them were wild about books.

He was especially interested in the interview printed by Camera with that world favourite, Harold Parmalee. For this was the screen artist whom Merton most envied, and whom he conceived himself most to resemble in feature. The lady interviewer, Miss Augusta Blivens, had gone trembling into the presence of Harold Parmalee, to be instantly put at her ease by the young artist's simple, unaffected manner. He chatted of his early struggles when he was only too glad to accept the few paltry hundreds of dollars a week that were offered him in minor parts; of his quick rise to eminence; of his unceasing effort to give the public something better and finer; of his love for the great out-of-doors; and of his daily flight to the little nest that sheltered his pal wife and the kiddies. Here he could be truly himself, a man's man, loving the simple things of life. Here, in his library, surrounded by his books, or in the music room playing over some little Chopin prelude, or on the lawn romping with the giant police dog, he could forget the public that would not let him rest. Nor had he been spoiled in the least, said the interviewer, by the adulation poured out upon him by admiring women and girls in volume sufficient to turn the head of a less sane young man.

"There are many beautiful women in the world." pursued the writer, "and I dare say there is not one who meets Harold Parmalee who does not love him in one way or another. He has mental brilliancy for the intellectuals, good looks for the empty-headed, a strong vital appeal, a magnetism almost overwhelming to the susceptible, and an easy and supremely appealing courtesy for every woman he encounters."

Merton drew a long breath after reading these earnest words. Would an interviewer some day be writing as much about him? He studied the pictures of Harold Parmalee that abundantly spotted the article. The full face, the profile, the symmetrical shoulders, the jaunty bearing, the easy, masterful smile. From each of these he would raise his eyes to his own pictured face on the wall above him. Undoubtedly he was not unlike Harold Parmalee. He noted little similarities. He had the nose, perhaps a bit more jutting than Harold's, and the chin, even more prominent.

Possibly a director would have told him that his Harold Parmalee beauty was just a trifle overdone; that his face went just a bit past the line of pleasing resemblance and into something else. But at this moment the aspirant was reassured. His eyes were pale, under pale brows, yet they showed well in the prints. And he was slightly built, perhaps even thin, but a diet rich in fats would remedy that. And even if he were quite a little less comely than Parmalee, he would still be impressive. After all, a great deal depended upon the acting, and he was learning to act.

Months ago, the resolution big in his heart, he had answered the advertisement in Silver Screenings, urging him to "Learn Movie Acting, a fascinating profession that pays big. Would you like to know," it demanded, "if you are adapted to this work? If so, send ten cents for our Ten-Hour Talent-Prover, or Key to Movie-Acting Aptitude, and find whether you are suited to take it up."

Merton had earnestly wished to know this, and had sent ten cents to the Film Incorporation Bureau, Station N, Stebbinsville, Arkansas. The Talent-Prover, or Key to Movie-Acting Aptitude, had come; he had mailed his answers to the questions and waited an anguished ten days, fearing that he would prove to lack the required aptitude for this great art. But at last the cheering news had come. He had every aptitude in full measure, and all that remained was to subscribe to the correspondence course.

He had felt weak in the moment of his relief from this torturing anxiety. Suppose they had told him that he wouldn't do? And he had studied the lessons with unswerving determination. Night and day he had held to his ideal. He knew that when you did this your hour was bound to come.

He yawned now, thinking, instead of the anger expressions he should have been practising, of the sordid things he must do to-morrow. He must be up at five, sprinkle the floor, sweep it, take down the dust curtains from the shelves of dry goods, clean and fill the lamps, then station outside the dummies in their raiment. All day he would serve customers, snatching a hasty lunch of crackers and cheese behind the grocery counter. And at night, instead of twice watching The Hazards of Hortense, he must still unreasonably serve late customers until the second unwinding of those delectable reels.

He suddenly sickened of it all. Was he not sufficiently versed in the art he had chosen to practise? And old Gashwiler every day getting harder to bear! His resolve stiffened. He would not wait much longer—only until the savings hidden out under the grocery counter had grown a bit. He made ready for bed, taking, after he had undressed, some dumb-bell exercises that would make his shoulders a trifle more like Harold Parmalee's. This rite concluded, he knelt by his narrow cot and prayed briefly.

"Oh, God, make me a good movie actor! Make me one of the best! For Jesus'sake, amen!"

CHAPTER
III.
WESTERN
STUFF

Saturday proved all that his black forebodings had pictured it—a day of sordid, harassing toil; toil, moreover, for which Gashwiler, the beneficiary, showed but the scantest appreciation. Indeed, the day opened with a disagreement between the forward-looking clerk and his hide-bound reactionary. Gashwiler had reached the store at his accustomed hour of 8:30 to find Merton embellishing the bulletin board in front with legends setting forth especial bargains of the day to be had within.

Chalk in hand, he had neatly written, "See our new importation of taffetas, $2.59 the yard." Below this he was in the act of putting down, "Try our choice Honey-dew spinach, 20 cts. the can." "Try our Preferred Chipped Beef, 58 cts. the pound."

He was especially liking that use of "the." It sounded modern. Yet along came Gashwiler, as if seeking an early excuse to nag, and criticized this.

"Why don't you say 'a yard,' 'a can,' 'a pound'?" he demanded harshly. "What's the sense of that there 'the' stuff? Looks to me like just putting on a few airs. You keep to plain language and our patrons'll like it a lot better." Viciously Merton Gill rubbed out the modern "the" and substituted the desired "a."

"Very well," he assented, "if you'd rather stick to the old-fashioned way; but I can tell you that's the way city stores do it. I thought you might want to be up to date, but I see I made a great mistake."

"Humph!" said Gashwiler, unbitten by this irony. "I guess the old way's good enough, long's our prices are always right. Don't forget to put on that canned salmon. I had that in stock for nearly a year now—and say it's twenty cents 'a' can, not 'the' can. Also say it's a grand reduction from thirty-five cents."

That was always the way. You never could please the old grouch. And so began the labour that lasted until nine that night. Merton must count out eggs and weigh butter that was brought in. He must do up sugar and grind coffee and measure dress goods and match silks; he must with the suavest gentility ask if there would not be something else to-day; and he must see that babies hazardously left on counters did not roll off.

He lived in a vortex of mental confusion, performing his tasks mechanically. When drawing a gallon of kerosene or refolding the shown dress goods, or at any task not requiring him to be genially talkative, he would be saying to Miss Augusta

Blivens in far-off Hollywood, "Yes, my wife is more than a wife. She is my best pal, and, I may also add, my severest critic."

There was but one break in the dreary monotony, and that was when Lowell Hardy, Simsbury's highly artistic photographer, came in to leave an order for groceries. Lowell wore a soft hat with rakish brim, and affected low collars and flowing cravats, the artistic effect of these being heightened in his studio work by a purple velvet jacket. Even in Gashwiler's he stood out as an artist. Merton received his order, and noting that Gashwiler was beyond earshot bespoke his services for the following afternoon.

"Say, Lowell, be on the lot at two sharp to-morrow, will you? I want to shoot some Western stuff—some stills."

Merton thrilled as he used these highly technical phrases. He had not read his magazines for nothing.

Lowell Hardy considered, then consented. He believed that he, too, might some day be called to Hollywood after they had seen the sort of work he could turn out. He always finished his art studies of Merton with great care, and took pains to have the artist's signature entirely legible. "All right, Mert, I'll be there. I got some new patent paper I'll try out on these."

"On the lot at two sharp to shoot Western stuff," repeated Merton with relish.

"Right—o!" assented Lowell, and returned to more prosaic studio art.

The day wore itself to a glad end. The last exigent customer had gone, the curtains were up, the lights were out, and at five minutes past nine the released slave, meeting Tessie Kearns at her front door, escorted her with a high heart to the second show at the Bijou Palace. They debated staying out until after the wretched comedy had been run, but later agreed that they should see this, as Tessie keenly wished to know why people laughed at such things. The antics of the painfully cross-eyed man distressed them both, though the mental inferiors by whom they were surrounded laughed noisily. Merton wondered how any producer could bring himself to debase so great an art, and Tessie wondered if she hadn't, in a way, been aiming over the public's head with her scenarios. After all, you had to give the public what it wanted. She began to devise comedy elements for her next drama.

But The Hazards of Hortense came mercifully to soothe their annoyance. The slim little girl with a wistful smile underwent a rich variety of hazards, each threatening a terrible death. Through them all she came unscathed, leaving behind her a trail of infuriated scoundrels whom she had thwarted. She escaped from an underworld den in a Chicago slum just in the nick of time, cleverly concealing herself in the branches of the great eucalyptus tree that grew hard by, while her maddened pursuers scattered in their search for the prize. Again she was captured, this time to be conveyed by aeroplane, a helpless prisoner and subject to the most fiendish insults by Black Steve, to the frozen North. But in the far Alaskan wilds she eluded the fiends and drove swiftly over the frozen wastes with their only dog team. Having left her pursuers far behind, she decided to rest for the night in a deserted cabin along the way. Here a blizzard drove snow through the chinks between the logs, and a pack of fierce wolves besieged her. She tried to bar the door, but the bar was gone. At that moment she heard a call. Could it be Black Steve again? No, thank heaven! The door was pushed open and there stood Ralph Murdock, her fiance. There was a quick embrace and words of cheer from Ralph. They must go on.

But no, the wind cut like a knife, and the wolves still prowled. The film here showed a running insert of cruel wolves exposing all their fangs. Ralph had lost his rifle. He went now to put his arm through the iron loops in place of the missing bar. The wolves sought to push open the door, but Ralph's arm foiled them.

Then the outside of the cabin was shown, with Black Steve and his three ugly companions furtively approaching. The wolves had gone, but human wolves, ten thousand times more cruel, had come in their place. Back in the cabin Ralph and Hortense discovered that the wolves had gone. It had an ugly look. Why should the wolves go? Ralph opened the door and they both peered out. There in the shadow of a eucalyptus tree stood Black Steve and his dastardly crew. They were about to storm the cabin. All was undoubtedly lost.

Not until the following week would the world learn how Hortense and her manly fiance had escaped this trap. Again had Beulah Baxter striven and suffered to give the public something better and finer.

"A wonder girl," declared Merton when they were again in the open. "That's what I call her—a wonder girl. And she owes it all to hard, unceasing struggle and work and pains and being careful. You ought to read that new interview with her in this month's Silver Screenings."

"Yes, yes, she's wonderful," assented Tessie as they strolled to the door of her shop. "But I've been thinking about comedy. You know my new one I'm writing— of course it's a big, vital theme, all about a heartless wife with her mind wholly on society and bridge clubs and dancing and that sort of dissipation, and her husband is Hubert Glendenning, a studious young lawyer who doesn't like to go out evenings but would rather play with the kiddies a bit after their mother has gone to a party, or read over some legal documents in the library, which is very beautifully furnished; and her old school friend, Corona Bartlett, comes to stay at the house, a very voluptuous type, high coloured, with black hair and lots of turquoise jewellery, and she's a bad woman through and through, and been divorced and everything by a man whose heart she broke, and she's become a mere adventuress with a secret vice—she takes perfume in her tea, like I saw that one did—and all her evil instincts are aroused at once by Hubert, who doesn't really care deeply for her, as she has only a surface appeal of mere sensuous beauty; but he sees that his wife is neglecting him and having an affair with an Italian count—I found such a good name for him, Count Ravioli—and staying out with him until all hours; so in a moment of weakness he gives himself to Corona Bartlett, and then sees that he must break up his home and get a divorce and marry Corona to make an honest woman of her; but of course his wife is brought to her senses, so she sees that she has been in the wrong and has a big scene with Corona in which she scorns her and Corona slinks away, and she forgives Hubert his one false step because it was her fault. It's full of big situations, but what I'm wondering—I'm wondering if I couldn't risk some comedy in it by having the faithful old butler a cross-eyed man. Nothing so outrageous as that creature we just saw, but still noticeably cross-eyed. Do you think it would lighten some of the grimmer scenes, perhaps, and wouldn't it be good pathos to have the butler aware of his infirmity and knowing the greatest surgeons in the world can't help him?"

"Well," Merton considered, "if I were you I shouldn't chance it. It would be mere acrobatic humour. And why do you want any one to be funny when you have a big gripping thing of love and hate like that? I don't believe I'd have him cross-eyed. I'd have him elderly and simple and dignified. And you don't want your audience to laugh, do you, when he holds up both hands to show how shocked he is at the way things are going on in that house?"

"Well, maybe I won't then. It was just a thought. I believe you have the right instinct in those matters, Merton. I'll leave him as he is."

"Good-night, then," said Merton. "I got to be on the lot to-morrow. My camera man's coming at two. Shooting some Western stuff."

"Oh, my! Really?"

Tessie gazed after him admiringly. He let himself into the dark store, so lately the scene of his torment, and on the way to his little room stopped to reach under the grocery counter for those hidden savings. To-night he would add to them the fifteen dollars lavished upon him by Gashwiler at the close of a week's toil. The money was in a tobacco pouch. He lighted the lamp on his table, placed the three new bills beside it and drew out the hoard. He would count it to confirm his memory of the grand total.

The bills were frayed, lacking the fresh green of new ones; weary looking, with an air of being glad to rest at last after much passing from hand to hand as symbols of wealth. Their exalted present owner tenderly smoothed out several that had become crumpled, secured them in a neat pile, adding the three recently acquired five-dollar bills, and proceeded to count, moistening the ends of a thumb and finger in defiance of the best sanitary teaching. It was no time to think of malignant bacteria.

By his remembered count he should now be possessed of two hundred and twelve dollars. And there was the two-dollar bill, a limp, gray thing, abraded almost beyond identification. He placed this down first, knowing that the remaining bills should amount to two hundred and ten dollars. Slowly he counted, to finish with a look of blank, hesitating wonder. He made another count, hastily, but taking greater care. The wonder grew. Again he counted, slowly this time, so that there could be no doubt. And now he knew! He possessed thirty-three dollars more than he had thought. Knowing this was right, he counted again for the luxury of it. Two hundred and forty-five obvious dollars!

How had he lost count? He tried to recall. He could remember taking out the money he had paid Lowell Hardy for the last batch of Clifford Armytage stills—for Lowell, although making professional rates to Merton, still believed the artist to be worth his hire—and he could remember taking some more out to send to the mail-order house in Chicago for the cowboy things; but it was plain that he had twice, at least, crowded a week's salary into the pouch and forgotten it.

It was a pleasurable experience; it was like finding thirty-three dollars. And he was by that much nearer to his goal; that much sooner would he be released from bondage; thirty-three dollars sooner could he look Gashwiler in the eye and say what he thought of him and his emporium. In his nightly prayer he did not neglect to render thanks for this.

He dressed the next morning with a new elation. He must be more careful about keeping tab on his money, but also it was wonderful to find more than you expected. He left the storeroom that reeked of kerosene and passed into the emporium to replace his treasure in its hiding place. The big room was dusky behind the drawn front curtains, but all the smells were there—the smell of ground coffee and spices at the grocery counter, farther on, the smothering smell of prints and woolens and new leather.

The dummies, waiting down by the door to be put outside, regarded each other in blank solemnity. A few big flies droned lazily about their still forms. Merton eyed the dusty floor, the gleaming counters, the curtains that shielded the shelves, with a new disdain. Sooner than he had thought he would bid them a last farewell. And to-day, at least, he was free of them—free to be on the lot at two, to shoot Western stuff. Let to-morrow, with its old round of degrading tasks, take care of itself.

At 10:30 he was in church. He was not as attentive to the sermon as he should have been, for it now occurred to him that he had no stills of himself in the garb of a clergyman. This was worth considering, because he was not going to be one of those one-part actors. He would have a wide range of roles. He would be able to play anything. He wondered how the Rev. Otto Carmichael would take the request for a brief loan of one of his pulpit suits. Perhaps he was not so old as he looked; perhaps he might remember that he, too, had once been young and fired with high ideals. It would be worth trying. And the things could be returned after a brief studio session with Lowell Hardy. He saw himself cast in such a part, the handsome young clergyman, exponent of a muscular Christianity. He comes to the toughest cattle town in all the great Southwest, determined to make honest men and good women of its sinning derelicts. He wins the hearts of these rugged but misguided souls. Though at first they treat him rough, they learn to respect him, and they call him the fighting parson. Eventually he wins the hand in marriage of the youngest of the dance-hall denizens, a sweet young girl who despite her evil surroundings has remained as pure and good as she is beautiful.

Anyway, if he had those clothes for an hour or two while the artist made a few studies of him he would have something else to show directors in search of fresh talent.

After church he ate a lonely meal served by Metta Judson at the Gashwiler residence. The Gashwilers were on their accustomed Sabbath visit to the distant farm of Mrs. Gashwiler's father. But as he ate he became conscious that the Gashwiler influence was not wholly withdrawn. From above the mantel he was sternly regarded by a tinted enlargement of his employer's face entitled Photographic Study by Lowell Hardy. Lowell never took photographs merely. He made photographic studies, and the specimen at hand was one of his most daring efforts. Merton glared at it in free hostility—a clod, with ideals as false as the artist's pink on his leathery cheeks! He hurried his meal, glad to be relieved from the inimical scrutiny.

He was glad to be free from this and from the determined recital by Metta Judson of small-town happenings. What cared he that Gus Giddings had been fined ten dollars and costs by Squire Belcher for his low escapade, or that Gus's father had sworn to lick him within an inch of his life if he ever ketched him touching stimmilints again?

He went to the barn, climbed to the hayloft, and undid the bundle containing his Buck Benson outfit. This was fresh from the mail-order house in Chicago. He took out almost reverently a pair of high-heeled boots with purple tops, a pair of spurs, a gay shirt, a gayer neckerchief, a broad-brimmed hat, a leather holster, and—most impressive of all—a pair of goatskin chaps dyed a violent maroon. All these he excitedly donned, the spurs last. Then he clambered down the ladder from the loft, somewhat impeded by the spurs, and went into the kitchen. Metta Judson, washing dishes, gave a little cry of alarm. Nothing like this had ever before invaded the Gashwiler home by front door or back.

"Why, Mert' Gill, whatever you dressed up like that for? My stars, you look like a cowboy or something! Well, I must say!"

"Say, Metta, do me a favour. I want to see how these things look in a glass. It's a cowboy outfit for when I play regular Buck Benson parts, and everything's got to be just so or the audience writes to the magazines about it and makes fun of you."

"Go ahead," said Metta. "You can git a fine look at yourself in the tall glass in the old lady's bedroom."

Forthwith he went, profaning a sanctuary, to survey himself in a glass that had never reflected anything but the discreet arraying of his employer's lady. He looked long and earnestly. The effect was quite all he had hoped. He lowered the front of the broad-brimmed hat the least bit, tightened his belt another notch and moved the holster to a better line. He looked again. From feet to head he was perfect.

Then, slightly crouching, he drew his revolver from the holster and held it forward from the hip, wrist and forearm rigidly straight.

"Throw up your hands!"

He uttered the grim words in a low tone, but one facing him would not have been deceived by low tones. Steely-eyed, grim of face, relentless in all his bearing, the most desperate adversary would have quailed. Probably even Gashwiler himself would have quailed. When Buck Benson looked and spoke thus he meant it.

He held it a long, breathless moment before relaxing. Then he tiptoed softly from the hallowed confines of a good woman's boudoir and clattered down the back stairs to the kitchen. He was thinking: "I certainly got to get me another gun if I'm ever going to do Two-Gun Benson parts, and I got to get the draw down better. I ain't quick enough yet."

"Well, did you like your rig?" inquired Metta genially.

"Oh, it'll do for the stills we're shooting to-day," replied the actor. "Of course I ought to have a rattlesnake-skin band on my hat, and the things look too new yet. And say, Metta, where's the clothesline? I want to practise roping a little before my camera man gets here."

"My stars! You're certainly goin' to be a real one, ain't you?"

She brought him the clothesline, in use only on Mondays. He re-coiled it carefully and made a running noose in one end.

At two Lowell Hardy found his subject casting the rope at an inattentive Dexter. The old horse stood in the yard, head down, one foot crossed nonchalantly before the other. A slight tremor, a nervous flickering of his skin, was all that ensued when the rope grazed him. When it merely fell in his general neighbourhood, as it oftener did, Dexter did not even glance up.

"Good stuff!" applauded the artist. "Now just stand that way, holding the noose out. I want to make a study of that."

He rapidly mounted his camera on a tripod and put in a plate. The study was made. Followed several studies of the fighting face of Two-Gun Benson, grim and rigid, about to shoot from the hip. But these were minor bits. More important would be Buck Benson and his old pal, Pinto. From the barn Merton dragged the saddle, blanket, and bridle he had borrowed from the Giddings House livery stable. He had never saddled a horse before, but he had not studied in vain. He seized Dexter by a wisp of his surviving mane and simultaneously planted a hearty kick in the beast's side, with a command, "Get around there, you old skate!" Dexter sighed miserably and got around as ordered. He was both pained and astonished.

He knew that this was Sunday. Never had he been forced to work on this day. But he meekly suffered the protrusion of a bit between his yellow teeth, and shuddered but slightly when a blanket and then a heavy saddle were flung across his back. True, he looked up in some dismay when the girth was tightened. Not once in all his years had he been saddled. He was used to having things loose around his waist.

The girth went still tighter. Dexter glanced about with genuine concern. Someone was intending to harm him. He curved his swanlike neck and snapped savagely at the shoulder of his aggressor, who kicked him again in the side and yelled, "Whoa, there, dang you!"

Dexter subsided. He saw it was no use. Whatever queer thing they meant to do to him would be done despite all his resistance. Still his alarm had caused him to hold up his head now. He was looking much more like a horse.

"There!" said Merton Gill, and as a finishing touch he lashed the coiled clothesline to the front of the saddle. "Now, here! Get me this way. This is one of the best things I do—that is, so far." Fondly he twined his arms about the long, thin neck of Dexter, who tossed his head and knocked off the cowboy hat. "Never mind that—it's out," said Merton. "Can't use it in this scene." He laid his cheek to the cheek of his pet. "Well, old pal, they're takin' yuh from me, but we got to keep a stiff upper lip. You an' me has been through some purty lively times together, but we got to face the music at last—there, Lowell, did you get that?"

The artist had made his study. He made three others of the same affecting scene at different angles. Dexter was overwhelmed with endearments. Doubtless he was puzzled—to be kicked in the ribs at one moment, the next to be fondled. But Lowell Hardy was enthusiastic. He said he would have some corking studies. He made another of Buck Benson preparing to mount good old Pinto; though, as a matter of fact, Buck, it appeared, was not even half prepared to mount.

"Go on, jump on him now," suggested the artist. "I'll get a few more that way."

"Well, I don't know," Merton hesitated. He was twenty-two years old, and he had never yet been aboard a horse. Perhaps he shouldn't try to go too far in one lesson. "You see, the old boy's pretty tired from his week's work. Maybe I better not mount him. Say, I'll tell you, take me rolling a cigarette, just standing by him. I darned near forgot the cigarettes."

From the barn he brought a sack of tobacco and some brown papers. He had no intention of smoking, but this kind of cigarette was too completely identified with Buck Benson to be left out. Lolling against the side of Dexter, he poured tobacco from the sack into one of the papers. "Get me this way," he directed, "just pouring it out."

He had not yet learned to roll a cigarette, but Gus Giddings, the Simsbury outlaw, had promised to teach him. Anyway, it was enough now to be looking keenly out from under his hat while he poured tobacco into the creased paper against the background of good old Pinto. An art study of this pose was completed. But Lowell Hardy craved more action, more variety.

"Go on. Get up on him," he urged. "I want to make a study of that."

"Well"—again Merton faltered—"the old skate's tired out from a hard week, and I'm not feeling any too lively myself."

"Shucks! It won't kill him if you get on his back for a minute, will it? And you'll want one on him to show, won't you? Hurry up, while the light's right."

Yes, he would need a mounted study to show. Many times he had enacted a scene in which a director had looked over the art studies of Clifford Armytage and handed them back with the remark, "But you seem to play only society parts, Mr. Armytage. All very interesting, and I've no doubt we can place you very soon; but just at present we're needing a lead for a Western, a man who can look the part and ride."

Thereupon he handed these Buck Benson stills to the man, whose face would instantly relax into an expression of pleased surprise.

"The very thing," he would say. And among those stills, certainly, should be one of Clifford Armytage actually on the back of his horse. He'd chance it.

"All right; just a minute."

He clutched the bridle reins of Dexter under his drooping chin, and overcoming a feeble resistance dragged him alongside the watering trough. Dexter at first thought he was wished to drink, but a kick took that nonsense out of him. With extreme care Merton stood upon the edge of the trough and thrust a leg blindly over the saddle. With some determined clambering he was at last seated. His feet were in the stirrups. There was a strange light in his eyes. There was a strange light in Dexter's eyes. To each of them the experience was not only without precedent but rather unpleasant.

"Ride him out in the middle here, away from that well," directed the camera man.

"You—you better lead him out," suggested the rider. "I can feel him tremble already. He—he might break down under me."

Metta Judson, from the back porch, here came into the piece with lines that the author had assuredly not written for her.

"Giddap, there, you Dexter Gashwiler," called Metta loudly and with the best intentions.

"You keep still," commanded the rider severely, not turning his head. What a long way it seemed to the ground! He had never dreamed that horses were so lofty. "Better lead him," he repeated to his camera man.

Lowell Hardy grasped the bridle reins, and after many vain efforts persuaded Dexter to stumble away from the well. His rider grasped the horn of his saddle.

"Look out, don't let him buck," he called.

But Dexter had again become motionless, except for a recurrent trembling under this monstrous infliction.

"Now, there," began the artist. "Hold that. You're looking off over the Western hills. Atta boy! Wait till I get a side view."

"Move your camera," said the rider. "Seems to me he doesn't want to turn around."

But again the artist turned Dexter half around. That wasn't so bad. Merton began to feel the thrill of it. He even lounged in the saddle presently, one leg over the pommel, and seemed about to roll another cigarette while another art study was made. He continued to lounge there while the artist packed his camera. What had he been afraid of? He could sit a horse as well as the next man; probably a few little tricks about it he hadn't learned yet, but he'd get these, too.

"I bet they'll come out fine," he called to the departing artist. "Leave that to me. I dare say I'll be able to do something good with them. So long."

"So long," returned Merton, and was left alone on the back of a horse higher than people would think until they got on him. Indeed he was beginning to like it. If you just had a little nerve you needn't be afraid of anything. Very carefully he clambered from the saddle. His old pal shook himself with relief and stood once more with bowed head and crossed forelegs.

His late burden observed him approvingly. There was good old Pinto after a hard day's run over the mesa. He had borne his beloved owner far ahead of the sheriff's posse, and was now securing a moment's much-needed rest. Merton undid the riata and for half an hour practised casting it at his immobile pet. Once the noose settled unerringly over the head of Dexter, who still remained immobile.

Then there was the lightning draw to be practised. Again and again the trusty weapon of Buck Benson flashed from its holster to the damage of a slower adversary. He was getting that draw down pretty good. From the hip with straight wrist and forearm Buck was ready to shoot in no time at all. Throughout that villain-infested terrain along the border he was known for his quick draw. The most desperate of them would never molest him except they could shoot him from behind. With his back to a wall, they slunk from the encounter.

Elated from this practice and from the memory of that one successful rope cast, Merton became daring in the extreme. He considered nothing less than remounting his old pal and riding, in the cool of early evening, up and down the alley upon which the barnyard gave. He coiled the rope and again lashed it to the left front of the saddle. Then he curved an affectionate arm over the arched neck of Pinto, who sighed deeply.

"Well, old pal, you and me has still got some mighty long miles to git over between now and sunup to-morrow. I reckon we got to put a right smart of distance between us and that pesky sheriff's posse, but I know yuh ain't lost heart, old pal."

Dexter here tossed his head, being cloyed with these embraces, and Two-Gun Benson caught a look in the desperate eyes of his pet which he did not wholly like. Perhaps it would be better not to ride him any more to-day. Perhaps it would be better not to ride him again until next Sunday. After all, wasn't Dexter practically a wild horse, caught up from the range and broken to saddle only that afternoon? No use overdoing it. At this moment the beast's back looked higher than ever.

It was the cutting remark of a thoughtless, empty-headed girl that confirmed Merton in his rash resolve. Metta Judson, again on the back steps, surveyed the scene with kindling eyes.

"I bet you daresn't get on him again," said Metta.

These were strong words; not words to be flung lightly at Two-Gun Benson.

"You know a lot about it, don't you?" parried Merton Gill.

"Afraid of that old skate!" murmured Metta, counterfeiting the inflections of pity.

Her target shot her a glance of equal pity for her lack of understanding and empty-headed banter. He stalked to the barnyard gate and opened it. The way to his haven over the border was no longer barred. He returned to Dexter, firmly grasped the bridle reins under his weak chin and cajoled him again to the watering trough. Metta Judson was about to be overwhelmed with confusion. From the edge of the trough he again clambered into the saddle, the new boots groping a way to the stirrups. The reins in his left hand, he swept off his ideal hat with a careless gesture—he wished he had had an art study made of this, but you can't think of everything at one time. He turned loftily to Metta as one who had not even heard her tasteless taunts.

"Well, so long! I won't be out late." Metta was now convinced that she had in her heart done this hero a wrong.

"You better be here before the folks get back!" she warned.

Merton knew this as well as she did, but the folks wouldn't be back for a couple of hours yet, and all he meant to venture was a ride at sober pace the length of the alley.

"Oh, I'll take care of that!" he said. "A few miles' stiff gallop'll be all I want." He jerked Dexter's head up, snapped the reins on his neck, and addressed him in genial, comradely but authoritative tones.

"Git up there, old hoss!"

Dexter lowered his head again and remained as if posing conscientiously for the statue of a tired horse.

"Giddap, there, you old skate!" again ordered the rider.

The comradely unction was gone from his voice and the bony neck received a smarter wallop with the reins. Dexter stood unmoved. He seemed to be fearing that the worst was now coming, and that he might as well face it on that spot as elsewhere. He remained deaf to threats and entreaties alike. No hoof moved from its resting place.

"Giddap, there, you old Dexter Gashwiler!" ordered Metta, and was not rebuked. But neither would Dexter yield to a woman's whim.

"I'll tell you!" said Merton, now contemptuous of his mount. "Get the buggy whip and tickle his ribs."

Metta sped on his errand, her eyes shining with the lust for torture. With the frayed end of the whip from the delivery wagon she lightly scored the exposed ribs of Dexter, tormenting him with devilish cunning. Dexter's hide shuttled back and forth. He whinnied protestingly, but did not stir even one hoof.

"That's the idea," said Merton, feeling scornfully secure on the back of this spiritless animal. "Keep it up! I can feel him coming to life."

Metta kept it up. Her woman's ingenuity contrived new little tricks with the instrument of torture. She would doubtless have had a responsible post with the Spanish Inquisition. Face set, absorbed in her evil work, she tickled the ribs crosswise and tickled between them, up and down, always with the artist's light touch.

Dexter's frame grew tense, his head came up. Once more he looked like a horse. He had been brave to face destruction, but he found himself unable to face being tickled to death. If only they had chosen some other method for his execution he would have perished gamely, but this was exquisitely poignant— beyond endurance. He tossed his head and stepped into a trot toward the open gate.

Metta yelled in triumph. The rider tossed his own head in rhythm to Dexter's trot. His whole body tossed in the saddle; it was a fearsome pace; the sensations were like nothing he had ever dreamed of. And he was so high above the good firm ground! Dexter continued his jolting progress to the applause of Metta. The rider tried to command Metta to keep still, and merely bit his tongue.

Stirred to life by the tickling, Dexter now became more acutely aware of that strange, restless burden on his back, and was inspired to free himself from it. He increased his pace as he came to the gate, and managed a backward kick with both heels. This lost the rider his stirrups and left him less securely seated than he wished to be. He dropped the reins and grasped the saddle's pommel with both hands.

He strangely seemed to consider the pommel the steering wheel of a motor car. He seemed to be twisting it with the notion of guiding Dexter. All might have been well, but on losing his stirrups the rider had firmly clasped his legs about the waist of the animal. Again and again he tightened them, and now Dexter not only

243

looked every inch a horse but very painfully to his rider felt like one, for the spurs were goring him to a most seditious behavior. The mere pace was slackened only that he might alarmingly kick and shake himself in a manner as terrifying to the rider as it was unseemly in one of Dexter's years.

But the thing was inevitable, because once in his remote, hot youth Dexter, cavorting innocently in an orchard, had kicked over a hive of busy bees which had been attending strictly to their own affairs until that moment. After that they had attended to Dexter with a thoroughness that had seared itself to this day across his memory. He now sincerely believed that he had overturned another hive of bees, and that not but by the most strenuous exertion could he escape from their harrying. They were stinging him venomously along his sides, biting deeper with every jump. At last he would bear his rider safely over the border.

The rider clasped his mount ever more tightly. The deep dust of the alley road mounted high over the spirited scene, and through it came not only the hearty delight of Metta Judson in peals of womanly laughter, but the shrill cries of the three Ransom children whom Merton had not before noticed. These were Calvin Ransom, aged eight; Elsie Ransom, aged six; and little Woodrow Ransom, aged four. Their mother had lain down with a headache, having first ordered them to take their picture books and sit quietly in the parlour as good children should on a Sabbath afternoon. So they had noisily pretended to obtain the picture books and then quietly tiptoed out into the backyard, which was not so stuffy as the parlour.

Detecting the meritorious doings in the Gashwiler barnyard, they perched in a row on the alley fence and had been excited spectators from the moment that Merton had mounted his horse.

In shrill but friendly voices they had piped, "Oh, Merton Gill's a cowboy, Merton Gill's a cowboy! Oh, looka the cowboy on the big horse!"

For of course they were motion-picture experts and would know a cowboy when they saw one. Wide-eyed, they followed the perilous antics of Dexter as he issued from the alley gate, and they screamed with childish delight when the spurs had recalled to his memory that far-off dreadful day with the busy bees. They now balanced precariously on the alley fence, the better to trace Merton's flight through the dust cloud. "Merton's in a runaway, Merton's in a runaway, Merton's in a runaway!" they shrieked, but with none of the sympathy that would have become them. They appeared to rejoice in Merton's plight. "Merton's in a runaway," they joyously chanted.

Suddenly they ceased, frozen with a new and splendid wonder, for their descriptive phrase was now inexact. Merton was no longer in a runaway. But only for a moment did they hesitate before taking up the new chant.

"Looky, looky. He's throwed Merton right off into the dirt. He's throwed Merton right off into the dirt. Oh, looky Merton Gill right down there in the dirt!"

Again they had become exact. Merton was right down there in the dirt, and a frantic, flashing-heeled Dexter was vanishing up the alley at the head of a cloud of dust. The friendly Ransom tots leaped from the fence to the alley, forgetting on her bed of pain the mother who supposed them to be engrossed with picture books in the library. With one accord they ran toward the prostrate horseman, Calvin ahead and Elsie a close second, holding the hand of little Woodrow.

They were presently able to observe that the fleeing Dexter had narrowly escaped running down a motor car inopportunely turning at that moment into the alley. The gallant animal swerved in time, leaving the car's driver and his wife aghast at their slight margin of safety. Dexter vanished to the right up shaded Spruce Street on a Sabbath evening as the first call to evening worship pealed from a neighbouring church tower.

His late rider had erected himself and was beating dust from the new chaps and the front of the new shirt. He picked up the ideal hat and dusted that. Underneath all the flurry of this adventure he was still the artist. He had been set afoot in the desert by a treacherous horse; he must find a water hole or perish with thirst. He replaced the hat, and it was then he observed the motor car bearing down the alley upon him.

"My good gosh!" he muttered.

The Gashwilers had returned a full two hours before their accustomed time. The car halted beside him and his employer leaned out a warmly hostile face.

"What's this mean?" he demanded.

The time was not one to tell Gashwiler what he thought of him. Not only was there a lady present, but he felt himself at a disadvantage. The lady saved him from an instant necessity for words.

"That was our new clothesline; I recognized it at once." The woman seemed to pride herself on this paltry feat.

"What's this mean?" again demanded Gashwiler. He was now a man of one idea.

Again was Merton Gill saved from the need of instant speech, though not in a way he would have chosen to be saved. The three Ransom children ran up, breathless, shouting.

"Oh, Merton, here's your pistol. I found it right in the road there." "We found your pistol right in the dirt there. I saw it first." "You did not; I saw it first. Merton, will you let me shoot it off, Merton? I found your pistol, didn't I, Merton? Didn't I find it right in the road there?" The friendly tots did little step dances while they were thus vocal.

"Be quiet, children," commanded Merton, finding a voice. But they were not to be quelled by mere tones.

"He throwed Merton right off into the dirt, didn't he, Merton? Merton, didn't he throw you right off into the dirt, Merton? Did he hurt you, Merton?" "Merton, will you let me shoot it off just once—just once, and I'll never ask again?" "He didn't either find it first, Merton." "He throwed you off right into the dirt—didn't he throw you right off into the dirt, Merton?"

With a harsher show of authority, or perhaps merely because he was bearded—so unreasoning are the inhibitions of the young—Gashwiler stilled the tumult. The dancing died. "What's this mean?" he repeated.

"We nearly had an accident," said the lady.

"What's this mean?"

An answer of sorts could no longer be delayed.

"Well, I thought I'd give Dexter a little exercise, so I saddled him up and was going to ride him around the block, when—when these kids here yelled and scared him so he ran away."

"Oh, what a story!" shouted the tots in unison. "What a bad story! You'll go to the bad place," intoned little Elsie.

"I swear, I don't know what's gettin' into you," declared Gashwiler. "Don't that horse get exercise enough during the week? Don't he like his day of rest? How'd you like me to saddle you up and ride you round the block? I guess you'd like that pretty well, wouldn't you?" Gashwiler fancied himself in this bit of sarcasm, brutal though it was. He toyed with it. "Next Sunday I'll saddle you up and ride you round the block—see how you like that, young man."

"It was our clothesline," said the lady. "I could tell it right off."

With a womanish tenacity she had fastened to a minor inconsequence of the outrage. Gashwiler became practical.

"Well, I must say, it's a pretty how-de-do, That horse'll make straight back for the farm; we won't have any delivery horse to-morrow. Sue, you get out; I'll go down the road a piece and see if I can head him off."

"He turned the other way," said Merton.

"Well, he's bound to head around for the farm. I'll go up the road and you hurry out the way he went. Mebbe you can catch him before he gets out of town."

Mrs. Gashwiler descended from the car.

"You better have that clothesline back by seven o'clock to-morrow morning," she warned the offender.

"Yes, ma'am, I will."

This was not spoken in a Buck Benson manner.

"And say"—Gashwiler paused in turning the car—"what you doing in that outlandish rig, anyhow? Must think you're one o' them Wild West cowboys or something. Huh!" This last carried a sneer that stung.

"Well, I guess I can pick out my own clothes if I want to."

"Fine things to call clothes, I must say. Well, go see if you can pick out that horse if you're such a good picker-out."

Again Gashwiler was pleased with himself. He could play venomously with words.

"Yes, sir," said Merton, and plodded on up the alley, followed at a respectful distance by the Ransom kiddies, who at once resumed their vocal exercises.

"He throwed you off right into the dirt, didn't he, Merton? Mer-tun, didn't he throw you off right into the dirt?"

If it were inevitable he wished that they would come closer. He would even have taken little Woodrow by the hand. But they kept far enough back of him to require that their voices should be raised. Incessantly the pitiless rain fell upon him—"Mer-tun, he throwed you off right into the dirt, didn't he, Merton?"

He turned out of the alley up Spruce Street. The Ransom children lawlessly followed, forgetting their good home, their poor, sick mother and the rules she had laid down for their Sabbath recreation. At every moment the shrill cry reached his burning ears, "Mer-tun, didn't he throw you off?" The kiddies appeared to believe that Merton had not heard them, but they were patient. Presently he would hear and reassure them that he had, indeed, been thrown off right into the dirt.

Now he began to meet or pass early churchgoers who would gaze at him in wonder or in frank criticism. He left the sidewalk and sought the centre of the road, pretending that out there he could better search for a valuable lost horse. The Ransom children were at first in two minds about following him, but they soon found it more interesting to stay on the sidewalk. They could pause to acquaint the churchgoers with a matter of common interest. "He throwed Merton off right into the dirt."

If the people they addressed appeared to be doubting this, or to find it not specific enough, they would call ahead to Merton to confirm their simple tale. With rapt, shining faces, they spread the glad news, though hurrying always to keep pace with the figure in the road.

Spruce Street was vacant of Dexter, but up Elm Street, slowly cropping the wayside herbage as he went, was undoubtedly Merton's good old pal. He quickened his pace. Dexter seemed to divine his coming and broke into a kittenish gallop until he reached the Methodist Church. Here, appearing to believe that he had again eluded pursuit, he stopped to graze on a carefully tended square of grass before the sacred edifice. He was at once shooed by two scandalized old ladies, but paid them no attention. They might perhaps even have tickled him, for this was the best grass he had found since leaving home. Other churchgoers paused in consternation, looking expectantly at the approaching Merton Gill. The three happy children who came up with him left no one in doubt of the late happening.

Merton was still the artist. He saw himself approach Dexter, vault into the saddle, put spurs to the beast, and swiftly disappear down the street. People would be saying that he should not be let to ride so fast through a city street. He was worse than Gus Giddings. But he saw this only with his artist's eye. In sordid fact he went up to Dexter, seized the trailing bridle reins and jerked savagely upon them. Back over the trail he led his good old pal. And for other later churchgoers there were the shrill voices of friendly children to tell what had happened—to appeal confidently to Merton, vaguely ahead in the twilight, to confirm their interesting story.

Dexter, the anarchist, was put to bed without his goodnight kiss. Good old Pinto had done his pal dirt. Never again would he be given a part in Buck Benson's company. Across the alley came the voices of tired, happy children, in the appeal for an encore. "Mer-tun, please let him do it to you again." "Mer-tun, please let him do it to you again."

And to the back porch came Mrs. Gashwiler to say it was a good thing he'd got that clothesline back, and came her husband wishing to be told what outlandish notion Merton Gill would next get into the thing he called his head. It was the beginning of the end.

Followed a week of strained relations with the Gashwiler household, including Dexter, and another week of relations hardly more cordial. But thirty dollars was added to the hoard which was now counted almost nightly. And the cruder wits of the village had made rather a joke of Merton's adventure. Some were tasteless enough to rally him coarsely upon the crowded street or at the post office while he awaited his magazines.

And now there were two hundred and seventy-five dollars to put him forever beyond their jibes. He carefully rehearsed a scathing speech for Gashwiler. He would tell him what he thought of him. That merchant would learn from it some things that would do him good if he believed them, but probably he wouldn't believe them. He would also see that he had done his faithful employee grave injustices. And he would be left, in some humiliation, having found, as Merton Gill took himself forever out of retail trade, that two could play on words as well as one. It was a good warm speech, and its author knew every word of it from mumbled rehearsal during the two weeks, at times when Gashwiler merely thought he was being queer again.

At last came the day when he decided to recite it in full to the man for whom it had been composed. He confronted him, accordingly, at a dull moment on the third Monday morning, burning with his message.

He looked Gashwiler firmly in the eye and said in halting tones, "Mr. Gashwiler, now, I've been thinking I'd like to go West for a while—to California, if you could arrange to let me off, please." And Mr. Gashwiler had replied, "Well, now, that is a surprise. When was you wishing to go, Merton?"

"Why, I would be much obliged if you'd let me get off to-night on No. 4, Mr. Gashwiler, and I know you can get Spencer Grant to take my place, because I asked him yester-day."

"Very well, Merton. Send Spencer Grant in to see me, and you can get off to-night. I hope you'll have a good time."

"Of course, I don't know how long I'll be gone. I may locate out there. But then again—"

"That's all right, Merton. Any time you come back you can have your same old job. You've been a good man, and they ain't so plenty these days."

"Thank you, Mr. Gashwiler."

No. 4 was made to stop at Simsbury for a young man who was presently commanding a meal in the palatial diner, and who had, before this meal was eaten, looked out with compassion upon two Simsbury-like hamlets that the train rushed by, a blur of small-towners standing on their depot platforms to envy the inmates of that splendid structure.

At last it was Western Stuff and no fooling.

CHAPTER IV. THE WATCHER AT THE GATE

The street leading to the Holden motion-picture studio, considered by itself, lacks beauty. Flanking it for most of the way from the boulevard to the studio gate are vacant lots labelled with their prices and appeals to the passer to buy them. Still their prices are high enough to mark the thoroughfare as one out of the common, and it is further distinguished by two rows of lofty eucalyptus trees. These have a real feathery beauty, and are perhaps a factor in the seemingly exorbitant prices demanded for the choice bungalow and home sites they shade. Save for a casual pioneer bungalow or two, there are no buildings to attract the notice until one reaches a high fence that marks the beginning of the Holden lot. Back of this fence is secreted a microcosmos, a world in little, where one may encounter strange races of people in their native dress and behold, by walking a block, cities actually apart by league upon league of the earth's surface and separated by centuries of time.

To penetrate this city of many cities, and this actual present of the remote past, one must be of a certain inner elect. Hardly may one enter by assuming the disguise of a native, as daring explorers have sometimes overcome the difficulty of entering other strange cities. Its gate, reached after passing along an impressive expanse of the reticent fence, is watched by a guardian. He is a stoatish man of middle age, not neatly dressed, and of forbidding aspect. His face is ruthless, with a very knowing cynicism. He is there, it would seem, chiefly to keep people out of the delightful city, though from time to time he will bow an assent or wave it with the hand clutching his evening newspaper to one of the favoured lawful inmates, who will then carelessly saunter or drive an expensive motor car through the difficult portal.

Standing across the street, one may peer through this portal into an avenue of the forbidden city. There is an exciting glimpse of greensward, flowering shrubbery, roses, vines, and a vista of the ends of enormous structures painted yellow. And this avenue is sprightly with the passing of enviable persons who are rightly there, some in alien garb, some in the duller uniform of the humble artisan, some in the pressed and garnished trappings of rich overlords.

It is really best to stand across the street for this clandestine view of heart-shaking delights. If you stand close to the gate to peer past the bulky shape of the warder he is likely to turn and give you a cold look. Further, he is averse to light conversation, being always morosely absorbed—yet with an eye ever alert for intrusive outlanders—in his evening paper. He never reads a morning paper, but has some means of obtaining at an early hour each morning a pink or green evening paper that shrieks with crimson headlines. Such has been his reading through all time, and this may have been an element in shaping his now inveterate hostility toward those who would engage him in meaningless talk. Even in accepting the gift of an excellent cigar he betrays only a bored condescension. There is no relenting of countenance, no genial relaxing of an ingrained suspicion toward all who approach him, no cordiality, in short, such as would lead you to believe that he might be glad to look over a bunch of stills taken by the most artistic photographer in all Simsbury, Illinois. So you let him severely alone after a bit, and go to stand across the street, your neatly wrapped art studies under your arm, and leaning against the trunk of a eucalyptus tree, you stare brazenly past him into the city of wonders.

It is thus we first observe that rising young screen actor, Clifford Armytage, beginning the tenth day of his determined effort to become much more closely identified with screen activities than hitherto. Ten days of waiting outside the guarded gate had been his, but no other ten days of his life had seemed so eventful or passed so swiftly. For at last he stood before his goal, had actually fastened his eyes upon so much of it as might be seen through its gate. Never had he achieved so much downright actuality.

Back in Simsbury on a Sunday morning he had often strolled over to the depot at early train time for a sight of the two metal containers housing the films shown at the Bijou Palace the day before. They would be on the platform, pasted over with express labels. He would stand by them, even touch them, examine the padlocks, turn them over, heft them; actually hold within his grasp the film wraith of Beulah Baxter in a terrific installment of The Hazards of Hortense. Those metal containers imprisoned so much of beauty, of daring, of young love striving against adverse currents—held the triumphant fruiting of Miss Baxter's toil and struggle and sacrifice to give the public something better and finer. Often he had caressed the crude metal with a reverent hand, as if his wonder woman herself stood there to receive his homage.

That was actuality, in a way. But here it was in full measure, without mental subterfuge or vain imaginings. Had he not beheld from this post—he was pretty sure he had—Miss Baxter herself, swathed in costly furs, drive a robin's-egg-blue roadster through the gate without even a nod to the warder? Indeed, that one glimpse of reality had been worth his ten days of waiting—worth all his watching of the gate and its keeper until he knew every dent in the keeper's derby hat, every bristle in his unkempt mustache, every wrinkle of his inferior raiment, and every pocket from which throughout the day he would vainly draw matches to relight an apparently fireproof cigar. Surely waiting thus rewarded could not be called barren. When he grew tired of standing he could cross the street and rest on a low bench that encircled one of the eucalyptus trees. Here were other waiters without the pale, usually men of strongly marked features, with a tendency to extremes in stature or hair or beards or noses, and not conspicuously neat in attire. These, he discovered, were extras awaiting employment, many of them Mexicans or strange-appearing mongrels, with a sprinkling of Negroes. Often he could have recruited there a band of outlaws for desperate deeds over the border. He did not fraternize with these waifs, feeling that his was another plane.

He had spent three days thus about the studio gate when he learned of the existence of another entrance. This was a door almost opposite the bench. He ventured through it and discovered a bare room with a wooden seat running about its sides. In a partition opposite the entrance was a small window and over it the words "Casting Director." One of the two other doors led to the interior, and through this he observed pass many of the chosen. Another door led to the office of the casting director, glimpses of which could be obtained through the little window.

The waiting room itself was not only bare as to floor and walls, but was bleak and inhospitable in its general effect. The wooden seat was uncomfortable, and those who sat upon it along the dull-toned walls appeared depressed and unhopeful, especially after they had braved a talk through the little window with someone who seemed always to be saying, "No, nothing to-day. Yes, perhaps next week. I have your address." When the aspirants were women, as they mostly were, the someone back of the window would add "dear" to the speech: "No, nothing to-day, dear."

There seemed never to be anything to-day, and Clifford Armytage spent very little of his waiting time in this room. It made him uncomfortable to be stared at by other applicants, whether they stared casually, incuriously, or whether they seemed to appraise him disparagingly, as if telling him frankly that for him there would never be anything to-day.

Then he saw that he, too, must undergo that encounter at the little window. Too apparently he was not getting anywhere by loitering about outside. It was exciting, but the producers would hardly look there for new talent.

He chose a moment for this encounter when the waiting room was vacant, not caring to be stared at when he took this first step in forming a connection that was to be notable in screen annals. He approached the window, bent his head, and encountered the gaze of a small, comely woman with warm brown eyes, neat reddish hair, and a quick manner. The gaze was shrewd; it seemed to read all that was needed to be known of this new candidate.

"Yes?" said the woman.

She looked tired and very businesslike, but her manner was not unkind. The novice was at once reassured. He was presently explaining to her that he wished to act in the pictures at this particular studio. No, he had not had much experience; that is, you could hardly call it experience in actual acting, but he had finished a course of study and had a diploma from the General Film Production Company of Stebbinsville, Arkansas, certifying him to be a competent screen actor. And of course he would not at first expect a big part. He would be glad to take a small part to begin with—almost any small part until he could familiarize himself with studio conditions. And here was a bunch of stills that would give any one an idea of the range of parts he was prepared to play, society parts in a full-dress suit, or soldier parts in a trench coat and lieutenant's cap, or juveniles in the natty suit with the belted coat, and in the storm-king model belted overcoat. And of course Western stuff—these would give an idea of what he could do—cowboy outfit and all that sort of thing, chaps and spurs and guns and so forth. And he was prepared to work hard and struggle and sacrifice in order to give the public something better and finer, and would it be possible to secure some small part at once? Was a good all-round actor by any chance at that moment needed in the company of Miss Beulah Baxter, because he would especially like such a part, and he would be ready to start to work at any time—to-morrow, or even to-day.

The tired little woman beyond the opening listened patiently to this, interrupting several times to say over an insistent telephone, "No, nothing to-day, dear." She looked at the stills with evident interest and curiously studied the face of the speaker as she listened. She smiled wearily when he was through and spoke briskly.

"Now, I'll tell you, son; all that is very nice, but you haven't had a lick of real experience yet, have you?—and things are pretty quiet on the lot just now. To-day there are only two companies shooting. So you couldn't get anything to-day or to-morrow or probably for a good many days after that, and it won't be much when you get it. You may get on as an extra after a while when some of the other companies start shooting, but I can't promise anything, you understand. What you do now—leave me your name and address and telephone number."

"Yes, ma'am," said the applicant, and supplied these data.

"Clifford Armytage!" exclaimed the woman. "I'll say that's some warm name!"

"Well, you see"—he paused, but resolved to confide freely in this friendly seeming person—"you see, I picked that out for a good name to act under. It sounds good, doesn't it? And my own right name is only Merton Gill, so I thought I'd better have something that sounded a little more—well, you know."

"Sure!" said the woman. "All right, have any name you want; but I think I'll call you Merton when you come again. You needn't act with me, you know. Now, let's see—name, age, height, good general wardrobe, house address, telephone number—oh, yes, tell me where I can find you during the day."

"Right out here," he replied firmly. "I'm going to stick to this studio and not go near any of the others. If I'm not in this room I'll be just outside there, on that bench around the tree, or just across the street where you can see through the gate and watch the people go through."

"Say!" Again the woman searched his face and broke into her friendly smile. "Say, you're a real nut, aren't you? How'd you ever get this way?"

And again he was talking, telling now of his past and his struggles to educate himself as a screen actor—one of the best. He spoke of Simsbury and Gashwiler and of Lowell Hardy who took his stills, and of Tessie Kearns, whose sympathy and advice had done so much to encourage him. The woman was joyously attentive. Now she did more than smile. She laughed at intervals throughout the narrative, though her laughter seemed entirely sympathetic and in no way daunted the speaker.

"Well, Merton, you're a funny one—I'll say that. You're so kind of ignorant and appealing. And you say this Bughalter or Gigwater or whatever his name is will take you back into the store any time? Well, that's a good thing to remember, because the picture game is a hard game. I wouldn't discourage a nice clean boy like you for the world, but there are a lot of people in pictures right now that would prefer a steady job like that one you left."

"It's Gashwiler—that name."

"Oh, all right, just so you don't forget it and forget the address."

The new applicant warmly reassured her.

"I wouldn't be likely to forget that, after living there all those years."

When he left the window the woman was again saying into the telephone, "No, dear, nothing to-day. I'm sorry."

It was that night he wrote to Tessie Kearns:

Dear Friend Tessie:

Well, Tessie, here I am safe and sound in Hollywood after a long ride on the cars that went through many strange and interesting cities and different parts of the country, and I guess by this time you must have thought I was forgetting my old friends back in Simsbury; but not so, I can assure you, for I will never forget our long talks together and how you cheered me up often when the sacrifice and struggle seemed more than any man could bear. But now I feel repaid for all that sacrifice and struggle, for I am here where the pictures are made, and soon I will be acting different parts in them, though things are quiet on the lot now with only two companies shooting to-day; but more companies will be shooting in a few days more and then will come the great opportunity for me as soon as I get known, and my different capabilities, and what I can do and everything.

I had a long talk to-day with the lady out in front that hires the actors, and she was very friendly, but said it might be quite some time, because only two companies on the lot were shooting to-day, and she said if Gashwiler had promised to keep my old job for me to be sure and not forget his address, and it was laughable that she should say such a thing, because I would not be liable to forget his address when I lived there so long. She must have thought I was very forgetful, to forget that address.

There is some great scenery around this place, including many of the Rocky Mtns. etc. that make it look beautiful, and the city of Los Angeles is bigger than Peoria. I am quite some distance out of the centre of town, and I have a nice furnished room about a mile from the Holden studios, where I will be hired after a few more companies get to shooting on the lot. There is an electric iron in the kitchen where one can press their clothes. And my furnished room is in the house of a Los Angeles society woman and her husband who came here from Iowa. Their little house with flowers in front of it is called a bungalow. The husband, Mr. Patterson, had a farm in Iowa, six miles out from Cedar Falls, and he cares little for society; but the wife goes into society all the time, as there is hardly a day just now that some society does not have its picnic, and one day it will be the Kansas Society picnic and the next day it will be the Michigan Society having a picnic, or some other state, and of course the Iowa Society that has the biggest picnic of all, and Mr. Patterson says his wife can go to all these society functions if she wants, but he does not care much for society, and he is thinking of buying a half interest in a good soft-drink place just to pass the time away, as he says after the busy life he has led he needs something to keep him busy, but his wife thinks only of society.

I take my meals out at different places, especially at drug stores. I guess you would be surprised to see these drug stores where you can go in and sit at the soda counter and order your coffee and sandwiches and custard pie and eat them right there in the drug store, but there are other places, too, like cafeterias, where you put your dishes on a tray and carry it to your own table. It is all quite different from Simsbury, and I have seen oranges growing on the trees, and there are palm trees, and it does not snow here; but the grass is green and the flowers bloom right through the winter, which makes it very attractive with the Rocky Mtns. standing up in the distance, etc.

Well, Tessie, you must excuse this long letter from your old friend, and write me if any company has accepted Passion's Perils and I might have a chance to act in that some day, and I will let you know when my first picture is released and the title of it so you can watch out for it when it comes to the Bijou Palace. I often think of the old town, and would like to have a chat with you and my other old friends, but I am not homesick, only sometimes I would like to be back there, as there are not many people to chat with here and one would almost be lonesome sometimes if they could not be at the studio. But I must remember that work and struggle and sacrifice are necessary to give the public something better and finer and become a good screen actor. So no more at present, from your old friend, and address Clifford Armytage at above number, as I am going by my stage name, though the lady at the Holden lot said she liked my old name better and called me that, and it sounded pretty good, as I have not got used to the stage name yet.

He felt better after this chat with his old friend, and the following morning he pressed a suit in the Patterson kitchen and resumed his vigil outside the gate.

But now from time to time, at least twice a day, he could break the monotony of this by a call at the little window.

Sometimes the woman beyond it would be engrossed with the telephone and would merely look at him to shake her head. At others, the telephone being still, she would engage him in friendly talk. She seemed to like him as an occasional caller, but she remained smilingly skeptical about his immediate success in the pictures. Again and again she urged him not to forget the address of Giggenholder or Gooshswamp or whoever it might be that was holding a good job for him. He never failed to remind her that the name was Gashwiler, and that he could not possibly forget the address because he had lived at Simsbury a long time. This always seemed to brighten the woman's day. It puzzled him to note that for some reason his earnest assurance pleased her.

As the days of waiting passed he began to distinguish individuals among the people who went through the little outer room or sat patiently around its walls on the hard bench, waiting like himself for more companies to start shooting. Among the important-looking men that passed through would be actors that were now reaping the reward of their struggle and sacrifice; actors whom he thrilled to recognize as old screen friends. These would saunter in with an air of fine leisure, and their manner of careless but elegant dress would be keenly noted by Merton. Then there were directors. These were often less scrupulously attired and seemed always to be solving knotty problems. They passed hurriedly on, brows drawn in perplexity. They were very busy persons. Those on the bench regarded them with deep respect and stiffened to attention as they passed, but they were never observed by these great ones.

The waiting ones were of all ages; mostly women, with but a sprinkling of men. Many of the women were young or youngish, and of rare beauty, so Merton Gill thought. Others were elderly or old, and a few would be accompanied by children, often so young that they must be held on laps. They, too, waited with round eyes and in perfect decorum for a chance to act. Sometimes the little window would be pushed open and a woman beckoned from the bench. Some of them greeted the casting director as an old friend and were still gay when told that there was nothing to-day. Others seemed to dread being told this, and would wait on without daring an inquiry. Sometimes there would be a little flurry of actual business. Four society women would be needed for a bridge table at 8:30 the next morning on Stage Number Five. The casting director seemed to know the wardrobe of each of the waiters, and would select the four quickly. The gowns must be smart—it was at the country house of a rich New Yorker—and jewels and furs were not to be forgotten. There might be two days' work. The four fortunate ladies would depart with cheerful smiles. The remaining waiters settled on the bench, hoping against hope for another call.

Among the waiting-room hopefuls Merton had come to know by sight the Montague family. This consisted of a handsome elderly gentleman of most impressive manner, his wife, a portly woman of middle age, also possessing an impressive manner, and a daughter. Mr. Montague always removed his hat in the waiting room, uncovering an abundant cluster of iron-gray curls above a noble brow. About him there seemed ever to linger a faint spicy aroma of strong drink, and he would talk freely to those sharing the bench with him. His voice was full and rich in tone, and his speech, deliberate and precise, more than hinted that he had once been an ornament of the speaking stage. His wife, also, was friendly of manner, and spoke in a deep contralto somewhat roughened by wear but still notable.

The daughter Merton did not like. She was not unattractive in appearance, though her features were far off the screen-heroine model, her nose being too short, her mouth too large, her cheekbones too prominent, and her chin too square. Indeed, she resembled too closely her father, who, as a man, could carry such things more becomingly. She was a slangy chit, much too free and easy in her ways, Merton considered, and revealing a self-confidence that amounted almost to impudence. Further, her cheeks were brown, her brief nose freckled, and she did not take the pains with her face that most of the beautiful young women who waited there had so obviously taken. She was a harum-scarum baggage with no proper respect for any one, he decided, especially after the day she had so rudely accosted one of the passing directors. He was a more than usually absorbed director, and with drawn brows would have gone unseeing through the waiting room when the girl hailed him.

"Oh, Mr. Henshaw, one moment please!"

He glanced up in some annoyance, pausing with his hand to the door that led on to his proper realm.

"Oh, it's you, Miss Montague! Well, what is it? I'm very, very busy."

"Well, it's something I wanted to ask you." She quickly crossed the room to stand by him, tenderly flecking a bit of dust from his coat sleeve as she began, "Say, listen, Mr. Henshaw: Do you think beauty is a curse to a poor girl?"

Mr. Henshaw scowled down into the eyes so confidingly lifted to his.

"That's something you won't ever have to worry about," he snapped, and was gone, his brows again drawn in perplexity over his work.

"You're not angry with poor little me, are you, Mr. Henshaw?"

The girl called this after him and listened, but no reply came from back of the partition.

Mrs. Montague, from the bench, rebuked her daughter.

"Say, what do you think that kidding stuff will get you? Don't you want to work for him any more?"

The girl turned pleading eyes upon her mother.

"I think he might have answered a simple question," said she.

This was all distasteful to Merton Gill. The girl might, indeed, have deserved an answer to her simple question, but why need she ask it of so busy a man? He felt that Mr. Henshaw's rebuke was well merited, for her own beauty was surely not excessive.

Her father, from the bench, likewise admonished her.

"You are sadly prone to a spirit of banter," he declared, "though I admit that the so-called art of the motion picture is not to be regarded too seriously. It was not like that in my day. Then an actor had to be an artist; there was no position for the little he-doll whippersnapper who draws the big money to-day and is ignorant of even the rudiments of the actor's profession."

He allowed his glance to rest perceptibly upon Merton Gill, who felt uncomfortable.

"We were with Looey James five years," confided Mrs. Montague to her neighbours. "A hall show, of course—hadn't heard of movies then—doing Virginius and Julius Caesar and such classics, and then starting out with The Two Orphans for a short season. We were a knock-out, I'll say that. I'll never forget the night we opened the new opera house at Akron. They had to put the orchestra under the stage."

"And the so-called art of the moving picture robs us of our little meed of applause," broke in her husband. "I shall never forget a remark of the late Lawrence Barrett to me after a performance of Richelieu in which he had fairly outdone himself. 'Montague, my lad,' said he 'we may work for the money, but we play for the applause.' But now our finest bits must go in silence, or perhaps be interrupted by a so-called director who arrogates to himself the right to instill into us the rudiments of a profession in which we had grounded ourselves ere yet he was out of leading strings. Too often, naturally, the results are discouraging."

The unabashed girl was meantime having sprightly talk with the casting director, whom she had hailed through the window as Countess. Merton, somewhat startled, wondered if the little woman could indeed be of the nobility.

"Hello, Countess! Say, listen, can you give the camera a little peek at me to-day, or at pa or ma? 'No, nothing to-day, dear.'" She had imitated the little woman's voice in her accustomed reply. "Well, I didn't think there would be. I just thought I'd ask. You ain't mad, are you? I could have gone on in a harem tank scene over at the Bigart place, but they wanted me to dress the same as a fish, and a young girl's got to draw the line somewhere. Besides, I don't like that Hugo over there so much. He hates to part with anything like money, and he'll gyp you if he can. Say, I'll bet he couldn't play an honest game of solitaire. How'd you like my hair this way? Like it, eh? That's good. And me having the only freckles left in all Hollywood. Ain't I the little prairie flower, growing wilder every hour?

"Say, on the level, pa needs work. These days when he's idle he mostly sticks home and tries out new ways to make prime old Kentucky sour mash in eight hours. If he don't quit he is going to find himself seeing some moving pictures that no one else can. And he's all worried up about his hair going off on top, and trying new hair restorers. You know his latest? Well, he goes over to the Selig place one day and watches horse meat fed to the lions and says to himself that horses have plenty of hair, and it must be the fat under the skin that makes it grow, so he begs for a hunk of horse from just under the mane and he's rubbing that on. You can't tell what he'll bring home next. The old boy still believes you can raise hair from the dead. Do you want some new stills of me? I got a new one yesterday that shows my other expression. Well, so long, Countess."

The creature turned to her parents.

"Let's be on our way, old dears. This place is dead, but the Countess says they'll soon be shooting some tenement-house stuff up at the Consolidated. Maybe there'll be something in it for someone. We might as well have a look-in."

Merton felt relieved when the Montague family went out, the girl in the lead. He approved of the fine old father, but the daughter lacked dignity in speech and manner. You couldn't tell what she might say next.

The Montagues were often there, sometimes in full, sometimes represented by but one of their number. Once Mrs. Montague was told to be on Stage Six the next morning at 8:30 to attend a swell reception.

"Wear the gray georgette, dearie," said the casting director, "and your big pearls and the lorgnon."

"Not forgetting the gold cigarette case and the chinchilla neck piece," said Mrs. Montague. "The spare parts will all be there, Countess, and thanks for the word."

The elder Montague on the occasion of his calls often found time to regale those present with anecdotes of Lawrence Barrett.

"A fine artist in his day, sir; none finer ever appeared in a hall show."

And always about his once superb frock coat clung the scent of forbidden beverages. On one such day he appeared with an untidy sprouting of beard, accompanied by the talkative daughter.

"Pa's landed a part," she explained through the little window. "It's one of those we-uns mountaineer plays with revenooers and feuds; one of those plays where the city chap don't treat our Nell right—you know. And they won't stand for the crepe hair, so pop has got to raise a brush and he's mad. But it ought to give him a month or so, and after that he may be able to peddle the brush again; you can never tell in this business, can you, Countess?"

"It's most annoying," the old gentleman explained to the bench occupants. "In the true art of the speaking stage an artificial beard was considered above reproach. Nowadays one must descend to mere physical means if one is to be thought worthy."

CHAPTER V. A BREACH IN THE CITY WALLS

During these weeks of waiting outside the gate the little woman beyond the window had continued to be friendly but not encouraging to the aspirant for screen honours late of Simsbury, Illinois. For three weeks had he waited faithfully, always within call, struggling and sacrificing to give the public something better and finer, and not once had he so much as crossed the line that led to his goal.

Then on a Monday morning he found the waiting-room empty and his friend beyond the window suffering the pangs of headache. "It gets me something fierce right through here," she confided to him, placing her finger-tips to her temples.

"Ever use Eezo Pain Wafers?" he demanded in quick sympathy. She looked at him hopefully.

"Never heard of 'em."

"Let me get you some."

"You dear thing, fly to it!"

He was gone while she reached for her purse, hurrying along the eucalyptus-lined street of choice home sites to the nearest drug store. He was fearing someone else might bring the little woman another remedy; even that her headache might go before he returned with his. But he found her still suffering.

"Here they are." He was breathless. "You take a couple now and a couple more in half an hour if the ache hasn't stopped." "Bless your heart! Come around inside." He was through the door and in the dimly lit little office behind that secretive partition. "And here's something else," he continued. "It's a menthol pencil and you take this cap off—see?—and rub your forehead with it. It'll be a help." She swallowed two of the magic wafers with the aid of water from the cooler, and applied the menthol.

"You're a dear," she said, patting his sleeve. "I feel better already. Sometimes these things come on me and stay all day." She was still applying the menthol to throbbing temples. "Say, don't you get tired hanging around outside there? How'd you like to go in and look around the lot? Would you like that?"

Would he! "Thanks!" He managed it without choking, "If I wouldn't be in the way."

"You won't. Go on—amuse yourself." The telephone rang. Still applying the menthol she held the receiver to her ear. "No, nothing to-day, dear. Say, Marie, did you ever take Eezo Pain Wafers for a headache? Keep 'em in mind—they're great. Yes, I'll let you know if anything breaks. Goo'-by, dear."

Merton Gill hurried through a narrow corridor past offices where typewriters clicked and burst from gloom into the dazzling light of the Holden lot. He paused on the steps to reassure himself that the great adventure was genuine. There was the full stretch of greensward of which only an edge had shown as he looked through the gate. There were the vast yellow-brick, glass-topped structures of which he had seen but the ends. And there was the street up which he had looked for so many weeks, flanked by rows of offices and dressing rooms, and lively with the passing of many people. He drew a long breath and became calculating. He must see everything and see it methodically. He even went now along the asphalt walk to the corner of the office building from which he had issued for the privilege of looking back at the gate through which he had so often yearningly stared from across the street.

Now he was securely inside looking out. The watchman sat at the gate, bent low over his paper. There was, it seemed, more than one way to get by him. People might have headaches almost any time. He wondered if his friend the casting director were subject to them. He must carry a box of the Eezo wafers.

He strolled down the street between the rows of offices and the immense covered stages. Actors in costume entered two of these and through their open doors he could see into their shadowy interiors. He would venture there later. Just now he wished to see the outside of things. He contrived a pace not too swift but business-like enough to convey the impression that he was rightfully walking this forbidden street. He seemed to be going some place where it was of the utmost importance that he should be, and yet to have started so early that there was no need for haste.

He sounded the far end of that long street visible from outside the gate, discovering its excitements to wane gently into mere blacksmith and carpenter shops. He retraced his steps, this time ignoring the long row of offices for the opposite line of stages. From one dark interior came the slow, dulled strains of an orchestra and from another shots rang out. He met or passed strangely attired people, bandits, priests, choir boys, gentlemen in evening dress with blue-black eyebrows and careful hair. And he observed many beautiful young women, variously attired, hurrying to or from the stages. One lovely thing was in bridal dress of dazzling white, a veil of lace floating from her blonde head, her long train held up by a coloured maid. She chatted amiably, as she crossed the street, with an evil-looking Mexican in a silver-corded hat—a veritable Snake de Vasquez.

But the stages could wait. He must see more streets. Again reaching the office that had been his secret gateway to these delights, he turned to the right, still with the air of having business at a certain spot to which there was really no need for him to hurry. There were fewer people this way, and presently, as if by magic carpet, he had left all that sunlight and glitter and cheerful noise and stood alone in the shadowy, narrow street of a frontier town. There was no bustle here, only an intense stillness. The street was deserted, the shop doors closed. There was a ghostlike, chilling effect that left him uneasy. He called upon himself to remember that he was not actually in a remote and desolate frontier town from which the inhabitants had fled; that back of him but a few steps was abounding life, that outside was the prosaic world passing and repassing a gate hard to enter. He whistled the fragment of a tune and went farther along this street of uncanny silence and vacancy, noting, as he went, the signs on the shop windows. There was the Busy Bee Restaurant, Jim's Place, the Hotel Renown, the Last Dollar Dance Hall, Hank's Pool Room. Upon one window was painted the terse announcement, "Joe—Buy or Sell." The Happy Days Bar adjoined the General Store.

He moved rapidly through this street. It was no place to linger. At the lower end it gave insanely upon a row of three-story brownstone houses which any picture patron would recognize as being wholly of New York. There were the imposing steps, the double-doored entrances, the broad windows, the massive lines of the whole. And beyond this he came to a many-coloured little street out of Bagdad, overhung with gay balconies, vivacious with spindled towers and minarets, and small reticent windows, out of which veiled ladies would glance. And all was still with the stillness of utter desertion.

Then he explored farther and felt curiously disappointed at finding that these structures were to real houses what a dicky is to a sincere, genuine shirt. They were pretentiously false.

One had but to step behind them to discover them as poor shells.

Their backs were jutting beams carried but little beyond the fronts and their stout-appearing walls were revealed to be fragile contrivances of button-lath and thin plaster. The ghost quality departed from them with this discovery.

He left these cities of silence and came upon an open space and people. They were grouped before a railway station, a small red structure beside a line of railway track. At one end in black letters, on a narrow white board, was the name Boomerville.

The people were plainly Western: a dozen cowboys, a sprinkling of bluff ranchers and their families. An absorbed young man in cap and khaki and puttees came from a distant group surrounding a camera and readjusted the line of these people. He placed them to his liking. A wagon drawn by two horses was driven up and a rancher helped a woman and girl to alight. The girl was at once sought out by the cowboys. They shook hands warmly under megaphoned directions from a man back by the camera. The rancher and his wife mingled with the group. The girl was drawn aside by one of the cowboys. He had a nobler presence than the others; he was handsome and his accoutrements seemed more expensive. They looked into each other's eyes a long time, apparently pledging an eternal fidelity. One gathered that there would have been an embrace but for the cowboy's watchful companions. They must say good-by with a mere handshake, though this was a slow, trembling, long-drawn clasp while they steadily regarded each other, and a second camera was brought to record it at a distance of six feet. Merton Gill thrilled with the knowledge that he was beholding his first close-up. His long study of the photo-drama enabled him to divine that the rancher's daughter was going to Vassar College to be educated, but that, although returning a year later a poised woman of the world, she would still long for the handsome cowboy who would marry her and run the Bar-X ranch. The scene was done. The camera would next be turned upon a real train at some real station, while the girl, with a final look at her lover, entered a real car, which the camera would show moving off to Vassar College. Thus conveying to millions of delighted spectators the impression that a real train had steamed out of the station, which was merely an imitation of one, on the Holden lot. The watcher passed on. He could hear the cheerful drone of a sawmill where logs were being cut. He followed the sound and came to its source. The saw was at the end of an oblong pool in which logs floated. Workmen were poling these toward the saw. On a raised platform at one side was a camera and a man who gave directions through a megaphone; a neighbouring platform held a second camera. A beautiful young girl in a print dress and her thick hair in a braid came bringing his dinner in a tin pail to the handsomest of the actors. He laid down his pike-pole and took both the girl's hands in his as he received the pail. One of the other workmen, a hulking brute with an evil face, scowled darkly at this encounter and a moment later had insulted the beautiful young girl. But the first actor felled him with a blow. He came up from this, crouchingly, and the fight was on. Merton was excited by this fight, even though he was in no doubt as to which actor would win it. They fought hard, and for a time it appeared that the handsome actor must lose, for the bully who had insulted the girl was a man of great strength, but the science of the other told. It was the first fight Merton had ever witnessed. He thought these men must really be hating each other, so bitter were their expressions. The battle grew fiercer. It was splendid. Then, at the shrill note of a whistle, the panting combatants fell apart.

"Rotten!" said an annoyed voice through the megaphone. "Can't you boys give me a little action? Jazz it, jazz it! Think it's a love scene? Go to it, now—plenty of jazz—understand what I mean?" He turned to the camera man beside him. "Ed, you turn ten—we got to get some speed some way. Jack"—to the other camera man—"you stay on twelve. All ready! Get some life into it, now, and Lafe"—this to the handsome actor—"don't keep trying to hold your front to the machine. We'll get you all right. Ready, now. Camera!"

Again the fight was on. It went to a bitter finish in which the vanquished bully was sent with a powerful blow backward into the water, while the beautiful young girl ran to the victor and nestled in the protection of his strong arms.

Merton Gill passed on. This was the real thing. He would have a lot to tell Tessie Kearns in his next letter. Beyond the sawmill he came to an immense wooden structure like a cradle on huge rockers supported by scaffolding. From the ground he could make nothing of it, but a ladder led to the top. An hour on the Holden lot had made him bold. He mounted the ladder and stood on the deck of what he saw was a sea-going yacht. Three important-looking men were surveying the deckhouse forward. They glanced at the newcomer but with a cheering absence of curiosity or even of interest. He sauntered past them with a polite but not-too-keen interest. The yacht would be an expensive one. The deck fittings were elaborate. A glance into the captain's cabin revealed it to be fully furnished, with a chart and a sextant on the mahogany desk.

"Where's the bedding for this stateroom?" asked one of the men.

"I got a prop-rustler after it," one of the others informed him.

They strolled aft and paused by an iron standard ingeniously swung from the deck.

"That's Burke's idea," said one of the men. "I hadn't thought about a steady support for the camera; of course if we stood it on deck it would rock when the ship rocked and we'd get no motion. So Burke figures this out. The camera is on here and swings by that weight so it's always straight and the rocking registers. Pretty neat, what?"

"That was nothing to think of" said one of the other men, in apparent disparagement. "I thought of it myself the minute I saw it." The other two grinned at this, though Merton Gill, standing by, saw nothing to laugh at. He thought the speaker was pretty cheeky; for of course any one could think of this device after seeing it. He paused for a final survey of his surroundings from this elevation. He could see the real falseness of the sawmill he had just left, he could also look into the exposed rear of the railway station, and could observe beyond it the exposed skeleton of that New York street. He was surrounded by mockeries.

He clambered down the ladder and sauntered back to the street of offices. He was by this time confident that no one was going to ask him what right he had in there. Now, too, he became conscious of hunger and at the same moment caught the sign "Cafeteria" over a neat building hitherto unnoticed. People were entering this, many of them in costume. He went idly toward the door, glanced up, looked at his watch, and became, to any one curious about him, a man who had that moment decided he might as well have a little food. He opened the screen door of the cafeteria, half expecting it to prove one of those structures equipped only with a front. But the cafeteria was practicable. The floor was crowded with little square polished tables at which many people were eating. A railing along the side of the room made a passage to the back where food was served from a counter to the proffered tray. He fell into line. No one had asked him how he dared try to eat with real actors and actresses and apparently no one was going to. Toward the end of the passage was a table holding trays and napkins the latter wrapped about an equipment of cutlery. He took his tray and received at the counter the foods he designated. He went through this ordeal with difficulty because it was not easy to keep from staring about at other patrons. Constantly he was detecting some remembered face. But at last, with his laden tray he reached a vacant table near the centre of the room and took his seat. He absently arranged the food before him. He could stare at leisure now. All about him were the strongly marked faces

264

of the film people, heavy with makeup, interspersed with hungry civilians, who might be producers, directors, camera men, or mere artisans, for the democracy of the cafeteria seemed ideal.

At the table ahead of his he recognized the man who had been annoyed one day by the silly question of the Montague girl. They had said he was a very important director. He still looked important and intensely serious. He was a short, very plump man, with pale cheeks under dark brows, and troubled looking gray hair. He was very seriously explaining something to the man who sat with him and whom he addressed as Governor, a merry-looking person with a stubby gray mustache and little hair, who seemed not too attentive to the director.

"You see, Governor, it's this way: the party is lost on the desert—understand what I mean—and Kempton Ward and the girl stumble into this deserted tomb just at nightfall. Now here's where the big kick comes—"

Merton Gill ceased to listen for there now halted at his table, bearing a laden tray, none other than the Montague girl, she of the slangy talk and the regrettably free manner. She put down her tray and seated herself before it. She had not asked permission of the table's other occupant, indeed she had not even glanced at him, for cafeteria etiquette is not rigorous. He saw that she was heavily made up and in the costume of a gypsy, he thought, a short vivid skirt, a gay waist, heavy gold hoops in her ears, and dark hair massed about her small head. He remembered that this would not be her own hair. She fell at once to her food. The men at the next table glanced at her, the director without cordiality; but the other man smiled upon her cheerfully.

"Hello, Flips! How's the girl?"

"Everything's jake with me, Governor. How's things over at your shop?"

"So, so. I see you're working."

"Only for two days. I'm just atmosphere in this piece. I got some real stuff coming along pretty soon for Baxter. Got to climb down ten stories of a hotel elevator cable, and ride a brake-beam and be pushed off a cliff and thrown to the lions, and a few other little things."

"That's good, Flips. Come in and see me some time. Have a little chat. Ma working?"

"Yeah—got a character bit with Charlotte King in Her Other Husband." "Glad to hear it. How's Pa Montague?"

"Pa's in bed. They've signed him for Camillia of the Cumberlands, providing he raises a brush, and just now it ain't long enough for whiskers and too long for anything else, so he's putterin' around with his new still."

"Well, drop over sometime, Flips, I'm keeping you in mind."

"Thanks, Governor. Say—" Merton glanced up in time to see her wink broadly at the man, and look toward his companion who still seriously made notes on the

265

back of an envelope. The man's face melted to a grin which he quickly erased. The girl began again:

"Mr. Henshaw—could you give me just a moment, Mr. Henshaw?" The serious director looked up in quite frank annoyance.

"Yes, yes, what is it, Miss Montague?"

"Well, listen, Mr. Henshaw, I got a great idea for a story, and I was thinking who to take it to and I thought of this one and I thought of that one, and I asked my friends, and they all say take it to Mr. Henshaw, because if a story has any merit he's the one director on the lot that can detect it and get every bit of value out of it, so I thought—but of course if you're busy just now—"

The director thawed ever so slightly. "Of course, my girl, I'm busy—but then I'm always busy. They run me to death here. Still, it was very kind of your friends, and of course—"

"Thank you, Mr. Henshaw." She clasped her hands to her breast and gazed raptly into the face of her coy listener.

"Of course I'll have to have help on the details, but it starts off kind of like this. You see I'm a Hawaiian princess—" She paused, gazing aloft.

"Yes, yes, Miss Montague—an Hawaiian princess. Go on, go on!"

"Oh, excuse me; I was thinking how I'd dress her for the last spool in the big fire scene. Well, anyway, I'm this Hawaiian princess, and my father, old King Mauna Loa, dies and leaves me twenty-one thousand volcanoes and a billiard cue—"

Mr. Henshaw blinked rapidly at this. For a moment he was dazed. "A billiard cue, did you say?" he demanded blankly.

"Yes. And every morning I have to go out and ram it down the volcanoes to see are they all right—and—"

"Tush, tush!" interrupted Mr. Henshaw scowling upon the playwright and fell again to his envelope, pretending thereafter to ignore her.

The girl seemed to be unaware that she had lost his attention. "And you see the villain is very wealthy; he owns the largest ukelele factory in the islands, and he tries to get me in his power, but he's foiled by my fiance, a young native by the name of Herman Schwarz, who has invented a folding ukelele, so the villain gets his hired Hawaiian orchestra to shove Herman down one of the volcanoes and me down another, but I have the key around my neck, which Father put there when I was a babe and made me swear always to wear it, even in the bath-tub, so I let myself out and unlock the other one and let Herman out and the orchestra discovers us and chases us over the cliff, and then along comes my old nurse who is now running a cigar store in San Pedro and she—" Here she affected to discover that Mr. Henshaw no longer listened.

"Why, Mr. Henshaw's gone!" she exclaimed dramatically. "Boy, boy, page Mr. Henshaw." Mr. Henshaw remained oblivious.

"Oh, well, of course I might have expected you wouldn't have time to listen to my poor little plot. Of course I know it's crude, but it did seem to me that something might be made out of it." She resumed her food. Mr. Henshaw's companion here winked at her and was seen to be shaking with emotion. Merton Gill could not believe it to be laughter, for he had seen nothing to laugh at. A busy man had been bothered by a silly girl who thought she had the plot for a photodrama, and even he, Merton Gill, could have told her that her plot was impossibly wild and inconsequent. If she were going into that branch of the art she ought to take lessons, the way Tessie Kearns did. She now looked so mournful that he was almost moved to tell her this, but her eyes caught his at that moment and in them was a light so curious, so alive with hidden meanings, so eloquent of some iron restraint she put upon her own emotions, that he became confused and turned his gaze from hers almost with the rebuking glare of Henshaw. She glanced quickly at him again, studying his face for the first time. There had been such a queer look in this young man's eyes; she understood most looks, but not that one.

Henshaw was treating the late interruption as if it had not been. "You see, Governor, the way we got the script now, they're in this tomb alone for the night—understand what I mean—and that's where the kick comes for the audience. They know he's a strong young fellow and she's a beautiful girl and absolutely in his power—see what I mean?—but he's a gentleman through and through and never lays a hand on her. Get that? Then later along comes this Ben Ali Ahab—"

The Montague girl glanced again at the face of the strange young man whose eyes had held a new expression for her, but she and Mr. Henshaw and the so-called governor and all those other diners who rattled thick crockery and talked unendingly had ceased to exist for Merton Gill. A dozen tables down the room and nearer the door sat none other than Beulah Baxter. Alone at her table, she gazed raptly aloft, meditating perhaps some daring new feat. Merton Gill stared, entranced, frozen. The Montague girl perfectly understood this look and traced it to its object. Then she surveyed Merton Gill again with something faintly like pity in her shrewd eyes. He was still staring, still rapt.

Beulah Baxter ceased to look aloft. She daintily reached for a wooden toothpick from the bowl before her and arose to pay her check at the near-by counter. Merton Gill arose at the same moment and stumbled a blind way through the intervening tables. When he reached the counter Miss Baxter was passing through the door. He was about to follow her when a cool but cynical voice from the counter said, "Hey, Bill—ain't you fergittin' somepin'."

He looked for the check for his meal; it should have been in one hand or the other. But it was in neither. He must have left it back on his tray. Now he must return for it. He went as quickly as he could. The Montague girl was holding it up as he approached. "Here's the little joker, Kid," she said kindly.

"Thanks!" said Merton. He said it haughtily, not meaning to be haughty, but he was embarrassed and also fearful that Beulah Baxter would be lost. "Exit limping," murmured the girl as he turned away. He hurried again to the door, paid the check and was outside. Miss Baxter was not to be seen. His forgetfulness about the check had lost her to him. He had meant to follow, to find the place where she was working, and look and look and look! Now he had lost her. But she might be on one of those stages within the big barns. Perhaps the day was not yet lost. He crossed the street, forgetting to saunter, and ventured within the cavernous gloom beyond an open door. He stood for a moment, his vision dulled by the dusk. Presently he saw that he faced a wall of canvas backing. Beyond this were low voices and the sound of people moving. He went forward to a break in the canvas wall and at the same moment there was a metallic jar and light flooded the enclosure. From somewhere outside came music, principally the low, leisurely moan of a 'cello. A beautiful woman in evening dress was with suppressed emotion kneeling at the bedside of a sleeping child. At the doorway stood a dark, handsome gentleman in evening dress, regarding her with a cynical smile. The woman seemed to bid the child farewell, and arose with hands to her breast and quivering lips. The still-smiling gentleman awaited her. When she came to him, glancing backward to the sleeping child, he threw about her an elaborate fur cloak and drew her to him, his cynical smile changing to one of deceitful tenderness. The woman still glanced back at the child, but permitted herself to be drawn through the doorway by the insistent gentleman. From a door the other side of the bed came a kind-faced nurse. She looked first at the little one then advanced to stare after the departing couple. She raised her hands tragically and her face became set in a mask of sorrow and despair. She clasped the hands desperately.

Merton Gill saw his nurse to be the Montague mother. "All right," said an authoritative voice. Mrs. Montague relaxed her features and withdrew, while an unkempt youth came to stand in front of the still-grinding camera and held before it a placard on which were numbers. The camera stopped, the youth with the placard vanished. "Save it," called another voice, and with another metallic jar the flood of light was turned off. The 'cello ceased its moan in the middle of a bar.

The watcher recalled some of the girl's chat. Her mother had a character bit in Her Other Husband. This would be it, one of those moving tragedies not unfamiliar to the screen enthusiast. The beautiful but misguided wife had been saying good-by to her little one and was leaving her beautiful home at the solicitation of the false friend in evening dress—forgetting all in one mad moment. The watcher was a tried expert, and like the trained faunal naturalist could determine a species from the shrewd examination of one bone of a photoplay. He knew that the wife had been ignored by a husband who permitted his vast business interests to engross his whole attention, leaving the wife to seek solace in questionable quarters. He knew that the shocked but faithful nurse would presently discover the little one to be suffering from a dangerous fever; that a hastily summoned physician would shake his head and declare in legible words,

"Naught but a mother's love can win that tiny soul back from the brink of Eternity." The father would overhear this, and would see it all then: how his selfish absorption in Wall Street had driven his wife to another. He would pursue her, would find her ere yet it was too late. He would discover that her better nature had already prevailed and that she had started back without being sent for. They would kneel side by side, hand in hand, at the bedside of the little one, who would recover and smile and prattle, and together they would face an untroubled future.

This was all thrilling to Merton Gill; but Beulah Baxter was not here, her plays being clean and wholesome things of the great outdoors. Far down the great enclosure was another wall of canvas backing, a flood of light above it and animated voices from within. He stood again to watch. But this drama seemed to have been suspended. The room exposed was a bedroom with an open window facing an open door; the actors and the mechanical staff as well were busily hurling knives at various walls. They were earnest and absorbed in this curious pursuit. Sometimes they made the knife penetrate the wall, oftener it merely struck and clattered to the floor. Five knives at once were being hurled by five enthusiasts, while a harried-looking director watched and criticised.

"You're a clumsy bunch," he announced at last. "It's a simple thing to do, isn't it?" The knife-throwers redoubled their efforts, but they did not find it a simple thing to do.

"Let me try it, Mr. Burke." It was the Montague girl still in her gipsy costume. She had been standing quietly in the shadow observing the ineffective practice.

"Hello, Flips! Sure, you can try it. Show these boys something good, now. Here, Al, give Miss Montague that stickeree of yours." Al seemed glad to relinquish the weapon. Miss Montague hefted it, and looked doubtful.

"It ain't balanced right," she declared. "Haven't you got one with a heavier handle?"

"Fair enough," said the director. "Hey, Pickles, let her try that one you got." Pickles, too, was not unwilling to oblige.

"That's better," said the girl. "It's balanced right." Taking the blade by its point between thumb and forefinger she sent it with a quick flick of the wrist into the wall a dozen feet away. It hung there quivering.

"There! That's what we want. It's got to be quivering when Jack shoots at Ramon who threw it at him as he leaps through the window. Try it again, Flips." The girl obliged and bowed impressively to the applause.

"Now come here and try it through the doorway." He led her around the set. "Now stand here and see can you put it into the wall just to the right of the window. Good! Some little knife-thrower, I'll say. Now try it once with Jack coming through. Get set, Jack."

Jack made his way to the window through which he was to leap. He paused there to look in with some concern. "Say, Mr. Burke, will you please make sure she understands? She isn't to let go of that thing until I'm in and crouched down ready to shoot—understand what I mean? I don't want to get nicked nor nothing."

"All right, all right! She understands."

Jack leaped through the window to a crouch, weapon in hand. The knife quivered in the wall above him as he shot.

"Fine and dandy. Some class, I'll say. All right, Jack. Get back. We'll gun this little scene right here and now. All ready, Jack, all ready Miss Montague—camera!—one, two, three—come in, Jack." Again the knife quivered in the wall above his head even while he crouched to shoot at the treacherous Mexican who had thrown it.

"Good work, Flips. Thanks a whole lot. We'll do as much for you some time."

"You're entirely welcome, Mr. Burke. No trouble to oblige. How you coming?"

"Coming good. This thing's going to be a knockout. I bet it'll gross a million. Nearly done, too, except for some chase stuff up in the hills. I'll do that next week. What you doing?"

"Oh, everything's jake with me. I'm over on Number Four—Toys of Destiny—putting a little pep into the mob stuff. Laid out for two hours, waiting for something—I don't know what."

Merton Gill passed on. He confessed now to a reluctant admiration for the Montague girl. She could surely throw a knife. He must practise that himself sometime. He might have stayed to see more of this drama but he was afraid the girl would break out into more of her nonsense. He was aware that she swept him with her eyes as he turned away but he evaded her glance. She was not a person, he thought, that one ought to encourage.

He emerged from the great building and crossed an alley to another of like size. Down toward its middle was the usual wall of canvas with half-a-dozen men about the opening at one corner. A curious whirring noise came from within. He became an inconspicuous unit of the group and gazed in. The lights were on, revealing a long table elaborately set as for a banquet, but the guests who stood about gave him instant uneasiness. They were in the grossest caricatures of evening dress, both men and women, and they were not beautiful. The gowns of the women were grotesque and the men were lawless appearing, either as to hair or beards or both. He divined the dreadful thing he was stumbling upon even before he noted the sign in large letters on the back of a folding chair: "Jeff Baird's Buckeye Comedies." These were the buffoons who with their coarse pantomime, their heavy horse-play, did so much to debase a great art. There, even at his side, was the arch offender, none other than Jeff Baird himself, the man whose regrettable sense of so-called humour led him to make these low appeals to the witless. And even as he looked the cross-eyed man entered the scene. Garbed in

270

the weirdly misfitting clothes of a waiter, holding aloft a loaded tray of dishes, he entered on roller skates, to halt before Baird with his uplifted tray at a precarious balance.

"All right, that's better," said Baird. "And, Gertie, listen: don't throw the chair in front of him. That's out. Now we'll have the entrance again. You other boys on the rollers, there—" Three other basely comic waiters on roller skates came to attention.

"Follow him in and pile up on him when he makes the grand spill—see what I mean? Get your trays loaded now and get off. Now you other people, take your seats. No, no, Annie, you're at the head, I told you. Tom, you're at the foot and start the rough-house when you get the tray in the neck. Now, all set."

Merton Gill was about to leave this distressing scene but was held in spite of himself by the voice of a newcomer.

"Hello, Jeff! Atta boy!"

He knew without turning that the Montague girl was again at his elbow. He wondered if she could be following him.

"Hello, Flips! How's the kid?" The producer had turned cordially to her. "Just in time for the breakaway stuff. See how you like it."

"What's the big idea?"

"Swell reception at the Maison de Glue, with the waiters on roller skates in honour of rich Uncle Rollo Glue. The head waiter starts the fight by doing a fall with his tray. Tom gets the tray in the neck and soaks the nearest man—banquet goes flooey. Then we go into the chase stuff."

"Which is Uncle Rollo?"

"That's him at the table, with the herbaceous border under his chin."

"Is he in the fight?"

"I think so. I was going to rehearse it once more to see if I could get a better idea. Near as I can see now, everybody takes a crack at him."

"Well, maybe." Montague girl seemed to be considering. "Say, how about this, Jeff? He's awful hungry, see, and he's begun to eat the celery and everything he can reach, and when the mix-up starts he just eats on and pays no attention to it. Never even looks up, see what I mean? The fight spreads the whole length of the table; right around Rollo half-a-dozen murders are going on and he just eats and pays no attention. And he's still eating when they're all down and out, and don't know a thing till Charlie or someone crowns him with the punch-bowl. How about it? Ain't there a laugh in that?" Baird had listened respectfully and now patted the girl on a shoulder.

"Good work, Kid! That's a gag, all right. The little bean's sparking on all six, ain't it? Drop around again. We need folks like you. Now, listen, Rollo—you there, Rollo, come here and get this. Now, listen—when the fight begins—"

Merton Gill turned decisively away. Such coarse foolery as this was too remote from Beulah Baxter who, somewhere on that lot, was doing something really, as her interview had put it, distinctive and worth while.

He lingered only to hear the last of Baird's instructions to Rollo and the absurd guests, finding some sinister fascination in the man's talk. Baird then turned to the girl, who had also started off.

"Hang around, Flips. Why the rush?"

"Got to beat it over to Number Four."

"Got anything good there?"

"Nothing that will get me any billing. Been waiting two hours now just to look frenzied in a mob."

"Well, say, come around and see me some time."

"All right, Jeff. Of course I'm pretty busy. When I ain't working I've got to think about my art."

"No, this is on the level. Listen, now, sister, I got another two reeler to pull off after this one, then I'm goin' to do something new, see? Got a big idea. Probably something for you in it. Drop in t' the office and talk it over. Come in some time next week. 'F I ain't there I'll be on the lot some place. Don't forget, now."

Merton Gill, some distance from the Buckeye set, waited to note what direction the Montague girl would take. She broke away presently, glanced brazenly in his direction, and tripped lightly out the nearest exit. He went swiftly to one at the far end of the building, and was again in the exciting street. But the afternoon was drawing in and the street had lost much of its vivacity. It would surely be too late for any glimpse of his heroine. And his mind was already cluttered with impressions from his day's adventure. He went out through the office, meaning to thank the casting director for the great favour she had shown him, but she was gone. He hoped the headache had not driven her home. If she were to suffer again he hoped it would be some morning. He would have the Eezo wafers in one pocket and a menthol pencil in the other. And she would again extend to him the freedom of that wonderful city.

In his room that night he tried to smooth out the jumble in his dazed mind. Those people seemed to say so many things they considered funny but that were not really funny to any one else. And moving-picture plays were always waiting for something, with the bored actors lounging about in idle apathy. Still in his ears sounded the drone of the sawmill and the deep purr of the lights when they were put on. That was a funny thing. When they wanted the lights on they said "Kick it," and when they wanted the lights off they said "Save it!" And why did a boy

272

come out after every scene and hold up a placard with numbers on it before the camera? That placard had never shown in any picture he had seen. And that queer Montague girl, always turning up when you thought you had got rid of her. Still, she had thrown that knife pretty well. You had to give her credit for that. But she couldn't be much of an actress, even if she had spoken of acting with Miss Baxter, of climbing down cables with her and falling off cliffs. Probably she was boasting, because he had never seen any one but Miss Baxter do these things in her pictures. Probably she had some very minor part. Anyway, it was certain she couldn't be much of an actress because she had almost promised to act in those terrible Buckeye comedies. And of course no one with any real ambition or capacity could consider such a thing—descending to rough horse-play for the amusement of the coarser element among screen patrons.

But there was one impression from the day's whirl that remained clear and radiant: He had looked at the veritable face of his heroine. He began his letter to Tessie Kearns. "At last I have seen Miss Baxter face to face. There was no doubt about its being her. You would have known her at once. And how beautiful she is! She was looking up and seemed inspired, probably thinking about her part. She reminded me of that beautiful picture of St. Cecelia playing on the piano...."

CHAPTER VI. UNDER THE GLASS TOPS

He approached the office of the Holden studios the following morning with a new air of assurance. Formerly the mere approach had been an adventure; the look through the gate, the quick glimpse of the privileged ones who entered, the mingling, later, with the hopeful and the near-hopeless ones who waited. But now his feeling was that he had, somehow, become a part of that higher life beyond the gate. He might linger outside at odd moments, but rightfully he belonged inside. His novitiate had passed. He was one of those who threw knives or battled at the sawmill with the persecuter of golden-haired innocence, or lured beautiful women from their homes. He might be taken, he thought, for an actor resting between pictures.

At the gate he suffered a momentary regret at an error of tactics committed the evening before. Instead of leaving the lot by the office he should have left by the gate. He should have strolled to this exit in a leisurely manner and stopped, just inside the barrier, for a chat with the watchman; a chat, beginning with the gift of a cigar, which should have impressed his appearance upon that person. He should have remarked casually that he had had a hard day on Stage Number Four, and must now be off to a good night's rest because of the equally hard day to-morrow. Thus he could now have approached the gate with confidence and passed freely in, with a few more pleasant words to the watchman who would have no difficulty in recalling him.

But it was vain to wish this. For all the watchman knew this young man had never been beyond the walls of the forbidden city, nor would he know any reason why the besieger should not forever be kept outside. He would fix that next time.

He approached the window of the casting office with mingled emotions. He did not hope to find his friend again stricken with headache, but if it chanced that she did suffer he hoped to be the first to learn of it. Was he not fortified with the potent Eezo wafers, and a new menthol pencil, even with an additional remedy of tablets that the druggist had strongly recommended? It was, therefore, not with any actual, crude disappointment that he learned of his friend's perfect well-being. She smiled pleasantly at him, the telephone receiver at one ear. "Nothing to-day, dear," she said and put down the instrument.

Yes, the headache was gone, vanquished by his remedies. She was fine, thank you. No, the headaches didn't come often. It might be weeks before she had another attack. No, of course she couldn't be certain of this. And indeed she would be sure to let him know at the very first sign of their recurrence.

He looked over his patient with real anxiety, a solicitude from the bottom of which he was somehow unable to expel the last trace of a lingering hope that would have dismayed the little woman—not hope, exactly, but something almost like it which he would only translate to himself as an earnest desire that he might be at hand when the dread indisposition did attack her. Just now there could be no doubt that she was free from pain.

He thanked her profusely for her courtesy of the day before. He had seen wonderful things. He had learned a lot. And he wanted to ask her something, assuring himself that he was alone in the waiting room. It was this: did she happen to know—was Miss Beulah Baxter married?

The little woman sighed in a tired manner. "Baxter married? Let me see." She tapped her teeth with the end of a pencil, frowning into her vast knowledge of the people beyond the gate. "Now, let me think." But this appeared to be without result. "Oh, I really don't know; I forget. I suppose so. Why not? She often is."

He would have asked more questions, but the telephone rang and she listened a long time, contributing a "yes, yes," of understanding at brief intervals. This talk ended, she briskly demanded a number and began to talk in her turn. Merton Gill saw that for the time he had passed from her life. She was calling an agency. She wanted people for a diplomatic reception in Washington. She must have a Bulgarian general, a Serbian diplomat, two French colonels, and a Belgian captain, all in uniform and all good types. She didn't want just anybody, but types that would stand out. Holden studios on Stage Number Two. Before noon, if possible. All right, then. Another bell rang, almost before she had hung up. "Hello, Grace. Nothing to-day, dear. They're out on location, down toward Venice, getting some desert stuff. Yes, I'll let you know."

Merton Gill had now to make way at the window for a youngish, weary-looking woman who had once been prettier, who led an elaborately dressed little girl of five. She lifted the child to the window. "Say good-morning to the beautiful lady, Toots. Good-morning, Countess. I'm sure you got something for Toots and me to-day because it's our birthday—both born on the same day—what do you think of that? Any little thing will help us out a lot—how about it?"

He went outside before the end of this colloquy, but presently saw the woman and her child emerge and walk on disconsolately toward the next studio. Thus began another period of waiting from which much of the glamour had gone. It was not so easy now to be excited by those glimpses of the street beyond the gate. A certain haze had vanished, leaving all too apparent the circumstance that others were working beyond the gate while Merton Gill loitered outside, his talent, his training, ignored. His early air of careless confidence had changed to one not at all careless or confident. He was looking rather desperate and rather unbelieving. And it daily grew easier to count his savings. He made no mistakes now. His hoard no longer enjoyed the addition of fifteen dollars a week. Only subtractions were made.

There came a morning when but one bill remained. It was a ten-dollar bill, bearing at its centre a steel-engraved portrait of Andrew Jackson. He studied it in consternation, though still permitting himself to notice that Jackson would have made a good motion-picture type—the long, narrow, severe face, the stiff uncomprising mane of gray hair; probably they would have cast him for a feuding mountaineer, deadly with his rifle, or perhaps as an inventor whose device was stolen on his death-bed by his wicked Wall Street partner, thus leaving his motherless daughter at the mercy of Society's wolves.

But this was not the part that Jackson played in the gripping drama of Merton Gill. His face merely stared from the last money brought from Simsbury, Illinois, and the stare was not reassuring. It seemed to say that there was no other money in all the world. Decidedly things must take a turn. Merton Gill had a quite definite feeling that he had already struggled and sacrificed enough to give the public something better and finer. It was time the public realized this.

Still he waited, not even again reaching the heart of things, for his friend beyond the window had suffered no relapse. He came to resent a certain inconsequence in the woman. She might have had those headaches oftener. He had been led to suppose that she would, and now she continued to be weary but entirely well.

More waiting and the ten-dollar bill went for a five and some silver. He was illogically not sorry to be rid of Andrew Jackson, who had looked so tragically skeptical. The five-dollar bill was much more cheerful. It bore the portrait of Benjamin Harrison, a smooth, cheerful face adorned with whiskers that radiated success. They were little short of smug with success. He would almost rather have had Benjamin Harrison on five dollars than the grim-faced Jackson on ten. Still, facts were facts. You couldn't wait as long on five dollars as you could on ten.

Then on the afternoon of a day that promised to end as other days had ended, a wave of animation swept through the waiting room and the casting office. "Swell cabaret stuff" was the phrase that brought the applicants to a lively swarm about the little window. Evening clothes, glad wraps, cigarette cases, vanity-boxes—the Victor people doing The Blight of Broadway with Muriel Mercer—Stage Number Four at 8:30 to-morrow morning. There seemed no limit to the people desired. Merton Gill joined the throng about the window. Engagements were rapidly made, both through the window and over the telephone that was now ringing those people who had so long been told that there was nothing to-day. He did not push ahead of the women as some of the other men did. He even stood out of the line for the Montague girl who had suddenly appeared and who from the rear had been exclaiming: "Women and children first!"

"Thanks, old dear," she acknowledged the courtesy and beamed through the window. "Hullo, Countess!" The woman nodded briefly. "All right, Flips; I was just going to telephone you. Henshaw wants you for some baby-vamp stuff in the cabaret scene and in the gambling hell. Better wear that salmon-pink chiffon and the yellow curls. Eight-thirty, Stage Four. Goo'-by."

"Thanks, Countess! Me for the jumping tintypes at the hour named. I'm glad enough to be doing even third business. How about Ma?"

"Sure! Tell her grand-dame stuff, chaperone or something, the gray georgette and all her pearls and the cigarette case."

"I'll tell her. She'll be glad there's something doing once more on the perpendicular stage. Goo'-by."

She stepped aside with "You're next, brother!" Merton Gill acknowledged this with a haughty inclination of the head. He must not encourage this hoyden. He glanced expectantly through the little window. His friend held a telephone receiver at her ear. She smiled wearily. "All right, son. You got evening clothes, haven't you? Of course, I remember now. Stage Four at 8:30. Goo'-by."

"I want to thank you for this opportunity—" he began, but was pushed aside by an athletic young woman who spoke from under a broad hat. "Hullo, dearie! How about me and Ella?"

"Hullo, Maizie. All right. Stage Four, at 8:30, in your swellest evening stuff."

At the door the Montague girl called to an approaching group who seemed to have heard by wireless or occult means the report of new activity in the casting office. "Hurry, you troupers. You can eat to-morrow night, maybe!" They hurried. She turned to Merton Gill. "Seems like old times," she observed.

"Does it?" he replied coldly. Would this chit never understand that he disapproved of her trifling ways?

He went on, rejoicing that he had not been compelled to part, even temporarily, with a first-class full-dress suit, hitherto worn only in the privacy of Lowell Hardy's studio. It would have been awkward, he thought, if the demand for it had been much longer delayed. He would surely have let that go before sacrificing his Buck Benson outfit. He had traversed the eucalyptus avenue in this ecstasy, and was on a busier thoroughfare. Before a motion-picture theatre he paused to study the billing of Muriel Mercer in Hearts Aflame. The beauteous girl, in an alarming gown, was at the mercy of a fiend in evening dress whose hellish purpose was all too plainly read in his fevered eyes. The girl writhed in his grasp. Doubtless he was demanding her hand in marriage. It was a tense bit. And to-morrow he would act with this petted idol of the screen. And under the direction of that Mr. Henshaw who seemed to take screen art with proper seriousness. He wondered if by any chance Mr. Henshaw would call upon him to do a quadruple transition, hate, fear, love, despair. He practised a few transitions as he went on to press his evening clothes in the Patterson kitchen, and to dream, that night, that he rode his good old pal, Pinto, into the gilded cabaret to carry off Muriel Mercer, Broadway's pampered society pet, to the clean life out there in the open spaces where men are men.

At eight the following morning he was made up in a large dressing room by a grumbling extra who said that it was a dog's life plastering grease paint over the maps of dubs. He was presently on Stage Four in the prescribed evening regalia for gentlemen. He found the cabaret set, a gilded haunt of pleasure with small tables set about an oblong of dancing floor. Back of these on three sides were raised platforms with other tables, and above these discreet boxes, half masked by drapery, for the seclusion of more retiring merry-makers. The scene was deserted as yet, but presently he was joined by another early comer, a beautiful young woman of Spanish type with a thin face and eager, dark eyes. Her gown was glistening black set low about her polished shoulders, and she carried a red rose. So exotic did she appear he was surprised when she addressed him in the purest English.

"Say, listen here, old timer! Let's pick a good table right on the edge before the mob scene starts. Lemme see—" She glanced up and down the rows of tables. "The cam'ras'll be back there, so we can set a little closer, but not too close, or we'll be moved over. How 'bout this here? Let's try it." She sat, motioning him to the other chair. Even so early in his picture career did he detect that in facing this girl his back would be to the camera. He hitched his chair about.

"That's right," said the girl, "I wasn't meaning to hog it. Say, we was just in time, wasn't we?"

Ladies and gentlemen in evening dress were already entering. They looked inquiringly about and chose tables. Those next to the dancing space were quickly filled. Many of the ladies permitted costly wraps of fur or brocade to spill across the backs of their chairs. Many of the gentlemen lighted cigarettes from gleaming metal cases. There was a lively interchange of talk.

"We better light up, too," said the dark girl. Merton Gill had neglected cigarettes and confessed this with some embarrassment. The girl presented an open case of gold attached to a chain pendent from her girdle. They both smoked. On their table were small plates, two wine glasses half filled with a pale liquid, and small coffee-cups. Spirals of smoke ascended over a finished repast. Of course if the part called for cigarettes you must smoke whether you had quit or not.

The places back of the prized first row were now filling up with the later comers. One of these, a masterful-looking man of middle age—he would surely be a wealthy club-man accustomed to command tables—regarded the filled row around the dancing space with frank irritation, and paused significantly at Merton's side. He seemed about to voice a demand, but the young actor glanced slowly up at him, achieving a superb transition—surprise, annoyance, and, as the invader turned quickly away, pitying contempt.

"Atta boy!" said his companion, who was, with the aid of a tiny gold-backed mirror suspended with the cigarette case, heightening the crimson of her full lips.

Two cameras were now in view, and men were sighting through them. Merton saw Henshaw, plump but worried looking, scan the scene from the rear. He gave hurried direction to an assistant who came down the line of tables with a running glance at their occupants. He made changes. A couple here and a couple there would be moved from the first row and other couples would come to take their places. Under the eyes of this assistant the Spanish girl had become coquettish. With veiled glances, with flashing smiles from the red lips, with a small gloved hand upon Merton Gill's sleeve, she allured him. The assistant paused before them. The Spanish girl continued to allure. Merton Gill stared moodily at the half-empty wine glass, then exhaled smoke as he glanced up at his companion in profound ennui. If it was The Blight of Broadway probably they would want him to look bored.

"You two stay where you are," said the assistant, and passed on.

"Good work," said the girl. "I knew you was a type the minute I made you."

Red-coated musicians entered an orchestra loft far down the set. The voice of Henshaw came through a megaphone: "Everybody that's near the floor fox-trot." In a moment the space was thronged with dancers. Another voice called "Kick it!" and a glare of light came on.

"You an' me both!" said the Spanish girl, rising.

Merton Gill remained seated. "Can't," he said. "Sprained ankle." How was he to tell her that there had been no chance to learn this dance back in Simsbury, Illinois, where such things were frowned upon by pulpit and press? The girl resumed her seat, at first with annoyance, then brightened. "All right at that," she said. "I bet we get more footage this way." She again became coquettish, luring with her wiles one who remained sunk in ennui.

A whistle blew, a voice called "Save it!" and the lights jarred off. Henshaw came trippingly down the line. "You people didn't dance. What's the matter?" Merton Gill glanced up, doing a double transition, from dignified surprise to smiling chagrin. "Sprained ankle," he said, and fell into the bored look that had served him with the assistant. He exhaled smoke and raised his tired eyes to the still luring Spanish girl. Weariness of the world and women was in his look. Henshaw scanned him closely.

"All right, stay there—keep just that way—it's what I want." He continued down the line, which had become hushed. "Now, people. I want some flashes along here, between dances—see what I mean? You're talking, but you're bored with it all. The hollowness of this night life is getting you; not all of you—most of you girls can keep on smiling—but The Blight of Broadway shows on many. You're beginning to wonder if this is all life has to offer—see what I mean?" He continued down the line.

From the table back of Merton Gill came a voice in speech to the retreating back of Henshaw: "All right, old top, but it'll take a good lens to catch any blight on this bunch—most of 'em haven't worked a lick in six weeks, and they're tickled pink." He knew without turning that this was the Montague girl trying to be funny at the expense of Henshaw who was safely beyond hearing. He thought she would be a disturbing element in the scene, but in this he was wrong, for he bent upon the wine glass a look more than ever fraught with jaded world-weariness. The babble of Broadway was resumed as Henshaw went back to the cameras.

Presently a camera was pushed forward. Merton Gill hardly dared look up, but he knew it was halted at no great distance from him. "Now, here's rather a good little bit," Henshaw was saying. "You, there, the girl in black, go on—tease him the way you were, and he's to give you that same look. Got that cigarette going? All ready. Lights! Camera!" Merton was achieving his first close-up. Under the hum of the lights he was thinking that he had been a fool not to learn dancing, no matter how the Reverend Otto Carmichael denounced it as a survival from the barbaric Congo. He was also thinking that the Montague girl ought to be kept away from people who were trying to do really creative things, and he was bitterly regretting that he had no silver cigarette case. The gloom of his young face was honest gloom. He was aware that his companion leaned vivaciously toward him with gay chatter and gestures. Very slowly he inhaled from a cigarette that was already distasteful—adding no little to the desired effect—and very slowly he exhaled as he raised to hers the bored eyes of a soul quite disillusioned. Here, indeed, was the blight of Broadway.

"All right, first rate!" called Henshaw. "Now get this bunch down here." The camera was pushed on.

"Gee, that was luck!" said the girl. "Of course it'll be cut to a flash, but I bet we stand out, at that." She was excited now, no longer needing to act.

From the table back of Merton came the voice of the Montague girl: "Yes, one must suffer for one's art. Here I got to be a baby-vamp when I'd rather be simple little Madelon, beloved by all in the village."

He restrained an impulse to look around at her. She was not serious and should not be encouraged. Farther down the set Henshaw was beseeching a table of six revellers to give him a little hollow gayety. "You're simply forcing yourselves to have a good time," he was saying; "remember that. Your hearts aren't in it. You know this night life is a mockery. Still, you're playing the game. Now, two of you raise your glasses to drink. You at the end stand up and hold your glass aloft. The girl next to you there, stand up by him and raise your face to his—turn sideways more. That's it. Put your hand up to his shoulder. You're slightly lit, you know, and you're inviting him to kiss you over his glass. You others, you're drinking gay enough, but see if you can get over that it's only half-hearted. You at the other end there—you're staring at your wine glass, then you look slowly up at your partner but without any life. You're feeling the blight, see? A chap down the line here just did it perfectly. All ready, now! Lights! Camera! You blonde girl, stand up, face raised to him, hand up to his shoulder. You others, drinking, laughing. You at the end, look up slowly at the girl, look away—about there—bored, weary of it all— cut! All right. Not so bad. Now this next bunch, Paul."

Merton Gill was beginning to loathe cigarettes. He wondered if Mr. Henshaw would mind if he didn't smoke so much, except, of course, in the close-ups. His throat was dry and rough, his voice husky. His companion had evidently played more smoking parts and seemed not to mind it.

Henshaw was now opposite them across the dancing floor, warning his people to be gay but not too gay. The glamour of this night life must be a little dulled.

"Now, Paul, get about three medium shots along here. There's a good table—get that bunch. And not quite so solemn, people; don't overdo it. You think you're having a good time, even if it does turn to ashes in your mouth—now, ready; lights! Camera!"

"I like Western stuff better," confided Merton to his companion. She considered this, though retaining her arch manner. "Well, I don't know. I done a Carmencita part in a dance-hall scene last month over to the Bigart, and right in the mi'st of the fight I get a glass of somethin' all over my gown that practically rooned it. I guess I rather do this refined cabaret stuff—at least you ain't so li'ble to roon a gown. Still and all, after you been warmin' the extra bench for a month one can't be choosy. Say, there's the princ'ples comin' on the set."

He looked around. There, indeed, was the beautiful Muriel Mercer, radiant in an evening frock of silver. At the moment she was putting a few last touches to her perfect face from a make-up box held by a maid. Standing with her was another young woman, not nearly so beautiful, and three men. Henshaw was instructing these. Presently he called through his megaphone: "You people are excited by the entrance of the famous Vera Vanderpool and her friends. You stop drinking, break off your talk, stare at her—see what I mean?—she makes a sensation. Music, lights, camera!"

Down the set, escorted by a deferential head-waiter, came Muriel Mercer on the arm of a middle-aged man who was elaborately garnished but whose thin dyed mustaches, partially bald head, and heavy eyes, proclaimed him to Merton Gill as one who meant the girl no good. They were followed by the girl who was not so beautiful and the other two men. These were young chaps of pleasing exterior who made the progress laughingly. The five were seated at a table next the dancing space at the far end. They chatted gayly as the older man ordered importantly from the head-waiter. Muriel Mercer tapped one of the younger men with her plumed fan and they danced. Three other selected couples danced at the same time, though taking care not to come between the star and the grinding camera. The older man leered at the star and nervously lighted a gold-tipped cigarette which he immediately discarded after one savage bite at it. It could be seen that Vera Vanderpool was the gayest of all that gay throng. Upon her as yet had come no blight of Broadway, though she shrank perceptibly when the partially bald one laid his hand on her slender wrist as she resumed her seat. Food and wine were brought. Vera Vanderpool drank, with a pretty flourish of her glass.

Now the two cameras were moved forward for close-ups. The older man was caught leering at Vera. It would surely be seen that he was not one to trust. Vera was caught with the mad light of pleasure in her beautiful eyes. Henshaw was now speaking in low tones to the group, and presently Vera Vanderpool did a transition. The mad light of pleasure died from her eyes and the smile froze on her beautiful mouth. A look almost of terror came into her eyes, followed by a pathetic lift of the upper lip. She stared intently above the camera. She was beholding some evil thing far from that palace of revels.

"Now they'll cut back to the tenement-house stuff they shot last week," explained the Spanish girl.

"Tenement house?" queried Merton. "But I thought the story would be that she falls in love with a man from the great wind-swept spaces out West, and goes out there to live a clean open life with him—that's the way I thought it would be— out there where she could forget the blight of Broadway."

"No, Mercer never does Western stuff. I got a little girl friend workin' with her and she told me about this story. Mercer gets into this tenement house down on the east side, and she's a careless society butterfly; but all at once she sees what a lot of sorrow there is in this world when she sees these people in the tenement house, starving to death, and sick kids and everything, and this little friend of mine does an Italian girl with a baby and this old man here, he's a rich swell and prominent in Wall Street and belongs to all the clubs, but he's the father of this girl's child, only Mercer don't know that yet. But she gets aroused in her better nature by the sight of all this trouble, and she almost falls in love with another gentleman who devotes all his time to relieving the poor in these tenements—it was him who took her there—but still she likes a good time as well as anybody, and she's stickin' around Broadway and around this old guy who's pretty good company in spite of his faults. But just now she got a shock at remembering the horrible sights she has seen; she can't get it out of her mind. And pretty soon she'll see this other gentleman that she nearly fell in love with, the one who hangs around these tenements doing good—he'll be over at one of them tables and she'll leave her party and go over to his table and say, 'Take me from this heartless Broadway to your tenements where I can relieve their suffering,' so she goes out and gets in a taxi with him, leaving the old guy with not a thing to do but pay the check. Of course he's mad, and he follows her down to the tenements where she's relieving the poor—just in a plain black dress—and she finds out he's the real father of this little friend of mine's child, and tells him to go back to Broadway while she has chosen the better part and must live her life with these real people. But he sends her a note that's supposed to be from a poor woman dying of something, to come and bring her some medicine, and she goes off alone to this dive in another street, and it's the old guy himself who has sent the note, and he has her there in this cellar in his power. But the other gentleman has found the note and has follered her, and breaks in the door and puts up a swell fight with the old guy and some toughs he has hired, and gets her off safe and sound, and so
282

they're married and live the real life far away from the blight of Broadway. It's a swell story, all right, but Mercer can't act it. This little friend of mine can act all around her. She'd be a star if only she was better lookin'. You bet Mercer don't allow any lookers on the same set with her. Do you make that one at the table with her now? Just got looks enough to show Mercer off. Mercer's swell-lookin', I'll give her that, but for actin'—say, all they need in a piece for her is just some stuff to go in between her close-ups. Don't make much difference what it is. Oh, look! There comes the dancers. It's Luzon and Mario."

Merton Gill looked. These would be hired dancers to entertain the pleasure-mad throng, a young girl with vine leaves in her hair and a dark young man of barbaric appearance. The girl was clad in a mere whisp of a girdle and shining breast plates, while the man was arrayed chiefly in a coating of dark stain. They swirled over the dance floor to the broken rhythm of the orchestra, now clinging, now apart, working to a climax in which the man poised with his partner perched upon one shoulder. Through the megaphone came instructions to applaud the couple, and Broadway applauded—all but Merton Gill, who stared moodily into his coffee cup or lifted bored eyes to the scene of revelry. He was not bored, but his various emotions combined to produce this effect very plausibly. He was dismayed at this sudden revelation of art in the dance so near him. Imogene Pulver had once done an art dance back in Simsbury, at the cantata of Esther in the vestry of the Methodist church, and had been not a little criticised for her daring; but Imogene had been abundantly clad, and her gestures much more restrained. He was trying now to picture how Gashwiler would take a thing like this, or Mrs. Gashwiler, for that matter! One glimpse of those practically unclad bodies skipping and bounding there would probably throw them into a panic. They couldn't have sat it through. And here he was, right up in front of them, and not turning a hair.

This reflection permitted something of the contemptuous to show in the random glances with which he swept the dancers? He could not look at them steadily, not when they were close, as they often were. Also, he loathed the cigarette he was smoking. The tolerant scorn for the Gashwilers and his feeling for the cigarette brought him again into favourable notice. He heard Henshaw, but did not look up.

"Get another flash here, Paul. He's rather a good little bit." Henshaw now stood beside him. "Hold that," he said. "No, wait." He spoke to Merton's companion. "You change seats a minute with Miss Montague, as if you'd got tired of him—see what I mean? Miss Montague—Miss Montague." The Spanish girl arose, seeming not wholly pleased at this bit of directing. The Montague girl came to the table. She was a blithesome sprite in a salmon-pink dancing frock. Her blonde curls fell low over one eye which she now cocked inquiringly at the director.

"You're trying to liven him up," explained Henshaw. "That's all—baby-vamp him. He'll do the rest. He's quite a good little bit."

The Montague girl flopped into the chair, leaned roguishly toward Merton Gill, placed a small hand upon the sleeve of his coat and peered archly at him through beaded lashes, one eye almost hidden by its thatch of curls. Merton Gill sunk low in his chair, cynically tapped the ash from his tenth cigarette into the coffee cup and raised bored eyes to hers. "That's it—shoot it, Paul, just a flash."

The camera was being wheeled toward them. The Montague girl, with her hand still on his arm, continued her wheedling, though now she spoke.

"Why, look who's here. Kid, I didn't know you in your stepping-out clothes. Say, listen, why do you always upstage me? I never done a thing to you, did I? Go on, now, give me the fishy eye again. How'd you ace yourself into this first row, anyway? Did you have to fight for it? Say, your friend'll be mad at me putting her out of here, won't she? Well, blame it on the gelatin master. I never suggested it. Say, you got Henshaw going. He likes that blighted look of yours."

He made no reply to this chatter. He must keep in the picture. He merely favoured her with a glance of fatigued indifference. The camera was focused.

"All ready, you people. Do like I said, now. Lights, camera!"

Merton Gill drew upon his cigarette with the utmost disrelish, raised the cold eyes of a disillusioned man to the face of the leering Montague girl, turned aside from her with every sign of apathy, and wearily exhaled the smoke. There seemed to be but this one pleasure left to him.

"Cut!" said Henshaw, and somewhere lights jarred off. "Just stick there a bit, Miss Montague. We'll have a couple more shots when the dancing begins."

Merton resented this change. He preferred the other girl. She lured him but not in so pronounced, so flagrant a manner. The blight of Broadway became more apparent than ever upon his face. The girl's hand still fluttered upon his sleeve as the music came and dancers shuffled by them.

"Say, you're the actin' kid, all right." She was tapping the floor with the heel of a satin slipper. He wished above all things that she wouldn't call him "Kid." He meditated putting a little of Broadway's blight upon her by saying in a dignified way that his real name was Clifford Armytage. Still, this might not blight her—you couldn't tell about the girl.

"You certainly are the actin'est kid on this set, I'll tell the lot that. Of course these close-ups won't mean much, just about one second, or half that maybe. Or some hick in the cuttin' room may kill 'em dead. Come on, give me the fish-eye again. That's it. Say, I'm glad I didn't have to smoke cigarettes in this scene. They wouldn't do for my type, standin' where the brook and river meet up. I hate a cigarette worse'n anything. You—I bet you'd give up food first."

"I hate 'em, too," he muttered grudgingly, glad to be able to say this, even though only to one whose attentions he meant to discourage. "If I have to smoke one more it'll finish me."

"Now, ain't that the limit? Too bad, Kid!"

"I didn't even have any of my own. That Spanish girl gave me these."

The Montague girl glanced over his shoulder at the young woman whose place she had usurped. "Spanish, eh? If she's Spanish I'm a Swede right out of Switzerland. Any-way, I never could like to smoke. I started to learn one summer when I was eight. Pa and Ma and I was out with a tent Tom-show, me doing Little Eva, and between acts I had to put on pants and come out and do a smoking song, all about a kid learning to smoke his first cigar and not doin' well with it, see? But they had to cut it out. Gosh, what us artists suffer at times! Pa had me try it a couple of years later when I was doin' Louise the blind girl in the Two Orphans, playin' thirty cents top. It was a good song, all right, with lots of funny gags. I'd 'a' been the laughing hit of the bill if I could 'a' learned not to swallow. We had to cut it out again after the second night. Talk about entering into your part. Me? I was too good."

If the distant camera glanced this way it caught merely the persistent efforts of a beautiful debutante who had not yet felt the blight of Broadway to melt the cynicism of one who suffered it more and more acutely each moment. Her hand fluttered on his sleeve and her left eye continuously beguiled him from under the overhanging curl. As often as he thought it desirable he put the bored glance upon her, though mostly he stared in dejection at the coffee cup or the empty wine glass. He was sorry that she had had that trouble with the cigar, but one who as Little Eva or poor persecuted Louise, the blind girl, had to do a song and dance between the acts must surely come from a low plane of art. He was relieved when, at megaphoned directions, an elderly fop came to whirl her off in the dance. Her last speech was: "That poor Henshaw—the gelatin master'll have megaphone-lip by to-night."

He was left alone at his table. He wondered if they might want a close-up of him this way, uncompanioned, jaded, tired of it all, as if he would be saying: "There's always the river!" But nothing of this sort happened. There was more dancing, more close-ups of Muriel Mercer being stricken with her vision of tenement misery under the foul glare of a middle-aged roue inflamed with wine. And there was a shot of Muriel perceiving at last the blight of Broadway and going to a table at which sat a pale, noble-looking young man with a high forehead, who presently led her out into the night to the real life of the worthy poor. Later the deserted admirer became again a roue inflamed with wine and submitted to a close-up that would depict his baffled rage. He clenched his hands in this and seemed to convey, with a snarling lift of his lip, that the girl would yet be his. Merton Gill had ceased to smoke. He had sounded on Broadway even the shallow pleasure of cigarettes. He was thoroughly blighted.

At last a megaphoned announcement from the assistant director dismissing the extras, keeping the star, the lead, and a few small-part people, to clean up medium shots, "dramatics," and other work requiring no crowd. "All you extra people here to-morrow morning, eight-thirty, same clothes and make-up." There was a quick breaking up of the revelry. The Broadway pleasure-seekers threw off the blight and stormed the assistant director for slips of paper which he was now issuing. Merton Gill received one, labelled "Talent check." There was fine print upon it which he took no pains to read, beyond gathering its general effect that the Victor Film-art Company had the full right to use any photographs of him that its agents might that day have obtained. What engrossed him to the exclusion of this legal formality was the item that he would now be paid seven dollars and fifty cents for his day's work—and once he had been forced to toil half a week for this sum! Emerging from the stage into the sunlight he encountered the Montague girl who hailed him as he would have turned to avoid her.

"Say, trouper, I thought I'd tell you in case you didn't know—we don't take our slips to that dame in that outside cafeteria any more. She always pinches off a quarter or may be four bits. They got it fixed now so the cash is always on tap in the office. I just thought I'd tell you."

"Thanks," he said, still with the jaded air of the disillusioned. He had only the vaguest notion of her meaning, but her intention had been kindly. "Thank you very much."

"Oh, don't mention it. I just thought I'd tell you." She glanced after him shrewdly.

Nearing the office he observed a long line of Broadway revellers waiting to cash their slips. Its head was lost inside the building and it trailed far outside. No longer was any blight to be perceived. The slips were ready in hand. Instead of joining the line Merton decided upon luncheon. It was two o'clock, and though waiters with trays had been abundant in the gilded cabaret, the best screen art had not seemed to demand a serving of actual food. Further, he would eat in the cafeteria in evening dress, his make-up still on, like a real actor. The other time he had felt conspicuous because nothing had identified him with the ordinary clientele of the place.

The room was not crowded now. Only a table here and there held late comers, and the choice of foods when he reached the serving counter at the back was limited. He permitted himself to complain of this in a practised manner, but made a selection and bore his tray to the centre of the room. He had chosen a table and was about to sit, when he detected Henshaw farther down the room, and promptly took the one next him. It was probable that Henshaw would recall him and praise the work he had done. But the director merely rolled unseeing eyes over him as he seated himself, and continued his speech to the man Merton had before seen him with, the grizzled dark man with the stubby gray mustache whom he called

Governor. Merton wondered if he could be the governor of California, but decided not. Perhaps an ex-governor.

"She's working out well," he was saying. "I consider it one of the best continuities Belmore has done. Not a line of smut in it, but to make up for that we'll have over thirty changes of costume."

Merton Gill coughed violently, then stared moodily at his plate of baked beans. He hoped that this, at least, would recall him to Henshaw who might fix an eye on him to say: "And, by the way, here is a young actor that was of great help to me this morning." But neither man even glanced up. Seemingly this young actor could choke to death without exciting their notice. He stared less moodily at the baked beans. Henshaw would notice him sometime, and you couldn't do everything at once.

The men had finished their luncheon and were smoking. The animated Henshaw continued his talk. "And about that other thing we were discussing, Governor, I want to go into that with you. I tell you if we can do Robinson Crusoe, and do it right, a regular five-thousand-foot program feature, the thing ought to gross a million. A good, clean, censor-proof picture—great kid show, run forever. Shipwreck stuff, loading the raft, island stuff, hut stuff, goats, finding the footprint, cannibals, the man Friday—can't you see it?"

The Governor seemed to see it. "Fine—that's so!" He stared above the director's head for the space of two inhalations from his cigarette, imbuing Merton Gill with gratitude that he need not smoke again that day. "But say, look here, how about your love interest?"

Henshaw waved this aside with his own cigarette and began to make marks on the back of an envelope. "Easy enough—Belmore can fix that up. We talked over one or two ways. How about having Friday's sister brought over with him to this island? The cannibals are going to eat her, too. Then the cannibals run to their canoes when they hear the gun, just the same as in the book. And Crusoe rescues the two. And when he cuts the girl's bonds he finds she can't be Friday's real sister, because she's white—see what I mean? Well, we work it out later that she's the daughter of an English Earl that was wrecked near the cannibal island, and they rescued her, and Friday's mother brought her up as her own child. She's saved the papers that came ashore, and she has the Earl's coat-of-arms tattooed on her shoulder blade, and finally, after Crusoe has fallen in love with her, and she's remembered a good deal of her past, along comes the old Earl, her father, in a ship and rescues them all. How about that?" Henshaw, brightly expectant, awaited the verdict of his chief.

"Well—I don't know." The other considered. "Where's your conflict, after the girl is saved from the savages? And Crusoe in the book wears a long beard. How about that? He won't look like anything—sort of hairy, and that's all."

Henshaw from the envelope on which he drew squares and oblongs appeared to gain fresh inspiration. He looked up with new light in his eyes. "I got it—got the whole thing. Modernize it. This chap is a rich young New Yorker, cruising on his yacht, and he's wrecked on this island and gets a lot of stuff ashore and his valet is saved, too—say there's some good comedy, see what I mean?—valet is one of these stiff English lads, never been wrecked on an island before and complains all the time about the lack of conveniences. I can see a lot of good gags for him, having to milk the goats, and getting scared of the other animals, and no place to press his master's clothes—things like that, you know. Well, the young fellow explores the island and finds another party that's been wrecked on the other side, and it's the girl and the man that got her father into his power and got all of his estate and is going to make beggars of them if the girl won't marry him, and she comes on the young fellow under some palms and they fall in love and fix it up to double-cross the villain—Belmore can work it out from there. How about that? And say, we can use a lot of trims from that South Sea piece we did last year, all that yacht and island stuff—see what I mean?"

The other considered profoundly. "Yes, you got a story there, but it won't be Robinson Crusoe, don't you see?"

Again Henshaw glanced up from his envelope with the light of inspiration. "Well, how about this? Call it Robinson Crusoe, Junior! There you are. We get the value of the name and do the story the way we want it, the young fellow being shaved every day by the valet, and he can invite the other party over to dine with him and receive them in evening dress and everything. Can't you see it? If that story wouldn't gross big then I don't know a story. And all easy stuff. We can use the trims for the long shots, and use that inlet, toward the other end of Catalina for the hut and the beach; sure-fire stuff, Governor—and Robinson Crusoe, Junior is a cinch title."

"Well, give Belmore as much dope as you've got, and see what he can work out."

They arose and stood by the counter to pay their checks.

"If you want to see the rushes of that stuff we shot this morning be over to the projection room at five," said Henshaw as they went out. Neither had observed the rising young screen actor, Clifford Armytage, though he had coughed violently again as they left. He had coughed most plausibly, moreover, because of the cigarettes.

At the cashier's window, no longer obstructed, he received his money, another five-dollar bill adorned with the cheerfully prosperous face of Benjamin Harrison and half that amount in silver coin. Then, although loath to do this, he went to the dressing room and removed his make-up. That grease paint had given him a world of confidence.

At the casting office he stopped to tell his friend of the day's camera triumph, how the director had seemed to single him out from a hundred or so revellers to portray facially the deadly effect of Broadway's night life.

"Good work!" she applauded. "Before long you'll be having jobs oftener. And don't forget, you're called again to-morrow morning for the gambling-house scene."

She was a funny woman; always afraid he would forget something he could not possibly forget. Once more in the Patterson kitchen he pressed his suit and dreamt of new eminences in his chosen art.

The following morning he was again the first to reach the long dressing room, the first to be made up by the grumbling extra, the first to reach the big stage. The cabaret of yesterday had overnight been transformed into a palatial gambling hell. Along the sides of the room and at its centre were tables equipped for strange games of chance which only his picture knowledge enabled him to recognize. He might tarry at these tables, he thought, but he must remember to look bored in the near presence of Henshaw. The Spanish girl of yesterday appeared and he greeted her warmly. "I got some cigarettes this time," he said, "so let me pay you back all those I smoked of yours yesterday." Together they filled the golden case that hung from her girdle.

"It's swell, all right," said the girl, gazing about the vast room now filling with richly clad gamblers.

"But I thought it was all over except the tenement-house scenes where Vera Vanderpool has gone to relieve the poor," he said.

The girl explained. "This scene comes before the one we did yesterday. It's where the rich old boy first sees Vera playing roulette, and she loses a lot of money and is going to leave her string of pearls, but he says it's a mere trifle and let him pay her gambling losses, so in a weak moment she does, and that's how he starts to get her into his power. You'll see how it works out. Say, they spent some money on this set, all right."

It was indeed a rich set, as the girl had said. It seemed to Merton Gill that it would be called on the screen "One of those Plague Spots that Eat like a Cancer at the Heart of New York." He lighted a cigarette and leaned nonchalantly against a pillar to smile a tired little smile at the pleasure-mad victims of this life who were now grouping around the roulette and faro tables. He must try for his jaded look.

"Some swell shack!" The speaker was back of him, but he knew her for the Montague girl, and was instantly enabled to increase the blighted look for which he had been trying. "One natty little hovel, I'll tell the world," the girl continued. "Say, this puts it all over the Grand Central station, don't it? Must be right smack at the corner of Broadway and Fifth Avenue. Well, start the little ball rolling, so I can make a killing." He turned his head slightly and saw her dance off to one of the roulette tables, accompanied by the middle-aged fop who had been her companion yesterday.

Henshaw and his assistant now appeared and began grouping the players at the various tables. Merton Gill remained leaning wearily against his massive pillar, trying to appear blase under the chatter of the Spanish girl. The groups were arranged to the liking of Henshaw, though only after many trials. The roulette ball was twirled and the lively rattle of chips could be heard. Scanning his scene, he noted Merton and his companion.

"Oh, there you are, you two. Sister, you go and stand back of that crowd around the faro table. Keep craning to look over their shoulders, and give us your side view. I want to use this man alone. Here." He led Merton to a round table on which were a deck of cards and some neatly stacked chips. "Sit here, facing the camera. Keep one hand on the cards, sort of toying with 'em, see what I mean?"

He scattered the piled chips loosely about the table, and called to a black waiter: "Here, George, put one of those wine glasses on his left."

The wine glass was placed. "Now kind of slump down in your chair, like you saw the hollowness of it all—see what I mean?"

Merton Gill thought he saw. He exhaled smoke, toyed contemptuously with the cards at his right hand and, with a gesture of repulsion, pushed the wine glass farther away. He saw the hollowness of it all. The spirit of wine sang in his glass but to deaf ears. Chance could no longer entice him. It might again have been suspected that cigarettes were ceasing to allure.

"Good work! Keep it up," said Henshaw and went back to his cameras.

The lights jarred on; desperate gaming was filmed. "More life at the roulette tables," megaphoned Henshaw. "Crowd closer around that left-hand faro table. You're playing for big stakes." The gaming became more feverish. The mad light of pleasure was in every eye, yet one felt that the blight of Broadway was real.

The camera was wheeled forward and Merton Gill joyously quit smoking while Henshaw secured flashes of various groups, chiefly of losers who were seeing the hollowness of it all. He did not, however, disdain a bit of comedy.

"Miss Montague."

"Yes, Mr. Henshaw." The Montague girl paused in the act of sprinkling chips over a roulette lay-out.

"Your escort has lost all his chips and you've lost all he bought for you—"

The girl and her escort passed to other players the chips before them, and waited.

"Your escort takes out his wallet, shows it to you empty, and shrugs his shoulders. You shrug, too, but turn your back on him, facing the camera, and take some bills out of your stocking—see what I mean? Give her some bills, someone."

"Never mind, Mr. Henshaw; I already got some there." The pantomime was done, the girl turned, stooped, withdrew flattened bills from one of the salmon-pink stockings and flourished them at her escort who achieved a transition from gloom to joy. Merton Gill, observing this shameless procedure, plumbed the nether depths of disgust for Broadway's night life.

The camera was now wheeled toward him and he wearily lighted another cigarette. "Get a flash of this chap," Henshaw was saying. The subject leaned forward in his chair, gazing with cynical eyes at the fevered throng. Wine, women, song, all had palled. Gambling had no charm—he looked with disrelish at the cigarette he had but just lighted.

"All right, Paul, that's good. Now get that bunch over at the crap table."

Merton Gill lost no time in relinquishing his cigarette. He dropped it into the wine glass which became a symbol of Broadway's dead-sea fruit. Thereafter he smoked only when he was in the picture. He felt that he was becoming screen wise. And Henshaw had remembered him. The cast of The Blight of Broadway might not be jewelled with his name, but his work would stand out. He had given the best that was in him.

He watched the entrance of Muriel Mercer, maddest of all the mad throng, accompanied by the two young men and the girl who was not so beautiful. He watched her lose steadily, and saw her string of pearls saved by the elderly scoundrel who had long watched the beautiful girl as only the Wolf of Wall Street could watch one so fair. He saw her leave upon his arm, perhaps for further unwholesome adventure along Broadway. The lights were out, the revelry done.

Merton Gill beyond a doubt preferred Western stuff, some heart-gripping tale of the open spaces, or perhaps of the frozen north, where he could be the hard-riding, straight-shooting, two-fisted wonder-man, and not have to smoke so many cigarettes—only one now and then, which he would roll himself and toss away after a few puffs. Still, he had shown above the mob of extra people, he thought. Henshaw had noticed him. He was coming on.

The Montague girl hailed him as he left the set. "Hullo, old trouper. I caught you actin' again to-day, right out before the white folks. Well, so far so good. But say, I'm glad all that roulette and stuff was for the up-and-down stage and not on the level. I'd certainly have lost everything but my make-up. So long, Kid!" She danced off to join a group of other women who were leaving. He felt a kindly pity for the child. There could be little future in this difficult art for one who took it so lightly; who talked so frankly to strangers without being introduced.

At luncheon in the cafeteria he waited a long time in the hope of encountering Henshaw, who would perhaps command his further services in the cause of creative screen art. He meant to be animated at this meeting, to show the director that he could be something more than an actor who had probed the shams of

Broadway. But he lingered in vain. He thought Henshaw would perhaps be doing without food in order to work on the scenario for Robinson Crusoe, Junior.

He again stopped to thank his friend, the casting director, for securing him his first chance. She accepted his thanks smilingly, and asked him to drop around often. "Mind, you don't forget our number," she said.

He was on the point of making her understand once for all that he would not forget the number, that he would never forget Gashwiler's address, that he had been coming to this studio too often to forget its location. But someone engaged her at the window, so he was obliged to go on without enlightening the woman. She seemed to be curiously dense.

CHAPTER VII. "NOTHING TO-DAY, DEAR!"

The savings had been opportunely replenished. In two days he had accumulated a sum for which, back in Simsbury, he would have had to toil a week. Yet there was to be said in favour of the Simsbury position that it steadily endured. Each week brought its fifteen dollars, pittance though it might be, while the art of the silver screen was capricious in its rewards, not to say jumpy. Never, for weeks at a stretch, had Gashwiler said with a tired smile, "Nothing to-day—sorry!" He might have been a grouch and given to unreasonable nagging, but with him there was always a very definite something to-day which he would specify, in short words if the occasion seemed to demand. There was not only a definite something every day but a definite if not considerable sum of money to be paid over every Saturday night, and in the meantime three very definite and quite satisfying meals to be freely partaken of at stated hours each day.

The leisure enforced by truly creative screen art was often occupied now with really moving pictures of Metta Judson placing practicable food upon the Gashwiler table. This had been no table in a gilded Broadway resort, holding empty coffee cups and half empty wine glasses, passed and repassed by apparently busy waiters with laden trays who never left anything of a practicable nature. Doubtless the set would not have appealed to Henshaw. He would never have been moved to take close-ups, even for mere flashes, of those who ate this food. And yet, more and more as the days went by, this old-time film would unreel itself before the eager eyes of Merton Gill. Often now it thrilled him as might have an installment of The Hazards of Hortense, for the food of his favourite pharmacy was beginning to pall and Metta Judson, though giving her shallow mind to base village gossip, was a good cook. She became the adored heroine of an apparently endless serial to be entitled The Hazards of Clifford Armytage, in which the hero had tragically little to do but sit upon a bench and wait while tempting repasts were served.

Sometimes on the little bench around the eucalyptus tree he would run an entire five-thousand-foot program feature, beginning with the Sunday midday dinner of roast chicken, and abounding in tense dramatic moments such as corned-beef and cabbage on Tuesday night, and corned-beef hash on Wednesday morning. He would pause to take superb closeups of these, the corned beef on its spreading platter hemmed about with boiled potatoes and turnips and cabbage, and the corned beef hash with its richly browned surface. The thrilling climax would be the roast of beef on Saturday night, with close-ups taken in the very eye of the camera, of the mashed potatoes and the apple pie drenched with cream. And there were close-ups of Metta Judson, who had never seriously contemplated a screen career, placing upon the table a tower of steaming hot cakes, while a platter of small sausages loomed eloquently in the foreground.

With eyes closed he would run this film again and again, cutting here, rearranging sequences, adding trims from suddenly remembered meals of the dead past, devising more intimate close-ups, such as the one of Metta withdrawing pies from the oven or smoothing hot chocolate caressingly over the top of a giant cake, or broiling chops, or saying in a large-lettered subtitle—artistically decorated with cooked foods—"How about some hot coffee, Merton?"

He became an able producer of this drama. He devised a hundred sympathetic little touches that Henshaw would probably never have thought of. He used footage on a mere platter of steak that another director might have ignored utterly. He made it gripping—the supreme heart-interest drama of his season a big thing done in a big way, and yet censor-proof. Not even the white-souled censors of the great state of Pennsylvania could have outlawed its realism, brutal though this was in such great moments as when Gashwiler carved the roast beef. So able was his artistry that Merton's nostrils would sometimes betray him—he could swear they caught rich aromas from that distant board.

Not only had the fare purveyed by his favourite pharmacy put a blight upon him equal to Broadway's blight, but even of this tasteless stuff he must be cautious in his buying. A sandwich, not too meaty at the centre, coffee tasting strangely of other things sold in a pharmacy, a segment of pie fair—seeming on its surface, but lacking the punch, as he put it, of Metta Judson's pie, a standardized, factory-made, altogether formal and perfunctory pie—these were the meagre items of his accustomed luncheon and dinner.

He had abandoned breakfast, partly because it cost money and partly because a gentleman in eastern Ohio had recently celebrated his hundred and third birthday by reason, so he confided to the press, of having always breakfasted upon a glass of clear cold water. Probably ham and eggs or corned—beef hash would have cut him off at ninety, and water from the tap in the Patterson kitchen was both clear and cold. It was not so much that he cared to live beyond ninety or so, but he wished to survive until things began to pick up on the Holden lot, and if this did bring him many more years, well and good. Further, if the woman in the casting office persisted, as she had for ten days, in saying "Nothing yet" to inquiring screen artists, he might be compelled to intensify the regime of the Ohio centenarian. Perhaps a glass of clear cold water at night, after a hearty midday meal of drug—store sandwiches and pie, would work new wonders.

It seemed to be the present opinion of other waiters on the extra bench that things were never going to pick up on the Holden lot nor on any other lot. Strongly marked types, ready to add distinction to the screen of painted shadows, freely expressed a view that the motion-picture business was on the rocks. Unaffected by the optimists who wrote in the picture magazines, they saw no future for it. More than one of them threatened to desert the industry and return to previous callings. As they were likely to put it, they were going to leave the pictures flat and go back to type-writing or selling standard art-works or waiting on table or something where you could count on your little bit every week.

Under the eucalyptus tree one morning Merton Gill, making some appetizing changes in the fifth reel of Eating at Gashwiler's, was accosted by a youngish woman whom he could not at first recall. She had come from the casting office and paused when she saw him.

"Hello, I thought it was you, but I wasn't sure in them clothes. How they coming?"

He stared blankly, startled at the sudden transposition he had been compelled to make, for the gleaming knife of Gashwiler, standing up to carve, had just then hovered above the well-browned roast of beef. Then he placed the speaker by reason of her eyes. It was the Spanish girl, his companion of the gilded cabaret, later encountered in the palatial gambling hell that ate like a cancer at the heart of New York—probably at the corner of Broadway and Fifth Avenue.

He arose and shook hands cordially. He had supposed, when he thought of the girl at all, that she would always be rather Spanish, an exotic creature rather garishly dressed, nervously eager, craving excitement such as may be had in cabarets on Broadway, with a marked inclination for the lighter life of pleasure. But she wore not so much as a rose in her smoothly combed hair. She was not only not excited but she was not exciting. She was plainly dressed in skirt and shirtwaist of no distinction, her foot-gear was of the most ordinary, and well worn, and her face under a hat of no allure was without make-up, a commonplace, somewhat anxious face with lines about the eyes. But her voice as well as her eyes helped him to recall her.

She spoke with an effort at jauntiness after Merton had greeted her. "That's one great slogan, 'Business as Usual!' ain't it? Well, it's business as usual here, so I just found out from the Countess—as usual, rotten. I ain't had but three days since I seen you last."

"I haven't had even one," he told her.

"No? Say, that's tough. You're registered with the Service Bureau, ain't you?"

"Well, I didn't do that, because they might send me any place, and I sort of wanted to work on this particular lot." Instantly he saw himself saving Beulah Baxter, for the next installment, from a fate worse than death, but the one-time Spanish girl did not share this vision.

"Oh, well, little I care where I work. I had two days at the Bigart in a hop-joint scene, and one over at the United doin' some board-walk stuff. I could 'a' had another day there, but the director said I wasn't just the type for a chick bathing-suit. He was very nice about it. Of course I know my legs ain't the best part of me— I sure ain't one of them like the girl that says she's wasted in skirts." She grinned ruefully.

He felt that some expression of sympathy would be graceful here, yet he divined that it must be very discreetly, almost delicately, worded. He could easily be too blunt.

"I guess I'd be pretty skinny in a bathing-suit myself, right now. I know they won't be giving me any such part pretty soon if I have to cut down on the meals the way I been doing."

"Oh, of course I don't mean I'm actually skinny—"

He felt he had been blunt, after all.

"Not to say skinny." she went on, "but—well, you know—more like home-folks, I guess. Anyway, I got no future as a bathing beauty—none whatever. And this walkin' around to the different lots ain't helpin' me any, either. Of course it ain't as if I couldn't go back to the insurance office. Mr. Gropp, he's office manager, he was very nice about it. He says, 'I wish you all the luck in the world, girlie, and remember your job as filin' clerk will always be here for you.' Wasn't that gentlemanly of him? Still, I'd rather act than stand on my feet all day filing letters. I won't go back till I have to."

"Me either," said Merton Gill, struggling against the obsession of Saturday-night dinner at Gashwiler's.

Grimly he resumed his seat when the girl with a friendly "So long!" had trudged on. In spite of himself he found something base in his nature picturing his return to the emporium and to the thrice-daily encounter with Metta Judson's cookery. He let his lower instincts toy with the unworthy vision. Gashwiler would advance him the money to return, and the job would be there. Probably Spencer Grant had before this tired of the work and gone into insurance or some other line, and probably Gashwiler would be only too glad to have the wanderer back. He would get off No. 3 just in time for breakfast.

He brushed the monstrous scene from his eyes, shrugged it from his shoulders. He would not give up. They had all struggled and sacrificed, and why should he shrink from the common ordeal? But he wished the Spanish girl hadn't talked about going back to her job. He regretted not having stopped her with words of confident cheer that would have stiffened his own resolution. He could see her far down the street, on her way to the next lot, her narrow shoulders switching from light to shadow as she trudged under the line of eucalyptus trees. He hoped she wouldn't give up. No one should ever give up—least of all Merton Gill.

The days wore wearily on. He began to feel on his own face the tired little smile of the woman in the casting office as she would look up to shake her head, often from the telephone over which she was saying: "Nothing to-day, dear. Sorry!" She didn't exactly feel that the motion-picture business had gone on the rocks, but she knew it wasn't picking up as it should. And ever and again she would have Merton Gill assure her that he hadn't forgotten the home address, the town where lived Gighampton or Gumwash or whoever it was that held the good old job open for him. He had divined that it was a jest of some sort when she warned him not to forget the address and he would patiently smile at this, but he always put her right about the name of Gashwiler. Of course it was a name any one might forget, though the woman always seemed to make the most earnest effort to remember it.

Each day, after his brief chat with her in which he learned that there would be nothing to-day, he would sit on the waiting-room bench or out under the eucalyptus tree and consecrate himself anew to the art of the perpendicular screen. And each day, as the little hoard was diminished by even those slender repasts at the drug store, he ran his film of the Gashwiler dining room in action.

From time to time he would see the Montague girl, alone or with her mother, entering the casting office or perhaps issuing from the guarded gate. He avoided her when possible. She persisted in behaving as if they had been properly introduced and had known each other a long time. She was too familiar, and her levity jarred upon his more serious mood. So far as he could see, the girl had no screen future, though doubtless she was her own worst enemy. If someone had only taught her to be serious, her career might have been worth while. She had seemed not wholly negligible in the salmon-pink dancing frock, though of course the blonde curls had not been true.

Then the days passed until eating merely at a drug-store lunch counter became not the only matter of concern. There was the item of room rent. Mrs. Patterson, the Los Angeles society woman, had, upon the occasion of their first interview, made it all too clear that the money, trifling though it must seem for a well-furnished room with the privilege of electric iron in the kitchen, must be paid each week in advance. Strictly in advance. Her eye had held a cold light as she dwelt upon this.

There had been times lately when, upon his tree bench, he would try to dramatize Mrs. Patterson as a woman with a soft heart under that polished society exterior, chilled by daily contact with other society people at the Iowa or Kansas or other society picnics, yet ready to melt at the true human touch. But he had never quite succeeded in this bit of character work. Something told him that she was cold all through, a society woman without a flaw in her armour. He could not make her seem to listen patiently while he explained that only one company was now shooting on the lot, but that big things were expected to be on in another week or so. A certain skeptic hardness was in her gaze as he visioned it.

He decided, indeed, that he could never bring himself even to attempt this scene with the woman, so remote was he from seeing her eye soften and her voice warm with the assurance that a few weeks more or less need not matter. The room rent, he was confident, would have to be paid strictly in advance so long as their relations continued. She was the kind who would insist upon this formality even after he began to play, at an enormous salary, a certain outstanding part in the

Hazards of Hortense. The exigencies, even the adversities, of art would never make the slightest appeal to this hardened soul. So much for that. And daily the hoard waned.

Yet his was not the only tragedy. In the waiting room, where he now spent more of his time, he listened one day to the Montague girl chat through the window with the woman she called Countess.

"Yeah, Pa was double-crossed over at the Bigart. He raised that lovely set of whiskers for Camillia of the Cumberlands and what did he get for it?—just two weeks. Fact! What do you know about that? Hugo has him killed off in the second spool with a squirrel rifle from ambush, and Pa thinking he would draw pay for at least another three weeks. He kicked, but Hugo says the plot demanded it. I bet, at that, he was just trying to cut down his salary list. I bet that continuity this minute shows Pa drinking his corn out of a jug and playing a fiddle for the dance right down to the last scene. Don't artists get the razz, though. And that Hugo, he'd spend a week in the hot place to save a thin dime. Let me tell you, Countess, don't you ever get your lemon in his squeezer."

There were audible murmurs of sympathy from the Countess.

"And so the old trouper had to start out Monday morning to peddle the brush. Took him three days to land anything at all, and then it's nothing but a sleeping souse in a Western bar-room scene. In here now he is—something the Acme people are doing. He's had three days, just lying down with his back against a barrel sleeping. He's not to wake up even when the fight starts, but sleep right on through it, which they say will be a good gag. Well, maybe. But it's tough on his home. He gets all his rest daytimes and keeps us restless all night making a new kind of beer and tending his still, and so on. You bet Ma and I, the minute he's through with this piece, are going pronto to get that face of his as naked as the day he was born. Pa's so temperamental—like that time he was playing a Bishop and never touched a drop for five weeks, and in bed every night at nine-thirty. Me? Oh, I'm having a bit of my own in this Acme piece—God's Great Outdoors, I think it is—anyway, I'm to be a little blonde hussy in the bar-room, sitting on the miners' knees and all like that, so they'll order more drinks. It certainly takes all kinds of art to make an artist. And next week I got some shipwreck stuff for Baxter, and me with bronchial pneumonia right this minute, and hating tank stuff, anyway. Well, Countess, don't take any counterfeit money. So long."

She danced through a doorway and was gone—she was one who seldom descended to plain walking. She would manage a dance step even in the short distance from the casting—office door to the window. It was not of such material, Merton Gill was sure, that creative artists were moulded. And there was no question now of his own utter seriousness. The situation hourly grew more desperate. For a week he had foregone the drug-store pie, so that now he recalled it as very wonderful pie indeed, but he dared no longer indulge in this luxury. An occasional small bag of candy and as much sugar as he could juggle into his coffee must satisfy his craving for sweets. Stoically he awaited the end—some end. The moving-picture business seemed to be still on the rocks, but things must take a turn.

He went over the talk of the Montague girl. Her father had perhaps been unfairly treated, but at least he was working again. And there were other actors who would go unshaven for even a sleeping part in the bar-room scene of God's Great Outdoors. Merton Gill knew one, and rubbed his shaven chin. He thought, too, of the girl's warning about counterfeit money. He had not known that the casting director's duties required her to handle money, but probably he had overlooked this item in her routine. And was counterfeit money about? He drew out his own remaining bill and scrutinized it anxiously. It seemed to be genuine. He hoped it was, for Mrs. Patterson's sake, and was relieved when she accepted it without question that night.

Later he tested the handful of silver that remained to him and prayed earnestly that an increase of prosperity be granted to producers of the motion picture. With the silver he eked out another barren week, only to face a day the evening of which must witness another fiscal transaction with Mrs. Patterson. And there was no longer a bill for this heartless society creature. He took a long look at the pleasant little room as he left it that morning. The day must bring something but it might not bring him back that night.

At the drug store he purchased a bowl of vegetable soup, loaded it heavily with catsup at intervals when the attendant had other matters on his mind, and seized an extra half—portion of crackers left on their plate by a satiated neighbour. He cared little for catsup, but it doubtless bore nourishing elements, and nourishment was now important. He crumpled his paper napkin and laid upon the marble slab a trifling silver coin. It was the last of his hoard. When he should eat next and under what circumstances were now as uncertain as where he should sleep that night, though he was already resolving that catsup would be no part of his meal. It might be well enough in its place, but he had abundantly proved that it was not, strictly speaking, a food.

He reached the Holden studios and loitered outside for half an hour before daring the daily inquiry at the window. Yet, when at last he did approach it, his waning faith in prayer was renewed, for here in his direst hour was cheering news. It seemed even that his friend beyond the window had been impatient at his coming.

"Just like you to be late when there's something doing!" she called to him with friendly impatience. "Get over to the dressing rooms on the double-quick. It's the Victor people doing some Egyptian stuff—they'll give you a costume. Hurry along!"

And he had lingered over a bowl of soggy crackers soaked, at the last, chiefly in catsup! He hurried, with a swift word of thanks.

In the same dressing room where he had once been made up as a Broadway pleasure seeker he now donned the flowing robe and burnoose of a Bedouin, and by the same grumbling extra his face and hands were stained the rich brown of children of the desert. A dozen other men of the paler race had undergone the same treatment. A sheik of great stature and noble mien smoked an idle cigarette in the doorway. He was accoutred with musket and with pistols in his belt.

An assistant director presently herded the desert men down an alley between two of the big stages and to the beginning of the oriental street that Merton had noticed on his first day within the Holden walls. It was now peopled picturesquely with other Bedouins. Banners hung from the walls and veiled ladies peeped from the latticed balconies. A camel was led excitingly through the crowded way, and donkeys and goats were to be observed. It was a noisy street until a whistle sounded at the farther end, then all was silence while the voice of Henshaw came through the megaphone.

It appeared that long shots of the street were Henshaw's first need. Up and down it Merton Gill strolled in a negligent manner, stopping perhaps to haggle with the vendor who sold sweetmeats from a tray, or to chat with a tribal brother fresh from the sandy wastes, or to purchase a glass of milk from the man with the goats. He secured a rose from the flower seller, and had the inspiration to toss it to one of the discreet balconies above him, but as he stepped back to do this he was stopped by the watchful assistant director who stood just inside a doorway. "Hey, Bill, none of that! Keep your head down, and pay no attention to the dames. It ain't done."

He strolled on with the rose in his hand. Later, and much nearer the end of the street where the cameras were, he saw the sheik of noble mien halt the flower seller, haggle for another rose, place this daintily behind his left ear and stalk on, his musket held over one shoulder, his other hand on a belted pistol. Merton disposed of his rose in the same manner. He admired the sheik for his stature, his majestic carriage, his dark, handsome, yet sinister face with its brooding eyes. He thought this man, at least, would be a true Arab, some real son of the desert who had wandered afar. His manner was so much more authentic than that of the extra people all about.

A whistle blew and the street action was suspended. There was a long wait while cameras were moved up and groups formed under the direction of Henshaw and his assistant. A band of Bedouins were now to worship in the porch of a mosque. Merton Gill was among these. The assistant director initiated them briefly into Moslem rites. Upon prayer rugs they bowed their foreheads to earth in the direction of Mecca.

"What's the idea of this here?" demanded Merton Gill's neighbour in aggrieved tones.

"Ssh!" cautioned Merton. "It's Mass or something like that." And they bent in unison to this noon-tide devotion.

When this was done Henshaw bustled into the group. "I want about a dozen or fifteen good types for the cafe," he explained to his assistant. Merton Gill instinctively stood forward, and was presently among those selected. "You'll do," said Henshaw, nodding. The director, of course, had not remembered that this was the actor he had distinguished in The Blight of Broadway, yet he had again chosen him for eminence. It showed, Merton felt, that his conviction about the screen value of his face was not ill founded.

The selected types were now herded into a dark, narrow, low-ceiled room with a divan effect along its three walls. A grizzled Arab made coffee over a glowing brazier. Merton Gill sat cross-legged on the divan and became fearful that he would be asked to smoke the narghileh which the assistant director was now preparing. To one who balked at mere cigarettes, it was an evil-appearing device. His neighbour who had been puzzled at prayer-time now hitched up his flowing robe to withdraw a paper of cigarettes from the pocket of a quite occidental garment.

"Go on, smoke cigarettes," said the assistant director.

"Have one?" said Merton's neighbour, and he took one. It seemed you couldn't get away from cigarettes on the screen. East and West were here one. He lighted it, though smoking warily. The noble sheik, of undoubtedly Asiatic origin, came to the doorway overlooking the assistant director's work on the narghileh. A laden camel halted near him, sneered in an evil manner at the bystanders, and then, lifting an incredible length of upper lip, set his yellow teeth in the nearest shoulder. It was the shoulder of the noble sheik, who instantly rent the air with a plaintive cry: "For the love of Mike!—keep that man-eater off'n me, can't you?"

His accent had not been that of the Arabian waste-land. Merton Gill was disappointed. So the fellow was only an actor, after all. If he had felt sympathy at all, it would now have been for the camel. The beast was jerked back with profane words and the sheik, rubbing his bitten shoulder, entered the cafe, sitting cross-legged at the end of the divan nearest the door.

"All right, Bob." The assistant director handed him the tube of the water pipe, and the sheik smoked with every sign of enjoyment. Merton Gill resolved never to play the part of an Arab sheik—at the mercy of man-eating camels and having to smoke something that looked murderous.

Under Henshaw's direction the grizzled proprietor now served tiny cups of coffee to the sheik and his lesser patrons. Two of these played dominoes, and one or two reclined as in sleep. Cameras were brought up. The interior being to his satisfaction, Henshaw rehearsed the entrance of a little band of European tourists. A beautiful girl in sports garb, a beautiful young man in khaki and puttees, a fine old British father with gray side whiskers shaded by a sun-hat with a flowing veil twined about it. These people sat and were served coffee, staring in a tourist manner at their novel surroundings. The Bedouins, under stern command, ignored them, conversing among themselves over their coffee—all but the sheik.

The sheik had been instantly struck by the fair young English girl. His sinister eyes hung constantly upon her, shifting only when she regarded him, furtively returning when she ceased. When they left the cafe, the sheik arose and placed himself partly in the girl's way. She paused while his dark eyes caught and held hers. A long moment went before she seemed able to free herself from the hypnotic tension he put upon her. Then he bowed low, and the girl with a nervous laugh passed him.

It could be seen that the sheik meant her no good. He stepped to the door and looked after the group. There was evil purpose in his gaze.

Merton Gill recalled something of Henshaw's words the first day he had eaten at the cafeteria: "They find this deserted tomb just at nightfall, and he's alone there with the girl, and he could do anything, but the kick for the audience is that he's a gentleman and never lays a finger on her."

This would be the story. Probably the sheik would now arrange with the old gentleman in the sun-hat to guide the party over the desert, and would betray them in order to get the beautiful girl into his power. Of course there would be a kick for the audience when the young fellow proved to be a gentleman in the deserted tomb for a whole night—any moving-picture audience would expect him under these propitious circumstances to be quite otherwise, if the girl were as beautiful as this one. But there would surely be a greater kick when the sheik found them in the tomb and bore the girl off on his camel, after a fight in which the gentleman was momentarily worsted. But the girl would be rescued in time. And probably the piece would be called Desert Passion.

He wished he could know the ending of the story. Indeed he sincerely wished he could work in it to the end, not alone because he was curious about the fate of the young girl in the bad sheik's power. Undoubtedly the sheik would not prove to be a gentleman, but Merton would like to work to the end of the story because he had no place to sleep and but little assurance of wholesome food. Yet this, it appeared, was not to be. Already word had run among the extra people. Those hired to-day were to be used for to-day only. Tomorrow the desert drama would unfold without them.

Still, he had a day's pay coming. This time, though, it would be but five dollars—his dress suit had not been needed. And five dollars would appease Mrs. Patterson for another week. Yet what would be the good of sleeping if he had nothing to eat? He was hungry now. Thin soup, ever so plenteously spiced with catsup, was inadequate provender for a working artist. He knew, even as he sat there cross-legged, an apparently self-supporting and care-free Bedouin, that this ensuing five dollars would never be seen by Mrs. Patterson.

There were a few more shots of the cafe's interior during which one of the inmates carefully permitted his half—consumed cigarette to go out. After that a few more shots of the lively street which, it was now learned, was a street in Cairo. Earnest efforts were made by the throngs in these scenes to give the murderous camel plenty of head room. Some close-ups were taken of the European tourists while they bargained with a native merchant for hammered brassware and rare shawls.

The bad sheik was caught near the group bending an evil glare upon the beauteous English girl, and once the camera turned while she faced him with a little shiver of apprehension. Later the sheik was caught bargaining for a camel train with the innocent-looking old gentleman in the sun-hat. Undoubtedly the sheik was about to lead them into the desert for no good purpose. A dreadful fate seemed in store for the girl, but she must be left to face it without the support of Merton Gill.

The lately hired extras were now dismissed. They trooped back to the dressing room to doff their flowing robes and remove the Bedouin make-up. Merton Gill went from the dressing room to the little window through which he had received his robe and his slip was returned to him signed by the assistant director. It had now become a paper of value, even to Mrs. Patterson; but she was never to know this, for its owner went down the street to another window and relinquished it for a five-dollar bill.

The bill was adorned with a portrait of Benjamin Harrison smugly radiating prosperity from every hair in his beard. He was clearly one who had never gone hungry nor betrayed the confidence of a society woman counting upon her room rent strictly in advance. The portrait of this successful man was borne swiftly to the cafeteria where its present owner lavishly heaped a tray with excellent food and hastened with it to a table. He ate with but slight regard for his surroundings. Beulah Baxter herself might have occupied a neighbouring table without coming to his notice at once. He was very hungry. The catsup-laden soup had proved to be little more than an appetizer.

In his first ardour he forgot his plight. It was not until later in the meal that the accusing face of Mrs. Patterson came between him and the last of his stew which he secured with blotters of bread. Even then he ignored the woman. He had other things to think of. He had to think of where he should sleep that night. But for once he had eaten enough; his optimism was again enthroned.

Sleeping, after all, was not like eating. There were more ways to manage it. The law of sleep would in time enforce itself, while eating did nothing of the sort. You might sleep for nothing, but someone had to be paid if you ate. He cheerfully paid eighty cents for his repast. The catsup as an appetizer had been ruinous.

It was late in the afternoon when he left the cafeteria and the cheerful activities of the lot were drawing to a close. Extra people from the various stages were hurrying to the big dressing room, whence they would presently stream, slips in hand, toward the cashier's window. Belated principals came in from their work to resume their choice street garments and be driven off in choice motor cars.

Merton Gill in deep thought traversed the street between the big stages and the dressing rooms. Still in deep thought he retraced his steps, and at the front office turned off to the right on a road that led to the deserted street of the Western town. His head bowed in thought he went down this silent thoroughfare, his footsteps echoing along the way lined by the closed shops. The Happy Days Saloon and Joe—Buy or Sell, the pool-room and the restaurant, alike slept for want of custom. He felt again the eeriness of this desertion, and hurried on past the silent places.

Emerging from the lower end of this street he came upon a log cabin where activity still survived. He joined the group before its door. Inside two cameras were recording some drama of the rude frontier. Over glowing coals in the stone fireplace a beautiful young girl prepared food in a long-handled frying pan. At a table in the room's centre two bearded miners seemed to be appraising a buckskin pouch of nuggets, pouring them from hand to hand. A candle stuck in a bottle flickered beside them. They were honest, kindly faced miners, roughly dressed and heavily bearded, but it could be seen that they had hearts of gold. The beautiful young girl, who wore a simple dress of blue calico, and whose hair hung about her fair face in curls of a radiant buff, now served them food and poured steaming coffee from a large pot.

The miners seemed loth to eat, being excited by the gold nuggets. They must have struck it rich that day, Merton Gill divined, and now with wealth untold they would be planning to send the girl East to school. They both patted her affectionately, keeping from her the great surprise they had in store.

The girl was arch with them, and prettily kissed each upon his bald head. Merton at once saw that she would be the daughter of neither; she would be their ward. And perhaps they weren't planning to send her to school. Perhaps they were going to send her to fashionable relatives in the East, where she would unwittingly become the rival of her beautiful but cold-hearted cousin for the hand of a rich young stock-broker, and be ill-treated and long for the old miners who would get word of it and buy some fine clothes from Joe—Buy or Sell, and go East to the consternation of the rich relatives and see that their little mountain flower was treated right.

As he identified this photo-play he studied the interior of the cabin, the rough table at which the three now ate, the makeshift chairs, the rifle over the fireplace, the picks and shovels, the shelf along the wall with its crude dishes, the calico curtain screening off what would be the dressing room of the little mountain flower. It was a home-like room, for all its roughness. Along one wall were two bunks, one above the other, well supplied with blankets.

The director, after a final shot of one of the miners being scalded by his coffee which he drank from a saucer, had said, "All right, boys! We'll have the fight first thing in the morning."

Merton Gill passed on. He didn't quite know what the fight would be about. Surely the two miners wouldn't fight. Perhaps another miner of loose character would come along and try to jump their claim, or attempt some dirty work with the little girl. Something like that. He carried with him the picture of the homey little ulterior, the fireplace with its cooking utensils, the two bunks with their ample stock of blankets—the crude door closed with a wooden bar and a leather latch-string, which hung trustfully outside.

In other circumstances—chiefly those in which Merton Gill had now been the prominent figure in the film world he meant one day to become—he would on this night have undoubtedly won public attention for his mysterious disappearance. The modest room in the Patterson home, to which for three months he had unfailingly come after the first picture show, on this night went untenanted. The guardian at the Holden gate would have testified that he had not passed out that way, and the way through the offices had been closed at five, subsequent to which hour several witnesses could have sworn to seeing him still on the lot.

In the ensuing search even the tank at the lower end of the lot might have been dragged—without result.

Being little known to the public, however, and in the Patterson home it being supposed that you could never tell about motion-picture actors, his disappearance for the night caused absolutely no slightest ripple. Public attention as regarded the young man remained at a mirror-like calm, unflawed by even the mildest curiosity. He had been seen, perhaps, though certainly not noted with any interest, to be one of the group watching a night scene in front of one of the Fifth Avenue mansions.

Lights shone from the draped windows of this mansion and from its portals issued none other than Muriel Mercer, who, as Vera Vanderpool, freed at last from the blight of Broadway, was leaving her palatial home to cast her lot finally with the ardent young tenement worker with the high forehead. She descended the brown-stone steps, paused once to look back upon the old home where she had been taught to love pleasure above the worth-while things of life, then came on to the waiting limousine, being greeted here by the young man with the earnest forehead who had won her to the better way.

The missing youth might later have been observed, but probably was not, walking briskly in the chill night toward the gate that led to the outer world. But he wheeled abruptly before reaching this gate, and walked again briskly, this time debouching from the main thoroughfare into the black silence of the Western village. Here his pace slackened, and halfway down the street he paused irresolutely. He was under the wooden porch of the Fashion Restaurant—Give our Tamales a Trial. He lingered here but a moment, however, then lurked on down the still thoroughfare, keeping well within the shadow of the low buildings. Just beyond the street was the log cabin of the big-hearted miners. A moment later he could not have been observed even by the keenest eye.

305

Nothing marked his disappearance, at least nothing that would have been noted by the casual minded. He had simply gone. He was now no more than the long-vanished cowboys and sheriffs and gamblers and petty tradesmen who had once peopled this street of silence and desolation.

A night watchman came walking presently, flashing an electric torch from side to side. He noticed nothing. He was, indeed, a rather imaginative man, and he hoped he would not notice anything. He did not like coming down this ghostly street, which his weak mind would persist in peopling with phantom crowds from long-played picture dramas. It gave him the creeps, as he had more than once confessed. He hurried on, flashing his torch along the blind fronts of the shops in a perfunctory manner. He was especially nervous when he came to corners. And he was glad when he issued from the little street into the wider one that was well lighted.

How could he have been expected to notice a very trifling incongruous detail as he passed the log cabin? Indeed many a keener-eyed and entirely valorous night watchman might have neglected to observe that the leathern latch-string of the cabin's closed door was no longer hanging outside.

CHAPTER VIII. CLIFFORD ARMYTAGE, THE OUTLAW

Dawn brought the wide stretches of the Holden lot into gray relief. It lightened the big yellow stages and crept down the narrow street of the Western town where only the ghosts of dead plays stalked. It burnished the rich fronts of the Fifth Avenue mansions and in the next block illumined the rough sides of a miner's cabin.

With more difficulty it seeped through the blurred glass of the one window in this structure and lightened the shadows of its interior to a pale gray. The long-handled frying-pan rested on the hearth where the little girl had left it. The dishes of the overnight meal were still on the table; the vacant chairs sprawled about it; and the rifle was in its place above the rude mantel; the picks and shovels awaited the toil of a new day. All seemed as it had been when the director had closed the door upon it the previous night.

But then the blankets in the lower bunk were seen to heave and to be thrust back from the pale face of Merton Gill. An elbow came into play, and the head was raised. A gaze still vague with sleep travelled about the room in dull alarm. He was waking up in his little room at the Patterson house and he couldn't make it look right. He rubbed his eyes vigorously and pushed himself farther up. His mind resumed its broken threads. He was where he had meant to be from the moment he had spied the blankets in those bunks.

In quicker alarm, now, he reached for his watch. Perhaps he had slept too late and would be discovered—arrested, jailed! He found his watch on the floor beside the bunk. Seven o'clock. He was safe. He could dress at leisure, and presently be an early-arriving actor on the Holden lot. He wondered how soon he could get food at the cafeteria. Sleeping in this mountain cabin had cursed him with a ravenous appetite, as if he had indeed been far off in the keen air of the North Woods.

He crept from the warm blankets, and from under the straw mattress—in which one of the miners had hidden the pouch of nuggets—he took his newly pressed trousers. Upon a low bench across the room was a battered tin wash-basin, a bucket of water brought by the little girl from the spring, and a bar of yellow soap. He made a quick toilet, and at seven-thirty, a good hour before the lot would wake up, he was dressed and at the door.

It might be chancy, opening that door; so he peered through a narrow crack at first, listening intently. He could hear nothing and no one was in sight. He pushed the latch—string through its hole, then opened the door enough to emit his slender shape.

A moment later, ten feet from the closed door, he stood at ease, scanning the log cabin as one who, passing by, had been attracted by its quaint architecture. Then glancing in both directions to be again sure that he was unobserved, he walked away from his new home.

He did not slink furtively. He took the middle of the street and there was a bit of swagger to his gait. He felt rather set up about this adventure. He reached what might have been called the lot's civic centre and cast a patronizing eye along the ends of the big stages and the long, low dressing—room building across from them. Before the open door of the warehouse he paused to watch a truck being loaded with handsome furniture—a drawing room was evidently to be set on one of the stages. Rare rugs and beautiful chairs and tables were carefully brought out. He had rather a superintending air as he watched this process. He might have been taken for the owner of these costly things, watching to see that no harm befell them. He strolled on when the truck had received its load. Such people as he had met were only artisans, carpenters, electricians, property-men. He faced them all confidently, with glances of slightly amused tolerance. They were good men in their way but they were not actors—not artists.

In the neatly landscaped little green place back of the office building a climbing rose grew on a trellis. He plucked a pink bud, fixed it in his lapel, and strolled down the street past the dressing rooms. Across from these the doors of the big stages were slid back, and inside he could see that sets were being assembled. The truckload of furniture came to one of these doors and he again watched it as the stuff was carried inside.

For all these workmen knew, he might presently be earning a princely salary as he acted amid these beautiful objects, perhaps attending a reception in a Fifth Avenue mansion where the father of a beautiful New York society girl would tell him that he must first make good before he could aspire to her hand. And he would make good—out there in the great open spaces, where the girl would come to him after many adventures and where they would settle to an untroubled future in the West they both loved.

He had slept; he knew where—with luck—he could sleep again; and he had money in his pocket for several more ample meals. At this moment he felt equal to anything. No more than pleasantly aware of his hunger, sharpened by the walk in this keen morning air, he made a nonchalant progress toward the cafeteria. Motor cars were now streaming through the gate, disgorging other actors—trim young men and beautiful young women who must hurry to the dressing rooms while he could sit at ease in a first-class cafeteria and eat heavily of sustaining foods. Inside he chose from the restricted menu offered by the place at this early hour and ate in a leisurely, almost condescending manner. Half-a-dozen other early comers wolfed their food as if they feared to be late for work, but he suffered no such anxiety. He consumed the last morsel that his tray held, drained his cup of coffee, and jingled the abundant silver coin in his pocket.

True, underneath it, as he plumed himself upon his adventure, was a certain pestering consciousness that all was not so well with him as observers might guess. But he resolutely put this away each time it threatened to overwhelm him. He would cross no bridge until he came to it. He even combated this undercurrent of sanity by wording part of an interview with himself some day to appear in Photo Land:

"Clifford Armytage smiled that rare smile which his admirers have found so winning on the silver screen—a smile reminiscent, tender, eloquent of adversities happily surmounted. 'Yes,' he said frankly in the mellow tones that are his, 'I guess there were times when I almost gave up the struggle. I recall one spell, not so many years ago, when I camped informally on the Holden lot, sleeping where I could find a bed and stinting myself in food to eke out my little savings. Yet I look back upon that time'—he mischievously pulled the ears of the magnificent Great Dane that lolled at his feet—'as one of the happiest in my career, because I always knew that my day would come. I had done only a few little bits, but they had stood out, and the directors had noticed me. Not once did I permit myself to become discouraged, and so I say to your readers who may feel that they have in them the stuff for truly creative screen art—'"

He said it, dreaming above the barren tray, said it as Harold Parmalee had said it in a late interview extorted from him by Augusta Blivens for the refreshment of his host of admirers who read Photo Land. He was still saying it as he paid his check at the counter, breaking off only to reflect that fifty-five cents was a good deal to be paying for food so early in the day. For of course he must eat again before seeking shelter of the humble miner's cabin.

It occurred to him that the blankets might be gone by nightfall. He hoped they would have trouble with the fight scene. He hoped there would be those annoying delays that so notoriously added to the cost of producing the screen drama—long waits, when no one seemed to know what was being waited for, and bored actors lounged about in apathy. He hoped the fight would be a long fight. You needed blankets even in sunny California.

He went out to pass an enlivening day, fairly free of misgiving. He found an abundance of entertainment. On one stage he overlooked for half an hour a fragment of the desert drama which he had assisted the previous day. A covered incline led duskily down to the deserted tomb in which the young man and the beautiful English girl were to take shelter for the night. They would have eluded the bad sheik for a little while, and in the tomb the young man would show himself to be a gentleman by laying not so much as a finger upon the defenceless girl.

But this soon palled upon the watching connoisseur. The actual shots were few and separated by barren intervals of waiting for that mysterious something which photoplays in production seemed to need. Being no longer identified with this drama he had lost much of his concern over the fate in store for the girl, though he knew she would emerge from the ordeal as pure as she was beautiful—a bit foolish at moments, perhaps, but good.

He found that he was especially interested in bedroom scenes. On Stage Four a sumptuous bedroom, vacant for the moment, enchained him for a long period of contemplation. The bed was of some rare wood ornately carved, with a silken canopy, spread with finest linen and quilts of down, its pillows opulent in their embroidered cases. The hide of a polar bear, its head mounted with open jaws, spread over the rich rug beside the bed. He wondered about this interestingly. Probably the stage would be locked at night. Still, at a suitable hour, he could descreetly find out. On another stage a bedroom likewise intrigued him, though this was a squalid room in a tenement and the bed was a cheap thing sparsely covered and in sad disorder. People were working on this set, and he presently identified the play, for Muriel Mercer in a neat black dress entered to bring comfort to the tenement dwellers. But this play, too, had ceased to interest him. He knew that Vera Vanderpool had escaped the blight of Broadway to choose the worthwhile, the true, the vital things of life, and that was about all he now cared to know of the actual play. This tenement bed had become for him its outstanding dramatic value. He saw himself in it for a good night's rest, waking refreshed in plenty of time to be dressed and out before the tenement people would need it. He must surely learn if the big sliding doors to these stages were locked overnight.

He loitered about the stages until late afternoon, with especial attention to sleeping apartments. In one gripping drama he felt cheated. The set showed the elaborately fitted establishment of a fashionable modiste. Mannequins in wondrous gowns came through parted curtains to parade before the shop's clientele, mostly composed of society butterflies. One man hovered attentive about the most beautiful of these, and whispered entertainingly as she scanned the gowns submitted to her choice. He was a dissolute—looking man, although faultlessly arrayed. His hair was thin, his eyes were cruel, and his face bespoke self-indulgence.

The expert Merton Gill at once detected that the beautiful young woman he whispered to would be one of those light—headed wives who care more for fashionable dress than for the good name of their husbands. He foresaw that the creature would be trapped into the power of this villain by her love of finery, though he was sure that the end would find her still a good woman. The mannequins finished their parade and the throng of patrons broke up. The cameras were pushed to an adjoining room where the French proprietor of the place figured at a desk. The dissolute pleasure-seeker came back to question him. His errant fancy had been caught by one of the mannequins—the most beautiful of them, a blonde with a flowerlike face and a figure whose perfection had been boldly attested by the gowns she had worn. The unprincipled proprietor at once demanded from a severe-faced forewoman that this girl be sent for, after which he discreetly withdrew. The waiting scoundrel sat and complacently pinched the ends of his small dark mustache. It could be seen that he was one of those who believe that money will buy anything.

The fair girl entered and was leeringly entreated to go out to dinner with him. It appeared that she never went out to dinner with any one, but spent her evenings with her mother who was very, very ill. Her unworthy admirer persisted. Then the telephone on the manager's desk called her. Her mother was getting worse. The beautiful face was now suffused with agony, but this did not deter the man from his loathsome advances. There was another telephone call. She must come at once if she were to see her mother alive. The man seized her. They struggled. All seemed lost, even the choice gown she still wore; but she broke away to be told over the telephone that her mother had died. Even this sad news made no impression upon the wretch. He seemed to be a man of one idea. Again he seized her, and the maddened girl stabbed him with a pair of long gleaming shears that had lain on the manager's desk. He fell lifeless at her feet, while the girl stared in horror at the weapon she still grasped.

Merton Gill would not have lingered for this. There were tedious waits, and scenes must be rehearsed again and again. Even the agony of the girl as she learned of her mother's passing must be done over and over at the insistence of a director who seemed to know what a young girl should feel at these moments. But Merton had watched from his place back of the lights with fresh interest from the moment it was known that the girl's poor old mother was an invalid, for he had at first believed that the mother's bedroom would be near by. He left promptly when it became apparent that the mother's bedroom would not be seen in this drama. They would probably show the doctor at the other telephone urging the girl to hurry home, and show him again announcing that all was over, but the expense of mother and her deathbed had been saved. He cared little for the ending of this play. Already he was becoming a little callous to the plight of beautiful young girls threatened with the loss of that which they held most dear.

Purposely all day he had avoided the neighbourhood of his humble miner's home. He thought it as well that he should not be seen much around there. He ate again at four o'clock, heartily and rather expensively, and loafed about the stages until six. Then he strolled leisurely down the village street and out the lower end to where he could view the cabin. Work for the day was plainly over. The director and his assistant lingered before the open door in consultation. A property man and an electrician were engaged inside, but a glance as he passed showed that the blankets were still in the bunks. He did not wait to see more, but passed on with all evidences of disinterest in this lowly abode.

He ascertained that night that the fight must have been had. The table was overturned, one of the chairs wrecked, and there were other signs of disorder. Probably it had been an excellent fight; probably these primitive men of the woods had battled desperately. But he gave little consideration to the combat, and again slept warmly under the blankets. Perhaps they would fight again to-morrow, or perhaps there would be less violent bits of the drama that would secure him another night of calm repose.

The following morning found him slightly disturbed by two unforeseen needs arising from his novel situation. He looked carefully at his collar, wondering how many days he would be able to keep it looking like a fresh collar, and he regretted that he had not brought his safety-razor to this new home. Still the collar was in excellent shape as yet, and a scrutiny of his face in the cracked mirror hanging on the log wall determined that he could go at least another day without shaving. His beard was of a light growth, gentle in texture, and he was yet far from the plight of Mr. Montague. Eventually, to be sure, he would have to go to the barber shop on the lot and pay money to be shaved, which seemed a pity, because an actor could live indefinitely unshaven but could live without food for the merest fragment of time.

He resolved to be on the lookout that day for a barber-shop set. He believed they were not common in the photodrama, still one might be found.

He limited himself to the lightest of breakfasts. He had timidly refrained from counting his silver but he knew he must be frugal. He rejoiced at this economy until late afternoon when, because of it, he simply had to eat a heavier dinner than he had expected to need. There was something so implacable about this demand for food. If you skimped in the morning you must make amends at the next meal. He passed the time as on the previous day, a somewhat blase actor resting between pictures, and condescending to beguile the tedium by overlooking the efforts of his professional brethren. He could find no set that included a barber shop, although they were beds on every hand. He hoped for another night in the cabin, but if that were not to be, there was a bed easy of access on Stage Three. When he had observed it, a ghastly old father was coughing out his life under its blankets, nursed only by his daughter, a beautiful young creature who sewed by his bedside, and who would doubtless be thrown upon the world in the very next reel, though—Merton was glad to note—probably not until the next day.

Yet there was no need for this couch of the tubercular father, for action in the little cabin was still on. After making the unhappy discovery in the cafeteria that his appetite could not be hoodwinked by the clumsy subterfuge of calling coffee and rolls a breakfast some six hours previously, he went boldly down to stand before his home. Both miners were at work inside. The room had been placed in order again, though the little mountain flower was gone. A letter, he gathered, had been received from her, and one of the miners was about to leave on a long journey.

Merton could not be sure, but he supposed that the letter from the little girl told that she was unhappy in her new surroundings, perhaps being ill-treated by the supercilious Eastern relatives. The miner who was to remain helped the other to pack his belongings in a quaint old carpet sack, and together they undid a bundle which proved to contain a splendid new suit. Not only this, but now came

312

a scene of eloquent appeal to the watcher outside the door. The miner who was to remain expressed stern disapproval of the departing miner's beard. It would never do, he was seen to intimate, and when the other miner portrayed helplessness a new package was unwrapped and a safety razor revealed to his shocked gaze.

At this sight Merton Gill felt himself growing too emotional for a mere careless bystander, and withdrew to a distance where he could regain better control of himself. When he left the miner to be shorn was betraying comic dismay while the other pantomimed the correct use of the implement his thoughtfulness had provided. When he returned after half—an-hour's rather nervous walk up another street, the departing miner was clean shaven and one might note the new razor glittering on the low bench beside the battered tin basin.

They worked late in his home that night; trifling scenes were taken and retaken. The departing miner had to dress in his splendid but ill-fitting new garments and to bid an affectionate farewell to his partner, then had to dress in his old clothes again for some bit that had been forgotten, only to don the new suit for close-ups. At another time Merton Gill might have resented this tediously drawn-out affair which was keeping him from his rest, for he had come to look upon this structure as one having rights in it after a certain hour, but a sight of the razor which had not been touched allayed any possible feeling of irritation.

It was nine-thirty before the big lights jarred finally off and the director said, "That's all, boys." Then he turned to call, "Jimmie! Hey, Jimmie! Where's that prop-rustler gone to now?"

"Here, Mr. Burke, yes, sir."

"We've finished the shack stuff. Let's see—" He looked at the watch on his wrist—"That'll be all for tonight. Strike this first thing tomorrow morning."

"Yes, sir," said Jimmie. The door was closed and the men walked away. Merton trailed them a bit, not remaining too pointedly near the cabin. He circled around through Fifth Avenue to regain the place.

Softly he let himself in and groped through the dark until his hand closed upon the abandoned razor. Satisfying himself that fresh blades had accompanied it, he made ready for bed. He knew it was to be his last night in this shelter. The director had told Jimmie to strike it first thing in the morning. The cabin would still be there, but it would contain no homely furniture, no chairs, no table, no wash-basin, no safety-razor and, most vital of lacks—it would be devoid of blankets.

Yet this knowledge did not dismay him. He slept peacefully after praying that something good would happen to him. He put it that way very simply. He had placed himself, it seemed, where things could only happen to him. He was, he felt, beyond bringing them about.

CHAPTER IX. MORE WAYS THAN ONE

Early he was up to bathe and shave. He shaved close to make it last longer, until his tender face reddened under the scraping. Probably he would not find another cabin in which a miner would part with his beard for an Eastern trip. Probably he would have to go to the barber the next time. He also succeeded, with soap and water, in removing a stain from his collar. It was still a decent collar; not immaculate, perhaps, but entirely possible.

This day he took eggs with his breakfast, intending to wheedle his appetite with a lighter second meal than it had demanded the day before. He must see if this would not average better on the day's overhead.

After breakfast he was irresistibly drawn to view the moving picture of his old home being dismantled. He knew now that he might stand brazenly there without possible criticism. He found Jimmy and a companion property-boy already busy. Much of the furniture was outside to be carted away. Jimmy, as Merton lolled idly in the doorway, emptied the blackened coffee pot into the ashes of the fireplace and then proceeded to spoon into the same refuse heap half a kettle of beans upon which the honest miners had once feasted. The watcher deplored that he had not done more than taste the beans when he had taken his final survey of the place this morning. They had been good beans, but to do more than taste them would have been stealing. Now he saw them thrown away and regretted that he could not have known what their fate was to be. There had been enough of them to save him a day's expenses.

He stood aside as the two boys brought out the cooking utensils, the rifle, the miners' tools, to stow them in a waiting handcart. When they had loaded this vehicle they trundled it on up the narrow street of the Western town. Yet they went only a little way, halting before one of the street's largest buildings. A sign above its wooden porch flaunted the name Crystal Palace Hotel. They unlocked its front door and took the things from the cart inside.

From the street the watcher could see them stowing these away. The room appeared to contain a miscellaneous collection of articles needed in the ruder sort of photodrama. Emptying their cart, they returned with it to the cabin for another load. Merton Gill stepped to the doorway and peered in from apparently idle curiosity. He could see a row of saddles on wooden supports; there were kitchen stoves, lamps, painted chairs, and heavy earthenware dishes on shelves. His eyes wandered over these articles until they came to rest upon a pile of blankets at one side of the room. They were neatly folded, and they were many.

Down before the cabin he could see the handcart being reloaded by Jimmie and his helper. Otherwise the street was empty. The young man at the doorway stepped lightly in and regarded the windows on either side of the door. He sauntered to the street and appeared to be wondering what he would examine next in this curious world. He passed Jimmie and the other boy returning with the last load from the cabin. He noted at the top of the load the mattress on which he had lain for three nights and the blankets that had warmed him. But he was proved not to be so helpless as he had thought. Again he knew where a good night's rest might be had by one using ordinary discretion.

Again that day, the fourth of his double life, he went the mad pace, a well-fed, carefree youth, sauntering idly from stage to stage, regarding nonchalantly the joys and griefs, the twistings of human destiny there variously unfolded. Not only was he this to the casual public notice; to himself he was this, at least consciously. True, in those nether regions of the mind so lately discovered and now being so expertly probed by Science, in the mind's dark basement, so to say, a certain unlovely fronted dragon of reality would issue from the gloom where it seemed to have been lurking and force itself upon his notice.

This would be at oddly contented moments when he least feared the future, when he was most successfully being to himself all that he must seem to others. At such times when he leisurely walked a world of plenty and fruition, the dragon would half-emerge from its subconscious lair to chill him with its head composed entirely of repellent facts. Then a stout effort would be required to send the thing back where it belonged, to those lower, decently hidden levels of the mind—life.

And the dragon was cunning. From hour to hour, growing more restive, it employed devices of craft and subtlety. As when Merton Gill, carefree to the best of his knowledge, strolling lightly to another point of interest, graciously receptive to the pleasant life about him, would suddenly discover that a part of his mind without superintendence had for some moments been composing a letter, something that ran in effect:

"Mr. Gashwiler, dear sir, I have made certain changes in my plans since I first came to sunny California and getting quite a little homesick for good old Simsbury and I thought I would write you about taking back my old job in the emporium, and now about the money for the ticket back to Simsbury, the railroad fare is—"

He was truly amazed when he found this sort of thing going on in that part of his mind he didn't watch. It was scandalous. He would indignantly snatch the half-finished letter and tear it up each time he found it unaccountably under way.

It was surely funny the way your mind would keep doing things you didn't want it to do. As, again, this very morning when, with his silver coin out in his hand, he had merely wished to regard it as a great deal of silver coin, a store of plenty against famine, which indeed it looked to be under a not-too-minute scrutiny. It looked like as much as two dollars and fifty cents, and he would have preferred to pocket it again with this impression. Yet that rebellious other part of

315

his mind had basely counted the coin even while he eyed it approvingly, and it had persisted in shouting aloud that it was not two dollars and fifty cents but one dollar and eighty—five cents.

The counting part of the mind made no comment on this discrepancy; it did not say that this discovery put things in a very different light. It merely counted, registered the result, and ceased to function, with an air of saying that it would ascertain the facts without prejudice and you could do what you liked about them. It didn't care.

That night a solitary guest enjoyed the quiet hospitality of the Crystal Palace Hotel. He might have been seen—but was not—to effect a late evening entrance to this snug inn by means of a front window which had, it would seem, at some earlier hour of the day, been unfastened from within. Here a not-too-luxurious but sufficing bed was contrived on the floor of the lobby from a pile of neatly folded blankets at hand, and a second night's repose was enjoyed by the lonely patron, who again at an early hour of the morning, after thoughtfully refolding the blankets that had protected him, was at some pains to leave the place as he had entered it without attracting public notice, perchance of unpleasant character.

On this day it would not have been possible for any part of the mind whatsoever to misvalue the remaining treasure of silver coin. It had become inconsiderable, and even if kept from view could be, and was, counted again and again by mere blind fingertips. They contracted, indeed, a senseless habit of confining themselves in a trouser's pocket to count the half-dollar, the quarter, and the two dimes long after the total was too well known to its owner.

Nor did this total, unimpressive at best, long retain even these poor dimensions. A visit to the cafeteria, in response to the imperious demands of a familiar organic process, resulted in less labour, by two dimes, for the stubbornly reiterative fingertips.

An ensuing visit to the Holden lot barber, in obedience to social demands construed to be equally imperious with the physical, reduced all subsequent counting, whether by fingertips or a glance of the eye, to barest mechanical routine. A single half-dollar is easy to count. Still, on the following morning there were two coins to count. True, both were dimes.

A diligent search among the miscellany of the Crystal Palace Hotel had failed to reveal a single razor. The razor used by the miner should in all reason have been found, but there was neither that nor any other. The baffled seeker believed there must have been crooked work somewhere. Without hesitation he found either Jimmie or his companion to be guilty of malfeasance in office. But at least one item of more or less worried debate was eliminated. He need no longer weigh mere surface gentility against the stern demands of an active metabolism. A shave cost a quarter. Twenty cents would not buy a shave, but it would buy at the cafeteria something more needful to any one but a fop.

He saw himself in the days to come—if there were very many days to come, of which he was now not too certain—descending to the unwholesome artistic level of the elder Montague. He would, in short, be compelled to peddle the brush. And of course as yet it was nothing like a brush—nothing to kindle the eye of a director needing genuine brushes. In the early morning light he fingered a somewhat gaunt chin and wondered how long "they" would require to grow. Not yet could he be taken for one of those actors compelled by the rigorous exactions of creative screen art to let Nature have its course with his beard. At present he merely needed a shave.

And the collar had not improved with usage. Also, as the day wore on, coffee with one egg proved to have been not long-enduring fare for this private in the army of the unemployed. Still, his morale was but slightly impaired. There were always ways, it seemed. And the later hours of the hungry afternoon were rather pleasantly occupied in dwelling upon one of them.

The sole guest of the Crystal Palace Hotel entered the hostelry that night somewhat earlier than was usual; indeed at the very earliest moment that foot traffic through the narrow street seemed to have diminished to a point where the entry could be effected without incurring the public notice which he at these moments so sincerely shunned. After a brief interval inside the lobby he issued from his window with certain objects in hand, one of which dropped as he clambered out. The resulting clamour seemed to rouse far echoes along the dead street, and he hastily withdrew, with a smothered exclamation of dismay, about the nearest corner of the building until it could be ascertained that echoes alone had been aroused.

After a little breathless waiting he slunk down the street, keeping well within friendly shadows, stepping softly, until he reached the humble cabin where so lately the honest miners had enacted their heart-tragedy. He jerked the latch-string of the door and was swiftly inside, groping a way to the fireplace. Here he lighted matches, thoughtfully appropriated that morning from the cafeteria counter. He shielded the blaze with one hand while with the other he put to use the articles he had brought from his hotel.

Into a tin cooking pot with a long handle he now hastily ladled well-cooked beans from the discarded heap in the fireplace, by means of an iron spoon. He was not too careful. More or less ashes accompanied the nutritious vegetables as the pot grew to be half full. That was a thing to be corrected later, and at leisure. When the last bean had been salvaged the flame of another match revealed an unsuspected item—a half-loaf of bread nestled in the ashes at the far corner of the fireplace. It lacked freshness; was, in truth, withered and firm to the touch, but doubtless more wholesome than bread freshly baked.

He was again on his humble cot in the seclusion of the Crystal Palace Hotel. Half-reclining, he ate at leisure. It being inadvisable to light matches here he ate chiefly by the touch system. There was a marked alkaline flavour to the repast, not unpleasantly counteracted by a growth of vegetable mould of delicate lavender tints which Nature had been decently spreading over the final reduction of this provender to its basic elements. But the time was not one in which to cavil about minor infelicities. Ashes wouldn't hurt any one if taken in moderation; you couldn't see the mould in a perfectly dark hotel; and the bread was good.

The feast was prolonged until a late hour, but the finger—tips that had accurately counted money in a dark pocket could ascertain in a dark hotel that a store of food still remained. He pulled the blankets about him and sank comfortably to rest. There was always some way.

Breakfast the next morning began with the promise of only moderate enjoyment. Somehow in the gray light sifting through the windows the beans did not look as good as they had tasted the night before, and the early mouthfuls were less blithesome on the palate than the remembered ones of yesterday. He thought perhaps he was not so hungry as he had been at his first encounter with them. He delicately removed a pocket of ashes from the centre, and tried again. They tasted better now. The mould of tender tints was again visible but he made no effort to avoid it. For his appetite had reawakened. He was truly hungry, and ate with an entire singleness of purpose.

Toward the last of the meal his conscious self feebly prompted him to quit, to save against the inevitable hunger of the night. But the voice was ignored. He was now clay to the moulding of the subconscious. He could have saved a few of the beans when reason was again enthroned, but they were so very few that he fatuously thought them not worth saving. Might as well make a clean job of it. He restored the stewpan and spoon to their places and left his hotel. He was fed. To-day something else would have to happen.

The plush hat cocked at a rakish angle, he walked abroad with something of the old confident swagger. Once he doubtfully fingered the sprouting beard, but resolutely dismissed a half-formed notion of finding out how the Holden lot barber would regard a proposition from a new patron to open a charge account. If nothing worse than remaining unshaven was going to happen to him, what cared he? The collar was still pretty good. Why let his beard be an incubus? He forgot it presently in noticing that the people arriving on the Holden lot all looked so extremely well fed. He thought it singular that he should never before have noticed how many well-fed people one saw in a day.

Late in the afternoon his explorations took him beyond the lower end of his little home street, and he was attracted by sounds of the picture drama from a rude board structure labelled the High Gear Dance Hall. He approached and entered with that calm ease of manner which his days on the lot had brought to a perfect bloom. No one now would ever suppose that he was a mere sightseer or chained to the Holden lot by circumstances over which he had ceased to exert the slightest control.

The interior of the High Gear Dance Hall presented nothing new to his seasoned eye. It was the dance-hall made familiar by many a smashing five-reel Western. The picture was, quite normally, waiting. Electricians were shoving about the big light standards, cameras were being moved, and bored actors were loafing informally at the round tables or chatting in groups about the set.

One actor alone was keeping in his part. A ragged, bearded, unkempt elderly man in red shirt and frayed overalls, a repellent felt hat pulled low over his brow, reclined on the floor at the end of the bar, his back against a barrel. Apparently he slept. A flash of remembrance from the Montague girl's talk identified this wretched creature. This was what happened to an actor who had to peddle the brush. Perhaps for days he had been compelled to sleep there in the interests of dance-hall atmosphere.

He again scanned the group, for he remembered, too, that the Montague girl would also be working here in God's Great Outdoors. His eyes presently found her. She was indeed a blonde hussy, short-skirted, low-necked, pitifully rouged, depraved beyond redemption. She stood at the end of the piano, and in company with another of the dance-hall girls who played the accompaniment, she was singing a ballad the refrain of which he caught as "God calls them Angels in Heaven, we call them Mothers here."

The song ended, the Montague girl stepped to the centre of the room, looked aimlessly about her, then seized an innocent bystander, one of the rough characters frequenting this unsavoury resort, and did a dance with him among the tables. Tiring of this, she flitted across the room and addressed the bored director who impatiently awaited the changing of lights. She affected to consider him a reporter who had sought an interview with her. She stood erect, facing him with one hand on a hip, the other patting and readjusting her blonde coiffure.

"Really," she began in a voice of pained dignity, "I am at a loss to understand why the public should be so interested in me. What can I say to your readers—I who am so wholly absorbed in my art that I can't think of hardly anything else? Why will not the world let us alone? Hold on—don't go!"

She had here pretended that the reporter was taking her at her word. She seized him by a lapel to which she clung while with her other arm she encircled a post, thus anchoring the supposed intruder into her private affairs. "As I was saying," she resumed, "all this publicity is highly distasteful to the artist, and yet since you have forced yourself in here I may as well say a few little things about how good I am and how I got that way. Yes, I have nine motor cars, and I just bought a lace tablecloth for twelve hundred bones—"

She broke off inconsequently, poor victim of her constitutional frivolity. The director grinned after her as she danced away, though Merton Gill had considered her levity in the worst of taste. Then her eye caught him as he stood modestly back of the working electricians and she danced forward again in his direction. He would have liked to evade her but saw that he could not do this gracefully.

She greeted him with an impudent grin. "Why, hello, trouper! As I live, the actin' Kid!" She held out a hand to him and he could not well refuse it. He would have preferred to "up-stage" her once more, as she had phrased it in her low jargon, but he was cornered. Her grip of his hand quite astonished him with its vigour.

"Well, how's everything with you? Everything jake?" He tried for a show of easy confidence. "Oh, yes, yes, indeed, everything is."

"Well, that's good, Kid." But she was now without the grin, and was running a practised eye over what might have been called his production. The hat was jaunty enough, truly a hat of the successful, but all below that, the not-too-fresh collar, the somewhat rumpled coat, the trousers crying for an iron despite their nightly compression beneath their slumbering owner, the shoes not too recently polished, and, more than all, a certain hunted though still-defiant look in the young man's eyes, seemed to speak eloquently under the shrewd glance she bent on him.

"Say, listen here, Old-timer, remember I been trouping man and boy for over forty year and it's hard to fool me—you working?"

He resented the persistent levity of manner, but was coerced by the very apparent real kindness in her tone. "Well," he looked about the set vaguely in his discomfort, "you see, right now I'm between pictures—you know how it is."

Again she searched his eyes and spoke in a lower tone: "Well, all right—but you needn't blush about it, Kid." The blush she detected became more flagrant.

"Well, I—you see—" he began again, but he was saved from being explicit by the call of an assistant director.

"Miss Montague. Miss Montague—where's that Flips girl—on the set, please." She skipped lightly from him. When she returned a little later to look for him he had gone.

He went to bed that night when darkness had made this practicable, and under his blankets whiled away a couple of wakeful hours by running tensely dramatic films of breakfast, dinner, and supper at the Gashwiler home. It seemed that you didn't fall asleep so quickly when you had eaten nothing since early morning. Never had he achieved such perfect photography as now of the Gashwiler corned-beef hash and light biscuits, the Gashwiler hot cakes and sausage, and never had Gashwiler so impressively carved the Saturday night four-rib roast of tender beef. Gashwiler achieved a sensational triumph in the scene, being accorded all the close—ups that the most exacting of screen actors could wish. His knife-work was perfect. He held his audience enthralled by his technique.

Mrs. Gashwiler, too, had a small but telling part in the drama to-night; only a character bit, but one of those poignant bits that stand out in the memory. The subtitle was, "Merton, won't you let me give you another piece of the mince pie?"

That was all, and yet, as screen artists say, it got over. There came very near to being not a dry eye in the house when the simple words were flashed beside an insert of thick, flaky-topped mince pies with quarters cut from them to reveal their noble interiors

Sleep came at last while he was regretting that lawless orgy of the morning. He needn't have cleaned up those beans in that silly way. He could have left a good half of them. He ran what might have been considered a split-reel comedy of the stew-pan's bottom still covered with perfectly edible beans lightly protected with Nature's own pastel-tinted shroud for perishing vegetable matter and diversified here and there with casual small deposits of ashes.

In the morning something good really did happen. As he folded his blankets in the gray light a hard object rattled along the floor from them. He picked this up before he recognized it as a mutilated fragment from the stale half—loaf of bread he had salvaged. He wondered how he could have forgotten it, even in the plenitude of his banquet. There it was, a mere nubbin of crust and so hard it might almost have been taken for a petrified specimen of prehistoric bread. Yet it proved to be rarely palatable. It's flavour was exquisite. It melted in the mouth.

Somewhat refreshed by this modest cheer, he climbed from the window of the Crystal Palace with his mind busy on two tracks. While the letter to Gashwiler composed itself, with especially clear directions about where the return money should be sent, he was also warning himself to remain throughout the day at a safe distance from the door of the cafeteria. He had proved the wisdom of this even the day before that had started with a bounteous breakfast. To-day the aroma of cooked food occasionally wafted from the cafeteria door would prove, he was sure, to be more than he could bear.

He rather shunned the stages to-day, keeping more to himself. The collar, he had to confess, was no longer, even to the casual eye, what a successful screen-actor's collar should be. The sprouting beard might still be misconstrued as the whim of a director sanctified to realism—every day it was getting to look more like that—but no director would have commanded the wearing of such a collar except in actual work where it might have been a striking detail in the apparel of an underworldling, one of those creatures who became the tools of rich but unscrupulous roues who are bent upon the moral destruction of beautiful young screen heroines. He knew it was now that sort of collar. No use now in pretending that it had been worn yesterday for the first time.

CHAPTER X. OF SHATTERED ILLUSIONS

The next morning he sat a long time in the genial sunlight watching carpenters finish a scaffolding beside the pool that had once floated logs to a sawmill. The scaffolding was a stout affair supporting an immense tank that would, evidently for some occult reason important to screen art, hold a great deal of water. The sawmill was gone; at one end of the pool rode a small sail-boat with one mast, its canvas flapping idly in a gentle breeze. Its deck was littered with rigging upon which two men worked. They seemed to be getting things shipshape for a cruise.

When he had tired of this he started off toward the High Gear Dance Hall. Something all day had been drawing him there against his will. He hesitated to believe it was the Montague girl's kindly manner toward him the day before, yet he could identify no other influence. Probably it was that. Yet he didn't want to face her again, even if for a moment she had quit trying to be funny, even if for a moment her eyes had searched his quite earnestly, her broad, amiable face glowing with that sudden friendly concern. It had been hard to withstand this yesterday; he had been in actual danger of confiding to her that engagements of late were not plentiful—something like that. And it would be harder to-day. Even the collar would make it harder to resist the confidence that he was not at this time overwhelmed with offers for his art.

He had for what seemed like an interminable stretch of time been solitary and an outlaw. It was something to have been spoken to by a human being who expressed ever so fleeting an interest in his affairs, even by someone as inconsequent, as negligible in the world of screen artistry as this lightsome minx who, because of certain mental infirmities, could never hope for the least enviable eminence in a profession demanding seriousness of purpose. Still it would be foolish to go again to the set where she was. She might think he was encouraging her.

So he passed the High Gear, where a four-horse stage, watched by two cameras, was now releasing its passengers who all appeared to be direct from New York, and walked on to an outdoor set that promised entertainment. This was the narrow street of some quaint European village, Scotch he soon saw from the dress of its people. A large automobile was invading this remote hamlet to the dismay of its inhabitants. Rehearsed through a megaphone they scurried within doors at its approach, ancient men hobbling on sticks and frantic mothers grabbing their little ones from the path of the monster. Two trial trips he saw the car make the length of the little street.

At its lower end, brooding placidly, was an ancient horse rather recalling Dexter in his generously exposed bones and the jaded droop of his head above a low stone wall. Twice the car sped by him, arousing no sign of apprehension nor even of interest. He paid it not so much as the tribute of a raised eyelid.

The car went back to the head of the street where its entrance would be made. "All right—ready!" came the megaphoned order. Again the peaceful street was thrown into panic by this snorting dragon from the outer world. The old men hobbled affrightedly within doors, the mothers saved their children. And this time, to the stupefaction of Merton Gill, even the old horse proved to be an actor of rare merits. As the car approached he seemed to suffer a painful shock. He tossed his aged head, kicked viciously with his rear feet, stood absurdly aloft on them, then turned and fled from the monster. As Merton mused upon the genius of the trainer who had taught his horse not only to betray fright at a motor car but to distinguish between rehearsals and the actual taking of a scene, he observed a man who emerged from a clump of near-by shrubbery. He carried a shotgun. This was broken at the breech and the man was blowing smoke from the barrels as he came on.

So that was it. The panic of the old horse had been but a simple reaction to a couple of charges of—perhaps rock—salt. Merton Gill hoped it had been nothing sterner. For the first time in his screen career he became cynical about his art. A thing of shame, of machinery, of subterfuge. Nothing would be real, perhaps not even the art.

It is probable that lack of food conduced to this disparaging outlook; and he recovered presently, for he had been smitten with a quick vision of Beulah Baxter in one of her most daring exploits. She, at least, was real. Deaf to entreaty, she honestly braved her hazards. It was a comforting thought after this late exposure of a sham.

In this slightly combative mood he retraced his steps and found himself outside the High Gear Dance Hall, fortified for another possible encounter with the inquiring and obviously sympathetic Montague girl. He entered and saw that she was not on the set. The bar-room dance-hall was for the moment deserted of its ribald crew while an honest inhabitant of the open spaces on a balcony was holding a large revolver to the shrinking back of one of the New York men who had lately arrived by the stage. He forced this man, who was plainly not honest, to descend the stairs and to sign, at a table, a certain paper. Then, with weapon still in hand, the honest Westerner forced the cowardly New Yorker in the direction of the front door until they had passed out of the picture.

On this the bored director of the day before called loudly, "Now, boys, in your places. You've heard a shot—you're running outside to see what's the matter. On your toes, now—try it once." From rear doors came the motley frequenters of the place, led by the elder Montague.

They trooped to the front in two lines and passed from the picture. Here they milled about, waiting for further orders.

"Rotten!" called the director. "Rotten and then some. Listen. You came like a lot of children marching out of a public school. Don't come in lines, break it up, push each other, fight to get ahead, and you're noisy, too. You're shouting. You're saying, 'What's this? What's it all about? What's the matter? Which way did he go?' Say anything you want to, but keep shouting—anything at all. Say 'Thar's gold in them hills!' if you can't think of anything else. Go on, now, boys, do it again and pep it, see. Turn the juice on, open up the old mufflers."

The men went back through the rear doors. The late caller would here have left, being fed up with this sort of stuff, but at that moment he descried the Montague girl back behind a light-standard. She had not noted him, but was in close talk with a man he recognized as Jeff Baird, arch perpetrator of the infamous Buckeye comedies. They came toward him, still talking, as he looked.

"We'll finish here to-morrow afternoon, anyway," the girl was saying.

"Fine," said Baird. "That makes everything jake. Get over on the set whenever you're through. Come over tonight if they don't shoot here, just to give us a look-in."

"Can't," said the girl. "Soon as I get out o' this dump I got to eat on the lot and everything and be over to Baxter's layout—she'll be doing tank stuff till all hours—shipwreck and murder and all like that. Gosh, I hope it ain't cold. I don't mind the water, but I certainly hate to get out and wait in wet clothes while Sig Rosenblatt is thinking about a retake."

"Well"—Baird turned to go—"take care of yourself—don't dive and forget to come up. Come over when you're ready."

"Sure! S'long!" Here the girl, turning from Baird, noted Merton Gill beside her. "Well, well, as I live, the actin' kid once more! Say, you're getting to be a regular studio hound, ain't you?"

For the moment he had forgotten his troubles. He was burning to ask her if Beulah Baxter would really work in a shipwreck scene that night at the place where he had watched the carpenters and the men on the sailboat; but as he tried to word this he saw that the girl was again scanning him with keen eyes. He knew she would read the collar, the beard, perhaps even a look of mere hunger that he thought must now be showing.

"Say, see here, Trouper, what's the shootin' all about, anyway? You up against it—yes." There was again in her eye the look of warm concern, and she was no longer trying to be funny. He might now have admitted a few little things about his screen career, but again the director interrupted.

"Miss Montague—where are you? Oh! Well, remember you're behind the piano during that gun play just now, and you stay hid till after the boys get out. We'll shoot this time, so get set."

She sped off, with a last backward glance of questioning. He waited but a moment before leaving. He was almost forgetting his hunger in the pretty certain knowledge that in a few hours he would actually behold his wonder-woman in at least one of her daring exploits. Shipwreck! Perhaps she would be all but drowned. He hastened back to the pool that had now acquired this high significance. The carpenters were still puttering about on the scaffold. He saw that platforms for the cameras had been built out from its side.

He noted, too, and was puzzled by an aeroplane propeller that had been stationed close to one corner of the pool, just beyond the stern of the little sailing-craft. Perhaps there would be an aeroplane wreck in addition to a shipwreck. Now he had something besides food to think of. And he wondered what the Montague girl could be doing in the company of a really serious artist like Beulah Baxter. From her own story she was going to get wet, but from what he knew of her she would be some character not greatly missed from the cast if she should, as Baird had suggested, dive and forget to come up. He supposed that Baird had meant this to be humorous, the humour typical of a man who could profane a great art with the atrocious Buckeye comedies, so called.

He put in the hours until nightfall in aimless wandering and idle gazing, and was early at the pool-side where his heroine would do her sensational acting. It was now a scene of thrilling activity. Immense lights, both from the scaffolding and from a tower back of the sailing-craft, flooded its deck and rigging from time to time as adjustments were made. The rigging was slack and the deck was still littered, intentionally so, he now perceived. The gallant little boat had been cruelly buffeted by a gale. Two sailors in piratical dress could be seen to emerge at intervals from the cabin.

Suddenly the gale was on with terrific force, the sea rose in great waves, and the tiny ship rocked in a perilous manner. Great billows of water swept its decks. Merton Gill stared in amazement at these phenomena so dissonant with the quiet starlit night. Then he traced them without difficulty to their various sources. The gale issued from the swift revolutions of that aeroplane propeller he had noticed a while ago. The flooding billows were spilled from the big tank at the top of the scaffold and the boat rocked in obedience to the tugging of a rope—tugged from the shore by a crew of helpers—that ran to the top of its mast. Thus had the storm been produced.

A spidery, youngish man from one of the platforms built out from the scaffold, now became sharply vocal through a megaphone to assistants who were bending the elements to the need of this particular hazard of Hortense. He called directions to the men who tugged the rope, to the men in control of the lights, and to another who seemed to create the billows. Among other items he wished more action for the boat and more water for the billows. "See that your tank gets full-up this time," he called, whereupon an engine under the scaffold, by means of a large rubber hose reaching into the pool, began to suck water into the tank above.

The speaker must be Miss Baxter's director, the enviable personage who saw her safely through her perils. When one of the turning reflectors illumined him Merton saw his face of a keen Semitic type. He seemed to possess not the most engaging personality; his manner was aggressive, he spoke rudely to his doubtless conscientious employees, he danced in little rages of temper, and altogether he was not one with whom the watcher would have cared to come in contact. He wondered, indeed, that so puissant a star as Beulah Baxter should not be able to choose her own director, for surely the presence of this unlovely, waspishly tempered being could be nothing but an irritant in the daily life of the wonder-woman. Perhaps she had tolerated him merely for one picture. Perhaps he was especially good in shipwrecks.

If Merton Gill were in this company he would surely have words with this person, director or no director. He hastily wrote a one-reel scenario in which the man so far forgot himself as to speak sharply to the star, and in which a certain young actor, a new member of the company, resented the ungentlemanly words by pitching the offender into a convenient pool and earned even more than gratitude from the starry-eyed wonder-woman.

The objectionable man continued active, profuse of gesture and loud through the megaphone. Once more the storm. The boat rocked threateningly, the wind roared through its slack rigging, and giant billows swept the frail craft. Light as from a half-clouded moon broke through the mist that issued from a steam pipe. There was another lull, and the Semitic type on the platform became increasingly offensive. Merton saw himself saying, "Allow me, Miss Baxter, to relieve you of the presence of this bounder." The man was impossible. Constantly he had searched the scene for his heroine. She would probably not appear until they were ready to shoot, and this seemed not to be at once if the rising temper of the director could be thought an indication.

The big hose again drew water from the pool to the tank, whence, at a sudden release, it would issue in billows. The big lights at last seemed to be adjusted to the director's whim. The aeroplane propeller whirred and the gale was found acceptable. The men at the rope tugged the boat into grave danger. The moon lighted the mist that overhung the scene.

Then at last Merton started, peering eagerly forward across the length of the pool. At the far end, half illumined by the big lights, stood the familiar figure of his wonder—woman, the slim little girl with the wistful eyes. Plainly he could see her now as the mist lifted. She was chatting with one of the pirates who had stepped ashore from the boat. The wonderful golden hair shone resplendent under the glancing rays of the arcs. A cloak was about her shoulders, but at a word of command from the director she threw it off and stepped to the boat's deck. She

326

was dressed in a short skirt, her trim feet and ankles lightly shod and silken clad. The sole maritime touch in her garb was a figured kerchief at her throat similar to those worn by the piratical crew.

"All ready, Hortense—all ready Jose and Gaston, get your places."

Miss Baxter acknowledged the command with that characteristic little wave of a hand that he recalled from so many of her pictures, a half-humorous, half-mocking little defiance. She used it often when escaping her pursuers, as if to say that she would see them in the next installment.

The star and the two men were now in the cabin, hidden from view. Merton Gill was no seaman, but it occurred to him that at least one of the crew would be at the wheel in this emergency. Probably the director knew no better. Indeed the boat, so far as could be discerned, had no wheel. Apparently when a storm came up all hands went down into the cabin to get away from it.

The storm did come up at this moment, with no one on deck. It struck with the full force of a tropic hurricane. The boat rocked, the wind blew, and billows swept the deck. At the height of the tempest Beulah Baxter sprang from the cabin to the deck, clutching wildly at a stanchion. Buffeted by the billows she groped a painful way along the side, at risk of being swept off to her death.

She was followed by one of the crew who held a murderous knife in his hand, then by the other sailor who also held a knife. They, too, were swept by the billows, but seemed grimly determined upon the death of the heroine. Then, when she reached midships and the foremost fiend was almost upon her, the mightiest of all the billows descended and swept her off into the cruel waters. Her pursuers, saving themselves only by great effort, held to the rigging and stared after the girl. They leaned far over the ship's rocking side and each looked from under a spread hand.

For a distressing interval the heroine battled with the waves, but her frail strength availed her little. She raised a despairing face for an instant to the camera and its agony was illumined. Then the dread waters closed above her. The director's whistle blew, the waves were stilled, the tumult ceased. The head of Beulah Baxter appeared halfway down the tank. She was swimming toward the end where Merton stood.

He had been thrilled beyond words at this actual sight of his heroine in action, but now it seemed that a new emotion might overcome him. He felt faint. Beulah Baxter would issue from the pool there at his feet. He might speak to her, might even help her to climb out. At least no one else had appeared to do this. Seemingly no one now cared where Miss Baxter swam to or whether she were offered any assistance in landing. She swam with an admirable crawl stroke, reached the wall, and put up a hand to it. He stepped forward, but she was out before he reached her side. His awe had delayed him. He drew back then, for the star, after vigorously shaking herself, went to a tall brazier in which glowed a charcoal fire.

Here he now noticed for the first time the prop-boy Jimmie, he who had almost certainly defaulted with an excellent razor. Jimmie threw a blanket about the star's shoulders as she hovered above the glowing coals. Merton had waited for her voice. He might still venture to speak to her—to tell her of his long and profound admiration for her art. Her voice came as she shivered over the fire:

"Murder! That water's cold. Rosenblatt swore he'd have it warmed but I'm here to say it wouldn't boil an egg in four minutes."

He could not at first identify this voice with the remembered tones of Beulah Baxter. But of course she was now hoarse with the cold. Under the circumstances he could hardly expect his heroine's own musical clearness. Then as the girl spoke again something stirred among his more recent memories. The voice was still hoarse, but he placed it now. He approached the brazier. It was undoubtedly the Montague girl. She recognized him, even as she squeezed water from the hair of wondrous gold.

"Hello, again, Kid. You're everywhere, ain't you? Say, wha'd you think of that Rosenblatt man? Swore he'd put the steam into that water and take off the chill. And he never." She threw aside the blanket and squeezed water from her garments, then began to slap her legs, arms, and chest.

"Well, I'm getting a gentle glow, anyhow. Wha'd you think of the scene?"

"It was good—very well done, indeed." He hoped it didn't sound patronizing, though that was how he felt. He believed now that Miss Baxter would have done it much better. He ventured a question. "But how about Miss Baxter—when does she do something? Is she going to be swept off the boat, too?"

"Baxter? Into that water? Quit your kidding!"

"But isn't she here at all—won't she do anything here?"

"Listen here, Kid; why should she loaf around on the set when she's paying me good money to double for her?"

"You—double for Beulah Baxter?" It was some more of the girl's nonsense, and a blasphemy for which he could not easily forgive her.

"Why not? Ain't I a good stunt actress? I'll tell the lot she hasn't found any one yet that can get away with her stuff better than what I do."

"But she—I heard her say herself she never allowed any one to double for her—she wouldn't do such a thing."

Here sounded a scornful laugh from Jimmie, the prop—boy. "Bunk!" said he at the laugh's end. "How long you been doublin' for her, Miss Montague? Two years, ain't it?—I know it was before I come here, and I been on the lot a year and a half. Say, he ought to see some the stuff you done for her out on location, like jumpin' into the locomotive engine from your auto and catchin' the brake beams

328

when the train's movin', and goin' across that quarry on the cable, and ridin' down that lumber flume sixty miles per hour and ridin' some them outlaw buckjumpers—he'd ought to seen some that stuff, hey, Miss Montague?"

"That's right, Jimmie, you tell him all about me. I hate to talk of myself." Very wonderfully Merton Gill divined that this was said with a humorous intention. Jimmy was less sensitive to values. He began to obey.

"Well, I dunno—there's that motorcycle stuff. Purty good, I'll say. I wouldn't try that, no, sir, not for a cool million dollars. And that chase stuff on the roofs down town where you jumped across that court that wasn't any too darned narrow, an' say, I wisht I could skin up a tree the way you can. An' there was that time—"

"All right, all right, Jimmie. I can tell him the rest sometime. I don't really hate to talk about myself—that's on the level. And say, listen here, Jimmie, you're my favourite sweetheart, ain't you?"

"Yes, ma'am," assented Jimmie, warmly. "All right. Beat it up and get me about two quarts of that hot coffee and about four ham sandwiches, two for you and two for me. That's a good kid."

"Sure!" exclaimed Jimmie, and was off.

Merton Gill had been dazed by these revelations, by the swift and utter destruction of his loftiest ideal. He hardly cared to know, now, if Beulah Baxter were married. It was the Montague girl who had most thrilled him for two years. Yet, almost as if from habit, he heard himself asking, "Is—do you happen to know if Beulah Baxter is married?"

"Baxter married? Sure! I should think you'd know it from the way that Sig Rosenblatt bawls everybody out."

"Who is he?"

"Who is he? Why, he's her husband, of course—he's Mr. Beulah Baxter."

"That little director up on the platform that yells so?" This unspeakable person to be actually the husband of the wonder-woman, the man he had supposed she must find intolerable even as a director. It was unthinkable, more horrible, somehow, than her employment of a double. In time he might have forgiven that—but this!

"Sure, that's her honest-to-God husband. And he's the best one out of three that I know she's had. Sig's a good scout even if he don't look like Buffalo Bill. In fact, he's all right in spite of his rough ways. He'd go farther for you than most of the men on this lot. If I wanted a favour I'd go to Sig before a lot of Christians I happen to know. And he's a bully director if he is noisy. Baxter's crazy about him, too. Don't make any mistake there."

"I won't," he answered, not knowing what he said.

She shot him a new look. "Say, Kid, as long as we're talking, you seem kind of up against it. Where's your overcoat a night like this, and when did you last—"

"Miss Montague! Miss Montague!" The director was calling.

"Excuse me," she said. "I got to go entertain the white folks again." She tucked up the folds of her blanket and sped around the pool to disappear in the mazes of the scaffolding. He remained a moment staring dully into the now quiet water. Then he walked swiftly away.

Beulah Baxter, his wonder-woman, had deceived her public in Peoria, Illinois, by word of mouth. She employed a double at critical junctures. "She'd be a fool not to," the Montague girl had said. And in private life, having been unhappily wed twice before, she was Mrs. Sigmund Rosenblatt. And crazy about her husband!

A little while ago he had felt glad he was not to die of starvation before seeing his wonder-woman. Reeling under the first shock of his discoveries he was now sorry. Beulah Baxter was no longer his wonder-woman. She was Mr. Rosenblatt's. He would have preferred death, he thought, before this heart-withering revelation.

CHAPTER XI. THE MONTAGUE GIRL INTERVENES

He came to life the next morning, shivering under his blankets. It must be cold outside. He glanced at his watch and reached for another blanket, throwing it over himself and tucking it in at the foot. Then he lay down again to screen a tense bit of action that had occurred late the night before. He had plunged through the streets for an hour, after leaving the pool, striving to recover from the twin shocks he had suffered. Then, returning to his hotel, he became aware that The Hazards of Hortense were still on. He could hear the roar of the aeroplane propeller and see the lights over the low buildings that lined his street.

Miserably he was drawn back to the spot where the most important of all his visions had been rent to tatters. He went to the end of the pool where he had stood before. Mr. Rosenblatt-hardly could he bring his mind to utter the hideous syllables-was still dissatisfied with the sea's might. He wanted bigger billows and meant to have them if the company stayed on the set all night. He was saying as much with peevish inflections. Merton stood warming himself over the fire that still glowed in the brazier.

To him from somewhere beyond the scaffold came now the Montague girl and Jimmie. The girl was in her blanket, and Jimmie bore a pitcher, two tin cups, and a package of sandwiches. They came to the fire and Jimmie poured coffee for the girl. He produced sugar from a pocket.

"Help yourself, James," said the girl, and Jimmie poured coffee for himself. They ate sandwiches as they drank. Merton drew a little back from the fire. The scent of the hot coffee threatened to make him forget he was not only a successful screen actor but a gentleman.

"Did you have to do it again?" he asked.

"I had to do it twice again," said the girl from over her tin cup. "They're developing the strips now, then they'll run them in the projection room, and they won't suit Sig one little bit, and I'll have to do it some more. I'll be swimming here till daylight doth appear."

She now shot that familiar glance of appraisal at Merton. "Have a sandwich and some coffee, Kid-give him your cup, Jimmie."

It was Merton Gill's great moment, a heart-gripping climax to a two-days' drama that had at no time lacked tension. Superbly he arose to it. Consecrated to his art, Clifford Armytage gave the public something better and finer. He drew himself up and spoke lightly, clearly, with careless ease:

"No, thanks-I couldn't eat a mouthful." The smile with which he accompanied the simple words might be enigmatic, it might hint of secret sorrows, but it was plain enough that these could not ever so distantly relate to a need for food.

Having achieved this sensational triumph, with all the quietness of method that should distinguish the true artist, he became seized with stage fright amounting almost to panic. He was moved to snatch the sandwich that Jimmie now proffered, the cup that he had refilled with coffee. Yet there was but a moment of confusion. Again he wielded an iron restraint. But he must leave the stage. He could not tarry there after his big scene, especially under that piercing glance of the girl. Somehow there was incredulity in it.

"Well, I guess I'll have to be going," he remarked jauntily, and turned for his exit.

"Say, Kid." The girl halted him a dozen feet away.

"Say, listen here. This is on the level. I want to have a talk with you to-morrow. You'll be on the lot, won't you?"

He seemed to debate this momentarily, then replied, "Oh, yes. I'll be around here somewhere." "Well, remember, now. If I don't run into you, you come down to that set where I was working to-day. See? I got something to say to you."

"All right. I'll probably see you sometime during the day."

He had gone on to his hotel. But he had no intention of seeing the Montague girl on the morrow, nor of being seen by her. He would keep out of that girl's way whatever else he did. She would ask him if everything was jake, and where was his overcoat, and a lot of silly questions about matters that should not concern her.

He was in two minds about the girl now. Beneath an unreasonable but very genuine resentment that she should have doubled for Beulah Baxter-as if she had basely cheated him of his most cherished ideal-there ran an undercurrent of reluctant but very profound admiration for her prowess. She had done some thrilling things and seemed to make nothing of it. Through this admiration there ran also a thread of hostility because he, himself, would undoubtedly be afraid to attempt her lightest exploit. Not even the trifling feat he had just witnessed, for he had never learned to swim. But he clearly knew, despite this confusion, that he was through with the girl. He must take more pains to avoid her. If met by chance, she must be snubbed-up-staged, as she would put it.

Under his blankets now, after many appealing close-ups of the sandwich which Jimmie had held out to him, he felt almost sorry that he had not taken the girl's food. All his being, save that part consecrated to his art, had cried out for it. Art, had triumphed, and now he was near to regretting that it had not been beaten down. No good thinking about it, though.

He reached again for his watch. It was seven-thirty and time to be abroad. Once more he folded his blankets and placed them on the pile, keeping an alert glance, the while, for another possible bit of the delicious bread. He found nothing of this sort. The Crystal Palace Hotel was bare of provender. Achieving a discreet retirement from the hostelry he stood irresolute in the street. This morning there was no genial sun to warm him. A high fog overcast the sky, and the air was chill. At intervals he shivered violently. For no reason, except that he had there last beheld actual food, he went back to the pool.

Evidently Mr. Rosenblatt had finally been appeased. The place was deserted and lay bare and ugly in the dull light. The gallant ship of the night before was seen to be a poor, flimsy make-shift. No wonder Mr. Rosenblatt had wished billows to engulf it and mist to shroud it. He sat on a beam lying at the ship end of the pool and stared moodily at the pitiful make-believe.

He rounded his shoulders and pulled up the collar of his coat. He knew he should be walking, but doubted his strength. The little walk to the pool had made him strangely breathless. He wondered how long people were in starving to death. He had read of fasters who went for weeks without food, but he knew he was not of this class. He lacked talent for it. Doubtless another day would finish him. He had no heart now for visions of the Gashwiler table. He descended tragically to recalling that last meal at the drug store-the bowl of soup with its gracious burden of rich, nourishing catsup.

He began to alter the scenario of his own life. Suppose he had worked two more weeks for Gashwiler. That would have given him thirty dollars. Suppose he had worked a month. He could have existed a long time on sixty dollars. Suppose he had even stuck it out for one week more-fifteen dollars at this moment! He began to see a breakfast, the sort of meal to be ordered by a hungry man with fifteen dollars to squander.

The shivering seized him again and he heard his teeth rattle. He must move from this spot, forever now to be associated with black disillusion. He arose from his seat and was dismayed to hear a hail from the Montague girl. Was he never to be free from her? She was poised at a little distance, one hand raised to him, no longer the drenched victim of a capricious Rosenblatt, but the beaming, joyous figure of one who had triumphed over wind and wave. He went almost sullenly to her while she waited. No good trying to escape her for a minute or so.

"Hello, old Trouper! You're just in time to help me hunt for something." She was in the familiar street suit now, a skirt and jacket of some rough brown goods and a cloth hat that kept close to her small head above hair that seemed of no known shade whatever, though it was lighter than dark. She flashed a smile at him from her broad mouth as he came up, though her knowing gray eyes did not join in this smile. He knew instantly that she was taking him in.

This girl was wise beyond her years, he thought, but one even far less knowing could hardly have been in two minds about his present abject condition. The pushed-up collar of his coat did not entirely hide the once-white collar beneath it, the beard had reached its perhaps most distressing stage of development, and the suit was rumpled out of all the nattiness for which it had been advertised. Even the plush hat had lost its smart air.

Then he plainly saw that the girl would, for the moment at least, ignore these phenomena. She laughed again, and this time the eyes laughed, too. "C'mon over and help me hunt for that bar pin I lost. It must be at this end, because I know I had it on when I went into the drink. Maybe it's in the pool, but maybe I lost it after I got out. It's one of Baxter's that she wore in the scene just ahead of last night, and she'll have to have it again to-day. Now—" She began to search the ground around the cold brazier. "It might be along here." He helped her look. Pretty soon he would remember an engagement and get away. The search at the end of the pool proved fruitless. The girl continued to chatter. They had worked until one-thirty before that grouch of a Rosenblatt would call it a day. At that she'd rather do water stuff than animal stuff-especially lions. "Lions? I should think so!" He replied to this. "Dangerous, isn't it?"

"Oh, it ain't that. They're nothing to be afraid of if you know 'em, but they're so hot and smelly when you have to get close to 'em. Anything I really hate, it's having to get up against a big, hot, hairy, smelly lion."

He murmured a sympathetic phrase and extended his search for the lost pin to the side of the pool. Almost under the scaffold he saw the shine of precious stones and called to her as he picked up the pin, a bar pin splendidly set with diamonds. He was glad that he had found it for her. It must have cost a great deal of money and she would doubtless be held responsible for its safe-keeping.

She came dancing to him. "Say, that's fine-your eyes are working, ain't they? I might 'a' been set back a good six dollars if you hadn't found that." She took the bauble and fastened it inside her jacket. So the pin, too, had been a tawdry makeshift. Nothing was real any more. As she adjusted the pin he saw his moment for escape. With a gallant striving for the true Clifford Armytage manner he raised the plush hat.

"Well, I'm glad you found Mrs. Rosenblatt's pin-and I guess I'll be getting on."

The manner must have been defective. She looked through him and said with great firmness, "Nothing like that, old pippin." Again he was taken with a violent fit of shivering. He could not meet her eyes. He was turning away when she seized him by the wrist. Her grip was amazingly forceful. He doubted if he could break away even with his stoutest effort. He stood miserably staring at the ground. Suddenly the girl reached up to pat his shoulder. He shivered again and she continued to pat it. When his teeth had ceased to be castanets she spoke:

"Listen here, old Kid, you can't fool any one, so quit trying. Don't you s'pose I've seen 'em like you before? Say, boy, I was trouping while you played with marbles. You're up against it. Now, c'mon"—with the arm at his shoulder she pulled him about to face her-"c'mon and be nice-tell mother all about it."

The late Clifford Armytage was momentarily menaced by a complete emotional overthrow. Another paroxysm of shivering perhaps averted this humiliation. The girl dropped his wrist, turned, stooped, and did something. He recalled the scene in the gambling hell, only this time she fronted away from the camera. When she faced him again he was not surprised to see bills in her hand. It could only have been the chill he suffered that kept him from blushing. She forced the bills into his numb fingers and he stared at them blankly. "I can't take these," he muttered.

"There, now, there, now! Be easy. Naturally I know you're all right or I wouldn't give up this way. You're just having a run of hard luck. The Lord knows, I've been helped out often enough in my time. Say, listen, I'll never forget when I went out as a kid with Her First False Step-they had lions in that show. It was a frost from the start. No salaries, no nothing. I got a big laugh one day when I was late at rehearsal. The manager says: 'You're fined two dollars, Miss Montague.' I says, 'All right, Mr. Gratz, but you'll have to wait till I can write home for the money.' Even Gratz had to laugh. Anyway, the show went bust and I never would 'a' got any place if two or three parties hadn't of helped me out here and there, just the same as I'm doing with you this minute. So don't be foolish."

"Well-you see-I don't—" He broke off from nervous weakness. In his mind was a jumble of incongruous sentences and he seemed unable to manage any of them.

The girl now sent a clean shot through his armour. "When'd you eat last?"

He looked at the ground again in painful embarrassment. Even in the chill air he was beginning to feel hot. "I don't remember," he said at last quite honestly.

"That's what I thought. You go eat. Go to Mother Haggin's, that cafeteria just outside the gate. She has better breakfast things than the place on the lot." Against his will the vision of a breakfast enthralled him, yet even under this exaltation an instinct of the wariest caution survived.

"I'll go to the one on the lot, I guess. If I went out to the other one I couldn't get in again."

She smiled suddenly, with puzzling lights in her eyes. "Well, of all things! You want to get in again, do you? Say, wouldn't that beat the hot place a mile? You want to get in again? All right, Old-timer, I'll go out with you and after you've fed I'll cue you on to the lot again."

"Well-if it ain't taking you out of your way." He knew that the girl was somehow humouring him, as if he were a sick child. She knew, and he knew, that the lot was no longer any place for him until he could be rightly there.

"No, c'mon, I'll stay by you." They walked up the street of the Western village. The girl had started at a brisk pace and he was presently breathless.

"I guess I'll have to rest a minute," he said. They were now before the Crystal Palace Hotel and he sat on the steps.

"All in, are you? Well, take it easy."

He was not only all in, but his mind still played with incongruous sentences. He heard himself saying things that must sound foolish.

"I've slept in here a lot," he volunteered. The girl went to look through one of the windows.

"Blankets!" she exclaimed. "Well, you got the makings of a trouper in you, I'll say that. Where else did you sleep?"

"Well, there were two miners had a nice cabin down the street here with bunks and blankets, and they had a fight, and half a kettle of beans and some bread, and one of them shaved and I used his razor, but I haven't shaved since because I only had twenty cents day before yesterday, and anyway they might think I was growing them for a part, the way your father did, but I moved up here when I saw them put the blankets in, and I was careful and put them back every morning. I didn't do any harm, do you think? And I got the rest of the beans they'd thrown into the fireplace, and if I'd only known it I could have brought my razor and overcoat and some clean collars, but somehow you never seem to know when—"

He broke off, eyeing her vaguely. He had little notion what he had been saying or what he would say next.

"This is going to be good," said the Montague girl. "I can see that from here. But now you c'mon-we'll walk slow-and you tell me the rest when you've had a little snack."

She even helped him to rise, with a hand under his elbow, though he was quick to show her that he had not needed this help. "I can walk all right," he assured her.

"Of course you can. You're as strong as a horse. But we needn't go too fast." She took his arm in a friendly way as they completed the journey to the outside cafeteria.

At this early hour they were the only patrons of the place. Miss Montague, a little with the air of a solicitous nurse, seated her charge at a corner table and took the place opposite him.

"What's it going to be?" she demanded.

Visions of rich food raced madly through his awakened mind, wide platters heaped with sausage and steaks and ham and corned-beef hash.

"Steak," he ventured, "and something like ham and eggs and some hot cakes and coffee and—" He broke off. He was becoming too emotional under this golden spread of opportunity. The girl glanced up from the bill of fare and appraised the wild light in his eyes.

"One minute, Kid-let's be more restful at first. You know-kind of ease into the heavy eats. It'll prob'ly be better for you."

"Anything you say," he conceded. Her words of caution had stricken him with a fear that this was a dream; that he would wake up under blankets back in the Crystal Palace. It was like that in dreams. You seemed able to order all sorts of food, but something happened; it never reached the table. He would take no further initiative in this scene, whether dream or reality. "You order something," he concluded. His eyes trustfully sought the girl's.

"Well, I think you'll start with one orange, just to kind of hint to the old works that something good is coming. Then—lemme see"—she considered gravely. "Then I guess about two soft-boiled eggs—no, you can stand three—and some dry toast and some coffee. Maybe a few thin strips of bacon wouldn't hurt. We'll see can you make the grade." She turned to give the order to a waitress. "And shoot the coffee along, sister. A cup for me, too."

Her charge shivered again at the mere mention of coffee. The juncture was critical. He might still be dreaming, but in another moment he must know. He closely, even coolly, watched the two cups of coffee that were placed before them. He put a benumbed hand around the cup in front of him and felt it burn. It was too active a sensation for mere dreaming. He put sugar into the cup and poured in the cream from a miniature pitcher, inhaling a very real aroma. Events thus far seemed normal. He stirred the coffee and started to raise the cup. Now, after all, it seemed to be a dream. His hand shook so that the stuff spilled into the saucer and even out on to the table. Always in dreams you were thwarted at the last moment.

The Montague girl had noted the trembling and ineffective hand. She turned her back upon him to chat with the waitress over by the food counter. With no eye upon him, he put both hands about the cup and succeeded in raising it to his lips. The hands were still shaky, but he managed some sips of the stuff, and then a long draught that seemed to scald him. He wasn't sure if it scalded or not. It was pretty hot, and fire ran through him. He drained the cup—still holding it with both hands. It was an amazing sensation to have one's hand refuse to obey so simple an order. Maybe he would always be that way now, practically a cripple.

The girl turned back to him. "Atta boy," she said. "Now take the orange. And when the toast comes you can have some more coffee." A dread load was off his mind. He did not dream this thing. He ate the orange, and ate wonderful toast to the accompaniment of another cup of coffee. The latter half of this he managed with but one hand, though it was not yet wholly under control. The three eggs seemed like but one. He thought they must have been small eggs. More toast was commanded and more coffee.

"Easy, easy!" cautioned his watchful hostess from time to time. "Don't wolf it—you'll feel better afterwards."

"I feel better already," he announced.

"Well," the girl eyed him critically, "you certainly got the main chandelier lighted up once more."

A strange exhilaration flooded all his being. His own thoughts babbled to him, and he presently began to babble to his new friend.

"You remind me so much of Tessie Kearns," he said as he scraped the sides of the egg cup.

"Who's she?"

"Oh, she's a scenario writer I know. You're just like her." He was now drunk—maudlin drunk—from the coffee. Sober, he would have known that no human beings could be less alike than Tessie Kearns and the Montague girl. Other walls of his reserve went down.

"Of course I could have written to Gashwiler and got some money to go back there—"

"Gashwiler, Gashwiler?" The girl seemed to search her memory. "I thought I knew all the tank towns, but that's a new one. Where is it?"

"It isn't a town; it's a gentleman I had a position with, and he said he'd keep it open for me." He flew to another thought with the inconsequence of the drunken. "Say, Kid"—He had even caught that form of address from her—"I'll tell you. You can keep this watch of mine till I pay you back this money." He drew it out. "It's a good solid-gold watch and everything. My uncle Sylvester gave it to me for not smoking, on my eighteenth birthday. He smoked, himself; he even drank considerable. He was his own worst enemy. But you can see it's a good solid—gold watch and keeps time, and you hold it till I pay you back, will you?"

The girl took the watch, examining it carefully, noting the inscription engraved on the case. There were puzzling glints in her eyes as she handed it back to him. "No; I'll tell you, it'll be my watch until you pay me back, but you keep it for me. I haven't any place to carry it except the pocket of my jacket, and I might lose it, and then where'd we be?"

"Well, all right." He cheerfully took back the watch. His present ecstasy would find him agreeable to all proposals.

"And say," continued the girl, "what about this Gashweiler, or whatever his name is? He said he'd take you back, did he? A farm?"

"No, an emporium—and you forgot his name just the way that lady in the casting office always does. She's funny. Keeps telling me not to forget the address, when of course I couldn't forget the town where I lived, could I? Of course it's a little town, but you wouldn't forget it when you lived there a long time—not when you got your start there."

"So you got your start in this town, did you?"

He wanted to talk a lot now. He prattled of the town and his life there, of the eight-hour talent-tester and the course in movie-acting. Of Tessie Kearns and her scenarios, not yet prized as they were sure to be later. Of Lowell Hardy, the artistic photographer, and the stills that he had made of the speaker as Clifford Armytage. Didn't she think that was a better stage name than Merton Gill, which didn't seem to sound like so much? Anyway, he wished he had his stills here to show her. Of course some of them were just in society parts, the sort of thing that Harold Parmalee played—had she noticed that he looked a good deal like Harold Parmalee? Lots of people had.

Tessie Kearns thought he was the dead image of Parmalee. But he liked Western stuff better—a lot better than cabaret stuff where you had to smoke one cigarette after another—and he wished she could see the stills in the Buck Benson outfit, chaps and sombrero and spurs and holster. He'd never had two guns, but the one he did have he could draw pretty well. There would be his hand at his side, and in a flash he would have the gun in it, ready to shoot from the hip. And roping—he'd need to practise that some. Once he got it smack over Dexter's head, but usually it didn't go so well.

Probably a new clothesline didn't make the best rope—too stiff. He could probably do a lot better with one of those hair ropes that the real cowboys used. And Metta Judson—she was the best cook anywhere around Simsbury. He mustn't forget to write to Metta, and to Tessie Kearns, to be sure and see The Blight of Broadway when it came to the Bijou Palace. They would be surprised to see those close—ups that Henshaw had used him in. And he was in that other picture. No close-ups in that, still he would show pretty well in the cage-scene— he'd had to smoke a few cigarettes there, because Arabs smoke all the time, and he hadn't been in the later scene where the girl and the young fellow were in the deserted tomb all night and he didn't lay a finger on her because he was a perfect gentleman.

He didn't know what he would do next. Maybe Henshaw would want him in Robinson Crusoe, Junior, where Friday's sister turned out to be the daughter of an English earl with her monogram tattooed on her left shoulder. He would ask Henshaw, anyway.

The Montague girl listened attentively to the long, wandering recital. At times she would seem to be strongly moved, to tears or something. But mostly she listened with a sympathetic smile, or perhaps with a perfectly rigid face, though at such moments there would be those curious glints of light far back in her gray eyes. Occasionally she would prompt him with a question.

In this way she brought out his version of the Sabbath afternoon experience with Dexter. He spared none of the details, for he was all frankness now. He even told how ashamed he had felt having to lead Dexter home from his scandalous grazing before the Methodist Church. He had longed to leap upon the horse and ride him back at a gallop, but he had been unable to do this because there was nothing from which to climb on him, and probably he would have been afraid to gallop the beast, anyway.

This had been one of the bits that most strangely moved his listener. Her eyes were moist when he had finished, and some strong emotion seemed about to overpower her, but she had recovered command of herself, and become again the sympathetic provider and counsellor.

He would have continued to talk, apparently, for the influence of strong drink had not begun to wane, but the girl at length stopped him.

"Listen here, Merton—" she began; her voice was choked to a peculiar hoarseness and she seemed to be threatened with a return of her late strong emotion. She was plainly uncertain of her control, fearing to trust herself to speech, but presently, after efforts which he observed with warmest sympathy, she seemed to recover her poise. She swallowed earnestly several times, wiped her moisture—dimmed eyes with her handkerchief, and continued, "It's getting late and I've got to be over at the show shop. So I'll tell you what to do next. You go out and get a shave and a haircut and then go home and get cleaned up—you said you had a room and other clothes, didn't you?"

Volubly he told her about the room at Mrs. Patterson's, and, with a brief return of lucidity, how the sum of ten dollars was now due this heartless society woman who might insist upon its payment before he would again enjoy free access to his excellent wardrobe.

"Well, lemme see—" She debated a moment, then reached under the table, fumbled obscurely, and came up with more money. "Now, here, here's twenty more besides that first I gave you, so you can pay the dame her money and get all fixed up again, fresh suit and clean collar and a shine and everything. No, no—this is my scene; you stay out."

He had waved protestingly at sight of the new money, and now again he blushed.

"That's all understood," she continued. "I'm staking you to cakes till you get on your feet, see? And I know you're honest, so I'm not throwing my money away. There—sink it and forget it. Now, you go out and do what I said, the barber first. And lay off the eats until about noon. You had enough for now. By noon you can stoke up with meat and potatoes—anything you want that'll stick to the merry old slats. And I'd take milk instead of any more coffee. You've thinned down some—you're not near so plump as Harold Parmalee. Then you rest up for the balance of the day, and you show here to-morrow morning about this time. Do you get it?

The Countess'll let you in. Tell her I said to, and come over to the office building. See?"

He tried to tell her his gratitude, but instead he babbled again of how much she was like Tessie Kearns. They parted at the gate.

With a last wondering scrutiny of him, a last reminder of her very minute directions, she suddenly illumined him with rays of a compassion that was somehow half-laughter. "You poor, feckless dub!" she pronounced as she turned from him to dance through the gate. He scarcely heard the words; her look and tone had been so warming.

Ten minutes later he was telling a barber that he had just finished a hard week on the Holden lot, and that he was glad to get the brush off at last. From the barber's he hastened to the Patterson house, rather dreading the encounter with one to whom he owed so much money. He found the house locked. Probably both of the Pattersons had gone out into society. He let himself in and began to follow the directions of the Montague girl. The bath, clean linen, the other belted suit, already pressed, the other shoes, the buttoned, cloth-topped ones, already polished! He felt now more equal to the encounter with a heartless society woman. But, as she did not return, he went out in obedience to a new hunger.

In the most sumptuous cafeteria he knew of, one patronized only in his first careless days of opulence, he ate for a long time. Roast beef and potatoes he ordered twice, nor did he forget to drink the milk prescribed by his benefactress. Plenty of milk would make him more than ever resemble Harold Parmalee. And he commanded an abundance of dessert: lemon pie and apple pie and a double portion of chocolate cake with ice-cream. His craving for sweets was still unappeased, so at a near-by drug store he bought a pound box of candy.

The world was again under his feet. Restored to his rightful domain, he trod it with lightness and certainty. His mind was still a pleasant jumble of money and food and the Montague girl. Miles of gorgeous film flickered across his vision. An experienced alcoholic would have told him that he enjoyed a coffee "hang-over." He wended a lordly way to the nearest motion-picture theatre.

Billed there was the tenth installment of The Hazards of Hortense. He passed before the lively portrayal in colours of Hortense driving a motor car off an open drawbridge. The car was already halfway between the bridge and the water beneath. He sneered openly at the announcement: "Beulah Baxter in the Sensational Surprise Picture of the Century." A surprise picture indeed, if those now entering the theatre could be told what he knew about it! He considered spreading the news, but decided to retain the superiority his secret knowledge gave him.

Inside the theatre, eating diligently from his box of candy, he was compelled to endure another of the unspeakable Buckeye comedies. The cross-eyed man was a lifeguard at a beach and there were social entanglements involving a bearded father, his daughter in an inconsiderable bathing suit, a confirmed dipsomaniac, two social derelicts who had to live by their wits, and a dozen young girls also arrayed in inconsiderable bathing suits. He could scarcely follow the chain of events, so illogical were they, and indeed made little effort to do so. He felt far above the audience that cackled at these dreadful buffooneries. One subtitle read: "I hate to kill him—murder is so hard to explain."

This sort of thing, he felt more than ever, degraded an art where earnest people were suffering and sacrificing in order to give the public something better and finer. Had he not, himself, that very day, completed a perilous ordeal of suffering and sacrifice? And he was asked to laugh at a cross—eyed man posing before a camera that fell to pieces when the lens was exposed, shattered, presumably, by the impact of the afflicted creature's image! This, surely, was not art such as Clifford Armytage was rapidly fitting himself, by trial and hardship, to confer upon the public.

It was with curiously conflicting emotions that he watched the ensuing Hazards of Hortense. He had to remind himself that the slim little girl with the wistful eyes was not only not performing certain feats of daring that the film exposed, but that she was Mrs. Sigmund Rosenblatt and crazy about her husband. Yet the magic had not wholly departed from this wronged heroine. He thought perhaps this might be because he now knew, and actually liked, that talkative Montague girl who would be doing the choice bits of this drama. Certainly he was loyal to the hand that fed him.

Black Steve and his base crew, hirelings of the scoundrelly guardian who was "a Power in Wall Street," again and again seemed to have encompassed the ruin, body and soul, of the persecuted Hortense. They had her prisoner in a foul den of Chinatown, whence she escaped to balance precariously upon the narrow cornice of a skyscraper, hundreds of feet above a crowded thoroughfare. They had her, as the screen said, "Depressed by the Grim Menace of Tragedy that Impended in the Shadows." They gave her a brief respite in one of those gilded resorts "Where the Clink of Coin Opens Wide the Portals of Pleasure, Where Wealth Beckons with Golden Fingers," but this was only a trap for the unsuspecting girl, who was presently, sewed in a plain sack, tossed from the stern of an ocean liner far out at sea by creatures who would do anything for money—who, so it was said, were Remorseless in the Mad Pursuit of Gain.

At certain gripping moments it became apparent to one of the audience that Mrs. Sigmund Rosenblatt herself was no longer in jeopardy. He knew the girl who was, and profoundly admired her artistry as she fled along the narrow cornice of the skyscraper. For all purposes she was Beulah Baxter. He recalled her figure as being—not exactly stubby, but at least not of marked slenderness. Yet in the distance she was indeed all that an audience could demand. And she was honest, while Mrs. Rosenblatt, in the Majestic Theatre at Peoria, Illinois, had trifled airily with his faith in women and deceived him by word of mouth.

He applauded loudly at the sensational finish, when Hortense, driving her motor car at high speed across the great bridge, ran into the draw, that opened too late for her to slow down, and plunged to the cruel waters far below.

Mrs. Rosenblatt would possibly have been a fool to do this herself. The Montague girl had been insistent on that point; there were enough things she couldn't avoid doing, and all stars very sensibly had doubles for such scenes when distance or action permitted. At the same time, he could never again feel the same toward her. Indeed, he would never have felt the same even had there been no Rosenblatt. Art was art!

It was only five o'clock when he left the picture theatre, but he ate again at the luxurious cafeteria. He ate a large steak, drank an immense quantity of milk, and bought another box of candy on his way to the Patterson home. Lights were on there, and he went in to face the woman he had so long kept out of her money. She would probably greet him coldly and tell him she was surprised at his actions.

Yet it seemed that he had been deceived in this society woman. She was human, after all. She shook hands with him warmly and said they were glad to see him back; he must have been out on location, and she was glad they were not to lose him, because he was so quiet and regular and not like some other motion-picture actors she had known.

He told her he had just put in a hard week on the Holden lot, where things were beginning to pick up. He was glad she had missed him, and he certainly had missed his comfortable room, because the accommodations on the lot were not of the best. In fact, they were pretty unsatisfactory, if you came right down to it, and he hoped they wouldn't keep him there again. And, oh, yes—he was almost forgetting. Here was ten dollars—he believed there were two weeks' rent now due. He passed over the money with rather a Clifford Armytage flourish.

Mrs. Patterson accepted the bill almost protestingly. She hadn't once thought about the rent, because she knew he was reliable, and he was to remember that any time convenient to him would always suit her in these matters. She did accept the bill, still she was not the heartless creature he had supposed her to be.

As he bade her good-night at the door she regarded him closely and said, "Somehow you look a whole lot older, Mr. Armytage."

"I am," replied Mr. Armytage.

* * * * * *

Miss Montague, after parting with her protege had walked quickly, not without little recurrent dance steps—as if some excess of joy would ever and again overwhelm her—to the long office building on the Holden lot, where she entered a door marked "Buckeye Comedies. Jeff Baird, Manager." The outer office was vacant, but through the open door to another room she observed Baird at his desk, his head bent low over certain sheets of yellow paper. He was a bulky, rather phlegmatic looking man, with a parrot-like crest of gray hair. He did not look up as the girl entered. She stood a moment as if to control her excitement, then spoke.

"Jeff, I found a million dollars for you this morning."

"Thanks!" said Mr. Baird, still not looking up. "Chuck it down in the coal cellar, will you? We're littered with the stuff up here."

"On the level, Jeff."

Baird looked up. "On the level?"

"You'll say so."

"Shoot!"

"Well, he's a small-town hick that saved up seventy-two dollars to come here from Goosewallow, Michigan, to go into pictures-took a correspondence course in screen—acting and all that, and he went broke and slept in a property room down in the village all last week; no eats at all for three, four days. I'd noticed him around the lot on different sets; something about him that makes you look a second time. I don't know what it is-kind of innocent and bug-eyed the way he'd rubber at things, but all the time like as if he thought he was someone. Well, I keep running across him and pretty soon I notice he's up against it. He still thinks he's someone, and is very up-stage if you start to kid him the least bit, but the signs are there, all right. He's up against it good and hard.

"All last week he got to looking worse and worse. But he still had his stage presence. Say, yesterday he looked like the juvenile lead of a busted road show that has walked in from Albany and was just standing around on Broadway wondering who he'd consent to sign up with for forty weeks—see what I mean?-hungry but proud. He was over on the Baxter set last night while I was doing the water stuff, and you'd ought to see him freeze me when I suggested a sandwich and a cup o' coffee. It was grand.

"Well, this morning I'm back for a bar pin of Baxter's I'd lost, and there he is again, no overcoat, shivering his teeth loose, and all in. So I fell for him. Took him up for some coffee and eggs, staked him to his room rent, and sent him off to get cleaned and barbered. But before he went he cut loose and told me his history from the cradle to Hollywood.

"I'd 'a' given something good if you'd been at the next table. I guess he got kind of jagged on the food, see? He'd tell me anything that run in his mind, and most of it was good. You'll say so. I'll get him to do it for you sometime. Of all the funny nuts that make this lot! Well, take my word for it; that's all I ask. And listen here, Jeff—I'm down to cases. There's something about this kid, like when I tell you I'd always look at him twice. And it's something rich that I won't let out for a minute or two. But here's what you and me do, right quick:

"The kid was in that cabaret and gambling-house stuff they shot last week for The Blight of Broadway, and this something that makes you look at him must of struck Henshaw the way it did me, for he let him stay right at the edge of the dance floor and took a lot of close-ups of him looking tired to death of the gay night life. Well, you call up the Victor folks and ask can you get a look at that stuff because you're thinking of giving a part to one of the extras that worked in it. Maybe we can get into the projection room right away and you'll see what I mean. Then I won't have to tell you the richest thing about it. Now!"—she took a long breath—"will you?"

Baird had listened with mild interest to the recital, occasionally seeming not to listen while he altered the script before him. But he took the telephone receiver from its hook and said briefly to the girl: "You win. Hello! Give me the Victor office. Hello! Mr. Baird speaking—"

The two were presently in the dark projection room watching the scenes the girl had told of.

"They haven't started cutting yet," she said delightedly. "All his close-ups will be in. Goody! There's the lad-get him? Ain't he the actin'est thing you ever saw? Now wait-you'll see others."

Baird watched the film absorbedly. Three times it was run for the sole purpose of exposing to this small audience Merton Gill's notion of being consumed with ennui among pleasures that had palled. In the gambling-hall bit it could be observed that he thought not too well of cigarettes. "He screens well, too," remarked the girl. "Of course I couldn't be sure of that."

"He screens all right," agreed Baird.

"Well, what do you think?"

"I think he looks like the first plume on a hearse."

"He looks all of that, but try again. Who does he remind you of? Catch this next one in the gambling hell—get the profile and the eyebrows and the chin—there!"

"Why—" Baird chuckled. "I'm a Swede if he don't look like—"

"You got it!" the girl broke in excitedly. "I knew you would. I didn't at first, this morning, because he was so hungry and needed a shave, and he darned near had me bawling when he couldn't hold his cup o' coffee except with two hands. But what d'you think?—pretty soon he tells me himself that he looks a great deal like Harold Parmalee and wouldn't mind playing parts like Parmalee, though he prefers Western stuff. Wouldn't that get you?"

The film was run again so that Baird could study the Gill face in the light of this new knowledge.

"He does, he does, he certainly does—if he don't look like a No. 9 company of Parmalee I'll eat that film. Say, Flips, you did find something."

"Oh, I knew it; didn't I tell you so?"

"But, listen—does he know he's funny?"

"Not in a thousand years! He doesn't know anything's funny, near as I can make him."

They were out in the light again, walking slowly back to the Buckeye offices.

"Get this," said Baird seriously. "You may think I'm kidding, but only yesterday I was trying to think if I couldn't dig up some guy that looked more like Parmalee than Parmalee himself does—just enough more to get the laugh, see? And you spring this lad on me. All he needs is the eyebrows worked up a little bit. But how about him—will he handle? Because if he will I'll use him in the new five-reeler."

"Will he handle?" Miss Montague echoed the words with deep emphasis. "Leave him to me. He's got to handle. I already got twenty-five bucks invested in his screen career. And, Jeff, he'll be easy to work, except he don't know he's funny. If he found out he was, it might queer him—see what I mean? He's one of that kind—you can tell it. How will you use him? He could never do Buckeye stuff."

"Sure not. But ain't I told you? In this new piece Jack is stage struck and gets a job as valet to a ham that's just about Parmalee's type, and we show Parmalee acting in the screen, but all straight stuff, you understand. Unless he's a wise guy he'll go all through the piece and never get on that it's funny. See, his part's dead straight and serious in a regular drama, and the less he thinks he's funny the bigger scream he'll be. He's got to be Harold Parmalee acting right out, all over the set, as serious as the lumbago—get what I mean?"

"I got you," said the girl, "and you'll get him to-morrow morning. I told him to be over with his stills. And he'll be serious all the time, make no mistake there. He's no wise guy. And one thing, Jeff, he's as innocent as a cup—custard, so you'll have to keep that bunch of Buckeye roughnecks from riding him. I can tell you that much. Once they started kidding him, it would be all off."

"And, besides—" She hesitated briefly. "Somehow I don't want him kidded. I'm pretty hard-boiled, but he sort of made me feel like a fifty-year-old mother watching her only boy go out into the rough world. See?"

"I'll watch out for that," said Baird.

CHAPTER XII. ALIAS HAROLD PARMALEE

Merton Gill awoke to the comforting realization that he was between sheets instead of blankets, and that this morning he need not obscurely leave his room by means of a window. As he dressed, however, certain misgivings, to which he had been immune the day before, gnawed into his optimism. He was sober now. The sheer intoxication of food after fasting, of friendly concern after so long a period when no one had spoken him kindly or otherwise, had evaporated. He felt the depression following success.

He had been rescued from death by starvation, but had anything more than this come about? Had he not fed upon the charity of a strange girl, taking her money without seeing ways to discharge the debt? How could he ever discharge it? Probably before this she had begun to think of him as a cheat. She had asked him to come to the lot, but had been vague as to the purpose. Probably his ordeal of struggle and sacrifice was not yet over. At any rate, he must find a job that would let him pay back the borrowed twenty-five dollars.

He would meet her as she had requested, assure her of his honest intentions, and then seek for work. He would try all the emporiums in Hollywood. They were numerous and some one of them would need the services of an experienced assistant. This plan of endeavour crystallized as he made his way to the Holden lot. He had brought his package of stills, but only because the girl had insisted on seeing them.

The Countess made nothing of letting him in. She had missed him, she said, for what seemed like months, and was glad to hear that he now had something definite in view, because the picture game was mighty uncertain and it was only the lucky few nowadays that could see something definite. He did not confide to her that the definite something now within his view would demand his presence at some distance from her friendly self.

He approached the entrance to Stage Five with head bent in calculation, and not until he heard her voice did he glance up to observe that the Montague girl was dancing from pleasure, it would seem, at merely beholding him. She seized both his hands in her strong grasp and revolved him at the centre of a circle she danced. Then she held him off while her eyes took in the details of his restoration.

"Well, well, well! That shows what a few ham and eggs and sleep will do. Kid, you gross a million at this minute. New suit, new shoes, snappy cravat right from the Men's Quality Shop, and all shaved and combed slick and everything! Say— and I was afraid maybe you wouldn't show."

He regarded her earnestly. "Oh, I would have come back, all right; I'd never forget that twenty-five dollars I owe you; and you'll get it all back, only it may take a little time. I thought I'd see you for a minute, then go out and find a job—you know, a regular job in a store."

"Nothing of the sort, old Trouper!" She danced again about him, both his hands in hers, which annoyed him because it was rather loud public behaviour, though he forgave her in the light of youth and kindliness. "No regular job for you, old Pippin—nothing but acting all over the place—real acting that people come miles to see."

"Do you think I can really get a part?" Perhaps the creature had something definite in view for him.

"Sure you can get a part! Yesterday morning I simply walked into a part for you. Come along over to the office with me. Goody—I see you brought the stills. I'll take a peek at 'em myself before Baird gets here." "Baird? Not the Buckeye comedy man?" He was chilled by a sudden fear.

"Yes, Jeff Baird. You see he is going to do some five—reelers and this first one has a part that might do for you. At least, I told him some things about you, and he thinks you can get away with it."

He went moodily at her side, thinking swift thoughts. It seemed ungracious to tell her of his loathing for the Buckeye comedies, those blasphemous caricatures of worth-while screen art. It would not be fair. And perhaps here was a quick way to discharge his debt and be free of obligation to the girl. Of course he would always feel a warm gratitude for her trusting kindness, but when he no longer owed her money he could choose his own line of work. Rather bondage to some Hollywood Gashwiler than clowning in Baird's infamies!

"Well, I'll try anything he gives me," he said at last, striving for the enthusiasm he could not feel.

"You'll go big, too," said the girl. "Believe, me Kid, you'll go grand."

In Baird's offices he sat at the desk and excitedly undid the package of stills. "We'll give 'em the once-over before he comes," she said, and was presently exclaiming with delight at the art study of Clifford Armytage in evening dress, two straight fingers pressing the left temple, the face in three-quarter view.

"Well, now, if that ain't Harold Parmalee to the life! If it wasn't for that Clifford Armytage signed under it, you'd had me guessing. I knew yesterday you looked like him, but I didn't dream it would be as much like him as this picture is. Say, we won't show Baird this at first. We'll let him size you up and see if your face don't remind him of Parmalee right away. Then we'll show him this and it'll be a cinch. And my, look at these others—here you're a soldier, and here you're a-a-a polo player—that is polo, ain't it, or is it tennis? And will you look at these stunning Westerns! These are simply the best of all—on horseback, and throwing a rope, and the fighting face with the gun drawn, and rolling a cigarette—and, as I live, saying good-by to the horse. Wouldn't that get you—Buck Benson to the life!"

Again and again she shuffled over the stills, dwelling on each with excited admiration. Her excitement was pronounced. It seemed to be a sort of nervous excitement. It had caused her face to flush deeply, and her manner, especially over the Western pictures, at moments oddly approached hysteria. Merton was deeply gratified. He had expected the art studies to produce no such impression as this. The Countess in the casting office had certainly manifested nothing like hysteria at beholding them. It must be that the Montague girl was a better judge of art studies.

"I always liked this one, after the Westerns," he observed, indicating the Harold Parmalee pose.

"It's stunning," agreed the girl, still with her nervous manner. "I tell you, sit over there in Jeff's chair and take the same pose, so I can compare you with the photo."

Merton obliged. He leaned an elbow on the chair-arm and a temple on the two straightened fingers. "Is the light right?" he asked, as he turned his face to the pictured angle.

"Fine," applauded the girl. "Hold it." He held it until shocked by shrill laughter from the observer. Peal followed peal. She had seemed oddly threatened with hysteria; perhaps now it had come. She rocked on her heels and held her hands to her sides. Merton arose in some alarm, and was reassured when the victim betrayed signs of mastering her infirmity. She wiped her eyes presently and explained her outbreak.

"You looked so much like Parmalee I just couldn't help thinking how funny it was—it just seemed to go over me like anything, like a spasm or something, when I got to thinking what Parmalee would say if he saw someone looking so much like him. See? That was why I laughed."

He was sympathetic and delighted in equal parts. The girl had really seemed to suffer from her paroxysm, yet it was a splendid tribute to his screen worth.

It was at this moment that Baird entered. He tossed his hat on a chair and turned to the couple.

"Mr. Baird, shake hands with my friend Merton Gill. His stage name is Clifford Armytage."

"Very pleased to meet you," said Merton, grasping the extended hand. He hoped he had not been too dignified, too condescending. Baird would sometime doubtless know that he did not approve of those so-called comedies, but for the present he must demean himself to pay back some money borrowed from a working girl.

"Delighted," said Baird; then he bent a suddenly troubled gaze upon the Gill lineaments. He held this a long moment, breaking it only with a sudden dramatic turning to Miss Montague.

"What's this, my child? You're playing tricks on the old man." Again he incredulously scanned the face of Merton. "Who is this man?" he demanded.

"I told you, he's Merton Gill from Gushwomp, Ohio," said the girl, looking pleased and expectant.

"Simsbury, Illinois," put in Merton quickly, wishing the girl could be better at remembering names.

Baird at last seemed to be convinced. He heavily smote an open palm with a clenched fist. "Well, I'll be swoshed! I thought you must be kidding. If I'd seen him out on the lot I'd 'a' said he was the twin brother of Harold Parmalee."

"There!" exclaimed the girl triumphantly. "Didn't I say he'd see it right quick? You can't keep a thing from this old bey. Now you just came over here to this desk and look at this fine batch of stills he had taken by a regular artist back in Cranberry."

"Ah!" exclaimed Baird unctuously, "I bet they're good. Show me." He went to the desk. "Be seated, Mr. Gill, while I have a look at these."

Merton Gill, under the eye of Baird which clung to him with something close to fascination, sat down. He took the chair with fine dignity, a certain masterly deliberation. He sat easily, and seemed to await a verdict confidently foreknown. Baird's eyes did not leave him for the stills until he had assumed a slightly Harold Parmalee pose. Then his head with the girl's bent over the pictures, he began to examine them.

Exclamations of delight came from the pair. Merton Gill listened amiably. He was not greatly thrilled by an admiration which he had long believed to be his due. Had he not always supposed that things of precisely this sort would be said about those stills when at last they came under the eyes of the right people?

Like the Montague girl, Baird was chiefly impressed with the Westerns. He looked a long time at them, especially at the one where Merton's face was emotionally averted from his old pal, Pinto, at the moment of farewell. Regarding Baird, as he stood holding this art study up to the light, Merton became aware for the first time that Baird suffered from some nervous affliction, a peculiar twitching of the lips, a trembling of the chin, which he had sometimes observed in senile persons. All at once Baird seemed quite overcome by this infirmity. He put a handkerchief to his face and uttered a muffled excuse as he hastily left the room. Outside, the noise of his heavy tread died swiftly away down the hall.

The Montague girl remained at the desk. There was a strange light in her eyes and her face was still flushed. She shot a glance of encouragement at Merton.

"Don't be nervous, old Kid; he likes 'em all right." He reassured her lightly: "Oh, I'm not a bit nervous about him. It ain't as if he was doing something worth while, instead of mere comedies."

The girl's colour seemed to heighten. "You be sure to tell him that; talk right up to him. Be sure to say 'mere comedies.' It'll show him you know what's what. And as a matter of fact, Kid, he's trying to do something worth while, right this minute, something serious. That's why he's so interested in you."

"Well, of course, that's different." He was glad to learn this of Baird. He would take the man seriously if he tried to be serious, to do something fine and distinctive.

Baird here returned, looking grave. The Montague girl seemed more strangely intense. She beckoned the manager to her side.

"Now, here, Jeff, here was something I just naturally had to laugh at."

Baird had not wholly conquered those facial spasms, but he controlled himself to say, "Show me!"

"Now, Merton," directed the girl, "take that same pose again, like you did for me, the way you are in this picture."

As Merton adjusted himself to the Parmalee pose she handed the picture to Baird. "Now, Jeff, I ask you—ain't that Harold to the life—ain't it so near him that you just have to laugh your head off?"

It was even so. Baird and the girl both laughed convulsively, the former with rumbling chuckles that shook his frame. When he had again composed himself he said, "Well, Mr. Gill, I think you and I can do a little business. I don't know what your idea about a contract is, but—"

Merton Gill quickly interrupted. "Well, you see I'd hardly like to sign a contract with you, not for those mere comedies you do. I'll do anything to earn a little money right now so I can pay back this young lady, but I wouldn't like to go on playing in such things, with cross-eyed people and waiters on roller skates, and all that. What I really would like to do is something fine and worth while, but not clowning in mere Buckeye comedies."

Mr. Baird, who had devoted the best part of an active career to the production of Buckeye comedies, and who regarded them as at least one expression of the very highest art, did not even flinch at these cool words. He had once been an actor himself. Taking the blow like a man, he beamed upon his critic. "Exactly, my boy; don't you think I'll ever ask you to come down to clowning. You might work with me for years and I'd never ask you to do a thing that wasn't serious. In fact, that's why I'm hoping to engage you now. I want to do a serious picture, I want to get out of all that slap-stick stuff, see? Something fine and worth while, like you say. And you're the very actor I need in this new piece."

"Well, of course, in that case—" This was different; he made it plain that in the case of a manager striving for higher things he was not one to withhold a helping hand. He was beginning to feel a great sympathy for Baird in his efforts for the worth while. He thawed somewhat from the reserve that Buckeye comedies had put upon him. He chatted amiably. Under promptings from the girl he spoke freely of his career, both in Simsbury and in Hollywood. It was twelve o'clock before they seemed willing to let him go, and from time to time they would pause to gloat over the stills.

At last Baird said cheerily, "Well, my lad, I need you in my new piece. How'll it be if I put you on my payroll, beginning to-day, at forty a week? How about it, hey?"

"Well, I'd like that first rate, only I haven't worked any to-day; you shouldn't pay me for just coming here."

The manager waved a hand airily. "That's all right, my boy; you've earned a day's salary just coming here to cheer me up. These mere comedies get me so down in the dumps sometimes. And besides, you're not through yet. I'm going to use you some more. Listen, now—" The manager had become coldly businesslike. "You go up to a little theatre on Hollywood Boulevard—you can't miss it—where they're running a Harold Parmalee picture. I saw it last night and I want you to see it to-day. Better see it afternoon and evening both."

"Yes, sir," said Merton.

"And watch Parmalee. Study him in this picture. You look like him already, but see if you can pick up some of his tricks, see what I mean? Because it's a regular Parmalee part I'm going to have you do, see? Kind of a society part to start with, and then we work in some of your Western stuff at the finish. But get Parmalee as much as you can. That's all now. Oh, yes, and can you leave these stills with me? Our publicity man may want to use them later."

"All right, Mr. Baird, I'll do just what you say, and of course you can keep the stills as long as I got an engagement with you, and I'm very glad you're trying to do something really worth while."

"Thanks," said Baird, averting his face.

The girl followed him into the hall. "Great work, boy, and take it from me, you'll go over. Say, honest now, I'm glad clear down into my boots." She had both his hands again, and he could see that her eyes were moist. She seemed to be an impressionable little thing, hysterical one minute while looking at a bunch of good stills, and sort of weepy the next. But he was beginning to like her, in spite of her funny talk and free ways.

"And say," she called after him when he had reached the top of the stairs, "you know you haven't had much experience yet with a bunch of hard-boiled troupers; many a one will be jealous of you the minute you begin to climb, and maybe they'll get fresh and try to kid you, see? But don't you mind it—give it right back to them. Or tell me if they get too raw. Just remember I got a mean right when I swing free."

"All right, thank you," he replied, but his bewilderment was plain.

She stared a moment, danced up to him, and seized a hand in both of hers. "What I mean son, if you feel bothered any time—by anything—just come to me with it, see? I'm in this piece, and I'll look out for you. Don't forget that." She dropped his hand, and was back in the office while he mumbled his thanks for what he knew she had meant as a kindness.

So she was to be in the Baird piece; she, too, would be trying to give the public something better and finer. Still, he was puzzled at her believing he might need to be looked out for. An actor drawing forty dollars a week could surely look out for himself. He emerged into the open of the Holden lot as one who had at last achieved success after long and gruelling privation. He walked briefly among the scenes of this privation, pausing in reminiscent mood before the Crystal Palace Hotel and other outstanding spots where he had so stoically suffered the torments of hunger and discouragement.

He remembered to be glad now that no letter of appeal had actually gone to Gashwiler. Suppose he had built up in the old gentleman's mind a false hope that he might again employ Merton Gill? A good thing he had held out! Yesterday he was starving and penniless; to-day he was fed and on someone's payroll for probably as much money a week as Gashwiler netted from his entire business. From sheer force of association, as he thus meditated, he found himself hungry, and a few moments later he was selecting from the food counter of the cafeteria whatever chanced to appeal to the eye—no weighing of prices now.

Before he had finished his meal Henshaw and his so-called Governor brought their trays to the adjoining table. Merton studied with new interest the director who would some day be telling people that he had been the first to observe the aptitude of this new star—had, in fact, given him a lot of footage and close-ups and medium shots and "dramatics" in The Blight of Broadway when he was a mere extra—before he had made himself known to the public in Jeff Baird's first worth-while piece.

He was strongly moved, now, to bring himself to Henshaw's notice when he heard the latter say, "It's a regular Harold Parmalee part, good light comedy, plenty of heart interest, and that corking fight on the cliff."

He wanted to tell Henshaw that he himself was already engaged to do a Harold Parmalee part, and had been told, not two hours ago, that he would by most people be taken for Parmalee's twin brother. He restrained this impulse, however, as Henshaw went on to talk of the piece in hand.

It proved to be Robinson Crusoe, which he had already discussed. Or, rather, not Robinson Crusoe any longer. Not even Robinson Crusoe, Junior. It was to have been called Island Passion, he learned, but this title had been amended to Island Love.

"They're getting fed up on that word 'passion,'" Henshaw was saying, "and anyhow, 'love' seems to go better with 'island,' don't you think, Governor? 'Desert

Passion' was all right—there's something strong and intense about a desert. But 'island' is different."

And it appeared that Island Love, though having begun as Robinson Crusoe, would contain few of the outstanding features of that tale. Instead of Crusoe's wrecked sailing-ship, there was a wrecked steam yacht, a very expensive yacht stocked with all modern luxuries, nor would there be a native Friday and his supposed sister with the tattooed shoulder, but a wealthy young New Yorker and his valet who would be good for comedy on a desert island, and a beautiful girl, and a scoundrel who would in the last reel be thrown over the cliffs.

Henshaw was vivacious about the effects he would get. "I've been wondering, Governor," he continued, "if we're going to kill off the heavy, whether we shouldn't plant it early that besides wanting this girl who's on the island, he's the same scoundrel that wronged the young sister of the lead that owns the yacht. See what I mean?-it would give more conflict."

"But here—" The Governor frowned and spoke after a moment's pause. "Your young New Yorker is rich, isn't he? Fine old family, and all that, how could he have a sister that would get wronged? You couldn't do it. If he's got a wronged sister, he'd have to be a workingman or a sailor or something. And she couldn't be a New York society girl; she'd have to be working some place, in a store or office—don't you see? How could you have a swell young New Yorker with a wronged sister? Real society girls never get wronged unless their father loses his money, and then it's never anything serious enough to kill a heavy for. No—that's out." "Wait, I have it." Henshaw beamed with a new inspiration. "You just said a sailor could have his sister wronged, so why not have one on the yacht, a good strong type, you know, and his little sister was wronged by the heavy, and he'd never known who it was, because the little girl wouldn't tell him, even on her death-bed, but he found the chap's photograph in her trunk, and on the yacht he sees that it was this same heavy—and there you are. Revenge—see what I mean? He fights with the heavy on the cliff, after showing him the little sister's picture, and pushes him over to death on the rocks below—get it? And the lead doesn't have to kill him. How about that?" Henshaw regarded his companion with pleasant anticipation.

The Governor again debated before he spoke. He still doubted. "Say, whose show is this, the lead's or the sailor's that had the wronged sister? You'd have to show the sailor and his sister, and show her being wronged by the heavy—that'd take a big cabaret set, at least—and you'd have to let the sailor begin his stuff on the yacht, and then by the time he'd kept it up a bit after the wreck had pulled off the fight, where would your lead be? Can you see Parmalee playing second to this sailor? Why, the sailor'd run away with the piece. And that cabaret set would cost money when we don't need it—just keep those things in mind a little."

"Well," Henshaw submitted gracefully, "anyway, I think my suggestion of Island Love is better than Island Passion—kind of sounds more attractive, don't you think?"

The Governor lighted a cigarette. "Say, Howard, it's a wonderful business, isn't it? We start with poor old Robinson Crusoe and his goats and parrot and man Friday, and after dropping Friday's sister who would really be the Countess of Kleig, we wind up with a steam-yacht and a comic butler and call it Island Love. Who said the art of the motion picture is in its infancy? In this case it'll be plumb senile. Well, go ahead with the boys and dope out your hogwash. Gosh! Sometimes I think I wouldn't stay in the business if it wasn't for the money. And remember, don't you let a single solitary sailor on that yacht have a wronged sister that can blame it on the heavy, or you'll never have Parmalee playing the lead."

Again Merton Gill debated bringing himself to the notice of these gentlemen. If Parmalee wouldn't play the part for any reason like a sailor's wronged sister, he would. It would help him to be known in Parmalee parts. Still, he couldn't tell how soon they might need him, nor how soon Baird would release him. He regretfully saw the two men leave, however. He might have missed a chance even better than Baird would give him.

He suddenly remembered that he had still a professional duty to perform. He must that afternoon, and also that evening, watch a Harold Parmalee picture. He left the cafeteria, swaggered by the watchman at the gate-he had now the professional standing to silence that fellow-and made his way to the theatre Baird had mentioned.

In front he studied the billing of the Parmalee picture. It was "Object, Matrimony-a Smashing Comedy of Love and Laughter." Harold Parmalee, with a gesture of mock dismay, seemed to repulse a bevy of beautiful maidens who wooed him. Merton took his seat with a dismay that was not mock, for it now occurred to him that he had no experience in love scenes, and that an actor playing Parmalee parts would need a great deal of such experience. In Simsbury there had been no opportunity for an intending actor to learn certain little niceties expected at sentimental moments. Even his private life had been almost barren of adventures that might now profit him.

He had sometimes played kissing games at parties, and there had been the more serious affair with Edwina May Pulver-nights when he had escorted her from church or sociables to the Pulver gate and lingered in a sort of nervously worded ecstasy until he could summon courage to kiss the girl. Twice this had actually happened, but the affair had come to nothing, because the Pulvers had moved away from Simsbury and he had practically forgotten Edwina May; forgotten even the scared haste of those embraces. He seemed to remember that he had grabbed her and kissed her, but was it on her cheek or nose?

Anyway, he was now quite certain that the mechanics of this dead amour were not those approved of in the best screen circles. Never had he gathered a beauteous girl in his arms and very slowly, very accurately, very tenderly, done what Parmalee and other screen actors did in their final fade-outs. Even when Beulah Baxter had been his screen ideal he had never seen himself as doing more than save her from some dreadful fate. Of course, later, if he had found out that she was unwed—

He resolved now to devote special study to Parmalee's methods of wooing the fair creature who would be found in his arms at the close of the present film. Probably Baird would want some of that stuff from him.

From the very beginning of "Object, Matrimony" it was apparent that the picture drama would afford him excellent opportunities for studying the Parmalee technique in what an early subtitle called "The Eternal Battle of the Sexes." For Parmalee in the play was Hubert Throckmorton, popular screen idol and surfeited with the attentions of adoring women. Cunningly the dramatist made use of Parmalee's own personality, of his screen triumphs, and of the adulation lavished upon him by discriminating fair ones. His breakfast tray was shown piled with missives amply attesting the truth of what the interviewer had said of his charm. All women seemed to adore Hubert Throckmorton in the drama, even as all women adored Harold Parmalee in private life.

The screen revealed Throckmorton quite savagely ripping open the letters, glancing at their contents and flinging them from him with humorous shudders. He seemed to be asking why these foolish creatures couldn't let an artist alone. Yet he was kindly, in this half-humorous, half-savage mood. There was a blending of chagrin and amused tolerance on his face as the screen had him murmur, casting the letter aside, "Poor, Silly Little Girls!"

From this early scene Merton learned Parmalee's method of withdrawing the gold cigarette case, of fastidiously selecting a cigarette, of closing the case and of absently—thinking of other matters—tamping the gold-tipped thing against the cover. This was an item that he had overlooked. He should have done that in the cabaret scene. He also mastered the Parmalee trick of withdrawing the handkerchief from the cuff of the perfectly fitting morning coat. That was something else he should have done in The Blight of Broadway. Little things like that, done right, gave the actor his distinction.

The drama progressed. Millionaire Jasper Gordon, "A Power in Wall Street," was seen telephoning to Throckmorton. He was entreating the young actor to spend the week-end at his palatial Long Island country home to meet a few of his friends. The grim old Wall Street magnate was perturbed by Throckmorton's refusal, and renewed his appeal. He was one of those who always had his way in Wall Street, and he at length prevailed upon Throckmorton to accept his invitation. He than manifested the wildest delight, and he was excitedly kissed by his beautiful daughter who had been standing by his side in the sumptuous library while he telephoned. It could be seen that the daughter, even more than her grim old father, wished Mr. Throckmorton to be at the Long Island country home.

Later Throckmorton was seen driving his high-powered roadster, accompanied only by his valet, to the Gordon country home on Long Island, a splendid mansion surrounded by its landscaped grounds where fountains played and roses bloomed against the feathery background of graceful eucalyptus trees. Merton Gill here saw that he must learn to drive a high-powered roadster. Probably Baird would want some of that stuff, too.

A round of country-house gaieties ensued, permitting Throckmorton to appear in a series of perfectly fitting sports costumes. He was seen on his favourite hunter, on the tennis courts, on the first tee of the golf course, on a polo pony, and in the mazes of the dance. Very early it was learned that the Gordon daughter had tired of mere social triumphs and wished to take up screen acting in a serious way. She audaciously requested Throckmorton to give her a chance as leading lady in his next great picture.

He softened his refusal by explaining to her that acting was a difficult profession and that suffering and sacrifice were necessary to round out the artist. The beautiful girl replied that within ten days he would be compelled to admit her rare ability as an actress, and laughingly they wagered a kiss upon it. Merton felt that this was the sort of thing he must know more about.

Throckmorton was courteously gallant in the scene. Even when he said, "Shall we put up the stakes now, Miss Gordon?" it could be seen that he was jesting. He carried this light manner through minor scenes with the beautiful young girl friends of Miss Gordon who wooed him, lay in wait for him, ogled and sighed. Always he was the laughingly tolerant conqueror who had but a lazy scorn for his triumphs.

He did not strike the graver note until it became suspected that there were crooks in the house bent upon stealing the famous Gordon jewels. That it was Throckmorton who averted this catastrophe by sheer nerve and by use of his rare histrionic powers—as when he disguised himself in the coat and hat of the arch crook whom he had felled with a single blow and left bound and gagged, in order to receive the casket of jewels from the thief who opened the safe in the library, and that he laughed away the thanks of the grateful millionaire, astonished no one in the audience, though it caused Merton Gill to wonder if he could fell a crook with one blow. He must practice up some blows.

Throckmorton left the palatial country home wearied by the continuous adulation. The last to speed him was the Gordon daughter, who reminded him of their wager; within ten days he would acknowledge her to be an actress fit to play as his leading woman.

Throckmorton drove rapidly to a simple farm where he was not known and would be no longer surfeited with attentions. He dressed plainly in shirts that opened wide at the neck and assisted in the farm labours, such as pitching hay and leading horses into the barn. It was the simple existence that he had been craving—away from it all! No one suspected him to be Hubert Throckmorton, least of all the simple country maiden, daughter of the farmer, in her neat print dress and heavy braid of golden hair that hung from beneath her sunbonnet. She knew him to be only a man among men, a simple farm labourer, and Hubert

Throckmorton, wearied by the adulation of his feminine public, was instantly charmed by her coy acceptance of his attentions.

That this charm should ripen to love was to be expected. Here was a child, simple, innocent, of a wild-rose beauty in her print dress and sunbonnet, who would love him for himself alone. Beside a blossoming orange tree on the simple Long Island farm he declared his love, warning the child that he had nothing to offer her but two strong arms and a heart full of devotion.

The little girl shyly betrayed that she returned his love but told him that he must first obtain the permission of her grandmother without which she would never consent to wed him. She hastened into the old farmhouse to prepare Grandmother for the interview.

Throckmorton presently faced the old lady who sat huddled in an armchair, her hands crooked over a cane, a ruffled cap above her silvery hair. He manfully voiced his request for the child's hand in marriage. The old lady seemed to mumble an assent. The happy lover looked about for his fiance when, to his stupefaction, the old lady arose briskly from her chair, threw off cap, silvery wig, gown of black, and stood revealed as the child herself, smiling roguishly up at him from beneath the sunbonnet. With a glad cry he would have seized her, when she stayed him with lifted hand. Once more she astounded him. Swiftly she threw off sunbonnet, blonde wig, print dress, and stood before him revealed as none other than the Gordon daughter.

Hubert Throckmorton had lost his wager. Slowly, as the light of recognition dawned in his widening eyes, he gathered the beautiful girl into his arms. "Now may I be your leading lady?" she asked.

"My leading lady, not only in my next picture, but for life," he replied.

There was a pretty little scene in which the wager was paid. Merton studied it. Twice again, that evening, he studied it. He was doubtful. It would seem queer to take a girl around the waist that way and kiss her so slowly. Maybe he could learn. And he knew he could already do that widening of the eyes. He could probably do it as well as Parmalee did.

     * * * * * * *

Back in the Buckeye office, when the Montague girl had returned from her parting with Merton, Baird had said:

"Kid, you've brightened my whole day."

"Didn't I tell you?"

"He's a lot better than you said."

"But can you use him?"

"You can't tell. You can't tell till you try him out. He might be good, and he might blow up right at the start."

358

"I bet he'll be good. I tell you. Jeff, that boy is just full of acting. All you got to do—keep his stuff straight, serious. He can't help but be funny that way."

"We'll see. To-morrow we'll kind of feel him out. He'll see this Parmalee film to-day—I caught it last night—and there's some stuff in it I want to play horse with, see? So I'll start him to-morrow in a quiet scene, and find out does he handle. If he does, we'll go right into some hokum drama stuff. The more serious he plays it the better. It ought to be good, but you can't ever tell in our trade. You know that as well as I do."

The girl was confident. "I can tell about this lad," she insisted.

CHAPTER XIII. GENIUS COMES INTO ITS OWN

Merton Gill, enacting the part of a popular screen idol, as in the play of yesterday, sat at breakfast in his apartments on Stage Number Five. Outwardly he was cool, wary, unperturbed, as he peeled the shell from a hard-boiled egg and sprinkled salt upon it. For the breakfast consisted of hard-boiled eggs and potato salad brought on in a wooden dish.

He had been slightly disturbed by the items of this meal; it was not so elegant a breakfast as Hubert Throckmorton's, but he had been told by Baird that they must be a little different.

He had been slightly disturbed, too, at discovering the faithful valet who brought on the simple repast was the cross—eyed man. Still, the fellow had behaved respectfully, as a valet should. He had been quietly obsequious of manner, revealing only a profound admiration for his master and a constant solicitude for his comfort. Probably he, like Baird, was trying to do something distinctive and worth while.

Having finished the last egg—glad they had given him no more than three—the popular screen idol at the prompting of Baird, back by the cameras, arose, withdrew a metal cigarette case, purchased that very morning with this scene in view, and selected a cigarette. He stood negligently, as Parmalee had stood, tapped the end of the cigarette on the side of the case, as Parmalee had done, lighted a match on the sole of his boot, and idly smoked in the Parmalee manner.

Three times the day before he had studied Parmalee in this bit of business. Now he idly crossed to the centre-table upon which reposed a large photograph album. He turned the pages of this, pausing to admire the pictures there revealed. Baird had not only given him general instructions for this scene, but now prompted him in low, encouraging tones.

"Turn over slowly; you like 'em all. Now lift the album up and hold it for a better light on that one. It's one of the best, it pleases you a lot. Look even more pleased—smile! That's good. Put down the album; turn again, slowly; turn twice more, that's it; pick it up again. This one is fine—"

Baird took him through the album in this manner, had him close it when all the leaves were turned, and stand a moment with one hand resting on it. The album had been empty. It had been deemed best not to inform the actor that later close-ups of the pages would show him to have been refreshed by studying photographs of himself—copies, in fact, of the stills of Clifford Armytage at that moment resting on Baird's desk.

As he stood now, a hand affectionately upon the album, a trace of the fatuously admiring smile still lingering on his expressive face, a knock sounded upon the door. "Come in," he called.

The valet entered with the morning mail. This consisted entirely of letters. There were hundreds of them, and the valet had heaped them in a large clothes-basket which he now held respectfully in front of him.

The actor motioned him, with an authentic Parmalee gesture, to place them by the table. The valet obeyed, though spilling many letters from the top of the overflowing basket. These, while his master seated himself, he briskly swept up with a broom.

The chagrined amusement of Harold Parmalee, the half-savage, half-humorous tolerance for this perhaps excusable weakness of woman, was here accurately manifested. The actor yawned slightly, lighted another cigarette with flawless Parmalee technique, withdrew a handkerchief from his sleeve-cuff, lightly touched his forehead with it, and began to open the letters. He glanced at each one in a quick, bored manner, and cast it aside.

When a dozen or so had been thus treated he was aroused by another knock at the door. It opened to reveal the valet with another basket overflowing with letters. Upon this the actor arose, spread his arms wide in a gesture of humorous helplessness. He held this briefly, then drooped in humorous despair.

He lighted another cigarette, eyed the letters with that whimsical lift of the brows so characteristic of Parmalee, and lazily blew smoke toward them. Then, regarding the smoke, he idly waved a hand through it. "Poor, silly little girls!" But there was a charming tolerance in his manner. One felt his generous recognition that they were not wholly without provocation.

This appeared to close the simple episode. The scenes, to be sure, had not been shot without delays and rehearsals, and a good two hours of the morning had elapsed before the actor was released from the glare of light and the need to remember that he was Harold Parmalee. His peeling of an egg, for example, had not at first been dainty enough to please the director, and the scene with the album had required many rehearsals to secure the needed variety of expressions, but Baird had been helpful in his promptings, and always kind.

"Now, this one you've turned over—it's someone you love better than anybody. It might be your dear old mother that you haven't seen for years. It makes you kind of solemn as you show how fond you were of her. You're affected deeply by her face. That's it, fine! Now the next one, you like it just as much, but it pleases you more. It's someone else you're fond of, but you're not so solemn.

"Now turn over another, but very slow—slow—but don't let go of it. Stop a minute and turn back as if you had to have another peek at the last one, see what I mean? Take plenty of time. This is a great treat for you. It makes you feel kind of religious. Now you're getting it—that's the boy! All right—"

The scene where he showed humorous dismay at the quantity of his mail had needed but one rehearsal. He had here been Harold Parmalee without effort. Also he had not been asked to do again the Parmalee trick of lighting a cigarette nor of withdrawing the handkerchief from its cuff to twice touch his forehead in moments of amused perplexity. Baird had merely uttered a low "Fine!" at beholding these bits.

He drew a long breath of relief when released from the set. Seemingly he had met the test. Baird had said that morning, "Now we'll just run a little kind of test to find out a few things about you," and had followed with a general description of the scenes. It was to be of no great importance—a minor detail of the picture. Perhaps this had been why the wealthy actor breakfasted in rather a plainly furnished room on hard-boiled eggs and potato salad. Perhaps this had been why the costume given him had been not too well fitting, not too nice in detail. Perhaps this was why they had allowed the cross-eyed man to appear as his valet. He was quite sure this man would not do as a valet in a high-class picture. Anyway, however unimportant the scene, he felt that he had acquitted himself with credit.

The Montague girl, who had made him up that morning, with close attention to his eyebrows, watched him from back of the cameras, and she seized both his hands when he left the set. "You're going to land," she warmly assured him. "I can tell a trouper when I see one."

She was in costume. She was apparently doing the part of a society girl, though slightly overdressed, he thought.

"We're working on another set for this same picture," she explained, "but I simply had to catch you acting. You'll probably be over with us to-morrow. But you're through for the day, so beat it and have a good time."

"Couldn't I come over and watch you?"

"No, Baird doesn't like to have his actors watching things they ain't in; he told me specially that you weren't to be around except when you're working. You see, he's using you in kind of a special part in this multiple-reeler, and he's afraid you might get confused if you watched the other parts. I guess he'll start you to-morrow. You're to be in a good, wholesome heart play. You'll have a great chance in it."

"Well, I'll go see if I can find another Parmalee picture for this afternoon. Say, you don't think I was too much like him in that scene, do you? You know it's one thing if I look like him—I can't help that—but I shouldn't try to imitate him too closely, should I? I got to think about my own individuality, haven't I?"

"Sure, sure you have! But you were fine—your imitation wasn't a bit too close. You can think about your own individuality this afternoon when you're watching him." Late that day in the projection room Baird and the Montague girl watched the "rush" of that morning's episode.

"The squirrel's done it," whispered the girl after the opening scene. It seemed to her that Merton Gill on the screen might overhear her comment.

Even Baird was low-toned. "Looks so," he agreed.

"If that ain't Parmalee then I'll eat all the hard-boiled eggs on the lot."

Baird rubbed his hands. "It's Parmalee plus," he corrected.

"Oh, Mother, Mother!" murmured the girl while the screen revealed the actor studying his photographs.

"He handled all right in that spot," observed Baird.

"He'll handle right—don't worry. Ain't I told you he's a natural born trouper?"

The mail was abandoned in humorous despair. The cigarette lighted in a flawless Parmalee manner, the smoke idly brushed aside. "Poor, silly little girls," the actor was seen to say. The girl gripped Baird's arm until he winced. "There, old Pippin! There's your million, picked right up on the lot!"

"Maybe," assented the cooler Baird, as they left the projection room.

"And say," asked the girl, "did you notice all morning how he didn't even bat an eye when you spoke to him, if the camera was still turning? Not like a beginner that'll nearly always look up and get out of the picture."

"What I bet," observed Baird, "I bet he'd 'a' done that album stuff even better than he did if I'd actually put his own pictures in, the way I'm going to for the close-ups. I was afraid he'd see it was kidding if I did, or if I told him what pictures they were going to be. But I'm darned now if I don't think he'd have stood for it. I don't believe you'll ever be able to peeve that boy by telling him he's good."

The girl glanced up defensively as they walked.

"Now don't get the idea he's conceited, because he ain't. Not one bit."

"How do you know he ain't?"

She considered this, then explained brightly, "Because I wouldn't like him if he was. No, no—now you listen here" as Baird had grinned. "This lad believes in himself, that's all. That's different from conceit. You can believe a whole lot in yourself, and still be as modest as a new—hatched chicken. That's what he reminds me of, too." The following morning Baird halted him outside the set on which he would work that day. Again he had been made up by the Montague girl, with especial attention to the eyebrows so that they might show the Parmalee lift.

"I just want to give you the general dope of the piece before you go on," said Baird, in the shelter of high canvas backing. "You're the only son of a widowed mother and both you and she are toiling to pay off the mortgage on the little home. You're the cashier of this business establishment, and in love with the proprietor's daughter, only she's a society

363

girl and kind of looks down on you at first. Then, there's her brother, the proprietor's only son. He's the clerk in this place. He doesn't want to work, but his father has made him learn the business, see? He's kind of a no-good; dissipated; wears flashy clothes and plays the races and shoots craps and drinks. You try to reform him because he's idolized by his sister that you're in love with.

"But you can't do a thing with him. He keeps on and gets in with a rough crowd, and finally he steals a lot of money out of the safe, and just when they are about to discover that he's the thief you see it would break his sister's heart so you take the crime on your own shoulders. After that, just before you're going to be arrested, you make a getaway—because, after all, you're not guilty—and you go out West to start all over again—"

"Out there in the big open spaces?" suggested Merton, who had listened attentively.

"Exactly," assented Baird, with one of those nervous spasms that would now and again twitch his lips and chin. "Out there in the big open spaces where men are men—that's the idea. And you build up a little gray home in the West for yourself and your poor old mother who never lost faith in you. There'll be a lot of good Western stuff in this—Buck Benson stuff, you know, that you can do so well— and the girl will get out there some way and tell you that her brother finally confessed his crime, and everything'll be Jake, see what I mean?"

"Yes, sir; it sounds fine, Mr. Baird. And I certainly will give the best that is in me to this part." He had an impulse to tell the manager, too, how gratified he was that one who had been content with the low humour of the Buckeye comedies should at last have been won over to the better form of photodrama. But Baird was leading him on to the set; there was no time for this congratulatory episode.

Indeed the impulse was swept from his mind in the novelty of the set now exposed, and in the thought that his personality was to dominate it. The scene of the little drama's unfolding was a delicatessen shop. Counters and shelves were arrayed with cooked foods, salads, cheeses, the latter under glass or wire protectors. At the back was a cashier's desk, an open safe beside it. He took his place there at Baird's direction and began to write in a ledger.

"Now your old mother's coming to mop up the place," called Baird. "Come on, Mother! You look up and see her, and rush over to her. She puts down her bucket and mop, and takes you in her arms. She's weeping; you try to comfort her; you want her to give up mopping, and tell her you can make enough to support two, but she won't listen because there's the mortgage on the little flat to be paid off. So you go back to the desk, stopping to give her a sad look as she gets down on the floor. Now, try it."

A very old, bent, feeble woman with a pail of water and cloths tottered on. Her dress was ragged, her white hair hung about her sad old face in disorderly strands. She set down her bucket and raised her torn apron to her eyes.

"Look up and see her," called Baird. "A glad light comes into her eyes. Rush forward—say 'Mother' distinctly, so it'll show. Now the clench. You're crying on his shoulder, Mother, and he's looking down at you first, then off, about at me. He's near crying himself. Now he's telling you to give up mopping places, and you're telling him every little helps.

"All right, break. Get to mopping, Mother, but keep on crying. He stops for a long look at you. He seems to be saying that some day he will take you out of such work. Now he's back at his desk. All right. But we'll do it once more. And a little more pathos, Merton, when you take the old lady in your arms. You can broaden it. You don't actually break down, but you nearly do."

The scene was rehearsed again, to Baird's satisfaction, and the cameras ground. Merton Gill gave the best that was in him. His glad look at first beholding the old lady, the yearning of his eyes when his arms opened to enfold her, the tenderness of his embrace as he murmured soothing words, the lingering touch of his hand as he left her, the manly determination of the last look in which he showed a fresh resolve to release her from this toil, all were eloquent of the deepest filial devotion and earnestness of purpose.

Back at his desk he was genuinely pitying the old lady. Very lately, it was evident, she had been compelled to play in a cabaret scene, for she smelled strongly of cigarettes, and he could not suppose that she, her eyes brimming with anguished mother love, could have relished these. He was glad when it presently developed that his own was not to be a smoking part.

"Now the dissipated brother's coming on," explained Baird. "He'll breeze in, hang up his hat, offer you a cigarette, which you refuse, and show you some money that he won on the third race yesterday. You follow him a little way from the desk, telling him he shouldn't smoke cigarettes, and that money he gets by gambling will never do him any good. He laughs at you, but you don't mind. On your way back to the desk you stop by your mother, and she gets up and embraces you again.

"Take your time about it—she's your mother, remember."

The brother entered. He was indeed dissipated appearing, loudly dressed, and already smoking a cigarette as he swaggered the length of the shop to offer Merton one. Merton refused in a kindly but firm manner. The flashy brother now pulled a roll of bills from his pocket and pointed to his winning horse in a racing extra. The line in large type was there for the close-up—"Pianola Romps Home in Third Race."

Followed the scene in which Merton sought to show this youth that cigarettes and gambling would harm him. The youth remained obdurate. He seized a duster and, with ribald action, began to dust off the rows of cooked food on the counters. Again the son stopped to embrace his mother, who again wept as she enfolded him. The scene was shot.

Step by step, under the patient coaching of Baird, the simple drama unfolded. It was hot beneath the lights, delays were frequent and the rehearsals tedious, yet Merton Gill continued to give the best that was in him. As the day wore on, the dissipated son went from bad to worse. He would leave the shop to place money on a horse race, and he would seek to induce the customers he waited on to play at dice with him. A few of them consented, and one, a coloured man who had come to purchase pigs'-feet, won at this game all the bills which the youth had shown to Merton on entering.

There were moments during this scene when Merton wondered if Baird were not relapsing into Buckeye comedy depths, but he saw the inevitable trend of the drama and the justification for this bit of gambling. For the son, now penniless, became desperate. He appealed to Merton for a loan, urging it on the ground that he had a sure thing thirty—to-one shot at Latonia. At least these were the words of Baird, as he directed Merton to deny the request and to again try to save the youth from his inevitable downfall. Whereupon the youth had sneered at Merton and left the place in deep anger.

There followed the scene with the boy's sister, only daughter of the rich delicatessen merchant, who Merton was pleased to discover would be played by the Montague girl. She entered in a splendid evening gown, almost too splendid, Merton thought, for street wear in daylight, though it was partially concealed by a rich opera cloak. The brother being out, Merton came forward to wait upon her.

"It's like this," Baird explained. "She's just a simple New York society girl, kind of shallow and heartless, because she has never been aroused nor anything, see? You're the first one that's really touched her heart, but she hesitates because her father expects her to marry a count and she's come to get the food for a swell banquet they're giving for him. She says where's her brother, and if anything happened to him it would break her heart. Then she orders what she wants and you do it up for her, looking at her all the time as if you thought she was the one girl in the world.

"She kind of falls for you a little bit, still she is afraid of what her father would say. Then you get bolder, see? You come from behind the counter and begin to make love, talking as you come out—so-and-so, so-and-so, so-and-so—Miss Hoffmeyer, I have loved you since the day I first set eyes on you—so-and-so, so-and-so, so-and-so, I have nothing to offer but the love of an honest man—she's falling for it, see? So you get up close and grab her—cave-man stuff. Do a good hard clench—she's yours at last; she just naturally sags right down on to you. You've got her.

"Do a regular Parmalee. Take your time. You're going to kiss her and kiss her right. But just as you get down to it the father busts in and says what's the meaning of this, so you fly apart and the father says you're discharged, because his daughter is the affianced wife of this Count Aspirin, see? Then he goes back to the safe and finds all the money has been taken, because the son has sneaked in and grabbed out the bundle and hid it in the ice-box on his way out, taking only a few bills to get down on a horse. So he says call the police—but that's enough for now. Go ahead and do that love scene for me."

Slowly the scene was brought to Baird's liking. Slowly, because Merton Gill at first proved to be diffident at the crisis. For three rehearsals the muscular arm of Miss Montague had most of the clenching to do. He believed he was being rough and masterful, but Baird wished a greater show of violence. They had also to time this scene with the surreptitious entrance of the brother, his theft of the money which he stuffed into a paper sack and placed in the ice-box, and his exit.

The leading man having at last proved that he could be Harold Parmalee even in this crisis, the scene was extended to the entrance of the indignant father. He was one of those self-made men of wealth, Merton thought, a short, stout gentleman with fiery whiskers, not at all fashionably dressed. He broke upon the embrace with a threatening stick. The pair separated, the young lover facing him, proud, erect, defiant, the girl drooping and confused.

The father discharged Merton Gill with great brutality, then went to the safe at the back of the room, returning to shout the news that he had been robbed by the man who would have robbed him of his daughter. It looked black for Merton. Puzzled at first, he now saw that the idolized brother of the girl must have taken the money. He seemed about to declare this when his nobler nature compelled him to a silence that must be taken for guilt.

The erring brother returned, accompanied by several customers. "Bring a detective to arrest this man," ordered the father. One of the customers stepped out to return with a detective. Again Merton was slightly disquieted at perceiving that the detective was the cross-eyed man. This person bustled about the place, tapping the cooked meats and the cheeses, and at last placed his hand upon the shoulder of the supposed thief. Merton, at Baird's direction, drew back and threatened him with a blow. The detective cringed and said: "I will go out and call a policeman."

The others now turned their backs upon the guilty man. Even the girl drew away after one long, agonized look at the lover to whose embrace she had so lately submitted. He raised his arms to her in mute appeal as she moved away, then dropped them at his side.

"Give her all you got in a look," directed Baird. "You're saying: 'I go to a felon's cell, but I do it all for you.' Dream your eyes at her." Merton Gill obeyed.

The action progressed. In this wait for the policeman the old mother crept forward. She explained to Merton that the money was in the ice-box where the real thief had placed it, and since he had taken the crime of another upon his shoulders he should also take the evidence, lest the unfortunate young man be later convicted by that; she also urged him to fly by the rear door while there was yet time. He did these things, pausing for a last embrace of the weeping old lady, even as the hand of the arriving policeman was upon the door.

"All for to-day, except some close-ups," announced Baird when this scene had been shot. There was a breaking up of the group, a relaxation of that dramatic tension which the heart-values of the piece had imposed. Only once, while Merton was doing some of his best acting, had there been a kind of wheezy tittering from certain members of the cast and the group about the cameras.

Baird had quickly suppressed this. "If there's any kidding in this piece it's all in my part," he announced in cold, clear tones, and there had been no further signs of levity. Merton was pleased by this manner of Baird's. It showed that he was finely in earnest in the effort for the worth-while things. And Baird now congratulated him, seconded by the Montague girl. He had, they told him, been all that could be expected.

"I wasn't sure of myself," he told them, "in one scene, and I wanted to ask you about it, Mr. Baird. It's where I take that money from the ice-box and go out with it. I couldn't make myself feel right. Wouldn't it look to other people as if I was actually stealing it myself? Why couldn't I put it back in the safe?"

Baird listened respectfully, considering. "I think not," he announced at length. "You'd hardly have time for that, and you have a better plan. It'll be brought out in the subtitles, of course. You are going to leave it at the residence of Mr. Hoffmeyer, where it will be safe. You see, if you put it back where it was, his son might steal it again. We thought that out very carefully."

"I see," said Merton. "I wish I had been told that. I feel that I could have done that bit a lot better. I felt kind of guilty."

"You did it perfectly," Baird assured him.

"Kid, you're a wonder," declared the Montague girl. "I'm that tickled with you I could give you a good hug," and with that curious approach to hysteria she had shown while looking at his stills, she for a moment frantically clasped him to her. He was somewhat embarrassed by this excess, but pardoned it in the reflection that he had indeed given the best that was in him. "Bring all your Western stuff to the dressing room tomorrow," said Baird.

Western stuff—the real thing at last! He was slightly amazed later to observe the old mother outside the set. She was not only smoking a cigarette with every sign of relish, but she was singing as she did a little dance step. Still she had been under a strain all day, weeping, too, almost continuously. He remembered this, and did not judge her harshly as she smoked, danced, and lightly sang,

> *Her mother's name was Cleo,   Her father's name was Pat;   They called her Cleopatra,   And let it go at that.*

CHAPTER XIV. OUT THERE WHERE MEN ARE MEN

From the dressing room the following morning, arrayed in the Buck Benson outfit, unworn since that eventful day on the Gashwiler lot, Merton accompanied Baird to a new set where he would work that day. Baird was profuse in his admiration of the cowboy embellishments, the maroon chaps, the new boots, the hat, the checked shirt and gay neckerchief.

"I'm mighty glad to see you so sincere in your work," he assured Merton. "A lot of these hams I hire get to kidding on the set and spoil the atmosphere, but don't let it bother you. One earnest leading man, if he'll just stay earnest, will carry the piece. Remember that—you got a serious part."

"I'll certainly remember," Merton earnestly assured him.

"Here we are; this is where we begin the Western stuff," said Baird. Merton recognized the place. It was the High Gear Dance Hall where the Montague girl had worked. The name over the door was now "The Come All Ye," and there was a hitching rack in front to which were tethered half-a—dozen saddled horses.

Inside, the scene was set as he remembered it. Tables for drinking were about the floor, and there was a roulette wheel at one side. A red-shirted bartender, his hair plastered low over his brow, leaned negligently on the bar. Scattered around the room were dance-hall girls in short skirts, and a number of cowboys.

"First, I'll wise you up a little bit," said Baird. "You've come out here to work on a ranche in the great open spaces, and these cowboys all love you and come to town with you every time, and they'll stand by you when the detective from New York gets here. Now—let's see—I guess first we'll get your entrance. You come in the front door at the head of them. You've ridden in from the ranche. We get the horseback stuff later. You all come in yelling and so on, and the boys scatter, some to the bar and some to the wheel, and some sit down to the tables to have their drinks and some dance with the girls. You distribute money to them from a paper sack. Here's the sack." From a waiting property boy he took a paper sack. "Put this in your pocket and take it out whenever you need money.

"It's the same sack, see, that the kid put the stolen money in, and you saved it after returning the money. It's just a kind of an idea of mine," he vaguely added, as Merton looked puzzled at this.

"All right, sir." He took the sack, observing it to contain a rude imitation of bills, and stuffed it into his pocket.

"Then, after the boys scatter around, you go stand at the end of the bar. You don't join in their sports and pastimes, see? You're serious; you have things on your mind. Just sort of look around the place as if you were holding yourself above such things, even if you do like to give the boys a good time. Now we'll try the entrance."

Cameras were put into place, and Merton Gill led through the front door his band of rollicking good fellows. He paused inside to give them bills from the paper sack. They scattered to their dissipations. Their leader austerely posed at one end of the bar and regarded the scene with disapproving eyes. Wine, women, and the dance were not for him. He produced again the disillusioned look that had won Henshaw.

"Fine," said Baird. "Gun it, boys."

The scene was shot, and Baird spoke again: "Hold it, everybody; go on with your music, and you boys keep up the dance until Mother's entrance, then you quit and back off."

Merton was puzzled by this speech, but continued his superior look, breaking it with a very genuine shock of surprise when his old mother tottered in at the front door. She was still the disconsolate creature of the day before, bedraggled, sad-eyed, feeble, very aged, and still she carried her bucket and the bundle of rags with which she had mopped. Baird came forward again.

"Oh, I forgot to tell you. Of course you had your old mother follow you out here to the great open spaces, but the poor old thing has cracked under the strain of her hard life, see what I mean? All her dear ones have been leaving the old nest and going out over the hills one by one-you were the last to go-and now she isn't quite right, see?

"You have a good home on the ranche for her, but she won't stay put. She follows you around, and the only thing that keeps her quiet is mopping, so you humour her; you let her mop. It's the only way. But of course it makes you sad. You look at her now, then go up and hug her the way you did yesterday; you try to get her to give up mopping, but she won't, so you let her go on. Try it."

Merton went forward to embrace his old mother. Here was tragedy indeed, a bit of biting pathos from a humble life. He gave the best that was in him as he enfolded the feeble old woman and strained her to his breast, murmuring to her that she must give it up-give it up.

The old lady wept, but was stubborn. She tore herself from his arms and knelt on the floor. "I just got to mop, I just got to mop," she was repeating in a cracked voice. "If I ain't let to mop I git rough till I'm simply a scandal."

It was an affecting scene, marred only by one explosive bit of coarse laughter from an observing cowboy at the close of the old mother's speech. Merton Gill glanced up in sharp annoyance at this offender. Baird was quick in rebuke.

"The next guy that laughs at this pathos can get off the set," he announced, glaring at the assemblage. There was no further outbreak and the scene was filmed.

There followed a dramatic bit that again involved the demented mother. "This ought to be good if you can do it the right way," began Baird. "Mother's mopping along there and slashes some water on this Mexican's boot-where are you, Pedro? Come here and get this. The old lady sloshes water on you while you're playing monte here, so you yell Carramba or something, and kick at her. You don't land on her, of course, but her son rushes up and grabs your arm—here, do it this way." Baird demonstrated. "Grab his wrist with one hand and his elbow with the other and make as if you broke his arm across your knee-you know, like you were doing joojitsey. He slinks off with his broken arm, and you just dust your hands off and embrace your mother again.

"Then you go back to the bar, not looking at Pedro at all. See? He's insulted your mother, and you've resented it in a nice, dignified, gentlemanly way. Try it."

Pedro sat at the table and picked up his cards. He was a foul-looking Mexican and seemed capable even of the enormity he was about to commit. The scene was rehearsed to Baird's satisfaction, then shot. The weeping old lady, blinded by her tears, awkward with her mop, the brutal Mexican, his prompt punishment.

The old lady was especially pathetic as she glared at her insulter from where she lay sprawled on the floor, and muttered, "Carramba, huh? I dare you to come outside and say that to me!"

"Good work," applauded Baird when the scene was finished. "Now we're getting into the swing of it. In about three days here we'll have something that exhibitors can clean up on, see if we don't."

The three days passed in what for Merton Gill was a whirlwind of dramatic intensity. If at times he was vaguely disquieted by a suspicion that the piece was not wholly serious, he had only to remember the intense seriousness of his own part and the always serious manner of Baird in directing his actors. And indeed there were but few moments when he was even faintly pricked by this suspicion. It seemed a bit incongruous that Hoffmeyer, the delicatessen merchant, should arrive on a bicycle, dressed in cowboy attire save for a badly dented derby hat, and carrying a bag of golf clubs; and it was a little puzzling how Hoffmeyer should have been ruined by his son's mad act, when it would have been shown that the money was returned to him. But Baird explained carefully that the old man had been ruined some other way, and was demented, like the poor old mother who had gone over the hills after her children had left the home nest. And assuredly in Merton's own action he found nothing that was not deeply earnest as well as strikingly dramatic. There was the tense moment when a faithful cowboy broke upon the festivities with word that a New York detective was coming to search for the man who had robbed the Hoffmeyer establishment. His friends gathered loyally about Merton and swore he would never be taken from them alive. He was induced to don a false mustache until the detective had gone. It was a long, heavy black mustache with curling tips, and in this disguise he stood aloof from his companions when the detective entered.

The detective was the cross-eyed man, himself now disguised as Sherlock Holmes, with a fore-and-aft cloth cap and drooping blond mustache. He smoked a pipe as he examined those present. Merton was unable to overlook this scene, as he had been directed to stand with his back to the detective. Later it was shown that he observed in a mirror the Mexican whom he had punished creeping forward to inform the detective of his man's whereabouts. The coward's treachery cost him dearly. The hero, still with his back turned, drew his revolver and took careful aim by means of the mirror.

This had been a spot where for a moment he was troubled. Instead of pointing the weapon over his shoulder, aiming by the mirror, he was directed to point it at the Mexican's reflection in the glass, and to fire at this reflection. "It's all right," Baird assured him. "It's a camera trick, see? It may look now as if you were shooting into the mirror but it comes perfectly right on the film. You'll see. Go on, aim carefully, right smack at that looking-glass—fire!" Still somewhat doubting, Merton fired. The mirror was shattered, but a dozen feet back of him the treacherous Mexican threw up his arms and fell lifeless, a bullet through his cowardly heart. It was a puzzling bit of trick-work, he thought, but Baird of course would know what was right, so the puzzle was dismissed. Buck Benson, silent man of the open, had got the scoundrel who would have played him false.

A thrilling struggle ensued between Merton and the hellhound of justice. Perceiving who had slain his would-be informant, the detective came to confront Merton. Snatching off his cap and mustache he stood revealed as the man who had not dared to arrest him at the scene of his crime. With another swift movement he snatched away the mustache that had disguised his quarry. Buck Benson, at bay, sprang like a tiger upon his antagonist. They struggled while the excited cowboys surged about them. The detective proved to be no match for Benson. He was borne to earth, then raised aloft and hurled over the adjacent tables.

This bit of acting had involved a trick which was not obscure to Merton like his shot into the mirror that brought down a man back of him. Moreover, it was a trick of which he approved. When he bore the detective to earth the cameras halted their grinding while a dummy in the striking likeness of the detective was substituted. It was a light affair, and he easily raised it for the final toss of triumph.

"Throw it high as you can over those tables and toward the bar," called Baird. The figure was thrown as directed.

"Fine work! Now look up, as if he was still in the air, now down, now brush your left sleeve lightly with your right hand, now brush your right sleeve lightly with your left hand.

"All right—cut. Great, Merton! If that don't get you a hand I don't know what will. Now all outside for the horseback stuff!"

Outside, the faithful cowboys leaped into their saddles and urged their beloved leader to do the same. But he lingered beside his own horse, pleading with them to go ahead. He must remain in the place of danger yet awhile for he had forgotten to bring out his old mother. They besought him to let them bring her out, but he would not listen. His alone was the task.

Reluctantly the cowboys galloped off. As he turned to re-enter the dance-hall he was confronted by the detective, who held two frowning weapons upon him. Benson was at last a prisoner.

The detective brutally ordered his quarry inside. Benson, seeing he was beaten, made a manly plea that he might be let to bid his horse good-by. The detective seemed moved. He relented. Benson went to his good old pal.

"Here's your chance for a fine bit," called Baird. "Give it to us now the way you did in that still. Broaden it all you want to. Go to it."

Well did Merton Gill know that here was his chance for a fine bit. The horse was strangely like Dexter upon whom he had so often rehearsed this bit. He was a bony, drooping, sad horse with a thin neck. "They're takin' ye frum me, old pal—takin' ye frum me. You an' me has seen some tough times an' I sort o' figgered we'd keep on together till the last—an' now they got me, old pal, takin' me far away where ye won't see me no more—"

"Go to it, cowboy—take all the footage you want!" called Baird in a curiously choked voice.

The actor took some more footage. "But we got to keep a stiff upper lip, old pal, you and me both. No cryin', no bustin' down. We had our last gallop together, an' we're at the forkin' of th' trail. So we got to be brave—we got to stand the gaff."

Benson released his old pal, stood erect, dashed a bit of moisture from his eyes, and turned to the waiting detective who, it seemed, had also been strangely moved during this affecting farewell. Yet he had not forgotten his duty. Benson was forced to march back into the Come All Ye Dance Hall. As he went he was wishing that Baird would have him escape and flee on his old pal.

And Baird was a man who seemed to think of everything, or perhaps he had often seen the real Buck Benson's play, for it now appeared that everything was going to be as Merton Gill wished. Baird had even contrived an escape that was highly spectacular.

Locked by the detective in an upper room, the prisoner went to the window and glanced out to find that his loyal horse was directly beneath him. He would leap from the window, alight in the saddle after a twenty-foot drop, and be off over the border. The window scene was shot, including a flash of the horse below. The mechanics of the leap itself required more time. Indeed, it took the better part of a morning to satisfy Baird that this thrilling exploit had been properly achieved. From a lower window, quite like the high one, Merton leaped, but only to the ground a few feet below.

"That's where we get your take-off," Baird explained.

"Now we get you lighting in the saddle." This proved to be a more delicate bit of work. From a platform built out just above the faithful horse Merton precariously scrambled down into the saddle. He glanced anxiously at Baird, fearing he had not alighted properly after the supposed twenty-foot drop, but the manager appeared to be delighted with his prowess after the one rehearsal, and the scene was shot.

"It's all jake," Baird assured him. "Don't feel worried. Of course we'll trick the bit where you hit the saddle; the camera'll look out for that."

One detail only troubled Merton. After doing the leap from the high window, and before doing its finish where he reached the saddle, Baird directed certain changes in his costume. He was again to don the false mustache, to put his hat on, and also a heavy jacket lined with sheep's wool worn by one of the cowboys in the dance-hall. Merton was pleased to believe he had caught the manager napping here. "But Mr. Baird, if I leap from the window without the hat or mustache or jacket and land on my horse in them, wouldn't it look as if I had put them on as I was falling?"

Baird was instantly overcome with confusion. "Now, that's so! I swear I never thought of that, Merton. I'm glad you spoke about it in time. You sure have shown me up as a director. You see I wanted you to disguise yourself again—I'll tell you; get the things on, and after we shoot you lighting in the saddle we'll retake the window scene. That'll fix it."

Not until long afterward, on a certain dread night when the earth was to rock beneath him, did he recall that Baird had never retaken that window scene. At present the young actor was too engrossed by the details of his daring leap to remember small things. The leap was achieved at last. He was in the saddle after a twenty-foot drop. He gathered up the reins, the horse beneath him coughed plaintively, and Merton rode him out of the picture. Baird took a load off his mind as to this bit of riding.

"Will you want me to gallop?" he asked, recalling the unhappy experience with Dexter.

"No; just walk him beyond the camera line. The camera'll trick it up all right." So, safely, confidently, he had ridden his steed beyond the lens range at a curious shuffling amble, and his work at the Come All Ye Dance Hall was done.

Then came some adventurous days in the open. In motor cars the company of artists was transported to a sunny nook in the foothills beyond the city, and here in the wild, rough, open spaces, the drama of mother-love, sacrifice, and thrills was further unfolded.

First to be done here was the continuation of the hero's escape from the dance-hall. Upon his faithful horse he ambled along a quiet road until he reached the shelter of an oak tree. Here he halted at the roadside.

"You know the detective is following you," explained Baird, "and you're going to get him. Take your nag over a little so the tree won't mask him too much. That's it. Now, you look back, lean forward in the saddle, listen! You hear him coming. Your face sets—look as grim as you can. That's the stuff—the real Buck Benson stuff when they're after him. That's fine. Now you get an idea. Unlash your rope, let the noose out, give it a couple of whirls to see is everything all right. That's it— only you still look grim—not so worried about whether the rope is going to act right. We'll attend to that. When the detective comes in sight give about three good whirls and let her fly. Try it once. Good! Now coil her up again and go through the whole thing. Never mind about whether you're going to get him or not. Remember, Buck Benson never misses. We'll have a later shot that shows the rope falling over his head."

Thereupon the grim-faced Benson, strong, silent man of the open, while the cameras ground, waited the coming of one who hounded him for a crime of which he was innocent. His iron face was relentless. He leaned forward, listening. He uncoiled the rope, expertly ran out the noose, and grimly waited. Far up the road appeared the detective on a galloping horse. Benson twirled the rope as he sat in his saddle. It left his hand, to sail gracefully in the general direction of his pursuer.

"Cut!" called Baird. "That was bully. Now you got him. Ride out into the road. You're dragging him off his horse, see? Keep on up the road; you're still dragging the hound. Look back over your shoulder and light your face up just a little—that's it, use Benson's other expression. You got it fine. You're treating the skunk rough, but look what he was doing to you, trying to pinch you for something you never did. That's fine—go ahead. Don't look back any more."

Merton was chiefly troubled at this moment by the thought that someone would have to double for him in the actual casting of the rope that would settle upon the detective's shoulders. Well, he must practise roping. Perhaps, by the next picture, he could do this stuff himself. It was exciting work, though sometimes tedious. It had required almost an entire morning to enact this one simple scene, with the numerous close-ups that Baird demanded.

The afternoon was taken up largely in becoming accustomed to a pair of old Spanish spurs that Baird now provided him with. Baird said they were very rare old spurs which he had obtained at a fancy price from an impoverished Spanish family who had treasured them as heirlooms. He said he was sure that Buck Benson in all his vast collection did not possess a pair of spurs like these. He would doubtless, after seeing them worn by Merton Gill in this picture, have a pair made like them.

The distinguishing feature of these spurs was their size. They were enormous, and their rowels extended a good twelve inches from Merton's heels after he had donned them.

"They may bother you a little at first," said Baird, "but you'll get used to them, and they're worth a little trouble because they'll stand out."

The first effort to walk in them proved bothersome indeed, for it was made over ground covered with a low-growing vine and the spurs caught in this. Baird was very earnest in supervising this progress, and even demanded the presence of two cameras to record it.

"Of course I'm not using this stuff," he said, "but I want to make a careful study of it. These are genuine hidalgo spurs. Mighty few men in this line of parts could get away with them. I bet Benson himself would have a lot of trouble. Now, try it once more."

Merton tried once more, stumbling as the spurs caught in the undergrowth. The cameras closely recorded his efforts, and Baird applauded them. "You're getting it—keep on. That's better. Now try to run a few steps—go right toward that left-hand camera."

He ran the few steps, but fell headlong. He picked himself up, an expression of chagrin on his face.

"Never mind," urged Baird. "Try it again. We must get this right." He tried again to run; was again thrown. But he was determined to please the manager, and he earnestly continued his efforts. Benson himself would see the picture and probably marvel that a new man should have mastered, apparently with ease, a pair of genuine hidalgos.

"Maybe we better try smoother ground," Baird at last suggested after repeated falls had shown that the undergrowth was difficult. So the cameras were moved on to the front of a ranche house now in use for the drama, and the spur lessons continued. But on smooth ground it appeared that the spurs were still troublesome. After the first mishap here Merton discovered the cause. The long shanks were curved inward so that in walking their ends clashed. He pointed this out to Baird, who was amazed at the discovery.

"Well, well, that's so! They're bound to interfere. I never knew that about hidalgo spurs before."

"We might straighten them," suggested the actor.

"No, no," Baird insisted, "I wouldn't dare try that. They cost too much money, and it might break 'em. I tell you what you do, stand up and try this: just toe in a little when you walk—that'll bring the points apart. There—that's it; that's fine."

The cameras were again recording so that Baird could later make his study of the difficulties to be mastered by the wearer of genuine hidalgos. By toeing in

Merton now succeeded in walking without disaster, though he could not feel that he was taking the free stride of men out there in the open spaces.

"Now try running." directed Baird, and he tried running; but again the spurs caught and he was thrown full in the eyes of the grinding camera. He had forgotten to toe in. But he would not give up. His face was set in Buck Benson grimness. Each time he picked himself up and earnestly resumed the effort. The rowels were now catching in the long hair of his chaps.

He worked on, directed and cheered by the patient Baird, while the two camera men, with curiously strained faces, recorded his failures. Baird had given strict orders that other members of the company should remain at a distance during the spur lessons, but now he seemed to believe that a few other people might encourage the learner. Merton was directed to run to his old mother who, bucket at her side and mop in hand, knelt on the ground at a little distance. He was also directed to run toward the Montague girl, now in frontier attire of fringed buckskin. He made earnest efforts to keep his feet during these essays, but the spurs still proved treacherous.

"Just pick yourself up and go on," ordered Baird, and had the cameras secure close shots of Merton picking himself up and going carefully on, toeing in now, to embrace his weeping old mother and the breathless girl who had awaited him with open arms.

He was tired that night, but the actual contusions he had suffered in his falls were forgotten in the fear that he might fail to master the hidalgos. Baird himself seemed confident that his pupil would yet excite the jealousy of Buck Benson in this hazardous detail of the screen art. He seemed, indeed, to be curiously satisfied with his afternoon's work. He said that he would study the film carefully and try to discover just how the spurs could be mastered.

"You'll show 'em yet how to take a joke," he declared when the puzzling implements were at last doffed. The young actor felt repaid for his earnest efforts. No one could put on a pair of genuine hidalgos for the first time and expect to handle them correctly.

There were many days in the hills. Until this time the simple drama had been fairly coherent in Merton Gill's mind. So consecutively were the scenes shot that the story had not been hard to follow. But now came rather a jumble of scenes, not only at times bewildering in themselves, but apparently unrelated.

First it appeared that the Montague girl, as Miss Rebecca Hoffmeyer, had tired of being a mere New York society butterfly, had come out into the big open spaces to do something real, something worth while. The ruin of her father, still unexplained, had seemed to call out unsuspected reserves in the girl. She was stern and businesslike in such scenes as Merton was permitted to observe. And she had not only brought her ruined father out to the open spaces but the dissipated brother, who was still seen to play at dice whenever opportunity offered. He played with the jolly cowboys and invariably won.

Off in the hills there were many scenes which Merton did not overlook. "I want you to have just your own part in mind," Baird told him. And, although he was puzzled later, he knew that Baird was somehow making it right in the drama when he became again the successful actor of that first scene, which he had almost forgotten. He was no longer the Buck Benson of the open spaces, but the foremost idol of the shadowed stage, and in Harold Parmalee's best manner he informed the aspiring Montague girl that he could not accept her as leading lady in his next picture because she lacked experience. The wager of a kiss was laughingly made as she promised that within ten days she would convince him of her talent.

Later she herself, in an effective scene, became the grimfaced Buck Benson and held the actor up at the point of her two guns. Then, when she had convinced him that she was Benson, she appeared after an interval as her own father; the fiery beard, the derby hat with its dents, the chaps, the bicycle, and golf bag. In this scene she seemed to demand the actor's intentions toward the daughter, and again overwhelmed him with confusion, as Parmalee had been overwhelmed when she revealed her true self under the baffling disguise. The wager of a kiss was prettily paid. This much of the drama he knew. And there was an affecting final scene on a hillside.

The actor, arrayed in chaps, spurs, and boots below the waist was, above this, in faultless evening dress. "You see, it's a masquerade party at the ranche," Baird explained, "and you've thought up this costume to sort of puzzle the little lady."

The girl herself was in the short, fringed buckskin skirt, with knife and revolvers in her belt. Off in the hills day after day she had worn this costume in those active scenes he had not witnessed. Now she was merely coy. He followed her out on the hillside with only a little trouble from the spurs—indeed he fell but once as he approached her—and the little drama of the lovers, at last united, was touchingly shown.

In the background, as they stood entwined, the poor demented old mother was seen. With mop and bucket she was cleansing the side of a cliff, but there was a happier look on the worn old face.

"Glance around and see her," railed Baird. "Then explain to the girl that you will always protect your mother, no matter what happens. That's it. Now the clench—kiss her—slow! That's it. Cut!"

Merton's part in the drama was ended. He knew that the company worked in the hills another week and there were more close-ups to take in the dance-hall, but he was not needed in these. Baird congratulated him warmly.

"Fine work, my boy! You've done your first picture, and with Miss Montague as your leading lady I feel that you're going to land ace-high with your public. Now all you got to do for a couple of weeks is to take it easy while we finish up some rough ends of this piece. Then we'll be ready to start on the new one. It's pretty well doped out, and there's a big part in it for you—big things to be done in a big way, see what I mean."

"Well, I'm glad I suited you," Merton replied. "I tried to give the best that was in me to a sincere interpretation of that fine part. And it was a great surprise to me. I never thought I'd be working for you, Mr. Baird, and of course I wouldn't have been if you had kept on doing those comedies. I never would have wanted to work in one of them." "Of course not," agreed Baird cordially. "I realized that you were a serious artist, and you came in the nick of time, just when I was wanting to be serious myself, to get away from that slap-stick stuff into something better and finer. You came when I needed you. And, look here, Merton, I signed you on at forty a week—"

"Yes, sir: I was glad to get it."

"Well, I'm going to give you more. From the beginning of the new picture you're on the payroll at seventy-five a week. No, no, not a word—" as Merton would have thanked him. "You're earning the money. And for the picture after that—well, if you keep on giving the best that's in you, it will be a whole lot more. Now take a good rest till we're ready for you."

At last he had won. Suffering and sacrifice had told. And Baird had spoken of the Montague girl as his leading lady—quite as if he were a star. And seventy-five dollars a week! A sum Gashwiler had made him work five weeks for. Now he had something big to write to his old friend, Tessie Kearns. She might spread the news in Simsbury, he thought. He contrived a close-up of Gashwiler hearing it, of Mrs. Gashwiler hearing it, of Metta Judson hearing it.

They would all be incredulous until a certain picture was shown at the Bijou Palace, a gripping drama of mother-love, of a clean-limbed young American type wrongfully accused of a crime and taking the burden of it upon his own shoulders for the sake of the girl he had come to love; of the tense play of elemental forces in the great West, the regeneration of a shallow society girl when brought to adversity by the ruin of her old father; of the lovers reunited in that West they both loved.

And somehow—this was still a puzzle—the very effective weaving in and out of the drama of the world's most popular screen idol, played so expertly by Clifford Armytage who looked enough like him to be his twin brother.

Fresh from joyous moments in the projection room, the Montague girl gazed at Baird across the latter's desk, Baird spoke.

"Sis, he's a wonder."

"Jeff, you're a wonder. How'd you ever keep him from getting wise?"

Baird shrugged. "Easy! We caught him fresh."

"How'd you ever win him to do all those falls on the trick spurs, and get the close-ups of them? Didn't he know you were shooting?"

"Oh!" Baird shrugged again. "A little talk made that all jake. But what bothers me—how's he going to act when he's seen the picture?"

The girl became grave. "I'm scared stiff every time I think of it. Maybe he'll murder you, Jeff."

"Maybe he'll murder both of us. You got him into it."

She did not smile, but considered gravely, absently.

"There's something else might happen," she said at last. "That boy's got at least a couple of sides to him. I'd rather he'd be crazy mad than be what I'm thinking of now, and that's that all this stuff might just fairly break his heart. Think of it—to see his fine honest acting turned into good old Buckeye slap-stick! Can't you get that? How'd you like to think you were playing Romeo, and act your heart out at it, and then find out they'd slipped in a cross-eyed Juliet in a comedy make-up on you? Well, you can laugh, but maybe it won't be funny to him. Honest, Jeff, that kid gets me under the ribs kind of. I hope he takes it standing up, and goes good and crazy mad."

"I'll know what to say to him if he does that. If he takes it the other way, lying down, I'll be too ashamed ever to look him in the eye again. Say, it'll be like going up to a friendly baby and soaking it with a potato masher or something."

"Don't worry about it, Kid. Anyway, it won't be your fault so much as mine. And you think there's only two ways for him to take it, mad or heart broken? Well, let me tell you something about that lad—he might fool you both ways. I don't know just how, but I tell you he's an actor, a born one. What he did is going to get over big. And I never yet saw a born actor that would take applause lying down, even if it does come for what he didn't know he was doing. Maybe he'll be mad— that's natural enough. But maybe he'll fool us both. So cheerio, old Pippin! and let's fly into the new piece. I'll play safe by shooting the most of that before the other one is released. And he'll still be playing straight in a serious heart drama. Fancy that, Armand!"

CHAPTER XV. A NEW TRAIL

One genial morning a few days later the sun shone in across the desk of Baird while he talked to Merton Gill of the new piece. It was a sun of fairest promise. Mr. Gill's late work was again lavishly commended, and confidence was expressed that he would surpass himself in the drama shortly to be produced.

Mr. Baird spoke in enthusiastic terms of this, declaring that if it did not prove to be a knock-out—a clean-up picture—then he, Jeff Baird, could safely be called a Chinaman. And during the time that would elapse before shooting on the new piece could begin he specified a certain study in which he wished his actor to engage.

"You've watched the Edgar Wayne pictures, haven't you?"

"Yes, I've seen a number of them."

"Like his work?—that honest country-boy-loving-his—mother-and-little-sister stuff, wearing overalls and tousled hair in the first part, and coming out in city clothes and eight dollar neckties at the last, with his hair slicked back same as a seal?"

"Oh, yes, I like it. He's fine. He has a great appeal."

"Good! That's the kind of a part you're going to get in this new piece. Lots of managers in my place would say 'No-he's a capable young chap and has plenty of talent, but he lacks the experience to play an Edgar Wayne part.' That's what a lot of these Wisenheimers would say. But me—not so. I believe you can get away with this part, and I'm going to give you your chance."

"I'm sure I don't know how to thank you, Mr. Baird, and I'll try to give you the very best that is in me—"

"I'm sure of that, my boy; you needn't tell me. But now—what I want you to do while you got this lay-off between pieces, chase out and watch all the Edgar Wayne pictures you can find. There was one up on the Boulevard last week I'd like you to watch half-a-dozen times. It may be at another house down this way, or it may be out in one of the suburbs. I'll have someone outside call up and find where it is to-day and they'll let you know. It's called Happy Homestead or something snappy like that, and it kind of suggests a layout for this new piece of mine, see what I mean? It'll suggest things to you.

"Edgar and his mother and little sister live on this farm and Edgar mixes in with a swell dame down at the summer hotel, and a villain tries to get his old mother's farm and another villain takes his little sister off up to the wicked city, and Edgar has more trouble than would patch Hell a mile, see? But it all comes right in the end, and the city girl falls for him when she sees him in his stepping-out clothes.

"It's a pretty little thing, but to my way of thinking it lacks strength; not enough punch to it. So we're sort of building up on that general idea, only we'll put in the pep that this piece lacked. If I don't miss my guess, you'll be able to show Wayne a few things about serious acting—especially after you've studied his methods a little bit in this piece."

"Well, if you think I can do it," began Merton, then broke off in answer to a sudden thought. "Will my mother be the same actress that played it before, the one that mopped all the time?"

"Yes, the same actress, but a different sort of mother. She—she's more enterprising; she's a sort of chemist, in a way; puts up preserves and jellies for the hotel. She never touches a mop in the whole piece and dresses neat from start to finish."

"And does the cross-eyed man play in it? Sometimes, in scenes with him, I'd get the idea I wasn't really doing my best."

"Yes, yes, I know." Baird waved a sympathetic hand. "Poor old Jack. He's trying hard to do something worth while, but he's played in those cheap comedy things so long it's sort of hard for him to get out of it and play serious stuff, if you know what I mean."

"I know what you mean," said Merton.

"And he's been with me so long I kind of hate to discharge him. You see, on account of those eyes of his, it would be hard for him to get a job as a serious actor, so I did think I'd give him another part in this piece if you didn't object, just to sort of work him into the worth-while things. He's so eager for the chance. It was quite pathetic how grateful he looked when I told him I'd try him once more in one of the better and finer things. And a promise is a promise."

"Still, Merton, you're the man I must suit in this cast; if you say the word I'll tell Jack he must go, though I know what a blow it will be to him—"

"Oh, no, Mr. Baird," Merton interrupted fervently, "I wouldn't think of such a thing. Let the poor fellow have a chance to learn something better than the buffoonery he's been doing. I'll do everything I can to help him. I think it is very pathetic, his wanting to do the better things; it's fine of him. And maybe some day he could save up enough to have a good surgeon fix his eyes right. It might be done, you know."

"Now that's nice of you, my boy. It's kind and generous. Not every actor of your talent would want Jack working in the same scene with him. And perhaps, as you say, some day he can save up enough from his wages to have his eyes fixed. I'll mention it to him. And this reminds me, speaking of the cast, there's another member who might bother some of these fussy actors. She's the girl who will take the part of your city sweetheart. As a matter of fact, she isn't exactly the type I'd have picked for the part, because she's rather a large, hearty girl, if you know what I mean. I could have found a lot who were better lookers; but the poor thing has a bedridden father and mother and a little crippled brother and a little sister that isn't well, and she's working hard to send them all to school—I mean the children, not her parents; so I saw the chance to do her a good turn, and I hope you'll feel that you can work harmoniously with her. I know I'm too darned human to be in this business—" Baird looked aside to conceal his emotion.

"I'm sure, Mr. Baird, I'll get along fine with the young lady, and I think it's fine of you to give these people jobs when you could get better folks in their places."

"Well, well, we'll say no more about that," replied Baird gruffly, as one who had again hidden his too-impressionable heart. "Now ask in the outer office where that Wayne film is to-day and catch it as often as you feel you're getting any of the Edgar Wayne stuff. We'll call you up when work begins."

He saw the Edgar Wayne film, a touching story in which the timid, diffident country boy triumphed over difficulties and won the love of a pure New York society girl, meantime protecting his mother from the insulting sneers of the idle rich and being made to suffer intensely by the apparent moral wreck of his dear little sister whom a rich scoundrel lured to the great city with false promises that he would make a fine lady of her. Never before had he studied the acting method of Wayne with a definite aim in view. Now he watched until he himself became the awkward country boy. He was primed with the Wayne manner, the appealing ingenuousness, the simple embarrassments; the manly regard for the old mother, when word came that Baird was ready for him in the new piece.

This drama was strikingly like the Wayne piece he had watched, at least in its beginning. Baird, in his striving for the better things, seemed at first to have copied his model almost too faithfully. Not only was Merton to be the awkward country boy in the little hillside farmhouse, but his mother and sister were like the other mother and sister.

Still, he began to observe differences. The little sister—played by the Montague girl—was a simple farm maiden as in the other piece, but the mother was more energetic. She had silvery hair and wore a neat black dress, with a white lace collar and a cameo brooch at her neck, and she embraced her son tearfully at frequent intervals, as had the other mother; but she carried on in her kitchen an active business in canning fruits and putting up jellies, which, sold to the rich people at the hotel, would swell the little fund that must be saved to pay the mortgage. Also, in the present piece, the country boy was to become a great inventor, and this was different. Merton felt that this was a good touch; it gave him dignity.

He appeared ready for work on the morning designated. He was now able to make up himself, and he dressed in the country-boy costume that had been

383

provided. It was perhaps not so attractive a costume as Edgar Wayne had worn, consisting of loose-fitting overalls that came well above his waist and were fastened by straps that went over the shoulders; but, as Baird remarked, the contrast would be greater when he dressed in rich city clothes at the last. His hair, too, was no longer the slicked-back hair of Parmalee, but tousled in country disorder.

For much of the action of the new piece they would require an outside location, but there were some interiors to be shot on the lot. He forgot the ill-fitting overalls when shown his attic laboratory where, as an ambitious young inventor, sustained by the unfaltering trust of mother and sister, he would perfect certain mechanical devices that would bring him fame, fortune, and the love of a pure New York society girl. It was a humble little room containing a work-bench that held his tools and a table littered with drawings over which he bent until late hours of the night.

At this table, simple, unaffected, deeply earnest, he was shown as the dreaming young inventor, perplexed at moments, then, with brightening eyes, making some needful change in the drawings. He felt in these scenes that he was revealing a world of personality. And he must struggle to give a sincere interpretation in later scenes that would require more action. He would show Baird that he had not watched Edgar Wayne without profit.

Another interior was of the neat living room of the humble home. Here were scenes of happy family life with the little sister and the fond old mother. The Montague girl was a charming picture in her simple print dress and sunbonnet beneath which hung her braid of golden hair. The mother was a sweet old dear, dressed as Baird had promised. She early confided to Merton that she was glad her part was not to be a mopping part. In that case she would have had to wear knee-pads, whereas now she was merely, she said, to be a tired business woman.

Still another interior was of her kitchen where she busily carried on her fruit-canning activities. Pots boiled on the stove and glass jars were filled with her product. One of the pots, Merton noticed, the largest, had a tightly closed top from which a slender tube of copper went across one corner of the little room to where it coiled in a bucket filled with water, whence it discharged its contents into bottles.

This, it seemed, was his mother's improved grape juice, a cooling drink to tempt the jaded palates of the city folks up at the big hotel.

The laboratory of the young inventor was abundantly filmed while the earnest country boy dreamed hopefully above his drawings or tinkered at metal devices on the work-bench. The kitchen in which his mother toiled was repeatedly shot, including close-ups of the old mother's ingenious contrivances—especially of the closed boiler with its coil of copper tubing—by which she was helping to save the humble home.

And a scene in the neat living room with its old-fashioned furniture made it all too clear that every effort would be required to save the little home. The cruel money-lender, a lawyer with mean-looking whiskers, confronted the three shrinking inmates to warn them that he must have his money by a certain day or out they would go into the streets. The old mother wept at this, and the earnest boy took her in his arms. The little sister, terrified by the man's rough words, also flew to this shelter, and thus he defied the intruder, calm, fearless, dignified. The money would be paid and the intruder would now please remember that, until the day named, this little home was their very own.

The scoundrel left with a final menacing wave of his gnarled hand; left the group facing ruin unless the invention could be perfected, unless Mother could sell an extraordinary quantity of fruit or improved grape juice to the city folks, or, indeed, unless the little sister could do something wonderful.

She, it now seemed, was confident she also could help. She stood apart from them and prettily promised to do something wonderful. She asked them to remember that she was no longer a mere girl, but a woman with a woman's determination. They both patted the little thing encouragingly on the back.

The interiors possible on the Holden lot having been finished, they motored each day to a remote edge of the city where outside locations had been found for the humble farmhouse and the grand hotel. The farmhouse was excellently chosen, Merton thought, being the neat, unpretentious abode of honest, hard-working people; but the hotel, some distance off, was not so grand, he thought, as Baird's new play seemed to demand. It was plainly a hotel, a wooden structure with balconies; but it seemed hardly to afford those attractions that would draw wealthier element from New York. He forebore to warn Baird of this, however, fearing to discourage a manager who was honestly striving for the serious in photodrama.

His first exterior scene saw him, with the help of Mother and little sister, loading the one poor motor car which the family possessed with Mother's products. These were then driven to the hotel. The Montague girl drove the car, and scenes of it in motion were shot from a car that preceded them.

They arrived before the hotel; Merton was directed to take from the car an iron weight attached to a rope and running to a connection forward on the hood. He was to throw the weight to the ground, plainly with the notion that he would thus prevent the car from running away. The simple device was, in fact, similar to that used, at Gashwiler's strict orders, on the delivery wagon back in Simsbury, for Gashwiler had believed that Dexter would run away if untethered. But of course it was absurd, Merton saw, to anchor a motor car in such a manner, and he was somewhat taken aback when Baird directed this action.

"It's all right," Baird assured him. "You're a simple country boy, and don't know any better, so do it plumb serious. You'll be smart enough before the show's over. Go ahead, get out, grab the weight, throw it down, and don't look at it again,

385

as if you did this every time. That's it. You're not being funny; just a simple country boy like Wayne was at first." He performed the action, still with some slight misgiving. Followed scenes of brother and sister offering Mother's wares to the city folks idling on the porch of the hotel. Each bearing a basket they were caught submitting the jellies and jams. The brother was laughed at, even sneered at, by the supercilious rich, the handsomely gowned women and the dissipated looking men. No one appeared to wish his jellies.

The little sister had better luck. The women turned from her, but the men gathered about her and quickly bought out the stock. She went to the car for more and the men followed her. To Merton, who watched these scenes, the dramatist's intention was plain. These men did not really care for jellies and jams, they were attracted solely by the wild-rose beauty of the little country girl. And they were plainly the sort of men whose attentions could mean no good to such as she.

Left on the porch, he was now directed to approach a distinguished looking old gentleman, probably a banker and a power in Wall Street, who read his morning papers. Timidly he stood before this person, thrusting forward his basket. The old gentleman glanced up in annoyance and brutally rebuffed the country boy with an angry flourish of the paper he read.

"You're hurt by this treatment," called Baird, "and almost discouraged. You look back over your shoulder to where sister is doing a good business with her stuff, and you see the old mother back in her kitchen, working her fingers to the bone—we'll have a flash of that, see?—and you try again. Take out that bottle in the corner of the basket, uncork it, and try again. The old man looks up-he's smelled something. You hold the bottle toward him and you're saying so-and-so, so-and-so, so-and-so, 'Oh, Mister, if you knew how hard my poor old mother works to make this stuff! Won't you please take a little taste of her improved grape juice and see if you don't want to buy a few shillings' worth'—so-and-so, so-and-so, so-and-so—see what I mean? That's it, look pleading. Think how the little home depends on it."

The old gentleman, first so rude, consented to taste the improved grape juice. He put the bottle to his lips and tilted it. A camera was brought up to record closely the look of pleased astonishment that enlivened his face. He arose to his feet, tilted the bottle again, this time drinking abundantly. He smacked his lips with relish, glanced furtively at the group of women in the background, caught the country boy by a sleeve and drew him farther along the porch.

"He's telling you what fine stuff this grape juice is," explained Baird; "saying that your mother must be a wonderful old lady, and he'll drop over to meet her; and in the meantime he wants you to bring him all this grape juice she has. He'll take it; she can name her own price. He hands you a ten dollar bill for the bottle he has and for another in the basket—that's it, give it to him. The rest of the bottles are jams or something. You want him to take them, but he pushes them back. He's saying he wants the improved grape juice or nothing. He shows a big wad of bills

386

to show he can pay for it. You look glad now—the little home may be saved after all."

The scene was shot. Merton felt that he carried it acceptably. He had shown the diffident pleading of the country boy that his mother's product should be at least tasted, his frank rejoicing when the old gentleman approved of it. He was not so well satisfied with the work of the Montague girl as his innocent little sister. In her sale of Mother's jellies to the city men, in her acceptance of their attentions, she appeared to be just the least bit bold. It seemed almost as if she wished to attract their notice. He hesitated to admit it, for he profoundly esteemed the girl, but there were even moments when, in technical language, she actually seemed to "vamp" these creatures who thronged about her to profess for her jams and jellies an interest he was sure they did not feel.

He wondered if Baird had made it plain to her that she was a very innocent little country girl who should be unpleasantly affected by these advances. The scene he watched shot where the little sister climbed back into the motor car, leered at by the four New York club-men, he thought especially distasteful. Surely the skirt of her print dress was already short enough. She needed not to lift it under this evil regard as she put her foot up to the step.

It was on the porch of the hotel, too, that he was to have his first scene with the New York society girl whose hand he won. She proved to be the daughter of the old gentleman who liked the improved grape juice. As Baird had intimated, she was a large girl; not only tall and stoutly built, but somewhat heavy of face. Baird's heart must have been touched indeed when he consented to employ her, but Merton remembered her bedridden father and mother, the little crippled brother, the little sister who was also in poor health, and resolved to make their scenes together as easy for her as he could.

At their first encounter she appeared in a mannish coat and riding breeches, though she looked every inch a woman in this attire.

"She sees you, and it's a case of love at first sight on her part," explained Baird. "And you love her, too, only you're a bashful country boy and can't show it the way she can. Try out a little first scene now."

Merton stood, his basket on his arm, as the girl approached him. "Look down," called Baird, and Merton lowered his gaze under the ardent regard of the social butterfly. She tossed away her cigarette and came nearer. Then she mischievously pinched his cheek as the New York men had pinched his little sister's. Having done this, she placed her hand beneath his chin and raised his face to hers.

"Now look up at her," called Baird. "But she frightens you. Remember your country raising. You never saw a society girl before. That's it—look frightened while she's admiring you in that bold way. Now turn a little and look down again. Pinch his cheek once more, Lulu. Now, Merton, look up and smile, but kind of scared—you're still afraid of her—and offer her a bottle of Ma's preserves. Step back a little as you do it, because you're kind of afraid of what she might do next. That's fine. Good work, both of you."

He was glad for the girl's sake that Baird had approved the work of both. He had been afraid she was overdoing the New York society manner in the boldness of her advances to him, but of course Baird would know.

His conscience hurt him a little when the Montague girl added her praise to Baird's for his own work. "Kid, you certainly stepped neat and looked nice in that love scene," she warmly told him. He would have liked to praise her own work, but could not bring himself to. Perhaps she would grow more shrinking and modest as the drama progressed.

A part of the play now developed as he had foreseen it would, in that the city men at the hotel pursued the little sister to her own door-step with attentions that she should have found unwelcome. But even now she behaved in a way he could not approve. She seemed determined to meet the city men halfway. "I'm to be the sunlight arc of this hovel," she announced when the city men came, one at a time, to shower gifts upon the little wild rose.

Later it became apparent that she must in the end pay dearly for her too-ready acceptance of these favours. One after another the four city men, whose very appearance would have been sufficient warning to most girls, endeavoured to lure her up to the great city where they promised to make a lady of her. It was a situation notoriously involving danger to the simple country girl, yet not even her mother frowned upon it.

The mother, indeed, frankly urged the child to let all of these kind gentlemen make a lady of her. The brother should have warned her in this extremity; but the brother was not permitted any share in these scenes. Only Merton Gill, in his proper person, seemed to feel the little girl was all too cordially inviting trouble.

He became confused, ultimately, by reason of the scenes not being taken consecutively. It appeared that the little sister actually left her humble home at the insistence of one of the villains, yet she did not, apparently, creep back months later broken in body and soul. As nearly as he could gather, she was back the next day. And it almost seemed as if later, at brief intervals, she allowed herself to start for the great city with each of the other three scoundrels who were bent upon her destruction. But always she appeared to return safely and to bring large sums of money with which to delight the old mother.

It was puzzling to Merton. He decided at last—he did not like to ask the Montague girl—that Baird had tried the same scene four times, and would choose the best of these for his drama.

Brother and sister made further trips to the hotel with their offerings, only the sister now took jams and jellies exclusively, which she sold to the male guests,

388

while the brother took only the improved grape juice which the rich old New Yorker bought and generously paid for.

There were other scenes at the hotel between the country boy and the heavy-faced New York society girl, in which the latter was an ardent wooer. Once she was made to snatch a kiss from him as he stood by her, his basket on his arm. He struggled in her embrace, then turned to flee.

She was shown looking after him, laughing, carelessly slapping one leg with her riding crop.

"You're still timid," Baird told him. "You can hardly believe you have won her love."

In some following scenes at the little farmhouse it became impossible for him longer to doubt this, for the girl frankly told her love as she lingered with him at the gate.

"She's one of these new women," said Baird. "She's living her own life. You listen—it's wonderful that this great love should have come to you. Let us see the great joy dawning in your eyes."

He endeavoured to show this. The New York girl became more ardent. She put an arm about him, drew him to her. Slowly, almost in the manner of Harold Parmalee, as it seemed to him, she bent down and imprinted a long kiss upon his lips. He had been somewhat difficult to rehearse in this scene, but Baird made it all plain. He was still the bashful country boy, though now he would be awakened by love.

The girl drew him from the gate to her waiting automobile. Here she overcame a last reluctance and induced him to enter. She followed and drove rapidly off.

It was only now that Baird let him into the very heart of the drama.

"You see," he told Merton, "you've watched these city folks; you've wanted city life and fine clothes for yourself; so, in a moment of weakness, you've gone up to town with this girl to have a look at the place, and it sort of took hold of you. In fact, you hit up quite a pace for awhile; but at last you go stale on it—" "The blight of Broadway," suggested Merton, wondering if there could be a cabaret scene.

"Exactly," said Baird. "And you get to thinking of the poor old mother and little sister back here at home, working away to pay off the mortgage, and you decide to come back. You get back on a stormy night; lots of snow and wind; you're pretty weak. We'll show you sort of fainting as you reach the door. You have no overcoat nor hat, and your city suit is practically ruined. You got a great chance for some good acting here, especially after you get inside to face the folks. It'll be the strongest thing you've done, so far."

It was indeed an opportunity for strong acting. He could see that. He stayed late with Baird and his staff one night and a scene of the prodigal's return to the

389

door of the little home was shot in a blinding snow-storm. Baird warmly congratulated the mechanics who contrived the storm, and was enthusiastic over the acting of the hero. Through the wintry blast he staggered, half falling, to reach the door where he collapsed. The light caught the agony on his pale face. He lay a moment, half-fainting, then reached up a feeble hand to the knob of the door.

It was one of the annoyances incident to screen art that he could not go in at that moment to finish his great scene. But this must be done back on the lot, and the scene could not be secured until the next day.

Once more he became the pitiful victim of a great city, crawling back to the home shelter on a wintry night. It was Christmas eve, he now learned. He pushed open the door of the little home and staggered in to face his old mother and the little sister. They sprang forward at his entrance; the sister ran to support him to the homely old sofa. He was weak, emaciated, his face an agony of repentance, as he mutely pled forgiveness for his flight.

His old mother had risen, had seemed about to embrace him fondly when he knelt at her feet, but then had drawn herself sternly up and pointed commandingly to the door. The prodigal, anguished anew at this repulse, fell weakly back upon the couch with a cry of despair. The little sister placed a pillow under his head and ran to plead with the mother. A long time she remained obdurate, but at last relented. Then she, too, came to fall upon her knees before the wreck who had returned to her.

Not many rehearsals were required for this scene, difficult though it was. Merton Gill had seized his opportunity. His study of agony expressions in the film course was here rewarded. The scene closed with the departure of the little sister. Resolutely, showing the light of some fierce determination, she put on hat and wraps, spoke words of promise to the stricken mother and son, and darted out into the night. The snow whirled in as she opened the door.

"Good work," said Baird to Merton. "If you don't hear from that little bit you can call me a Swede."

Some later scenes were shot in the same little home, which seemed to bring the drama to a close. While the returned prodigal lay on the couch, nursed by the forgiving mother, the sister returned in company with the New York society girl who seemed aghast at the wreck of him she had once wooed. Slowly she approached the couch of the sufferer, tenderly she reached down to enfold him. In some manner, which Merton could not divine, the lovers had been reunited.

The New York girl was followed by her father—it would seem they had both come from the hotel—and the father, after giving an order for more of Mother's grape juice, examined the son's patents. Two of them he exclaimed with delight over, and at once paid the boy a huge roll of bills for a tenth interest in them.

Now came the grasping man who held the mortgage and who had counted upon driving the family into the streets this stormy Christmas eve. He was overwhelmed with confusion when his money was paid from an ample hoard, and slunk, shame-faced, out into the night. It could be seen that Christmas day would dawn bright and happy for the little group.

To Merton's eye there was but one discord in this finale. He had known that the cross-eyed man was playing the part of hotel clerk at the neighbouring resort, but he had watched few scenes in which the poor fellow acted; and he surely had not known that this man was the little sister's future husband. It was with real dismay that he averted his gaze from the embrace that occurred between these two, as the clerk entered the now happy home.

One other detail had puzzled him. This was the bundle to which he had clung as he blindly plunged through the storm. He had still fiercely clutched it after entering the little room, clasping it to his breast even as he sank at his mother's feet in physical exhaustion and mental anguish, to implore her forgiveness. Later the bundle was placed beside him as he lay, pale and wan, on the couch.

He supposed this bundle to contain one of his patents; a question to Baird when the scene was over proved him to be correct. "Sure," said Baird, "that's one of your patents." Yet he still wished the little sister had not been made to marry the cross-eyed hotel clerk.

And another detail lingered in his memory to bother him. The actress playing his mother was wont to smoke cigarettes when not engaged in acting. He had long known it. But he now seemed to recall, in that touching last scene of reconciliation, that she had smoked one while the camera actually turned. He hoped this was not so. It would mean a mistake. And Baird would be justly annoyed by the old mother's carelessness.

CHAPTER XVI. OF SARAH NEVADA MONTAGUE

They were six long weeks doing the new piece. The weeks seemed long to Merton Gill because there were so many hours, even days, of enforced idleness. To pass an entire day, his face stiff with the make-up, without once confronting a camera in action, seemed to him a waste of his own time and a waste of Baird's money. Yet this appeared to be one of the unavoidable penalties incurred by those who engaged in the art of photodrama. Time was needed to create that world of painted shadows, so swift, so nicely consecutive when revealed, but so incoherent, so brokenly inconsequent, so meaningless in the recording.

How little an audience could suspect the vexatious delays ensuing between, say, a knock at a door and the admission of a visitor to a neat little home where a fond old mother was trying to pay off a mortgage with the help of her little ones. How could an audience divine that a wait of two hours had been caused because a polished city villain had forgotten his spats? Or that other long waits had been caused by other forgotten trifles, while an expensive company of artists lounged about in bored apathy, or smoked, gossiped, bantered?

Yet no one ever seemed to express concern about these waits. Rarely were their causes known, except by some frenzied assistant director, and he, after a little, would cease to be frenzied and fall to loafing calmly with the others. Merton Gill's education in his chosen art was progressing. He came to loaf with the unconcern, the vacuous boredom, the practised nonchalance, of more seasoned artists.

Sometimes when exteriors were being taken the sky would overcloud and the sun be denied them for a whole day. The Montague girl would then ask Merton how he liked Sunny Cafeteria. He knew this was a jesting term that would stand for sunny California, and never failed to laugh.

The girl kept rather closely by him during these periods of waiting. She seemed to show little interest in other members of the company, and her association with them, Merton noted, was marked by a certain restraint. With them she seemed no longer to be the girl of free ways and speech. She might occasionally join a group of the men who indulged in athletic sports on the grass before the little farmhouse—for the actors of Mr. Baird's company would all betray acrobatic tendencies in their idle moments—and he watched one day while the simple little country sister turned a series of hand-springs and cart-wheels that evoked sincere applause from the four New York villains who had been thus solacing their ennui.

But oftener she would sit with Merton on the back seat of one of the waiting automobiles. She not only kept herself rather aloof from other members of the company, but she curiously seemed to bring it about that Merton himself would have little contact with them. Especially did she seem to hover between him and the company's feminine members. Among those impersonating guests at the hotel were several young women of rare beauty with whom he would have been not unwilling to fraternize in that easy comradeship which seemed to mark studio life. These were far more alluring than the New York society girl who wooed him and who had secured the part solely through Baird's sympathy for her family misfortunes.

They were richly arrayed and charmingly mannered in the scenes he watched; moreover, they not too subtly betrayed a pleasant consciousness of Merton's existence. But the Montague girl noticeably monopolized him when a better acquaintance with the beauties might have come about. She rather brazenly seemed to be guarding him. She was always there.

This very apparent solicitude of hers left him feeling pleasantly important, despite the social contacts it doubtless deprived him of. He wondered if the Montague girl could be jealous, and cautiously one day, as they lolled in the motor car, he sounded her.

"Those girls in the hotel scenes—I suppose they're all nice girls of good family?" he casually observed.

"Huh?" demanded Miss Montague, engaged with a pencil at the moment in editing her left eyebrow. "Oh, that bunch? Sure, they all come from good old Southern families—Virginia and Indiana and those places." She tightened her lips before the little mirror she held and renewed their scarlet. Then she spoke more seriously. "Sure, Kid, those girls are all right enough. They work like dogs and do the best they can when they ain't got jobs. I'm strong for 'em. But then, I'm a wise old trouper. I understand things. You don't. You're the real country wild rose of this piece. It's a good thing you got me to ride herd on you. You're far too innocent to be turned loose on a comedy lot.

"Listen, boy—" She turned a sober face to him—"the straight lots are fairly decent, but get this: a comedy lot is the toughest place this side of the bad one. Any comedy lot."

"But this isn't a comedy lot. Mr. Baird isn't doing comedies any more, and these people all seem to be nice people. Of course some of the ladies smoke cigarettes—"

The girl had averted her face briefly, but now turned to him again. "Of course that's so; Jeff is trying for the better things; but he's still using lots of his old people. They're all right for me, but not for you. You wouldn't last long if mother here didn't look out for you. I'm playing your dear little sister, but I'm playing your mother, too. If it hadn't been for me this bunch would have taught you a lot of things you'd better learn some other way. Just for one thing, long before this you'd probably been hopping up your reindeers and driving all over in a Chinese sleigh."

He tried to make something of this, but found the words meaningless. They merely suggested to him a snowy winter scene of Santa Claus and his innocent equipage. But he would intimate that he understood.

"Oh, I guess not," he said knowingly. The girl appeared not to have heard this bit of pretense.

"On a comedy lot," she said, again becoming the oracle, "you can do murder if you wipe up the blood. Remember that."

He did not again refer to the beautiful young women who came from fine old Southern homes. The Montague girl was too emphatic about them.

At other times during the long waits, perhaps while they ate lunch brought from the cafeteria, she would tell him of herself. His old troubling visions of his wonder-woman, of Beulah Baxter the daring, had well-nigh faded, but now and then they would recur as if from long habit, and he would question the girl about her life as a double.

"Yeah, I could see that Baxter business was a blow to you, Kid. You'd kind of worshiped her, hadn't you?"

"Well, I—yes, in a sort of way—"

"Of course you did; it was very nice of you—" She reached over to pat his hand. "Mother understands just how you felt, watching the films back there in Gooseberry "—He had quit trying to correct her as to Gashwiler and Simsbury. She had hit upon Gooseberry as a working composite of both names, and he had wearily come to accept it—"and I know just how you felt"—Again she patted his hand—"that night when you found me doing her stuff."

"It did kind of upset me."

"Sure it would! But you ought to have known that all these people use doubles when they can—men and women both. It not only saves 'em work, but even where they could do the stuff if they had to—and that ain't so often—it saves 'em broken bones, and holding up a big production two or three months. Fine business that would be. So when you see a woman, or a man either, doing something that someone else could do, you can bet someone else is doing it. What would you expect? Would you expect a high-priced star to go out and break his leg?

"And at that, most of the doubles are men, even for the women stars, like Kitty Carson always carries one who used to be a circus acrobat. She couldn't hardly do one of the things you see her doing, but when old Dan gets on her blonde transformation and a few of her clothes, he's her to the life in a long shot, or even in mediums, if he keeps his map covered.

"Yeah, most of the doublers have to be men. I'll hand that to myself. I'm about the only girl that's been doing it, and that's out with me hereafter, I guess, the way

I seem to be making good with Jeff. Maybe after this I won't have to do stunts, except of course some riding stuff, prob'ly, or a row of flips or something light. Anything heavy comes up—me for a double of my own." She glanced sidewise at her listener. "Then you won't like me any more, hey, Kid, after you find out I'm using a double?"

He had listened attentively, absorbed in her talk, and seemed startled by this unforeseen finish. He turned anxious eyes on her. It occurred to him for the first time that he did not wish the Montague girl to do dangerous things any more. "Say," he said quickly, amazed at his own discovery, "I wish you'd quit doing all those—stunts, do you call 'em?"

"Why?" she demanded. There were those puzzling lights back in her eyes as he met them. He was confused.

"Well, you might get hurt."

"Oh!"

"You might get killed sometime. And it wouldn't make the least difference to me, your using a double. I'd like you just the same."

"I see; it wouldn't be the way it was with Baxter when you found it out."

"No; you—you're different. I don't want you to get killed," he added, rather blankly. He was still amazed at this discovery.

"All right, Kid. I won't," she replied soothingly.

"I'll like you just as much," he again assured her, "no matter how many doubles you have."

"Well, you'll be having doubles yourself, sooner or later—and I'll like you, too." She reached over to his hand, but this time she held it. He returned her strong clasp. He had not liked to think of her being mangled perhaps by a fall into a quarry when the cable gave way—and the camera men would probably keep on turning!

"I always been funny about men," she presently spoke again, still gripping his hand. "Lord knows I've seen enough of all kinds, bad and good, but I always been kind of afraid even of the good ones. Any one might not think it, but I guess I'm just natural-born shy. Man-shy, anyway."

He glowed with a confession of his own. "You know, I'm that way, too. Girl-shy. I felt awful awkward when I had to kiss you in the other piece. I never did, really—" He floundered a moment, but was presently blurting out the meagre details of that early amour with Edwina May Pulver. He stopped this recital in a sudden panic fear that the girl would make fun of him. He was immensely relieved when she merely renewed the strength of the handclasp.

"I know. That's the way with me. Of course I can put over the acting stuff, even vamping, but I'm afraid of men off-stage. Say, would you believe it, I ain't ever had but one beau. That was Bert Stacy. Poor old Bert! He was lots older than me; about thirty, I guess. He was white all through. You always kind of remind me of him. Sort of a feckless dub he was, too; kind of honest and awkward—you know. He was the one got me doing stunts. He wasn't afraid of anything. Didn't know it was even in the dictionary. That old scout would go out night or day and break everything but his contract. I was twelve when I first knew him and he had me doing twisters in no time. I caught on to the other stuff pretty good. I wasn't afraid, either, I'll say that for myself. First I was afraid to show him I was afraid, but pretty soon I wasn't afraid at all.

"We pulled off a lot of stuff for different people. And of course I got to be a big girl and three years ago when I was eighteen Bert wanted us to be married and I thought I might as well. He was the only one I hadn't been afraid of. So we got engaged. I was still kind of afraid to marry any one, but being engaged was all right. I know we'd got along together, too, but then he got his with a motorcycle.

"Kind of funny. He'd do anything on that machine. He'd jump clean over an auto and he'd leap a thirty-foot ditch and he was all set to pull a new one for Jeff Baird when it happened. Jeff was going to have him ride his motorcycle through a plate-glass window. The set was built and everything ready and then the merry old sun don't shine for three days. Every morning Bert would go over to the lot and wait around in the fog. And this third day, when it got too late in the afternoon to shoot even if the sun did show, he says to me, 'c'mon, hop up and let's take a ride down to the beach.' So I hop to the back seat and off we start and on a ninety-foot paved boulevard what does Bert do but get caught in a jam? It was an ice wagon that finally bumped us over. I was shook up and scraped here and there. But Bert was finished. That's the funny part. He'd got it on this boulevard, but back on the lot he'd have rode through that plate-glass window probably without a scratch. And just because the sun didn't shine that day, I wasn't engaged any more. Bert was kind of like some old sea-captain that comes back to shore after risking his life on the ocean in all kinds of storms, and falls into a duck-pond and gets drowned."

She sat a long time staring out over the landscape, still holding his hand. Inside the fence before the farmhouse three of the New York villains were again engaged in athletic sports, but she seemed oblivious of these. At last she turned to him again with an illumining smile.

"But I was dead in love once before that, and that's how I know just how you feel about Baxter. He was the preacher where we used to go to church. He was a good one. Pa copied a lot of his stuff that he uses to this day if he happens to get a preacher part. He was the loveliest thing. Not so young, but dark, with wonderful eyes and black hair, and his voice would go all through you. I had an awful case on him. I was twelve, and all week I used to think how I'd see him the next Sunday. Say, when I'd get there and he'd be working—doing pulpit stuff—he'd have me in kind of a trance.

"Sometimes after the pulpit scene he'd come down right into the audience and shake hands with people. I'd almost keel over if he'd notice me. I'd be afraid if he would and afraid if he wouldn't. If he said 'And how is the little lady this morning?' I wouldn't have a speck of voice to answer him. I'd just tremble all over. I used to dream I'd get a job workin' for him as extra, blacking his shoes or fetching his breakfast and things.

"It was the real thing, all right. I used to try to pray the way he did—asking the Lord to let me do a character bit or something with him. He had me going all right. You must 'a' been that way about Baxter. Sure you were. When you found she was married and used a double and everything, it was like I'd found this preacher shooting hop or using a double in his pulpit stuff."

She was still again, looking back upon this tremendous episode.

"Yes, that's about the way I felt," he told her. Already his affair with Mrs. Rosenblatt seemed a thing of his childhood. He was wondering, rather, if the preacher could have been the perfect creature the girl was now picturing him. It would not have displeased him to learn that this refulgent being had actually used a double in his big scenes, or had been guilty of mere human behaviour at odd moments. Probably, after all, he had been just a preacher. "Uncle Sylvester used to want me to be a preacher," he said, with apparent irrelevance, "even if he was his own worst enemy." He added presently, as the girl remained silent, "I always say my prayers at night." He felt vaguely that this might raise him to the place of the other who had been adored. He was wishing to be thought well of by this girl.

She was aroused from her musing by his confession. "You do? Now ain't that just like you? I'd have bet you did that. Well, keep on, son. It's good stuff."

Her serious mood seemed to pass. She was presently exchanging tart repartee with the New York villains who had perched in a row on the fence to be funny about that long—continued holding of hands in the motor car. She was quite unembarrassed, however, as she dropped the hand with a final pat and vaulted to the ground over the side of the car.

"Get busy, there!" she ordered. "Where's your understander—where's your top-mounter?" She became a circus ringmaster. "Three up and a roll for yours," she commanded. The three villains aligned themselves on the lawn. One climbed to the shoulders of the other and a third found footing on the second. They balanced there, presently to lean forward from the summit. The girl played upon an imaginary snare drum with a guttural, throaty imitation of its roll, culminating in the "boom!" of a bass-drum as the tower toppled to earth. Its units, completing their turn with somersaults, again stood in line, bowing and smirking their acknowledgments for imagined applause.

The girl, a moment later, was turning hand-springs. Merton had never known that actors were so versatile. It was an astounding profession, he thought, remembering his own registration card that he had filled out at the Holden office.

His age, height, weight, hair, eyes, and his chest and waist measures; these had been specified, and then he had been obliged to write the short "No" after ride, drive, swim, dance—to write "No" after "Ride?" even in the artistically photographed presence of Buck Benson on horseback!

Yet in spite of these disabilities he was now a successful actor at an enormous salary. Baird was already saying that he would soon have a contract for him to sign at a still larger figure. Seemingly it was a profession in which you could rise even if you were not able to turn hand-springs or were more or less terrified by horses and deep water and dance music.

And the Montague girl, who, he now fervently hoped, would not be killed while doubling for Mrs. Rosenblatt, was a puzzling creature. He thought his hand must still be warm from her enfolding of it, even when work was resumed and he saw her, with sunbonnet pushed back, stand at the gate of the little farmhouse and behave in an utterly brazen manner toward one of the New York clubmen who was luring her up to the great city. She, who had just confided to him that she was afraid of men, was now practically daring an undoubted scoundrel to lure her up to the great city and make a lady of her. And she had been afraid of all but a clergyman and a stunt actor! He wondered interestingly if she were afraid of Merton Gill. She seemed not to be.

On another day of long waits they ate their lunch from the cafeteria box on the steps of the little home and discussed stage names. "I guess we better can that 'Clifford Armytage' stuff," she told him as she seriously munched a sandwich. "We don't need it. That's out. Merton Gill is a lot better name." She had used "we" quite as if it were a community name.

"Well, if you think so—" he began regretfully, for Clifford Armytage still seemed superior to the indistinction of Merton Gill.

"Sure, it's a lot better," she went on. "That 'Clifford Armytage'—say, it reminds me of just another such feckless dub as you that acted with us one time when we all trouped in a rep show, playing East Lynne and such things. He was just as wise as you are, and when he joined out at Kansas City they gave him a whole book of the piece instead of just his sides. He was a quick study, at that, only he learned everybody's part as well as his own, and that slowed him. They put him on in Waco, and the manager was laid up, so they told him that after the third act he was to go out and announce the bill for the next night, and he learned that speech, too.

"He got on fine till the big scene in the third act. Then he went bloody because that was as far as he'd learned, so he just left the scene cold and walked down to the foots and bowed and said, 'Ladies and gentlemen, we thank you for your attendance here this evening and to-morrow night we shall have the honour of presenting Lady Audley's Secret.'

"With that he gave a cold look to the actors back of him that were gasping like fish, and walked off. And he was like you in another way because his real name was Eddie Duffy, and the lovely stage name he'd picked out was Clyde Maltravers."

"Well, Clifford Armytage is out, then," Merton announced, feeling that he had now buried a part of his dead self in a grave where Beulah Baxter, the wonder-woman, already lay interred. Still, he was conscious of a certain relief. The stage name had been bothersome.

"It ain't as if you had a name like mine," the girl went on. "I simply had to have help."

He wondered what her own name was. He had never heard her called anything but the absurd and undignified "Flips." She caught the question he had looked.

"Well, my honest-to-God name is Sarah Nevada Montague; Sarah for Ma and Nevada for Reno where Ma had to stop off for me—she was out of the company two weeks—and if you ever tell a soul I'll have the law on you. That was a fine way to abuse a helpless baby, wasn't it?"

"But Sarah is all right. I like Sarah."

"Do you, Kid?" She patted his hand. "All right, then, but it's only for your personal use."

"Of course the Nevada—" he hesitated. "It does sound kind of like a geography lesson or something. But I think I'll call you Sarah, I mean when we're alone." "Well, that's more than Ma ever does, and you bet it'll never get into my press notices. But go ahead if you want to."

"I will, Sarah. It sounds more like a true woman than 'Flips.'"

"Bless the child's heart," she murmured, and reached across the lunch box to pat his hand again.

"You're a great little patter, Sarah," he observed with one of his infrequent attempts at humour.

On still another day, while they idled between scenes, she talked to him about salaries and contracts, again with her important air of mothering him.

"After this picture," she told him, "Jeff was going to sew you up with a long-time contract, probably at a hundred and fifty per. But I've told him plain I won't stand for it. No five-year contract, and not any contract at that figure. Maybe three years at two hundred and fifty, I haven't decided yet. I'll wait and see—" she broke off to regard him with that old puzzling light far back in her eyes—"wait and see how you get over in these two pieces."

"But I know you'll go big, and so does Jeff. We've caught you in the rushes enough to know that. And Jeff's a good fellow, but naturally he'll get you for as little as he can. He knows all about money even if he don't keep Yom Kippur. So

I'm watching over you, son—I'm your manager, see? And I've told him so, plain. He knows he'll have to give you just what you're worth. Of course he's entitled to consideration for digging you up and developing you, but a three-year contract will pay him out for that. Trust mother."

"I do," he told her. "I'd be helpless without you. It kind of scares me to think of getting all that money. I won't know what to do with it."

"I will; you always listen to me, and you won't be camping on the lot any more. And don't shoot dice with these rough-necks on the lot." "I won't," he assured her. "I don't believe in gambling." He wondered about Sarah's own salary, and was surprised to learn that it was now double his own. It was surprising, because her acting seemed not so important to the piece as his. "It seems like a lot of money for what you have to do," he said.

"There," she smiled warmly, "didn't I always say you were a natural-born trouper? Well, it is a lot of money for me, but you see I've helped Jeff dope out both of these pieces. I'm not so bad at gags—I mean the kind of stuff he needs in these serious dramas. This big scene of yours, where you go off to the city and come back a wreck on Christmas night—that's mine. I doped it out after the piece was started—after I'd had a good look at the truck driver that plays opposite you."

Truck driver? It appeared that Miss Montague was actually applying this term to the New York society girl who in private life was burdened with an ailing family. He explained now that Mr. Baird had not considered her ideal for the part, but had chosen her out of kindness.

Again there flickered far back in her eyes those lights that baffled him. There was incredulity in her look, but she seemed to master it.

"But I think it was wonderful of you," he continued, "to write that beautiful scene. It's a strong scene, Sarah. I didn't know you could write, too. It's as good as anything Tessie Kearns ever did, and she's written a lot of strong scenes."

Miss Montague seemed to struggle with some unidentified emotion. After a long, puzzling gaze she suddenly said: "Merton Gill, you come right here with all that make-up on and give mother a good big kiss!"

Astonishingly to himself, he did so in the full light of day and under the eyes of one of the New York villains who had been pretending that he walked a tight-rope across the yard. After he had kissed the girl, she seized him by both arms and shook him. "I'd ought to have been using my own face in that scene," she said. Then she patted his shoulder and told him that he was a good boy.

The pretending tight-rope walker had paused to applaud. "Your act's flopping, Bo," said Miss Montague. "Work fast." Then she again addressed the good boy: "Wait till you've watched that scene before you thank me," she said shortly.

"But it's a strong scene," he insisted.

"Yes," she agreed. "It's strong."

He told her of the other instance of Baird's kindness of heart.

"You know I was a little afraid of playing scenes with the cross-eyed man, but Mr. Baird said he was trying so hard to do serious work, so I wouldn't have him discharged. But shouldn't you think he'd save up and have his eyes straightened? Does he get a very small salary?"

The girl seemed again to be harassed by conflicting emotions, but mastered them to say, "I don't know exactly what it is, but I guess he draws down about twelve fifty a week."

"Only twelve dollars and fifty cents a week!"

"Twelve hundred and fifty," said the girl firmly.

"Twelve hundred and fifty dollars a week!" This was monstrous, incredible. "But then why doesn't he have his eyes—"

Miss Montague drew him to her with both her capable arms. "My boy, my boy!" she murmured, and upon his painted forehead she now imprinted a kiss of deep reverence. "Run along and play," she ordered. "You're getting me all nervous." Forthwith she moved to the centre of the yard where the tight-rope walker still endangered his life above the heads of a vast audience.

She joined him. She became a performer on the slack wire. With a parasol to balance her, she ran to the centre of an imaginary wire that swayed perilously, and she swung there, cunningly maintaining a precarious balance. Then she sped back to safety at the wire's end, threw down her parasol, caught the handkerchief thrown to her by the first performer, and daintily touched her face with it, breathing deeply the while and bowing.

He thought Sarah was a strange child—"One minute one thing and the next minute something else."

CHAPTER XVII. MISS MONTAGUE USES HER OWN FACE

Work on the piece dragged slowly to an end. In these latter days the earnest young leading man suffered spells of concern for his employer. He was afraid that Mr. Baird in his effort to struggle out of the slough of low comedy was not going to be wholly successful. He had begun to note that the actors employed for this purpose were not invariably serious even when the cameras turned. Or, if serious, they seemed perhaps from the earnestness of their striving for the worth-while drama, to be a shade too serious. They were often, he felt, over-emphatic in their methods. Still, they were, he was certain, good actors. One could always tell what they meant.

It was at these times that he especially wished he might be allowed to view the "rushes." He not only wished to assure himself for Baird's sake that the piece would be acceptably serious, but he wished, with a quite seemly curiosity, to view his own acting on the screen. It occurred to him that he had been acting a long time without a glimpse of himself. But Baird had been singularly firm in this matter, and the Montague girl had sided with him. It was best, they said, for a beginning actor not to see himself at first. It might affect his method before this had crystallized; make them self-conscious, artificial.

He was obliged to believe that these well-wishers of his knew best. He must not, then, trifle with a screen success that seemed assured. He tried to be content with this decision. But always the misgivings would return. He would not be really content until he had watched his own triumph. Soon this would be so securely his privilege that not even Baird could deny it, for the first piece in which he had worked was about to be shown. He looked forward to that.

It was toward the end of the picture that his intimacy with the Montague girl grew to a point where, returning from location to the studio late, they would dine together. "Hurry and get ungreased, Son," she would say, "and you can take an actress out to dinner." Sometimes they would patronize the cafeteria on the lot, but oftener, in a spirit of adventure, they would search out exotic restaurants. A picture might follow, after which by street-car he would escort her to the Montague home in a remote, flat region of palm-lined avenues sparsely set with new bungalows.

She would disquiet him at these times by insisting that she pay her share of the expense, and she proved to have no mean talent for petty finance, for she remembered every item down to the street-car fares. Even to Merton Gill she seemed very much a child once she stepped from the domain of her trade. She would stare into shop windows wonderingly, and never failed to evince the most childish delight when they ventured to dine at an establishment other than a cafeteria.

At times when they waited for a car after these dissipations he suffered a not unpleasant alarm at sight of a large-worded advertisement along the back of a bench on which they would sit. "You furnish the Girl, We furnish the House," screamed the bench to him above the name of an enterprising tradesman that came in time to bite itself deeply into his memory.

Of course it would be absurd, but stranger things, he thought, had happened. He wondered if the girl was as afraid of him as of other men. She seemed not to be, but you couldn't tell much about her. She had kissed him one day with a strange warmth of manner, but it had been quite publicly in the presence of other people. When he left her at her door now it was after the least sentimental of partings, perhaps a shake of her hard little hand, or perhaps only a "S'long—see you at the show-shop!"

It was on one of these nights that she first invited him to dine with the Montague family. "I tried last night to get you on the telephone," she explained, "but they kept giving me someone else, or maybe I called wrong. Ain't these six-figured Los Angeles telephone numbers the limit? When you call 208972 or something, it sounds like paging a box-car. I was going to ask you over. Ma had cooked a lovely mess of corned beef and cabbage. Anyway, you come eat with us to-morrow night, will you? She'll have something else cooked up that will stick to the merry old slats. You can come home with me when we get in from work."

So it was that on the following night he enjoyed a home evening with the Montagues. Mrs. Montague had indeed cooked up something else, and had done it well; while Mr. Montague offered at the sideboard a choice of amateur distillations and brews which he warmly recommended to the guest. While the guest timidly considered, having had but the slightest experience with intoxicants, it developed that the confidence placed in his product by the hospitable old craftsman was not shared by his daughter.

"Keep off it," she warned, and then to her father, "Say, listen, Pa, have a heart; that boy's got to work to-morrow." "So be it, my child," replied Mr. Montague with a visible stiffening of manner. "Sylvester Montague is not the man to urge strong drink upon the reluctant or the over-cautious. I shall drink my aperatif alone."

"Go to it, old Pippin," rejoined his daughter as she vanished to the kitchen.

"Still, a little dish of liquor at this hour," continued the host suggestively when they were alone.

"Well"—Merton wished the girl had stayed—"perhaps just a few drops."

"Precisely, my boy, precisely. A mere dram." He poured the mere dram and his guest drank. It was a colourless, fiery stuff with an elusive taste of metal. Merton contrived an expression of pleasure under the searching glance of his host.

"Ah, I knew you would relish it. I fancy I could amaze you if I told you how recently it was made. Now here"—He grasped another bottle purposely—"is something a full ten days older. It has developed quite a bouquet. Just a drop—"

The guest graciously yet firmly waved a negation.

"Thanks," he said, "but I want to enjoy the last—it—it has so much flavour."

"It has; it has, indeed. I'll not urge you, of course. Later you must see the simple mechanism by which I work these wonders. Alone, then, I drink to you."

Mr. Montague alone drank of two other fruits of his loom before the ladies appeared with dinner. He was clean—shaven now and his fine face glowed with hospitality as he carved roast chickens. The talk was of the shop: of what Mr. Montague scornfully called "grind shows" when his daughter led it, and of the legitimate hall-show when he gained the leadership. He believed that moving pictures had sounded the knell of true dramatic art and said so in many ways.

He tried to imagine the sensations of Lawrence Barrett or Louis James could they behold Sylvester Montague, whom both these gentlemen had proclaimed to be no mean artist, enacting the role of a bar-room rowdy five days on end by reclining upon a sawdust floor with his back supported by a spirits barrel. The supposititious comments of the two placed upon the motion-picture industry the black guilt of having degraded a sterling artist to the level of a peep-show mountebank. They were frankly disgusted at the spectacle, and their present spokesman thought it as well that they had not actually lived to witness it—even the happier phases of this so-called art in which a mere chit of a girl might earn a living wage by falling downstairs for a so-called star, or the he-doll whippersnapper—Merton Gill flinched in spite of himself—could name his own salary for merely possessing a dimpled chin.

Further, an artist in the so-called art received his payment as if he had delivered groceries at one's back door. "You, I believe—"—The speaker addressed his guest—"are at present upon a pay-roll; but there are others, your elders-possibly your betters, though I do not say that—"

"You better not," remarked his daughter, only to be ignored.

"—others who must work a day and at the close of it receive a slip of paper emblazoned 'Talent Pay Check.' How more effectively could they cheapen the good word 'talent'? And at the foot of this slip you are made to sign, before receiving the pittance you have earned, a consent to the public exhibition for the purpose of trade or advertising, of the pictures for which you may have posed. Could tradesmen descend to a lower level, I ask you?"

"I'll have one for twelve fifty to-morrow night," said Mrs. Montague, not too dismally. "I got to do a duchess at a reception, and I certainly hope my feet don't hurt me again."

"Cheer up, old dears! Pretty soon you can both pick your parts," chirped their daughter. "Jeff's going to give me a contract, and then you can loaf forever for all I care. Only I know you won't, and you know you won't. Both of you'd act for nothing if you couldn't do it for money. What's the use of pretending?"

"The chit may be right, she may be right," conceded Mr. Montague sadly.

Later, while the ladies were again in the kitchen, Mr. Montague, after suggesting, "Something in the nature of an after-dinner cordial," quaffed one for himself and followed it with the one he had poured out for a declining guest who still treasured the flavour of his one aperitif.

He then led the way to the small parlour where he placed in action on the phonograph a record said to contain the ravings of John McCullough in his last hours. He listened to this emotionally.

"That's the sort of technique," he said, "that the so—called silver screen has made but a memory." He lighted his pipe, and identified various framed photographs that enlivened the walls of the little room. Many of them were of himself at an earlier age.

"My dear mother-in-law," he said, pointing to another. "A sterling artist, and in her time an ornament of the speaking stage. I was on tour when her last days came. She idolized me, and passed away with my name on her lips. Her last request was that a photograph of me should be placed in her casket before it went to its final resting place."

He paused, his emotion threatening to overcome him. Presently he brushed a hand across his eyes and continued, "I discovered later that they had picked out the most wretched of all my photographs—an atrocious thing I had supposed was destroyed. Can you imagine it?"

Apparently it was but the entrance of his daughter that saved him from an affecting collapse. His daughter removed the record of John McCullough's ravings, sniffed at it, and put a fox-trot in its place.

"He's got to learn to dance," she explained, laying hands upon the guest.

"Dancing—dancing!" murmured Mr. Montague, as if the very word recalled bitter memories.

With brimming eyes he sat beating time to the fox-trot measure while Merton Gill proved to all observers that his mastery of this dance would, if ever at all achieved, be only after long and discouraging effort.

"You forget all about your feet," remarked the girl as they paused, swaying to the rhythm. "Remember the feet—they're important in a dance. Now!—" But it was hard to remember his feet or, when he did recall them, to relate their movements even distantly to the music. When this had died despairingly, the girl surveyed her pupil with friendly but doubting eyes.

"Say, Pa, don't he remind you of someone? Remember the squirrel that joined out with us one time in the rep show and left 'East Lynne' flat right in the middle of the third act while he went down and announced the next night's play—the one that his name was Eddie Duffy and he called himself Clyde Maltravers?"

"In a way, in a way," agreed Mr. Montague dismally. "A certain lack of finish in the manner, perhaps."

"Remember how Charlie Dickman, the manager, nearly murdered him for it in the wings? Not that Charlie didn't have a right to. Well, this boy dances like Eddie Duffy would have danced."

"He was undeniably awkward and forgetful," said Mr. Montague. "Well do I recall a later night. We played Under the Gaslight; Charlie feared to trust him with a part, so he kept the young man off stage to help with the train noise when the down express should dash across. But even in this humble station he proved inefficient. When the train came on he became confused, seized the cocoanut shells instead of the sand-paper, and our train that night entered to the sound of a galloping horse. The effect must have been puzzling to the audience. Indeed, many of them seemed to consider it ludicrous. Charlie Dickman confided in me later. 'Syl, my boy,' says he, 'this bird Duffy has caused my first gray hairs.' It was little wonder that he persuaded young Duffy to abandon the drama. He was not meant for the higher planes of our art. Now our young friend here"—he pointed to the perspiring Merton Gill—"doesn't even seem able to master a simple dance step. I might say that he seems to out-Duffy Duffy—for Duffy could dance after a fashion."

"He'll make the grade yet," replied his daughter grimly, and again the music sounded. Merton Gill continued unconscious of his feet, or, remembering them, he became deaf to the music. But the girl brightened with a sudden thought when next they rested.

"I got it!" she announced. "We'll have about two hundred feet of this for the next picture—you trying to dance just the way you been doing with me. If you don't close to a good hand I'll eat my last pay-check."

The lessons ceased. She seemed no longer to think it desirable that her pupil should become proficient in the modern steps. He was puzzled by her decision. Why should one of Baird's serious plays need an actor who forgot his feet in a dance?

There were more social evenings at the Montague home. Twice the gathering was enlarged by other members of the film colony, a supper was served and poker played for inconsiderable stakes. In this game of chance the Montague girl proved to be conservative, not to say miserly, and was made to suffer genuinely when Merton Gill displayed a reckless spirit in the betting. That he amassed winnings of ninety-eight cents one night did not reassure her. She pointed out that he might easily have lost this sum.

She was indeed being a mother to the defenceless boy. It was after a gambling session that she demanded to be told what he was doing with his salary. His careless hazarding of poker-chips had caused her to be fearful of his general money sense.

Merton Gill had indeed been reckless. He was now, he felt, actually one of the Hollywood set. He wondered how Tessie Kearns would regard his progress. Would she be alarmed to know he attended those gay parties that so often brought the film colony into unfavourable public notice? Jolly dinners, dancing, gambling, drinking with actresses—for Mr. Montague had at last turned out a beer that met with the approval not only of his guests but of his own more exacting family. The vivacious brew would now and again behave unreasonably at the moment of being released, but it was potable when subdued.

It was a gay life, Merton felt. And as for the Montague girl's questions and warnings about his money, he would show her! He had, of course, discharged his debt to her in the first two weeks of his work with Baird. Now he would show her what he really thought of money.

He would buy her a gift whose presentation should mark a certain great occasion. It should occur on the eve of his screen debut, and would fittingly testify his gratitude. For the girl, after all, had made him what he was. And the first piece was close to its premiere. Already he had seen advance notices in the newspapers. The piece was called Hearts On Fire, and in it, so the notices said, the comedy manager had at last realized an ambition long nourished. He had done something new and something big: a big thing done in a big way. The Montague girl would see that the leading man who had done so much to insure the success of Baird's striving for the worth-while drama was not unforgetful of her favours and continuous solicitude.

He thought first of a ring, but across the blank brick wall of the jewellery shop he elected to patronize was an enormous sign in white: The House of Lucky Wedding Rings. This staring announcement so alarmed him that he not only abandoned the plan for a ring-any sort of ring might be misconstrued, he saw-but in an excess of caution chose another establishment not so outspoken. If it kept wedding rings at all, it was decently reticent about them, and it did keep a profusion of other trinkets about which a possible recipient could entertain no false notions. Wrist watches, for example. No one could find subtle or hidden meanings in a wrist watch.

He chose a bauble that glittered prettily on its black silk bracelet, and was not shocked in the least when told by the engaging salesman that its price was a sum for which in the old days Gashwiler had demanded a good ten weeks of his life. Indeed it seemed rather cheap to him when he remembered the event it should celebrate. Still, it was a pleasing trifle and did not look cheap.

"Do you warrant it to keep good time?" he sternly demanded.

The salesman became diplomatic, though not without an effect of genial man-to-man frankness. "Well, I guess you and I both know what women's bracelet-watches are." He smiled a superior masculine smile that drew his customer within the informed brotherhood. "Now here, there's a platinum little thing that costs seven hundred and fifty, and this one you like will keep just as good time as that one that costs six hundred more. What could be fairer than that?"

"All right," said the customer. "I'll take it." During the remaining formalities attending the purchase the salesman, observing that he dealt with a tolerant man of the world, became even franker. "Of course no one," he remarked pleasantly while couching the purchase in a chaste bed of white satin, "expects women's bracelet-watches to keep time. Not even the women."

"Want 'em for looks," said the customer.

"You've hit it, you've hit it!" exclaimed the salesman delightedly, as if the customer had expertly probed the heart of a world-old mystery.

He had now but to await his great moment. The final scenes of the new piece were shot. Again he was resting between pictures. As the date for showing the first piece drew near he was puzzled to notice that both Baird and the Montague girl curiously avoided any mention of it. Several times he referred to it in their presence, but they seemed resolutely deaf to his "Well, I see the big show opens Monday night."

He wondered if there could be some recondite bit of screen etiquette which he was infringing. Actors were superstitious, he knew. Perhaps it boded bad luck to talk of a forthcoming production. Baird and the girl not only ignored his reference to Hearts on Fire, but they left Baird looking curiously secretive and the Montague girl looking curiously frightened. It perplexed him. Once he was smitten with a quick fear that his own work in this serious drama had not met the expectations of the manager.

However, in this he must be wrong, for Baird not only continued cordial but, as the girl had prophesied, he urged upon his new actor the signing of a long-time contract. The Montague girl had insisted upon being present at this interview, after forbidding Merton to put his name to any contract of which she did not approve. "I told Jeff right out that I was protecting you," she said. "He understands he's got to be reasonable."

It appeared, as they set about Baird's desk in the Buckeye office, that she had been right. Baird submitted rather gracefully, after but slight demur, to the terms which Miss Montague imposed in behalf of her protege. Under her approving eye Merton Gill affixed his name to a contract by which Baird was to pay him a salary of two hundred and fifty dollars a week for three years.

It seemed an incredible sum. As he blotted his signature he was conscious of a sudden pity for the manager. The Montague girl had been hard—hard as nails, he thought—and Baird, a victim to his own good nature, would probably lose a great deal of money. He resolved never to press his advantage over a man who had been caught in a weak moment.

"I just want to say, Mr. Baird," he began, "that you needn't be afraid I'll hold you to this paper if you find it's too much money to pay me. I wouldn't have taken it at all if it hadn't been for her." He pointed an almost accusing finger at the girl.

Baird grinned; the girl patted his hand. Even at grave moments she was a patter. "That's all right, Son," she said soothingly. "Jeff's got all the best of it, and Jeff knows it, too. Don't you, Jeff?"

"Well—" Baird considered. "If his work keeps up I'm not getting any the worst of it."

"You said it. You know very well what birds will be looking for this boy next week, and what money they'll have in their mitts.

"Maybe," said Baird.

"Well, you got the best of it, and you deserve to have. I ain't ever denied that, have I? You've earned the best of it the way you've handled him. All I'm here for, I didn't want you to have too much the best of it, see? I think I treated you well."

"You're all right, Flips." "Well, everything's jake, then?"

"Everything's jake with me."

"All right! And about his work keeping up—trust your old friend and well-wisher. And say, Jeff—" Her eyes gleamed reminiscently. "You ain't caught him dancing yet. Well—wait, that's all. We'll put on a fox-trot in the next picture that will sure hog the footage."

As this dialogue progressed, Merton had felt more and more like a child in the presence of grave and knowing elders. They had seemed to forget him, to forget that the amazing contract just signed bore his name. He thought the Montague girl was taking a great deal upon herself. Her face, he noted, when she had stated terms to Baird, was the face she wore when risking a small bet at poker on a high hand. She seemed old, indeed. But he knew how he was going to make her feel younger. In his pocket was a gift of rare beauty, even if you couldn't run railway trains by it. And pretty things made a child of her.

Baird shook hands with him warmly at parting. "It'll be a week yet before we start on the new piece. Have a good time. Oh, yes, and drop around some time next week if there's any little thing you want to talk over—or maybe you don't understand."

He wondered if this were a veiled reference to the piece about to be shown. Certainly nothing more definite was said about it. Yet it was a thing that must be of momentous interest to the manager, and the manager must know that it would be thrilling to the actor.

He left with the Montague girl, who had become suddenly grave and quiet. But outside the Holden lot, with one of those quick transitions he had so often remarked in her, she brightened with a desperate sort of gaiety.

"I'll tell you what!" she exclaimed. "Let's go straight down town—it'll be six by the time we get there—and have the best dinner money can buy: lobster and chicken and vanilla ice-cream and everything, right in a real restaurant—none of this tray stuff—and I'll let you pay for it all by yourself. You got a right to, after that contract. And we'll be gay, and all the extra people that's eating in the restaurant'll think we're a couple o' prominent film actors. How about it?" She danced at his side.

"We'll have soup, too," he amended. "One of those thick ones that costs about sixty cents. Sixty cents just for soup!" he repeated, putting a hand to the contract that now stiffened one side of his coat.

"Well, just this once," she agreed. "It might be for the last time."

"Nothing like that," he assured her. "More you spend, more you make—that's my motto."

They waited for a city-bound car, sitting again on the bench that was so outspoken. "You furnish the girl, we furnish the home," it shouted. He put his back against several of the bold words and felt of the bracelet-watch in his pocket.

"It might be the last time for me," insisted the girl. "I feel as if I might die most any time. My health's breaking down under the strain. I feel kind of a fever coming on right this minute."

"Maybe you shouldn't go out."

"Yes, I should."

They boarded the car and reached the real restaurant, a cozy and discreet resort up a flight of carpeted stairs. Side by side on a seat that ran along the wall they sat at a table for two and the dinner was ordered. "Ruin yourself if you want to," said the girl as her host included celery and olives in the menu. "Go on and order prunes, too, for all I care. I'm reckless. Maybe I'll never have another dinner, the way this fever's coming on. Feel my hand."

Under the table she wormed her hand into his, and kept it there until food came. "Do my eyes look very feverish?" she asked.

"Not so very," he assured her, covering an alarm he felt for the first time. She did appear to be feverish, and the anxiety of her manner deepened as the meal progressed. It developed quickly that she had but scant appetite for the choice food now being served. She could only taste bits here and there. Her plates were removed with their delicacies almost intact. Between courses her hand would seek his, gripping it as if in some nameless dread. He became worried about her state; his own appetite suffered.

Once she said as her hot hand clung to his, "I know where you'll be to-morrow night." Her voice grew mournful, despairing. "And I know perfectly well it's no good asking you to stay away."

He let this pass. Could it be that the girl was already babbling in delirium?

"And all the time," she presently went on, "I'll simply be sick a-bed, picking at the covers, all blue around the gills. That'll be me, while you're off to your old motion picture—'the so-called art of the motion picture,'" she concluded with a careful imitation of her father's manner.

He tried to determine whether she were serious or jesting. You never could tell about this girl. Whatever it was, it made him uneasy.

Outside he wished to take her home in a taxi-cab, but she would not hear to this. "We'll use the town-car, Gaston," she announced with a flash of her old manner as she waved to an on-coming street-car. During the long ride that followed she was silent but restless, tapping her foot, shifting in her seat, darting her head about. The one thing she did steadily was to clutch his arm.

During the walk from the car to the Montague house she twice indulged in her little dance step, even as she clung to the arm, but each time she seemed to think little of it and resumed a steady pace, her head down. The house was dark. Without speaking she unlocked the door and drew him into the little parlour.

"Stand right on that spot," she ordered, with a final pat of his shoulder, and made her way to the dining room beyond where she turned on a single light that faintly illumined the room in which he waited. She came back to him, removed the small cloth hat, tossed it to a chair, and faced him silently.

The light from the other room shone across her eyes and revealed them to him shadowy and mysterious. Her face was set in some ominous control. At last she looked away from him and began in a strained voice, "If anything happens to me—"

He thought it time to end this nonsense. She might be feverish, but it could be nothing so serious as she was intimating. He clutched the gift. "Sarah," he said lightly, "I got a little something for you—see what I mean?" He thrust the package into her weakly yielding hands.

She studied it in the dusk, turning it over and over. Then with no word to him she took it to the dining room where under the light she opened it. He heard a smothered exclamation that seemed more of dismay than the delight he expected, though he saw that she was holding the watch against her wrist. She came back to the dusk of the parlour, beginning on the way one of her little skipping dance steps, which she quickly suppressed. She was replacing the watch on its splendid couch of satin and closing the box.

"I never saw such a man!" she exclaimed with an irritation that he felt to be artificial. "After all you've been through, I should think you'd have learned the value of money. Anyway, it's too beautiful for me. And anyway, I couldn't take it—not to-night, anyway. And anyway—" Her voice had acquired a huskiness in this speech that now left her incoherent, and the light revealed a wetness in her eyes. She dabbed at them with a handkerchief. "Of course you can take it to-night," he said in masterful tones, "after all you've done for me."

"Now you listen," she began. "You don't know all I've done for you. You don't know me at all. Suppose something came out about me that you didn't think I'd 'a' been guilty of. You can't ever tell about people in this business. You don't know me at all-not one little bit. I might 'a' done lots of things that would turn you against me. I tell you you got to wait and find out about things. I haven't the nerve to tell you, but you'll find out soon enough—"

The expert in photoplays suffered a sudden illumination. This was a scene he could identify—a scene in which the woman trembled upon the verge of revealing to the man certain sinister details of her past, spurred thereto by a scoundrel who blackmailed her. He studied the girl in a new light. Undoubtedly, from her words, he saw one panic-stricken by the threatened exposure of some dreadful complication in her own past. Certainly she was suffering.

"I don't care if this fever does carry me off," she went on. "I know you could never feel the same toward me after you found out—"

Again she was dabbing at her eyes, this time with the sleeve of her jacket. A suffering woman stood before him. She who had always shown herself so competent to meet trouble with laughing looks was being overthrown by this nameless horror. Suddenly he knew that to him it didn't matter so very much what crime she had been guilty of.

"I don't care what you've done," he said, his own voice husky. She continued to weep.

He felt himself grow hot. "Listen here, Kid"—He now spoke with more than a touch of the bully in his tone—"stop this nonsense. You—you come here and give me a good big kiss—see what I mean?"

She looked up at him from wet eyes, and amazingly through her anguish she grinned. "You win!" she said, and came to him.

He was now the masterful one. He took her protectingly in his arms. He kissed her though with no trace of the Parmalee technique. His screen experience might never have been. It was more like the dead days of Edwina May Pulver.

"Now you stop it," he soothed—"all this nonsense!" His cheek was against hers and his arms held her. "What do I care what you've done in your past—what do I care? And listen here, Kid"—There was again the brutal note of the bully in his voice—"don't ever do any more of those stunts—see what I mean? None of that falling off streetcars or houses or anything. Do you hear?"

He felt that he was being masterful indeed. He had swept her off her feet. Probably now she would weep violently and sob out her confession. But a moment later he was reflecting, as he had so many times before reflected, that you never could tell about the girl. In his embrace she had become astoundingly calm. That emotional crisis threatening to beat down all her reserves had passed. She reached up and almost meditatively pushed back the hair from his forehead, regarding him with eyes that were still shadowed but dry. Then she gave him a quick little hug and danced away. It was no time for dancing, he thought.

"Now you sit down," she ordered. She was almost gay again, yet with a nervous, desperate gaiety that would at moments die to a brooding solemnity. "And listen," she began, when he had seated himself in bewilderment at her sudden change of mood, "you'll be off to your old motion picture to-morrow night, and I'll be here sick in bed—"

"I won't go if you don't want me to," he put in quickly.

"That's no good; you'd have to go sometime. The quicker the better, I guess. I'll go myself sometime, if I ever get over this disease that's coming on me. Anyway, you go, and then if you ever see me again you can give me this—" She quickly came to put the watch back in his hands. "Yes, yes, take it. I won't have it till you give it to me again, if I'm still alive." She held up repulsing hands. "Now we've had one grand little evening, and I'll let you go." She went to stand by the door.

He arose and stood by her. "All this nonsense!" he grumbled. "I—I won't stand for it—see what I mean?" Very masterfully again he put his arms about her. "Say," he demanded, "are you afraid of me like you said you'd always been afraid of men?"

"Yes, I am. I'm afraid of you a whole lot. I don't know how you'll take it." "Take what?"

"Oh, anything—anything you're going to get."

"Well, you don't seem to be afraid of me."

"I am, more than any one."

"Well, Sarah, you needn't be—no matter what you've done. You just forget it and give me a good big—"

"I'm glad I'm using my own face in this scene," murmured Sarah.

Down at the corner, waiting for his car, he paced back and forth in front of the bench with its terse message—"You furnish the girl, we furnish the house"— Sarah was a funny little thing with all that nonsense about what he would find out. Little he cared if she'd done something—forgery, murder, anything.

He paused in his stride and addressed the vacant bench: "Well, I've done my part."

CHAPTER XVIII. "FIVE REELS-500 LAUGHS"

It occurred to him the next morning that he might have taken too lightly Sarah's foreboding of illness. Reviewing her curious behaviour he thought it possible she might be in for something serious.

But a midday telephone call at the Montague home brought assurances from the mother that quieted this fear. Sarah complained of not feeling well, and was going to spend a quiet day at home. But Mrs. Montague was certain it was nothing serious. No; she had no temperature. No fever at all. She was just having a spell of thinking about things, sort of grouchy like. She had been grouchy to both her parents. Probably because she wasn't working. No, she said she wouldn't come to the telephone. She also said she was in a bad way and might pass out any minute. But that was just her kidding. It was kind of Mr. Gill to call up. He wasn't to worry.

He continued to worry, however, until the nearness of his screen debut drove Sarah to the back of his mind. Undoubtedly it was just her nonsense. And in the meantime, that long—baffled wish to see himself in a serious drama was about to be gratified in fullest measure. He was glad the girl had not suggested that she be with him on this tremendous occasion. He wanted to be quite alone, solitary in the crowd, free to enjoy his own acting without pretense of indifference.

The Pattersons, of course, were another matter. He had told them of his approaching debut and they were making an event of it. They would attend, though he would not sit with them. Mr. Patterson in his black suit, his wife in society raiment, would sit downstairs and would doubtless applaud their lodger; but he would be remote from them; in a far corner of the topmost gallery, he first thought, for Hearts on Fire was to be shown in one of the big down-town theatres where a prominent member of its cast could lose himself.

He had told the Pattersons a little about the story. It was pretty pathetic in spots, he said, but it all came right in the end, and there were some good Western scenes. When the Pattersons said he must be very good in it, he found himself unable to achieve the light fashion of denial and protestation that would have become him. He said he had struggled to give the world something better and finer. For a moment he was moved to confess that Mrs. Patterson, in the course of his struggles, had come close to losing ten dollars, but he mastered the wild impulse. Some day, after a few more triumphs, he might laughingly confide this to her.

The day was long. Slothfully it dragged hours that seemed endless across the company of shining dreams that he captained. He was early at the theatre, first of early comers, and entered quickly, foregoing even a look at the huge lithographs in front that would perhaps show his very self in some gripping scene.

With an empty auditorium to choose from, he compromised on a balcony seat. Down below would doubtless be other members of the company, probably Baird himself, and he did not wish to be recognized. He must be alone with his triumph. And the loftier gallery would be too far away.

The house filled slowly. People sauntered to their seats as if the occasion were ordinary; even when the seats were occupied and the orchestra had played, there ensued the annoying delays of an educational film and a travelogue. Upon this young actor's memory would be forever seared the information that the conger eel lays fifteen million eggs at one time and that the inhabitants of Upper Burmah have quaint native pastimes. These things would stay with him, but they were unimportant. Even the prodigal fecundity of the conger eel left him cold.

He gripped the arms of his seat when the cast of Hearts on Fire was flung to the screen. He caught his own name instantly, and was puzzled. "Clifford Armytage—By Himself." Someone had bungled that, but no matter. Then at once he was seeing that first scene of his. As a popular screen idol he breakfasted in his apartment, served by a valet who was a hero worshipper.

He was momentarily disquieted by the frank adoration of the cross-eyed man in this part. While acting the scene, he remembered now that he had not always been able to observe his valet. There were moments when he seemed over-emphatic. The valet was laughed at. The watcher's sympathy went out to Baird, who must be seeing his serious effort taken too lightly.

There came the scene where he looked at the photograph album. But now his turning of the pages was interspersed with close-ups of the portraits he regarded so admiringly. And these astonishingly proved to be enlarged stills of Clifford Armytage, the art studies of Lowell Hardy. It was puzzling. On the screen he capably beamed the fondest admiration, almost reverent in its intensity—and there would appear the still of Merton bidding an emotional farewell to his horse. The very novelty of it held him for a moment—Gashwiler's Dexter actually on the screen! He was aroused by the hearty laughter of an immense audience.

"It's Parmalee," announced a hoarse neighbour on his right. "He's imitatin' Harold! Say, the kid's clever!"

The laughter continued during the album scene. He thought of Baird, somewhere in that audience, suffering because his play was made fun of. He wished he could remind him that scenes were to follow which would surely not be taken lightly. For himself, he was feeling that at least his strong likeness to Parmalee had been instantly admitted. They were laughing, as the Montague girl had laughed that first morning, because the resemblance was so striking. But now on the screen, after the actor's long fond look at himself, came the words, "The Only Man He Ever Loved."

Laughter again. The watcher felt himself grow hot. Had Baird been betrayed by one of his staff?

The scene with the letters followed. Clothes baskets of letters. His own work, as he opened a few from the top, was all that he could have wished. He was finely Harold Parmalee, and again the hoarse neighbour whispered, "Ain't he got Parmalee dead, though?"

"Poor, silly little girls!" the screen exclaimed, and the audience became noisy. Undoubtedly it was a tribute to his perfection in the Parmalee manner. But he was glad that now there would come acting at which no one could laugh. There was the delicatessen shop, the earnest young cashier and his poor old mother who mopped. He saw himself embrace her and murmur words of encouragement, but incredibly there were giggles from the audience, doubtless from base souls who were impervious to pathos. The giggles coalesced to a general laugh when the poor old mother, again mopping on the floor, was seen to say, "I hate these mopping mothers. You get took with house-maid's knee in the first reel."

Again he was seized with a fear that one of Baird's staff had been clumsy with subtitles. His eyes flew to his own serious face when the silly words had gone.

The drama moved. Indeed the action of the shadows was swifter than he supposed it would be. The dissolute son of the proprietor came on to dust the wares and to elicit a laugh when he performed a bit of business that had escaped Merton at the time. Against the wire screen that covered the largest cheese on the counter he placed a placard, "Dangerous. Do not Annoy."

Probably Baird had not known of this clowning. And there came another subtitle that would dismay Baird when the serious young bookkeeper enacted his scene with the proprietor's lovely daughter, for she was made to say: "You love above your station. Ours is 125th Street; you get off at 59th."

He was beginning to feel confused. A sense of loss, of panic, smote him. His own part was the intensely serious thing he had played, but in some subtle way even that was being made funny. He could not rush to embrace his old mother without exciting laughter.

The robbery of the safe was effected by the dissolute son, the father broke in upon the love scene, discovered the loss of his money, and accused an innocent man. Merton felt that he here acted superbly. His long look at the girl for whom he was making the supreme sacrifice brought tears to his own eyes, but still the witless audience snickered. Unobserved by the others, the old mother now told her son the whereabouts of the stolen money, and he saw himself secure the paper sack of bills from the ice-box. He detected the half-guilty look of which he had spoken to Baird. Then he read his own incredible speech—"I better take this cool million. It might get that poor lad into trouble!" Again the piece had been hurt by a wrong subtitle. But perhaps the audience laughed because it was accustomed to laugh at Baird's productions. Perhaps it had not realized that he was now attempting one of the worth-while things. This reasoning was refuted as he watched what occurred after he had made his escape.

His flight was discovered, policemen entered, a rapid search behind counters ensued. In the course of this the wire screen over the biggest cheese was knocked off the counter. The cheese leaped to the floor, and the searchers, including the policemen, fled in panic through the front door. The Montague girl, the last to escape, was seen to announce, "The big cheese is loose—it's eating all the little ones!"

A band of intrepid firemen, protected by masks and armed with axes, rushed in. A terrific struggle ensued. The delicatessen shop was wrecked. And through it all the old mother continued to mop the floor. Merton Gill, who had first grown hot, was now cold. Icy drops were on his chilled brow. How had Hearts on Fire gone wrong?

Then they were in the great open spaces of the Come All Ye dance hall. There was the young actor in his Buck Benson costume, protecting his mother from the brutality of a Mexican, getting his man later by firing directly into a mirror—Baird had said it would come right in the exposure, but it hadn't. And the witless cackled.

He saw his struggle with the detective. With a real thrill he saw himself bear his opponent to the ground, then hurl him high and far into the air, to be impaled upon the antlers of an elk's head suspended back of the bar. He saw himself lightly dust his sleeves after this feat, and turn aside with the words, "That's one Lodge he can join."

Then followed a scene he had not been allowed to witness. There swung Marcel, the detective, played too emphatically by the cross-eyed man. An antler point suspended him by the seat of his trousers. He hung limply a moment, then took from his pocket a saw with which he reached up to contrive his release. He sawed through the antler and fell. He tried to stand erect, but appeared to find this impossible. A subtitle announced: "He had put a permanent wave in Marcel."

This base fooling was continuously blown upon by gales of stupid laughter. But not yet did Merton Gill know the worst. The merriment persisted through his most affecting bit, the farewell to his old pal outside—how could they have laughed at a simple bit of pathos like that? But the watching detective was seen to weep bitterly.

"Look a' him doin' Buck Benson," urged the hoarse neighbour gleefully. "You got to hand it to that kid—say, who is he, anyway?"

Followed the thrilling leap from a second-story window to the back of the waiting pal. The leap began thrillingly, but not only was it shown that the escaping man had donned a coat and a false mustache in the course of his fall, but at its end he was revealed slowly, very slowly, clambering into the saddle!

They had used here, he saw, one of those slow cameras that seem to suspend all action interminably, a cruel device in this instance. And for his actual escape, when he had ridden the horse beyond camera range at a safe walk, they had used another camera that gave the effect of intense speed. The old horse had walked, but with an air of swiftness that caused the audience intense delight.

Entered Marcel, the detective, in another scene Merton had not watched. He emerged from the dance-hall to confront a horse that remained, an aged counterpart of the horse Merton had ridden off. Marcel stared intently into the beast's face, whereupon it reared and plunged as if terrified by the spectacle of the cross-eyed man.

Merton recalled the horse in the village that had seemed to act so intelligently. Probably a shot-gun had stimulated the present scene. The detective thereupon turned aside, hastily donned his false mustache and Sherlock Holmes cap, and the deceived horse now permitted him to mount. He, too, walked off to the necromancy of a lens that multiplied his pace a thousandfold. And the audience rocked in its seats.

One horse still remained before the dance-hall. The old mother emerged. With one anguished look after the detective, she gathered up her disreputable skirts and left the platform in a flying leap to land in the saddle. There was no trickery about the speed at which her horse, belaboured with the mop-pail, galloped in pursuit of the others. A subtitle recited—"She has watched her dear ones leave the old nest flat. Now she must go out over the hills and mop the other side of them!"

Now came the sensational capture by lasso of the detective. But the captor had not known that, as he dragged his quarry at the rope's end, the latter had somehow possessed himself of a sign which he later walked in with, a sign reading, "Join the Good Roads Movement!" nor that the faithful old mother had ridden up to deposit her inverted mop-pail over his head.

Merton Gill had twice started to leave. He wanted to leave. But each time he found himself chained there by the evil fascination of this monstrous parody. He remained to learn that the Montague girl had come out to the great open spaces to lead a band of train-robbers from the "Q.T. ranche."

He saw her ride beside a train and cast her lasso over the stack of the locomotive. He saw her pony settle back on its haunches while the rope grew taut and the train was forced to a halt. He saw the passengers lined up by the wayside and forced to part with their valuables. Later, when the band returned to the ranche with their booty, he saw the dissolute brother, after the treasure was divided, winning it back to the family coffers with his dice. He saw the stricken father playing golf on his bicycle in grotesque imitation of a polo player.

And still, so incredible the revealment, he had not in the first shock of it seemed to consider Baird in any way to blame. Baird had somehow been deceived by his actors. Yet a startling suspicion was forming amid his mental flurries, a suspicion that bloomed to certainty when he saw himself the ever-patient victim of the genuine hidalgo spurs.

Baird had said he wanted the close-ups merely for use in determining how the spurs could be mastered, yet here they were. Merton Gill caught the spurs in undergrowth and caught them in his own chaps, arising from each fall with a look of gentle determination that appealed strongly to the throng of lackwits. They shrieked at each of his failures, even when he ran to greet his pictured sweetheart and fell headlong. They found the comedy almost unbearable when at Baird's direction he had begun to toe in as he walked. And he had fallen clumsily again when he flew to that last glad rendezvous where the pair were irised out in a love triumphant, while the old mother mopped a large rock in the background. An intervening close-up of this rock revealed her tearful face as she cleansed the granite surface. Above her loomed a painted exhortation to "Use Wizard Spine Pills." And of this pathetic old creature he was made to say, even as he clasped the beloved in his arms—"Remember, she is my mother. I will not desert her now just because I am rich and grand!"

At last he was free. Amid applause that was long and sincere he gained his feet and pushed a way out. His hoarse neighbour was saying, "Who is the kid, anyway? Ain't he a wonder!"

He pulled his hat down, dreading he might be recognized and shamed before these shallow fools. He froze with the horror of what he had been unable to look away from. The ignominy of it! And now, after those spurs, he knew full well that Baird had betrayed him. As the words shaped in his mind, a monstrous echo of them reverberated through its caverns—the Montague girl had betrayed him!

He understood her now, and burned with memories of her uneasiness the night before. She had been suffering acutely from remorse; she had sought to cover it with pleas of physical illness. At the moment he was conscious of no feeling toward her save wonder that she could so coolly have played him false. But the thing was not to be questioned. She—and Baird—had made a fool of him.

As he left the theatre, the crowd about him commented approvingly on the picture: "Who's this new comedian?" he heard a voice inquire. But "Ain't he a wonder!" seemed to be the sole reply.

He flushed darkly. So they thought him a comedian. Well, Baird wouldn't think so—not after to-morrow. He paused outside the theatre now to study the lithograph in colours. There he hurled Marcel to the antlers of the elk. The announcement was "Hearts on Fire! A Jeff Baird Comedy. Five Reels-500 Laughs."

Baird, he sneeringly reflected, had kept faith with his patrons if not with one of his actors. But how he had profaned the sunlit glories of the great open West and its virile drama! And the spurs, as he had promised the unsuspecting wearer, had stood out! The horror of it, blinding, desolating!

And he had as good as stolen that money himself, taking it out to the great open spaces to spend in a bar-room. Baird's serious effort had turned out to be a wild, inconsequent farrago of the most painful nonsense.

But it was over for Merton Gill. The golden bowl was broken, the silver cord was loosed. To-morrow he would tear up Baird's contract and hurl the pieces in Baird's face. As to the Montague girl, that deceiving jade was hopeless. Never again could he trust her.

In a whirling daze of resentment he boarded a car for the journey home. A group seated near him still laughed about Hearts on Fire. "I thought he'd kill me with those spurs," declared an otherwise sanely behaving young woman—"that hurt, embarrassed look on his face every time he'd get up!"

He cowered in his seat. And he remembered another ordeal he must probably face when he reached home. He hoped the Pattersons would be in bed, and walked up and down before the gate when he saw the house still alight. But the light stayed, and at last he nerved himself for a possible encounter. He let himself in softly, still hoping he could gain his room undiscovered; but Mrs. Patterson framed herself in the lighted door of the living room and became exclamatory at sight of him.

And he who had thought to stand before these people in shame to receive their condolences now perceived that his trial would be of another but hardly less-distressing sort. For somehow, so dense were these good folks, that he must seem to be not displeased with his own performance. Amazingly they congratulated him, struggling with reminiscent laughter as they did so.

"And you never told us you was one of them funny comedians," chided Mrs. Patterson. "We thought you was just a beginner, and here you got the biggest part in the picture! Say, the way you acted when you'd pick yourself up after them spurs threw you—I'll wake up in the night laughing at that."

"And the way he kept his face so straight when them other funny ones was cutting their capers all around him," observed Mr. Patterson.

"Yes! wasn't it wonderful, Jed, the way he never let on, keeping his face as serious as if he'd been in a serious play?"

"I like to fell off my seat," added Mr. Patterson.

"I'll tell you something, Mr. Armytage," began Mrs. Patterson with a suddenly serious manner of her own, "I never been one to flatter folks to their faces unless I felt it from the bottom of my heart—I never been that kind; when I tell a person such-and-such about themselves they can take it for the truth's own truth; so you can believe me now—I saw lots of times in that play to-night when you was even funnier than the cross-eyed man."

The young actor was regarding her strangely; seemingly he wished to acknowledge this compliment but could find no suitable words. "Yes, you can blush and hem and haw," went on his critic, "but any one knows me I'll tell you I mean it when I talk that way—yes, sir, funnier than the cross-eyed man himself. My, I guess the neighbours'll be talking soon's they find out we got someone as important as you be in our spare-room—and, Mr. Armytage, I want you to give me a signed photograph of yourself, if you'll be so good."

He escaped at last, dizzy from the maelstrom of conflicting emotions that had caught and whirled him. It had been impossible not to appear, and somehow difficult not to feel, gratified under this heartfelt praise. He had been bound to appear pleased but incredulous, even when she pronounced him superior, at times, to the cross-eyed man—though the word she used was "funnier."

Betrayed by his friends, stricken, disconsolate, in a panic of despair, he had yet seemed glad to hear that he had been "funny." He flew to the sanctity of his room. Not again could he bear to be told that the acting which had been his soul's high vision was a thing for merriment.

He paced his room a long time, a restless, defenceless victim to recurrent visions of his shame. Implacably they returned to torture him. Reel after reel of the ignoble stuff, spawned by the miscreant, Baird, flashed before him; a world of base painted shadows in which he had been the arch offender.

Again and again he tried to make clear to himself just why his own acting should have caused mirth. Surely he had been serious; he had given the best that was in him.

And the groundlings had guffawed!

Perhaps it was a puzzle he could never solve. And now he first thought of the new piece.

This threw him into fresh panic. What awful things, with his high and serious acting, would he have been made to do in that? Patiently, one by one, he went over the scenes in which he had appeared. Dazed, confused, his recollection could bring to him little that was ambiguous in them. But also he had played through Hearts on Fire with little suspicion of its low intentions.

He went to bed at last, though to toss another hour in fruitless effort to solve this puzzle and to free his eyes of those flashing infamies of the night. Ever and again as he seemed to become composed, free at last of tormenting visions, a mere subtitle would flash in his brain, as where the old mother, when he first punished her insulter, was made by the screen to call out, "Kick him on the knee-cap, too!"

But the darkness refreshed his tired eyes, and sun at last brought him a merciful outlet from a world in which you could act your best and still be funnier than a cross-eyed man.

He awakened long past his usual hour and occupied his first conscious moments in convincing himself that the scandal of the night before had not been a bad dream. The shock was a little dulled now. He began absurdly to remember the comments of those who had appeared to enjoy the unworthy entertainment. Undoubtedly many people had mentioned him with warm approval. But such praise was surely nothing to take comfort from. He was aroused from this retrospection by a knock on his door. It proved to be Mr. Patterson bearing a tray. "Mrs. P. thought that you being up so late last night mebbe would like a cup of coffee and a bite of something before you went out." The man's manner was newly respectful. In this house, at least, Merton Gill was still someone.

He thanked his host, and consumed the coffee and toast with a novel sense of importance. The courtesy was unprecedented. Mrs. Patterson had indeed been sincere. And scarcely had he finished dressing when Mr. Patterson was again at the door.

"A gentleman downstairs to see you, Mr. Armytage. He says his name is Walberg but you don't know him. He says it's a business matter."

"Very well, I'll be down." A business matter? He had no business matters with any one except Baird.

He was smitten with a quick and quite illogical fear. Perhaps he would not have to tear up that contract and hurl it in the face of the manager who had betrayed him. Perhaps the manager himself would do the tearing. Perhaps Baird, after seeing the picture, had decided that Merton Gill would not do. Instantly he felt resentful. Hadn't he given the best that was in him? Was it his fault if other actors had turned into farce one of the worth-while things?

He went to meet Mr. Walberg with this resentment so warm that his greeting of the strange gentleman was gruff and short. The caller, an alert, businesslike man, came at once to his point. He was, it proved, not the representative of a possibly repenting Baird. He was, on the contrary, representing a rival producer. He extended his card—The Bigart Comedies.

"I got your address from the Holden office, Mr. Armytage. I guess I routed you out of bed, eh? Well, it's like this, if you ain't sewed up with Baird yet, the Bigart people would like to talk a little business to you. How about it?"

"Business?" Mr. Armytage fairly exploded this. He was unhappy and puzzled; in consequence, unamiable.

"Sure, business," confirmed Mr. Walberg. "I understand you just finished another five-reeler for the Buckeye outfit, but how about some stuff for us now? We can give you as good a company as that one last night and a good line of comedy. We got a gag man that simply never gets to the end of his string. He's doping out something right now that would fit you like a glove—and say, it would be a great idea to kind a' specialize in that spur act of yours. That got over big. We could work it in again. An act like that's good for a million laughs."

Mr. Armytage eyed Mr. Walberg coldly. Even Mr. Walberg felt an extensive area of glaciation setting in.

"I wouldn't think of it," said the actor, still gruffly.

"Do you mean that you can't come to the Bigart at all—on any proposition?"

"That's what I mean," confirmed Mr. Armytage.

"Would three hundred and fifty a week interest you?"

"No," said Mr. Armytage, though he gulped twice before achieving it.

Mr. Walberg reported to his people that this Armytage lad was one hard-boiled proposition. He'd seen lots of 'em in his time, but this bird was a wonder.

Yet Mr. Armytage was not really so granitic of nature as the Bigart emissary had thought him. He had begun the interview with a smouldering resentment due to a misapprehension; he had been outraged by a suggestion that the spurs be again put to their offensive use; and he had been stunned by an offer of three hundred and fifty dollars a week. That was all.

Here was a new angle to the puzzles that distracted him. He was not only praised by the witless, but he had been found desirable by certain discerning overlords of filmdom. What could be the secret of a talent that caused people, after viewing it but once, to make reckless offers?

And another thing—why had he allowed Baird to "sew him up"? The Montague girl again occupied the foreground of his troubled musings. She, with her airs of wise importance, had helped to sew him up. She was a helpless thing, after all, and false of nature. He would have matters out with her this very day. But first he must confront Baird in a scene of scorn and reprobation.

On the car he became aware that far back in remote caverns of his mind there ran a teasing memory of some book on the shelves of the Simsbury public library. He was sure it was not a book he had read. It was merely the title that hid itself. Only this had ever interested him, and it but momentarily. So much he knew. A book's title had lodged in his mind, remained there, and was now curiously stirring in some direct relation to his present perplexities.

But it kept its face averted. He could not read it. Vaguely he identified the nameless book with Tessie Kearns; he could not divine how, because it was not her book and he had never seen it except on the library shelf.

The nameless book persistently danced before him. He was glad of this. It kept him at moments from thinking of the loathly Baird.

CHAPTER XIX. THE TRAGIC COMEDIAN

Penetrating the Holden lot he was relieved to find that he created no immediate sensation. People did not halt to point derisive fingers at him; he had half feared they would. As he approached the office building he was almost certain he saw Baird turn in ahead of him. Yet when he entered the outer room of the Buckeye offices a young woman looked up from her typewriter to tell him that Mr. Baird was not in.

She was a serious-eyed young woman of a sincere manner; she spoke with certainty of tone. Mr. Baird was not only out, but he would not be in for several days. His physician had ordered him to a sanitarium.

The young woman resumed her typing; she did not again, glance up. The caller seemed to consider waiting on a chance that she had been misinformed. He was now sure he had seen Baird enter the building, and the door of his private office was closed. The caller idled outside the railing, absently regarding stills of past Buckeye atrocities that had been hung upon the walls of the office by someone with primitive tastes in decoration. He was debating a direct challenge of the young woman's veracity.

What would she say if told that the caller meant to wait right there until Mr. Baird should convalesce? He managed some appraising side-glances at her as she bent over her machine. She seemed to believe he had already gone.

Then he did go. No good talking that way to a girl. If it had been a man, now—"You tell Mr. Baird that Mr. Gill's got to see him as soon as possible about something important," he directed from the open door.

The young woman raised her serious eyes to his and nodded. She resumed her work. The door closed. Upon its closing the door of Baird's private office opened noiselessly to a crack that sufficed for the speaking voice at very moderate pitch to issue.

"Get Miss Montague on the 'phone," directed the voice. The door closed noiselessly. Beyond it Mr. Baird was presently speaking in low, sweet tones.

"'Lo, Sister! Listen; that squirrel just boiled in here, and I ducked him. I told the girl I wasn't to be in unless he was laughing all over, and he wasn't doing the least little thing that was anywheres near laughing. See what I mean? It's up to you now. You started it; you got to finish it. I've irised out. Get me?"

On the steps outside the rebuffed Merton Gill glanced at his own natty wrist-watch, bought with some of the later wages of his shame. It was the luncheon hour; mechanically he made his way to the cafeteria. He had ceased to rehearse the speech a doughtier Baird would now have been hearing.

Instead he roughly drafted one that Sarah Nevada Montague could not long evade. Even on her dying bed she would be compelled to listen. The practising orator with bent head mumbled as he walked. He still mumbled as he indicated a choice of foods at the cafeteria counter; he continued to be thus absorbed as he found a table near the centre of the room.

He arranged his assortment of viands. "You led me on, that's what you did," he continued to the absent culprit. "Led me on to make a laughing-stock of myself, that's what you did. Made a fool of me, that's what you did."

"All the same, I can't help thinking he's a harm to the industry," came the crisp tones of Henshaw from an adjoining table. The rehearsing orator glanced up to discover that the director and the sunny-faced brown and gray man he called Governor were smoking above the plates of their finished luncheon.

"I wouldn't worry too much," suggested the cheerful governor.

"But see what he does: he takes the good old reliable, sure-fire stuff and makes fun of it. I admit it's funny to start with, but what'll happen to us if the picture public ever finds that out? What'll we do then for drama—after they've learned to laugh at the old stuff?"

"Tush, tush, my boy!" The Governor waved a half—consumed cigarette until its ash fell. "Never fear. Do you think a thousand Jeff Bairds could make the picture public laugh at the old stuff when it's played straight? They laughed last night, yes; but not so much at the really fine burlesque; they guffawed at the slap-stick stuff that went with it. Baird's shrewd. He knows if he played straight burlesque he'd never make a dollar, so notice how he'll give a bit of straight that is genuine art, then a bit of slap-stick that any one can get. The slap-stick is what carries the show. Real burlesque is criticism, my boy; sometimes the very high-browest sort. It demands sophistication, a pretty high intelligence in the man that gets it.

"All right. Now take your picture public. Twenty million people every day; not the same ones every day, but with same average cranial index, which is low for all but about seven out of every hundred. That's natural because there aren't twenty million people in the world with taste or real intelligence—probably not five million. Well, you take this twenty million bunch that we sell to every day, and suppose they saw that lovely thing last night—don't you know they'd all be back to-night to see a real mopping mother with a real son falsely accused of crime— sure they'd be back, their heads bloody but unbowed. Don't worry; that reliable field marshal, old General Hokum, leads an unbeatable army."

Merton Gill had listened to the beginning of this harangue, but now he savagely devoured food. He thought this so—called Governor was too much like Baird.

"Well, Governor, I hope you're right. But that was pretty keen stuff last night. That first bit won't do Parmalee any good, and that Buck Benson stuff—you can't tell me a little more of that wouldn't make Benson look around for a new play."

"But I do tell you just that. It won't hurt Parmalee a bit; and Benson can go on Bensoning to the end of time—to big money. You keep forgetting this twenty-million audience. Go out and buy a picture magazine and read it through, just to remind you. They want hokum, and pay for it. Even this thing of Baird's, with all the saving slapstick, is over the heads of a good half of them. I'll make a bet with you now, anything you name, that it won't gross two thirds as much as Benson's next Western, and in that they'll cry their eyes out when he kisses his horse good-bye. See if they don't. Or see if they don't bawl at the next old gray-haired mother with a mop and a son that gets in bad.

"Why, if you give 'em hokum they don't even demand acting. Look at our own star, Mercer. You know as well as I do that she not only can't act, but she's merely a beautiful moron. In a world where right prevailed she'd be crowned queen of the morons without question. She may have an idea that two and two make four, but if she has it's only because she believes everything she hears. And look at the mail she gets. Every last one of the twenty million has written to tell her what a noble actress she is. She even believes that.

"Baird can keep on with the burlesque stuff, but his little old two-reelers'll probably have to pay for it, especially if he keeps those high-priced people. I'll bet that one new man of his sets him back seven hundred and fifty a week. The Lord knows he's worth every cent of it. My boy, tell me, did you ever in all your life see a lovelier imitation of a perfectly rotten actor? There's an artist for you. Who is he, anyway? Where'd he come from?" Merton Gill again listened; he was merely affecting to busy himself with a fork. It was good acting.

"I don't know," replied Henshaw. "Some of the crowd last night said he was just an extra that Baird dug up on the lot here. And, on the subject of burlesque, they also said Baird was having him do some Edgar Wayne stuff in a new one."

"Fine!" The Governor beamed. "Can't you see him as the honest, likable country boy? I bet he'll be good to his old mother in this one, too, and get the best of the city slickers in the end. For heaven's sake don't let me miss it! This kid last night handed me laughs that were better than a month's vacation for this old carcass of mine. You say he was just an extra?"

"That's what I heard last night. Anyway, he's all you say he is as an artist. Where do you suppose he got it? Do you suppose he's just the casual genius that comes along from time to time? And why didn't he stay 'straight' instead of playing horse with the sacred traditions of our art? That's what troubled me as I watched him. Even in that wild business with the spurs he was the artist every second. He must have tricked those falls but I couldn't catch him at it. Why should such a man tie up with Baird?"

"Ask me something hard. I'd say this bird had been tried out in serious stuff and couldn't make the grade. That's the way he struck me. Probably he once thought he could play Hamlet—one of those boys. Didn't you get the real pathos he'd turn on now and then? He actually had me kind of teary a couple of times. But I could see he'd also make me laugh my head off any time he showed in a straight piece.

"To begin with, look at that low-comedy face of his. And then—something peculiar—even while he's imitating a bad actor you feel somehow that it isn't all imitation. It's art, I grant you, but you feel he'd still be a bad actor if he'd try to imitate a good one. Somehow he found out his limits and decided to be what God meant him to be. Does that answer you? It gives you acting-plus, and if that isn't the plus in this case I miss my guess."

"I suppose you're right—something like that. And of course the real pathos is there. It has to be. There never was a great comedian without it, and this one is great. I admit that, and I admit all you say about our audience. I suppose we can't ever sell to twenty million people a day pictures that make any demand on the human intelligence. But couldn't we sell something better to one million—or a few thousand?"

The Governor dropped his cigarette end into the dregs of his coffee. "We might," he said, "if we were endowed. As it is, to make pictures we must make money. To make money we must sell to the mob. And the mob reaches full mental bloom at the age of fifteen. It won't buy pictures the average child can't get."

"Of course the art is in its infancy," remarked Henshaw, discarding his own cigarette.

"Ours is the Peter Pan of the arts," announced the Governor, as he rose.

"The Peter Pan of the arts—"

"Yes. I trust you recall the outstanding biological freakishness of Peter."

"Oh!" replied Henshaw.

When Merton Gill dared to glance up a moment later the men were matching coins at the counter. When they went out he left a half-eaten meal and presently might have been observed on a swift-rolling street-car. He mumbled as he blankly surveyed palm-bordered building sites along the way. He was again rehearsing a tense scene with the Montague girl. In actor parlance he was giving himself all the best of it. But they were new lines he mumbled over and over. And he was no longer eluded by the title of that book he remembered on the library shelf at Simsbury. Sitting in the cafeteria listening to strange talk, lashed by cruel memories, it had flashed upon his vision with the stark definition of a screened subtitle. He rang the Montague bell twice before he heard a faint summons to enter. Upon the parlour couch, under blankets that reached her pillowed head, lay Sarah. She was pale and seemed to suffer. She greeted him in a feeble voice, lids fluttering over the fires of that mysterious fever burning far back in her eyes.

"Hullo, Kid," he began brightly. "Here's your watch." Her doubting glance hovered over him as he smiled down at her. "You giving it to me again, Merton?" She seemed unable to conquer a stubborn incredulity.

"Of course I'm giving it to you again. What'd you think I was going to do?"

She still surveyed him with little veiled glances. "You look so bright you give me Kleig eyes," she said. She managed a wan smile at this.

"Take it," he insisted, extending the package. "Of course it won't keep Western Union time, but it'll look good on you."

She appeared to be gaining on her incredulity, but a vestige of it remained. "I won't touch it," she declared with more spirit than could have been expected from the perishing, "I won't touch it till you give me a good big kiss."

"Sure," he said, and leaned down to brush her pale cheek with his lips. He was cheerfully businesslike in this ceremony.

"Not till you do it right," she persisted. He knelt beside the couch and did it right. He lingered with a hand upon her pale brow.

"What you afraid of?" he demanded.

"You," she said, but now she again brought the watch to view, holding it away from her, studying its glitter from various angles. At last she turned her eyes up to his. They were alive but unrevealing. "Well?"

"Well?" he repeated coolly.

"Oh, stop it!" Again there was more energy than the moribund are wont to manifest. There was even a vigorous impatience in her tone as she went on, "You know well enough what I was afraid of. And you know well enough what I want to hear right now. Shoot, can't you?"

He shot. He stood up, backed away from the couch to where he could conveniently regard its stricken occupant, and shot gaily.

"Well, it'll be a good lesson to you about me, this thing of your thinking I was fooled over that piece. I s'pose you and Baird had it between you all the time, right down to the very last, that I thought he was doin' a serious play. Ho, ho!" He laughed gibingly. It was a masterful laugh. "A serious play with a cross-eyed man doing funny stuff all through. I thought it was serious, did I? Yes, I did!" Again the dry, scornful laugh of superiority. "Didn't you people know that I knew what I could do and what I couldn't do? I should have thought that little thing would of occurred to you all the time. Didn't you s'pose I knew as well as any one that I got a low-comedy face and couldn't ever make the grade in a serious piece?

"Of course I know I got real pathos—look how I turned it on a couple o' times in that piece last night—but even when I'm imitating a bad actor you can see it ain't all acting. You'd see soon enough I was a bad actor if I tried to imitate a good one. I guess you'd see that pretty quick. Didn't you and Baird even s'pose I'd found out my limits and decided to be what God meant me to be?

"But I got the pathos all right, and you can't name one great comedian that don't need pathos more'n he needs anything else. He just has to have it—and I got it. I got acting-plus; that's what, I got. I knew it all the time; and a whole lot of other people knew it last night. You could hear fifty of 'em talking about it when I came out of the theatre, saying I was an artist and all like that, and a certain Los Angeles society woman that you can bet never says things she don't mean, she told me she saw lots of places in this piece that I was funnier than any cross-eyed man that ever lived. And what happens this morning?" Hands in pockets he swaggered to and fro past the couch.

"Well, nothing happens this morning except people coming around to sign me up for three hundred and fifty a week. One of 'em said not an hour ago—he's a big producer, too—that Baird ought to be paying me seven hundred and fifty because I earned every cent of it. Of course I didn't want to say anything the other day, with you pretending to know so much about contracts and all that—I just thought I'd let you go on, seeing you were so smart—and I signed what you told me to. But I know I should have held off—with this Bamberger coming over from the Bigart when I was hardly out of bed, and says will three hundred and fifty a week interest me and promising he'll give me a chance to do that spur act again that was the hit of the piece—"

He broke off, conscious suddenly that the girl had for some time been holding a most peculiar stare rigidly upon him. She had at first narrowed her right eye at a calculating angle as she listened; but for a long time now the eyes had been widened to this inexplicable stare eloquent of many hidden things.

As he stopped his speech, made ill at ease by the incessant pressing of the look, he was caught and held by it to a longer silence than he had meant to permit. He could now read meanings. That unflinching look incurred by his smooth bluster was a telling blend of pity and of wonder.

"So you know, do you," she demanded, "that you look just enough too much like Harold Parmalee so that you're funny? I mean." she amended, seeing him wince, "that you look the way Parmalee would look if he had brains?"

He faltered but made a desperate effort to recover his balance.

"And besides, what difference does it make? If we did good pictures we'd have to sell 'em to a mob. And what's a mob? It's fifteen years old and nothing but admirers, or something like that, like Muriel Mercer that wouldn't know how much are two times two if the neighbours didn't get it to her—"

Again he had run down under her level look. As he stopped, the girl on the couch who had lain with the blankets to her neck suddenly threw them aside and sat up. Surprisingly she was not garbed in sick-bed apparel. She seemed to be fully dressed.

A long moment she sat thus, regarding him still with that slow look, unbelieving yet cherishing. His eyes fell at last.

"Merton!" he heard her say. He looked up but she did not speak. She merely gave a little knowing nod of the head and opened her arms to him. Quickly he knelt beside her while the mothering arms enfolded him. A hand pulled his head to her breast and held it there. Thus she rocked gently, the hand gliding up to smooth his hair. Without words she cherished him thus a long time. The gentle rocking back and forth continued.

"It's—it's like that other time you found me—" His bluster had gone. He was not sure of his voice. Even these few words had been hard. He did not try more.

"There, there, there!" she whispered. "It's all right, everything's all right. Your mother's got you right here and she ain't ever going to let you go—never going to let you go."

She was patting his head in rhythm with her rocking as she snuggled and soothed him. There was silence for another interval. Then she began to croon a song above him as she rocked, though the lyric was plainly an improvisation.

"Did he have his poor old mother going for a minute? Yes, he did. He had her going for a minute, for a minute. Yes, he had her going good for a minute.

"But oh, he won't ever fool her very long, very long, not very long, because he can't fool his dear old mother very long, very long; and he can bet on that, bet on that, so he can, bet a lot of money on that, that, that!" Her charge had grown still again, but she did not relax her tightened arms.

"Say," he said at last.

"Well, honey."

"You know those benches where we wait for the cars?"

"Do I know them?" The imperative inference was that she did.

"I looked at the store yesterday. The sign down there says 'Himebaugh's dignified system of deferred payments.'"

"Yes, yes, I know."

"Well, I saw another good place—it says 'The house of lucky rings'—you know—rings!"

"Sure, I know. That's all right."

"Well," he threw off the arms and got to his feet. She stood up then.

"Well, all right!"

They were both constrained now. Both affected an ease that neither felt. It seemed to be conceded without words that they must very lightly skirt the edges of Merton Gill's screen art. They talked a long tune volubly of other things: of the girl's illness from which she now seemed most happily to have recovered, of whether she was afraid of him—she professed still to be—of the new watch whose beauties were newly admired when it had been adjusted to its owner's wrist; of finances they talked, and even, quite simply, of accessible homes where two could live as cheaply as one.

It was not until he was about to go, when he stood at the door while the girl readjusted his cravat, smoothed his hair, and administered a final series of pats where they seemed most needed, that he broke ever so slightly through the reserve which both had felt congealing about a certain topic.

"You know," he said, "I happened to remember the title of a book this morning; a book I used to see back in the public library at home. It wasn't one I ever read. Maybe Tessie Kearns read it. Anyway, she had a poem she likes a lot written by the same man. She used to read me good parts of it. But I never read the book because the title sounded kind of wild, like there couldn't be any such thing. The poem had just a plain name; it was called 'Lucile,' but the book by the same man was called 'The Tragic Comedians.' You wouldn't think there could be a tragic comedian would you?—well, look at me."

She looked at him, with that elusive, remote flickering back in her eyes, but she only said, "Be sure and come take me out to dinner. To-night I can eat. And don't forget your overcoat. And listen—don't you dare go into Himebaugh's till I can go with you."

One minute after he had gone the Montague girl was at the telephone.

"Hello! Mr. Baird, please. Is this Mr. Baird? Well, Jeff, everything's jake. Yeah. The poor thing was pretty wild when he got here. First he began to bluff. He'd got an earful from someone, probably over on the lot. And he put it over on me for a minute, too. But he didn't last good. He was awful broke up when the end came. Bless his heart. But you bet I kissed the hurt place and made it well. How about him now? Jeff, I'm darned if I can tell except he's right again. When he got here he was some heart-broke and some mad and some set up on account of things he hears about himself. I guess he's that way still, except I mended the heart-break. I can't quite make him out—he's like a book where you can't guess what's coming in the next chapter, so you keep on reading. I can see we ain't ever going to talk much about it—not if we live together twenty years. What's that? Yeah. Didn't I tell you he was always getting me, somehow? Well, now I'm got. Yeah. We're gonna do an altar walk. What? Oh, right away. Say, honest, Jeff, I'll never have an easy minute again while he's out of my sight. Helpless! You said it. Thanks, Jeff. I know that, old man. Good-by!"

CHAPTER XX. ONWARD
AND UPWARD

At the first showing of the Buckeye company's new five-reel comedy—Five Reels-500 Laughs—entitled Brewing Trouble, two important members of its cast occupied balcony seats and one of them throughout the piece brazenly applauded the screen art of her husband. "I don't care who sees me," she would reply ever and again to his whispered protests.

The new piece proved to be a rather broadly stressed burlesque of the type of picture drama that has done so much to endear the personality of Edgar Wayne to his public. It was accorded a hearty reception. There was nothing to which it might be compared save the company's previous Hearts on Fire, and it seemed to be felt that the present offering had surpassed even that masterpiece of satire.

The Gills, above referred to, watched the unwinding celluloid with vastly different emotions. Mrs. Gill was hearty in her enjoyment, as has been indicated. Her husband, superficially, was not displeased. But beneath that surface of calm approval—beneath even the look of bored indifference he now and then managed—there still ran a complication of emotions, not the least of which was honest bewilderment. People laughed, so it must be funny. And it was good to be known as an artist of worth, even if the effects of your art were unintended.

It was no shock to him to learn now that the mechanical appliance in his screen-mother's kitchen was a still, and that the grape juice the honest country boy purveyed to the rich New Yorker had been improved in rank defiance of a constitutional amendment. And even during the filming of the piece he had suspected that the little sister, so engagingly played by the present Mrs. Gill, was being too bold. With slight surprise, therefore, as the drama unfolded, he saw that she had in the most brazen manner invited the attentions of the city villains.

She had, in truth, been only too eager to be lured to the great city with all its pitfalls, and had bidden the old home farewell in her simple country way while each of the villains in turn had awaited her in his motor-car. What Merton had not been privileged to watch were the later developments of this villainy. For just beyond the little hamlet at a lonely spot in the road each of the motor-cars had been stopped by a cross-eyed gentleman looking much like the clerk in the hotel, save that he was profusely bewhiskered and bore side-arms in a menacing fashion.

Declaring that no scoundrel could take his little daughter from him, he deprived the villains of their valuables, so that for a time at least they should not bring other unsuspecting girls to grief. As a further precaution he compelled them to abandon their motor-cars, in which he drove off with the rescued daughter. He was later seen to sell the cars at a wayside garage, and, after dividing their spoils with his daughter, to hail a suburban trolley upon which they both returned to the home nest, where the little girl would again languish at the gate, a prey to any designing city man who might pass.

She seemed so defenceless in her wild-rose beauty, her longing for pretty clothes and city ways, and yet so capably pro by this opportune father who appeared to foresee the moment of her flights.

He learned without a tremor that among the triumphs of his inventive genius had been a machine for making ten—dollar bills, at which the New York capitalist had exclaimed that the state right for Iowa alone would bring one hundred thousand dollars. Even more remunerative, it would seem, had been his other patent—the folding boomerang. The manager of the largest boomerang factory in Australia stood ready to purchase this device for ten million dollars. And there was a final view of the little home after prosperity had come to its inmates so long threatened with ruin. A sign over the door read "Ye Olde Fashioned Gifte Shoppe," and under it, flaunted to the wayside, was the severely simple trade-device of a high boot.

These things he now knew were to be expected among the deft infamies of a Buckeye comedy. But the present piece held in store for him a complication that, despite his already rich experience of Buckeye methods, caused him distressing periods of heat and cold while he watched its incredible unfolding. Early in the piece, indeed, he had begun to suspect in the luring of his little sister a grotesque parallel to the bold advances made him by the New York society girl. He at once feared some such interpretation when he saw himself coy and embarrassed before her down-right attack, and he was certain this was intended when he beheld himself embraced by this reckless young woman who behaved in the manner of male screen idols during the last dozen feet of the last reel. But how could he have suspected the lengths to which a perverted spirit of satire would lead the Buckeye director?

For now he staggered through the blinding snow, a bundle clasped to his breast. He fell, half fainting, at the door of the old home. He groped for the knob and staggered in to kneel at his mother's feet. And she sternly repulsed him, a finger pointing to the still open door.

Unbelievably the screen made her say, "He wears no ring. Back to the snow with 'em both! Throw 'em Way Down East!"

And Baird had said the bundle would contain one of his patents!

Mrs. Gill watched this scene with tense absorption. When the mother's iron heart had relented she turned to her husband. "You dear thing, that was a beautiful piece of work. You're set now. That cinches your future. Only, dearest, never, never, never let it show on your face that you think it's funny. That's all you'll ever have to be afraid of in your work."

"I won't," he said stoutly.

He shivered—or did he shudder?—and quickly reached to take her hand. It was a simple, direct gesture, yet somehow it richly had the quality of pleading.

"Mother understands," she whispered. "Only remember, you mustn't seem to think it's funny."

"I won't," he said again. But in his torn heart he stubbornly cried, "I don't, I don't!"

* * * * * * *

Some six months later that representative magazine, Silver Screenings, emblazoned upon its front cover a promise that in the succeeding number would appear a profusely illustrated interview by Augusta Blivens with that rising young screen actor, Merton Gill.

The promise was kept. The interview wandered amid photographic reproductions of the luxurious Hollywood bungalow, set among palms and climbing roses, the actor and his wife in their high-powered roadster (Mrs. Gill at the wheel); the actor in his costume of chaps and sombrero, rolling a cigarette; the actor in evening dress, the actor in his famous scene of the Christmas eve return in Brewing Trouble; the actor regaining his feet in his equally famous scene of the malignant spurs; the actor and his young wife, on the lawn before the bungalow, and the young wife aproned, in her kitchen, earnestly busy with spoon and mixing bowl.

"It is perhaps not generally known," wrote Miss Blivens, "that the honour of having discovered this latest luminary in the stellar firmament should be credited to Director Howard Henshaw of the Victor forces. Indeed, I had not known this myself until the day I casually mentioned the Gills in his presence. I lingered on a set of Island Love, at present being filmed by this master of the unspoken drama, having but a moment since left that dainty little reigning queen of the celluloid dynasty, Muriel Mercer. Seated with her in the tiny bijou boudoir of her bungalow dressing room on the great Holden lot, its walls lined with the works of her favourite authors—for one never finds this soulful little girl far from the books that have developed her mentally as the art of the screen has developed her emotionally—she had referred me to the director when I sought further details of her forthcoming great production, an idyl of island romance and adventure. And presently, when I had secured from him the information I needed concerning this unique little drama of the great South Seas, I chanced to mention my approaching encounter with the young star of the Buckeye forces, an encounter to which I looked forward with some dismay.

"Mr. Henshaw, pausing in his task of effecting certain changes in the interior of the island hut, reassured me. 'You need have no fear about your meeting with Gill,' he said. 'You will find him quite simple and unaffected, an artist, and yet sanely human.' It was now that he revealed his own part in the launching of this young star. 'I fancy it is not generally known,' he continued, 'that to me should go the honour of having "discovered" Gill. It is a fact, however. He appeared as an extra one morning in the cabaret scene we used in Miss Mercer's tremendous hit, The Blight of Broadway. Instantly, as you may suppose, I was struck by the extraordinary distinction of his face and bearing. In that crowd composed of average extra people he stood out to my eye as one made for big things. After only a moment's chat with him I gave him a seat at the edge of the dancing floor and used him most effectively in portraying the basic idea of this profoundly stirring drama in which Miss Mercer was to achieve one of her brightest triumphs.

"'Watch that play to-day; you will discover young Gill in many of the close-ups where, under my direction, he brought out the psychological, the symbolic—if I may use the term—values of the great idea underlying our story. Even in these bits he revealed the fine artistry which he has since demonstrated more broadly under another director.

"'To my lasting regret the piece was then too far along to give him a more important part, though I intended to offer him something good in our next play for Muriel Mercer—you may recall her gorgeous success in Her Father's Wife—but I was never able to find the chap again. I made inquiries, of course, and felt a really personal sense of loss when I could get no trace of him. I knew then, as well as I know now, that he was destined for eminence in our world of painted shadows. You may imagine my chagrin later when I learned that another director was to reap the rewards of a discovery all my own.'

"And so," continued Miss Blivens, "it was with the Henshaw words still in my ears that I first came into the presence of Merton Gill, feeling that he would-as he at once finely did—put me at my ease. Simple, unaffected, modest, he is one whom success has not spoiled. Both on the set where I presently found him—playing the part of a titled roue in the new Buckeye comedy—to be called, one hears, 'Nearly Sweethearts or Something'-and later in the luxurious but homelike nest which the young star has provided for his bride of a few months-she was 'Flips' Montague, one recalls, daughter of a long line of theatrical folk dating back to days of the merely spoken drama-he proved to be finely unspoiled and surprisingly unlike the killingly droll mime of the Buckeye constellation. Indeed one cannot but be struck at once by the deep vein of seriousness underlying the comedian's surface drollery. His sense of humour must be tremendous; and yet only in the briefest flashes of his whimsical manner can one divine it.

"'Let us talk only of my work,' he begged me. 'Only that can interest my public.' And so, very seriously, we talked of his work.

"'Have you ever thought of playing serious parts?' I asked, being now wholly put at my ease by his friendly, unaffected ways.

"He debated a moment, his face rigidly set, inscrutable to my glance. Then he relaxed into one of those whimsically appealing smiles that somehow are acutely eloquent of pathos. 'Serious parts—with this low-comedy face of mine!' he responded. And my query had been answered. Yet he went on, 'No, I shall never play Hamlet. I can give a good imitation of a bad actor but, doubtless, I should give a very bad imitation of a good one.

"Et vailet, Messieurs." I remarked to myself. The man with a few simple strokes of the brush had limned me his portrait. And I was struck again with that pathetic appeal in face and voice as he spoke so confidingly. After all, is not pure pathos the hall-mark of great comedy? We laugh, but more poignantly because our hearts are tugged at. And here was a master of the note pathetic.

"Who that has roared over the Gill struggle with the dreadful spurs was not even at the climax of his merriment sympathetically aware of his earnest persistence, the pained sincerity of his repeated strivings, the genuine anguish distorting his face as he senses the everlasting futility of his efforts? Who that rocked with laughter at the fox-trot lesson in Object, Alimony, could be impervious to the facial agony above those incompetent, disobedient, heedless feet?

"Here was honest endeavour, an almost prayerful determination, again and again thwarted by feet that recked not of rhythm or even of bare mechanical accuracy. Those feet, so apparently aimless, so little under control, were perhaps the most mirthful feet the scored failure in the dance. But the face, conscious of their clumsiness, was a mask of fine tragedy.

"Such is the combination, it seems to me, that has produced the artistry now so generally applauded, an artistry that perhaps achieved its full flowering in that powerful bit toward the close of Brewing Trouble—the return of the erring son with his agony of appeal so markedly portrayed that for the moment one almost forgot the wildly absurd burlesque of which it formed the joyous yet truly emotional apex. I spoke of this.

"'True burlesque is, after all, the highest criticism, don't you think?' he asked me. 'Doesn't it make demands which only a sophisticated audience can meet-isn't it rather high-brow criticism?' And I saw that he had thought deeply about his art.

"'It is because of this,' he went on, 'that we must resort to so much of the merely slap-stick stuff in our comedies. For after all, our picture audience, twenty million people a day—surely one can make no great demands upon their intelligence.' He considered a moment, seemingly lost in memories of his work. 'I dare say,' he concluded, 'there are not twenty million people of taste and real intelligence in the whole world.'

"Yet it must not be thought that this young man would play the cynic. He is superbly the optimist, though now again he struck a note of almost cynic whimsicality. 'Of course our art is in its infancy—' He waited for my nod of agreement, then dryly added, 'We must, I think, consider it the Peter Pan of the arts. And I dare say you recall the outstanding biological freakishness of Peter.' But a smile—that slow, almost puzzled smile of his—accompanied the words.

436

"'You might,' he told me at parting, 'call me the tragic comedian.' And again I saw that this actor is set apart from the run of his brethren by an almost uncanny gift for introspection. He has ruthlessly analysed himself. He knows, as he put it, 'what God meant him to be.' Was here a hint of poor Cyrano?

"I left after some brief reference to his devoted young wife, who, in studio or home, is never far from his side. "'It is true that I have struggled and sacrificed to give the public something better and finer,' he told me then; 'but I owe my real success all to her.' He took the young wife's hand in both his own, and very simply, unaffectedly, raised it to his cheek where he held it a moment, with that dreamy, remembering light in his eyes, as of one striving to recall bits of his past.

"'I think that's all,' he said at last. But on the instant of my going he checked me once more. 'No, it isn't either.' He brightened. 'I want you to tell your readers that this little woman is more than my wife—she is my best pal; and, I may also add, my severest critic.'"

BOOK THREE

BUNKER BEAN

To H.G. WELLS

CHAPTER I

Bunker Bean was wishing he could be different. This discontent with himself was suffered in a moment of idleness as he sat at a desk on a high floor of a very high office-building in "downtown" New York. The first correction he would have made was that he should be "well over six feet" tall. He had observed that this was the accepted stature for a hero.

And the name, almost any name but "Bunker Bean!" Often he wrote good ones on casual slips of paper and fancied them his; names like Trevellyan or Montressor or Delancey, with musical prefixes; or a good, short, beautiful, but dignified name like "Gordon Dane." He liked that one. It suggested something. But Bean! And Bunker Bean, at that! True, it also suggested something, but this had never been anything desirable. Just now the people in the outside office were calling him "Boston."

"Gordon Dane," well over six feet, abundant dark hair, a bit inclined to "wave" and showing faint lines of gray "above the temples"; for Bean also wished to be thirty years old and to have learned about women; in short, to have suffered. Gordon Dane's was a face before which the eyes of women would fall in half-frightened, half-ecstatic subjection, and men would feel the inexplicable magnetism of his presence. He would be widely remarked for his taste in dress. He would don stripes or checks without a trace of timidity. He would quail before no violence of colour in a cravat.

A certain insignificant Bunker Bean was not like this. With a soul aspiring to stripes and checks that should make him a man to be looked at twice in a city street, he lacked courage for any but the quietest patterns. Longing for the cravat of brilliant hue, he ate out his heart under neutral tints. Had he not, in the intoxication of his first free afternoon in New York, boldly purchased a glorious thing of silk entirely, flatly red, an article to stamp its wearer with distinction; and had he not, in the seclusion of his rented room, that night hidden the flaming thing at the bottom of a bottom drawer, knowing in his sickened soul he dared not flaunt it?

Once, truly, had he worn it, but only for a brief stroll on a rainy Sunday, with an entirely opaque raincoat buttoned closely under his chin. Even so, he fancied that people stared through and through that guaranteed fabric straight to his red secret. The rag burned on his breast. Afterward it was something to look at beyond the locked door; perhaps to try on behind drawn shades, late of a night. And how little Gordon Dane would have made of such a matter! Floated in Bean's mind the refrain of a clothing advertisement. "The more advanced dressers will seek this fashion." "Something dignified yet different!" Gordon Dane would be "an advanced dresser."

But if you have been afraid of nearly everything nearly all your life, how then? You must be "dignified" only. The brave only may be "different." It was all well enough to gaze at striking fabrics in windows; but to buy and to wear openly, and get yourself pointed at—laughed at! Again sounded the refrain of the hired bard of dress. "*It is cut to give the wearer the appearance of perfect physical development. And the effect so produced so improves his form that he unconsciously strives to attain the appearance which the garment gives him; he expands his chest, draws in his waist and stands erect.*"

A rustling of papers from the opposite side of the desk promised a diversion of his thoughts. Bean was a hireling and the person who rustled the papers was his master, but the youth bestowed upon the great man a look of profound, albeit not unkindly, contempt. It could be seen, even as he sat in the desk-chair, that he was a short man; not an inch better than Bean, there. He was old. Bean, when he thought of the matter, was satisfied to guess him as something between fifty and eighty. He didn't know and didn't care how many might be the years of little Jim Breede. Breede was the most negligible person he knew.

He was nearly nothing, in Bean's view, if you came right down to it. Besides being of too few inches for a man and unspeakably old, he was unsightly. Nothing of the Gordon Dane about Breede. The little hair left him was an atrocious foggy gray; never in order, never combed, Bean thought. The brows were heavy, and still curiously dark, which made them look threatening. The eyes were the coldest of gray, a match for the hair in colour, and set far back in caverns. The nose was blunt, the chin a mere knobby challenge, and between them was the unloveliest moustache Bean had ever been compelled to observe; short, ragged, faded in streaks. And wrinkles—wrinkles wheresoever there was room for them: across the forehead that lost itself in shining yellow scalp; under the eyes, down the cheeks, about the traplike mouth. He especially loathed the smaller wrinkles that made tiny squares and diamonds around the back of Breede's neck.

Sartorially, also, Bean found Breede objectionable. He forever wore the same kind of suit. The very same suit, one might have thought, only Bean knew it was renewed from time to time; it was the kind called "a decent gray," and it had emphatically not been cut "to give the wearer the appearance of perfect physical development." So far as Bean could determine the sole intention had been to give the wearer plenty of room under the arms and at the waist. Bean found it disgusting—a man who had at least enough leisure to give a little thought to such matters.

Breede's shoes offended him. Couldn't the man pick out something natty, a shapelier toe, buttons, a neat upper of tan or blue cloth—patent leather, of course? But nothing of the sort; a strange, thin, nameless leather, never either shiny or quite dull, as broad at the toe as any place, no buttons; not even laces; elastic at the sides! Not *shoes*, in any dressy sense. Things to be pulled on. And always the same, like the contemptible suits of clothes.

He might have done a little something with his shirts, Bean thought; a stripe or crossed lines, a bit of gay colour; but no! Stiff-bosomed white shirts, cuffs that "came off," cuffs that fastened with hideous metallic devices that Bean had learned to scorn. A collar too loose, a black satin cravat, *and* no scarf-pin; not even a cluster of tiny diamonds.

From Breede and his ignoble attire Bean shifted the disfavour of his glance to Breede's luncheon tray on the desk between them. Breede's unvarying luncheon consisted of four crackers composed of a substance that was said, on the outside of the package, to be "predigested," one apple, and a glass of milk moderately inflated with seltzer. Bean himself had fared in princely fashion that day on two veal cutlets bathed in a German sauce of oily richness, a salad of purple cabbage, a profusion of vegetables, two cups of coffee and a German pancake that of itself would have disabled almost any but the young and hardy, or, presumably, a German.

Bean guessed the cost of Breede's meal to be a bit under eight cents. His own had cost sixty-five. He despised Breede for a petty economist.

Breede glanced up from his papers to encounter in Bean's eyes only a look of respectful waiting.

"Take letter G.S. Hubbell gen' traffic mag'r lines Wes' Chicago dear sir your favour twen'th instant—"

The words came from under that unacceptable moustache of Breede's like a series of exhausts from a motorcycle. Bean recorded them in his note-book. His shorthand was a marvel of condensed neatness. Breede had had trouble with stenographers; he was not easy to "take." He spoke swiftly, often indistinctly, and it maddened him to be asked to repeat. Bean had never asked him to repeat, and he inserted the a's and the's and all the minor words that Breede could not pause to utter. The letter continued:

"—mus' have report at your earl's' convenience of earnings and expenses of Grand Valley branch for las' four months with engineer's est'mate of prob'le cost of repairs and maintenance for nex' year—"

Breede halted to consult a document. Bean glanced up with his look of respectful waiting. Then he glanced down at his notes and wrote two other lines of shorthand. Breede might have supposed these to record the last sentence he had spoken, but one able to decipher the notes could have read: "That is one rotten suit of clothes. For God's sake, why not get some decent shoes next time—"

The letter was resumed. It came to its end with a phrase that almost won the difficult respect of Bean. Of a rumour that the C. & G.W. would build into certain coveted territory Breede exploded: "I can imagine nothing of less consequence!" Bean rather liked the phrase and the way Breede emitted it. That was a good thing to say to some one who might think you were afraid. He treasured the words; fondled them with the point of his pencil. He saw himself speaking them pithily to various persons with whom he might be in conflict. There was a thing now that Gordon Dane might have hurled at his enemies a dozen times in his adventurous career. Breede must have something in him—but look at his shiny white cuffs with the metal clasps, on the desk at his elbow!

Bean had lately read of Breede in a newspaper that "Conservative judges estimate his present fortune at a round hundred million." Bean's own stipend was thirty dollars a week, but he pitied Breede. Bean could learn to make millions if he should happen to want them; but poor old Breede could never learn to *look* like anybody.

There you have Bunker Bean at a familiar, prosaic moment in an afternoon of his twenty-third year. But his prosaic moments are numbered. How few they are to be! Already the door of Enchantment has swung to his scared touch. The times will show a scar or two from Bean. Bean the prodigious! The choicely perfect toy of Destiny at frolic! Bean the innocent—the monstrous!

Those who long since gave Bean up as an insoluble problem were denied the advantages of an early association with him. Only an acquaintance with his innermost soul of souls could permit any sane understanding of his works, and this it is our privilege, and our necessity, to make, if we are to comprehend with any sympathy that which was later termed his "madness." The examination shall be made quickly and with all decency.

Let us regard Bean through the glass of his earliest reactions to an environment that was commonplace, unstimulating, dull—the little wooden town set among cornfields, "Wellsville" they called it, where he came from out of the Infinite to put on a casual body.

Of Bean at birth, it may be said frankly that he was not imposing. He was not chubby nor rosy; had no dimples. His face was a puckered protest at the infliction of animal life. In the white garments conventional to his age he was a distressing travesty, even when he gurgled. In the nude he was quite impossible to all but the most hardened mothers, and he was never photographed thus in a washbowl. Even his own mother, before he had survived to her one short year, began to harbour the accursed suspicion that his beauty was not flawless nor his intelligence supreme. To put it brutally, she almost admitted to herself that he was not the most remarkable child in all the world. To be sure, this is a bit less incredible when we know that Bean's mother, at his advent, thought far less highly of Bean's father than on the occasion, seven years before, when she had consented to be endowed with all his worldly goods. In the course of those years she came to believe that she had married beneath her, a fact of which she made no secret to

442

her intimates and least of all to her mate, who, it may be added, privately agreed with her. Alonzo Bean, after that one delirious moment at the altar, had always disbelieved in himself pathetically. Who was he—to have wed a Bunker!

When little Bean's years began to permit small activities it was seen that his courage was amazing: a courage, however, that quickly overreached itself, and was sapped by small defeats. Tumbles down the slippery stairway, burns from the kitchen stove, began it. When a prized new sailor hat was blown to the centre of a duck-pond he sought to recover it without any fearsome self-communing. If faith alone could uphold one, Bean would have walked upon the face of the waters that day. But the result was a bald experience of the sensations of the drowning, and a lasting fear of any considerable body of water. Ever after it was an adventure not to be lightly dared to cross even the stoutest bridge.

And flying! A belief that we can fly as the birds is surely not unreasonable at the age when he essayed it. Nor should a mere failure to rise from the ground destroy it. One must leap from high places, and Bean did so. The roof of the chicken house was the last eminence to have an experimental value. On his bed of pain he realized that we may not fly as the birds; nor ever after could he look without tremors from any high place.

Such domestic animals as he encountered taught him further fear. Even the cat became contemptuous of him, knowing itself dreaded. That splendid courage he was born with had faded to an extreme timidity. Before physical phenomena that pique most children to cunning endeavour, little Bean was aghast.

And very soon to this burden of fear was added the graver problems of human association. From being the butt of capricious physical forces he became a social unit and found this more terrifying than all that had gone before. At least in the physical world, if you kept pretty still, didn't touch things, didn't climb, stayed away from edges and windows and water and cows and looked carefully where you stepped, probably nothing would hurt you. But these new terrors of the social world lay in wait for you; clutched you in moments of the most inoffensive enjoyment.

His mother seemed to be director-general of these monsters, a ruthless deviser of exquisite tortures. There were unseasonable washings, dressings, combings and curlings—admonitions to be "a little gentleman." Loathsomely garbed, he was made to sit stiffly on a chair in the presence of falsely enthusiastic callers; or he was taken to call on those same callers and made to sit stiffly again while they, with feverish affectations of curiosity, asked him what his name was, something they already knew at least as well as he did; made to overhear their ensuing declarations that the cat had got his tongue, which he always denied bitterly until he came to see through the plot and learned to receive the accusation in stony silence.

Boys of his own age took hold of him roughly and laid him in the dust, jeeringly threw his hat to some high roof, spat on his new shoes. Even little girls, divining his abjectness, were prone to act rowdyish with him. And this especially made him suffer. He comprehended, somehow, that it was ignoble for a man child to be afraid of little girls.

Money was another source of grief. Not an exciting thing in itself, he had yet learned that people possessing desirable objects would insanely part with them for money. Then came one of the Uncle Bunkers from over Walnut Shade way, who scowled at him when leaving and gave him a dime. He voiced a wish to exchange this for sweets with a certain madman in the village who had no understanding of the value of his stock. His mother demurred; not alone because candy was unwholesome, but because the only right thing to do with money was to "save" it. And his mother prevailed, even though his father coarsely suggested that all the candy he could ever buy with Bunker money wouldn't hurt him none. The mother said that this was "low," and the father retorted with equal lowness that a rigid saving of all Bunker-given money wouldn't make no one a "Croosus," neither, if you come down to *that*.

It resulted in his being told that he could play freely with his dime one whole afternoon before the unexciting process of saving it began. Well enough, that! He had grown too fearful of life to lose that coin vulgarly out in the grass, as another would almost surely have done.

But he was beguiled in the mart of the money changers. To him, standing safely within the front gate where nothing could burn him, fall upon him, or chase him, "playing" respectfully with his new dime, came one of slightly superior years and criminal instincts demanding to inspect the treasure. The privilege was readily accorded, to arouse only contempt. The piece was too small. The critic himself had a bigger one, and showed it.

The two coins were held side by side. Bean was envious. The small coin was of silver, the larger of copper, but he was no petty metallurgist. He wanted to trade and said so. The newcomer assented with a large air of benevolence, snatched the despised smaller coin and ran hastily off—doubtless into a life of prosperous endeavour. And little Bean, presently found by his mother crooning over a large copper cent, was appalled by what followed. He had brought back "a bigger money," yet he had done something infamous. It was the first gleam of an incapacity for finance that was one day to become brilliant. He came to think money was a pretty queer thing. People cheated it from you or took it away for your own good. Anyhow, it was not a matter to bother about. You never had it long enough.

Then there was language. Language was words, and politeness. Certain phrases had to be mouthed to strangers, designed to imply a respect he was generally far from feeling. This was bad enough, but what was worse was that you couldn't use just any word you might hear, however beautiful it sounded. For example, there was the compelling utterance he got from the two merry gentlemen who passed him at the gate one day. So jolly were they with their songs and laughter that he followed them a little way to where they sat under a tree and drank turn by turn from a bottle. His ear caught the thing and his lips shaped it so cunningly that they laughed more than ever. He returned to his gate, intoning it; the fresh voice rose higher as the phrasing became more familiar. Then he was on the porch, chanting as a bard from the mere sensuous beauty of the words. Through the open door he saw three faces. The minister and his wife were calling on his mother.

The immediate happenings need not be set down. After events again became coherent he was choking back sobs and listening to the minister pray for those of unclean lips. And the minister prayed especially for one among them that he might cease to pervert the right ways of the Lord. He knew this to mean himself, for his mother glared over at him where he knelt; he was grateful for the kneeling posture at that moment; he would not have cared to sit. But all he had learned was that if you are going to use words freely it had much better be when you are alone; this, and that the minister had enormous feet, kneeling there with the toes of his boots dug into the carpet.

No sooner was this language spectre laid than another confronted him; that of class distinction. Certain people were "low" and must be shunned by the high, unless the high perversely wished to be thought equally low. His mother was again the arbiter. Her rule as applied to children of his own age wrought but little hardship. She considered other children generally to be low, and her son feared them for their deeds of coarsely humorous violence. But he was never quite able to believe that his father was an undesirable associate.

In all his young life he had found no sport so good as riding on the seat beside that father while he drove the express wagon; a shiny green wagon with a seat close to the front and a tilted rest for one's feet, drawn by a grand black horse with a high-flung head, that would make nothing of eating a small boy if it ever had the chance. You drove to incoming trains, which was high adventure. But that was not all. You loaded the wagon with packages from the trains and these you proceeded to deliver in a leisurely and important manner. And some citizen of weight was sure to halt the wagon and ask if that there package of stuff from Chicago hadn't showed up yet, and it was mighty funny if it hadn't, because it was ordered special. Whereupon you said curtly that you didn't know anything about *that*—you couldn't fetch any package if it hadn't come, could you? And you drove on with pleased indignation.

Yet so fine a game as this was held by his mother to be unedifying. He would pick up a fashion of speech not genteel; he would grow to be a "rough." She, the inconsequent fair, who had herself been captivated by the driver of that very wagon, a gay blade directing his steed with a flourish! To be sure, she had found him doing this in a mist of romance, as one who must have his gallant fling at life before settling down. But the mist had cleared. Alonzo Bean, no longer the gay blade, had settled down upon the seat of his wagon. Once he had touched the guitar, sung an acceptable tenor, jested with life. Now he drove soberly, sang no more, and was concerned chiefly that his meals be served at set hours.

Small wonder, perhaps, that the mother should have feared the Bean and laboured to cultivate the true Bunker strain in her offspring. Small wonder that she kept him when she could from the seat of that wagon and from the deadening influence of a father to whom Romance had broken its fine promises. Little Bean distressed her enough by playing at express-wagon in preference to all other games. He meant to drive a real one when he was big enough—that is, at first. Secretly he aspired beyond that. Some day, when he would not be afraid to climb to a higher seat, he meant to drive the great yellow 'bus that also went to trains. But that was a dream too splendid to tell.

In the summer of his seventh year, when his mother was finding it increasingly difficult to supply antidotes for this poison, she even consented to his visiting some other Beans. Unfortunately, there were no Bunkers to harbour the child of one who had made so palpable a mésalliance; but the elder Beans would gladly receive him, and they at least had never driven express wagons.

To the little boy, who had no sense of their relationship, they were persons named "Gramper" and "Grammer" whom he would do well to look down upon because they were not Bunkers. So much he understood, and that he was to ride in a stage and find them on a remote farm. It was to be the summer of his first feat of daring since he had reached years of moral discretion.

He was still so timid at the beginning of the wonderful journey that when the kind old gentleman who drove the stage stopped his horses at a point on the road where ripe red apples hung thickly on a tree, climbed the fence and returned with a capacious hat full of the fruit, he was chilled with horror at the crime. He had been freely told what was thought of people, and what was done with them, who took things not their own. Afraid to decline the two apples proffered by the robber, who resumed his seat and ate brazenly of his loot, the solitary passenger would still be no party to the outrage. He presently dropped his own two apples over the back of the stage, and later, lacking the preacher's courage, averred that he had eaten them—and couldn't eat another one, thank you. He was not a little affected by the fine bravado with which the old man ate apple after apple along miles of the road, full in the gaze of passersby, to whom he nodded in open-faced greeting, as might an honest man; but he was disappointed that there was no quick dragging to a jail, nor smiting by the hand of God, which quite as often occurred, if his mother and the minister knew anything about such matters. He decided that at least the elderly reprobate would wake up in the dark that very night and cry out in mortal agony under the realization of his sin.

And yet he, the unsullied, the fine theoretical moralist, was to return along that road a thief. A thief of parts, of depraved daring.

"Gramper" and "Grammer" proved to be an incredibly old couple, brown and withered and gray of locks, shrunken in stature, slow and feeble in action, and

446

even rather timid themselves in their greetings. They made much of this grandchild, but they were diffident. Slowly it came to his knowledge that he was set up as a creature to adore. He enjoyed a blissful new sensation of being deferred to. Thereafter he lorded it over them, speaking in confident tones and making wild demands of entertainment. His mother had been right. They were Beans and, therefore, not much. He had brought his own silver napkin-ring and had meant to show them how wonderfully he folded and rolled his napkin after each meal. But it seemed they possessed no napkins whatever. Even his mother hadn't thought anything so repulsive as that of these people. He now boldly played the new game at table that his mother had frowned on. This was to measure off your meat and potatoes into an equal number of "bites," so that they would "come out even." If you were careful and counted right, the thing could be done every time.

And for the first time in all his years he asked for more pie. Of course this was anarchy. He knew well enough that one piece of pie is the heaven-allotted portion; that no one, even partly a Bunker, should crave beyond it; yet this fatuous old pair seemed to invite just that licentiousness, and they watched him with doting eyes while he swaggered through his second helping.

If more had been needed to show the Beanish lowness, it would have come after the first supper, for Gramper and Grammer sat out on a little vine-covered porch and smoked cob-pipes which they refilled at intervals from a sack of tobacco passed companionably back and forth. His own father was supposed to smoke but once a week, on Sunday, and then a cigar such as even a male Bunker might reputably burn. But a *pipe*, and between the lips of Grammer! She managed it with deftness and exhaled clouds of smoke into the still air of evening with a relish most painful to her amazed descendant. Yet she inspired him with an unholy ambition.

Asked the next day about the habit of smoking, Gramper said it was a bad habit; that it stunted people and shortened their days. Both he and Grammer were victims and warnings. Grammer had lumbago sometimes so you wouldn't hardly believe any one could suffer that way and live. As for Gramper himself, he had a cough brought on by tobacco that would carry him off dead one of these days; yes, sir, just like that! And then, to point his warning, Gramper coughed falsely. Even to the unpractised ear of his grandson the cough did not ring true. It lacked poignance.

Late that afternoon, when both the old ones slept, he abstracted a pipe, stuffed it with the rich black flakes and fled with matches to a nook of charming secrecy in the midst of the lilac clump. Thence arose presently clouds of smoke from the strongest tobacco money could buy.

At last he had dared something that didn't hurt him. He puffed valiantly, blowing out the smoke even as Grammer had done. Up to a certain moment his exaltation was intense, his scared soul expanding to greater deeds.

Then he coughed rather alarmingly. But that was to be expected. He drew in another breath of the stuff and coughed again. It was an honest cough; no doubt about that. Perhaps Gramper's cough had been honest. Perhaps the pipe he had selected was Gramper's own pipe, the one that made coughs. He became conscious of something more than throaty discomfort. Tiny beads of sweat bejewelled his brow, the lilac bush began to revolve swiftly about him. He must have taken Grammer's pipe after all—the one that led to lumbago. From revolving with a mere horizontal motion the lilacs now began also to whirl vertically. He had eaten a great deal at dinner....

A pallid remnant of himself declined supper that night. Never could he sit at table again to eat of food. Gramper and Grammer were at first alarmed and there was talk of sending for a veterinary, the nearest to a professional man of medicine within miles and miles. But this talk died out after Gramper had made a cursory examination of the big yard, with especial attention to the lilac clump, where a pipe and other evidence was noticed. After that they not only became strangely reassured, but during their evening smoke on the little porch they often chuckled as if relishing in secret some rare jest. It did not occur to Bean that they laughed at him. He did not suspect that any one could laugh at a little boy who had nearly died of lumbago. And he sat far away that night. The sight of the fuming pipes made him dizzy. His lesson had told. He was never to become an accomplished smoker.

His new spirit of adventure being thus blunted, he spent much of the next day indoors. Grammer opened the "front room" for him, no small concession, for this room was never put to vulgar use; rarely entered, indeed, save once a month for dusting. Here he found an atmosphere in keeping with his own chastened gloom, a musty air of mortality and twilight.

Such poor elegance as could be achieved by Beans alone, unaided by any Bunker, was here concentrated; a melodeon that groaned to his touch, with the startling effect of a voice from a long-closed tomb; a centre-table, luminous with varnish; gilded chairs in formal array; portraits in gilded frames; and best of all, a "whatnot," a thing to fit a corner, having many shelves and each shelf loaded with fascinating objects that maddened one because they must not be touched. Varnished pine-cones, flint arrow-heads, statuettes set on worsted mats, tiny strange boxes rarely ornamented—you mustn't even shake them to see if they contained anything—a small stuffed alligator in the act of climbing a pole; a frail cup and saucer; a watch-chain fashioned from Grammer's hair probably long before she fell into evil habits; a pink china dog that simpered; a dusty black cigar with a gay red-and-gold belt that had once upon a time been given to Gramper by a gentleman in Chicago; a silver cup inscribed "Baby"; a ball of clearest glass, bigger than any marble, with a white camel at its centre looking out unconcernedly; a gilded horseshoe adorned with a bow of blue ribbon; an array of treasure, in short, that made one suspect the Beans might have been something after all if only they had tried.

448

Then on the lower shelf, when Grammer, relying on his honour, had left the room, he made his wondrous discovery—a thing more beautiful than ever he had dreamed of beauty; a thing that caught all the light in the room and shot it back like a risen sun; a thing that excited, enchained, satisfied with a satisfaction so deep that somehow it became pain. It was a shell from the sea, polished to a dazzling brilliance of opal and jade, amethyst and sapphire, delicately subdued, blending as the tints in the western sky at sunset, soft, elusive, fluent. To his rapturously shocked soul, it was a living thing. Instantly a spell was upon him; long he gazed into its depths. It was more than deep; it was bottomless. In some magic solution he there beheld himself and all the world; imperiously it commanded his being. To his ear utterance came from that lucent abyss, a murmur of voices, a confusion of tones; and then invisible presences seemed to reach out greedy hands for him. It was no place for a small boy, and his short legs twinkled as he fled.

Out in the friendly, familiar yard, he looked curiously about him, basking in the sudden peace of it. A light wind stirred in the trees, the sky was a void of blue, the scent of the lilacs came to him. That was all reassuring; but something more came: a consciousness that he could translate only as something vast, yet without shape or substance, that opened to him, enfolded him, lifted him. It was a vision of boundless magnitudes and himself among them—among them and with a power he could put upon them. While it lasted he had a child's dim vision of the knowledge that life would be big for him. He heard again the confusion of voices, and his own among them, in far spacious places. He always remembered this moment. In after years he knew it had been given him then to run an eye along the line of his destiny.

The moment passed; his mind was again vacant. He picked a green apple from the low tree under which he stood, bit into it, chewed without enthusiasm, then hurled the remnant at an immature rabbit that he saw regarding him from the edge of the lilac clump. The missile went wild, but the rabbit fled and Bean pursued it. He was not afraid of a rabbit—not of a young rabbit.

Returning from the chase, an unavailing one, he believed, only because the game used quite unfair tactics of concealment, he remembered the shell. A longing for possession seized him. It was more than that. The thing was already his; had always been his. Yet he foresaw complications. His ownership might be stupidly denied.

He went in to drag Grammer again before the whatnot, his mind sharpened to subtlety.

"Are everything there yours?" He pointed to the top shelf.

"Everything!"

He lowered the pointing finger to the second shelf.

"Are everything there yours?"

"All of 'em!"

"Everything *there*?"

"Yes, yes!"

"And this one, too?"

"For the land's sake, yes!" averred Grammer of the choice contents of the fourth shelf. She was baking pies and found herself a bit impatient of this new game.

"Well, that's all, now!" and he dismissed her, not daring to inquire as to the lower shelf. He had seen the way things were going—a sickening way. But, having shrewdly stopped at the lower shelf, having prevented Grammer from saying that those valuable objects were also hers, he had still the right to come into his own. If the shell mightn't belong to her it might belong to him; therefore it did belong to him; which, as logic, is not so lame as it sounds. At least it is a workaday average.

It occurred to him once to ask for the shell bluntly. But reason forbade this. It was not conceivable that any one having so celestial a treasure would willingly part with it. When a thing was yours you took it, with dignity, but quietly.

During the remainder of his stay he was not conspicuously an occupant of the front room. No day passed that he did not contrive at least one look at his wonderful shell, but he craftily did not linger there, nor did he ever utter words about the thing, though these often crowded perilously to his lips.

A later day brought a letter to Grammer, and Gramper delightedly let it be known that the doctor at Wellsville had brought little Bean a fine new baby brother. Bean himself was not delighted at this. He had suffered the ministrations of that same doctor and he could imagine no visit of his to result in a situation at all pleasant to any one concerned. If he had brought a baby it was doubtless not a baby that people would care to have around the house. He was not cheered when told that he might now go home.

He meant to stay on, and said so.

But the second day brought another letter that had a curious effect on Gramper and Grammer. Grammer cried, and Gramper told him with a strange, grave manner that now he must go. He knew that he was not told why; something, he overheard them agree, needn't be told "just yet." This was rather exciting and reconciled him to leaving.

He crept softly down the narrow stairs that night, alleging, when called to by Grammer, the need of a drink of water. When he returned his hands trembled about the shell. Swiftly it went to the bottom of his small box, his extra clothing, all his little belongings, being packed cleverly about it.

They kissed him many times the next morning, and when he looked back under the trees to where the old couple stood in front of the little weather-beaten house he saw that Grammer was crying again. His conscience hurt him a little; he wondered how they would get along without the shell. But they couldn't have it, because it was his shell.

The stage turned after a bit, and suddenly there was Gramper at the roadside, breathless after his run across a corner of the east forty. Instantly he was in the clutch of a great fear; the loss had been discovered. He sat frozen, waiting.

But Gramper only flourished the napkin-ring, and humorously taunted him with not having packed everything, after all. The stage drove on, but for the next mile his breathing was jerky.

Toward the end of the day-long ride—Gramper couldn't be running after them *that* far—he surrendered to his exultation, opened the box and drew out the shell, fondling it, fascinated anew by its varying sheen, excited by the freedom with which he now might touch it. Again he was the sole passenger and he called to the old driver, to whom nothing at all seemed to have happened because of his filching fruit.

"See my shell I found at Grammer's!"

But the old man was blind to beauty. He turned a careless eye upon the treasure, turned it off again with a formless grunt that might have been perfunctory praise, and resumed his half-muttered talk to himself, marked by little oblique nods of triumph—some endless dispute that he seemed to hold with an invisible opponent.

The owner of the shell was chilled but not daunted. There would surely be others less benighted who must acclaim the shell's charm.

Presently he was at the familiar front gate and his father, looking unusual, somehow, came to lift him down.

"See my shell I found at Grammer's!"

"Your mother is dead."

"See my shell I found at Grammer's!"

"Your mother is dead."

It was the sinister iteration by which he was stricken, rather than the news itself. The latter only stunned. His hand in his father's, he went up the walk and into the house. There were women inside, women who moved with an effect of bustling stillness, the same women who had so often asked him what his name was. They seemed to know it well enough now. He was aware that his entrance created no little sensation. One of them kissed him and told him not to cry, but he had no thought of crying. He became aware of the thing in his hands.

"See my shell I found at Grammer's!"

The invitation was a general one. They looked in silence and some of them moved about, and then through a doorway he saw in the next room an object long and dark and shining set on two chairs.

He had never seen anything like it, but its suggestion was evil. The women waited. Something seemed to be expected of some one. His father led him into that room and lifted him up to see. His mother's face was there under a glass. He could see that she wore her pretty blue dress, and on one arm beside her was something covered with white. He called softly to her.

"Mamma! Mamma!"

But she did not open her eyes.

Then he was out again where the people were, and the people seemed to forget about him. He went to his little room under the sloping roof. He had not let go of the shell and now, in the fading light from the low window, he lost himself once more in its depths. Inwardly he knew that a terror lurked near, but he had not yet felt it. Only when bedtime came did the continued silence of his mother become meaningful. When he was left alone, he cried for her, still clutching his shell.

The minister came the next day, and many people, and the minister talked to them about his mother. The two Uncle Bunkers were there, grim, hard-mouthed, glaring, for they hated each other as only brothers can hate. He wondered if they would still let him be partly a Bunker, now that his mother was gone. He wondered also at the novel consideration he saw being shown to his father. Dressed in a new suit of black, with an unaccustomed black hat, his father was plainly become a man of importance. He was one apart, and people of undoubted consequence deferred to him—to the very last. He earnestly wished his mother could see that; his nervous little mother with the flushed face and tired eyes, always terrifically concerned about one small matter or another. He thought she would have liked to see that his father was some one, after all.

CHAPTER II

The Chicago epoch began a year later. The true nature of its causes never lay quite clearly in the mind of Bean. There was, first, an entirely new Uncle Bunker whom he had never seen, but whom he at once liked very much. He was a younger, more beautiful uncle, with a gay, light manner and expensive clothing. He wore a magnificent gold watch and chain, and jewelled rings flashed from his white fingers as he, in absent moments, daintily passed a small pocket-comb through the meshes of his lustrous brown side-whiskers. Little Bean knew that he did something on a board in Chicago; that he "operated" on the Board of Trade was the accustomed phrasing. He liked the word, and tried to picture what "operating" might mean in relation to a board.

The good people of Wellsville regarded this uncle with quite all the respect so flashing a figure deserved. Not so the two other Uncle Bunkers from over Walnut Shade way. Their first known agreement, voiced of this financier, was in saying something wise about a fool and his money.

Later, and perhaps for the last time on earth, they agreed once more. That was when the news of his marriage came to them—for what was she? Nothing but his landlady's daughter! Snip of a girl that helped her mother run a cheap Chicago boarding-house! Him that could have taken his pick, if he was going to be a fool and tie himself up! You could bet that the pair had "worked" him, that mother and the girl; landed him for his money, that was plain! Well, he'd made his bed!

Bean was not slow to liken this uncle to his mother, who had also "made her bed." He had at first a misty notion that the bride might a little resemble his father, a notion happily dispelled when he saw her. For the pair came to Wellsville. It was a sort of honeymoon combined vaguely with business. The bride was wonderfully pretty, Bean thought; dark and dainty and laughing, forever talking the most irresistible "baby-talk" to her adoring mate. Her name for him was "Boo'ful."

Bean at once fell deeply in love with this bride, a passion that was to endure beyond the life of most such affairs. She professed an infatuation equal to his own, and regretted that an immediate marriage, which he timidly advocated in the course of their first interview, was not practicable. That she was frivolous, light-minded, and would never settle down to be a good worker, was a village verdict he scorned. Who would have her otherwise? Not he, nor the adoring Boo'ful, it is certain. He determined to go to live at her house, and, strangely enough—for these sudden plans of his were most often discouraged—the thing seemed feasible. For one thing, his father was going to bring home a new mother; a lady, he gathered, who had not only settled down to be a good worker, but who, in espousing his father, would curiously not marry beneath her. Without being told so, he had absorbed from his first mother a conviction that this was possible to but few women. He felt a little glow of pride for his father in this affair.

Another matter that seemed to bear on his going away was that this brilliant and human Uncle Bunker was a "trustee." Not only a trustee, but *his* trustee; his very own, like his shell, or anything. This led to his discovery that he had money. His mother, it seemed, had left it to him; Bunker money that the two older uncles had sought and failed to divert from her on the occasion of her wedding one below her station. Money! and the capable Uncle Bunker as trustee of that money! Money one could buy things with! He was pleasantly conscious of being rather important under the glance of familiars. Even his father spoke formal words of counsel to him, as if a gulf was between them—his father now bereft of all Bunker prestige, legal or social.

And the new uncle was to "educate" him, though this was to be paid for out of that money of his very own. He was rudely shocked to learn that you had to pay money to go to school. Loathing school as he did, to pay money for your own torture—money that would buy things—seemed unutterably silly. But despite this imbecility the prospect retained its glamour.

He would have suffered punishments even worse than school for the privilege of existing near that beautiful bride, whom he was now calling, at her especial request, "Aunt Clara." She readily understood any affair that he chose to explain to her; understood about his shell and said it was the most beautiful thing in all the world. She understood, too, and was deeply sympathetic about Skipper, the dog. Skipper was one of a series of puppies that Bean had appropriated from the public highway. Some had shamefully deserted him after a little time of pampering. Others, and these were the several that had howled untimely in the far night, had mysteriously disappeared. Bean had sometimes a hurt suspicion that his father knew more than he cared to tell about these vanishings. But Skipper had stayed and had not howled. Buffeted wastrel of a thousand casual amours, soft-haired, confiding, ungainly, he was rich in understanding if not in beauty. And yet he must be left. Even the discriminating and ever-just Aunt Clara felt that Skipper would not do well in a great city. Of course she was not clumsy enough to suggest that there were other dogs in the world, as did her less discerning husband. But she said that it would come out all right, and Bean trusted her. She knew, too, what would happen on his first night away, and came softly to his bed and solaced him as he lay crying for Skipper.

Those first Chicago days were rich in flavour. The city was a marvel of many terrors, a place of weird sounds, strange shapes and swift movements, among which—having been made timid by much adversity—you had need to be very, very careful if your hand was in no one's. The house itself was wonderful: a house of real brick and very lofty. If you started in the basement you could go "upstairs" three distinct times in it before you reached the top. He had never imagined such a house for any but kings to live in. Within were many rooms; he hardly could count them all; and regal furnishings, gay with colour; and, permeating it all, a most appetizing odour of cooked food, eloquent tale of long-eaten banquets, able reminder of those to come.

Out beside the front door was a rather dingy sign that said "Boarders Wanted." His deduction after reading the sign was that the person who wanted the boarders was Aunt Clara's mother. She was like Aunt Clara in that she was dark and small, but in nothing else. She did not wear pretty dresses nor laugh nor address baby talk to "Boo'ful." She was very old and not nice to look at, Bean thought; and an uneasy woman, not knowing how to be quiet. Mostly she worked in the kitchen, after a hasty morning tour of the house to "do" the rooms. Bean was much surprised to learn that her name, too, was Clara. She did not look at all like any one whose name would be Clara.

And presently there was to be a house even more magnificent than this, where they would all live together and where, so they jested, the old Clara wouldn't know what to do, because there would be nothing to do. The house would be ready just as soon as Boo'ful made his "next turn," and that was so near in time that there was already a fascinating picture of the lines of the house, white lines on blue paper, over which Boo'ful and Aunt Clara spent many an evening in loving dispute. It seemed that you could change the house by merely changing those lines. Sometimes they put a curve into the main stairway or doubled the area of stained-glass window in the music-room; sometimes it was a mere detail of alteration in the butler's pantry, or the coachman's room over the stable. The old Clara displayed no interest in these details. She seemed to be content to go on wanting boarders.

This was not, as he saw it, an unlovely want. It surrounded her with gay companions at meal-time; they were "like one big family," as one of the number would frequently observe. He was the one that most often set them all to laughing by his talk like that of a German who speaks English imperfectly, which he didn't have to do at all. It was only make-believe, but very funny.

After this joyous group and his Aunt Clara, who really came first, his preference in humans was for a lady who lived two doors away. If you rang her bell she might be one of three persons. It depended on what you were looking for. She might be the manicure and chiropodist whose sign was displayed; she might be Madam Wanda, the world-renowned clairvoyant, sittings from 9 A.M. to 5 P.M., Advice on Love, Marriage and Business; sign also displayed; or she might be merely Mrs. Jackson, with a choice front room for a single gentleman, as declared by the third sign. In any case she was a smiling, plump lady with a capable blue eye and abundant dark hair that was smooth and shiny.

It was in company with his uncle that he first made her acquaintance. His uncle knew all that one need know about Love and Marriage, but it seemed that his knowledge of Business could be extended. There were times when only the gifts of a world-renowned clairvoyant could enable one to say what May wheat was going to do.

The acquaintance, lightly enough begun, ripened soon to intimacy, and so were the eyes of Bean first opened to mysteries that would later affect his life so vitally. He was soon carrying wood and coal up the back stairs of Mrs. Jackson, in return for which the lady ministered to him in her professional capacities. At their first important session on a rainy Saturday of leisure she trimmed and polished each of his ten finger-nails, told his past, present and future—he was going to cross water and there was a dark gentleman he had need to beware of—and suggested that his feet might need attention.

He squirmingly demurred at this last operation, and successfully resisted it. But the bonds of their friendship were sealed over a light collation which she served. She was a vegetarian, she told him. You couldn't get on to a high spiritual plane if you ate the corpses of murdered animals. But her food seemed sufficing and she drank beer which he brought her in a neat pitcher from the cheerful store on the corner where they sold such things. Beer, she explained to him, was a strictly vegetable product, though not the thing for growing boys. The young must discriminate, even among vegetables.

They liked each other well and in a little time he had absorbed the simple tale of her activities. When you rented rooms, people sometimes left without paying you. So had gone Professor de Lavigne, the chiropodist; so had vanished the original Madam Wanda. They had left their signs, and nothing else. The rest was simple after you had been seeing how they did it—a little practice with a nail-file, a little observation of parties that came in with crêpe on, to whom you said, "Standing right there I see some one near and dear to you that has lately passed on to the spirit land"; or male parties that looked all fussed up and worried, to whom you said that the deal was coming out all right, only they were always to act on their first impulse and look out for a man with kind of brownish hair who carried a gold watch and sometimes wore gloves. She said it was strange how she could "hit it" sometimes, especially where there were initials in the hats they left outside in the hall, or a name inside the overcoat pocket. It was wonderful what she had been able to tell parties for a dollar.

Bean cared little for these details, but he was excited by the theory back of them; a world from which the unseen spirits of the dead will counsel and guide us in our daily affairs if we will listen. It was a new terror added to a world of terrors— they were all about you, striving with futile hands to touch you, whispering words of cheer or warning to your deaf ears.

Mrs. Jackson herself believed it implicitly and went each week to consult one or another of the more advanced mediums. The last one had seen the spirit of her Aunt Mary, a deceased person so remote in time that she had been clean forgotten. But it was a valuable pointer. When you come to think about it, at least seven parties out of ten, if they were any way along in years, had a dead Aunt Mary. And

456

it was best to go to the good ones. Mrs. Jackson admitted that. You paid more, but you got more.

Uncle Bunker became of this opinion very soon. What Mrs. Jackson disclosed to him about May wheat had seemed to be hardly worth the dollar she asked. He began going to the good ones, and Bean gathered that even their superior gifts left something to be desired. The brilliant uncle began to accustom his home circle to frowns. Bean and the older Clara (she was beginning to complain about not sleeping and a pain in her side) were sensible of this change, but the younger Clara only pouted when she noticed it at all, prettily accusing her splendid consort of not caring for her as he had once professed to. She spent more time over her hair and shopped extensively for feminine trappings.

Then one day his uncle came home, a slinking wreck of beauty, and told Aunt Clara that all was lost save honour. Bean heard the interesting announcement, and gathered, after a question from his aunt, that his own patrimony had been a part of that all which was lost save honour. He heard his uncle add tearfully that one shot would end it now.

He was frightened by this, but his Aunt Clara seemed not to be. He heard her say, "There, there! Did a nassy ol' martet do adainst 'ums!" And later she was seen to take him up tea and toast and chicken.

The years seemed to march more swiftly then—school and growing and little changes in the house. Boo'ful never fired the shot that would have ended all. The older Clara inconsequently died and the frivolous Clara took her place in the kitchen. She had not corrected her light manner, but slowly she changed with the years until she was almost as faded as the old Clara had been. More ambitious, however, and working to better purpose. They went to a new and finer house that would hold more boarders; and the sign, which was lettered in gold, said, "Boarders Taken," a far more dignified sign than the old with its frank appeal of "Boarders Wanted." That new sign intimated a noble condescension.

Aunt Clara had not only settled down to be a worker, but she had proved to be a manager. Boo'ful actually performed little services about the house, staying in the kitchen at meal-time to carve and help serve the food. Aunt Clara had been unexpected adamant in the matter of his taking a fine revenge on the market that had gone against him. She refused to provide the very modest sum he pleaded for to this end, and as the two old Uncle Bunkers were equally obdurate—they said they had known when he married that flutter-budget just how he would end—his leisure was never seriously menaced.

Aunt Clara was especially firm about the money because of the considerable life-insurance premium she soon began to pay. It was her whim that little Bean had not been of competent years to lose all save honour, and she had discovered a life-insurance company whose officers were mad enough to compute Boo'ful's loss to the world in dollars and cents. He was, in fact, considered an excellent risk. He did not fade after the manner of the busy Aunt Clara, that gay little wretch whose girlish graces lingered on incongruously—like jests upon a tombstone.

Bean grew to college years. Aunt Clara had been insistent about the college; it was to be the best business college in Chicago. Bean matriculated without formality and studied stenography and typewriting. Aunt Clara had been afraid that he might "get in" with a fast college set and learn to drink and smoke and gamble. It may be admitted that he wished to do just these things, but he had observed the effects of drink, his one experience with tobacco remained all too vivid, and gambling required more capital than the car fare he was usually provided with. Besides, you came to a bad end if you gambled. It led to other things.

Nor would he, on the public street, join with any number of his class in the college yell. He was afraid a policeman would arrest him. Even in the more mature years of a comparatively blameless life he remained afraid of policemen, and never passed one without a tremor. All of which conduced to his efficiency as a student. When others fled to their questionable pleasures he was as likely as not to remain in his chair before a typewriter, pounding out again and again, "*The swift brown fox jumps over the lazy dog—*" a dramatic enough situation ingeniously worded to utilize nearly all the letters of our alphabet.

At last he was pronounced competent, received a diploma (which Aunt Clara framed handsomely and hung in her own room beside the pastel portrait of Boo'ful in his opulent prime) and took up a man's work.

The veil that hangs between mortal eyes and the Infinite had many times been pierced for him by the able Mrs. Jackson. He was now to enter another and more significant stage of his spiritual development.

His first employer was a noble-looking old man, white-bearded, and vast of brow, who came to be a boarder at Aunt Clara's. He was a believer in the cult of theosophy and specialized on reincarnation. Neither word was luminous to Bean, but he learned that the old gentleman was writing a book and would need an amanuensis. They agreed upon terms and the work began. The book was a romance entitled, "Glimpses Through the Veil of Time," and it was to tell of a soul's adventures through a prolonged series of reincarnations. So much Bean grasped. The terminology of the author was more difficult. When you have chiefly

458

learned to write, "Your favour of the 11th inst. came duly to hand and in reply we beg to state—" it is confusing to be switched to such words as "anthropogenesis" and to chapter headings like "Substituting Variable Quantities for Fixed Extraordinary Theoretic Possibilities." Even when the author meant to be most lucid Bean found him not too easy. "In order to simplify the theory of the Karmic cycle," dictated the white-bearded one for his Introduction, "let us think of the subplanes of the astral plane as horizontal divisions, and of the types of matter belonging to the seven great planetary Logoi as perpendicular divisions crossing these others at right angles."

What Bean made of this in transcribing his notes need not be told. What is solely important is that, as the tale progressed, he became enthralled by the doctrine of reincarnation. It was of minor consequence that he became expert in shorthand.

Had he lived before, would he live again? There must be a way to know. "Alclytus," began an early chapter of the tale, "was born this time in 21976 B.C. in a male body as the son of a king, in what is now the Telugu country not far from Masulipatam. He was proficient in riding, shooting, swimming and the sports of his race. When he came of age he married Surya, the daughter of a neighbouring rajah and they were very happy together in their religious studies—"

Had he, Bunker Bean, perhaps once espoused the daughter of a rajah, and been happy in religious studies with her? Had he, perchance, been even the rajah himself? Why not?

The romance was never finished. A worried son of the old gentleman appeared one day, alleged that he had run off from a good home where he was kindly treated, and by mild force carried him back. But he had performed his allotted part in Bean's life.

A few books had been left and these were read. Death was a recurring incident in an endless life. Wise men he saw had found this an answer to all problems—founders of religions and philosophies—Buddha, Pythagoras, Plato, the Christ. Wise moderns had accepted it, Max Müller and Hume and Goethe, Fichte, Schelling, Lessing. Bean could not appraise these authorities, but the names somehow sounded convincing and the men had seemed to think that reincarnation was the only doctrine of immortality a philosopher could consider.

It remained, then, to explore the Karmic past of Bunker Bean; not in any mood of lightness. A verse quoted by the old man had given him pause:

"Who toiled a slave may come anew a prince

For gentle worthiness and merit won;

Who ruled a king may wander earth in rags
For things done and undone."

What might he have been? For ruling once as a king, a bad king, was he now merely Bunker Bean, not precisely roaming the earth in rags, but sidling timidly through its terrors, disbelieving in himself, afraid of policemen, afraid of life?

So he confronted and considered the thing, fascinated by its vistas as once he had been by the shell. If it were true that we cast away our worn bodies and ever reclothe ourselves with new, why should not the right member of Mrs. Jackson's profession one day unfold to him his beginningless past?

CHAPTER III

"The courts havin' decided," continued Breede, in staccato explosions, "that the 'quipment is nes'ry part of road, without which road would be tot'ly crippled, you will note these first moggige 'quipment bonds take pri'rty over first-moggige bonds, an' gov'n y'sef 'cordingly your ver' truly—"

He glanced up at Bean, contracted his brows to a black menace and emitted a final detonation.

"'S all for 's aft'noon!"

He bit savagely into his unlighted cigar and began to rifle through a new sheaf of documents. Bean deftly effaced himself, with a parting glare at the unlighted cigar. It was a feature of Breede that no reporter ever neglected to mention, but Bean thought you might as well chew tobacco and be done with it. Moreover, the cigars were not such as one would have expected to find between the lips of a man whose present wealth was estimated at a round hundred million. Bulger, in the outer office, had given up trying to smoke them. He declared them to be the very worst that could be had for any money.

Before beginning the transcription of his notes, Bean had to learn the latest telephone news from the ball-ground. During the last half-hour he had inwardly raged more than usual at Breede for being kept from this information. Bulger always managed to get it on time, beginning with the third inning, even when he took dictation from Breede's confidential secretary, or from Tully, the chief clerk.

Bean looked inquiringly at Bulger now. Bulger nodded and presently strolled from his own desk to Bean's, where he left a slip of paper bearing the words, "Cubs, 3; Giants, 2; 1st ½ 4th."

Bean had envied Bulger from the first for this man-of-the-world ease. In actual person not superior to Bean, he had a temperament of daring. In every detail he was an advanced dresser, specializing in flamboyant cravats. He would have been Bean's model if Bean had been less a coward. Bulger was nearly all that Bean wished to be. He condescended to his tasks with an air of elegant and detached leisure that raised them to the dignity of sports. He had quite the air of a wealthy amateur with a passion for typewriting.

He had once done Breede's personal work, but had been banished to the outer office after Bean's first try-out. Breede had found some mysterious objection to him. Perhaps it was because Bulger would always look up with pleased sagacity, as if he were helping to compose Breede's letters. It may have been simple envy in Breede for his advanced dressing. Bulger had felt no unkindness toward Bean for thus supplanting him in a desirable post. But he did confide to his successor that if he, Bulger, ever found Breede under his heel, Breede could expect no mercy. Bulger would grind him—just like that!

Bean dramatized this as he wrote his letters; Breede pleasantly disintegrating under the iron heel of Bulger: Breede "The Great Reorganizer," as he was said to be known "in the Street," old "steel and velvet," meeting a just fate! So nearly mechanical was his typewriting that he spoiled one sheet of paper by transcribing two lines of shorthand not meant to be a part of the letter. Only by chance did a certain traffic manager of lines west of Chicago escape reading a briefly worded opinion of the clothes he wore that would have puzzled and might have pained him, for Breede, such had come to be his confidence in Bean, always signed his letters without reading them over. Bean gasped and wisely dismissed the drama of Bulger's revenge from his mind.

At four-thirty the day's work ended and Bean was free to forget until another day the little he had been unable to avoid learning about high railroad finance; free to lead his own secret life, which was a thing apart from all that wordy foolery.

He changed from his office coat to one alleged by its maker to give him the appearance of perfect physical development, and descended to the street-level in company with Bulger. Bean would have preferred to walk down; he suffered the sensations of dying each time the elevator seemed to fall, but he could not confess this to the doggish and intrepid Bulger.

There were other weaknesses he had to cloak. Bulger proffered cigarettes from a silver case at their first meeting. Bean declined.

"Doctor's orders," said he.

"Nerves?" suggested Bulger, expertly.

"Heart—gets me something fierce."

"Come in here to Tommy's and take a bracer," now suggested the hospitable Bulger. But again the physician had been obdurate.

"Won't let me touch a thing—liver," said Bean. "Got to be careful of a breakdown."

"Tough," said Bulger. "Man needs a certain amount of it, down here in the street. Course, a guy can't *sop* it up, like you see some do. Other night, now—gang of us out, y'understand—come too fast for your Uncle Cuthbert. Say, goin' up those stairs where I live I cert'n'ly must 'a' sounded like a well-known clubman gettin' home from an Elks' banquet. Head, next A.M.?—ask me, *ask* me! Nothing of the kind! Don't I show up with a toothache and con old Tully into a day off at the dentist's to have the bridge-work tooled up. Ask me was I at the dentist's? Wow! Not!—little old William J. Turkish bath for mine!"

Bean was moved to raw envy. But he knew himself too well. The specialist he professed to have consulted had put a ban upon the simplest recreations. Otherwise how could he with any grace have declined those repeated invitations of Bulger's to come along and meet a couple of swell dames that'd like to have a good time? Bulger, considered in relation to the sex not his own, was what he himself would have termed "a smooth little piece of work." Bean was not this. Of all his terrors women, as objects of purely male attention, were the greatest. He longed for them, he looked upon such as were desirable with what he believed to be an evil eye, but he had learned not to go too close. They talked, they disconcerted him horribly. And if they didn't talk they looked dangerous, as if they knew too much. Some day, of course, he would nerve himself to it. Indeed he very determinedly meant to marry, and to have a son who should be trained from the cradle with the sole idea of making him a great left-handed pitcher; but that was far in the future. He longed tragically to go with Bulger and meet a couple of swell dames, but he knew how it would be. Right off they would find him out and laugh at him.

Bulger consumed another high-ball, filled his cigarette case, and the two stood a moment on Broadway. Breede, the last to leave his office, crossed the pavement to a waiting automobile.

"There's his foxy Rebates going to the arms of his family," said Bulger, disrespectfully applying to Breede a term that had more than once made him interesting to the Interstate Commerce Commission.

"See the three skirts in the back? That's the Missis and the two squabs. Young one's only a flapper, but the old one's a peacherine for looks. Go on, lamp her once!"

Bean turned his diffident gaze upon the occupants of the tonneau with a sudden wild dream that he would stare insolently. But his eyes unaccountably came to rest in the eyes of the young one—the flapper. He saw only the eyes, and he felt that the eyes were seeing him. The motor chugged slowly up Broadway, nosing for a path about a slowly driven truck; the flapper looked back.

"Not half bad, that!" said Bean, recovering, and speaking in what he felt was the correct Bulger tone.

"Not for mine," said Bulger firmly. "Big sister, though, not so worse. Met up with her one time out to the country place, takin' stuff for the old man the time he got kidneys in his feet. I made a hit with her, too, on the level, but say! nothin' doing there for old John W. me! I dropped the thing like it was poison ivy. Me doin' the nuptial in a family like that, and bein' under Pop's thumb the rest of my life? Ask me, that's all; *ask* me! Wake me up any time in the night and ask me."

Again Bean was thrilled, resolving then and there that no daughter of Breede's should ever wed him. Bulger was entirely right. It wouldn't do. Bulger looked at his watch.

"Well, s'long; got a date down in the next block. She's out at five. Say, I want you to get a flash at her some day. Broadway car, yesterday, me goin' uptown with Max, see? she lookin' at her gloves. 'Pipe the queen in black,' I says to Max, jes' so she could hear, y' understand. Say, did she gimme the eye. Not at all! Not at *all*! Old William H. Smoothy, I guess yes. Pretty soon a gink setting beside her beats it, and quick change for me. Had her all dated up by Fourteenth Street. Dinner and a show, if things look well. Some class to her, all right. One the manicures in that shop down there. Well, s'long!"

Looking over his shoulder with sickish envy after the invincible Bulger, Bean left the curb for a passing car and came to a jolting stop against the biggest policeman he had ever seen. He mumbled a horrified apology, but his victim did not even turn to look down upon him. He fled into the car and found a seat, still trembling from that collision. From across the aisle a pretty girl surveyed him with veiled insolence. He furtively felt of his neutral-tinted cravat and took his hat off to see if there could be a dent in it. The girl, having plumbed his insignificance, now unconcernedly read the signs above his head. There was bitterness in the stare he bestowed upon her trim lines. Some day Bulger would chance to be on that car with her—then she'd be taken down a bit—Bulger who, by Fourteenth Street, had them all dated up.

Presently he was embarrassed by a stout, aggressive man who clutched a strap with one hand and some evening papers with the other, a man who clearly considered it outrageous that he should be compelled to stand in a street car. He glared at Bean with a cold, questioning indignation, shifting from one foot to the other, and seeming to be on the point of having words about it. This was not long to be endured. Bean glanced out in feigned dismay, as if at a desired cross-street he had carelessly passed, sprang toward the door of the car and caromed heavily against a tired workingman who still, however, was not too tired to put his sense of injury into quick, pithy words of the street. The pretty girl tittered horribly and the stout man, already in Bean's seat, rattled his papers impatiently, implying that people in that state ought to be kept off in the first place.

He had meant to leave the car and try another, but there at the step was another too-large policeman helping an uncertain old lady to the ground, so he slinkingly insinuated himself to the far corner of the platform, where, for forty city blocks, a whistling messenger boy gored his right side with the corners of an unyielding box while a dreamy-eyed man who, as Bulger would have said, had apparently been sopping it up like you see some do, leaned a friendly elbow on his shoulder, dented his new hat and from time to time stepped elaborately on his natty shoes with the blue cloth uppers. Also, the conductor demanded and received a second fare from him. What was the use of saying you had paid inside? The conductor was a desperate looking man who would probably say he knew that game, and stop the car....

Something of the sort always happened to him in street cars. It was bad enough when you walked, with people jostling you and looking as if they wondered what right you had to be there.

At last came the street down which he made a daily pilgrimage and he popped from the crowd on the platform like a seed squeezed from an orange.

464

Reaching the curb alive—the crossing policeman graciously halted a huge motor-truck driven by a speed-enthusiast—he corrected the latest dent in his hat, straightened his cravat, readjusted the shoulder lines of the coat appertaining to America's greatest eighteen-dollar suit—"$18.00—No More; No Less!"—and with a fear-quickened hand discovered that his watch was gone, his gold hunting-case watch and horseshoe fob set with brilliants, that Aunt Clara had given him on his twenty-first birthday for not smoking!

A moment he stood, raging, fearing. His money was safe, but they might decide to come back for that. Or the policeman might come up and make an ugly row because he had let himself be robbed in a public conveyance. He would have to prove that the watch was his; probably have to tell why Aunt Clara had given it to him.

With a philosophy peculiarly his own, a spirit of wise submission that was more than once to serve him well, he pulled his hat sharply down, braced and squared such appearance of perfect physical development as the eighteen dollars had achieved, and walked away. He had always known the watch would go. Now it was gone, no more worry. Good enough! As he walked he rehearsed an explanation to Bulger: cleverly worded intimations that the watch had been pawned to meet a certain quick demand on his resources not morally to his credit. He made the implication as sinister as he could.

And then he stood once more before the shrine of Beauty. In the show-window of a bird-and-animal store on Sixth Avenue was a four-months-old puppy, a "Boston-bull," that was, of a certainty, the most perfect thing ever born of a mother-dog. Already the head was enormous, in contrast, yet somehow in a maddening harmony with the clean-lined slender body. The colour-scheme was golden brown on a background of pure white. On the body this golden brown was distributed with that apparent carelessness which is Art. Overlaying the sides and back were three patches of it about the size and somewhat the shape of maps of Africa as such are commonly to be observed. In the colouring of the noble brow and absurdly wide jaws a more tender care was evident. There was the same golden brown, beginning well back of the ears and flowing lustrously to the edge of the overhanging upper lip, where it darkened. Midway between the ears—erectly alert those ears were—a narrow strip of white descended a little way to open to a circle of white in the midst of which was the black muzzle. At the point of each nostril was the tiniest speck of pink, Beauty's last triumphant touch.

As he came to rest before the window the creature leaped forward with joyous madness, reared two clumsy white feet against the glass (those feet that seemed to have been meant for a larger dog), barked ably—he could hear it even above the din of an elevated train—and then fell to a frantic licking of the glass where Bean had provocatively spread a hand. Perceiving this intimacy to be thwarted by some mysterious barrier to be felt but not seen, he backed away, fell forward upon his chest, the too-big paws outspread, and smiled from a vasty pink cavern. Between the stiffened ears could be seen the crooked tail, tinged with just enough of the brown, in unbelievably swift motion. Discovering this pose to bring no desired result, he ran mad in the sawdust, excavating it feverishly with his forepaws, sending it expertly to the rear with the others.

The fever passed; he surveyed his admirer for a moment, then began to revolve slowly upon all four feet until he had made in the sawdust a bed that suited him. Into this he sank and was instantly asleep, his slenderness coiled, the heavy head at rest on a paw, one ear drooping wearily, the other still erect.

For two weeks this daily visit had been almost the best of Bean's secrets. For two weeks he had known that his passion was hopeless, yet had he yearned out his heart there before the endearing thing. In the shock of his first discovery, spurred to unwonted daring, he had actually penetrated the store meaning to hear the impossible price. But an angry-looking old man (so Bean thought) had come noisily from a back room and glowered at him threateningly over big spectacles. So he had hastily priced a convenient jar of goldfish for which he felt no affection whatever, mumbled something about the party's calling, himself, next day, and escaped to the street. Anyway, it would have been no good, asking the price; it was bound to be a high price; and he couldn't keep a dog; and if he did, a policeman would shoot it for being mad when it was only playing.

But some time—yet, would it be this same animal? In all the world there could not be another so acceptable. He shivered with apprehension each day as he neared the place, lest some connoisseur had forestalled him. He quickened to a jealous distrust of any passerby who halted beside him to look into the window, and felt a great relief when these passed on.

Once he had feared the worst. A man beside him holding a candy-eating child by the hand had said, "Now, now, sir!" and, "Well, well, *was*he a nice old doggie!" Then they had gone into the store, very businesslike, and Bean had felt that he might be taking his last look at a loved one. Lawless designs throbbed in his brain—a wild plan to shadow the man to his home—to have that dog, *no matter how*. But when they came out the child carried nothing more than a wicker cage containing two pink-eyed white rabbits that were wrinkling their noses furiously.

With a last cherishing look at most of the beauty in all the world—it still slept despite the tearing clatter of a parrot with catarrhal utterance that shrieked over and over, "Oh, what a fool! Oh, what a fool!"—he turned away. What need to say that, with half the opportunity, his early infamy of the shell would have been repeated. He wondered darkly if the old man left that dog in the window nights!

He reached for his watch before he remembered its loss. Then he reminded himself bitterly that street clocks were abundant and might be looked at by simpletons who couldn't keep watches. He bought an evening paper that shrieked with hydrocephalic headlines and turned into a dingy little restaurant advertising a "Regular Dinner de luxe with Dessert, 35 cts."

There was gloom rather than gusto in his approach to the table. He expected little; everything had gone wrong; and he was not surprised to note that the cloth on the table must also have served that day for a "Business Men's Lunch, 35 cts.," as advertised on a wall placard. Several business men seemed to have eaten there—careless men, their minds perhaps on business while they ate. A moody waiter took his order, feebly affecting to efface all stains from the tablecloth by one magic sweep of an already abused napkin.

Bean read his paper. One shriek among the headlines was for a railroad accident in which twenty-eight lives had been lost. He began to go down the list of names hopefully, but there was not one that he knew. Although he wished no evil to any person, he was yet never able to suppress a strange, perverse thrill of disappointment at this result—that there should be the name of no one he knew in all those lists of the mangled. His food came and he ate, still striving—the game of childhood had become unconscious habit with him now—to make his meat and potatoes "come out even." The dinner de luxe was too palpably a soggy residue of that Business Men's Lunch. It fittingly crowned the afternoon's catastrophes. He turned from it to his paper and Destiny tied another knot on his bonds. There it was in bold print:

COUNTESS   CASANOVA
Clairvoyant   ...   Clairaudient
Psychometric.
Fresh   from   Unparalleled   European   Triumphs.
Answers the Unasked Question.

There was more of it. The Countess had been "prevailed upon by eminent scientists to give a brief series of tests in this city." Evening tests might be had from 8 to 10 P.M. Ring third bell.

The old query came back, the old need to know what he had been before putting on this present very casual body. Was his present state a reward or a penance? From the time of leaving the office to the last item in that sketchy dinner, he had been put upon by persons and circumstances. It was time to know what life meant by him.

And here was one who answered the unasked question!

Precisely at eight he rang the third bell, climbed two flights of narrow stairs and faced a door that opened noiselessly and without visible agency. He entered a small, dimly lighted room and stood there uncertainly. After a moment two heavy curtains parted at the rear of the room and the Countess Casanova stood before him. It could have been no other; her lustrous, heavy-lidded dark eyes swept him soothingly. Her hair was a marvellously piled storm-cloud above a full, well-rounded face. Her complexion was wonderful. One very plump, very white hand rested at the neck of the flowing scarlet robe she wore. A moment she posed thus, beyond doubt a being capable of expounding all wingy mysteries of any soul whatsoever.

467

Then she became alert and voluble. She took his hat and placed it in the hall, seated him before the table at the room's centre and sat confronting him from the other side. She filled her chair. It could be seen that she was no slave to tight lacing.

Although foreign in appearance, the Countess spoke with a singularly pure and homelike American accent. It was the speech he was accustomed to hear in Chicago. It reassured him.

The Countess searched his face with those wonderful eyes.

"You are intensely psychic," she announced.

Bean was aware of this. Every medium he had ever consulted had told him so.

The Countess gazed dreamily above his head.

"Your spiritual aura is clouded by troubled curnts, as it were. I see you meetin' a great loss, but you mus' take heart, for a very powerful hand on the other side is guardin' you night an' day. They tell me your initials is 'B.B.' You are employed somewheres in the daytime. I see a big place with lots of other people employed there—"

The Countess paused. Bean waited in silence.

"Here"—she came out of the clouds that menaced her sitter—"take this pad an' write a question on it. Don't lemme see it, mind! When you got it all wrote out, fold it up tight an' hold it against your forehead. Never leggo of it, not once!"

Bean wrote, secretly, well below the table's edge.

"Who was I in my last incarnation?"

He tore the small sheet from the pad, folded it tightly and, with elbows on the table, pressed it to his brow. If the Countess answered that question, then indeed was she a seer.

She took up the pad from which he had torn the sheet.

"Concentrate," she admonished him. "Let the whole curnt of your magnetism flow into that question. Excuse me! I left the slate in the nex' room. My control will answer you on the slate."

She withdrew between the curtains, but reappeared very soon. Bean was concentrating.

"That'll do," said the Countess. "Here!" She presented him with a double slate and a moist sponge. "Wipe it clean."

He washed the surfaces of the slate and the seer placed it upon the table between them, enclosing within its two sections a tiny fragment of slate pencil. She placed her hands upon the slate and bade her sitter do likewise.

468

"You often hear skeptics say they is sometimes trickery in this," said the Countess, "but say, listen now, how could it be? I leave it to you, friend. I ain't seen your question; you held it a minute and then put it in your pocket. An' you seen the slate was clean. Now concentrate; go into the Silence!"

Bean went into the Silence without suspicion, believing the Countess would fail. She couldn't know his question and no human power could write on the inside of that slate without detection. He waited with sympathy for the woman who had overestimated her gifts.

Then he was startled by the faintest sound of scratching, as of a pencil on a slate. It seemed to issue from beneath their hands at rest there in plain sight. The medium closed her eyes. Bean waited, his breath quickening. Little nervous crinklings began at the roots of his hair and descended his spine—that scratching, faint, yet vigorous, did it come from beyond the veil?

The scratching ceased. The ensuing silence was portentous.

"Open it and look!" commanded the Countess. And Bean forthwith opened it and looked a little way into his dead and dread past. Apparently upon the very surface he had washed clean were words that seemed to have been hurriedly inscribed:

"The last time you was Napolen Bonopart."

He stared wonderingly at those marks made by no mortal hand. He thrilled with a vast elation; and yet instantly a suspicion formed that here was something to his discredit, something one wouldn't care to have known. He had read as little history as possible, yet there floated in his mind certain random phrases, "A Corsican upstart," "An assassin," "No gentleman!"

"I—I suppose—you're sure there can't be any doubt about this?"

He looked pleadingly at the Countess. But the Countess was a mere psychic instrument, it seemed, and had to be told, first of the question—he produced it with a suspicion that she might doubt his honesty—and then of the astounding answer. Thus enlightened, she protested that there could be no doubt about the truth of the answer; she was ready to stake her professional reputation on its truth. She regarded Bean with an awe which she made no attempt to conceal.

"You had your *day*," she said significantly; "pomps and powers and—and attentions!"

Bean was excitedly piecing together what fragments of data his reading had left him.

"Emperor of France—"

But some one else had rung the third bell, perhaps one of those scientists coming to be dumfounded.

"He was," the Countess replied hurriedly, "the husban' of Mary Antonett, an' they both got arrested and gilletined in the great French revolution."

He was pretty certain that this was incorrect, but the Countess, after all, was a mere instrument of higher intelligence, and she now made no pretence of speaking otherwise than humanly.

"An' my controls say they'll leave me in a body if I take a cent less 'n three dollars."

One of the controls seemed to be looking this very threat or something like it from the medium's sharpened eyes.

Bean paid hastily, thus averting what would have been a calamity to all earnest students of the occult. The advertisement, it is true, had specifically mentioned one dollar as the accustomed honorarium, but this was no time to haggle.

Napoleon!

"Don't furgit the number," urged the Countess, "an' if you got any friends, I'd appreciate—"

"Certainly! Sure thing!" said the palpitating one, and blindly felt his way into the night.

The same stars shone above the city street; the same heedless throng disregarded them; disregarded, too, the slight figure that paused a moment to survey the sky and the world beneath it through a new pair of eyes.

Napoleon!

CHAPTER IV

He walked buoyantly home. He had a room at the top of a house in an uptown cross-street. Having locked his door and lighted a gas-jet he stood a long time before his mirror. It was a friendly young face he saw there, but troubled. The hair was pale, the eyes were pale, the nose small. The mouth was rather fine, cleanly cut and a little feminine. The chin was not a fighter's chin, yet neither chin nor mouth revealed any weakness. He scanned the features eagerly, striving to relate them with vaguely remembered portraits of Napoleon. He was about the same height as the Little Corporal, he seemed to recall, but an eagle boldness was lacking. Did he possess it latently? Could he develop it? He must have books about this possible former self of his. He had early become impatient of written history because when it says sixteen hundred and something it means the seventeenth century. If historians had but agreed to call sixteen hundred and something the sixteenth century, he would have read more of them. It was annoying to have to stop to figure.

Before retiring he went through certain exercises with an unusual vehemence. He was taking a course in jiu-jitsu from a correspondence school. Aforetime he had dreamed of a street encounter, with some blustering bully twice his size, from which, thanks to his skill, he would emerge unscarred, unruffled, perhaps flecking a bit of dust from one slight but muscular shoulder while his antagonist lay screaming with pain.

With the approach of sleep all his half-doubts were swept away. Of course he had been Napoleon. He could almost remember Marengo—or was it Austerlitz? There was a vague but not distressing uncertainty as to which of these conflicts he had directed, but he could—almost—remember.

And he had been one who commanded, and who, therefore, would make nothing of pricing a dog. He would enter that store boldly to-morrow, give its proprietor glare for glare, and demand to be told the price of the creature in the window. Napoleon would have made nothing of it.

The old man came noisily from his back room and again glowered above his spectacles. But this time he faced no weakling who made a subterfuge of undesired goldfish.

Bean gulped once, it is true, before words would come.

"I—uh—what's the price of that dog in the window?"

The old man removed his spectacles, ran a hand through upstanding white hair, and regarded his questioner suspiciously.

"You vant him, hey? Vell, I tell. Fifdy dollars, you bed your life!"

The blood leaped in his veins. He had expected to hear a hundred at least. Still, fifty was a difficult enough sum. He hesitated.

"Er—what's his name?"

"Naboleon."

"*What?*" He could not believe this thing.

"Naboleon. It comes in his bedigree when I giddim. You bed your life I gif him nod such names—robber, killer, Frenchman!"

Bean felt assaulted.

"He was a fighter?"

"Yah, fider—a killer unt a sdealer. You know what?"—his face lightened a little with garrulity—"my granmutter she seen him, yah, sure she seen him, seddin' on his horse when he gone ridin' into Utrecht in eighdeen hunderd fife, with soljus. Sure she seen him; she loogs outer a winda' so she could touch him if she been glose to him, unt a soljus rides oop unt says, 'Ve gamp right here, not?' unt Naboleon he shneer awful unt say, 'Gamp here vere dey go inter dem cellus from der ganal-side unt get unter us unt blow us high wit bowder—you sheep's head! No; we gamp back in der Malibaan vere is old linden drees hundred years old, eighd rows vun mile long, dere is vere we gamp, you gread fool!' Sure my granmutter seen him. He pull his nose mit t'um unt finger, so! Muddy boods, vun glofe off, seddin' oop sdraighd on a horse. Sure, she seen him. Robber unt big killer-sdealer! She vas olt lady, but she remember it lige it was to-morrow."

Excitement engendered by this reminiscence had well-nigh made Bean forget the dog. Once he had made people afraid. The world had trembled before him. Policemen had been as insects.

"I'll take that dog," he announced royally—then faltered—"but I haven't the money now. You keep him for me till I get it."

"Yah, you know vot? A olt man, lige me, say that same ofer lasd mont' ago, unt I nefer see him until yet!"

It was a time for extreme measures. Bean pressed seven dollars upon the dog's owner.

"And ten dollars every week; maybe more!"

The old man stowed the bills in a pocket under his apron and scratched the head of the parrot that was incisively remarking, "Oh! What a fool!" and giggling fatuously at its own jest.

"I guess you giddim. I guess mebbe you lige him, hey! He iss a awful glutton to eat!"

Napoleon!

And in the street car the first headline he saw in his morning paper was, "Young Napoleon of Finance Flutters Wall Street!"

The thing was getting uncanny.

A Napoleon of Finance!

Something, Napoleonic at least for Bunker Bean, had to be done in finance immediately. He had reached the office penniless. He first tried Bulger, who owed him ten dollars. But this was a Waterloo.

"Too bad, old top!" sympathized Bulger. "If you'd only sejested it yesterday. But you know how it is when a man's out; he's got to make a flash; got to keep up his end."

He considered the others in the office. Most of them, he decided, would, like Bulger, have been keeping their ends up. Of course, there was Breede. But Napoleon at his best would never have tried to borrow money of Breede, not even on the day of his coronation. Tully, the chief clerk, was equally impossible. Tully's thick glasses magnified his eyes so that they were terrible to look at. Tully would reach out a nerveless hand and draw forth the quivering heart of his secret. Tully would know right off that a man could have no respectable reason for borrowing five dollars on Thursday.

There remained old Metzeger who worked silently all day over a set of giant ledgers, interminably beautifying their pages with his meticulous figures. True, Bean had once heard Bulger fail interestingly to borrow five dollars of Metzeger until Saturday noon, but a flash of true Napoleonic genius now enabled him to see precisely why Bulger had not succeeded. Metzeger lived for numerals, for columned digits alone. He carried thousands of them in his head and apparently little else. He could tell to the fraction of a cent what Union Pacific had opened at on any day you chose to name. He had a passion for odd amounts. A flat million as a sum interested him far less than one like $107.69¾. He could remember it longer. It was necessary then to appeal to the poetry in the man.

A long time from across his typewriter he studied old Metzeger, tall, angular, his shoulders lovingly rounded above one of the ledgers, a green shade pulled well over his eyes, perhaps to conceal the too-flagrant love-light that shone there for his figures. Napoleon had won most of his battles in his tent.

Bean arose, moved toward the other and spoke in clear, cool tones.

"Mr. Metzeger, I want to borrow five dollars—"

The old man perceptibly stiffened and bent his head lower.

"—five dollars and eighty-seven cents until Saturday at ten minutes past twelve."

Metzeger looked up, surveying him keenly from under the green shade.

"*How* much?'

"Five eighty-seven."

There was a curious relenting in the sharpened old face. The man had been struck in a vital spot. With his fine-pointed pen he affectionately wrote the figures on a pad: "$5.87—12:10." They were ideal; they vanquished him. Slowly he counted out money from various pockets, but the sum was $5.90.

"Bring me the change," he said.

Bean brought it from the clerk who kept the stamp-box. Metzeger replaced three pennies in a pocket, and Bean moved off with the sum he had demanded, feeling almost as once he might have felt after Marengo.

It must be true! He couldn't have done the thing yesterday.

He omitted his visit to the dog that day and loitered for an hour in a second-hand bookshop he had often passed. He remembered it because of a coloured print that hung in the window, "The Retreat from Moscow." He had glanced carelessly enough at this, hardly noting who it was that headed the gloomy procession. Now he felt the biting cold, and shivered, though the day was warm. There were pleasanter prints inside. In one, Napoleon with sternly folded arms gazed down at a sleeping sentry. In another he reviewed troops at Fontainebleau, and again, from an eminence, he overlooked a spirited battle, directing it with a masterly wave of his sabre. These things were a little disconcerting to one in whom the blood-lust had diminished. He was better pleased with a steel engraving of the coronation, and this he secured for a trifle. It was a thing to nourish an ailing ego, a scene to draw sustenance from when people overwhelmed you in street cars and took your gold watch.

Then there were books about Napoleon, a whole shelf of them. A lot of authors had thought him worth writing about. He examined several volumes. One was full of dreadful caricatures that the English had delighted in. He found this most offensive and closed it quickly. Probably that explained why he had always felt an instinctive antipathy for the English.

"If you're interested in Napoleon things—" said the officious clerk, and Bean went cold. He wondered if the fellow suspected something.

"Not at all, not at all!" he protested, and refused to look at any more books.

He took his print of the coronation, securely wrapped, and went to another store several blocks away. He could get a Napoleon book there, where they wouldn't be suspicious. He found one that looked promising, "Napoleon, Man and Lover," and still another entitled "The Hundred Days." The latter had illustrations of the tomb, which he noted was in Paris. Its architecture impressed him, and his hands trembled as he held the book open. He had been buried with pomp, even with flamboyance. Robber and killer he might have been, but the picture showed a throng of admiring spectators looking down to where the dead colossus was chested, and on the summit of the dome that rounded above that kingly sarcophagus, a discriminating nation had put the cross of Christ in gold.

474

Let people say what they would! With all this glory of sepulchre there must be something in the man not to be wholly ashamed of.

And yet "Napoleon, Man and Lover," which he read that night, confirmed his first impression that this strangely uncovered incident in his Karmic past was, on the whole, scandalous; not a thing he would like to have "get about." He sympathized with the poor boy driven from his Corsican home, with the charity student of Brienne, with the young artillery officer, dreaming impossible dreams. But as lover—he blushed for that ruthless dead self of his; the Polish woman, the little actress, sending for them as if they were merchandise. It seemed to him that even the not too-fastidious Bulger would have been offended by such direct brutality.

Well, he was paying dearly for it now; afraid to venture into the presence of a couple of swell dames not invincibly austere, lacking the touch-and-go gallantry of a mere Bulger who had probably never been anybody worth mentioning.

And there was the poor pathetic Louise of Prussia. Bean had already fallen in love with her face, observed in advertisements of the Queen Quality Shoe. He recalled the womanly dignity of the figure descending the shallow steps, the arch accost of the soft eyes, the dimple in the round check. She had been sent to sue him, the invader, to soften him with blandishments. He had kept her waiting like a lackey, then had sought cynically to discover how far her devotion to her country's safety would carry her. And when her pitiful little basket of tricks had been emptied, her little traps sprung, he had sent her back to her husband with a message that crushed her woman's pride and shattered the hopes of her people. He had heard the word "bounder." It seemed to him that Napoleon had shown himself to be just that—a fearful and impossible bounder. He tingled with shame. He wished he might speak to that Queen now as a gentleman would.

And yet he could not read the book without a certain evil quickening. Brutal though his method of approach had been, the man had conquered more than mere force may ever conquer. The Polish woman had come to love him; the little actress would have followed him to his lonely island. Others, too many others, had confessed his power.

He was ashamed of such a past, yet read it with a guilty relish. He recalled the flapper who had so boldly met his glance. He thought she would have been less bold if she could have known the man she looked at. He placed "Napoleon, Man and Lover" at the bottom of his trunk beside the scarlet cravat he had feared to wear. It was not a book to "leave around."

"The Hundred Days," which he read the following night, was a much less discouraging work. It told of defeat, but of how glorious a defeat! The escape from Elba, the landing in France and the march to Paris, conquering, where he passed, by the sheer magnetism of his personality! His spirit bounded as he read of this and of the frightened exit of that puny usurper before the mere rumour of his approach. Then that audacious staking of all on a throw of the dice—Waterloo and a deathless ignominy. He heard the sob-choked voices of the Old Guard as they bade their leader farewell—felt the despairing clasp of their hands!

Alone in his little room, high above the flaring night streets, the timid boy read of the Hundred Days, and thrilled to a fancied memory of them. The breath that checked on his lips, the blood that ran faster in his veins at the recital, went to nourish a body that contained the essential part of that hero—he was reading about himself! He forgot his mean surroundings—and the timidities of spirit that had brought him thus far through life almost with the feelings of a fugitive.

The Lords of Destiny had found him indeed untractable as the great Emperor, the world-figure, and, for his proudness of spirit, had decreed that he should affrightedly tread the earth again as Bunker Bean. Everything pointed to it. Even the golden bees of Napoleon! Were there not three B's in his own name? The shameful truth is that he had been christened "Bunker Bunker Bean." His fond and foolish mother had thus ingenuously sought to placate the two old Uncle Bunkers; unsuccessfully, be it added, for each had affected to believe that he took second place in the name. But the three B's were there; did they not point psychically to the golden bees of the Corsican? Indeed, an astrologist in Chicago had once told him, for a paltry half-dollar, that those B's in his name were of a profoundly mystic significance.

Again, he was of distinguished French origin. Over and over had his worried mother sought to impress this upon him. The family was an old and noble one, fleeing from France, during a Huguenot persecution, to Protestant England where the true name "de Boncoeur" had been corrupted to "Bunker." At the time of his earliest dissatisfaction with the name he had even essayed writing it in the French manner—"B. de Boncoeur Bien"—supposing "Bien" to be approximate French for "Bean."

What more natural than that the freed soul, striving for another body, should have selected one of distinguished French ancestry? The commoner would inevitably seek to become a patrician.

It was a big thing; a thing to dream and wonder and calculate about. When he was puzzled or disturbed he would resort to the shell—a thing he had clung tenaciously to through all the years—sitting before it a long time, his eyes fixed upon it with hypnotic tensity.

What should it mean to him? How was his life to be modified by it? He did not doubt that changes would now ensue. He was already bolder in the public eye. If people stared superciliously at him, he sometimes stared back. That aggressive stout man could not now have bullied him out of his seat in the car with any mere looks.

The phrase "Napoleon of Finance" had stayed in his mind. Modernly the name seemed briefly to suggest some one who made a lot of money out of nothing but audacity. Certainly it was not being applied to soldiers or statesmen. This was interesting. If he made a lot of money he could move to the country and have plenty of room for the dog. And it seemed about the only field of adventure left for this peculiar genius. He began to think about making money. He knew vaguely how this was done: you bought stocks and then waited for the melon to be cut. You got on the inside of things. You were found to have bought up securities that trebled in value over night. Those that decreased in value had been bought by people who were not Napoleons. That was the gist of it. A Napoleonic mind would divine the way. "Napoleon knew human nature like a book," said one of the inspired historians. That was all you needed to know. He resolved to study human nature.

At precisely ten minutes past twelve on the following Saturday he laid upon old Metzeger's desk the exact sum of five dollars and eighty-seven cents. One less gifted as to human nature would have said, "Thank you!" and laid down five dollars and ninety cents. Bean fell into neither trap. Metzeger looked quickly at the clock and silently took the money. He had become the prey of a man who surmised him accurately.

Then occurred one of those familiar tragedies of the wage slave. The whole week long he had looked forward to the ball game. In the box that afternoon would be the Greatest Pitcher the World Had Ever Known. This figure had loomed in his mind that week bigger at times than all his past incarnations. He was going to forego a sight of his dog in order to be early on the ground. He would see the practice and thrill to the first line-up. He had lived over and over that supreme moment when the umpire sweeps the plate with a stubby broom and adjusts his mask.

The correct coat was buttoned and the hat was being adjusted when the door of the inner office opened with a sharp rattle.

"Wantcha!" said Breede.

There was a fateful, trembling moment in which Breede was like to have been blasted; it was as if the magnate had wantonly affronted him who had once been the recipient of a second funeral in Paris. Keeping Bean from a ball game aroused that one-time self of his as perhaps nothing else would have done. But Breede was Breede, after all, and Bean swallowed the hot words that rose to his lips. His perturbation was such, however, that Breede caught something of it.

"Hadjer lunch?"

"No!" said Bean, murderously.

"Gitcha some quick. Hurry!"

He knew the worst now. The afternoon was gone.

"Don't want any!" It was a miniature explosion after the Breede manner.

"C'mon, then!"

He was at the desk and Breede dictated interminably. When pauses came he wrote scathing comments on Breede's attire, his parsimony in the matter of food, his facial defects, and some objectionable characteristics as a human being, now perceived for the first time. He grew careless of concealing his attitude. Once he stared at Breede's detached cuffs with a scorn so malevolent that Breede turned them about on the desk to examine them himself. Bean went white, feeling "ready for anything!" but Breede merely continued his babble about "Federal Express" stock, and "first mortgage refunding 4 per cent. gold bonds," and multifarious other imbecilities that now filled a darkened world.

He jealously watched the letters Breede answered and laid aside, and the sheaf of reports that he juggled from hand to hand. His hope had been that the session might be brief. There was no clock in the room and he several times felt for the absent watch. Then he tried to estimate the time. When he believed it to be one o'clock he diversified his notes with a swift summary of Breede's character which only the man's bitterest enemies would have approved. At what he thought was two o'clock he stripped him of the last shreds of moral decency. When three o'clock seemed to arrive he did not dare put down, even in secretive shorthand, what he felt could justly be said of Breede. After that it was no good hoping. He relaxed into the dullness of a big despair, merely reflecting that Bulger's picture of Breede under his heel had been too mushily humane. What Bean wished at the moment was to have Breede tied to a stake, and to be carving choice morsels from him with a dull knife. He made the picture vivacious.

At what he judged to be four-thirty a spirited rap sounded on the door.

"C'min," yelled Breede.

Entered the flapper. Breede looked up.

"Seddown! View of efforts bein' made b' cert'n parties t' s'cure 'trol of comp'ny by promise of creatin' stock script on div'dend basis, it is proper f'r d'rectors t' state policy has been—"

The flapper had sat down and was looking intently at Bean. There was no coquetry in the look. It was a look of interest and one wholly in earnest. Bean became aware of it at Breede's first pause. At any other time he would have lowered his eyes before an assault so direct and continuous. Now in his hot rage he included the flapper in the glare he put upon her unconscious father.

He saw that she was truly enough a flapper; not a day over eighteen, he was sure. Not tall; almost "pudgy," with a plump, browned face and gray eyes like old Breede's, that looked through you. He noted these details without enthusiasm. Then he relented a little because of her dress. The shoes—he always looked first at a woman's shoes and lost interest in her if those were not acceptable—were of tan leather and low, with decently high heels. (He loathed common-sense shoes on women.) The hose were of tan silk. So far he approved. She wore a tailored suit of blue and had removed the jacket. The shirtwaist—he knew they were called "lingerie waists" in the windows—was of creamy softness and had the lines of the thing called "style." Her hat was a straw that drooped becomingly. "Some dresser, all right!" he thought, and then, "Why don't she take a look at old Cufflets there, and get him in right?"

Again and again he hardened his gaze upon her. Her eyes always met his, not with any recognition of him as a human being, but with some curious interest that seemed remote yet not impersonal. He indignantly tried to out-stare her, but the thing was simply not to be done. Even looking down at her feet steadily didn't dash her brazenness. She didn't seem to care where *he* looked. After a very few minutes of this he kept his eyes upon his note-book with dignified absorption. But he could feel her glance.

"—to c'nserve investment rep'sented by this stock upon sound basis rather than th' spec'lative policy of larger an' fluc'chating div'dends yours ver' truly what time's 'at game called?"

Thus concluded Breede, with a sudden noisy putting away of papers in an open drawer at his side.

Bean looked up at him, in open-mouthed fear for his sanity.

"Hello, Pops!" said the flapper.

"'Lo, Sis! What time's 'at game called?"

"Three," said Bean, still alarmed.

Breede looked at his watch.

"Jus' got time to make it."

He arose from the desk. Bean arose. The flapper arose.

"Take y' up in car," said Breede, most amazingly.

Bean pulled his collar from about his suddenly constricted throat.

"Letters!" He pointed to the note-book.

"Have 'em ready Monday noon. C'mon! Two-thirty now."

The early hour was as incredible as this social phenomenon.

"Daughter!" said Breede, with half a glance at the flapper, and deeming that he had performed a familiar social rite.

"Pleased to meet you!" said Bean, dazedly. The flapper jerked her head in a double nod.

Of the interval that must have elapsed before he found himself seated in the grandstand between Breede and the flapper he was able to recall but little. It was as if a dense fog shut him in. Once it lifted and he suffered a vision of himself in a swiftly propelled motor-car, beside an absorbed mechanician. He half turned in his seat and met the cool, steady gaze of the flapper; she smiled, but quickly checked herself to resume the stare; he was aware that Breede was at her side. And the fog closed in again. It was too unbelievable.

A bell clanged twice and his brain cleared. He saw the scurry of uniformed figures to the field, the catcher adjusted his mask. The Greatest Pitcher the World Has Ever Known stood nonchalantly in the box, stooped for a handful of earth and with it polluted the fair surface of a new ball. A second later the ball shot over the plate. The batter fanned, the crowd yelled.

All at once Bean was coldly himself. He knew that Breede sat at his right; that on his left was a peculiar young woman. He promptly forgot their identities, and his own as well, and recalled them but seldom during the ensuing game.

It is a phenomenon familiar to most of us. The sons of men, under the magic of that living diamond, are no longer little units of souls jealously on guard. Heart speaks to heart naked and unashamed; they fraternize across deeps that are commonly impassable, thrilling as one man to the genius of the double-play, or with one voice hurling merited insults at a remote and contemptuous umpire. It is only there, on earth, that they love their neighbour. There they are fused, and welded into that perfect whole which is perhaps the only colourable imitation ever to be had on earth of the democracy said to prevail in Heaven.

There was no longer a Bean, a Breede, a flapper. Instead were three merged souls in three volatile bodies, three voices that blended in cheers or execration. At any crisis they instinctively laid gripping hands upon each other and, half-rising, with distended eyes and tense half-voices, besought some panting runner to "Come on! Come *on*, you! Oh, come *on*!" There were other moments of supreme joy when they were blown to their feet and backs were impartially pounded. More than once they might have been observed, with brandishing fists, shouting, "Robber! Robber! *Robber!!!*" at the unperturbed man behind the plate who merely looked at an indicator in his hand and resumed his professional crouch quite as if nothing had happened.

And there were moments of snappy, broken talk, comments on individual players, a raking over the records. It was not Breede who talked to Bean then. It was one freed soul communicating with another. He none too gently put Breede right in the matter of Wagner's batting average for the previous year and the price that had been paid for the new infielder. And Breede in spirit sat meekly at his feet, grateful for his lore.

Of an absent player, Breede said he was too old—all of thirty-five. He'd never come back.

"They come back when they learn to play ball above the ears," retorted Bean with crisp sapience. "How about old Cy Young? How about old Callahan of the Sox? How about Wagner out there—think he's only nineteen—hey? Tell me *that*!"

He looked pityingly at the man of millions thus silenced.

Two men scored from third and second, thanks to a wild throw.

"Inside play, there?" said Breede.

"Inside, nothing!" retorted Bean arrogantly. "Matty couldn't get back to second and they *had* to run. If that Silas up there hadn't gone foamy in the fighting-top and tried to hit that policeman over by the fence with the ball, where'd your inside play been? D'you think the Pirates are trying to help 'em play inside ball? Inside, nothing!"

Again Breede looked respectful, and the flapper listened, lustrous-eyed.

The finish was close. With two men out in the last half of the ninth and two strikes called on the batter, a none too certain single brought in the winning run. The clinging trio shrieked—then dazedly fell apart. Life had gone from the magic. The vast crowd also fell apart to units, flooding to the narrow gates.

Outside Breede looked at Bean as if, faintly puzzled, he was trying to recall the fellow's face. One could fancy him saying, "Prob'ly some chap works in m' office."

Father and daughter entered the car. Bean raised his dented hat. Breede was oblivious; the flapper permitted herself a severe double nod. The motor chugged violently. Bean, moving on a few steps, turned. The flapper was looking back. She stared an instant then most astonishingly smiled, a smile that seemed almost vocal with many glad words. Bean felt himself smile weakly in response.

He walked a long way before he took a car, his eyes on the pavement, his mind filled with a vision. When the flapper smiled it did something to him, but what it was he couldn't tell. She had a different face when she smiled; her parting lips made a new beauty in the world. He thought the golden brown of her hair rather wonderful. It was like the golden brown of the new dog. He recalled little details of her face, the short upper lip, the forward chin, the breadth of the brow. There was something disconcerting about that brow and the eyes like her father's— probably have her own way! Then he remembered that he must have noticed a badge pinned to the left lapel of a jacket that had been fashioned—with no great difficulty, he thought—to give its wearer the appearance of perfect physical development. He couldn't remember when he had precisely noted this badge, perhaps in some frenzied moment in the game's delirium, but it was vividly before him now—"VOTES FOR WOMEN!" What did that signify in her character? Perhaps something not too pleasant.

Still—he lived again through the smile that had seemed to speak.

Three days later, at the close of an afternoon's grinding work, the grim old man at the desk looked up as Bean was leaving the room.

"S'good game!"

"Fine!" said Bean, as he closed the door.

But for this reference and one other circumstance Bean might have supposed that Breede had forgotten the day. The other circumstance was an area of rich yellowish purple on the arm which Breede had madly gripped in moments of ecstasy, together with painful spots on his right side where the elbow of Breede had almost continuously jabbed him.

CHAPTER V

The latest Napoleonic dynasty was tottering. The more Bean read of that possible former self, the less he admired its manifestations. A Corsican upstart, an assassin, no gentleman! It was all too true. Very well, for that vaunted force of will, but to what base ends had it been applied! He was merciless to himself, an egotist and a vulgarian. How it would shock that woman, as yet unidentified, who was one day to be the mother of the world's greatest left-handed pitcher. Take the flapper—impossible, of course, but just as an example—suppose she ever came to know about the Polish woman and the actress, and the others! How she would loathe him! And you couldn't tell what minute it might become known. People were taking an interest in such matters. He wished he had cautioned the Countess Casanova to keep the thing quiet. Probably she had talked.

He must go further into that past of his. Doubtless there were lessons to be drawn from the Napoleonic episode, but just now, when he was all confused, the thing—he put it bluntly—was "pretty raw."

"With Napoleon, to think was to act." So he had read in one chronicle. Very well, he would act. Again he would stand, with fearless eyes, at the portal of the vaulted past.

At eight o'clock that night he once more rang the third bell. He had feared that the Countess Casanova might have returned to European triumphs, but the solicitations of the scientific world were still prevailing.

He stood in the little parlour and again the Countess appeared from behind the heavy curtains, a plump white hand at the throat of her scarlet gown.

He was obliged to recall himself to her, for the Countess began to tell him that his aura was clouded with evil curnts.

"You told me what I was—last time, don't you remember? You know, you said, it was written on the slate what I was—" He could not bring himself to utter the name. But the Countess remembered.

"Sure; perfectly! And what was you wishing to know now?"

She surveyed him with heavy-lidded eyes, a figure of mystery, of secret knowledge.

"I want you to tell me who I was before that—before *him*."

The Countess blinked her eyes rapidly, as if it hurried calculation.

"And I don't mean *just* before. I want to go 'way back, thousands of years—what I was *first*." He looked helplessly around the room, then glanced appealingly at the Countess. The flushed and friendly face was troubled.

"Well, I dunno." She pondered, eying her sitter closely. "Of course all things is possible to us, but sometimes the conditions ain't jest right and y'r c'ntrol can't git into rapport with them that has been gone more'n a few years. Now this thing you're after—I don't say it can't be done—f'r money."

"If I learned something good, I wouldn't care anything about the money," he ventured.

The Countess glanced up interestedly.

"That's the way to look at it, friend, but how much you got on you?"

"Twenty-two dollars," confessed Bean succinctly.

"Would you part from twenty, if you was told what you want to know?"

"Yes; I can't stand that other thing any longer."

The Countess narrowed her eyes briefly, then became animated.

"Say, listen here, friend! That's a little more delikit work than I been doin', but they's a party near here—lemme see—" She passed one of the plump white hands over her brow in the throes of recollection. "I think his name is Professor Balthasar. I ain't ever met him, understand what I mean? but they say he's a genuine wonder an' no mistake; tell you anything right off the reel. You set right there and lemme go see if I can't call him up by telephone."

She withdrew between the curtains, behind which she carefully pulled sliding doors. Bean heard the murmur of her voice.

He waited anxiously. His Napoleon self was already fading. If only they would tell him something "good." Little he cared for the twenty dollars. He could get along by borrowing seventeen-seventy-nine from Metzeger. The voice still murmured. Only the well-fitting doors prevented Bean from hearing something that would have been of interest to him.

"That you, Ed?" the Countess was saying. "Listen here. 'Member th' one I told you about, thinks he's the original N.B.—you know who—well he's a repeater; here now wantin' t' know who he was before then, who he was *first* y'understand. An' say, I ain't got the right dope for that an' I want you to get over here quick's you can an' give him about a ten-minute spiel. Wha's that? Well, they's twenty, an' I split with you. But listen here, Ed, I get the idee this party's worth nursin' along. I dunno, something *about* him. That's why I'm tellin' you. I want it done right. Course, I could do enough stallin' muself t' cop the twenty; tell him Julius Caesar or the King of China or somebody, but I ain't got the follow-up, an' you can't tell *how* much he might be good for later. Take my tip: he's a natural born believer. Sure, twenty! All right!"

The doors slid back and the Countess reappeared between the curtains.

"I'm 'fraid I'll have to disappoint you," she began. "The Professer was called out t' give some advice to one the Vandabilts. But I got his private secatary on the wire an' he's gone out to chase him up. We'll haf to wait an' see."

Bean was sorry to be causing this trouble.

484

"Perhaps I better come another night."

"No, you don't! You set right there!" She seemed to listen to unspoken words, looking far off. "There! My control says he's comin'; he's on the way."

Bean was aghast before this power.

"'Nother thing," pursued the Countess in her normal manner, "keep perfec'ly still when he comes. Don't tip him off what you want. Let him do the talkin'. If he's the real thing he'll know what you want. They say he's a wonder, but what do *we* know about it? Let him prove it!"

Bean felt that he and the Countess were a pair of shrewd skeptics.

The third bell rang and a heavy tread was heard on the stairs. The mere sound of its mounting was impressive. The Countess laid a reminding finger on her lips, as she moved toward the door.

There appeared an elderly man, in a black frockcoat, loose-fitting and not too garishly new, a student's coat rather than a fop's.

"Is this Perfesser Balthasar?" inquired the Countess in her best manner.

"At your service, Madam!" He permitted himself a courtly inclination, conferred upon the Countess a glistening tall hat, and then covered his expansive baldness with a skullcap of silk which he drew from an inner pocket.

"I feared we was discommoding you," ventured the Countess, elegantly apologetic; "your secatary said you was out advisin' one the Vandabilts—"

"A mere trifle in the day's work, Madam!" He brushed it aside with an eloquent hand. "My mission is to serve. You wished to consult me?"

"Not me; but this young gentaman here—"

"Ah!" He turned to face Bean, who had risen, regarding him with serious eyes and twirling a curled moustache meditatively.

"I see, I see! An imprisoned soul seeking the light!" He came nearer to Bean, staring intently, then started with dramatic suddenness as if at an electric shock from concealed wires.

"What is this—what is this—what *is* this?"

Bean backed away defensively. The professor seemed with difficulty to withdraw his fascinated gaze, and turned apologetically to the Countess.

"You will pardon me, Madam, but I must ask you to leave us. My control warns me that I am in the presence of an individuality stronger than my own. His powerful mind is projecting the most vital queries. I shall be compelled to disclose to him matters he would perhaps not wish a third person to overhear. I see a line of mighty rulers, ruthless, red-handed—the past of his soul."

The Countess murmurously withdrew. The two males faced each other.

The professor was a mere sketch of a man, random, rakish, with head aslant and shifty eyes forever dropping away from a questioner's face. He abounded in inhuman angles and impossible lines. It seemed that he must have been rather dashingly done in the first place, then half obliterated and badly mended with fumbling, indecisive touches. His restless hands unceasingly wrung each other as if he had that moment made his own acquaintance and was trying to infuse a false geniality into the meeting.

When he spoke he had a trick of opening his mouth for a word and holding it so, a not over-clean forefinger poised above an outheld palm. It seemed to the listener that the word when it came would mean much. His white moustache alone had a well-finished look, curving jauntily upward.

"Sit there!" An authoritative finger pointed Bean to the chair he had lately occupied.

He sat nervously, suffering that peculiar apprehension which physicians and dentists had always inspired.

"Most amazing! Most astounding!" muttered the professor as if to his own ear alone. He sat in a chair facing Bean and regarded him long and intently. At brief intervals his face twitched, his body stiffened, he seemed to writhe in some malign grasp.

Bean gripped the arms of his chair. His tingling nerves were accurately defining his spine. He waited, breathless.

"I see it all," breathed the professor in low, solemn tones, his eyes fixed above Bean's head. "First the pomp and glitter of a throne. You wrench it from a people whose weakness you play upon with a devilish cunning, you ascend to it over the bodies of countless men slain in battle. Power through blood! You are cruel, insatiable, a predatory monster. But retribution comes. You are hurled from your throne. Again you ascend it, but only for a brief time. You fight your last battle; you *lose*! You are captured and taken to a lonely island somewhere far to the south, there to be imprisoned until your death. Afterward I see your body returned to the city that was once your capital. It now lies in a heavy stone coffin. It is in a European city. I can almost hear the name, but not plainly. I cannot get the name under which you ruled. I look into the abyss and the cries of your victims drown it. Horror piles upon horror!"

Bean was leaning forward, tense with excitement, his mouth open. "Yes, that's just the way I felt about it," he murmured.

"But this was only a few paltry years ago, perhaps a hundred. It passes from my view. I am led back, away from it—far back—the cries of those you slaughtered echo but faintly—the scene changes—"

The professor paused. Bean had cowered in his chair, wincing under each blow. He wiped his face and crumpled the moist handkerchief tightly in one hand.

486

"Perhaps the name may come to me now," continued the professor. "But your superior personality overwhelmed me at first; you are so self-willed, so dominant, so ruthless. The name, the name!" He cried the last words commandingly and snapped his fingers at the delinquent control. "There! I seem to hear—"

"Never mind that name," broke in Bean hastily. "Let it go! I—I don't want to know it. Go on back farther!"

Again the professor's look became trancelike.

"Ah! What a relief to be free from that blood-lust!" He breathed deeply and his eyes rolled far up under their lids.

"What is this? A statesman, still crafty, still the lines of cunning cruelty about the mouth. The city is Venice in the fourteenth century. He is dressed in a richly bejewelled robe and toys with an inlaid dagger. He is plotting the assassination of a Doge—"

"Please get still farther back, can't you?" pleaded Bean.

The seer struggled once more with his control.

"I next see you at the head of a Roman legion, going forth to battle. You are a tyrant, ruling by fear alone, and with your own sword I see you cut off the heads of—"

"Farther back," beseeched the sitter. "I—I've had enough of all that battle and killing. I—I don't *like* it. Go on back to the very first."

Patiently the adept redirected his forces.

"I see a poet. He sings his deathless lay by a roadside in ancient Greece. He is an old man, feeble, blind—"

"Something else," broke in the persistent sitter, resolving not to pay twenty dollars for having been a blind poet.

The professor glanced sharply at him. Perhaps his control did not relish these interruptions. He seemed to suppress words of impatience and began anew.

"Ah! Now I see your very first appearance on this planet. You were born from another as yet unknown to our astronomers. You are now"—he lowered his eyes to the sitter's face—"an Egyptian king."

Detecting no sign of displeasure at this, he continued with refreshed enthusiasm.

"It is thousands of years ago. You are the last king of the pre-dynastic era—"

"What kind of a king—one of those fighters?"

"You are a wise and good king. I see a peaceful realm peopled by contented subjects."

"*That's* what I want to know. Go on; tell me more. Married?"

"Your wife is a princess of rare beauty from—from Mesopotamia. You have three lovely children, two boys and a girl, and your palace on the banks of the Nile is one of the most beautiful and grand palaces ever erected by the hand of man. You are ministered to by slaves, and your councillors of state come to you with their reports. You are tall, handsome and of a most kingly presence. Your personal bravery is unquestioned, you are an adept in all manly sports, but you will not go to war as you very properly detest all violence. For this reason there is little to relate of your reign. It was uneventful and distinguished only by your wise and humane statesmanship—"

"What name?" asked Bean, in low, reverent tones.

"The name—er—the name is—oh, yes, I get it—the name is Ram-tah."

"Can I find him in the histories?"

"You cannot," answered the seer emphatically. "I am probably the only living man that can tell you very much about him."

"When did he—pass on?"

"At the age of eighty-two years. He was deeply mourned by all his people. He had been a king of great strength of character, stern at moments, but ever just. His remains received the treatment customary in those times, and the mummy was interred in the royal sepulchre which is now covered by the sands of the centuries. Anything else?"

Bean was leaning forward in his chair, his eyes lost in that far, glorious past.

"Nothing else, now, I think. If I could see you again some time, I'd like to ask—"

"My mission is to serve," answered the other, caressing the moustache with a deft hand. "Anything I can do for you, any time, command me."

The Countess appeared from between the curtains.

"Was the conditions right?" she asked.

"They have been, at least *so* far," replied the professor crisply, with a side-glance at Bean who seemed on the point of leaving.

"Say, friend, I guess you're forgetting something, ain't you?" demanded the Countess archly.

And Bean perceived that he had indeed forgotten something. He rectified the oversight with blushing apologies, while the professor inspected the mantel ornaments with an absent air. What was twenty dollars to a king and a sire of kings? He bowed himself from the room.

They listened until the hall door closed.

"There's yours, Ed. You earned it all right, I'll say that. My! don't I wish I was up on that dope."

"You were the wise lady to send for me, Lizzie. You'd have killed him off right here. As it is, he'll come back. He's a clerk somewhere, drawing twenty-five a week or so. He ought to give up at least five of it every week; cigarette money, anyway. Anything loose in the house?"

"They's a couple bottles beer in the icebox. Gee! ain't he good, though! If he only had the roll some has!"

In his little room far up under the hunched shoulders of the house, Bunker Bean sat reviewing his Karmic past. Over parts of it he shuddered. That crafty Venetian plotting to kill, trifling wickedly with the inlaid dagger; the brutal Roman, ruling by fear, cutting off heads! And the blind poet! He would rather be Napoleon than a blind poet, if you came down to that. But the king, wise, humane, handsome, masterly, with a princess of rare beauty from Mesopotamia to be the mother of his three lovely children. That was a dazzling vision to behold, a life sane and proper, abounding in majesty both moral and material.

He sought to live over his long and peaceful but brilliant reign. Then he dwelt on his death and burial. They had made a mummy of him, of course. Somewhere that very night, at that very instant, his lifeless form reposed beneath the desert sands. Perhaps the face had changed but little during the centuries. He, Bunker Bean, lay there in royal robes, hands folded upon his breast, as lamenting subjects had left him.

And what did it mean to him now? He thought he saw. As King Ram-tah he had been *too* peaceful. For all his stern and kingly bearing might he not have been a little timid—afraid of people now and then? And the Karmic law had swept him on and on into lives that demanded violence, the Roman warrior, the Venetian plotter, the Corsican usurper!

He saw that he must have completed one of those vast Karmic cycles. What he had supposed to be timidity was a natural reaction from Napoleonic bravado. Now he had finished the circle and was ready to become again his kingly self, his Ram-tah self—able, reliant, fearless.

He expanded his chest, erected his shoulders and studied himself in the glass: there was undoubted majesty in the glance. He vibrated with some fresh, strange power.

Yes; but what about to-morrow—out in the world? in daylight, passing the policeman on the corner, down at the office? Would he remain a king in the presence of Breede, even in the lesser presence of Bulger, or of old Metzeger from whom he purposed to borrow seventeen dollars and seventy-nine cents? All right about being a king, but how were other people to know it? Well, he would have to make them feel it. He must know it himself, first; then impress it upon them.

But a sense of unreality was creeping back. It was almost better to remember the Napoleon past. There were books about that. He pictured again the dead Ramtah in trappings of royalty. If he could only *see* himself, and be sure. But that was out of the question. It was no good wishing. After all, he was Bunker Bean, a poor thing who had to fly when Breede growled "Wantcha." He sat at his table, staring moodily into vacancy. He idly speculated about Breede's ragged moustache; he thought it had been blasted and killed by the words Breede spoke. A moment later he was conscious that he stared at an unopened letter on the table before him.

He took it up without interest, perceiving that it came from his Aunt Clara in Chicago. She would ask if he had yet joined the Y.M.C.A., and warn him to be careful about changing his flannels.

"Dear Bunker" [it began], "my own dear husband passed to his final rest last Thursday at 5 p.m. He was cheerful to the last and did not seem to suffer much. The funeral was on Saturday and was very beautiful and impressive. I did not notify you at the time as I was afraid the shock would affect you injuriously and that you might be tempted to make the long trip here to be with me. Now that you know it is all over, you can take it peacefully, as I am already doing. The life-insurance people were very nice about it and paid the claim promptly. I enclose the money which wipes out all but—"

He opened the double sheet. There were many more of the closely written lines, but he read no farther, for a check was folded there. His trembling fingers pulled the ends apart and his astounded eyes rested on its ornate face.

It was for ten thousand dollars.

At six minutes after eight the following evening the Countess Casanova, moved from her professional calm, hurriedly closed the sliding doors between the two rooms of her apartment and sprang to the telephone where she frantically demanded a number. The delay seemed interminable to her, but at last she began to speak.

"That you, Ed? F'r God's sake, beat it over here quick. That boob las' night is back here an' *he's got it*. I dunno—but something *big*, I tell you. He's actin' like a crazy man. Listen here! He wants t' know can you *locate* it—see it lyin' there underground. Why, the mummy; yes. M-u-m-m-i-e. Yes, sure! He's afraid mebbe they already dug him up an' got him in a musée somewheres, but if it's still there he wants it. Yes, sure thing, dontchu un'stand? *Wants* it! How in—how can I tell? That's up to you. Git here! Sure—fifty-fifty!"

Bean glanced up feverishly as the Countess reappeared. She was smoothing her hair and readjusting the set of the scarlet wrapper. Her own excitement was apparent.

"It's all right. I think he'll come, but it was a close call. He was jes' packin' his grip f'r Wash'n'ton. Got a telegraph from the Pres'dent to-day t' come at once. Of course he'll miss a big fee. The Pres'dent don't care f'r money when it's a question of gittin' th' right advice—"

"Oh, money!" murmured Bean, and waved a contemptuous hand.

His manner was not lost upon his hearer.

"Lots of money made in a hurry, these days," she suggested, "or got hold of some way—gits left to parties—thousand dollars, mebbe—two, three, four thousand?"

Again he performed the pushing gesture, as if he were discommoded by money. He scarcely heard her voice.

The Countess did not venture another effort to appraise his wealth.

She fell silent, watching him. Bean gazed at a clean square on the wall-paper where a picture had once hung. Then the authoritative tread was again heard on the stairway, and again the Countess Casanova welcomed Professor Balthasar to her apartment. She expressed a polite regret for having annoyed him.

Professor Balthasar bestowed his shiny hat upon her, enveloped his equally shiny skull with the silken cap and assured her that his mission was to serve. Bean had not risen. He still stared at the wall.

"I'll jes' leave you alone with our friend here," said the Countess charmingly. The professor questioned her with a glance and she shook her head in response, yet her gesture as she vanished through the curtains was one of large encouragement.

The professor faced Bean and coughed slightly. Bean diverted his stare to the professor and seemed about to speak, but the other silenced him with a commanding forefinger.

"Not a word! I see it all. You impose your tremendous will upon me."

He took the chair facing Bean and began swiftly:

"I see the path over the desert. I stop beside a temple. Sand is all about. Beneath that temple is a stone sarcophagus. Within it lies the body of King Tam-rah—"

"Ram-tah!" corrected Bean gently.

"Did I not say Ram-tah?" pursued the seer. "There it has lain sealed for centuries, while all about it the tombs of other kings have been despoiled by curiosity hunters looking for objects of interest to place in their cabinets. But Ram-tah, last king of the pre-dynastic period, though others will tell you differently, but that's because he never got into history much, by reason of his uniformly gentlemanly conduct. He rests there to-day precisely as he was put. I see it all; I penetrate the heaped sands. At this moment the moon shines upon the spot, and a night bird is calling to its mate in the mulberry tree near the northeast corner of the temple. I see it all. I am there! What is this? What is this I get from you, my young friend?"

The professor seemed to cock a psychic ear toward Bean.

"You want—ah, yes, I see what you want, but that, of course, humanly, would be impossible. Oh, quite impossible, quite, quite!"

"*Why*, if you're sure it's there?"

"My dear sir, you descend to the material world. I will talk to you now as one practical man to another. Simply because it would take more money than you can afford. The thing is practicable but too expensive."

"How do you know?"

"It is true, I do not know. My control warned me when I came here that your circumstances had been suddenly bettered. I withdraw the words. I do not know, but—you will pardon the bluntness—*can* you afford it?"

"What'd it cost? That's what I want to know."

"Hum!" said the professor. He was unable to achieve more for a little time. He hum'd again.

"There's the labour and the risk," he ventured at last. "Of course my agents at Cairo—I have secret agents in every city on the globe—could proceed to the spot from my carefully worded directions. They could do the work of excavating. So far, so good! But they would have to work quietly and would be punished if discovered. Of course here and there they could bribe. Naturally, they would have to bribe, and that, as you are doubtless aware, requires money. Again, entering this port the custom-house officials would have to be bribed, and they've gone up in price the last few years. My control tells me that this mummy is one they've been looking hard for. It's about the only one they haven't found. The loss will be discovered and my men might be traced. It requires an enormous sum. Now, for instance, a thousand dollars"—he regarded Bean closely and was reassured—"a thousand dollars wouldn't any more than start the work. Two thousand"—his eyes were steadily upon Bean now—"would further it some. Three thousand might see it pretty well advanced. Four thousand, of course, would help still farther and five thousand"—he had seen the shadow of dismay creep over the face of his sitter— "five thousand, I *think*, might put the thing through."

Bean drew a long breath. The professor had correctly read the change in his face at "five thousand," but it had been a sudden fear that his whole ten thousand was not going to suffice for this prodigious operation.

"I can afford that," said Bean shortly. He hardly dared trust himself to say more. His emotion threatened to overcome him.

The professor suffered from the same danger. He, too, dared trust himself to say no more than the few necessary words.

"There must be a payment down," he said with forced coldness.

"How much?"

"A thousand wouldn't be any too much."

"Enough?"

"Well, perhaps not enough," the professor nerved himself to admit.

"I'll give you two, now. Give you the rest when you get—when you get It here."

"You move me, I confess," conceded the professor. "I will undertake it."

"How long will it be, do you think?"

"I shall give orders by cable. A month, possibly, if all goes well."

"I'll give you check." He gulped at that. It was the first time he had ever used the words.

The Countess parted the curtains. Curiously enough she carried a pen and ink, though no one remarked upon the circumstance.

Bean had that morning left a carefully written signature at the bank where his draft had been deposited. He later wondered how the scrawl he achieved now could ever be identified as by the same hand.

And he was conscious, even as he wrote, that the Countess Casanova and Professor Balthasar were labouring under an excitement equal to his own. It *was* a big feat to attempt.

As before, they waited until he had closed the lower door.

"Oh, Ed!" breathed the Countess emotionally.

"Anything loose in the house?" asked the professor.

"They's a couple bottles beer in the icebox, but *Oh, Ed!*"

CHAPTER VI

Again we chant pregnant phrases from the Bard of Dress: "It is cut to give the wearer the appearance of perfect physical development. And the effect produced so improves his form that he unconsciously strives to attain the appearance which the garment gives him; he expands his chest, draws in his waist, and stands erect."

A psychologist, that Bard! acutely divining a basic law of this absurd human nature. In a beggar's rags few men could be more than beggars. In kingly robes, most men could be kings; could achieve the finished and fearless behaviour that is said to distinguish royalty.

Bunker Bean, the divinely credulous, now daily arrayed himself in royal vestures, set a well-fashioned crown upon the brow of him and strode forth, sceptre in hand. Invisible were these trappings, to be sure; he was still no marked man in a city street. But at least they were there to his own truth-lit eyes, and he most truly did "expand his chest, draw in his waist, and stand erect." Yea, in the full gaze of inhumanly large policemen would he do these things.

This, indeed, was one of the first prerogatives his royalty claimed. He discovered that it was not necessary for any but criminals to fear policemen. It might still be true that an honest man of moderate physique and tender sensibilities could not pass one without slight tremors of self-consciousness; but by such they were—a most prodigious thought—to be regarded as one's paid employees; within the law one might even greet them pleasantly in passing, and be answered civilly. Bean was now equal to approaching one and saying, "Good evening, Officer!" He would sometimes cross a street merely to perform this apparently barren rite. It stiffened his spine. It helped him to realize that he had indeed been a king and the sire of kings; that kingly stuff was in him.

So marked an advance in his spirit was not made in a day, however. It came only after long dwelling in thought upon his splendid past. And, too, after he had envisioned the circumstance that he was now a man of means. The latter was not less difficult of realization than his kingship. He had thought little about money, save at destitute moments; had dreamed of riches as a vague, rather pleasant and not important possibility. But kings were rich; no sooner had his kingship been proclaimed than money was in his hand. And, of course, more money would come to him, as it had once come on the banks of the Nile. He did not question how nor whence. He only knew.

It was three days before he bethought himself to finish the reading of Aunt Clara's letter, suspended at sight of the astounding enclosure. He had begun that letter a harried and trivial unit of the toiling masses. He came to finish it a complacent and lordly figure!

"—I enclose the check which wipes out all but $7,000 of that money from your dear mother with which dearest Edward so rashly speculated years ago, in the hope of making you a wealthy man. I am happy to say that $5,000 of this I can pay at once out of the money I have saved. I have been investing for years, as I could spare it, in the stock of the Federal Express Company, and now have fifty shares, which I will transfer to you at par, though they are quoted a little above that, if you are willing to accept them. The balance I will pay when I have sold the house and furnishings, as with my dearest husband gone I no longer have any incentive to keep on working. I am tired. It is a good safe stock paying 4½ per cent. and I would advise you to keep it and also put the Ins. money into the same stock. A very nice man in the Life Ins. office said it ought to pay more if the business was better managed. If you turned your talents to the express business you might learn to manage it yourself because you always had a fine head for such things, and by owning a lot of their stock you could get the other stockholders to elect you to be one of their directors, which would be a fine occupation for you, not too hard work and plenty of time to read good books which I hope you find same now of evenings in place of frittering away your time with associations of a questionable character, and ruining your health by late hours and other dissipation though I know you were always of good habits.

"Affectionately,

"Aunt   Clara.

P.S.—It has rained hard for two days."

There it was! Money *came* to you. Federal Express was only a name to him; he had written it sometimes at Breede's dictation. But his Aunt Clara was old enough to know about such things, and he would follow her advice, though being a director of an express company seemed as unexciting as it was doubtless respectable: what he had at times been wild enough to dream was that he should be the principal owner of a major-league baseball club, and travel with the club— see every game! If he should, temporarily, become the director of an express company, he would have it plainly understood that he might resign at any moment.

Night and morning he surveyed himself in the glass. Not in the way of ordinary human conceit; he was clear sighted enough as to the pulchritude of his present encasement; but with the eyes of the young who see visions. Raptly scrutinizing his meagre form he chanted a line of verse that seemed apposite:

"Build thou more stately mansions, O my soul!"

He was already persuaded that his next incarnation would enrich the world with something far more stately than the mansion that he at present occupied; something on the Gordon Dane order, he suspected. And it was not too soon to begin laying those unseen foundations—to think the thought that must come before the thing. He was veritably a king, yet for a time must he masquerade as a wage-slave, a serf to Breede, and an inferior of Bulger's, considered as a mere spectacle.

He began to word long conversations with these two; noiseless conversations, be it understood, in which the snappy dialogue went unuttered. His sarcasm to Bulger in the matter of that ten-dollar loan was biting, ruthless, witty, invariably leaving the debtor in direst confusion with nothing to retort. Bean always had the last word, both with Bulger and Breede, turning from them with easy contempt.

He was less hard on Breede than on Bulger, because of the ball game. A man who could behave like that in the presence of baseball must have good in him. Nevertheless, in this silent way, he curtly apprised Breede of his intentions about working beyond stipulated hours, and when Breede was rash enough to adopt a tone of bluster, Bean silenced him with a magnificent "I can imagine nothing of less consequence!"

He carried this silent warfare into public conveyances and when stout aggressive men glared at him because he had a seat he quickly and wittily reduced them to such absurdity in the public eye that they had to flee in impotent rage. The once modest street row with a bully twice his size was enlarged in cast. There were now, as befitted a king, two bullies, who writhed in pain, each with a broken arm, while the slight but muscular youth with a knowledge of jiu-jitsu walked coolly off, flecking dust from one of his capable shoulders. Sometimes he paused long enough to explain the affair, in a few dignified words, to an admiring policeman who found it difficult to believe that this stripling had vanquished two such powerful brutes. Sometimes another act was staged in which he conferred his card upon the amazed policeman and later explained the finesse of his science to him, thereby winning his deathless gratitude. He became quite chummy with this officer and was never to be afraid of anything any more.

He glowed from this new exercise. He became more witty, more masterful, while the repartee of his adversaries sank to wretched piffle. He met disaster only once. That was when his conscience began to hurt him after a particularly bitter assault on Bulger in which the latter had been more than usually contemptible in the matter of the overdue debt. He felt that he had really been too hard on the fellow. And Bulger, who must have been psychically gifted himself, came over from his typewriter at that moment and borrowed an additional five without difficulty. In later justification, Bean reflected that he would almost certainly have refused this second loan had it not been for his softened mood of the moment. Still he was glad that, with his instinctive secrecy he had kept from Bulger any knowledge of his new fortune. With Bulger aware that he had thousands of dollars in the bank, something told him that distressing complications would have ensued.

He debated several days about this money. He resolved, at length, that a thousand dollars should be devoted to the worthy purpose of living up to his new condition. A thousand dollars would, for the present, give him an adequate sensation of wealth. Three thousand more must be paid to Professor Balthasar when his secret agents brought It from Its long-hidden resting-place. Suppose the professor pleaded unexpected outlays, officials not too easily bribed or something, and demanded a further sum? At once, in a crowded street, he brought about a heated interview with the professor, in which the seer was told that a bargain was a bargain, and that if he had thought Bean was a man to stand nonsense of any sort he was indeed wildly mistaken. Bean was going to hold him to the exact sum, and his parting sting was that the professor had better get a new lot of controls if his old ones hadn't been able to tell him this. After he had cooled a little he reflected that if there were really any small sums the professor would be out of pocket, he would of course not be mean.

This left him four thousand dollars with which to buy his way into the directorate of that express company, as suggested by Aunt Clara. He had learned a great deal about buying stocks. He knew there was a method called "buying on a margin" which was greatly superior to buying the shares outright: you received a great many more shares for a given sum. Therefore he would buy thus, and the sooner be a director. He liked to think of that position in his moments of lesser exaltation. He recalled his child-self sitting beside his father on the seat of an express wagon. It was queer how life turned out—sometimes you couldn't get away from a thing. Maybe he would always be a director; still he could go into baseball, too.

He did his business with the broker without a twinge of his old timidity. Indeed, he was rather bored by the affair. The broker took his money and later in the day he learned that he controlled a very large number of the shares of the Federal Express Company. He forgot how many, but he knew it was a number befitting his new dignity. Having done this much he thought the directorship could wait. Let them come to him if they wanted him. He had other affairs on.

There was the new dog.

It was not the least of many great days in Bean's life, that golden afternoon when he sped to the bird-and-animal store and paid the last installment of Napoleon's ransom. The creature greeted him joyously as of yore through the wall of glass, frantically essaying to lick the hand that was so close and yet so unaccountably withheld.

The money passed, and one dream, at least, had been made to come true. For the first time he was in actual contact with the wonderful animal.

"He knows me," said Bean, as the dog hurled itself delightedly upon him. "We've been friends a long time. I think he got so he expected me every afternoon."

Napoleon barked emphatically in confirmation of this. He seemed to be saying: "Hurry! Let's get out of here before he puts me back in that window!"

The old man confessed that he would miss the little fellow. He advised Bean to call him "Nap." "Napoleon" was no right name for a dog of any character.

"You know what that fellow been if he been here now," he volunteered at parting. "I dell you, you bed your life! He been a gompanion unt partner in full with that great American train-robber, Chessie Chames. Sure he would. My grantmutter she seen him like she could maybe reach out a finger unt touch him!"

"I'll call him Nap," promised Bean. He had ceased to feel blamable for the shortcomings of Napoleon I, but it was just as well not to have the name used too freely.

When he issued to the street, the excited dog on a leash, he was prouder than most kings have ever had occasion to be.

Now, he went to inspect flats. He would at last have "apartments," and in a neighbourhood suitable for a growing dog. He bestowed little attention on the premises submitted to his view, occupying himself chiefly with observing the effect of his dog on the various janitors. Some were frankly hostile; some covertly so. Some didn't mind dogs—but there was rules. And some defeated themselves by a display of over-enthusiasm that manifestly veiled indifference, or perhaps downright dislike.

But a janitor was finally encountered who met the test. In ten seconds Bean knew that Cassidy would be a friend to any dog. He did not fawn upon the animal nor explode with praise. He merely bestowed a glance or two upon the distinguished head, and later rubbed the head expertly just back of the erect ears; this, while he exposed to Bean the circumstances under which one steam-heated apartment, suitable for light housekeeping, chanced to be vacant. The parties, it appeared, was givin' a Dutch lunch to a gang of their friends at 5 A.M. of a morning, and that was bad enough in a place that was well kep' up; but in the sicin' place they got scrappin', which had swiftly resulted in an ambulance call for the host and lessee, and the patrol wagon for his friends that were not in much better shape thimselves, praise Gawd. But the place was all cleaned up again and would be a jool f'r anny young man that could take a drink, or maybe two, and then stop.

Bean knew Cassidy by that time, and his inspection of the apartment was perfunctory. Cassidy would be a buckler and shield to the dog, in his absence. Cassidy would love him. The dog, on his spread forefeet, touched his chest to the ground and with ears erect, eyes agleam, and inciting soprano gurgles invited the world to a mad, mad, game.

Cassidy only said, "Aw, g'wan! *Would* you, now!" But each word was a caress. And Cassidy became Bean's janitor.

498

He moved the next day, bringing his effects in a cab. The cabman professed never to have seen a dog as "classy" as Nap, and voiced the cheerful prophecy that in any bench show he would make them all look like mutts. He received a gratuity of fifty cents in addition to the outrageous fee he demanded for coming so far north, although he had the appearance of one who uses liquor to excess, and could probably not have qualified as a judge of dogs.

Bean's installation, under the guidance of Cassidy, was effected without delay. The apartment proved to be entirely suitable for a king in abeyance. There was a bedroom, a parlour, an alcove off the latter that Cassidy said was the libr'y an' a good place f'r a dawg t' sleep, and beyond this was a feminine diminutive of a kitchen, prettily called a "kitchenette."

Bean felt like an insect in such a labyrinth of a place. He forgot where he put things, and then, overcome by the vastness and number of rooms, forgot what he was looking for, losing himself in an abstracted and fruitless survey of the walls. He must buy things to hang on the walls, especially over certain stains on the wall of the parlour, or throne-room, to which in the heat of battle, doubtless, certain items of the late Dutch lunch had been misdirected.

But he knew what to buy. Etchings. In the magazine stories he read, aside from the very rich characters who had galleries of old masters, there were two classes: one without taste that littered its rooms with expensive but ill-advised bric-a-brac; and one that wisely contented itself with "a few good etchings." He bought a few good etchings at a department store for $1.97 each, and felt irreproachable. And when he had arranged his books—about Napoleon I and ancient Egypt—he was ready to play the game of living. Mrs. Cassidy "did" his rooms, and Cassidy already showed the devotion of an old and tried retainer. The Cassidys made him feel feudal.

At night, while Nap fought a never-decided battle with a sofa-pillow, or curled asleep on the couch with a half-inch of silly pink tongue projecting from between his teeth, he read of Egypt, the black land, where had been the first great people of the ancient world. He devoured the fruit of the lotus, the tamarisk, the pomegranate, and held cats to be sacred. (Funny, that feeling he had always had about cats—afraid of them even in childhood—it had survived in his being!) There he had lived and reigned in that flat valley of the Nile, between borders of low mountains, until his name had been put down in the book of the dead, and he had gone for a time to the hall of Osiris.

Or, perhaps, he read reports of psychical societies, signed by men with any number of capital letters after their names: cool-headed scientists, university professors, psychologists, grave students all, who were constantly finding new and wonderful mediums, and achieving communication with the disembodied. He could tell them a few things; only, of course, he wouldn't make a fool of himself. He could *show* them something, too, when the secret agents of Professor Balthasar came bringing It.

Or he looked into the opal depths of his shell, and saw visions of his greatness to come, while Nap, unregarded, wrenched away one of his slippers and pretended to find it something alive and formidable, to be growled at and shaken and savagely macerated.

There came, on a certain fair morning, a summons from Breede, who was detained at his country place by the same malady that Bulger had once so crudely diagnosed. Bean was to bring out the mail and do his work there. The car waited below.

At another time the expedition might have attracted him. He had studied pictures of that country place in the Sunday papers. Now it meant a separation from his dog, who was already betraying for the Cassidys a greater fondness than the circumstances justified; and it meant an absence from town at the very time when the secret agents might happen along with It. Of course he could refuse to go, but that would cost him his job, and he was not yet even the director of an express company. Dejectedly he prepared for the journey.

"Better take some things along," suggested Tully, who had conveyed the order to him. "He may keep you three or four days."

Bulger followed him to the hall.

"Look out for Grandma, the Demon!" warned Bulger. "'F I was the old man I'd slip something in her tea."

"Who—who is she?" demanded Bean.

"Just his dear, sweet old mother, that's all! Talk you to death—suffergette! Oh! say!"

Reaching the street, his gloom was not at all lightened by the discovery of the flapper in the waiting car. She gave him the little double-nod and regarded him with that peculiar steely kindness he so well remembered. It was undoubtedly kind, that look, yet there was an implacable something in its quality that dismayed him. He wondered what she exactly meant by it.

"Get in," commanded the flapper, and Bean got in.

"Tell him where to go for your things."

Bean told him.

"I'm glad it's on our way. Pops is in an awful state. He swore right out at his own mother this morning, and he wants you there in a hurry. Maybe we'll be arrested for speeding."

Bean earnestly hoped they would. Pops in health was ordeal enough. But he remained silent, trusting to the vigilance of an excellent constabulary. The car reached the steam-heated apartment without adventure, however, and he quickly secured his suit-case and consigned the dog for an uncertain period to a Cassidy, who was brazenly taking more than a friendly interest in him. Cassidy talked bluntly of how "we" ought to feed him, as if he were already a part owner of the animal.

The car flew on, increasing a speed that had been unlawful almost from the start. He wondered what the police were about. He might write a sharp letter to the newspapers, signed, "Indignant Pedestrian," only it would be too late. He was being volleyed at the rate of thirty-five miles an hour into the presence of a man who had that morning sworn at his mother. He wished he could, say for one day, have Breede back there on the banks of the Nile—set him to work building a pyramid, or weeding the lotus patch, foot or *no* foot! He'd show him!

He switched this resentment to the young female at his side. He wanted her to quit looking at him that way. It made him nervous. But a muffled glance or two at her disarmed this feeling. She was all right to look at, he thought, had pretty hands and "all that"—she had stripped off her gloves when they reached the open country—and she didn't talk, which was what he most feared in her sex. He recalled that she had said hardly a word since the start. He might have supposed himself forgotten had it not been for that look of veiled determination which he encountered as often as he dared.

A young dog dashed from a gateway ahead of them and threatened the car furiously. They both applied imaginary brakes to the car with feet and hands and taut nerves. The puppy escaping death by an inch, trotted back to his saved home with an air that comes from duty well performed. They looked from the dog to each other.

"I'd make them against the law," said Bean.

"How could you? The idea!"

"I mean motors, not dogs."

"Oh! Of course!"

They had been brought a little together.

"You go in for dogs?" asked the flapper.

He hesitated. "Going in" for dogs seemed to mean more. "I've got only one just now," he confessed.

Wooded hills flew by them, the white road flickered forward to their wheels.

"You interested in the movement?" demanded the flapper again.

"Yes," he said.

"Granny will be delighted to know that. So many young men aren't."

"What make is it?" he inquired, preparing to look enlightened when told the name of the vehicle in which they rode.

"Oh, I mean the Movement—*the* movement!"

"Oh, yes," he faltered. "Greatly interested!" He remembered the badge on her jacket, and Bulger's warning about Grandma, the Demon.

"Granny and I marched in the parade this year, clear down to Washington Square. If she wasn't so old we'd both run over to London and get arrested in the Strand for breaking windows."

Bean shuddered.

"We're making our flag now for the next parade—big blue cloth with a gold star for every state that has raised woman from her degradation by giving her a vote."

He shuddered again. Although of legal years for the franchise, he had never voted. If you tried to vote some ward-heeler would challenge you and you'd like as not be hauled off to the lock-up. And what was the good of it! The politicians got what they wanted. But this he kept to himself.

"Granny'll put a badge on you," promised the flapper. "We have to take advantage of every little means."

He was still puzzling over this when they turned through a gateway, imposing with its tangle of wrought iron and gilt, and at a decorously reduced speed crinkled up a wide drive to the vast pile of gray stone that housed the un-filial Breede.

A taller and, Bean thought, a prettier girl than the flapper stepped aside for them, looking at Bean as they passed. One could read her look as one could not read the flapper's. It was outrageously languishing.

"Flirts with every one, makes no difference *who*!" explained the flapper with a venomous sniff.

Bean laughed uneasily.

"She's my own dear sister, and I love her, but she's a perfect cat!"

Bean made deprecating sounds with his lips.

"I suppose people have been wondering where I was," confessed the flapper as they descended upon the granite steps. "I forgot to tell them I was going. Better hurry to Pops or he'll be murdering some one."

A man took his bag and preceded him into the big hall.

"Engaged, too!" called the flapper bitterly.

He found Breede imprisoned in a large, light room that looked to the west. Below the windows a green hill fell sheerly away to the bank of a lordly river, and beyond rose other hills that shimmered in the haze. A light breeze fluttered the gayly striped awnings. Breede, at a desk, turned his back upon the fair scene and fumed.

"Take letter G.M. Watkins, Pres'den I 'n' N.C. Rai'way," began Breede as Bean entered the room. "Dear sir repline yours of 23d instan' would say Ouch! damn that foot don't take that regardin' traffic 'greement now'n 'fect that 'casion may rise 'n near future to 'mend same in 'cordance with stip'lations inform'ly made at conf'rence held las' Janwary will not'fy you 'n due time 'f change is made yours very truly have some lunch brought here 'n a minute may haf' t' stay three four days t'll this Whoo! damn foot gets well take letter H.J. Hobbs secon' 'sistant vice Pres'den' D. 'n' L.S. Rai'way New York, New York, dear Hobbs mark it pers'nal repline yours even date stock purchases goin' forward as rapidly's thought wise under circumstances it is held mos'ly 'n small lots an' too active a market might give rise t' silly notions about it—"

The day's work was on, familiar enough, with the exception of Breede's interjections; he spoke words many times that were not to be "taken down." And yet Bean forebore to record his wonted criticisms of his employer's dress. There was ground for them. Breede had never looked less the advanced dresser. But Bean's mind was busy with that older sister, she of the marvellously drooping eyes. He had recognized her at once as the ideal person with whom to be wrecked on a desert island. A flirt, and engaged, too, was she? No matter. He wrecked himself with her, and they lived on mussels and edible roots and berries, and some canned stuff from the ship, and he built a hut of "native thatch," and found a deposit of rubies, gathering bushels of them, and he became her affianced the very day the smoke of the rescuing steamer blackened the horizon. And throughout an idyllic union they always thought rather regretfully of that island; they had had such a beautiful time there. And his oldest son, who was left-handed, pitched a ball that was the despair of every batter in both leagues!

Such had been the devastation of that one drooping glance. This vision, enjoyed while he ate of the luncheon brought to him, might have been prolonged. He hadn't remembered a quarter of the delightful contingencies that arise when the right man and woman are wrecked on an island, but he looked up from his plate to find Breede regarding him and his abundant food with a look of such stony malignance that he could eat no more—Breede with his glass of diluted milk and one intensely hygienic cracker!

But during pauses in the afternoon's work the island vision became blurred by the singular energies of the flapper. What did she mean by looking at him that way? There was something ominous about it. He had to admit that in some occult way she benumbed his will power. He did not believe he would dare be wrecked on a desert island with the other one, if the flapper knew about it.

At last there was surcease of Breede.

"Have 'em ready in the morning," he directed, referring to the letters he had dictated. "G'wout 'n' 'muse yourself when you get time," he added hospitably. "Now I got to hobble to my room. If you see any women outside, tell 'em g'wan downstairs if they don't want to hear me."

He stood balanced on one foot, a stout cane in either hand. Bean opened the door, but the hall was vacant. Breede grunted and began his progress. It was, perhaps, not more than reasonably vocal considering his provocation.

Bean uncovered a typewriter and sat to it, his note-book before him. For a moment he reverted to the island vision. They could be attacked by savages from another island, and he would fight them off with the rifles he had salvaged from the ship. *She* would reload the weapons for him, and bind up his head when he was wounded. He fought the last half of the desperate battle with a stained bandage over his brow.

There was a sharp rap at the door and it opened before he could call. The flapper entered.

"Don't let me disturb you," she said, and walked to the window, as if she found the place only scenically interesting.

Bean murmured politely and began upon his letters. The flapper was relentless. She sat in her father's chair and fastened the old look of implacable kindness upon him. He beat the keys of the machine. The flapper was disturbing him atrociously.

A few moments later another rap sounded on the door, and again it opened before he could call. A shrewd-looking, rather trim old lady with carefully coiffed hair stood in the doorway.

"Don't let me disturb you," she said, and again Bean murmured.

"Mr. Bean, my grandmother," said the flapper.

"Keep right on with your work, young man," said the old lady in commanding tones, when Bean had acknowledged the presentation. "I like to watch it."

She sat in another chair, very straight in her lavender dress, and joined with the flapper in her survey of the wage-slave. This was undoubtedly Grandma, the Demon.

Bean continued his work, thinking as best he could above the words of Breede, that she must be a pretty raw old party, going around, voting, smashing windows, leading her innocent young grandchild into the same reckless life. Nice thing, that! He was not surprised when he heard a match lighted a moment later, and knew that Grandma was smoking a cigarette. Expect anything of *that* sort!

He had wished they would go before he finished the last letter, but they sat on, and Grandma filled the room with smoke.

"Now he's through!" proclaimed the flapper.

"How old are you?" asked Grandma, as Bean arose nervously from the machine.

He tried jauntily to make it appear that he must "count up."

"Let me see. I'm—twenty-three last Tuesday."

The old lady nodded approvingly, as if this were something to his credit.

"Got any vicious habits?"

Bean weakly began an answer intended to be facetious, and yet leave much to be inferred regarding his habits. But the Demon would have none of this.

"Smoke?"

"No!"

"Drink?"

"No!" He desperately wondered if she would know where to stop.

"How's your health? Ever been sick much?"

"I can't remember. I had lumbago when I was seven."

"Humph! Gamble, play cards, bet on races, go around raising cain with a lot of young devils at night?"

"No, I don't," said Bean, with a hint of sullen defiance. He wanted to add: "And I don't go round voting and breaking windows, either," but he was not equal to this.

"Well, I don't know—" She deliberated, adjusting one of her many puffs of gray hair, and gazing dreamily at a thread of smoke that ascended from her cigarette. She seemed to be wondering whether or not she ought to let him off this time. "Well, I don't know. It looks to me as if you were too good to be true."

She rose and tossed her cigarette out of the window. He thought he was freed, but at the door she turned suddenly upon him once more.

"What in time *have* you done? Haven't you ever had any fun?"

But she waited for no answer.

"I knew she'd admire you," said the flapper. "Isn't she a perfectly old dear?"

"Oh, yes!" gasped Bean. "Yes, yes, yes, indeed! She is *that*!"

CHAPTER VII

Bean had once attended a magician's entertainment and there suffered vicariously the agony endured by one of his volunteer assistants. Suavely the entertainer begged the help of "some kind gentleman from the audience." He was insistent, exerting upon the reluctant ones the pressure of his best platform manner.

When the pause had grown embarrassing, a shamed looking man slouched forward from an aisle seat amid hearty cheers. He ascended the carpeted runway from aisle to stage, stumbled over footlights and dropped his hat. Then the magician harried him to the malicious glee of the audience. He removed playing-cards, white rabbits and articles of feminine apparel from beneath the coat of his victim. He seated him in a chair that collapsed. He gave him a box to hold and shocked him electrically. He missed his watch and discovered it in the abused man's pocket. And when the ordeal was over the recovered hat was found to contain guinea-pigs. The kind gentleman from the audience had been shown to be transcendently awkward, brainless, and to have a mania for petty thievery. With burning face and falling glance, he had stumbled back to his seat, where a lady who had before exhibited the public manner of wife to husband toward him, now pretended that he was an utter and offensive stranger.

Bean, I say, had once suffered vicariously with this altruistic dolt. His suffering now was not vicarious. For three days he endured on the raw of his own soul tortures even more ingeniously harrowing.

To be shut up for three hours a day with Breede was bad enough, but custom had a little dulled his sensitiveness to this. And he could look Breede over and write down in beautiful shorthand what he thought of him.

But the other Breedes!

Mrs. Breede, a member of one of the very oldest families in Omaha, he learned, terrified him exceedingly. She was an advanced dresser—he had to admit that—but she was no longer beautiful. She was a plucked rose that had been too long kept; the petals were rusting, crumpling at the edges. He wondered if Breede had ever wished to be wrecked on a desert island with her. She surveyed Bean through a glass-and-gold weapon with a long handle, and on the two subsequent occasions when she addressed him called him Mr. Brown. Once meeting him in the hall, she seemed to believe that he had been sent to fix the telephone.

And the flapper's taller sister of the languishing glance—how quickly had she awakened him from that golden dream of the low-lying atoll and the wrecked ship in a far sea. She *did* flirt with "any one," no doubt about that. She adroitly revealed to Bean an unshakable conviction that he was desperately enamoured of her, and that it served him right for a presumptuous nobody. She talked to him, preened herself in his gaze, and maddened him with a manner of deadly roguishness. Then she flew to exert the same charm upon any one of the resplendent young men who were constantly riding over or tooting over in big black motor-cars. They were young men who apparently had nothing to do but "go in" for things—riding, tennis, polo, golf. To all of them she was the self-confident charmer; just the kind of a girl to make a fool of you and tell about it.

Twenty-four hours after her first assault upon him he was still wrecking the ship at the entrance to that lagoon, but now he watched the big sister go down for the third time while he placidly rescued a stoker to share his romantic isolation.

The flapper and Grandma, the Demon, were even more objectionable, and, what was worse, they alarmed him. Puzzled as to their purpose, he knew not what defence to make. He was swept on some secret and sinister current to an end he could not divine.

The flapper lay in wait for him at all hours when he might appear. Did he open a door, she lurked in the corridor; did he seek refuge in the gloom of the library, she arose to confront him from its dimmest nook; did he plan a masterly escape by a rear stairway, she burst upon him from the ambush of some exotic shrub to demand which way he had thought of going. He had never thought of a way that did not prove to have been her own. The creature was a leech! If she had only talked, he believed that he could have thrown her off. But she would not talk. She merely walked beside him insatiably. Sometimes he thought he could detect a faint anxiety in the look she kept upon him, but, mostly, it was the look of something calm, secure, ruthless. Something! It unnerved him.

It was usually probable that Grandma, the Demon, would join them, the silver cigarette case dangling at her girdle. Then was he sorely beset. They would perhaps talk about him over his head, discuss his points as if he were some new beast from the stables.

"I tell you, he's over an inch taller than I am," announced the flapper.

"U-u-mm!" replied Grandma, measuring Bean's stature with narrowed eye. "U-u-mm!"

"You show her!" commanded flapper, in a louder voice, as if she believed him deaf. She grasped his arm and whirled him about to stand with his back to hers.

"There!" said the flapper tensely, her eyes staring ahead. "There!"

"You're scrooching!" accused the Demon.

"Not a bit!—and see how square his shoulders are!" She turned to point out this grace of the animal.

"Ever take any drugs? Ever get any habits like that?" queried the Demon. Plainly Bean's confession to an unusual virtue had aroused her suspicion. He might be a drug fiend!

He faltered wretchedly, wishing Breede would send for him.

"I—well, I used to be made to take sulphur and molasses every spring ... but I never kept it up after I left home."

"Hum!" said the old lady, looking as if he could tell a lot more if he chose.

She gripped one of his biceps. He was not ashamed of these. The night and morning drill with that home exerciser had told, even though he was not yet so impressive as the machine's inventor, who, in magazine advertisements, looked down so fondly upon his own flexed arm.

"For goodness' sake!" exclaimed the Demon respectfully.

Bean thrilled at this, feeling like a primitive brute of the cave times, accustomed to subduing women by force.

After that they seemed tacitly to agree that they would pretend to show him over the "grounds." Bean hated the grounds, which were worried to the last square inch into a chilling formality, and the big glass conservatory was stifling, like an overcrowded, overheated auditorium. And he knew they were "drawing him out." They looked meaningly at each other whenever he spoke.

They questioned him about his early life, but learned only that his father had been "engaged in the express business." He was ably reticent.

Did he believe that women ought to be classed legally with drunkards, imbeciles and criminals? He did not, if you came down to that. Let them vote if they wanted to. He had other things to think about, more important. He didn't care much, either way. Voting didn't do any good.

He had taken the ideal attitude to enrage the woman suffragist. She will respect opposition. Careless indifference she cannot brook. Grandma opened upon him and battered him to a pulpy mass. Within the half hour he was supinely promising to remind her to give him a badge before he left; and there was further talk of his marching at the next parade as a member of the Men's League for Woman's Suffrage, or, at the very least, in the column of Men Sympathizers.

He wondered, wondered! Were they trying to assure themselves that he was a fit man to be in the employ of old Breede? He could imagine it of them; as soon as they thought about voting they began to interfere in a man's business. Yet this suspicion slept when he was with the flapper alone. Sometimes he was conscious of liking very much to be with her. He decided that this was because she didn't talk.

The evening of his last day came. Breede, in a burst of garrulity, had said: "Had enough this; go town to-morrow!" The flapper, and even the Demon, had seemed to be stirred by the announcement. He resolved to be more than ever on his guard. But they caught him fairly in the open.

"How do you like his hair parted that way in the middle?" demanded the flapper, with the calculating eye of one who ponders changes in a dwelling-house.

"U-u-mm!" considered the Demon gravely. "Not bad. Still, perhaps—!"

508

"Exactly what I was thinking!" said the flapper cordially. Then, to Bean, her tone slightly raised:

"Which way?"

"Got to get off a bunch of telegrams," lied Bean.

"Oh, all right! We'll wait for you," said the flapper. "Right there," she added, pointing to the most expensive pergola on the place.

In the dusk of an hour later he slunk stealthily down a rear stairway and made a cautious detour into the grounds. He earnestly meant to keep far from that pergola. Wait for him, would they? Well, he'd show them! Always spying on a man; *hounding* him! What business was it of theirs whether he had habits or not ... any kind of habits?

But he was to find himself under a spell such as is said to bring the weak-willed bird to the serpent's maw. His traitorous feet dragged him toward the trap. The odour of a cigarette drew his revolted nostrils. He could hear the murmurous duet.

Talking about him! Of course! He would like to break in on them and for a little while be a certain Corsican upstart in one of his most objectionable moods. That would take them down a bit. But, instead, he became something entirely different. With the stealth of the red Indian he effaced himself against a background of well-groomed shrubbery and crept toward the murmur. At last he could hear words above the beating of his heart.

"How can you *know*?" the Demon was saying. "A child of your age?"

The flapper's tone was calm and confident as one who relates a phenomenon that has become a commonplace.

"I knew it the very first second I ever saw him—something went over me just like that—I can't tell how, but I knew."

"Well, how can you know about him?"

"Oh, him!" The words implied that the flapper had waved a deprecating hand. "Why, I know about him in just the same way; you can't tell how. It comes over you!"

The Demon: (A long-drawn) "U-u-mm!"

The flapper: "And he makes me perfectly furious sometimes, too!"

There was a stir as if they were leaving. Bean retreated a dozen feet before he breathed again. So that was their game, was it? He'd see about that!

He waited for them to emerge, but they had apparently settled to more of this high-handed talk. Then, like an icy wave to engulf him, came a name—"Tommy Hollins." It came in the Demon's voice, indistinguishable words preceding it. And in the flapper's voice came "Tommy Hollins!" gently, caressingly, it seemed. In truth, the flapper had sniffed before uttering it, and the sniff had meant good-natured contempt but Bean had lost the sniff.

Now he had it! Tommy Hollins! He identified the youth, a yellow-headed, pink-faced lout in flannels who was always riding over, and who seemed to "go in" for nearly everything. He had detected a romping intimacy between the two. So it was Tommy Hollins. At once he felt a great relief; he need worry no longer over the singular attentions of this young woman. Let Tommy Hollins worry! He could admit, now, how grave had been his alarm. And there was nothing in it. He could meet her without being afraid. He was almost ready to approach them genially and pass an hour in light conversation. He advanced a few steps with this intention, but again came the voice of the flapper replying, apparently, to some unheard admonition. It came, cold and terrible.

"I don't care. I've got the right to choose the father of my own children!"

He blushed for this language, a blush he could feel mantling his very toes. He fled from there. He saw that the moment was not for light conversation. And even as he fled he caught the Demon's prolonged "U-u-mmm!"

Yet when he left in the morning the flapper lurked for him as ever, materializing from an apparently vacant corridor. He greeted her for the first time without ulterior questioning. He thought he liked her pretty well now. And she was undeniably good to look at in the white of her tennis costume; the hair, like Nap's spots in its golden brown, was filleted with a scarlet ribbon, and her eyes shone from her freshened face with an unwonted sparkle—decision, certitude—what was it? He deemed that he knew.

"Tommy Hollins coming to play," she vouchsafed in explanation of the racquet she carried. "Are you glad to go?"

"Glad to see my dog again." He smiled as a man of the world. He was on the verge of coquetry, now that he knew it to be safe.

"We'll bring him along too, next time."

"Oh, the next time!" He put it carelessly aside.

"You'll be out again, soon enough. I simply know Pops is going to have another bad spell—in a week or so."

He could have sworn that the eyes of Breede's daughter gleamed with cold anticipatory malice. He shuddered for Breede. And he wished Tommy Hollins well of his bargain. Flirt, indeed! All alike!

"Chubbins!" called the unconscious father from afar.

"Yes, Pops!" She gripped his hand with a well-muscled fervour. "Oh, he'll have another in a little while, don't you worry!" And she was off, with this evil in her heart, to a father but now convalescent.

Marvelling, he walked on to the Demon's ambuscade. She pounced upon him from behind a half-opened door.

"I want to say one word, young man. Oh, you needn't think I don't see the way things are going. I'm not blind if I am seventy-six! If you're the tender and innocent thing you say you are, you look out for yourself. I know you all! If you don't break out one time you do another. I'd a good deal rather you'd had it over before now and put it all behind you—don't interrupt—but you're sound and clean as far as I can see, and you've got a good situation. I don't say it couldn't be worse. But if you are—well, you see that you *stay* that way. Don't try to tell me. I've seen enough of men in my time—"

He broke away from her at Breede's call. The flapper jerked her head twice at him, very neatly, as the car passed the tennis court. She was beginning a practise volley with Tommy Hollins, who was disporting himself like a young colt.

"Chubbins!" he thought. Not a bad name for her, though it had come queerly from Breede. For the first time he was pricked with the needle of suspicion that Hollins might not be the right man for the flapper. Hearing her called "Chubbins" somehow made it seem different. Maybe Hollins, who seemed all of twenty, wouldn't "make her happy." He thought it was something that the family ought to consider very seriously. He was conscious of a willingness to consider it himself, as a friend of the family and a well-wisher of Chubbins.

He was back in the apartment and in the presence of a document that swept his mind of all Breedes. Never had he in fancy ceased to be king Ram-tah, cheated of historic mention because of his wisdom and goodness. He had looked commiseratingly upon Breede's country-house, thinking of his own palace on the banks of the slow-moving Nile. "—probably made this place look like a shack!" he had exultantly thought. And the benign monarch had ended his reign in peace, to be laid magnificently away, to repose undisturbed while the sands drifted over him—until—

The hour had come. "My men have succeeded, after incredible hardships," wrote Professor Balthasar. "The *goods* will be delivered to you Thursday night, the tenth. I trust the final payment will be ready, as, relying on your honour, I have advanced—"

The rest did not matter. His honour was surely to be relied upon. The money had been richly earned. An able man, this Balthasar! He had achieved the thing with admirable secrecy. Bean had feared the hounds of the daily press. They might discover who It was, to whom It was going; discover the true identity of Bunker Bean. The whole thing might come out in the papers! But Balthasar had known how. He approved the caution that had led him to speak of "the *goods*"; there was something almost witty about it.

He leaned far out a window, listening, straining his eyes up and down the lighted avenue. There was confusion in his mind as to how It could most fittingly be brought to him. The sable vision of a hearse drawn by four lordly black horses at first possessed his mind. But this was dismissed; there was no death! And the spectacle would excite comment. The idea of an ambulance, which he next considered, seemed equally impracticable. It would have to be done quietly; Balthasar would know. Trust Balthasar!

He heard the rhythmic clump-clump of a horse's hoofs on the asphalt pavement. This was presently accompanied by the sounds of wheels. An express wagon came under the street-lights. Balthasar rode beside the driver, his frock coat and glossy tall hat having been relinquished for the garb of an ordinary citizen. Back of them in the wagon he could distinguish the lines of an Object. It had come to him in a common express wagon, in a common crate, and the driver did not even wear a black mask. Balthasar had cunningly eluded detection by pretending there was nothing to conceal.

He drew back from the window and with fast beating heart went to open the door. They were already on the stairway. Balthasar was coming first. With sublime effrontery he had impressed Cassidy to help carry It, and Cassidy was warning the expressman to look out for that turn an' not tear inta th' plashter.

It was lowered to the floor in the throne-room. Cassidy and the expressman puffed freely and looked at the thing as if wondering how two men had ever been equal to it.

"'Twould be brickybac," said Cassidy genially.

"That there hall's choked with dust," said the expressman with seeming irrelevance.

"I noticed it meself," said Cassidy.

"Clogged me throat up fur fair," continued the expressman huskily.

"Pay the men liberally and let them be on their way," said Balthasar. Bean pressed money upon both and they departed.

"You couldn't get me to do it again for twice the money," said Balthasar; "the nervous strain I've been under. A custom-house detective was on our trail, but one of my men took care of him—at a dark corner."

Bean shuddered.

"They didn't—"

"Oh, nothing serious. He'll be as well as ever in a few days. Got a hatchet." He gestured significantly toward the crate.

But this was too precipitate for Bean. He could not disinter himself—it seemed like that—under the eyes of Balthasar.

"Not now! Not now! You've done your part—here!" He passed Balthasar the check he had written earlier in the evening.

"I'll leave you, then," said the professor. "But one thing, don't handle it much. It might disintegrate. I bid you farewell, my young friend."

Bean, at the door, listened to his descending steps. The professor was whistling. He recognized the air, "Call Me Up Some Rainy Afternoon." It was a lively air and the professor rendered it ably but quite softly.

The door locked, he was back staring at the crate that concealed his dead self. He was helpless before it. The fleshly tenement of a great king who had later flashed upon the world as Napoleon I, and was now Bunker Bean! Could he bear to look? He trembled and knew himself weak. Yet it would be done, some time.

There was a vigorous knock at the door. All was discovered!

The crime of assault at the dark corner had been traced to his door. Balthasar had betrayed him. The Egyptian authorities had discovered their loss. The thing was there. He was caught red-handed.

He reached the door and cautiously opened it an inch. Cassidy stood there, armed with a hatchet. They would use violence!

"Hatchet!" said Cassidy, genially extending the weapon. He wiped his mouth with the back of his hand. The aroma of beer stole into the room.

"F'r brox brickybac!" insinuated Cassidy.

"Thanks!" said Bean, accepting the tool.

"We kem frum th' sem county, Mayo, him an' me," volunteered Cassidy. "G'night!"

Once more Bean faced the crate. It must be done at once. Discovery was too probable. Gingerly he forced the blade under one of the boards and pried. The nails screeched horribly as they were withdrawn. The task was simple enough; the crate was a flimsy affair to have withstood so difficult a journey. But after each board was removed he peered to the street from behind the closed blind, half expecting to find policemen drawn to the spot.

A smoothly packed layer of excelsior greeted his eyes. It was rather reassuring. He felt that he might be unpacking any casual object. Exposed at last was the wooden case that enveloped him!

Awestruck, he looked down at it for a long time. He recognized the workmanship, having seen a dozen such in the museum in the park. He knelt by it and ran a reverent hand over its painted surface. In many colours were birds and beasts, and men in profile, and queer marks that he knew to be picture-writing; processions of slaves and oxen, reapers and water-bearers. The tints were fresh under their overlaying lacquer. There was even a smell of varnish. He wondered if the contents—if It—were in the same remarkable state of preservation. He rapped on the thin wood—it was cedar, he thought, or perhaps sycamore. The sound was musical, resonant; the same note that had vibrated how many thousands of years before.

Nap came up to smell, seeming to suspect that the box might contain food. He stretched his forepaws to the top of the case and betrayed eagerness.

"Napoleon!" cried Bean sternly, putting the dog's complete name upon him for the first time. He was banished to his couch and made to know that leaving it would entail unpleasantness.

The thought of the Corsican came back with a new significance. In that embodiment he had felt, perhaps dimly recalled, his Egyptian life. Had he not been drawn irresistibly to Egypt? "In the shadow of the pyramids," he had read in a history, "the conqueror of Italy dreamed of the pomp and power of a crown and sceptre, and upon his return to France from the Egyptian expedition, with characteristic energy he set himself to work to bring the dream to pass—" It was plain enough. He knew now the inner meaning of that engraving he had bought, in which Napoleon stood in rapt meditation before the Sphinx. They had all— King, Emperor, Bean—been dreamers that brought their dreams to pass. He mused long, staring down at the case; a queerly shaped thing, fashioned to follow the lines of the human form. From the neck the shoulders rounded gracefully. They might have been cut to give the wearer the appearance of perfect physical development; at least they seemed to fit him neatly.

It occurred to Bean that the case should not lie prone. It suggested death where death was not. He pulled out more excelsior until he could raise the case. It was surprisingly light and he leaned it upright against the wall. He now tried to pretend that everything was over. He gathered boards, excelsior and the crate and piled them in the kitchenette, which they approximately filled.

But inevitably he was brought back. He stood with hands upon the cover of the upreared case, drew a long shivering breath and gently lifted it off. His eyes were upon the swathed figure within, then slowly they crept up the yellowed linen and came to rest upon the bared face.

He had tried feebly to prefigure this face, but never had his visioning approached the actual in its majestic, still beauty. The brow was nobly broad, the nose straight and purposeful, the chin bold yet delicate. The grimness of the mouth was relieved by a faint lift of the upper lip, perhaps an echo of the smile with which he greeted death. There was a gleam of teeth from under the lip. The eyes had closed peacefully; the lids lay light upon their secrets as if they might flutter and open again. On cheek and chin was a discernible growth of dark beard; the hair above the brow was black and abundant. It was a kingly face, a face of command, though benign. It was all too easy to believe that a crown had become it well. And there had been no weakening at the end, no sunken cheeks nor hollowed temples. The lines were full. The general colour was of rich red mahogany.

He ran a tremulous hand over the face, smoothed the thick hair, fingered the firm lips that almost smiled. Under the swathing of linen he could see where the hands were folded on the breast. Low down on the right jaw was unmistakably a mole, a thing that had strangely survived on Bean's own face. Again he ran a hand over the features, then a corroborating hand over his own. Intently and long he studied each detail, nostrils, eyebrows, ears, hair, the tips of the just-revealed teeth.

"God!" he breathed. It was hardly more than a whisper and was uttered in all reverence.

Then—

"God! how I've changed!"

CHAPTER VIII

On the following afternoon, among the Sunday throng in the Metropolitan Museum of Art, a slender young man of inconsiderable stature, alert as to movement, but with an expression of absent dreaming, might have been observed giving special attention to the articles in those rooms devoted to ancient Egypt. Doubtless, however, no one did observe him more than casually, for, though of singularly erect carriage, he was garbed inconspicuously in neutral tints, and his behaviour was never such as to divert attention from the surrounding spoils of the archaeologist.

Had his mind been as an open book, he would surely have become a figure of interest. His mental attitude was that of a professional beau of acknowledged preeminence; he was comparing the self at home in the mummy case with the remnants of defunct Pharaohs here exposed under glass, and he was sniffing, in spirit, at their lack of kingly dignity and their inferior state of preservation. Their wooden cases were often marred, faded, and broken. Their shrouding linen was frayed and stained. Their features were unimpressive and, in too many instances, shockingly incomplete. They looked very little like kings, and the laudatory recitals of their one-time greatness, translated for the contemporary eye, seemed to be only the vapourings of third-class pugilists.

Sneering openly at a damaged Pharaoh of the fourth dynasty, he reflected that some day he would confer upon that museum a relic transcending all others. He saw it enshrined in a room by itself; it should never be demeaned by association with those rusty cadavers he saw about him. This would be when he had passed on to another body, in accordance with the law of Karma. He would leave a sum to the museum authorities, specifically to build this room, and to it would come thousands, for a glimpse of the superior Ram-tah, last king of the pre-dynastic period, surviving in a state calculated to impress every beholder with his singular merits. Ram-tah, cheated of his place in history's pantheon, should here at last come into his own; serene, beauteous, majestic, looking every inch a king, where mere Pharaohs looked like—like the coffee-stained, untidy fragments they were.

He left the place in a tolerant mood. He had weighed himself with the other great dead of the world.

That night he sat again before this old king, staring until he lost himself, staring as he had before stared into the depths of his shell. The shell, when he had looked steadily at it for a long time, had always seemed to put him in close touch with unknown forces. He had once tried to explain this to his Aunt Clara, who understood nearly everything, but his effort had been clumsy enough and had brought her no enlightenment. "You look into it—and it makes you *feel*!" was all he had been able to tell her.

But the shell was now discarded for the puissant person of Ram-tah. The message was more pointed. He drew power from the old dead face that yet seemed so living. He was himself a wise and good king. No longer could he play the coward before trivial adversities. He would direct large affairs; he would live big. Never again would he be afraid of death or Breede or policemen or the mockery of his fellows—or women! He might still avoid the latter, but not in terror; only in a dignified dread lest they talk and spoil it all.

He would choose, in due time, a worthy consort, and a certain Crown Prince would, in further due time, startle the world with his left-handed pitching. It was a prospect all golden to dream upon. His spirit grew tall and its fibre toughened.

To be sure, he did not achieve a kingly disregard for public opinion all in one day. There was the matter of that scarlet cravat. Monday morning he excavated it from the bottom of the trunk, where it lay beside "Napoleon, Man and Lover." He even adjusted it, carelessly pretending that it was just any cravat, the first that had come to hand. But its colour was still too alarming. It—so he usually thought of the great Ram-tah—would have worn the cravat without a tremor, but It had been born a king. One glance at the thing about his neck had vividly recalled the awkward circumstance that, to the world at large, he was still Bunker Bean, a youth incapable of flaunt or flourish.

Let it not be thought, however, that his new growth showed no result above ground. He purchased and wore that very morning a cravat not entirely red, it is true, but one distinguished by a narrow red stripe on a backing of bronze, which the clerk who manoeuvred the sale assured him was "tasty." Also he commanded a suit of clothes of a certain light check in which the Bean of uninspired days would never have braved public scrutiny. Such were the immediate and actual fruits of Ram-tah's influence.

There were other effects, perhaps more subtle. Performing his accustomed work for Breede that day, he began to study his employer from the kingly, or Ram-tah, point of view. He conceived that Breede in the time of Ram-tah would have been a steward, a keeper of the royal granaries, a dependable accountant; a good enough man in his lowly station, but one who could never rise. His laxness in the manner of dress was seen to be ingrained, an incurable defect of soul. In the time of Ram-tah he had doubtless worn the Egyptian equivalent for detached cuffs, and he would be doing the like for a thousand incarnations to come. All too plainly Breede's Karmic future promised little of interest. His degree of ascent in the human scale was hardly perceptible.

Bean was pleased at this thought. It left him in a fine glow of superiority and sharpened his relish for the mad jest of their present attitudes—a jest demanding that he seem to be Breede's subordinate.

Naturally, this was a situation that would not long endure. It was too preposterous. Money came not only to kings but to the kingly. He troubled as little about details as would have any other king. Were there not steel kings, and iron kings, railway kings, oil kings—money kings? He thought it was not unlikely that he would first engage the world's notice as an express king. He had received those fifty shares of stock from Aunt Clara and regarded them as a presage of his coming directorship. But he took no pride in this thought. Baseball was to be his life work. He would own one major-league team, at least; perhaps three or four. He would be known as the baseball king, and the world would forget his petty triumphs as a director of express.

He deemed it significant that the present directors of that same Federal Express Company one day held a meeting in Breede's office. It showed, he thought, how life "worked around." The thing was coming to his very door. With considerable interest he studied the directors as they came and went. Most of them, like Breede, were men whose wealth the daily press had a habit of estimating in rotund millions. He regarded them knowingly, thinking he could tell them something that might surprise them. But they passed him, all unheeding, moneyed-looking men of good round girth, who seemed to have found the dollar-game worth while.

The most of them, he was glad to note, were in dress slightly more advanced than Breede. One of them, a small but important-looking old gentleman with a purple face and a white parted beard, became on the instant Bean's ideal for correctness. From his gray spats to his top-hat, he was "dignified yet different," although dressing, for example, in a more subdued key than Bulger. Yet he was a constantly indignant looking old gentleman, and Bean guessed that he would be a trouble-maker on any board of directors. It seemed to him that he would like to take this person's place on the board; oust him in spite of his compelling garments.

And Breede would know then that he was something more than a machine. On the whole, he felt sorry for Breede at times. Perhaps he would let him have a little of the baseball stock.

So he sat and dreamed of his great past and of his brilliant future. Perhaps, after all, Bean as the blind poet had been not the least authentic of Balthasar's visions.

And inevitably he encountered the flapper in this dreaming; "Chubbins," he liked to call her. More and more he was suspecting that Tommy Hollins was not the man for Chubbins. He would prefer to see her the bride of an older man, two or three, or even four, years older, who was settled in life. A young girl—a young girl's parents—couldn't be too careful!

He was not for many days at a time deprived of the sight of the young girl in question. She had formed a habit of calling for her father at the close of his day's hard work. And she did not wait for him in the big car; she sat in his office, where, after she had inquired solicitously about his poor foot, she settled her gaze upon Bean. And Bean no longer evaded this gaze. She was a clever, attractive little thing and he liked her well. He thought of things he would tell her for her own good at the first opportunity.

He wondered guiltily when Breede's next attack might be expected, and he had a lively impression that the flapper, too, was more curious than alarmed about this. He seemed to feel that she was actually wishing to be told things by him for her own good.

However that may be, his next summons to the country place came without undue delay, and it is not at all improbable that Breede fell a victim to what the terminology of one of our most popular cults identifies as "malicious animal magnetism."

On this occasion he was not oppressed by those attentions which the flapper and Grandma, the Demon, still bestowed upon him. Where he had once fled, he now put himself in the way of them. He listened with admirably simulated interest to Grandma's account of the suffrage play for which she was rehearsing. She was to appear in the mob scene. He was certain she would lend vivacity to any mob. But he was glad that the flapper was not to appear. Voting and smashing windows were bad enough.

He tried at first to talk to the flapper about Tommy Hollins, whom he airily designated as "that Hollins boy". It seemed to be especially needed, because the Hollins boy arrived after breakfast every day and left only in the late afternoon. But the flapper declined nevertheless to consider him as meat for serious converse.

Bean considered that this was sheer flirting, whereupon he flung principle to the winds and flirted himself.

"You show signs of life," declared Grandma, who was quick to note this changed demeanor. And Bean smirked like a man of the world.

"She never set her mind on anything yet that she didn't get it," added Grandma, naming no one. "She's like her father there."

And Bean strolled off to enjoy a vision of himself defeating her purpose to ensnare the Hollins youth. Once he would have considered it crass presumption, but that was before a certain sarcophagus on the left bank of the Nile had been looted of its imperial occupant. Now he merely recalled a story about a King Cophetua and a beggar maid. It was a comparison that would have intensely interested the flapper's mother, who was this time regarding Bean through her glazed weapon as if he were some queer growth the head gardener had brought from the conservatory.

Grandma deftly probed his past for affairs of the heart. She pointedly had him alone, and her intimation was that he might talk freely, as to a woman of understanding and broad sympathy. But Bean made a wretched mess of it.

Certainly there had been "affairs." There was the girl in Chicago, two doors down the street, whom he had once taken to walk in the park, but only once, because she talked; the girl in the business college who had pretty hair and always smiled when she looked at him; and another who, he was almost sure, had sent him an outspoken valentine; yes, there had been plenty of girls, but he hadn't bothered much about them.

And Grandma, plainly incredulous, averred that he was too deep for her. Bean was on the point of inventing a close acquaintance with an actress, which he considered would be scandalous enough to compel a certain respect he seemed to find lacking in the old lady, but he saw quickly that she would confuse and trip him with a few questions. He was obliged to content himself with looking the least bit smug when she said:

"You're a deep one—too deep for me!"

He tried hard to look deep and at least as depraved as the conventions of good society seemed to demand.

He was beginning to enjoy the sinful thing. The girl was of course plighted to the Hollins boy, and yet she was putting herself in his way. Very well! He would teach her the danger of playing with fire. He would bring all of his arts and wiles to bear. True, in behaving thus he was conscious of falling below the moral standards of a wise and good king who had never stooped to baseness of any sort. But he was now living in a different age, and somehow—

"I'm a dual nature," he thought. And he applied to himself another phrase he seemed to recall from his reading of magazine stories.

"I've got the artistic temper!" This, he gathered, was held to explain, if not to justify, many departures from the conventional in affairs of the heart. It was a kind of licensed madness. Endowed with the "artistic temper," you were not held accountable when you did things that made plain people gasp. That was it! That was why he was carrying on with Tommy Hollins' girl, and not caring *what* happened.

In his times of leisure they walked through the shaded aisles of those too well-kept grounds, or they sat in seats of twisted iron and honored the setting sun with their notice. They did not talk much, yet they were acutely aware of each other. Sometimes the silence was prolonged to awkwardness, and one of them would jestingly offer a penny for the other's thoughts. This made a little talk, but not much, and sometimes increased the awkwardness; it was so plain that what they were thinking of could not be told for money.

They did tell their wonderful ages and their full names and held their hands side by side to note the astonishing differences between the "lines." A palmist had revealed something quite amazing to the flapper, but she refused to tell what it was, with a significance that left Bean in a tumultuous and pleasurable whirl of cowardice. Their hands flew apart rather self-consciously. Bean felt himself a scoundrel—"leading on" a young thing like that who was engaged to another. It was flirting of the most reprehensible sort. But there was his dual nature; a strain of the errant Corsican had survived to debauch him.

And if she didn't want to be "led on," he thought indignantly, why did she so persistently put herself in the way of it? She was always there! Serve her right, then! Serve the Hollins boy right, too!

Grandma eyed them shrewdly with her Demon's glance of questioning, but did nothing to keep them apart. On the contrary, she would often brazenly leave them together after conducting them to remote nooks. She made no flimsy excuses. She seemed indifferent to the fate of this tender bud left at the mercy of one whom she affected to regard as a seasoned roué.

There were four days of this regrettable philandering. On the fifth Breede manifested alarming symptoms of recovery. He ceased to be the meek man he was under actual suffering, and was several times guilty of short-worded explosions that should never have reached the ears of good women.

Said the flapper in tones of genuine dismay that evening:

"I'm afraid Pops is going to be well enough to go to town to-morrow!"

Even Grandma, pacing a bit of choice turf near at hand, rehearsing her lines in the mob scene, was shocked at this.

"You are a selfish little pig!" she called.

"But *he* will have to go away, if Pops goes," said the flapper, in magnificent extenuation.

The words told. Grandma seemed to see things in a new light.

"You come with me," she commanded; "both of you."

Ahead of them she led the way to that pergola where Bean had once overheard their talk.

"Sit down," said Grandma, and herself sat between them.

"You are a couple of children," she began accusingly. "Why, when I was your age—" She broke off suddenly, and for some moments stared into the tracery of vines.

"When I was your age," she began once more, but in a curiously altered voice—"Lord! What a time of years!" She spoke slowly, softly, as one who would evoke phantoms. "Why, at your age," she turned slightly to the flapper, "I'd been married two years, and your father was crawling about under my feet as I did the housework."

She was still looking intently ahead to make her vision alive.

"What a time of years, and how different! Sixty years ago—why, it seems farther back than Noah's ark. The log cabins in the little clearings, and people marrying when they wanted to—always early, and working hard and raising big

521

families. I was the only girl, but I had nine brothers. And Jim, your father's father, my dear, I remember the very moment he began to take notice of me, coming out of the log church one Sabbath. He only looked at me, that was all, and I had to pretend I didn't know. Then he came nights and sat in front of the big open fire, with all of us, at first. But after a little, the others would climb up the ladder to the loft and leave us, and we'd maybe eat a mince pie that I'd made—I was a good cook at sixteen—and there would be a pitcher of cider, and outside, the wind would be driving the snow against the tiny windowpanes—I can hear that sound now, and the sputtering of the backlog, and Jim—oh, well!" She waved the scene back.

"When we were married, Jim had his eighty acres all cleared, a yoke of nice fat steers, a cow, two pigs, and a couple of sheep; not much, but it seemed enough then. The furniture was home-made, the table-ware was tin plates and pewter spoons and horn-handled knives, and a set of real china that Pa and Ma gave us— that was for company—and a feather-bed and patch-work quilts I'd made, and a long-barrelled rifle, and the best coon-dog, Jim said, in the whole of York State. Oh, well!"

Bean became aware that the old lady had grasped his hand, and he divined that she was also holding a hand of the flapper.

"And my! such excitement you never did see when little Jim came! We began to save right off to send him to a good seminary. We were going to make a preacher out of him; and see the way he's turned out! Lord, what would his father make of this place and our little Jim, if he was to come back?

"I lost him before he got to see many changes in the world. I remember we did go to a party in Fredonia one time, where a woman from Buffalo wore a low-necked gown, and Jim never got over it. He swore to the day of his death that any woman who'd wear 'a dug-out dress' was a hussy. He didn't know what the world could be coming to, when they allowed such goings-on. Poor Jim! I was still young when he went, and of course—but I couldn't. I'd had my man and I'd had my baby, and somehow I was through. I wanted to learn more about the world, and little Jim was growing up and had a nice situation in the store at Fredonia, working early and late, sleeping under the counter, and saving his fifty dollars clear every year. I knew he'd always provide for me—Dear me! how I run on! Where was I?"

Bean's hand was released, and Grandma rose to her feet, turning to look down upon them.

"I forgot what I started to say, but maybe it was this, that the world hasn't changed so much as folks often think. I get to watching young people sometimes— it seems as if they were like the young people in my day, and I think any young man that's steady and decent and has a good situation—what I mean is this, that he—well, it depends on the girl, as it always did."

She turned and walked to the end of the pergola, fifty feet away. There she threw up a clenched fist and began to emit groans, cries of hoarse rage and ragged phrases of abuse. She was again rehearsing her lines in the mob scene of the equal-suffrage play. At the head of her fellow mobs-women, she hurled harsh epithets at the Prime Minister of the oldest English-speaking nation on earth. There seemed to be no escape for the Prime Minister. They had him.

"We've broken windows, we'll break heads!" shouted the Demon, and a gardener crossing the grounds might have been seen to quicken his pace after one backward look.

The pair on the bench were inattentive. They had instinctively drawn together, but they were silent. In Bean's mind was a confusion of many matters: Breede sleeping under a counter—people in log-cabins getting married—the best coon-dog in York State—a yoke of nice fat steers—

But beneath this was a sharpened consciousness of the girl breathing at his side. She seemed curiously to be waiting—waiting! The silence and their stillness became unbearable. Something must break ... their breaths were too long drawn. He got to his feet and the flapper was unaccountably standing beside him. It was too dark to see her face, but he knew that for once she was not looking at him; for once that head was bent. And then, preposterously, without volition, without foreknowledge, he was holding her tightly in his arms; holding her tightly and kissing her with a simple directness that "Napoleon, Man and Lover," could never have bettered.

There is no record of Napoleon having studied jiu-jitsu.

For one frenzied moment he was out of himself, a mere conquering male, unthinking, ruthless, exigent. Then the sweet strange touch of her cheek brought him back to the awful thing he had done. His reason worked with a lightning quickness. Terrified by his violence she would wrench herself free and run screaming to the house. And then—it was too horrible!

He waited, breathless, for retribution. The flapper did not wrench herself away. Slowly he relaxed the embrace that had made a brute of him. The flapper had not screamed. She was facing him now, breathless herself. He put her a little way from him; he wanted her to see it as he did.

The flapper drew a long and rather catchy breath, then she adjusted a strand of hair misplaced by his violence.

"I *knew* it!" she began, in tones surprisingly cool. "I knew it ever so long ago, from the very first moment!"

He tried to speak, but had no words. His utterance was formless. "When did *you* first know?" she persisted. She was patting her hair into place with both hands.

He didn't know; he didn't know that he knew now; but recalling her speech he had overheard, he had the presence of mind to commit a soulful perjury.

"From the very first," he lied glibly. "Something went over me—just like *that*. I can't tell you how, but I knew!"

"You made me so afraid of you," confessed the flapper.

"I never meant to, couldn't help it."

"I'm horribly shy, but I knew it had to be. I felt powerless."

"I *know*," he sympathized.

"Our day has come!" roared Grandma from out of the gloom. "We know our rights! We've broken glass! We break heads!" This was followed by "Ar! Ar! Ar!" meant for sinister growls of rage. It seemed to be the united voice of the mob.

They drew apart, once more self-conscious. They walked slowly out, passed the mob scene, which ignored them, and went with awkward little hesitations up the wide walk to the Breede portal. To Bean's suddenly cooled eye, the vast gray house towered above him as a menace. He had a fear that it might fall upon him.

At the entrance they stood discreetly apart. Bean wondered what he ought to say. His sense of guilt was overwhelming. But the flapper seemed clear-headed enough.

"You leave it to me," she said, as if he had confided his perplexity to her. "Leave it all to me. *I've* always managed."

"Yes," said Bean, meaning nothing whatever.

She made little movements that suggested departure. She was regarding him now with the old curious look that had puzzled him.

"You're just as perfectly nice as I knew you were," she announced, with an obvious pride in this bit of proved wisdom.

"Good-night!"

From a distance of five feet she bestowed the little double-nod upon him and fled.

"Good-night!" he managed to call after her. Then he was aware that he had wanted to call her "Chubbins!" He liked that name for her. If he could only have said "Good-night, Chubbins—"

For that matter he basely wanted again to—but he thought with shame that he had done enough for once. A pretty night's work, indeed! If Breede ever found it out—

When he left with Breede in the morning, she was on the tennis-court. Brazenly she engaged in light conversation across the net with no other than Thomas Hollins, Junior. She did not look up as the car passed the court, though he knew that she knew. Something in the poise of her head told him that.

He didn't wonder she couldn't face him in the light of day. He smiled bitterly, in scorn for the betrayed Tommy.

CHAPTER IX

Back in the lofty office that Saturday morning he sat under the eye of Breede, in outward seeming a neat and efficient amanuensis. In truth he was pluming himself as a libertine of rare endowments. He openly and shamelessly wished he had kissed the creature again. When the next opportunity came she wouldn't get off so lightly, he could tell her that. It was base, but it was thrilling. He would abandon himself. He would take her hand and hold it the very first time they were alone together. Well might she be afraid of him, as she had confessed herself to be. She little knew!

It was, though, pretty light conduct on her part. It was possible that he would not see her again. Perhaps a baggage like that would already have forgotten him; would have treated the thing as trivial, an incident to laugh about, even to regale her intimates with. Probably he had done nothing more than make a fool of himself as usual. Votes for women, indeed! He thought they should first learn how to behave properly with young men who weren't expecting things of that sort.

"—this 'mount'll then become 'vailable f'r purpose shortenin' line an' reducin' heavy grades," dictated the unconscious father of the baggage.

"I kissed that smug-faced little brat of yours last night," wrote Bean immediately thereafter. He didn't care. He would put the thing down plainly, right under Breede's nose.

"With 'creased freight earnin's these 'provements may be 'spected t' pay f'r 'emselves," continued Breede.

"And I don't say I wouldn't do the same thing over again," Bean slipped in skilfully.

He winced to think he might some day have a daughter of his own that would "carry on" just so with young men who would be all right if they were only let alone. He found new comfort in the reflection that his first-born would be a boy— to grow up and be the idol of a nation.

But a little later he was again thinking of her as "Chubbins," wishing he had called her that, wishing she had stayed longer out in the scented night—the wonderful smoothness of her yielding cheek! Her little tricks of voice and manner came back to him, her quick little patting of Grandma's back at unexpected moments, the tilting of her head like a listening bird, that inexplicable look as her eyes enveloped him, a tiny scar at her temple, mark of an early fall from her pony.

He became sentimental to a maudlin degree. She would go on in her shallow way of life, smashing windows, voting, leading perfectly decent young men to do things they never meant to do; but he, the tender, the true, the ever-earnest, he would not recover from the wound that frail one had so carelessly inflicted. He would be a changed man, with hair prematurely graying at the temples, like Gordon Dane's, hiding his hurt under a mask of light cynicism to all but persons of superior insight. The heartless quip, the mad jest on his lips! And years afterward, a deeply serious and very beautiful woman would divine his sorrow and win him back to his true self.

The wedding! The drive from the church! The carriage is halted by a street crowd. A stalwart policeman appears. He has just arrested two women, confirmed window-smashers—Grandma, the Demon, and the flapper. The flapper gives him one long look, then bows her head. She sees all the nobility she has missed. Serve her right, too!

Noon came and he was about to leave the office. He was still the changed man of quip and jest. Desperately he jested with old Metzeger, who was regretfully, it seemed, relinquishing his adored ledgers from Saturday noon until Monday morning.

"Say, I want to borrow nineteen thousand eleven hundred and eighty-nine dollars and thirty-seven cents until the sixteenth at seven minutes to eleven."

Old Metzeger repeated the numbers accurately. He looked wistful, but he knew it was a jest.

"Telephone for Boston Bean!" cried an office boy, dryly affecting to be unconscious of his wit.

He rushed nervously for the booth. No one in the great city had ever before found occasion to telephone him. He thought of Professor Balthasar. Balthasar would warn him to fly at once; that all was discovered.

He held the receiver to his ear and managed a husky "Hello!"

At first there were many voices, mostly indignant: "I want the manager!" "Get off the line!" "A hundred and nine and three quarters!" "That you, Howard? Say, this is—" "Get—off—that—line!" "Or I'll know the reason why before to-morrow night!" And then from Bedlam pealed the voice of the flapper, silencing these evil spirits.

"Hello! Hello! This line makes me perfectly furious. To-morrow about three o'clock—you're to give us tea and things, some nice place—Granny and me. Be along in the car. I remember the number. Be there. Good-bye!"

There was the rattle of a receiver being hung up. But he stood there not believing it—tea and car and be there—The receiver rattled again.

"You knew who I was, *didn't* you?"

"Yes, right away," muttered Bean. Then he brightened. "I knew your voice the moment I heard it." The madness was upon him and he soared. "You're Chubbins!" He waited.

"Cut out the Chubbins stuff, Bill, and get off there!" directed a coarse masculine voice from the unseen wire-world.

He got off there with all possible quickness. His first thought was that she probably had not heard the magnificent piece of daring. It was too bad. Probably he never could do it again. Then he turned and discovered that he had left the door of the telephone booth ajar. Chubbins might not have heard him, but Bulger assuredly had.

"Well, well, well!" declaimed Bulger in his best manner. "Look whom we have with us here to-night! Old Mr. George W. Fox Bean, keeping it all under his hat. Chubbins, eh? Some name, that! Don't tell me you thought it up all by yourself, you word-painter! Miss Chubbsy Chubbins! Where's she work?"

Bean saw release.

"Little manicure party," he confessed; "certain shop not far from here. Think I'm going to put *you* wise?"

Bulger was pleased at the implication.

"Ain't got a friend, has she?"

"No," said Bean. "Never did have one. Some class, too," he added with a leer that won Bulger's complete respect. He breathed freely again and was humming, "Love Me and the World Is Mine," as they separated.

But when he was alone the song died. The thing was getting serious. And she was so assured. Telling him to be there as if she were Breede himself. How did she know he had time for all that tea and Grandma nonsense? Suppose he had had another engagement. She hadn't given him time to say. Hadn't asked him; just *told* him. Well, it showed one thing. It showed that Bunker Bean could bring women to his feet.

His afternoon recreation, there being no baseball, was to lead Nap triumphantly through Central Park to be seen of an envious throng. He affected a lordly unconsciousness of the homage Nap received. He left adoring women in his wake and covetous men; and children demanded bluntly if he would sell that dog; or if he wouldn't sell him would he give him away, because they wanted him.

Surfeited with this easily won attention, he sat by the driveway to watch the endless parade of carriage folk. His eye was for the women in those shining equipages. Young or old, they were to him newly exciting. His attitude was the rather scornful one of a conqueror whose victories have cost him too little. They had been mysteries to him, but now, all in a day, he understood women. They were vulnerable things, and men were their masters. Votes, indeed!

His own power over them was abundantly proved. Any of them passing heedlessly there would, under the right conditions, confess it. Let him be called to their notice and they'd be following him around, forgetting plighted vows, getting him into places screened with vines and letting themselves be led on; telephoning him to give them and Grandma tea and things of a Sunday in some nice place—hanging on his words. Of course it had always been that way, only he had never known it. Looking back over his barren past he surveyed minor incidents with new eyes. There was that girl with the pretty hair in the business college, who always smiled in the quick, confidential way at him. Maybe she wouldn't have been a talker!

And how far was this present affair going? Pretty far already: clandestine meetings and that sort of thing. Still, he couldn't help being a man, could he? And Tommy Hollins, poor dupe!

In the steam-heated apartment It had been locked in a closet, which in an upright position It fitted nicely. He did not open the door that night. He felt that he was venturing into ways that the wise and good king would not approve. He could not face the thing while guilt was in his heart. A woman had come between them.

———————————————

At three o'clock the next afternoon he lounged carelessly against the basement railing of the steam-heated apartment. With Nap on a leash he was keenly aware that he was "some class." He was arrayed in the new suit of a quiet check. The cravat with the red stripe shimmered in the sunlight. He had a new straw hat with a coloured band, bought the day before at a shop advertising "Snappy Togs for Dressy Men." He lightly twirled a yellow stick and carried yellow gloves in one hand. He was almost the advanced dresser, dignified but unquestionably a bit different. He seemed to be one who has tamed the world to his ends; but, though he stood erect, expanded his chest and drew in his waist, as instinctively do all those who wear America's greatest eighteen-dollar suit, he was nevertheless wondering with a lively apprehension just what was going to be done with him. This life of "affairs" was making him uncomfortable.

Taking Nap along, he somehow felt, was a wise precaution. He didn't know what mad thing you might expect of Grandma, the Demon, but surely nothing very discreditable could occur in the presence of that innocent dog. And he would play the waiting game; make 'em show their hands.

At twenty minutes after three he wondered if he mightn't reasonably disappear. He would walk in the park and say afterward—if there should be an afterward—that he had given them up. An easy way out. He would do it. Twenty minutes more passed and he still meant to do it, knowing he wouldn't.

Then came the blare of a motor horn and Breede's biggest and blackest car descended upon him, stopping neatly at the curb.

He retained his calm, nonchalantly doffing the new straw hat.

"Just strolling off," he said; "given you up."

"Pops wanted to come," explained the flapper. "I had a perfectly annoying time not letting him. What a darling child of a dog! *Does* he want to—well, he *shall*!"

And Nap did at once. He seemed in the flapper to be greeting an old friend. He interrogated his lawful owner from the flapper's embrace, then reached up to implant a moist salute upon the ear of Grandma, who at once removed herself from his immediate presence.

"Sit there yourself," she commanded Bean. And Bean sat there beside the flapper, with Nap between them. The car moved gently on under the gaze of the impressed Cassidy, who had clattered up the iron stairway. Cassidy's gaze seemed to say, "All right, me lad, but you want t' look out f'r that sort. I know th' kind well!"

The car was moving swiftly now, heading for the north and the open.

"They cut us off yesterday," said the flapper. "I know I shall simply make a lot of trouble for that operator some day."

He wondered if she had heard that mad "Chubbins!" But now the flapper smiled upon him with a wondrous content, and he could say nothing. Instead of talking he stroked the head of Nap, who was panting with the excitement of this celestial adventure.

"I like you in that," confided the flapper with an approving glance. He wondered if she meant the hat, the cravat or America's very best suit for the money.

"I like *you* in that," he retorted with equal vagueness, at last stung to speech.

"Oh, this!" explained the flapper in pleased deprecation. "It's just a little old rag. What's his darling name?"

"Eh? Name? Napoleon, Man and—I mean Napoleon. I call him Nap," he said shortly, feeling himself in chameleon-like sympathy with the cravat.

Grandma, on the seat in front of them, stared silently ahead, but there was something ominous in her rigidity. She had the air of a captor.

Once when his hand was on Nap the flapper brazenly patted it. He pretended not to notice.

"Everything's all right," she said.

"Of course," he answered, believing nevertheless that everything was all wrong.

They had come swiftly to the country and now swept along a wide highway that narrowed in perspective far and straight ahead of them. He watched the road, grateful for the slight hypnotic effect of its lines running toward him. He must play the waiting game.

"Here's the inn," said the flapper. They turned into a big green yard and drew up at the steps of a rambling old house begirt with wide piazzas on which tables were set. This would be the nice place where he was to give them tea and things. They descended from the car, and he was aware that they pleasantly drew the attention of many people who were already there having tea and things: the big car and Grandma and the flapper in her little old rag and Nap still panting ecstatically, and, not least, himself in dignified and a little bit different apparel, lightly grasping the yellow stick and the quite as yellow gloves. It was horribly open and conspicuous, he felt; still, getting out of a car like that—and the flapper's little old rag was something that had to be looked at—he was drunk with it. Following a waiter to a table he felt that the floor was not meeting his feet.

They were seated! The shocking affair was on. The waiter inclined a deferential ear to the gentleman from the large and costly car.

"Tea and things," said the gentleman with a very bored manner indeed, and turned to rebuke the rare and costly dog with harsh words for his excessive emotion at the prospect of food.

The waiter manifested delight at the command; one could not help seeing that he considered it precisely the right one. He moved importantly off. The three regarded each other a moment.

Bean played the waiting game. The flapper played her ancient game of looking at him in that curious way. Grandma looked at them both, then meaningly at Bean. She spoke.

"I'll say very frankly that I wouldn't marry you myself."

He blinked, then he pretended to search with his eyes for their vanished waiter. But it was no good. He had to face the Demon, helpless.

"But that's nothing to your discredit, and it isn't a question of me," she added dispassionately.

His inner voice chanted, "Play the waiting game; play the waiting game."

"Every woman with a head on her knows what she wants when she sees it. And nowadays, thanks to the efforts of a few noble leaders of our sex, she has the right and the courage to take it. I haven't wasted any time talking to *her*." She indicated the flapper, who still fixed the implacable look on Bean.

"If she doesn't know at nineteen, she never would—"

"We've settled all *that*," said the flapper loftily. "Haven't we?"

Bean nodded. All at once that look of the flapper's began to be intelligible. He could almost read it.

"I suppose you expect me to talk a lot of that stuff about marriage being a serious business," continued the Demon evenly. "But I shan't. Marriage isn't half as serious as living alone is. It's what we were made for in my time, and your time isn't a bit different, young man."

She raised an argumentative finger toward him, as if he had sought to contest this.

"I've always—" he began weakly. But the Demon would have none of it.

"Oh, don't tell *me* what you've 'always!' I know well enough what you've 'always.' That isn't the point."

What did the woman think she was talking about? Couldn't he say a word to her without being snapped at?

"What is the point?" he ventured. It was still the waiting game, and it showed he wasn't afraid of her.

"The point is—"

And in that instant Bean read the flapper's look, the look she had puzzled him with from their first meeting. It was like finally understanding an oft-heard phrase in a foreign tongue. How luminous that look was now! The simple look of proud and assured and most determined ownership! It lay quietly on her face now as always. It was the look he must have bestowed on his shell the first time he saw it. Ownership!

"—the point is," the Demon was saying terribly, "I don't believe in long engagements."

He had once been persuaded, yielding out of spineless bravado, to descend the shaft of a mine in a huge bucket. The sensations of that plunge were now reproduced. He looked up to the far circle of light that ever diminished as he went down and down.

"I don't believe in them either," said the flapper firmly. "They're perfectly no good."

"I never did believe in 'em," he heard himself saying. And added with firmness equal to the flapper's, "Silly!" He was wondering if they would ever pull him to the surface again; if the rope would break.

"Just what I think," chanted the flapper. "Silly, and then some!"

"Then some!" repeated the male being in helpless, terrified corroboration.

"Won't he ever come?" queried the Demon. "Oh, here he is!"

The waiter was neatly removing tea and things from the tray. Bean recalled how on that other occasion he had fearfully believed the earth would close upon him, how hope revived as he was precariously drawn upward, and what a novel view the earth's fair surface presented when he again stood firmly upon it.

It was the waiter who raised him from this other abyss where he had been like to perish, the waiter and the things, including tea: plates, forks, napkins, cups and saucers, tea and hot water, jam, biscuit, toast. There was something particularly reassuring about that plate of nicely matched triangles of buttered toast. It spoke of a sane and orderly world where you were never taken off your feet.

"How many lumps?" demanded the pouring flapper.

"Just as you like; I'm not fussy," he answered.

This was untrue. His preference in the matter was decided, but he could not remember what it was. Afterward he knew that he did not take sugar in his tea, but the flapper had sweetened it with three lumps. Grandma again addressed him, engaging his difficult attention with a brandished fragment of toast.

"I can't imagine how you were ever mad enough to think of it," she said, "but you were. I give you credit for that. And just let me tell you that you've won a treasure. Of course, I don't say you won't find her difficult now and then, but you mustn't be too overbearing; give in a bit now and then; 't won't hurt you. Remember she's got a will of her own, as well as you have. Don't try to ride rough-shod—"

"Oh, we've settled all *that*," broke in the flapper. "Haven't we?"

"We've settled all that," said Bean, grateful for the solid feel of a cup in his fingers.

"Don't be too domineering, that's all," warned the Demon. "She wouldn't put up with it."

"I understand all *that*," insisted Bean, resolutely seizing a fork for which he had no use. "I can look ahead!"

He began hurriedly to eat toast, hoping it would seem that he had more to say but was too hungry to say it.

"I know *you*," persisted the Demon. "Brow-beating, bound to have your own way, and, after all, she's nothing but a child."

"I'll *want* him to have his own way," declared the child. "I'll see that he just perfectly gets it, too!"

"Give and take, that's my motto," he muttered, wondering if more toast would choke him.

"Be a row back there, of course," said Grandma, "but Julia's going to marry off the other child after her own heart, and it's only right for me to have a little say about this one. You're a better man than he is. You have a good situation and he's just a waster; couldn't buy his own cigarettes if he had to work for the money, say nothing of his gloves and ties. Born to riches, born to folly, say I. Still, Julia will fuss just about so much. Of course, Jim—"

"Oh, poor old Pops!" The flapper gracefully destroyed him as a factor in the problem.

Bean was feeding toast to Nap, who didn't choke.

"She always has to come around though when the girl makes up her mind. I haven't had that child in my charge for nothing."

"I have a right to choose the—" The flapper broke her speech with tea. "I have the *right*," she concluded defiantly.

Bean shuddered. He recalled the terrific remainder of that speech.

"I thought we better have this little talk," said Grandma, "and get everything understood."

"'S the only way to do," said Bean, wrinkling his forehead, "have everything clear."

"I had it all perfectly planned out long ago," said the flapper. "I don't *want* a large place."

"Lots of trouble," conceded Bean. "Something always coming up," he added knowingly.

"Nice yard," said the flapper, "plenty of room for flowers and the tennis court, and I'll do the marketing when I motor in for you. They won't let me do it back there," she concluded with some acrimony; "and they get good and cheated and I'm perfectly glad of it. Eighteen cents a head for lettuce! I saw that very thing on a tag yesterday!"

"Rob you right and left," mumbled Bean. "All you can expect."

"Just leave it all to me," said the flapper with four of her double nods. "They'll soon learn better."

"Hardly seems as if it could all be true," ventured Bean in a genial effort at sanity.

"It's just perfectly true and true," insisted the flapper. "I knew it all the time." She placed the old relentless gaze upon him. He was hers.

"The beautiful, blind wants of youth!" said the Demon, who had been silent a long time, for her. "I remember—" But it seemed to come to nothing. She was silent again.

He paid the waiter.

"It was just as well to have this little talk," murmured Grandma as they arose.

The car throbbed before the steps. They were in and away. A reviving breeze swept them as the car gained speed. At least it partially revived one of them.

In the back seat he presently found a hand in his, but his own hand seemed no longer a part of him. He thought the serenity of the flapper was remarkable. She seemed to feel that nothing wonderful had happened. There was something awful about that calm.

The car stopped before the steam-heated apartment. There were but brief adieus before it went on. Cassidy sat at the head of his basement stairs with a Sunday paper. He was reading an article entitled, "My Secrets of Beauty," profusely illustrated.

"I wouldn't have one o' the things did ye give it t' me," said Cassidy. "Runnin' inta telegrapht poles an' trolley cairs."

"Couple of friends of mine took me out for a little spin," said Bean, clutching his stick, his gloves and Nap's leash.

He seemed to be still spinning.

In his own place he went quickly to Its closet, pulled open the door and shouted aloud:

"Well, what do you make of *that*?"

The sound of his own voice was startling as he caught the look of the serene Ram-tah. He softly closed the door upon what his living self had been. He was too violent.

But he could not be cool all at once. He tossed hat, stick, and gloves aside and paced the room.

Engaged to be married! That was all any one could make of it. All the agreeable iniquity had been extracted from the affair. It was fearsomely respectable. And it was deadly serious. How had he got into it? And yet he had always felt something ominous in that girl's look.

And there would be a row "back there." Julia would make the row. And Jim. They might think Jim wouldn't help in the row, but he knew better. Jim was old Jim Breede, who would of course take Bunker Bean's head off. He had been a fool all the time. In the car he had strained himself to the point of mentioning the Hollins boy. The flapper had laughed unaffectedly. Tommy Hollins was a perfectly darling boy, a good sport and all that, but he couldn't be anything important to the flapper if he were the perfectly last man on earth. How any one could ever have thought such an absurd thing was beyond the flapper, for one.

And she didn't want a large place: flowers and a tennis court, and she'd do the marketing herself when she motored in for him. Moreover, he was not to be brutally domineering. He was to curb that tendency in himself, at least now and then, and let her have an opinion or two of her own. She was nothing but a child, after all; he mustn't be harsh with her.

He was weak before it. Once more he opened the closet door, feeling the need for new strength. A long time he looked into the still face. He was a king. Was it strange that a woman had fallen before him?

He reduced the event to its rudiments. He was the affianced husband of Breede's youngest daughter, who didn't believe in long engagements.

The thing was incredible, even as he faced Ram-tah.

How had he ever done it?

"Gee!" he muttered, "how'd I ever have the nerve to *do* it!"

Ram-tah's sleeping face remained still. If the wise and good king knew the answer he gave no sign.

CHAPTER X

"Where maint'nance f'r both roadway an' 'quipment is clearly surcharged," Breede was exploding, "extent of excess of maintenance over normal 'quirements cannot be taken as present earnin' power, an' this'll haf t' be understood before nex' meetin' d'r'ectors—"

"No need of *you* making any fuss," wrote Bean. "Let Julia do that. I'm as good a man as anybody if you come right down to it."

"—these prior-lien bon's an' receiver's stiff-cuts mus' natchally come ahead of firs'-mortgage bon's—" continued Breede.

"Wouldn't care if she told you right now over that telephone," wrote Bean. "You wouldn't dare touch me, and you know it."

Later he wrote "Poor old Pops!" contemptuously, and put an evil sneer upon Breede's removed cuffs.

At the same time he wished that the flapper and Grandma hadn't been so set against long engagements. And how long had they meant? One day, a week, a month? Would they have *it* done the next time they took him out in that car for tea and things? They were capable of it. Why couldn't they be reasonable and let things stay quiet for a while?

And how about that small place with flowers and a tennis court and a motor to go marketing in? Did they believe he was made of money? About all he could do was to provide a place big enough for a growing dog. And Breede, of course, would cast the girl off penniless, as they always did, telling her never to darken his doors again. And he'd have to find a new job. Breede wouldn't think of keeping on the scoundrel who had lured his child away.

Still, the flapper's mind was set on an early marriage, and, for this once, at least, he would let her have her own way. No good being brutal at the start. They would get along; scrimp and save; even move to Brooklyn, maybe. He looked into the far years and saw his son, greatest of all left-handed pitchers, shutting out Pittsburgh without a single hit. A very aged couple in the grandstand tried to claim relationship with his pitching marvel, saying he was their grandson, but few of the yelling enthusiasts would credit it. One of the crowd would later question the phenomenon's father, who was none other than the owner of the home team, and he would say, "Oh, yes, quite true, but there has been no communication between the two families for more than twenty years."

There would now follow from the abject grandparents timid overtures for a reconciliation, they having at last seen their mistake. These overtures met with a varying response. Sometimes he was adamant and told them no; they had made their bed twenty years before, and now they could lie on it. Again, he would relent, allowing them to come to the house and associate with their superb descendant once every week. He didn't want to be too hard on them.

And he was not penniless. He would continue in the unexciting express business for a while, until he had amassed enough to buy the ball-team.

Out at his typewriter, turning off Breede's letters, his mind kept reverting to those nicely printed stock certificates Aunt Clara had sent to him, five of them for ten shares each, his own name written on them. Of course there were hundreds of shares at the brokers', but those seemed not to mean so much. And they had gone down a point, whatever that was, since his purchase. The broker had explained that this was because of an unexpectedly low dividend, 3 per cent. It showed bad management. All the more reason for getting a new man on the Board—a lot of old fossils!

He recalled the indignant-looking old gentleman who was so excessively well dressed. He wore choice gold-rimmed eyeglasses tethered by a black silk ribbon. They were intensely respectable things when adjusted to the nose, but he knew he should clash with that old party the moment he got on the Board. He would find him to be one of the sort that is always looking for trouble.

He wondered if he might not himself some day have sufficient excuse for wearing glasses like those, at the end of a silk ribbon. He thought they set off the face. And the old gentleman's white parted beard flowed down upon a waistcoat he wouldn't mind owning: black silk set with tiny white stars, a good background for a small gold chain. There would be a bunch of important keys on one end of that chain. Bean had yearned to wear one of those key-chains, but he had never had more than a trunk-key and a latch-key, and it would look silly to pull those out on a chain before people; they'd begin to make fun of you!

He worked on, narrowly omitting to have Breede inform the vice-president of an important trunk-line that it wouldn't hurt him any to have those trousers pressed once in a while; also that plenty of barbers would be willing to cut his hair.

Bulger condescendingly wrote at his own typewriter, as if he were the son of a millionaire pretending to work up from the bottom. Old Metzeger was deep in a dream of odd numerals. The half-dozen other clerks wrought at tasks not too absorbing to prevent frequent glances at the clock on the wall.

Tully, the chief clerk, marred the familiarity of the hour by approaching Bean's desk. He walked lightly. Tully always walked as if he felt himself to be on dangerously thin ice. He might get safely across; then again he mightn't. He leaned confidentially on the back of Bean's chair and Bean looked up and through the lenses that so alarmingly magnified Tully's eyes. Tully twitched the point of his blond beard with thumb and finger as if to reassure himself of its presence.

"By the way, Bean, I notice some fifty shares of Federal Express stock in your name. Now it is not impossible that the office would be willing to take them over for you."

That was Tully's way. He was bound to say "some" fifty shares instead of fifty, and of anything he knew to be true he could only aver "it is not impossible." Of a certain familiar enough event in the natural world he would have declared, "The sun sets not infrequently in the west."

Bean was for the moment uncertain of Tully's meaning.

"Shares," he said. "Right there in my desk."

"Quite so, quite so!" said Tully. "I'm not wholly uncertain, you know—this is between us—that I couldn't place them for you. I may say the office would not find even those few shares unwelcome."

"Well, you see, I don't know about that," said Bean. "You see, I had a kind of an idea—"

"I think I may say they would take it not unkindly," said Tully.

"—of holding on to them," concluded Bean.

"Your letting them go for a fair price might not inconceivably react to your advantage," suggested the luminous Tully.

"It is not impossible that I shall want them myself," responded Bean, unconsciously adopting the Tully indirection.

"The office is not unwilling—" began Tully.

"I'll keep 'em a while," said Bean. "I have a sort of plan."

"I should not like to think it possible—"

Bean was tired of Tully. What was the man trying to get at, anyway? He didn't know; but he would shut him off. His mind leaped with an inspiration.

"I can imagine nothing of less consequence," said Bean.

He was at once proud of the snappy way the words came out. Breede, he thought, could hardly have been snappier. He glared at Tully, who looked shocked, hurt, and disgusted. Tully sighed and walked back to his own desk, as if the ice cracked beneath his small feet at every step.

Bean resumed his work, with the air of one forgetting a past annoyance. But he was not forgetting. He might let them have the stock; he had never thought any too well of that express directorship; but let them send some one that could talk straight. He didn't care if he *had* been short with Tully. He was going to lose his job anyway, the day after that wedding, if not before.

He wrote many of Breede's letters, and was again interrupted, this time by Markham, Breede's confidential secretary. Markham's approach to Bean was emphatically footed, as that of a man unable to imagine ice being thin under *his* feet. He was bluff and open, where Tully lurked behind his "not impossibles." He was even jovial now. He smiled down at Bean.

"By the way, Bean, some one was telling me you have some Federal Express."

"Have the shares right there in my desk," admitted Bean, wonderingly. He was suspicious all at once. Tully and Markham had both opened on him with "By

538

the way." He had always felt it a shrewd thing to suspect people who began with "By the way."

"Ah, yes, fifty shares, I believe." Markham smiled again, but seemed to try not to smile. He apparently considered it a rare jest that Bean should own any shares of anything; a thing for smiles even though one must humour the fellow.

"Fifty shares! Well, well, that's good! Now the fact is, old man, I can place those for you this afternoon. Some of the Federal people going to meet informally here, and they happen to want a little block or two of the stuff, for voting purposes, you know. Not that it's worth anything. How'd you happen to get down on such a dead one?"

"Well, you know, I had a sort of a plan about that stock. I don't know—"

"Of course I can't get you what you paid for it," continued the affable Markham, "because it's poor stuff, but maybe they'll stand a point or two above to-day's quotations. Just let me have them and I'll get your check made out right away; you can go out of here with more money to-night than any one else will." Markham was prattling on amiably, still trying not to be overcome by the funny joke of Bean owning things.

"I don't want to sell," declared Bean. There had been a moment's hesitation, but that opening, "By the way," of Markham's had finally decided him. You couldn't tell anything about such a man.

"Oh, come now, old chap," cajoled Markham, "Be a good fellow. It's only needed for a technical purpose, you know."

"I guess I'll hold on to it," said Bean. "I've been thinking for a long time—"

"Last quarter's dividend was 3 per cent.," reminded Markham.

"I know," admitted Bean, "and that's just why. You see I've got an idea—"

"As a matter of fact, I think J.B. doesn't exactly approve of his people here in the office speculating. He doesn't consider it ... well, you know one of you chaps here, if you weren't all loyal, might very often take advantage—you get my point?"

"I guess I won't sell just now," observed Bean.

"I don't understand this at all," said Markham, allowing it to be seen that he was shocked.

Bean wavered, but he was nettled. He was going to lose his job anyway. You might as well be hung for a sheep as a lamb. To Markham standing there, hurt and displeased, he looked up and announced curtly:

"I can imagine nothing of less consequence!"

He had the felicity to see Markham wince as from an unseen blow. Then Markham walked back to his own room. His tread would have broken ice capable of sustaining a hundred Tullys.

He saw it all now. They were plotting against him. They had learned of his plan to become a director and they were trying to freeze him out. He had never spoken of this plan, but probably they had consulted some good medium who had warned them to look out for him. Very well, if they wanted fight they should have fight. He wouldn't sell that stock, not even to Breede himself—

"Buzz! Buzz! Buzz!" went the electric call over his desk. That meant Breede. Very well; he knew his rights. He picked up his note-book and answered the summons.

Breede, munching an innocent cracker, stared at him.

"How long you had that Federal stock?"

"Aunt bought it five years ago."

"Where?"

"Chicago."

"Want to sell?"

"I think I'd rather—"

"You won't sell?"

"No!"

"'S all!"

Back at his machine he tried to determine whether he would have "let out" at Breede as he had at Tully and at Markham. He had supposed that Breede would of course nag him as the other two had. And would he have said to Breede with magnificent impudence, "I can imagine nothing of less consequence?" He thought he would have said this; the masks were very soon bound to be off Breede and himself. The flapper might start the trouble any minute. But Breede had given him no chance for that lovely speech. No good saying it unless you were nagged.

He became aware that the "Federal people" Markham had mentioned were gathering in Breede's room. Several of them brushed by him. Let them freeze him out if they could. He wondered what they said at meetings. Did every one talk, or only the head director? Markham had said this was to be an informal meeting.

It is probable that Bean would not have been much enlightened by the immediate proceedings of this informal meeting. The large, impressive, moneyed-looking directors sat easily about the table in Breede's inner room, and said little of meaning to a tyro in the express business.

The stock was pretty widely held in small lots, it seemed, and the agents out buying it up were obliged to proceed with caution. Otherwise people would get silly ideas and begin to haggle over the price. But the shares were coming in as rapidly as could be expected.

Bean would have made nothing of that. He would have been bored, until Markham made a reference to fifty shares that happened to be owned by a young chap in the outer office.

"Take 'em over," said one heavy-jowled director who incongruously held a cigarette between lips that seemed to demand the largest and blackest of cigars.

"He won't sell," answered Markham. "I spoke to him."

"Tell him to," said the director to Breede.

"Tell him yourself," said Breede. "He said he wouldn't sell."

"Um! Well, well!" said the director.

"Exactly what I told him," remarked the conscientious Tully, who was present to take notes, "and he said to me, 'Mr. Tully, I am unwilling to imagine anything of less consequence.' He seemed, uh—I might say—decided."

"Gave me the same thing," said Markham.

"Leak in the office," announced the elderly advanced dresser. "Fifty shares!" he added, twirling the glasses on their silk ribbon. "Hell! Going to let him get away with it?"

"Got to be careful," suggested a quiet director who had listened. "Can't tell who's back of him."

"Call him in," ordered the advanced dresser, fixing the glasses firmly on his purple nose. "Call him in! Bluff him in a minute!"

"Buzz! Buzz! Buzz!" smote fatefully on Bean's ears. He had expected it. If they didn't let him alone, he would tell them all that he could imagine nothing of less consequence.

He entered the room. He hardly dared scan the faces of those directors in the flesh, but they were all scanning him. He stood at the end of the table and fastened his eyes on a railway map that bedecked the opposite wall, one of those mendacious maps showing a trans-continental line of unbroken tangent; three thousand miles of railway without a curve, the opposition lines being mere spirals.

"Here, boy!" It was the advanced dresser of the white parted beard and the constant indignation. Bean looked at him. He had known from the first that he must clash with this man.

"That sort of thing'll never do with *us*, you know," continued the old gentleman, when he had diverted Bean's attention from the interesting map. "Never do at all; not at all; *not-tat-tall*. Preposterous! My word! What rot!"

The last was, phonetically, "Wha' *trawt!*"

Bean was studying the old gentleman's faultless garments. He wore a particularly effective waistcoat of white piqué striped with narrow black lines, and there was a pink carnation in the lapel of the superbly tailored frock coat.

"Wha' trawt!" repeated the ornate director. Bean looked again at the map.

"Here, boy, your last chance. We happen to need those shares in a little matter of voting. I'll draw you a check for the full amount."

He produced the daintiest of check-books and a fountain pen of a chaste design in gold. Bean's look was the look of those who see visions.

"Now then, *now* then!" spluttered the old gentleman, the pen poised. "Don't keep me waiting; don't keep me, I say! What amount? Wha'*tamount*?"

Bean's eyes were withdrawn from the wall. He came briskly to life.

"I'll tell you in a moment. I'll get the shares."

"Shrimp!" said the old gentleman triumphantly, when Bean had gone.

"He told *me*," began Tully. But the advanced dresser wanted no more of that.

"Shrimp!" he repeated.

Bean reëntered with the certificates. The old gentleman glanced angrily over them.

"Bean!" he exclaimed humorously. "Vegetable after all; not a fish! Funny name that! Bunker Bean! Boston, by gad! Not bad that, I *say*! Come, come, *come*! Want par, of course—all do! There y'are, boy!"

He blotted the check, tore it from the book and waved it toward Bean as he turned to the director of the cigarette.

"About that proposition before us to-day, Mr. Chairman—" but Bean had gone. Observing this, the old gentleman looked about him.

"Shrimp!" he said contemptuously, with the convinced air of an expert in marine biology.

Bean, outside, once more addressed himself to typewriting. He wondered if he should be seized with a toothache or a fainting spell. Toothache was good, but perhaps Bulger had used that too often. Still Tully would "fall" for a toothache. It gave him a chance to say that if people would only go to a dentist once every three months—Then he remembered that Tully was inside. He wouldn't make any excuse at all.

"Going out a few minutes," he explained to old Metzeger as he swiftly changed from his office coat and adjusted the new straw hat.

Bulger glanced up from his machine, winked at him and shaped a word with his able mouth. An adept in lip-reading could have seen it to be "Chubbins." Bean in response leered confession at him.

The broker's office was in the adjoining block.

"I've just made a little deal," explained Bean to the person who inquired his business. "Here's the check. You know I've got a sort of an idea I'd like a little more of that Federal Express stuff. Just buy me some the same as you did before, as much as you can get on ten margins, er—I mean on ten points."

"Nothing much doing in that stock," suggested the expert. "Why don't you get down on some the live ones. Now there's Union Pacific—"

"I know, but I want Federal Express. That is, you see, I want it merely for a technical purpose." He felt happy at recalling Markham's phrase.

"All right," said the expert resignedly. "We'll do what we can. May take three or four days."

Bean started for the door.

"Say," called the expert, as if on second thought, "you're up at Breede's office, ain't you—old J.B.'s?"

"Oh, I'm there for a few days yet," said Bean.

"Ah, ha!" said the expert. "Have a cigar!"

Bean aimlessly accepted the proffer.

"Sit down and gas a while," urged the expert genially. "Things looking up any over your way?"

"Oh, so-so, only," said Bean. "But I can't stop, thanks! Got to hurry back to see a man."

"Drop in again any time," said the expert. "We try to make this little den a home for our customers."

"Thanks!" said Bean. "I'll be sure to."

"Ah ha, and ah ha!" said the expert to himself. "Now I wonder."

On his way back to the office Bean suddenly discovered that he was chewing an unlighted cigar. He stopped to observe in a polished window its effect on his face. He rather liked it. He pulled the front of his hat down a bit and held the cigar at a confident angle. He thought it made him look forceful. He wished he might pass the purple-faced old gentleman—the whole Breede gang, for that matter—and chew the cigar at them.

"I'll show them," he muttered, over and around the impeding cigar. "I'll show them they can't keep *me* off that board. I knew what to do in a minute. Napoleon of Finance, eh? I'll show them who's who!"

He was back at his desk finishing the last of Breede's letters for the day. Tully had not discovered his absence. He winked at Bulger to assure him that the worst interpretation could be put upon that absence. He wondered if anything else could happen before the day ended.

"Telephone for Boston Bean," called the wag of an office boy.

This time he closed the double door of the booth, letting Bulger think what he pleased.

"I forgot to ask what you take, mornings," pealed the flapper.

"Take—mornings?"

"For breakfast, silly! Because I think it's best for you to take just eggs and toast; a little fruit of course; not all that meat and things."

"Oh, yes, of course; eggs and—things. Never want much."

"Well, all right, I just perfectly knew you'd see it that way. I'm making up lists. Tell me, do you like a panelled dining-room, you know, fumed oak, or something?"

"Only kind I'd ever have."

"I knew you would. What are you doing all the time?"

"Oh, me? I'm getting things into shape. You see, I have an idea—"

"Don't you buy the least little thing until I know. We want to be sure everything harmonizes and I've just perfectly got everything in my head the way it will be."

"That's right; that's the only way."

"You didn't say anything about—you know—to poor old Pops, did you?"

"Why, no. I didn't. You see he's been pretty much thinking about other things all day, and I—"

"Well, that's right. I was afraid you'd be just perfectly impatient. But you leave it all to me. I'll manage. It's the dearest joke! I may not tell them for two or three days. Every time I get alone I just perfectly giggle myself into spasms. Isn't it the funniest?"

"Ha, ha, ha, ha! I should think it was." He was fearfully hoping her keen sense of humour might continue to rule.

"We *do*, don't we?"

"Do what?"

"*You* know, stupid!"

"Yes, *yes* indeed! We just perfectly *do*!"

"More than any two people ever did before, don't we?"

"Well, I should think so; and then some."

"I knew you'd feel that way. Well, good-bye!"

He could fancy her giving the double nod as she hung up the receiver.

During the ride uptown he talked large with a voluble gentleman who had finished his evening paper and who wished to recite its leading editorial from memory as something of his own. They used terms like "the tired business man," "increased cost of living," "small investor," "the common people," and "enemies of the Public Good." The man was especially bitter against the Wall Street ring, and remarked that any one wishing to draw a lesson from history need look no

544

farther back than the French Revolution. The signs were to be observed on every hand.

Bean felt a little guilty, though he tried to carry it off. Was he not one of that same Wall Street ring? He pictured himself as a tired business man eating boiled eggs of a morning in a dining-room panelled with fumed oak, the flapper across the table in some little old rag. He thought it sounded pretty luxurious—like a betrayal of the common people. Still he had to follow his destiny. You couldn't get around that.

He stood a long time before Ram-tah that night, grateful for the lesson he had drawn from him in the afternoon. Back there among those fierce-eyed directors, badgered by the most objectionable of them, nerving himself to say presently that he could imagine nothing of less consequence, there had come before his eyes the inspiring face of the wise and good king. But most unaccountably, as he gazed, it seemed to him that the great Ram-tah had opened those long-closed eyes; opened them full for a moment; then allowed the left eye to close swiftly.

CHAPTER XI

The day began with placid routine. Breede did his accustomed two-hours' monologue. And no one molested Bean. No one appeared to know that he was other than he seemed, and that big things were going forward. Tully ignored him. Markham, who had the day before called him "Old man!" whistled obliviously as they brushed past each other in the hall. No directors called him in to tell him that would never do with *them*.

He was grateful for the lull. He couldn't be "stirred up" that way every day. And he needed to gather strength against Breede when Breede should discover that exquisite joke of the flapper's. He suspected that the flapper wouldn't find it funny to keep the thing from poor old Pops more than a few days longer.

"I'll be drawing my last pay next Saturday," he told himself.

"Telephone for Boston Baked," called the office-boy wit, late in the afternoon.

Bulger looked sympathetic.

"Same trouble I have," he confided as Bean passed him, "Take 'em on once and they bother the life out of you."

"You'd never believe," came the voice of the flapper. "I found the darlingest old sideboard with claw-feet yesterday over on Fourth Avenue. He wants two hundred and eighty, but they're all robbers, and I just perfectly mean to make him come down five or ten dollars. Every little counts. You leave it to me."

"Sure! You fix it all up!"

"And maybe we won't want fumed oak in the dining-room—maybe a rich mahogany stain. Would that suit? I'm only thinking of you."

"I'll leave all that to you; you'll perfectly well manage."

"I just perfectly darling well knew you'd say that; and I'm sending you down a car—"

"A what? Car?" This was even more alarming than the darling old sideboard.

"Just a little old last year's car. Poor old Pops would give it to me now if I asked him—but it's just as well to have it away in case Moms could ever make him change his mind, only of course she perfectly well can't do anything of the sort. But anyway I'm sending it to that shop around the corner in the street below you, and they'll hold it there to your order. You never can tell; we might need it suddenly some time, and anyway you ought to have it, don't you see, because I'm just perfectly giving it to you this minute, and you can run about in it with that dearest dog, and it's the very first thing I ever gave you, isn't it? I'll always remember it just for that. It will do us all right for a few weeks, until we can look around. And there never was any one before, was there? You just needn't answer; you'd have to say 'No,' and anyway Granny says a young—you know what—should never ask silly questions about what happened before she met him, because it perfectly well makes rows, and I know she's right, but there never *was*, was there, and no matter anyway, because it's settled forever now, and we *do*, don't we? My! but I'm excited. Don't forget what I said about the brass andirons and the curtains for your den. Goo'-bye."

"Huh! yes, of course not!" said Bean, but the flapper had gone.

Back at the typewriter he tried to collect his memories of her message: sideboard with darling feet of some kind, no fumed oak, perhaps—brass andirons, curtains for his den. He couldn't recall what she had said about those. Maybe it would come to him. He wished he had told her that he already had a few good etchings. And the car! That was plain in his mind—little old last year's thing—at that shop around the corner. Did one say "garrash" or "garrige"? He heard both.

Anyway, he owned a motor car; you couldn't get around that. Maybe Bulger wouldn't open his eyes if he knew it. Bulger was an authority on cars, and spoke in detail of their strange insides with the aplomb of a man who has dissected them for years. He had violent disputes with the second bookkeeper about which was the best car for the money. The bookkeeper actually owned a motorcycle, or would, after he had paid five dollars a month a few more times, but Bulger would never allow this minor contrivance to be brought into their discussions. Bulger was intolerant of anything costing under five thou'—eat you up with repairs.

Bean longed to approach Bulger and say:

"Some dame, that! Just sent me a little old last year's car."

But he knew this would never do. Bulger would not only tell him why the car was of an inferior make, but he would want to borrow it to take a certain party, or maybe the gang, out for a spin, and get everybody killed or arrested or something. Bulger dressed fearlessly; no one with eyes could deny that; but he was tactless. Better keep that car under cover.

At seven-thirty that evening, with Nap on a leash, he strolled into the garage. He carried the yellow stick and the gloves, and he was prepared to make all sorts of a nasty row if they tried to tell him the car wasn't there, or so much as hinted that he might not be the right party. He knew how to deal with those automobile sharks.

"I believe you have a car here for me—Mr. Bean," he said briskly. It was the first time in all his life that he had spoken of himself as "Mr. Bean!" He threw his shoulders back even farther when he had achieved it.

The soiled person whom he addressed merely called to another soiled person who, near at hand, seemed to be beating an unruly car into subjection. The second person merely ducked his head backward and over his right shoulder.

"All right, all right!" said the first person, and then to Bean, "All right, all right!"

The car was before him, a large, an alarming car—and red! It was as red as the unworn cravat. Good thing it was getting dark. He wouldn't like to go out in the daytime in one as red as that, not at first.

He ran his eyes critically over it, trying to look disappointed.

"Good shape?" he demanded.

"How about it, Joe? She all right?"

Joe perceptibly stopped hammering.

"Garrumph-rumph!" he seemed to say.

"Well?" said the first person, eying Bean as if this explained everything.

"Take a little spin," said Bean.

"Paul!"

Paul issued from the office, a shock-headed, slouching youth in extreme negligée, a half-burned cigarette dangling from his lower lip. He yawned without dislodging the cigarette.

"Gentleman wants to g'wout." Paul vanished.

Nap had already leaped to a seat in the red car. He had learned what those things were for.

Paul reappeared, trim in leathern cap, well-fitting Norfolk jacket and shining puttees.

"Never know he only had on an undershirt," thought Bean, struck by this swiftly devised effect of correct dressing. He sat in the roomy rear seat beside Nap, leaning an elbow negligently on the arm-rest. He watched Paul shrewdly in certain mysterious preparations for starting the car. An observer would have said that one false move on Paul's part would have been enough.

The car rolled out and turned into the wide avenue half a block away.

"Where to, Boss?" asked Paul.

"Just around," said Bean. "Tea and things!"

They glided swiftly on.

"Oh, just a little old last year's car!" said Bean, frowning royally at a couple of mere foot people who turned to stare.

What would that flapper do next?

He surrendered to the movement. Drunkenly he mused upon a wild inspiration to bring Ram-tah out and give him a ride in this big red car. It appealed to him much. Ram-tah would almost open his eyes at the novelty of that progress. But he felt that this was no safe thing to do. He would be arrested. The whole secret might come out.

He had retained no sense of direction, but he was presently conscious of the river close at his side, and then the car, with warning blasts, curved up to a much lighted building and halted. A large man in uniform came solicitously to help him descend and gave him a fragment of cardboard which he knew would redeem his motor.

He was seated at a table looking down upon the shining river.

"Tea and things," he said to the waiter.

"Yes, sir; black or green, sir?"

"Bottle ginger ale!" How did he know whether he wanted black or green tea. No time to be fussy.

He began a lordly survey of the people at neighbouring tables—people who had doubtless walked there, or come in hired cabs, at the best. Hired cabs had yesterday seemed impressive to him; now they were rather vulgar. Of course, there might be circumstances—

He froze like a pointing dog. At a table not twenty feet distant, actually in the flesh, sat the Greatest Pitcher the World Has Ever Known. For a moment he could only stare fixedly. The man was simply *there*! He was talking volubly to two other men, and he was also eating a mere raspberry ice!

It showed how things "worked around," once you got started. Hadn't his whole life been a proof of this? How many times had he wished he might happen upon that Pitcher just as he was now, in street clothes—to look at him, study him! He wished *he* had ordered raspberry ice instead of ginger ale, which he didn't like. He would order one anyway.

It was all Ram-tah. If you knew you were a king, you needn't ever worry again. You sat still and let things come to you. After all, a king was greater than a pitcher, if you came down to it—in some ways, certainly.

He stared until the group left the table. He could actually have touched the Pitcher as he passed. Would wonders never cease?

Two men in uniform helped him into the big red car again, tenderly, as if he were fragile. He had meant to return to the garage, but now he saw the more dignified way was to stop at his own house. Further, Paul should take him to the office in the morning and call for him at four-thirty again. He wouldn't be afraid to ride in the red car even in daylight now. Sitting there not twenty feet from that Pitcher!

"Eight o'clock in the morning," he said curtly to Paul as he descended. And Paul touched his leather cap respectfully as the car moved off.

Cassidy lounged near in shirt sleeves.

"I see three was kilt-up in wan yistaday in th' Bur-ronx," said Cassidy interestedly.

"Good thing for the tired business man, though," said Bean, yawning in a bored way. "And that fellow of mine is careful."

Then his seeming boredom vanished.

"Say, you can't guess who I saw just now. Close to him as I am to you this minute—"

Solitary in the big red car, descending the crowded lanes of the city the next morning, Bean's sensations were conceivably those that had been Ram-tah's at the zenith of his power. There was the fragrant and cherished memory of the Greatest Pitcher, and a car to ride solitary in that simply blared the common herd from before it. People in street-cars looked enviously out at him. He lolled urbanely, with a large public manner. When you were a king you behaved like one, and the world knelt to you. Great pitchers sitting under the same roof with you; red motor-cars; fumed oak dining-rooms; flappers; brokers; shares. He wished he had thought to chew an unlighted cigar in this resplendent chariot. There seemed to be almost a public demand for it. Certain things were expected of a man!

"Be here at four-thirty," he directed.

And Paul, his fellow, glancing up along the twenty-two stories of the office building, was impressed. He considered it probable that the bored young man owned this building. "The guys that have gits!" thought Paul.

Bean was preposterously working once more, playing the part of a cog on the wheel. Another day, it seemed, of that grotesque nonsense, even after the world's Greatest Pitcher had sat not twenty feet from him the night before, eating raspberry ice. But events could not long endure *that* strain. Before the day was over Breede would undoubtedly "fire" him, with two or three badly chosen words; actually go through the form of discharging a man who had once ruled all Egypt with a kindly but an iron hand!

Of course, the fellow was unconscious of this, as he still must be of the rare joke the flapper was exquisitely holding over his head. His demeanour toward Bean betrayed no recognition of shares or pitchers or big red cars, nor of the ever-impending change in their relationship. He dictated fragments of English words, and Bean reconstructed them with the cunning of a Cuvier. He felt astute, robust, and disrespectful. Just one wrong word from Breede and all would be over between them. The poor old wreck didn't dream that he had nursed a flapper in his bosom, a flapper that would just perfectly have what she wanted—and no good fussing.

In the outer office, however, he was aware that his expansion was subtly making itself felt. Bulger had insensibly altered and was treating him after the manner of a fellow club man. Old Metzeger said "Good morning!" to him

550

affectionately—for Metzeger—and once he detected Tully staring at him through the enlarging glasses as if in an effort to read his very soul. But he knew his soul was not to be read by such as Tully. Tully, back there on the Nile, would have been a dancer—at the most, a fancy skater—if, indeed, he had risen to the human order, and were not still a slinking gazelle. Good name that, for Tully. He would remember it—gazelle!

At three o'clock he glanced aside from his typewriter to see a director enter Breede's room. He did not lift his look above the hem of the man's coat, but he knew him for the quiet one. And yet, when the door closed upon him, he seemed to become as noisy as any of them. Bean heard his voice rising.

Another director came, the big one who gripped a cigarette with an obviously cigar mouth. Once behind the shut door he seemed to approve of the noise and to be swelling its volume.

Three other directors hurried in, the elderly advanced dresser in the lead. He, of course, was always indignant, but now the other two were manifesting choler equal to his own. They puffed and glowered and, when the door had closed, they seemed to help skilfully with the uproar. It was a mob scene.

Bean was reminded of a newspaper line he had once or twice encountered: "The scene was one of indescribable confusion. Pandemonium reigned!" Pandemonium indubitably seemed to reign over those directors. He wondered. He wondered uncomfortably.

"Buzz-z-z-z! Buzz-z-z-z-z! Buzz-z-z-z-z-z!"

He quit wondering. He knew.

Yet for a moment after he stood in their presence they seemed to take no note of him. They were not sitting decorously in chairs as he conceived that directors should. The big one with the cigarette sat on the table, ponderously balanced with a fat knee between fat red hands. Another stood with one foot on a chair. Only the quiet one was properly sitting down. The elderly advanced dresser was not even stationary. With the faultless coat thrown back by pocketed hands, revealing a waist line greater than it should have been, he strutted and stamped. He seemed to be trying to step holes into the rug, and to be exploding intimately to himself.

"Plain enough," said the man who had been studying his foot on the chair. "Some one pulled the plug."

"And away she goes—shoosh!" said the big man dramatically.

"Kennedy & Balch buying right and left. Open at a hundred and twenty-five to-morrow, sure!" said the quiet one quietly.

"Placed an order yesterday for four hundred shares and got 'em," said another, not so quietly. "And to-day they're bidding Federal Express up to the ceiling."

"Plug pulled!"

The advanced-dressing director strutted to the fore with a visibly purpling face.

"Plug pulled? Want t' know *where* it was pulled? Right in this office. Want to know who pulled it? *That!*" He pointed unmistakably to the child among them taking notes. At another time Bean might have quailed, at least momentarily; but he had now discovered that the advanced-dressing old gentleman used scent on his clothes. He was afraid of no man who could do that in the public nostrils. He surveyed the old gentleman with frank hostility, noting with approval, however, the dignified yet different pattern of his waistcoat. But he knew the other directors were looking hard at him.

"Shrimp! snake!" added the old gentleman, like a shocked naturalist encountering a loathsome hybrid.

"Been plowing with our heifer?" asked Breede incisively.

Bean was familiar with that homely metaphor. He felt easier.

"*Your* heifer!" He would have liked to snort as the old gentleman did, but refrained from an unpractised effort! "Your heifer? No; I bought a good fat yoke of steers to do my plowing. Took *his* money to buy one of 'em with!" He waved a careless arm at the smouldering-vessel across the table. They were all gasping, in horror, in disgust. He was a little embarrassed. He sought to smooth the thing over a bit with his next words.

"Eagle shot down with its own feather," he said, hazily recalling something that had seemed very poetic when he read it.

"Wha'd I tell you? Wha'd I *tell* you!" shouted the oldest director, doing an intricate dance step.

"Hold 'ny Federal?" asked Breede.

"A block or two; several margins of it," said Bean.

"How many shares?"

"Have to ask Kennedy & Balch; they're my brokers. I guess about some seven or eight hundred shares."

"Wha'd I tell you? Wha'd I *tell* you?" again shouted the oldest director, and, as if despairing of an answer, he swore surprisingly for one of his refined garniture and aroma.

"Find out something in this office?" asked Breede, evenly.

"Why wouldn't I? I found out something the minute you sent people to me with that 'By the way—' stuff. I knew it as quick as you had them breaking their ankles trying to get my fifty shares. Knew it the very minute you sent that—that slinking gazelle to me." He pointed at Tully.

He had not meant to call Tully that. It rushed out. Tully wriggled uneasily in his chair at the desk, blushed well into his yellow beard, then drew out a kerchief of purest white silk and began nervously to polish his glasses.

"Hoo-shaw-Ha-ha-Hooshway!"

It was Breede, with, for the moment, a second purple face on the Board of Directors. Neither Bean nor Tully ever knew whether he had suppressed a laugh or a sneeze.

"Come, come, *come*!" broke in the oldest, sweeping the largest director aside with one finger as he pulled a chair to the table.

"This'll never do with *us*, you know! How much, how much, how much?"

He again poised the chastely wrought fountain pen of gold above the dainty check-book in Morocco leather.

"Have to give 'em up you know; can't allow *that* sort of underhand work; where'd the world be, where'd it be, where'd it *be*? Sign an order; tell me what you paid. Take your word for it!"

He was feeling for Bean the contempt which a really distinguished safe-blower is said to feel for the cheap thief who purloins bottles of milk from basement doorways in the gray of dawn.

"Now, now, *now*, boy!" The pen was still poised.

"Oh, put up your trinkets," said Bean with a fine affectation of weariness.

The old gentleman sat back and exhaled a scented but vicious breath. There was silence. It seemed to have become evident that the unprincipled young scoundrel must be taken seriously.

Then spoke the largest director, removing from his lips a cigarette which his own bulk seemed to reduce to something for a microscope only. He had been silent up to this moment, and his words now caused Bean the first discomfort he had felt.

"You will come here to-morrow morning," he began, slanting his entire facial area toward Bean, "and you will make restitution for this betrayal of trust. I think I speak for these gentlemen here, when I say we will do nothing with you to-night. Of course, if we chose—but no; you are a free man until to-morrow morning. After that all will depend on you. You are still young; I shall be sorry if we are forced to adopt extreme measures. I believe we shall all be sorry. But I am sure a night of sober reflection will bring you to your senses. You will come here to-morrow morning. You may go."

The slow, cool words had told. He tried to preserve his confident front, as he turned to the door. He would have left his banner on the field but for the oldest director, who had too long been silent.

"Snake in the grass!" hissed the oldest director, and instantly the colours waved again from Bean's lifted standard. He did not like the oldest director and he soared into the pure ether of verbal felicity, forgetful of all threats.

He stared pityingly at the speaker a moment, then cruelly said:

"You know they quit putting perfumery on their clothes right after the Chicago fire."

He left the room with faultless dignity.

"*Impertinent* young whelp!" spluttered the oldest director; but his first fellow-director who dared to look at him saw that he was gazing pensively from the high window, his back to the group.

"No good," said the quiet director to the largest. "A little man's always the hardest to bluff. Bet I could bluff you quicker than you could bluff him!"

"Well, I didn't know what else," answered the largest director, who was already feeling bluffed.

"Why didn't J.B. here assert himself then?"

"'Fraid he'd get mad's 'ell an' quit me," said Breede. "Only st'nogfer ever found gimme minute's peace. Dunno why—talk aw ri'. He un'stan's me; res' drive me 'sane."

"Plug's pulled, anyway," commented the quiet director. "Only thing to do is haul in what we can on a rising market. God knows where she'll stop."

"Pound her down," said the largest director sagely.

"Any pounding now will pound her up."

"Hold off and let it die down."

"Only make it worse. No use; we've got to cut that money up."

"Seven hundred shares, did he say?" asked the large director. "Very pretty indeed! J.B., I'll only give you one guess whether he quits his job or not."

"Thasso!" admitted Breede dejectedly.

"He'll show up all right in the morning, mark me," said the largest director, regaining confidence.

"Sneaking snake in the grass," muttered the oldest director, yet without his wonted vim.

"I'll telephone to McCurdy, right in the next block here," continued the largest director. "Might as well have this chap watched to-night and keep tight to him to-morrow until he shows up. We may find somebody's behind him."

"'S my idea," said Breede, "some one b'ind him."

"Grinning little ape!" remarked the oldest director bitterly.

To Bean in the outer office came the facetious boy.

"Telephone for Perfesser Bunker Hill Monument," he said, but spoiled it by laughing himself. It was extempore and had caught him unawares. The harried Bean fled to the telephone booth.

"I wanted to tell you," began the flapper, "not to eat anything out of cans unless I just perfectly have it on my pure-food list. They poison people, but the dearest grocer gave me a list of all the safe things, made up by a regular committee that tells how much poison each thing has in it, so you can know right off, or alcohol either. Now, remember! Oh, yes, what was I going to say? Granny says the first glamour soon fades, but after that you just perfectly settle down to solid companionship. And oh, yes, I want you to let me just perfectly have my own way about those hangings for the drawing-room, because you see I know, and, oh, I had something else. No matter. Won't I be glad when the deal is adjusted in the interests of all concerned, as poor old Pops says. Why don't you tell me something? I'm just perfectly waiting to hear."

"Uh, of course, of course; you're just perfectly a slinking gazelle. Ha, ha, ha!" answered Bean, laughing at his own jest after the manner of the office-boy.

He was back making a feeble effort to finish the last of Breede's letters. He glanced mechanically at his notes. Above that routine work he had so many things to think about. He'd fixed Tully for good. Tully wouldn't try that "by the way" and "not impossible" stuff with *him* any more. And that little old man—perfumery not used since the Chicago fire, or had he said the Mexican War? No matter. And talked to Breede about heifers. But there was the big-faced brute, speaking pretty seriously. Let him go free *to-night*! State's prison offence, maybe! Might be in jail this time to-morrow. Would the flapper telephone to him there? Send him unpoisoned canned food? Would he be disgraced? Breede—directors—glamour wearing off—slinking gazelles with yellow whiskers—rotten perfumery. So rushed the turbulent flood of his mind. But the letter was finished at last.

Two days later a certain traffic manager of lines west of Chicago read a paragraph in this letter many times:

"The cramped conditions of this terminal have been of course appreciably relieved by the completion of the westside cut-off. Nevertheless our traffic has not yet attained its maximum, and new problems of congestion will arise next year. I am engaged to that perfectly flapper daughter of yours, and we are going to marry each other when she gets perfectly good and ready. Better not fuss any. Let Julia do the fussing. To meet this emergency I dare say it will come to four-tracking the old main line over the entire division. It will cost high, but we must have a first-class freight-carrier if we are to get the business."

The traffic manager at first reached instinctively for his telegraphic cipher code. But he reflected that this was not code-phrasing. He read the paragraph again and was obliged to remind himself that his only daughter was already the wife of a man he knew to be in excellent health. Also he was acquainted with no one named Julia.

He copied from the letter that portion of it which seemed relevant, and destroyed the original. He had never heard it said of Breede; but he knew there are times when, under continued mental strain, the most abstemious of men will relax.

CHAPTER XII

When Bean emerged from the office-building that afternoon he was closely scrutinized by an inconspicuous man who, just inside the door by the cigar-stand, had been conversing with Tully. Bean saw Tully, but strode by that gentleman with head erect, chest expanded, and waist drawn in. Tully was cut. And Bean did not, of course, notice the inconspicuous man with whom Tully talked.

This person, however, followed Bean to the street, where he seemed a little taken aback to observe the young man very authoritatively enter a large red touring car and utter a command to its driver with an air of seasoned ownership. The red car moved slowly up Broadway. The inconspicuous man surveyed the passing vehicles, and seemed relieved when he discovered an empty taxi-cab going north. He hailed it and entered, giving directions to its guide that entailed much pointing to the large red touring car now a block distant.

Thereafter, until late at night, the red car was trailed by the taxi-cab. At six o'clock the car stopped at a place of refreshment overlooking the river, where the trailed youth consumed a modest dinner, which he concluded with a radiant raspberry ice. A little later he reëntered the red car and was driven aimlessly for a couple of hours through leafy by-ways. The inconspicuous man became of the opinion that the occupant of the red car was cunningly endeavouring to conceal his true destination.

The car returned to the place of refreshment at nine-thirty, where the young man again ordered a raspberry ice, with which he trifled for the better part of an hour. He betrayed to the alert but inconspicuous person who sat near him, by his expectant manner of scanning newcomers' faces, that he had hoped to meet some one here.

This expectation was disappointed. The watchful person suspected that the youth's confederates might have been warned. The quarry at length departed, in obvious disappointment, and was driven to his abode in a decent neighbourhood. The taxi-cab was near enough to the red car when this place was reached to enable its occupant to hear the young man request it for eight the following morning. The young man entered what a sign at the doorway declared to be "Choice Steam-heated Apartments," and the occupant of the taxi-cab was presently overheard by the janitor of the apartments expostulating with the vehicle's driver about the sum demanded for his evening's recreation. He was heard to denounce the fellow as "a thief and a robber!" and to make a vicious threat concerning his license.

Bean was face to face with Ram-tah, demanding whatever strength might flow to him from that august personage. A crisis had come. Either he was a king, or he was not a king. If a king, he must do as kings would do. If not a king, he would doubtless behave like a rabbit.

But strength flowed to him as always from that calm, strong face. In Ramtah's presence he could believe no weakness of himself. Put him in jail, would they? A man who had not only once ruled a mighty people in peace, but who had, some hundreds of centuries later, made Europe tremble under the tread of his victorious armies. Ram-tah had been no fighter—but Napoleon! He, Bunker Bean, was a wise king, yet a mighty warrior. Beat him down, would they? Merely because he wanted to become a director in their company! Well, they would find out who they were trying to keep off that Board. What if they did put him in jail? A good lawyer would get him out in a few minutes with a writ of something or other, a stay of proceedings, a demurrer, a legal technicality. He read the papers. Lawyers were always getting Wall Street speculators out of jail by some one of those devices; and if every other means failed a legal technicality did the work. And the papers always called the released man a Napoleon of Finance. It wasn't going to be so bad.

He hauled Ram-tah out of the closet and stood him at the foot of the bed for the night, so that courage might come to him as he slept. The plan proved to be an excellent one after Nap grew quiet. Nap had always been excited in Ram-tah's immediate presence, and now he insisted upon sniffing about the royal cadaver in a manner atrociously suggestive. Being dissuaded from this and consenting to sleep, Bean sank into dreams of mastery beneath Ram-tah's lofty aspect.

He awoke with a giant's strength. He arrayed himself in the newest check suit, and an especially beautiful shirt with a lavender stripe that bore his embroidered initials on one sleeve. He thought he would like to face them in his shirtsleeves, and give Breede and the fussy old gentlemen a good look at that lettered arm. He was almost persuaded to don the entirely red cravat, let the consequences be what they might. His refreshed spirit was equal to this audacity— but the red car. Wearing a red cravat in a very red car was just a little *too* loud— "different" enough, to be sure, but hardly "dignified." Too advanced, in short. At eight o'clock he went out upon the world, grasping his yellow stick and gloves. Most heroically would he enter the office with stick and gloves. Make Bulger stare! And if they put him in jail he must look right—papers get his picture, of course!

On the curb, before the car that vibrated so excitingly he had a happy thought. Was he to go down there and wait, pallid, perhaps trembling, until they came in and did things with him? Not he! A certain Corsican upstart would let them assemble first, let them miss him—wonder if he would come at all. Then he would saunter in, superbly define the extreme limits of his imagination, and coolly ask them what they were going to do about it. This would irritate them. It would irritate them all, and especially the little oldest director. He would swell up and grow purple. Perhaps he would have a stroke right there on the rug. Good work!

"Can't go to business this early," he said genially to the ever respectful Paul. "Too fine a day. And I got a deal on hand; have to think it over. Go on out that way for a nice little spin."

Paul directed the car out that way, spinning it nicely. It was a monstrous performance, to spin at that hour in a direction quite away from the place where you are expected by all the laws of business and common decency. This seemed to be the opinion of an inconspicuous man who followed discreetly in a taxi-cab. But Bean enjoyed it, thinking that the night might find him in a narrow cell. He looked with new interest on the street-cars full of office-bound people. They were meekly going to their tasks while he was affronting men with more millions than he had checks on the newest suit.

As they left the city and came to outlying villages, he saw that he was going in the direction of Breede's place. He thought it would be a fine thing to get the flapper and go and be just perfectly married. Then he could send a telegram to the office, telling them he could imagine nothing of less consequence, and that they might all go to the devil. It was easy to be "snappy" in a telegram. But he remembered that the flapper just perfectly wished to manage it herself; probably she wouldn't like his taking a hand in the game. Better not be rough with the child at the start.

They were miles away. The person in the taxi-cab might have been observed searching his pockets curiously, and to be counting what money he found therein as he cast anxious glances toward the dial of the taxi-metre.

Bean surveyed the landscape approvingly. Anyway, it was a fine enough performance to keep them waiting there. They would all be enraged. Perhaps the old one would have his stroke before the arrival of the spectator to whom it would give the most pleasure. They might be taking him out to the ambulance, and all the other directors would stand there and say, "This is *your* work. Officer, do your duty!" Well, it would be worth it. He'd tell them so, too!

Looking ahead, he became aware that an electric car had suffered an accident. The passengers streamed out and gathered around the motorman who was peering under the car. As Paul slowed down and turned aside to pass, the motorman declared, "She's burned out. Have to wait for the next car to push us."

There were annoyed stirrings in the group. A few passengers started for a suburban railway station that could be seen a half-mile distant. Bean looked down upon these delayed people with amused sympathy.

Then, astoundingly, his eye fell upon one of the passengers a little aloof from the group about the motorman. He, too, after a last look at the car, seemed to be resolving on that long tramp to the station. He was a sightly young man, tall, heavily built, and dressed in garments that would on any human form have won Bean's instant respect. But on the form of the Greatest Pitcher the World Has Ever Seen—!!

His mind was at once vacant of all the past, of all the future. There was no more a Breede, male or female, no more directors or shares or jails. There was only a big golden Present, subduing, enthralling, limitless!

"Stop car!" hissed Bean. The car halted three feet from the young man on foot.

"Jump in!" gasped Bean.

"Thanks," said the young man; "I'm going the other way."

"Me, too! I was turning around just here."

The young man hesitated, surveying his interlocutor.

"Well," he said, "if it won't be too much trouble?"

"Trouble!" The word was a caress as Bean uttered it. He pushed a door open, clumsy with excitement, and the World's Greatest Pitcher stepped in to sit beside him.

"Grounds?" asked Bean.

"Yes," said the Pitcher, "if it's convenient."

"Polo Grounds," called Bean to Paul. "Hurry and turn around there, someway." He was afraid his guest might reconsider.

But the guest sat contentedly enough, the car was turned, and presently was speeding back toward town. The person in a taxi-cab which made the same turn a moment later was heard to say, "What the devil now?" with no discernible relevance.

"Living out this way?" asked Bean when he was again certain of his voice-control.

"No; only went out to stay over night with some friends. Had to get back this morning. They told me to take that car and change at—"

"Ought to have one these," said Bean, "then you know where you are."

"This runs well," said the Pitcher affably.

"'S little old last year's car," said Bean with skilled ennui.

He was trying to remember—mustn't talk to a ball-player about ball; they're sick of it.

"Got a busy day ahead of me in the Street," he said brightly. "I was only taking a little spin to get my head cleared out. Have to keep your head clear down there!"

"Say, that's some suit you have on," said the Pitcher with frank admiration. "I like that check."

"Do you?" asked Bean, trying not to choke. Then, "Where'd you get yours? I was noticing that suit the other night; saw you up at Claremont—"

"Couple of pals of mine when I'm in town—"

"That white line against the blue comes out great in the day time. Cut well, too. I see you got one those patent neck-capes that prevents wrinkling below the coat-collar. And extension safety pockets, I suppose?"

"Match pockets, change pockets, pencil pockets, fountain pen pockets, improved secret money pocket, right here; see?" The speaker indicated the last mentioned item. "Flower holder up here under the lapel." He revealed it.

"I have 'em make a vestee," said Bean; "goes on with gold pins; adds dressiness, the man says."

The Pitcher revealed a vestee, adjusted with gold pins.

The red car moved as smoothly as if nothing had happened.

Next was made the momentous discovery that each wore a shirt with the identical lavender stripe.

"Initials!" said Bean, pulling up the sleeve of his coat and rotating his fore-arm under the Pitcher's approving glance.

"Got mine tattooed the same way," said the Pitcher, pulling up the sleeve of his coat in turn.

They discussed shirts.

"Funny thing," said Bean. "Chap down in the office with me, worth about a hundred million if he's worth a cent, wears separate cuffs; fastens 'em on with those nickel jiggers."

"Had a fellow on the team last year did the same thing," said the Pitcher. "He's back to the bush now, though. The hick used to wear a made-up neck tie, too, till the other lads kidded him out of it."

"You must get a lot of those Silases, one time and another," said Bean sympathetically. He was wondering; the fellow had referred at least indirectly to his calling.

"In the box, to-day?" he asked, feeling brazen.

The Pitcher nodded.

"You certainly pitched some air-tight ball last time I saw you. Say, I'll tell you something. If I ever have a kid, you know what's going to happen? Nothing used but his left hand from the cradle up; and, for toys one league ball and a light bat. That's all."

"Right way," said the Pitcher approvingly.

"I'm only afraid the managers will get wise to him and not let him finish out his college course," said Bean. "I don't know, though. I'll be in the business myself by that time; may sign him on myself."

"Like it?" asked the Pitcher, interestedly.

"*Like* it! Say, what else is there? *Like* it! I'm only keeping on down there in the Street till I put a certain deal through; then nothing but old Base B. Ball for mine! You'll see. I'll pick up one the big clubs somewhere if *money'll* do it!"

"Well, it's the one branch of the business where you don't have to treat your arm like a sick baby," said the Pitcher. "Say, you want to come inside a while?"

To Bean's amazement the car had stopped before the players' entrance. He had supposed himself miles back in the country. Did he want to go inside for a while! He was out of the car as quickly as Nap could have achieved it.

"What did you say your name was?" asked the Pitcher.

He was in a long room lined with lockers. He recognized several players lounging there. A big man with a hard face, half in a uniform, was singing, "Though Silver Threads Are 'Mong the Gold, I Love You Just the Same." These men were requested to shake hands with the Pitcher's friend, Mr. Bean. They were also told informally that his new check suit was some suit.

"I'll soon have one coming off the same piece," said the Pitcher.

They went through a little door and out upon the grounds. A few players were idling there, only two of the pitchers being in uniform. The vast empty stands and bleachers seemed to confer privacy upon an informal and friendly gathering.

Several more players shook hands with the Pitcher's friend, Mr. Bean, and the circumstance of his presence was explained.

"I found your twist-paw out in the brush with nothing but a bum trolley car between him and a long walk," said Bean jauntily.

"He's got the prettiest red car that ever made you jump at a crossing," added the Pitcher.

They sat on the bench together.

"He winds up like old Sycamore," said Bean expertly of a young pitcher who was working nearby.

"He does for a fact," testified one of the players. "Did you know old Syc?"

"Chicago," said Bean. "Down and out; coming in from some tank-team and having to wear his uniform for underclothes all winter."

They regarded him with respectful interest.

"Poor Syc could never learn to take water in it," said one.

"He lived in a boarding-house two doors away from me," said Bean. "And when he'd taken about six or seven in at Frank's Place, he'd start singing 'My Darling Nellie Gray,' only he'd have to cry at about the third verse; then he'd lick some man that was laughing at him."

"That's old Syc, all right. You *got* him, pal!"

The talk went to other stars of the past. Bean mostly listened, but when he spoke they heard one who knew whereof he spoke. He was familiar with the public performance of every player of prominence for ten years. He was at home, among equals, and easy in his mind.

562

An inconspicuous man who had gained admittance to the grounds, by alleging his need to inspect a sign that was to be "done over," above the fence beyond the outfield, passed closely to Bean and detected the true situation with one sweep of his eagle eyes.

Fifteen minutes later this man was saying over a telephone to the largest director who sat in Breed's office:

"Nothing doing last night but riding around in a big red car that was waiting for him down in front. This morning at eight he starts north and picks up a man just this side Fordham, from a trolley car that breaks down. They turn around and go to the baseball park. He's setting there now, gassing with a lot of the players, telling funny stories and the like. He looks as if he didn't have a trouble on earth. My taxi-cab bill is now, for last night and to-day, forty-six eighty-five. Shall I keep on him?"

"No!" shouted the largest director. "Let him go to—let him alone and come in."

"I forgot to say," added the inconspicuous man, "that the party he picked up on the road and brought back here looks like he might be a ball player himself."

"Come in," repeated the largest director; "on a street-car!"

"Looks to me," ventured the quiet director to the largest, "as if you didn't bluff him quite to death last night."

"Aut'mobile!" said Breede. "Knew he had some one b'ind him."

"Let's get to business. No good putting it off now," said the quiet director.

"Seven hundred shares! My God! This is monstrous!" said the little eldest director, who had been making noises like a heavy locomotive.

Bean would have sat forever on that bench of the mighty, world-forgetting, if not world-forgot. But the departure of several of the men drew his attention to the supreme obligation of a guest.

"Well," he said, rising.

"Look in on us again some day," urged the Pitcher cordially.

"Thanks, I surely will," said Bean. "I like to forget business this way, now and then. Good day!"

They waved him friendly adieus, and he was out where Paul waited.

"Forget business!" He had indeed for two hours forgotten business and people. Not once had he thought of those waiting directors.

Well, they could do their worst, now. He was ripe to laugh at any fate. What was prison? "The prisoner," he seemed to read, "betrayed no consciousness of the enormity of his crime, and had, indeed, spent the morning at the Polo Grounds, chatting with various members of the Giants, with which team he is a great favourite."

Let them bring their gyves. Let the barred door clang shut!

"Office!" he said to Paul. There was no doubt in Paul's mind as to the quality of his patron. He had at once recognized the Greatest Pitcher. He ceased to speculate as to whether this assured young man owned the high office-building. That was now of minor consequence.

On the way downtown he tried to remember what day it was. He thought it was Friday, but again it seemed to be Monday. He stopped the car and bought an afternoon paper to find out.

At the entrance to the big office-building he debated a moment.

"Wait!" he directed Paul.

He was uncertain how long he might be permitted to remain in that building. If he must go to jail, he would ride. He wondered if Paul knew the address of the best jail. He could have things sent in to him—magazines and fruit.

Inside the entrance he paused before the cigar-stand. He must think carefully what he would say to those men of round millions. He must keep up his front. His glance roamed to the beautifully illustrated boxes of cigars. A good idea!

"Gimme one those," he said to the clerk, indicating a box that flaunted the polychrome portrait of a distinguished-looking Spaniard. He was surprised at the price, but he bit the tip off violently and began to mouth it.

"I'm no penny-pincher," he muttered, thinking of the cigar's cost. He tilted the cigar to a fearless angle and slanted his hat over his left eye. He lolled against the cigar-case, gathering resolution for the ordeal.

The door of an elevator down the corridor shot open, and there emerged, in single file, a procession, headed by the little oldest director, who had allowed him to go free overnight. They marched toward the door, looking straight ahead. They must pass in front of him. He felt a sudden great relief. Something in their bearing told him they were powerless to restrict his liberty.

The oldest director deigned him no glance, but snorted accurately in his direction, nevertheless. The quiet one grinned faintly at him, but the two neutral directors passed him loftily, as if they were Virtue scorning Vice in a morality play. The largest director frowned at the stripling who was savagely chewing a fifty-cent cigar at the procession.

The moment was incontestably the stripling's. He was cool and meant to take the fullest advantage of it. He meant to say, contemptuously, "I can imagine nothing of less consequence!"

But the officious cigar-clerk held a lighted match to the choice cigar and the magnificent defiance was smothered by a cough. He was obliged to content himself with glaring at the expansive and well-rounded back of the biggest director.

He was alone on the field, pretending enjoyment of a cigar which was now lighted and loathsome.

Bulger entered from the street and viewed him with friendly alarm.

"Say, where you been?" demanded Bulger. "Old Pussy-foot's got a sore thumb right now from pounding that buzzer of yours all morning. He's hot at every one. I heard him call Tully a slinking something or other; couldn't get the word, but Tully got it. Say, you better get busy—regular old George W. Busy—if you want to hold that job."

"Job!" laughed Bean bitterly, and waved the expensive and lighted cigar in Bulger's face. "Job! Well, I may get busy, and then again I may not. All depends!"

"Gee!" said Bulger, profoundly moved by this admirable spirit of insubordination. "Well, I got to get back; I'm five minutes late myself."

Bean waited until he had gone. Then he strolled out to the street and furtively dropped an excellent and but slightly burned cigar into the gutter. He wished those fellows at cigar-stands would do only what they were put there for. Taking liberties with people!

He decided to go back as if nothing had happened. Let Breede do the talking, and if he talked rough, then tell him very simply that nothing of less consequence could be imagined. Continue to play the waiting game. That was it!

He entered the office, humming lightly. He seemed to be annoyed by the people he found there. He glared at Bulger, at old Metzeger, at the other clerks, and especially at Tully. Tully looked uncomfortable. He wasn't a gazelle after all. He was a startled fawn.

"Telephone for—" began the office boy humourist, but Bean was out of hearing in the direction of the telephone booth before the latest *mot* could be delivered.

"Been trying to get you all the morning," began the flapper in eager tones. "I should think you would stay there, when I may have to call you any minute. That grocer gave me the nicest little book, 'Why Did Your Husband Fail in Business?' with a picture of the poor man that failed on the cover. It's because he didn't get enough phosphorous to make him 100 per cent. efficient, and if he'd eaten 'Brain-more' mush for breakfast, nothing would have happened. We'll try it, anyway, and there's a triple-plate spoon in every package, so if I order a dozen ... and oh, yes, what was I going to say? Why, I'm perfectly going to pull off the funniest stunt this afternoon; you'd just deliciously die laughing if I told you, but it will be still funnier if you don't know. Are you paying attention? It's because I'd already spent my allowance for three years and seven months ahead—I figured it all out like a statement—and I've perfectly just got to have some money of my real own. I've enough to worry about without bringing money into it, with proper food for you and those patent laundry tubs I told you about, and the man says he wouldn't think of letting it go for less than two seventy-five, but that's five dollars saved.

Well, good-bye! I'll manage everything, and Granny says always to conceal little household worries from him, and just perfectly keep the future looking bright and interesting ... she says that's the secret. Good-bye! What am I?"

"Startled fawn," said Bean.

"Well, don't forget."

"I won't. I'll attend to my part all right."

He heard the fateful buzzing even before he opened the door of the telephone booth. Breede was at it again. He walked coolly to his desk for a note-book. Every one else in the office was showing nervousness. He was the only man who could still the troubled waters. He would play the waiting game; keep the future looking "bright and interesting." Breede could do the rest.

"Buzz! Buzz-z-z-z! Buzz-z-z-z-z!" It sounded pretty vicious.

He entered Breede's room with his accustomed air of quiet service. Breede did not glance at him. He began, as usual, to dictate before Bean was seated.

"Letter T.J. Williams 'sistant sup'ntendent M.P. 'n' C. department C. 'n' L.M. rai'way Sh'-kawgo dear sir please note 'closed schej'l car 'pairin' make two copies send one don't take that an' let me have at y'r earles c'nvenience—"

Apparently nothing at all had happened. He was at his old post, and Breede did nothing but explode fragments of words as ever. No talk of jail or betrayal of trust or of his morning's flagrant absence.

One might have thought that Breede himself played the waiting game. Or perhaps Breede only toyed with him. He fastened his gaze on the criminal cuffs. They were his rock of refuge in any cataclysm that might impend. If only he could keep those cuffs within his range of vision he would fear nothing. Patent laundry tubs; five dollars saved; why your husband failed in business; bright and interesting future—

"'Lo! 'Lo!" Breede was detonating into the desk-telephone which had sounded at his elbow.

"'Lo! Well? What? Run off! Stop nonsense! Busy!" He hung up the receiver.

"—also mus' be stipulated that case of div'dend bein' passed—"

The desk telephone again rang, this time more emphatically. Bean was chilled by a premonition that the flapper meant to pull off that funny stunt which was to cause him quite deliciously to die laughing.

Breede grasped the receiver again impatiently.

"Busy, tell you! No time nonsense! What! *What.* W-H-A-T!!!"

He listened another moment, then lessening his tone-production but losing nothing of intensity, he ripped out:

"*Gur—reat Godfrey!*"

His eyes, narrowed as he listened, now widened upon Bean who stared determinedly at the cuffs.

"You know what she *says*?"

"Yes," said Bean doggedly.

Then his eyes met Breede's and gave them blaze for blaze. The Great Reorganizer knew it not, but he no longer looked at Bunker Bean. Instead, he was trying to shrivel with his glare a veritable king of old Egypt who had enjoyed the power of life and death over his remotest subject. Bean did not shrivel. Breede glared his deadliest only a moment. He felt the sway of the great Ram-tah without identifying it. He divined that mere glaring would not shrivel this presumptuous atom. In truth, Bean outglared him. Breede leaned again to the telephone, listening. Bean lowered his eyes to the cuffs. He sneered at them now. The intention of the lifted upper lip was too palpable.

"Gur-reat stars above!" murmured Breede. "She says she's got it all reasoned out!" There was something almost plaintive in his tones; he shuddered. Then he rallied bravely once more.

"Tell you, no time nonsense. Busy."

But he seemed to know he was beaten. He listened again, then wilted.

"What next?" he demanded of Bean.

"Ask *her*!"

"Nice mess you got *me* into!"

Bean sneered resolutely at the cuffs. Again the telephone tinkled.

Breede listened and horror grew on his face.

"Now she's told her mother," he muttered. "My God!"

The transmitter was an excellent one, and Bean caught notes of hysteria. Julia was fussing back there.

"Now, now!" urged Breede. "No good. Better lie down. She says she's got it all reasoned *out*, don't I tell you?" He put a throttling hand over the anguished voice, and looked dumbly at Bean. He noted the evil sneer and traced it to the cuffs. Slowly he hung up the receiver and took one of the cuffs in his hands.

"Wha's matter these cuffs?" he demanded with a show of his true spirit.

"Right enough. Cuffs all right, if you like that kind. But why don't you wear 'em *on*—like this?" He luminously exposed his left forearm. It was by intention the one that carried the purple monogram.

"Sewed on, like that!" he added almost sharply.

Breede seemed to be impressed by the exhibit.

"Well," he began, awkwardly, as a man knowing himself in the wrong but still defiant, "I won't do it. *That's* all! Not for anybody."

Still, he seemed to consider that something more than mere apparent perverseness would become him.

"They get down 'round m' hands all the time. Can't think when they get down that way. Bother me. Take m' mind off. I won't do it, that's all. I don't care. Not for anybody't all!" He replaced the cuff beside its mate. He seemed to be saying that he had settled the matter—and no good talking any more about it.

Bean was silent and dignified. His own air seemed to disclose that when once you warned people in plain words, you could no longer be held responsible. For a moment they made a point of ignoring the larger matter.

"Say," Breede suddenly exploded, "I wish you'd tell me just how many kinds of a—no matter! Where was I? This reserve fund may be subject to draft f'r repairs an' betterment durin' 'suin' quarter or 'ntil such time as—"

The telephone again rang its alarm. Breede took the receiver and allowed dismay to be read on his face as he listened.

"Well, well, well," he at length began, soothingly, "go lie down; take something; take *something*; well, send over t' White Plains f'r s'more. Putcha t' sleep. What can *I* do?" Again the throttling hand.

He ruefully surveyed his littered desk, then drew the long sigh of the baffled.

"Take telegram m' wife. Sorry can't be home late, 'port'n board meet'n'. May be called out of town."

The telephone rang, but was ignored.

"Send it off," he directed Bean above the bell's clear call. "Then c'mon; go ball game. G'wup 'n subway."

"Got car downstairs," suggested Bean.

"You got your work cut out f'r you; 'sall I got t' say," growled Breede.

"'S little old last year's car," said Bean modestly.

CHAPTER XIII

As the little old last year's car bore them to the north, some long sleeping-image seemed to stir in Breede's mind.

"Got car like this m'self somewheres," he remarked.

Bean was relieved. He didn't want the name of a woman to be brought into the matter just then.

"'S all right for town work," he said. "Good enough for all I want of a car."

"'S awful!" said Breede, obviously forgetting the car for another subject.

"What can I do? She says she's got the right," suggested Bean.

"She'd take it anyway. *I* know her. Pack a suit-case. Had times with her already. Takes it from her mother."

"Can't be too rough at the start," declared Bean. "Manage 'em of course, but 'thout their finding it out—velvet glove." He looked quietly confident and Breede glanced at him almost respectfully.

"When?" he asked.

"Haven't made up my mind yet," said Bean firmly. "I may consult her, then again I may not; don't believe in long engagements."

Breede's glance this time was wholly respectful.

"You're a puzzle to me," he conceded.

Bean's shrug eloquently seemed to retort, "that's what they all say, sooner or later."

They were silent upon this. Bean wondered if Julia was still fussing back there. Or had she sent to White Plains for some more? And what was the flapper just perfectly doing at that moment? Life was wonderful! Here he was to witness a ball game on Friday!

They were in the grandstand, each willing and glad to forget, for the moment, just how weirdly wonderful life was. A bell clanged twice, the plate was swept with a stubby broom, the home team scurried to their places.

"There he is!" exclaimed Breede; "that's him!" Breede leaned out over the railing and pointed to the Greatest Pitcher the World Has Ever Seen. Bean sat coolly back.

The Pitcher scanned the first rows of faces in the grandstand. His glance came to rest on a slight, becomingly attired young man, who betrayed no emotion, and, in the presence of twenty thousand people, the Pitcher unmistakably saluted Bunker Bean. Bean gracefully acknowledged the attention.

"He know *you*?" queried Breede with animation.

"*Know* me!" He looked at Breede almost pityingly, then turned away.

The Pitcher sent the ball fairly over the plate.

"Stur-r-r-ike one!" bellowed the umpire.

"With him all morning," said Bean condescendingly to his admiring companion. "Get shirts same place," he added.

His cup had run over. He was on the point of confiding to his companion the supreme felicity in store for Breede as a grandfather. But the batter struck out and the moment was only for raw rejoicing. They forgot. Bean ceased to be a puzzle to any one, and Breede lapsed into unconsciousness of Julia.

The game held them for eleven innings. The Greatest Pitcher saved it to the home team.

"He was saying to me only this morning—" began Bean, as the Pitcher fielded the last bunt. But the prized quotation was lost in the uproar. Pandemonium truly reigned and the scene was unquestionably one of indescribable confusion.

Outside the gate they were again Breede and Bean; or, rather, Bean and Breede. The latter could not so quickly forget that public recognition by the Greatest Pitcher.

"You're a puzzle t'me," said Breede. "Lord! I can't g'ome yet. Have't take me club."

"Can't make y'out," admitted Breede once more, as they parted before the sanctuary he had indicated.

"Often puzzle myself," confessed the inscrutable one, as the little old last year's car started on. Breede stood on the pavement looking after it. For some reason the car puzzled him, too.

Bean was wondering if Julia herself wouldn't have been a little appeased if she could have seen the Pitcher single him out of that throng. Some day he might crush the woman by actually taking the Pitcher to call.

At his door he dismissed the car. He wanted quiet. He wanted to think it all out. That morning it had seemed probable that by this time he would have been occupying a felon's cell, inspecting the magazines and fruit sent to him. Instead, he was not only free, but he was keeping a man worth many millions from his own home, and perhaps he had caused that man's wife to send over to White Plains for some more. It was Ram-tah. All Ram-tah. If only every one could find his Ram-tah—

Cassidy was reading his favourite evening paper, the one that shrieked to the extreme limits of its first page in scarlet headlines and mammoth type. It was a paper that Bean never bought, because the red ink rubbed off to the peril of one's eighteen-dollar suit.

Cassidy, who for thirty years had voted as the ward-boss directed, was for the moment believing himself to be a rabid socialist.

"Wall Street crooks!" he began, in a fine orative frenzy. "Dur-r-rinkin' their champagne whilst th' honest poor's lucky t' git a shell av hops! Ruh-hobbin' th' tax-pay'r f'r' t' buy floozie gowns an' joold bresslets f'r their fancy wives an' such. I know th' kind well; not wan cud do a day's bakin' or windy-washin'!"

He held the noisy sheet before Bean and accusingly pointed a blunt forefinger. "Burly Blonde Divorcée, Routed Society Burglar," across the first two columns, but the proceeding was rather tamely typed and the Burly Blonde's portrait in evening dress was inconspicuous beside the headlines "Flurry in Federal Express! Wild Scenes on Stock Exchange. Millions made by Gentlemen's Agreement."

"Gentlemin!" hissed Cassidy. "The sem agreemint that two gentlemin porch-climbers has whin wan climbs whilst th' other watches t' see is th' cop at th' upper ind av th' beat! Millions med whilst I'm wur-r-kin' f'r twenty per month an' what's slipped me—th' sem not buyin' manny jools ner private steamboats! Millions med! I know th' kind well!" Bean felt his own indignation rise with Cassidy's. He was seeing why they had feared to have him on the board of directors. Apparently they were bent on wrecking the company by a campaign of extravagance. The substance of what he gleaned from Cassidy's newspaper was that those directors had declared a stock dividend of 200 per cent. and a cash dividend of 100 per cent.

They were madly wrecking the company in which he had invested his savings. Such was his first thought. And they were crooks, as Cassidy said, because for two years they had been quietly, through discreet agents, buying in the stock from unsuspecting holders.

"Rascals," agreed Bean with Cassidy, leaving but slight gifts for character analysis.

"Tellin' th' poor dubs th' stock was goin' down with one hand an' buyin' it in with th' other," said the janitor, lucidly.

Bean was suddenly troubled by a cross-current of thought. When you wrecked a company you didn't buy in the stock—you *sold*. He viewed the headlines from a new angle. Those directors were undoubtedly rascals, but was he not a rascal himself? What about his own shares?

"Maybe there's something we don't understand about it," he ventured to Cassidy.

"I know th' kind well," persisted Cassidy. "Th' idle rich! Small use have they f'r th' wur-r-r-kin' man! Souls no wider than th' black av y'r nail!"

"Might have had good reasons," said Bean, cautiously.

"Millions av thim," assented Cassidy with a pointed cynicism. "An' me own father dyin' twenty-three years ago fr'm ixposure contracted in County Mayo!"

Bean returned the paper to its owner and went slowly in to Ram-tah. One of the idle rich! Well, that is what kings mostly were, if you came down to it. At least they had to be rich to buy all those palaces. But not necessarily idle. The renewed Ram-tah would not be idle. It was not idleness to own a major-league club.

For the first time in their intercourse he felt that he faced the dead king almost as an equal. He was confronted by problems of administration, as Ram-tah must often have been. He must think.

If the flapper quite madly brought about an immediate marriage they would, for their honeymoon, follow the home club on its Western trip, and the groom would not be idle. He would be "looking over the ground." Then he would buy one of the clubs. If he proved to be not rich enough for that, not quite as rich as one of the idle rich, he would buy stock and become a director. He was feeling now that he knew how to be a director; that his experience with the express company had qualified him. He wondered how rich he would prove to be. Maybe he would have as much as thirty thousand dollars.

And he was a puzzle to Breede. He looked knowingly at Ram-tah when he remembered this. Ram-tah had probably puzzled people, too.

He went to the office in the morning still wondering how rich he might be. The newspaper he read did not enlighten him, though it spoke frankly of "Federal Express Scandal." If the thing was *very* scandalous, perhaps he had made a lot of money. But he could not be sure of this. It might be merely "newspaper vituperation," which was something he knew to be not uncommon. The paper had declared that those directors had juggled a twenty-million dollar surplus for years, lending it to one another at a low rate of interest, until, alarmed by clamouring stockholders, they had declared this enormous dividend, taking first, however, the precaution to buy for a low price all the stock they could. But the newspaper did not say how rich any one would be that had a whole lot of margins on that stock at Kennedy & Balch's. Maybe you had to hire a lawyer in those cases.

Entering the office, he was rudely shocked by Tully.

"Good-morning, Mr. Bean!" said Tully distinctly.

"Good-morning!" returned Bean, stunned by Tully's "Mr." "Uh! pleasant day," he added.

"Yes, sir!" said Tully, again distinctly.

Bean controlled himself and went to his desk.

"'Mr.' and 'Sir'! Gee! Am I as rich as *that*??" he thought.

Half an hour later it no longer seemed to him that he was rich at all. He was seated opposite Breede taking letters in shorthand as if he were merely a thirty-dollar-a-week Bunker Bean. Breede was refusing to recognize any change in their relationship. He made no reference to their talk of the day before and his detached cuffs stubbornly occupied their old position on the desk. Was it all a dream—and the flapper, too?

But the flapper soon called him to the telephone.

"Poor old Pops came home late, and he says you're just perfectly a puzzle to him," she began.

"I know," said Bean; "he says he can't make me out."

"And Moms began to say the silliest things about you, until I just had to take her seriously, so I perfectly told her that woman had come into her own in this generation, thanks to a few noble leaders of our sex—it's in Granny's last speech at the league—and that sent her up in the air. I don't think she can be as well as she used to be; and I told Pops he had to give me some money, and he said he knew it as well as I did, so what was the use of talking about it, and so he just perfectly gave me fifty or sixty thousand dollars and told me to make it go as far as I could, but I don't know, that grocer says the cost of living is going up every day because the Senate isn't insurgent enough; and anyway I'll get the tickets and a suite on that little old boat that sails Wednesday. I thought you'd want a day or two; and everything will be very quiet, only the family present, coming into town for it, you know, Wednesday morning, and the boat sails at noon, and I'll be so perfectly glad when it's all over because it's a very serious step for a young girl to take. Granny herself says it should never be taken lightly, unless you just perfectly know, but of course we do, don't we? I think you'll like fumed oak better, after all—and poor old Pops saying you're such a puzzle to him. He says he can't make out just how many kinds of a perfectly swear-word fool you are, but I can, and that's just deliciously enough for anybody. And you're to come out to-morrow and have tea and things in the afternoon, and *I'm* going to be before sister is, after all. She's perfectly furious about it and says I ought to be put back into short skirts, but I just perfectly knew it the very first time I ever looked at you. Stay around there, in case I think of something I've forgotten. G'bye."

Wednesday—a little old steamer sailing at noon! A steamer, and he couldn't swim a stroke and was always terrified by water. And the trip West with the home team! What about that? Why had he not the presence of mind to cut in and just perfectly tell her where they were going? But he had let the moment pass. It was too late. He didn't want to begin by making a row. And Breede was puzzled by him *that*way, was he? Couldn't make out how many kinds of perfectly swear-word fool he was?

He regretted that he had not been more emphatic about those cuffs. And Breede had said it after witnessing that salute from the pitcher's box! He must be a hard man to convince of anything. What more proof did he want?

Buzz! Buzz! Buzz!

The man who couldn't make him out was calling for him. For an hour longer he took down the man's words, not sneering pointedly at the cuffs, yet allowing it to be seen that he was conscious of them. A puzzle was he?

"—Hopin' t'ave promp' action accordin' 'bove 'structions, remain yours ver' truly she's got it all reasoned out," concluded Breede.

"She just told me," said Bean; "little old steamer sailing Wednesday."

"Can't make y' out," said Breede.

That thing was getting tiresome.

"You're a puzzle to me, too," said Bean.

"Hanh! Wha's 'at? What kinda puzzle?"

"Same kind," said Bean, brightly.

"Hum!" said Breede, and pretended to search for a missing document. Then he eyed Bean again.

"Know how much you made on that Federal stuff?"

"I was going to ask a lawyer," confessed Bean. "I got a whole lot of margins or whatever you call 'em around at that broker's. Maybe he wouldn't mind letting me know."

"Stock'll be up t' six hundred before week's out; net you 'round four hund' thous'n'," exploded Breede in his most vicious manner.

"Four hundred thousand margins?" He wanted to be cautious.

"*Dollars*, dammit!" shouted Breede.

Bean was able to remain cool. That amount of money would have meant nothing to him back on the Nile. Why should it now?

"It wasn't the money I was after," he began, loftily.

"*Hanh!*"

"Principle of the thing!" concluded Bean.

Breede had lost control of his capable under jaw. It sagged limply. At last he spoke, slowly and with awe in his tone.

"You don't puzzle me any more." He shook his head solemnly. "Not any more. I *know* now!"

"Little old steamer—can't swim a stroke," said Bean.

"'S all," said Breede, still shaking his head helplessly.

At his desk outside Bean feigned to be absorbed in an intricate calculation. In reality he was putting down "400,000," then "$400,000," then "$400,000.00" By noon he had covered several pages of his note-book with this instructive exercise. Once he had written it $398,973.87, with a half-formed idea of showing it to old Metzeger.

As he was going out Tully trod lightly over a sheet of very thin ice and accosted him.

"The market was not discouraging to-day," said Tully genially.

"'S good time to buy heavily in margins," said Bean.

"Yes, sir," said Tully respectfully.

In the street he chanted "four hundred thousand dollars" to himself. He was one of the idle rich. He hoped Cassidy would never hear of it. Then, passing a steamship office, he recalled the horror that lay ahead of him. Little old steamer. But was a financier who had been netted four hundred thousand dollars to be put afloat upon the waters at the whim of a flapper? She was going too far. He'd better tell her so in plain words; say, "Look here, I've just netted four hundred thousand dollars, and no little old steamer for mine. I don't care much for the ocean. We stay on land. Better understand who's who right at the start."

That is what he would tell the flapper; make it clear to her. She'd had her own way long enough. Marriage was a serious business. He was still resolving this when he turned into a shop.

"I want to get a steamer trunk—sailing Wednesday," he said in firm tones to the clerk.

It was midnight of Tuesday. In the steam-heated apartment Bean paced the floor. He was attired in the garments prescribed for gentlemen's evening wear, and he was still pleasantly fretted by the excitement of having dined with the Breede family at the ponderous town house up east of the park.

He tried to recall in their order the events of those three days since he had left the office on Saturday. His coolest efforts failed. It was like watching a screen upon which many and diverse films were superimposing scenes in which he was an actor of more or less consequence, but in which his figure was always blurred. It was confounding.

Yet he had certainly gone out to that country place Sunday for tea and things, taking Nap. And the flapper, with a sinful pride, had shown him off to the family. He and the flapper had clearly been of more consequence than the big sister and the affianced waster, who wouldn't be able to earn his own cigarettes, say nothing of his ties and gloves. Sister and the waster, who seemed to be an agreeable young man, were simply engaged in a prosaic way, and looked prosaically forward to a church wedding. No one thought anything about them, and sister was indeed made perfectly furious by the airs the flapper put on.

Mrs. Breede, from one of the very oldest families of Omaha, had displayed amazing fortitude. She had not broken down once, although she plainly regarded Bean as a malignant and fatal disease with which her latest-born had been infected. "I must be brave, brave!" she had seemed to be reminding herself. And when Nap had chased and chewed her toy spaniel, named "Rex," until it seemed that Rex might pass on, she had summoned all her woman's resignation and only murmured, "Nothing can matter now!"

There had seemed to be one fleeting epoch which he shared alone with the flapper, feeling the smooth yielding of her cheek and expanding under her very proudest gaze of ownership. And a little more about fumed oak panels and the patent laundry tubs.

Monday there had been a mere look-in at the office, with Tully saying "Sir"; with Breede exploding fragments of words to a middle-aged and severely gowned woman stenographer who was more formidable than a panorama of the Swiss Alps, and who plainly made Breede uncomfortable; and with Bulger saying, "Never fooled your Uncle Cuthbert for a minute. Did little old George W. Wisenham have you doped out right or not? Ask me, *ask* me; wake me up any time in the night and ask me!"

Tuesday afternoon he had walked with the flapper in the park and had learned of many things going forward with solely his welfare in view—little old house surrounded on all sides by just perfectly scenery—little old next year's car—little old going-away rag—little old perfectly just knew it the first moment she saw him—little old new rags to be bought in Paris—and sister only going to Asheville on *hers*.

And the dinner in town, where he had seemed to make an excellent impression, only that Mrs. Breede persisted in behaving as if the body was still upstairs and she must be brave, brave! And Grandma, the Demon, confiding to him over her after-dinner cigarette that he was in for it now, though she hadn't dared tell him so before; but he'd find that out for himself soon enough if he wasn't very careful about thwarting her. It made her perfectly furious to be thwarted.

Nor did he fail to note that the stricken mother was distinctly blaming the Demon for the whole dreadful affair. Her child had been allowed to associate with a grandmother who had gone radical at an age when most of her sex simmer in a gentle fireside conservatism and die respectably. But it was too late now. She could only be brave, brave!

And he was to be there at nine sharp, which was too early, but the flapper could be sure only after he came that nothing had happened to him, that he had neither failed in business, been poisoned by some article of food not on her list, nor diverted by that possible Other One who seemed always to lurk in the flapper's mental purlieus. She just perfectly wanted him there an hour too early; all there was about it!

These events had beaten upon him with the unhurried but telling impact of an ocean tide. Two facts were salient from the mass: whatever he had done he had done because of Ram-tah; and he was going to Paris, where he would see the actual tomb of that other outworn shell of his.

He thought he would not be able to sleep. He had the night in which to pack that steamer trunk. Leisurely he doffed the faultless evening garments—he was going to have a waistcoat pointed like the waster's, with four of those little shiny buttons, and studs and cuff-links to match—and donned a gayly flowered silk robe.

With extreme discomfort he surveyed the new steamer trunk. Merely looking at a steamer trunk left him with acute premonitions of what the voyage had in store for him. But the flapper was the flapper; and it was the only way ever to see that tomb.

The packing began, the choice garments were one by one neatly folded. A light tan overcoat hung in Ram-tah's closet, back of the case. Ram-tah was dragged forth and for the moment lay prone. He was to be left in the locked closet until a more suitable housing could be provided, and Cassidy had been especially warned not to let the steam-heated apartment take fire.

He found the coat and returned to the half-packed trunk in the bedroom where he resumed his wonderful task, stopping at intervals for always futile efforts at realization of this mad impossibility. It was all Ram-tah. Nothing but that kingly manifestation of himself could have brought him up to the thing. He dropped a choice new bit of haberdashery into the trunk and went for another look at It prone on the floor in that other room.

A long time he gazed down at the still face—his own still face, the brow back of which he had once solved difficult problems of administration, the eyes through which he had once beheld the glories of his court, the lips that had kissed his long dead queen, smiled with rapture upon his first-born and uttered the words that had made men call him wise. It was not strange—not unbelievable. It was sane and true. He was still a king.

He reached down and laid a tender, a fraternal hand upon the brow. The contact strengthened him, as always. He could believe anything wise and good of himself. He could be a true mate to that bewildering flapper, full of understanding kindness. He saw little intimate moments of their life together, her perplexities over fumed oak and patent tubs and marketing for pure food; always her terrific earnestness. Now and then he would laugh at that, but then she would laugh too; sometimes the flapper seemed to show, with an engaging little sense of shame, that she just perfectly knew how funny she was.

But she was staunch; she had perfectly well known the very first moment she saw him. And she had never spoiled it all, like that other one in Chicago, by asking him if he was fond of Nature and Good Music and such things. The flapper was capable but quiet. With his hand still upon Ram-tah's brow in that half-timid, strange caress, he was flooded with a sudden new gladness about the flapper. She was *dear*, if you came right down to it. And Ram-tah had brought her to him. He erected himself to look down once more. They *knew*, those two selves; understood each other and life.

It occurred to him for the first time that Ram-tah, too, must have liked dogs, must have been inexpressibly moved by the chained souls that were always trying to speak from their brown eyes. He looked over to Nap, who fiercely battled with a sofa cushion, and was now disembowelling it through a rent in the cover. He wondered what Ram-tah's favourite dog had been like.

He went back to the bedroom to finish his packing. Ram-tah could lie until the moment came to lock him again in the closet, to leave him once more in a seclusion to which he had long been accustomed.

He worked leisurely, stowing those almost advanced garments so that they should show as few wrinkles as possible after their confinement. Occasionally Nap diverted his thoughts by some louder growl than usual in the outer room, or by some noisier scramble.

The trunk was packed and locked for the final time. Thrice had it been unlocked and opened to receive slight forgotten objects. The last to be placed directly under the lid was the entirely scarlet cravat. He was equal to wearing it now, but a sense of the morrow's proprieties deterred him. The stricken mother! In deference to her he laid out for the morning's wear the nearest to a black cravat that he possessed, an article surely unassuming enough to be no offence in a house of mourning.

He fastened the straps of the trunk and sighed in relief. It was a steamer trunk, and he was to sail on a little old steamer, but other people had survived that ordeal. Ram-tah would have met it boldly. Ram-tah!

He stood in the doorway, his attention attracted to Nap, who had for some moments been more than usually vocal. In a far corner Nap had a roundish object between his paws and his sharp teeth tore viciously at it. He looked up and growled in fierce pretence that his master also wished to gnaw this delectable object.

A moment Bean stood there, looking, looking. Slowly certain details cleared to his vision: the details of an unspeakable atrocity. He felt his knees grow weak, and clutched at the doorway for support.

The body of Ram-tah was out of its case and half across the room, yards of the swathed linen unfurled; but, more terrible than all, the head of Ram-tah was not where it should have been.

In the far corner the crouching Nap gnawed at that head, tearing, mutilating, desecrating.

"Napoleon!" It was a cry of little volume, but tense and terrible. Napoleon, destroyer of kings! In this moment he once more put the creature's full name upon him. The dog found the name alarming; perceived that he had committed some one of those offences for which he was arbitrarily punished. He relaxed the stout jaws, crawled slinkingly to the couch, and leaped upon it. Once there, he whimpered protestingly. One of the few clear beliefs he had about a perplexing social system was that nothing hurtful could befall him once he had gained that couch. It was sanctuary.

Bean's next emotion was sympathy for the dog's fright. He tottered across to the couch, mumbling little phrases of reassurance to the abject Nap. He sat down beside him, and put a kindly arm about him.

"Why, why, Nappy! Yes, 'sall right, yes, he *was*—most beautiful doggie in the whole world; yes, he *was*."

He hardly dared look toward the scene of the outrage. The calamity was overwhelming, but how could dogs know any better? Timidly, at length, he raised his eyes, first to where the fragmentary head lay, then to the torn body.

Something about the latter electrified him. He leaped from the couch and seized an end of the linen that bound the mummy. He pulled, and the linen unwound. He curiously surveyed something at his feet. It was a tightly rolled wad of excelsior. The swathing of linen—he had unwound it to where the hands should have been folded on the breast—had enclosed excelsior.

Dazedly he looked into the empty case. Upon one of the new boards he saw marked with the careless brush of some shipping-clerk, "Watkins & Co., Hartford, Conn."

Again, as with the unstable lilac-bushes, his world spun about him; it drew in and darkened. He had the sensation of a grain of dust sucked down a vast black funnel.

Outside the quiet room, the city went on its ruthless, noisy way. In there where dynasties had fallen and a monarch lay prone, a spotted dog sporting with a *papier-mâché* something, came suddenly on a cold hand flung out on the rug. Nap instantly forsook the sham for the real, deserted the head of Ram-tah, and laved Bean's closed eyes with a lolloping pink tongue.

CHAPTER XIV

The next morning at eight-thirty the door of the steam-heated apartment resounded to sharp knocking. There being no response, the knocking was repeated and prolonged. Retreating footsteps were heard in the hallway. Five minutes later a key rattled in the door and Cassidy entered, followed by the waster.

Bean was discovered in a flowered dressing-gown gazing open-eyed at the shut door of a closet. He sat on the couch and one of his arms clasped a sleeping dog. The floor was littered with wisps of excelsior.

"My word, old top, had to have the chap let me into your diggin's you know. You were sleeping like the dead." The waster was bustling and breezy.

"Busy," said Bean. He arose and went into the hall where Cassidy stood.

"He *would* have in," explained Cassidy. "Say th' wor-r-d if he's no frind, an' he'll have out agin. I'll put him so. 'T would not be a refined thing to do, but nicissary if needed."

"'S all right," said Bean. "Friend of mine." He closed the door on Cassidy.

Inside, he found the waster interestedly poking with his stick at a roundish object on the floor.

"Dog's been at it," explained the waster brightly. "What's the idea? Private theatricals?"

"Yes," said Bean, "private theatricals," and resumed his place on the couch, staring dully at the closet door.

"But, look here, old chap, you must liven up. She would have it I should come for you. My word! I believe you're funking! You look absurdly rotten like it, you know."

"Toothache, right across here," muttered Bean. "Have to put it off."

"But that's not done, old top; really it's not done, you know. It ... it ... one doesn't do it at all, you know."

"Never?" asked Bean, brightening a little with alarm.

"Jolly well never," insisted the waster; "not for anything a dentist-fellow could manage. Come now!"

Bean was listless once more, deaf, unseeing.

"Righto," said the waster. "Bachelor dinner last night ... yes?"

The situation had become intelligible to him. He found the bathroom, and from it came the sound of running water. He had the air of a Master of Revels.

"Into it—only thing to do!"

He led Bean to the brink of the icy pool and skilfully flayed him of the flowered gown. He was thorough, the waster. He'd known chaps to pretend to get in by making a great splashing with one hand, after they were left alone. He overcame a few of the earlier exercises in jiu-jitsu and committed Bean's form to the deep.

"Righto!" he exclaimed. "Does it every time. Shiver all you like. Good for you! Now then—clothes! Clothes and things, Man! Oh, here they are to be sure! How stupid of me! Feel better already, yes? Knew it. Studs in shirt. My word! Studs! Studs! There! Let me tie it. Here! Look alive man! She would have it. She must have known you. There!"

He had finished by clamping Bean's hat tightly about his head. Bean was thinking that the waster possessed more executive talent than Grandma had given him credit for; also that he would find an excuse to break away once they were outside; also that Balthasar was keenly witty. Balthasar had *said* it would disintegrate if handled.

He would leave Nap with Cassidy. He would return for him that night, then flee. He would go back to Wellsville, which he should never have left.

The waster had him in the car outside, a firm grasp on one of his arms.

"I'll allow you only one," said the waster judicially as the car moved off. "I know where the chap makes them perfectly—brings a mummy back to life—"

"A mum—what mummy?" asked Bean dreamily.

"Your own, if you had one, you silly juggins!"

Bean winced, but made no reply.

The car halted before an uptown hotel.

"Come on!" said the waster.

"Bring it out," suggested Bean, devising flight.

The waster prepared to use force.

"Quit. I'll go," said Bean.

He was before a polished bar, the white-jacketed attendant of which not only recognized the waster but seemed to divine his errand.

"Two," commanded the waster. The attendant had already reached for a bottle of absinthe, and now busied himself with two eggs, a shaker, and cracked ice.

"White of an egg, delicate but nourishing after bachelor dinners," said the waster expertly.

Bean, in the polished mirror, regarded a pallid and shrinking youth whom he knew to be himself—not a reincarnation of the Egyptian king, but just Bunker

Bean. He could not endure a long look at the thing, and allowed his gaze to wander to the panelled woodwork of the bar.

"Fumed oak," he suggested to the waster.

But the waster pushed one of the slender-stemmed glasses toward him.

"There's the life-line, old top; cling to it! Here's a go!"

Bean drank. The beverage was icy, but it warmed him to life. The mere white of an egg mixed with a liquid of such perfect innocence that he recalled it from his soothing-syrup days.

"Have one with me," he said in what he knew to be a faultless bar manner.

"Oh, I say old top," the waster protested.

"One," said Bean stubbornly.

The attendant was again busy.

"Better be careful," warned the waster. "Those things come to you and steal their hands into yours like little innocent children, but—".

They drank. Bean felt himself bold for any situation. He would carry the farce through if they insisted on it. He no longer planned to elude the waster. They were in the speeding car.

"Fumed eggs!" murmured Bean approvingly.

They were inside that desolated house, the door closed fatefully upon them. The waster disappeared. Bean heard the flapper's voice calling cheerily to him from above stairs. A footman disapprovingly ushered him to the midst of an immense drawing-room of most ponderous grandeur, and left him to perish.

He sat on the edge of a chair and tried to clear his mind about this enormity he was going to commit. False pretenses! Nothing less. He was not a king at all. He was Bunker Bean, a stenographer, whose father drove an express wagon, and whose grandmother had smoked a pipe. He had never been anything more, nor ever would be. And here he was ... pretending.

No wonder Julia had fussed! She had seen through him. How they would all scorn him if they knew what that scoundrelly Balthasar knew. He'd made money, but he had no right to it. He had made that under false pretenses, too, believing money would come naturally to a king. Would they find him out at once, or not until it was too late? He shudderingly recalled a crisis in the ceremony of marriage where some one is invited to make trouble, urged to come forward and say if there isn't some reason why this man and this woman shouldn't be married at all. Could he live through that? Suppose a policeman rushed in, crying, "I forbid the banns! The man is an impostor!" He seemed to remember that banns were often forbidden in novels. Then would he indeed be a thing for contemptuous laughter.

Yet, in spite of this dismal foreboding, he was presently conscious of an unusual sense of well-being. It had been growing since they stopped for those eggs, in that fumed oak place. What about the Corsican? Better have been him than no one! He would look at that tomb. Then he would know. He was rather clinging to the idea of the Corsican. It gave him courage. Still, if he could get out peacefully ...

He stepped lightly to the hall and was on the point of seizing his hat when the flapper called down to him.

"You just perfectly don't leave this house again!"

"Not going to," he answered guiltily. "Looking to see what size hat I wear. Fumed eggs," he concluded triumphantly.

He was not again left alone. The waster came back and supposed he would do some golfing "over across."

Bean loathed golf and gathered the strange power to say so.

"Sooner be a mail-carrier than a golf-player," he answered stoutly. "Looks more fun, anyway."

"*My* word!" exclaimed the waster, "aren't you even keen on watching it?"

"Sooner watch a lot of Italians tearing up a street-car track," Bean persisted.

"Oh, come!" protested the waster.

"Like to have another fumed egg," said Bean.

"You've had one too many," declared the waster, knowing that no sober man could speak thus of the sport of kings.

Grandma, the Demon, entered and portentously shook hands with him. She seemed to have discovered that marriage was very serious.

"Fumed eggs," said Bean, regarding her shrewdly.

"What?" demanded Grandma.

"Fumed eggs, hundred p'cent efficient," he declared stoutly.

The Demon eyed him more closely.

"My grandmother smoked, too," said Bean, "but I never went in for it much."

"U-u-u-mmm!" said the Demon. It was to be seen that she felt puzzled.

Breede slunk into the room, garbed in an unaccustomed frock coat. He went through the form of shaking hands with Bean.

Bean felt a sudden necessity to tell Breede a lot of things. He wished to confide in the man.

"Principle of the thing's all I cared about," he began. "Anybody make money that wants to be a Wall Street crook and take it away from the tired business man. What I want to be is one of the idle rich ... only not idle much of the time, you know. Good major league club for mine. Been looking the ground over; sound 'vestment; keep you out of bad company, lots time to read good books."

"Hanh! Wha's 'at?" exploded Breede.

"Fumed eggs," said Bean, feeling witty. He affected to laugh at his own jest as he perceived that the mourning mother had entered the room. Breede drew cautiously away from him. Mrs. Breede nodded to him bravely.

He mentioned the name of the world's greatest pitcher, with an impulse to take the woman down a bit.

"Get our shirts same place; he's going to have a suit just like this—no, like another one I have in that little old steamer trunk."

He was aware that they all eyed him too closely. The waster winked at him. Then he found himself shaking hands with a soothing old gentleman in clerical garb who called him his young friend and said that this was indeed a happy moment.

The three Breedes and the waster stood apart, studying him queerly. He was feeling an embarrassed need to make light conversation, and he was still conscious of that strange power to make it. He was going to tell the old gentleman, whose young friend he was, that fumed eggs were a hundred p'cent efficient.

But the flapper saved him from that. She came in, quiet but businesslike, and in a low yet distinct voices said she wished it to be perfectly over at once. She did not relax her grasp of Bean's arm after she approached him, and he presently knew that something solemn was going on in which he was to be seriously involved.

"Say, 'I do,'" muttered the old gentleman, and Bean did so. The flapper had not to be told.

There followed a blurred and formal shaking of his hand by those present, and the big sister whom he had not noticed before came up and kissed him.

Then he was conscious of the flapper still at his side. He turned to her and was amazed to discover that she was blinking tears from her eyes.

"There, *there*!" he muttered soothingly, and took her in his arms quite as if they were alone. He held her closely a moment, with little mumbled endearments, softly patting her cheek.

"There, there! No one ever going to hurt *you*. You're *dear*; yes, you are!"

He was much embarrassed to discover those staring others still present. But the flapper swiftly revived. It seemed to be perfectly over for the flapper. She announced that every one must hurry.

Hurriedly, with every one, it seemed, babbling nonsense of remote matters, they sat at a table, and ate of cold food from around a bed of flowers. Bean ate frankly. He was hungry, but he took his part in the talk as a gentleman should.

They were toasting the bride in champagne.

"Never drink," protested Bean to the proffered glass.

"Won't happen every day, old top," suggested the waster.

He drank. The sparkling stuff brought him new courage. He drained the glass.

"I knew they were trying to keep me off that board of directors," he confided to Breede, "specially that oldest one."

"That your first drink s'morning?" asked Breede in discreet tones.

"First drink I ever took. Had two eggs's morning."

"What board of directors?" asked Breede suspiciously.

"Fed'l Express. I wanted that stock for a technical purpose—so I could get on board of directors."

Breede looked across the table to Grandma. There seemed to be alarm in his face.

"Given it up, though," continued Bean. "Can't be robbing tired business men. Rather be a baseball king if you come down to that. I'll own three four major league clubs before year's out. See 'f I don't! 'S only kind of king I want to be— wake me up any time in the night and ask me—old George W. Baseball King. 'S my name. I been other kings enough. Nothing in it. You wouldn't believe it if I told you I was a king of Egypt once, 'way back, thous'n's years before you were ever born. I had my day; pomps and attentions and powers. But I was laid away in a mummy case—did that in those days—thous'n's and thous'n's of years before you were ever born—an' that time I was Napoleon ..."

He stopped suddenly, feeling that the room had grown still. He had been hearing a voice, and the voice was his own. What had he said? Had he told them he was nothing, after all? He gazed from face to face with consternation. They looked at him so curiously. There was an embarrassing pause.

The flapper, he saw, was patting his hand at the table's edge.

"No one ever hurt you while I'm around," he said, and then he glared defiantly at the others. The old gentleman, whose young friend he was, began an anecdote, saying that of course he couldn't render the Irish dialect, also that if they had heard it before they were to be sure and let him know. Apparently no one had heard it before, although Breede left the table for the telephone.

Bean kept the flapper's hand in his. And when the anecdote was concluded everybody arose under cover of the applause, and they were in that drawing-room again where the thing had happened.

The waster chattered volubly to every one. Grandma and the bride's mother were in earnest but subdued talk in a far corner. Breede came to them.

"Chap's plain dotty," said Breede. "Knew something was wrong."

"Your mother's doing," said Mrs. Breede.

"U-u-u-mm!" said the Demon. "I'll go with them."

"I shall also go with my child," said the mother. "James, you will go too."

But Breede had acted without waiting to talk.

"Other car'll be here, 'n' I telephoned for quarters on boat. 'S full up, but they'll manage. Chap might cut her throat."

"U-u-u-mm!" said the Demon.

"Half pas' ten," reminded Breede. "Hurry!"

Bean had accosted the waster.

"Always take fumed eggs for breakfast," he cautioned. "Of course, little fruit an' tea an' things."

"Your father's had a sudden call to Paris. We're going with him," said the Demon, appearing bonneted.

"What boat?" demanded the flapper in quick alarm.

"Your's," said the Demon.

"Jolly party, all together," said Bean cordially. "He coming, too?" He pointed to the old gentleman, but this it seemed had not been thought of.

"He better come too," insisted Bean. "I'm his young friend, and this is indeed a happy moment. Jus' little ol' las' year's steamer."

"You're tagging," accused the flapper viciously, turning to the Demon.

———————————————————

Bean awoke late that night, believing he was dead—that he had fallen in sleep and been laid unto his fathers. But the narrow grave was unstable. It heaved and rolled as if to expel him.

Slowly he remembered. First he identified his present location. He was in an upper berth of that little old steamer. Outside a little round window was the whole big ocean and beneath him slept a man from Hartford, Conn. He had caught the city's name on the end of the man's steamer trunk and been enraged by it. Hartford was a city of rascals. The man himself looked capable of any infamy. He was tall and thin, and wore closely trimmed side-whiskers of a vicious iron gray. He regarded Bean with manifest hostility and had ostentatiously locked a suit-case upon his appearance.

So much for his whereabouts. How had he come there? Laboriously, he went over the events of the afternoon. They were hazy, but certain peaks jutted above the haze. They were "tagged," as the flapper had surmised they were going to be. Aboard the little old steamer had appeared Breede and Julia and the Demon. They had called the flapper aside and apparently told her something for her own good, though the flapper had not liked it, and had told them with much spirit that they were to perfectly mind their own affairs.

Bean had fled into the throng on deck. His hat had received many dents, and when he emerged to a clear space at the far end of the boat he had discovered that his perfectly new watch was gone. He was being put upon, and meekly submitting to it as in that other time when he had not believed himself to be somebody. He stared moodily over the rail as the little old steamer moved out. Thousands of people on the dock were waving handkerchiefs and hats. They seemed to be waving directly at him and yelling. Above it all, he was back in the bird-and-animal store, hearing the parrot shriek over and over, "Oh, what a fool! Oh, what a fool!"

He made an adventurous way through all kinds of hurried people, back to that group of queerly behaving Breedes. The flapper was showing traces of tears, but also a considerable acrimony. She was threatening to tell the captain to just perfectly turn the little old steamer back. But it came to nothing. At least to nothing more than Bean's sharing the stateroom of the Hartford man, who had covered the lower berth with his belongings so that there might be no foolish mistake.

And that was because there had been no provision made on the little old steamer for this invasion of casual Breedes. Pops and Moms had secured an officer's room; the Demon, rather than sit up in the smoking-room of nights, had consented to share the flapper's suite; and Bean had been taken in charge by a cold-blooded steward who left him in the narrow quarters of the Hartford person.

And there, in the far night, he was wishing he might be back in the steam-heated apartment with Nap. He had a violent headache, and he had awakened from a dream of falling into a well of cool, clear water of which he thirstily drank. His narrow bed behaved abominably, rolling him from side to side, then letting his head sink to some far-off terrifying depth. And there was no way of leaving that little old steamer ... not for a man who couldn't swim a stroke.

So he suffered for long miserable hours. Light broke through the little round windows, and outside he could see the appalling waste of water, foaming, seething, rising to engulf him. He couldn't recall mounting to that high place where he had slept. He wondered if the callous steward would sometime come to take him down. Perhaps the steward would forget.

The man from Hartford bestirred himself and was presently shaving before the small glass. Bean looked sullenly down at him. The man was running a wicked-looking razor perilously about his restless Adam's apple. He was also lightly humming "The Holy City."

"Watkins," said Bean distinctly, recalling the name that had revealed the fictitious and Hartford origin of It.

"Adams," said the man, breaking off his song and tightening a leathery cheek for the razor.

"Adam's apple," said Bean, scornfully. "Watkins!"

The man glanced at him and painfully twisted up a corner of his mouth while he applied the razor to the other corner. But he did not speak.

"Think there's a doctor on this little old steamer?" demanded Bean.

The man from Hartford laid down his weapon and began to lave his face.

"I believe," he spluttered, "that medical attendance is provided for those still in mortal error."

"'S'at *so*?" demanded Bean, sullenly.

The man achieved another bar of "The Holy City," and fondly dusted his face with talcum powder, critically observing the effect.

"If you will go into the silence," he at length said, "and there hold the thought of the all-good, you will be freed from your delusion."

"Humph!" said Bean and turned his face from the Hartford man.

The latter locked his razor into a toilet-case, locked the toilet-case into a suit-case, and seemed to debate locking the suit-case into a little old steamer trunk. Deciding, however, that his valuables were sufficiently protected, and that nothing was left out to excite the cupidity of a man to whom he had not been properly introduced, the person from Hartford went forth with a final retort.

"'As a man thinketh in his heart, so is he!'"

"'S'at *so*?" said Bean insolently to the closed door.

He roused himself and descended precariously from his shelf. Once upon his feet he was convinced that the ship was foundering. He hurriedly dressed and adjusted a life-belt from one of a number he saw behind a rack. Over the belt he put on a serviceable rain-coat. It seemed to be the coat to wear.

Outside he plunged through narrow corridors until he came to a stairway. He mounted this to be as far away from the ocean as possible. He came out upon a deck where people were strangely not excited by the impending disaster. Innocent children romped, oblivious to their fate, while callous elders walked the deck or reclined in little old steamer chairs.

He poised a moment, trying to prevent the steamer's deck from mounting by planting one foot firmly upon it. The device, sound enough in mechanical theory, proved unavailing. The vast hulk sank alternately at either end, and to fearsome depths of the sea. There would come a last plunge. He tightened the life-belt.

Then, through the compelling force of associated ideas, there seemed to come to him the faint sweet scent of lilac blossoms ... the vision of a lilac clump revolving both vertically and horizontally ... the noisome fumes of Grammer's own pipe.

"Too much for you, eh? Ha, ha, ha!" It was the scoundrel from Hartford, malignantly cheerful. He was inhaling a cubeb cigarette.

"Lumbago!" said Bean, both hands upon the life-belt.

"'As a man thinketh, so is he!' As simple as that," admonished the other.

Bean groped for the door and for ages fled down blind corridors, vainly seeking that little old stateroom. He did not find it as quickly as he should have; but he was there at last, and a deft steward quickly divested him of the life-belt and other garments for which there no longer seemed to be any need.

He lay weakly reflecting, with a sinister glee, that the boat was bound to sink in a moment. He wanted it to sink. Death was coming too slowly.

Later he knew that the flapper was there. She had come to die with him, though she was plainly not in a proper state of mind to pass on. She was saying that something was the nerviest piece of work she'd ever been up against, and that she would perfectly just fix them ... only give her a little time—they were snoop-cats!

"You'll perfectly manage; jus' leave it to you," breathed her moribund husband.

"If you'd try some fruit and two eggs," suggested the flapper.

He raised a futile hand defensively, and an expression of acute repugnance was to be seen upon his yellowed face.

"Please, please go 'way," he murmured. "Let Julia do fussing. Go way off to other end of little old steamer; stay there."

The flapper saw it was no time for woman's nursing. Sadly she went.

"Telephone to a drug-store," demanded Bean after her, but she did not hear.

He continued to die, mercifully unmolested, until the man from Hartford came in to ascertain if his locks had been tampered with.

"Hold to the all good!" urged the man at a moment when it was too poignantly, too openly certain that Bean could hold to very little indeed.

"Uh-hah!" gasped Bean.

"Go into the silence," urged the man kindly.

"You go—" retorted Bean swiftly; but he should not further be shamed by the recording of language which he lived to regret.

The Hartford man said, "Tut-tut-tut!" and went elsewhere than he had been told to go.

There ensued a dreadful time of alternating night and day, with recurrent visions of the flapper, who perfectly knew and said that he had been eating stuff out of the wrong cans.

"'As a man thinketh in his heart, so is he'," affirmed the Hartford person each morning as he shaved.

And a merry party gathered in the adjoining stateroom of afternoons and sang songs of the jolly sailor's life: "My Bonnie Lies Over the Ocean," and "Sailing, Sailing Over the Bounding Main."

On the morning of the fourth day he made the momentous discovery that the image of food was not repulsive to all his better instincts. Carefully he got upon his feet and they amazingly supported him. He dressed with but slight discomfort. He would audaciously experiment upon himself with the actual sight of food. It was the luncheon hour.

Outside the door he met the flapper on one of her daily visits of inspection.

"I perfectly well knew you'd never die," exclaimed the flapper, and laid glad hands upon him.

"Where do they eat?" asked Bean.

"How jolly! We'll eat together," rejoined the flapper. "The funniest thing! They all kept up till half an hour ago. Then it got rougher and rougher and now they're all three laid out. Poor Moms says it's the smell of the rubber matting, and Granny says she had too many of those perfectly whiffy old cigarettes, and Pops says he's plain seasick. Serves 'em rippingly well right—*taggers!*"

She convoyed him to the dining-room, where he was welcomed by a waiter who had sorrowfully thought not to come to his notice. He greedily scanned the menu card, while the waiter, of his own initiative, placed some trifles of German delicatessen before them.

"It is a lot rougher," said the flapper. "Isn't it too close for you in here?" She was fixedly regarding on a plate before her a limp, pickled fish with one glazed eye staring aloft.

"Never felt better in my life," declared Bean. "Don't care how this little old steamer teeters now. Got my sea-legs."

"Me, too," said the flapper, but with a curious diminution of spirit. She still hung on the hypnotic eye of the pickled fish.

"Ham and cabbage!" said Bean proudly to the waiter.

The flapper pushed her chair swiftly back.

"Forgot my handkerchief," said she.

"There it is," prompted Bean ineptly.

The flapper placed it to her lips and rose to her feet.

"'S perfe'ly old rubber mattin'," she uttered through the fabric, and started toward the doorway. Bean observed that incoming diners anxiously made way for her. He followed swiftly and overtook the flapper at her door.

"Maybe if you'd try a little—" he began.

"Please go away," pleaded the flapper.

Bean returned to the ham and cabbage.

"Ought to go into the silence," he reflected. "'S all she needs. Fixed me all right."

After his hearty luncheon he ventured on deck. It was undeniably rougher, but he felt no fear. The breeze being cold, he went below for his overcoat.

Watkins of Hartford—or Adams, as he persisted in calling himself—reclined in his berth, his unlocked treasures carelessly scattered about him.

"Hold fast to the all good," counselled Bean revengefully.

"Uh—hah!" said Watkins or Adams, not doing so.

Bean fled. Everybody was getting it. The little old steamer was becoming nothing but a plague-ship.

"'As a man thinketh in his heart, so is he'," he muttered, wondering if the words meant anything.

Then, in the fulness of his returned strength, he was appalled anew by the completeness of his own tragedy. He had become once more insignificant. Forever, now, he must be afraid of policemen and all earthly powers. People in crowds would dent his hat and take his new watches. He must never again carry anything but a dollar watch.

And the Breedes saw through him. He must have confessed everything back at that table when he had felt so inscrutably buoyant. Once in Paris they would have him arrested. They might even have him put in irons before the ship landed.

And back in the steam-heated apartment lay that mutilated head, a sheer fabrication of *papier-mâché*. He wondered if Mrs. Cassidy had swept it out ... the head that had meant so much to him. There was no hope any more. If he were still free in Paris he would have one look at that tomb, and then ... well, he had had his day.

Two days later the little old steamer debarked many passengers in the harbour of Cherbourg, carelessly confiding them to a much littler and much older steamer that transported them to the actual land. Among these were a feebly exploding father, a weak but faithful mother, and the swathed wrecks of the Demon and the flapper.

Then began a five-hour train-ride to the one-time capital of a famous upstart. There was but little talk among the members of the party. Bean kept grimly to himself because the only friendly member slept. He studied her pale, drawn face. She had indeed managed well, but his own downfall had thwarted her. He was a nobody. They were doubtless right in wanting to keep him from her. Yet he would see that tomb, and at the earliest possible moment.

At eleven that night they reached the capital. A dispiriting silence was maintained to the doors of a hotel. The women drooped in chairs. Breede acquainted the reception committee of a Paris hostelry with the party's needs as to chambers.

Thereupon they discovered one of the party to be missing. No one had seen him since entering. They were excited by this, all but the flapper.

"I don't blame him," averred the flapper ... "Tagging us! You let him alone! I shall perfectly not worry if he doesn't come home all night. Do you understand? And when he does come—"

"Not safe," snapped Breede. "King of Egypt, Napoleon ... not after money, just principle of thing. Chap's nutty—talk'n' like that!"

"Good *night*!" snapped the flapper in her turn.

CHAPTER XV

He had walked quickly away while porters were collecting the bags. "Keep on the main street," he thought, plunging ahead. He did not change this plan until he discovered himself again at the door of that hotel he meant to leave. It faced a circle, and he had traversed this. He fled down a cross-street and again felt free.

For hours he walked the lighted avenues, or sat moodily on wayside benches, and at length, on a rustic seat screened by shrubbery in a little park, he dozed.

He awoke in the early light, stretched legs and arms luxuriously and again walked. He saw it was five o'clock. He was thrilled now by the morning beauty of the Corsican's city, all gray and green in the flooding sun. And the streets had filled with a voluble traffic that affected him pleasantly. Every one seemed to speak gayly to every one. Two cab-drivers exchanged swift incivilities, but in a quite perfunctory way, with evident good-will.

Walking aimlessly as yet—it was too early for tombs—he came again to that hotel on the circle. They were asleep in there. Little they'd worried—glad to be so easily rid of him.

Then he noticed at the circle's centre a lofty column wrought in bronze with infinite small detail. Surmounting that column was the figure of the Corsican. An upstart who had prevailed!

He left the circle, lest he be apprehended by the Breedes. Soon he was again in that vast avenue of the park-places where he had slept. And now, far off on this splendid highway, he descried a mighty arch. Sternly gray and beautiful it was. And when, standing under it, he looked aloft to its mighty facade, its grandeur seemed threatening to him. He knew what that arch was—another monument imposed upon the city by the imperial assassin—without royal lineage since the passing of Ram-tah.

"Some class to *that* upstart!" he muttered. And if Napoleon had been no one, was it not probable that Bean had not been even Napoleon. The Countess Casanova had doubtless deceived him, though perhaps unintentionally. She had seemed a kind woman, he thought, but you couldn't tell about her controls.

His mind was being washed in that wondrous sunlight.

He was himself an upstart. No doubt about it. But what of it? Here were columns and arches to commemorate the most egregious of all upstarts. Upstarts were men who believed in themselves.

He retraced his steps from the arch.

Curious thing that scoundrel Watkins had kept saying on the boat. "As a man thinketh in his own heart, so is he." Must mean something. What?

Far down that wide avenue he came to a bridge of striking magnificence, beset with golden sculpture. He supposed it to be one more tribute to the sublime Corsican who had thought in his heart, and *was*.

He had the meaning of those words now.

He, Bunker Bean, had believed himself to be mean, insignificant. And so he had been that. Then he had come to believe himself a king, and straightway had he been kingly. The Corsican, detecting the falsity of some Ram-tah, would have gone on believing in himself none the less. It was all that mattered. "As a man thinketh—" If you came down to that, nobody needed a Ram-tah at all.

From the centre of the bridge he raised his eyes and there, far off, high above all those gray buildings, was the golden cross that he knew to surmount the tomb. Sharply it glittered against the blue of the sky.

"Be upstart enough," it seemed to say, "and all things are yours. Believe yourself kingly, though your Ram-tah come from Hartford."

He walked vigorously toward that cross. It often eluded him as he puzzled a way through the winding gray-walled streets. More than once he was forced to turn back, to make laborious circuits. But never for long was the cross out of sight.

Constantly as he walked that new truth ran in his mind, molten, luminous. Who knew of Ram-tah's fictive origin, or even of Ram-tah at all? No one but a witty scoundrel calling himself Balthasar.

Bean had become some one through a belief in himself. Ram-tah had been a crude bit of scaffolding, and was well out of the way. The confidence he had helped to build would now endure without his help. Be an upstart. A convinced upstart. Such the world accepts.

Then he issued from the maze of narrow streets and confronted the tomb. Through the open door, even at this early hour, people went and came. The Corsican's magnetism prevailed. And he, Bunker Bean, the lowly, had that same power to magnetize, to charm, to affront the world and yet evoke monuments—if he could only believe it.

He went quickly through the iron gateway, up the long walk and took the imposing stairway in leaps. Then, standing uncovered in that wonderfully lit room, he gazed down at the upstart's mighty urn.

Long he stood under that spell of line and colour and magnitude, lost in the spaciousness of it. No Balthasar had cheated here. There lay the mighty and little man who had never lost belief in himself—who had been only a little chastened by an adversity due to the craven world's fear of his prowess.

He was quite unconscious of others beside him who paid tribute there. He thought of those last sad days on that lonely island, the spirit still unbroken. His emotion surged to his eyes, threatening to overwhelm him. He gulped twice and angrily brushed away some surprising tears.

By his side stood a white-faced young Frenchman with a flowing brown beard. He became infected with Bean's emotion. He made no pretence of brushing his tears aside. He frankly wept.

Beyond this man a stout motherly woman, with two children in hand, was flooded by the current. She sobbed comfortably and companionably. The two children widened their eyes at her a moment, then fell to weeping noisily.

Farther around the railing a distinguished looking old gentleman of soldierly bearing, who wore a tiny red ribbon in the lapel of his frock coat, loudly blew his nose and pressed a kerchief of delicate weave to his brimming eyes.

Beyond him a young woman became stricken with grief and was led out by her solicitous husband, who seemed to feel that a tomb was no place for her at that time.

The exit of this couple aroused Bean. He cast a quick glance upon the havoc he had wrought and fled, wiping his eyes.

Halfway down the steps he encountered the alleged Adams of Hartford, who had stopped to open his Badaeker at the right page before entering the tomb.

"A magnificent bit of architecture," said the Hartford man instructively.

"Pretty loud for a tomb," replied Bean judicially. He was not going to let this Watkins, or whatever his name was, know what a fool he had made of himself in there. Then he remembered something.

"Say," he ventured, "how'd you happen to think up that thing you were always getting off to me back there on the boat—about as a man thinketh *is* he?"

"Tut-tut-tut! Really? But that is from the Holy Scriptures, which should always be read in connection with Science and Health."

"I must get it—something *in* that. Funny thing," he added genially, "getting good stuff like that out of Hartford, Connecticut."

He left Watkins or Adams staring after him in some bewilderment, a forgotten finger between the leaves of the Badaeker.

He began once more to lay a course through those puzzling streets. He was going to that hotel. He was going to be an upstart and talk to his own wife.

The tomb had cleared his brain.

"I'm no king," he thought; "never was a king; more likely a guinea-pig. But I'm some one now, all right! I'll show 'em; not afraid of the whole lot put together; face 'em all."

He came out upon the river at last and presently found himself back in that circle of the hotel. He stared a while at the bronze effigy surmounting that vainglorious column. Then he drew a long breath and went into the hotel.

A capable Swiss youth responded to his demand to be shown to his room, seeming to consider it not strange that Americans in Paris should now and then return to their rooms.

At the doorway of a drawing-room that looked out upon the column the Swiss suggested coffee—perhaps?

"And fruit and fumed ... boiled eggs and toast and all that meat and stuff," supplemented Bean firmly.

He tried one of two doors that opened from the drawing-room and exposed a bedroom. His, evidently. There was the little old steamer trunk. He discovered a bathroom adjoining and was presently suffering the celestial agonies of a cold bath with no waster to coerce him.

He dressed with indignant muttering, and with occasional glances out at that supreme upstart's memorial. He chose his suit of the most legible checks. He had been a little fearful about it in New York. It was rather advanced, even for one of that Wall Street gang that had netted himself four hundred thousand dollars. Now he donned it intrepidly.

And, with no emotion whatever but a certain grim sureness of himself, he at last adjusted the entirely red cravat. He gloated upon this flagrantly. He hastily culled seven cravats of neutral tint and hurled them contemptuously into a waste-basket. Done with that kind!

He heard a waiter in the drawing-room serving his breakfast. He drew on a dark-lined waistcoat of white piqué—like the one worn by the oldest director the day Ram-tah had winked—then the perfectly fitting coat of unmistakable checks, and went out to sit at the table. He was resolving at the moment that he would do everything he had ever been afraid to do. "'S only way show you're not afraid," he muttered. He was wearing a cravat he had always feared to wear, and now he would devour meat things for breakfast, whatever the flapper thought about it.

When he had a little dulled the edge of his hunger, he rang a bell.

"Find m' wife," he commanded the Swiss youth, only to be met with a look of blankness. He was considering if it might do him good to make a row about this—he had always been afraid to make rows—but the other door of the drawing-room opened. His wife was found.

"'S all for 's aft'noon," he exploded to the servitor, who seemed not displeased to withdraw from this authoritative presence. Then he engaged a slice of bacon with a ruthless fork.

"Where you *been*?" he demanded of the flapper. Only way to do—go at them hammer and tongs!

The flapper gazed at him from the doorway. She was still pale and there were reddened circles about her eyes. The little old rag of a morning robe she wore added to her pallor and gave her an unaccustomed look of fragility.

"Where you been all the time?" repeated her husband with the arrogance of a confirmed upstart.

The flapper seemed to be on the point of tears, but she came into the room and sat across the table from him. In spite of the blurring moisture in her eyes he could still read the old look of ownership. Time had not impaired it.

"I just perfectly wouldn't let them know I felt bad," she began. "I said I was going to sleep and wouldn't worry one bit if you perfectly never came home all night. And you never did, because I couldn't sleep and watched ... but I wouldn't let them know it for just perfectly old hundred thousand dollars. And this morning I said I'd had a bully sleep and felt fit and you had a right to go where you wanted to and they could please mind their own affairs, and I laughed so at them when they said they were going for the police—"

"Police, eh? Let 'em bring their old police. They think I'm afraid of police?" He valiantly attacked an egg.

"Of course not, stupid, but they thought you might wander off and get lost, like those people in the newspapers that wake up in Jersey City or some place and can't remember their own names or how it happened, and they wanted the police to just perfectly find you, and I wanted them to, too. I was deathly afraid—"

"I know my own name, all right. I'm little Tempest and Sunshine; that's my name.

"—but I wouldn't let them know I was afraid. And I laughed at them and told them they didn't know you at all and that you'd come home—come home."

He found he could strangely not be an upstart another moment in the presence of that flapper. He was over kneeling beside her, reaching his arms up about her, pressing her cheek down to his. The flapper held him tightly and wept.

"There, there!" he soothed her, smoothing the golden brown hair that spilled about her shoulders. "No one ever going to hurt you while I'm around. You're the just perfectly *dearest*, if you come right down to it. Now, now! 'S all right. Everything all right!"

"It's those perfectly old taggers," exploded the flapper, suddenly recovering her true form, "just furiously tagging."

"'S got to stop right now," declared Bean, rising. "Wipe that egg off your face, and let's get out of here."

"London," she suggested brightly. "Granny has always—"

"No London!" he broke in, visibly returning to the Corsican or upstart manner. "And no Grandma, no Pops, no Moms! You and me—us—understand what I mean? Think I'm going to have my wife sloshing around over there, voting, smashing windows, getting run in and sent to the island for thirty days. No! Not for little old George W. Me!"

"I never wanted to so very much," confessed the flapper with surprising meekness. "You tell where to go, then."

Bean debated. Baseball! Perhaps there would be a game on the home grounds that day. Paris might be playing London or St. Petersburg or Berlin or Venice.

"First we go see a ball game," he said.

The flapper astounded him.

"I don't think they have it over here—baseball," she observed.

No baseball? She must be crazy. He rang the bell.

The capable Swiss entered. In less than ten minutes he was able to convince the amazed American that baseball was positively not played on the continent of Europe. It was monstrous. It put a different aspect upon Europe.

"Makes no difference where we go, then," announced Bean. "Just any little old last year's place. We'll 'lope."

"Ripping," applauded the flapper, with brightening eyes.

"Hurry and dress. I'll get a little old car and we'll beat it before they get back. No time for trunk; take bag."

Down in the office he found they made nothing of producing little old cars for the right people. The car was there even as he was taking the precaution to secure a final assurance from the manager that Paris did not by any chance play London that day.

The two bags were installed in the ready car; then a radiant flapper beside an amateur upstart. The driver desired instructions.

"*Ally, ally!*" directed Bean, waving a vague but potent hand.

"We've done it," rejoiced the flapper. "Serve the perfectly old taggers good and plenty right!"

Bean lifted a final gaze to the laurel-crowned Believer. He knew that Believer's secret now.

"What a stunning tie," exclaimed the flapper. "It just perfectly does something to you."

"'S little old last year's tie," said her husband carelessly.

At six-thirty that evening they were resting on a balcony overlooking the garden of a hotel at Versailles. Back of them in the little parlour a waiter was setting a most companionable small table for two. Such little sounds as he made were thrilling. They

598

liked the hotel much. Its management seemed to have been expecting them ever since the building's erection, and to have reserved precisely that nest for them.

They had been "doing" the palace. A little self-conscious, in their first free solitude, they had agreed that the palace would be instructive. Through interminable galleries they had gone, inspecting portraits of the dead who had made and marred French history ... led on by a guide whose amiable delusion it was that he spoke English. The flapper had been chiefly exercised in comparing the palace, to its disadvantage, with a certain house to be surrounded on all sides by scenery and embellished with perfectly patent laundry tubs.

The flapper sighed in contentment, now.

"We needn't ever do it again," she said. "How they ever made it in that old barn—"

Bean had occupied himself in thinking it was funny about kings. To have been born a king meant not so much after all. He still dwelt upon it as they sat looking down into the shadowed garden.

"There was that last one," he said musingly. "Born as much a king as any ... and look what they did to him. Better man than the other two before him ... they had 'habits' enough, and he was decent. But he couldn't make them believe in him. He couldn't have believed in himself very hard. His picture looks like a man I know in New York named Cassidy .. always puttering around, dead serious about something that doesn't matter at all. You got to bluff people, and this poor old dub didn't know how ... so they clipped his head off for it. Two or three times a good bluff would have saved him."

"No bath, no furnace," murmured the flapper. "That perfectly reminds me, soon as we get back—"

"Then," pursued Bean, "along comes Mr. little old George W. Napoleon Bluff and makes them eat out of his hand in about five minutes. Didn't he walk over them, though? And they haven't quit thanking him for it yet. Saw a lot of 'em snivelling over him at that tomb this morning. Think he'd died only yesterday. You know, I don't blame him so much for a lot of things he did—fighting and women and all that. He knew what they'd do to him if he ever for one minute quit bluffing. You know, he was what I call an upstart."

The flapper stole a hand into his and sighed contentedly.

"You've perfectly worked it all out, haven't you?" she said.

"—and if you come right down to it, I'm nothing but 'n upstart myself."

"Oh, splash!" said the flapper, in loving refutation.

"'S all," he persisted; "just 'n upstart. Of course I don't have to be one with you. I wouldn't be afraid to tell you anything in the world; but those others, now; every one else in the world except you; I'll show 'em who's little old George W. Upstart—old man Upstart himself, that's what!"

"You're a king," declared the flapper in a burst of frankness.

"Eh?" said Bean, a little startled.

"Just a perfectly little old king," persisted the flapper with dreamy certitude. "Never fooled little George W. Me. Knew it the very first second. Went over me just like *that*."

"Oh, I'm no king; never was a king; rabbit, I guess. Little old perfectly upstart rabbit, that's what!"

"What am I?" asked the flapper pointedly.

"Little old flippant flapper, that's what! But you're my Chubbins just the same; my Chubbins!" and he very softly put his hand to her cheek.

"*Monsieur et Madame sont servi,*" said the waiter. He was in the doorway but discreetly surveyed the evening sky through an already polished wine-glass held well aloft.

The three perfectly taggers meeting their just due, consulted miserably as they gathered about a telephone in Paris the following morning. The Demon had answered the call.

"Says she has it all reasoned out," announced the Demon.

"'S what she said before," grunted Breede. "Tha's nothing new."

"And she says we're snoop-cats and we might as well go back home—now," continued the Demon. "Says she's got the—u-u-m-mm!—says to perfectly quit tagging."

"Nothing can matter now," said the bereaved mother.

"He's talking himself," said the Demon. "Mercy he's got a new voice ... sounds like another man. He says if we don't beat it out of here by the next boat—he can imagine nothing of less—something or other I can't hear—"

"—consequence," snapped Breede.

"Yes, that's it; and now he's laughing and telling her she's a perfectly flapper."

"Oh, my poor child," murmured the mother.

"Puzzle t' me," said Breede. "I swear I can't make out just how many kinds of a—"

"James!" said his wife sternly, and indicated the presence of several interested foreigners.

THE END

600

.

Made in the USA
Columbia, SC
18 January 2018